"In an era when the commodifying tendencies of capitalism are speeding up and the market extends its reach into multiple areas previously considered outside its domain, this much needed *Routledge Handbook of Commodification* provides invaluable insight into a hotly contested terrain."

Anne Phillips, *author of* Unconditional Equals, *Professor Emerita, LSE*

THE ROUTLEDGE HANDBOOK OF COMMODIFICATION

Some goods are freely traded as commodities without question or controversy. For other goods, their commodification – their being made available in exchange for money, or their being subject to market valuation and exchange – is hotly contested. "Contested" commodities range from labour and land, to votes, healthcare, and education, to human organs, gametes, and intimate services, to parks and emissions. But in the context of a market economy, what distinguishes these goods as non-commodifiable, or what defines them as contestable commodities? And why should their status as such justify restricting the market choices of rationally consenting parties to otherwise voluntary exchanges?

This volume draws together wide-ranging, interdisciplinary research on the legitimate scope of markets and the kinds of goods that should be exempt therefrom. In bringing diverse answers to this question together for the first time, it identifies commodification studies as a unique field of scholarly research in its own right. In so doing, it fosters interdisciplinary dialogue, advances scholarship, and enhances education in this controversial, important, and growing field of research. Contemporary theorists who examine this question do so from across the disciplinary spectrum and ground their answers in diverse scholarly literature and divergent methodological approaches. Their arguments will be of interest to scholars and students of philosophy, economics, law, political science, sociology, policy, feminist theory, and ecology, among others.

The contributors to this volume take diverse and divergent positions on the benefits of markets in general and on the possible harms of specific contested markets in particular. While some favour free markets and others regulation or prohibition, and while some engage in more normative and others in more empirical analysis, the contributors all advance nuanced and thoughtful arguments that engage deeply with the complex set of moral and empirical questions at the heart of commodification studies. This volume collects their new and provocative work together for the first time.

Elodie Bertrand is Associate Research Professor in economics at the French National Centre for Scientific Research, ISJPS (University Paris 1 Panthéon-Sorbonne and CNRS, UMR 8103). She co-edited the *Elgar Companion to Ronald Coase* (2016), and *The Limits of the Market: Commodification of Nature and Body* (2020).

Vida Panitch is Associate Professor of Philosophy and Director of Ethics and Public Affairs at Carleton University in Ottawa, Canada. Her research focuses on questions of commodification, exploitation, and distributive justice. She co-edited *Exploitation: from Theory to Practice* (2017).

THE ROUTLEDGE HANDBOOK OF COMMODIFICATION

Edited by Elodie Bertrand and Vida Panitch

Routledge
Taylor & Francis Group
LONDON AND NEW YORK

Designed cover image: image of a painting by Canadian Artist, Matt Durant, called *Dollars and Sense* (2007)

First published 2024
by Routledge
4 Park Square, Milton Park, Abingdon, Oxon OX14 4RN

and by Routledge
605 Third Avenue, New York, NY 10158

Routledge is an imprint of the Taylor & Francis Group, an informa business

British Library Cataloguing-in-Publication Data
A catalogue record for this book is available from the British Library

ISBN: 978-1-032-03737-0 (hbk)
ISBN: 978-1-032-03740-0 (pbk)
ISBN: 978-1-003-18874-2 (ebk)

DOI: 10.4324/9781003188742

Typeset in Times New Roman
by Newgen Publishing UK

CONTENTS

CONTRIBUTORS

Nathalie Berta is Professor of Economics at University Paris Cité, France. She is working on the history of environmental policies and carbon markets.

Elodie Bertrand (she) is Associate Research Professor in economics at the French National Centre for Scientific Research, ISJPS (University Paris 1 Panthéon-Sorbonne and CNRS, UMR 8103). She co-edited the *Elgar Companion to Ronald Coase* (2016), and *The Limits of the Market: Commodification of Nature and Body* (2020).

Jason Brennan is the Robert J and Elizabeth Flanagan Family Term Professor and Director at the Georgetown Institute for the Study of Markets and Ethics.

Harry Brighouse is the Mildred Fish Harnack Professor of Philosophy of Education and Carol Dickson Bascom Professor of the Humanities at University of Wisconsin-Madison.

Pierre Crétois is Associate Professor in Political Philosophy at Bordeaux-Montaigne University, France. His research, in the SPH (Sciences, Philosophy, Humanities, UMR 4574) research team, focuses on philosophical approaches to the problem of property rights.

Marie Daou is Associate Professor of Economics at the University of Montpellier, and member of Montpellier Research in Economics (MRE). Her research focuses on the history of recent economic thought, economic philosophy and law and economics.

Martha M. Ertman (she/her) is University of Maryland Carey Law School's Carole & Hanan Sibel Research Professor. She teaches Contracts, Commercial Law, and Transactional Skills, and writes about contracts that benefit have-nots in contexts such as family and reparations for racial injustice.

Christopher Freiman is Professor of General Business, John Chambers College of Business and Economics, West Virginia University.

Christine Frison is an Associate Research Professor at the University of Liège, Belgium. She is also an invited lecturer at the University of Louvain (UCLouvain). She is also an associate researcher in the Government & Law research group at the University of Antwerp (Belgium) and an associate legal fellow at the Centre for International Sustainable Development Law (McGill University, Canada). She published *Redesigning the Global Seed Commons: Law and Policy for Agrobiodiversity and Food Security* (Routledge, 2018).

Fabien Girard is Associate Professor in the Faculty of Law at Université Grenoble Alpes (UGA) and Junior Fellow at the Institut universitaire de France (IUF), France. When he was a research fellow at the Maison Française d'Oxford (MFO), he led a research program titled "Theory of Law and Legal Anthropology". He coedited *Biocultural Rights, Indigenous Peoples and Local Communities: Protecting Culture and the Environment* (Routledge, 2022).

Erik Gomez-Baggethun is Professor of Environmental Governance at the Norwegian University of Life Sciences (Norway) and a senior scientific advisor at the Norwegian Institute of Nature Research (NINA).

Ciaran Harte (he/his) is a MSc graduate on Ecological Economics by the University of Edinburgh (United Kingdom).

L. Chad Horne is Assistant Professor of Instruction in the Department of Philosophy at Northwestern University in Evanston, Illinois. He works in political philosophy and applied ethics.

Pierre Januard (he/his) is Research Fellow in Economics at University Paris 1 Panthéon-Sorbonne (PHARE), France. He has written his PhD and several academic papers on various aspects of Thomas Aquinas's economic thought.

Peter M. Jaworski is an associate teaching professor of Strategy, Ethics, Economics and Public Policy at Georgetown University's McDonough School of Business, USA.

Michael Joel Kessler (he/him) is the Raymond Pryke Chair at Trinity College in the University of Toronto. He is an assistant professor in the Ethics, Society, and Law program as well as the Director of the Margaret MacMillan Trinity One program.

Kimberly D. Krawiec is the Charles O. Gregory Professor of Law and Sullivan & Cromwell Professor of Law, University of Virginia, USA.

André Lapidus (he/his) is Professor of Economics at University Paris 1 Panthéon-Sorbonne (PHARE), France. His research interests include history of economic thought, decision theory, and methodology of the history of economic thought.

Catherine Larrère is Emeritus Professor of Philosophy at University Paris 1 Panthéon-Sorbonne (ISJPS). Her publications include *Les philosophies de l'environnement* (1997), *Du bon usage de la nature* (with Raphaël Larrère, 1st edition 1997), and *L'écoféminisme* (2023).

Alain Marciano is Professor of Economics at the University of Montpellier. He is also Senior Research Fellow, Karl Mittermaier Centre for Philosophy of Economics, University of Johannesburg, and Distinguished Affiliated Fellow, F. A. Hayek Program for Advanced Study in Philosophy, Politics, and Economics, Mercatus Center, George Mason University.

Julia Martin-Ortega (she/her) is Professor of Ecological Economics at the Sustainability Research Institute, School of Earth and Environment, University of Leeds (United Kingdom).

M. Azahara Mesa-Jurado (she/her) is a researcher/Lecturer at Sustainability Sciences Department in El Colegio de la Frontera Sur (Mexico) specializing in rural resources management and human-nature relationships.

Roldan Muradian (he/his) is Professor (Adjunct) at the Universidade Federal Fulminense (Brazil) with an interest in environmental governance and human-nature interactions.

Emily C. Nacol (she/her) is Associate Professor of Political Science at the University of Toronto, Canada. She is the author of *An Age of Risk: Politics and Economy in Early Modern Britain* (2016).

Jennifer Nedelsky is Professor of Law at Osgoode Hall Law School, York University, Toronto, Canada. She writes on feminist legal theory, restructuring work and care, judgment, and property. She is the author of *Private Property and the Limits of American Constitutionalism*, *Law's Relations: A Relational Theory of Self, Autonomy, and Law*, and *Part Time for All: A Care Manifesto*, co-authored with Tom Malleson.

Christine Noiville is Research Professor at the National Center for Scientific Research (CNRS), France. She chairs the CNRS ethics committee (COMETS) and serves as the director of the Institut des sciences juridiques et philosophiques de la Sorbonne (ISJPS–UMR 8103). Additionally, she is the Head of the Haut comité pour la transparence et l'information sur la sécurité nucléaire (HCTISN). Since 2019, she has been a co-editor of the review *Cahiers Droit, sciences et technologies*. She co-edited *Des enjeux d'intérêt public en temps de pandémie. Un double regard juridique et philosophique* (éditions, 2021).

Paula Novo (she/her) is Lecturer of Ecological Economics at the Sustainability Research Institute, School of Earth and Environment, University of Leeds (United Kingdom).

John O'Neill is Professor of Political Economy at Manchester University, UK. His books include *Markets, Deliberation and Environment* (Routledge, 2007), *The Market: Ethics, Knowledge and Politics* (1998) and *Ecology, Policy and Politics: Human Well-Being and the Natural World* (1993). He also co-authored *Environmental Values* (2008) with A. Holland and A. Light.

Vida Panitch (she/her) is Associate Professor of Philosophy and Director of Ethics and Public Affairs at Carleton University in Ottawa, Canada. Her research focuses on questions of commodification, exploitation, and distributive justice.

Jonathan Peterson (he/him) is an Associate Professor of Philosophy and Director of the University Honors Program at Loyola University New Orleans, USA.

Nicolas Postel is Professor of economics at the University of Lille (France), and member of the CLERSE (University of Lille and CNRS). His current research focuses on Corporate Social Responsibility from an institutionalist point of view and, more generally, he tries to define the foundations of an institutionalist paradigm in economics inspired by the work of Karl Polanyi.

Margaret Jane Radin is Professor Emerita of Law, University of Toronto, the Henry King Ransom Professor Emerita of Law, University of Michigan, and the William Benjamin Scott & Luna M. Scott Professor Emerita of Law, Stanford University. She is the author of *Contested Commodities* (1996), *Reinterpreting Property* (1993) and *Boilerplate* (2013).

Laurie J. Shrage is Professor Emeritus in Philosophy at Florida International University, USA. Her work employs political theory to evaluate the goals of contemporary social movements.

Richard Sobel is Professor of Economics at the University of Lille (France), and member of the CLERSE (University of Lille and CNRS). His current research focuses on the philosophical foundations of the concepts of political economy (commodity, value, wage relation, exploitation, capital accumulation) and its critique, particularly in Marx and Marxist/Marxian analysis.

Philippe Steiner is Emeritus Professor of sociology at Sorbonne university (GEMASS). He has published extensively on economic sociology and the history of social sciences. His last publications include *Faire la fête: sociologie de la joie* (2023), *Comment ça matche. Sociologie de l'appariement* (edited with M. Simioni, 2022), and *Calculation and Morality. The costs of slavery and the value of emancipation* (with C. Oudin-Bastide, 2019).

Aksel Braanen Sterri is a postdoctoral researcher in ethics at Harvard University's Department of Government and OsloMet's Faculty of Health Sciences. He is particularly interested in how we can design markets to improve animal welfare.

James Stacey Taylor is Professor of Philosophy at The College of New Jersey. His most recent book is *Markets with Limits: How the commodification of academia derails debate* (Routledge 2022).

Marie Trespeuch is Assistant Professor at Sorbonne University (GEMASS). Her works deal with digital transformations of markets, and relations between economic activities and moral issues. Her PhD dissertation (2011) analysed the liberalization of the French gambling market. With Ph. Steiner, she edited *Marchés contestés. Quand le marché rencontre la morale* (2015).

François Vatin is Professor of Sociology at University Paris Nanterre. He has published, among other books, *Le travail. Activité productive et ordre social* (2014), *In the flow. Working in Chemical and Nuclear Power Plants* (with G. Rot, 2021), *De l'économie. Le mot et la chose. La forme et la substance* (second edition, 2023).

Adrian Walsh (he/his) is Professor of Philosophy and Political Theory at the University of New England, Australia. He is also currently a research fellow in the Department of Philosophy, Linguistics and Theory of Science at the University of Gothenburg.

Stephen Wilkinson (he/his) is Professor of Bioethics at Lancaster University, UK.

PREFACE

Margaret Jane Radin

I

Money is widely used as a mechanism of exchange in our contemporary societies. The use of money to acquire goods and services entails the valuation of those goods in monetary terms as "products". However, a given product or good is not only an economic item, but often fulfills human needs and desires, such as nutrition, health, education, and family life. *Commodification* refers to the valuation of a product primarily in economic terms while minimizing or excluding other methods of valuation, such as in terms of human needs, justice, or equity.

The question thus arises: what things should not be bought and sold? Most contemporary societies have rejected the buying of slaves, for example. But how do we determine which commodification is acceptable and which should be contested, while still acknowledging that in most exchanges, money may be a morally benign and useful mode of exchange? *Contested commodification* refers to the commodification of a good which should properly be valued in non-commodified ways.

To examine commodification requires thought about which aspects of human society may be monetized freely, which conditionally, and which should be prohibited from monetary exchange. Sometimes these distinctions are not at all clear-cut and may provoke considerable debate. These debates motivate this volume and inspire the important and multifaceted work of its editors and contributors.

In this preface, I will argue that two classes of goods should be (to the greatest extent possible) non-commodified: first, *goods essential to flourishing*, and second, goods which are necessary to the functioning of a democratic society, that is, *democratic goods*. I will address each of these in turn and conclude with some remarks about the importance of this volume in addressing these and related questions of contested commodification.

II

In theory, if a society is to flourish, it must be organized such that all members may flourish. Although there are many philosophical definitions of flourishing, human flourishing may be defined as *a successful and worthy human life*. Therefore, when social institutions are organized so that members' human needs may be met, the society itself may flourish. These needs include physical and emotional well-being, the opportunity to pursue meaningful life projects, and full, meaningful participation in the political life of the society.

The goods and services necessary to meet these needs include: clean water, adequate food, safe housing, meaningful work, education, health care, and environmental preservation. That such *necessary goods* must be available to everyone is grounded in a society's commitment to the worth and development of each citizen. Some examples of necessary goods are health care, education, and family life.

Without health a person cannot pursue any of the goals essential to flourishing, nor participate fully in society. The provision of health care goods and services in the US is highly commodified, with private actors dominating the provision of insurance, the institutions (hospitals, pharmaceutical corporations, etc.) which supply these goods and services, and the delivery of health care itself. This arrangement may, in my view, truly be called "commodified", as apart from the necessary exchange value of these items, there is an overwhelming incentive to profit which both distorts and restricts the provision of these goods and services. The many negative consequences of this commodification include national health care spending far in excess of that of any other advanced nation, poorer outcomes than that of many nations on national indices of health, high numbers of uninsured citizens, and an overwhelming amount of personal medical debt, a category of debt largely unknown in other advanced nations. Probably the most troublesome commodification of medicine has been the US's refusal to allow medical care, or even insurance, to be organized and provided by the state. In such an environment corruption flourishes, as evidenced by the Sackler family's distribution of a dangerous drug (Oxycodone) that it marketed to doctors with considerable effort, and which resulted in (and continues to cause) many deaths and addictions throughout the world. Another result of the "profits over people" approach is to burden the delivery of health care services with unnecessary gatekeepers such as billing agents and eligibility consultants whose function is to restrict rather than to promote access to health services.

Education is essential to providing a person with the opportunity to develop their abilities, to create a life of value, and thus to flourish. If education were available only on the basis of the ability to pay, then so too would be the opportunity to flourish, which runs counter to a society's commitment to the equal worth of its citizens. Education is also essential for people to acquire the knowledge they need to make informed political decisions, to share ideas with those who hold different viewpoints, and to participate fully in the political life of their society.

When education is viewed as necessary to human flourishing, as it was in the US for the two generations following World War II, then public provision of primary, secondary and university education is heavily subsidized by the state. By contrast, as is increasingly the case in the US today, when education is seen as a "commodity", and the student as a "consumer" of the (educational) "product" who is making an "investment" in his or her future economic agency, then the costs of education are shifted to the student, education itself becomes more standardized, and (as in health care) middle agents serving to restrict and condition access proliferate. Consequences of this approach include declining state support, aging facilities, increased class sizes, and high student debt, which in the US stands at $1.75 trillion, outstripping credit card debt.

For many people, having a family seems essential to leading a flourishing life. Paid surrogacy is one way to help people achieve this if they otherwise cannot conceive or carry a child on their own. For those who are socially or biologically infertile, this method of family building is important to the leading of flourishing lives. This was a heavily debated question in early writings concerning contested commodification. Surrogacy is a practice whose commercialization was once thought to impede human flourishing, insofar as it was seen to treat women as breeders and to promote the view that their bodies could be used for service in the interests of men, and/or of the wealthy. In previous decades, commercial surrogacy was seen to undermine women's freedom to make their own choices whether to bring forth births, or not to do so. But the practice has changed and so must our attitudes to it.

What should be disallowed, in my view, is not payment to surrogates ("commercialization"), but rather high payments to lawyers or others presenting themselves as agents or providers of babies, that is, the commodification of this service. It is important to regulate costs so as to avoid converting an important opportunity for family building into a mechanism whereby lawyers and brokers reap profits off the needs of the childless and the labours of women. And although paid and well-regulated surrogacy may rightly be seen as defensible, burgeoning commodification increases the dangers of profiteering and exploitation in the realm of reproduction.

As illustrated above, excessive commodification may impede the satisfaction of fundamental human needs. Where markets threaten access to these goods for some on an arbitrary basis such as ability to pay, the state is not only permitted but, in my view, obliged to intervene. In the context of a society in which there is a very unequal distribution of money, commodification of those goods necessary to human flourishing may create a desperate underclass suffering starvation, poor health, and homelessness, for whom flourishing is out of reach. The commodification of the goods required to flourish in a society should receive the closest scrutiny, and the strictest regulation.

III

Societies are organized to take care of the human needs that persons cannot fulfill alone, and those whose fulfillment requires cooperation from others. This involves significant coordination, which may only be guaranteed through the enforcement of a known and established set of rules. Democratic societies rely on citizen participation, i.e., the consent of the governed, to provide the basis for social action. Mechanisms for this participation may be thought of as *democratic goods.* These include the right to vote, the right to a fair trial, free speech, and fair elections. These goods protect opportunities for people to have a say in how their society proceeds, how it is governed, and hence how they themselves are governed.

Law is mediated by caretakers (including voters, lawmakers, and judges), in whose custody lies the rule of law. A democratic society based on the rule of law depends on the service of trustworthy overseers, who can be called upon to keep the society in the realm of democracy, including keeping democratic goods appropriately available to all. The protection of the rule of law is in their hands. There are three democratic goods I will consider here briefly: votes, public offices, and the judiciary. The caretakers responsible for the protection of these goods – voters, officials, and members of the judiciary – must perform their roles free of monetary influence if the goods in their care are to remain truly democratic.

The voter is the primary caretaker of democracy. A democracy as a successful mode of government depends upon the ability of the governed to keep officials honest and committed to their jobs. A well-designed system of voting, free of commodification, would view all aspects of the voting process – campaigns, voting technology and the conduct of elections – as public goods, to be financed and supervised by the commons. Votes are themselves democratic goods but are also absolutely indispensable to the protection of other democratic goods. The sad fact is that the US voting system itself has been highly commodified, with campaigns run as private entities, and voting technologies being the province of private corporations.

Elections are increasingly being determined by private campaign financing. This may be the biggest current threat to democratic practices in the US. In 1976 the US Supreme Court ruled that political contributions are a form of free speech, and in 2010 that under the First Amendment corporations have the same rights to political speech as individuals. It thus found no compelling government interest in prohibiting corporations from using their general treasury funds to make election-related independent expenditures. Thus, money became political speech. This has led to many anti-democratic pathologies: ultra-wealthy people lavishly funding campaigns (often their own), and when successful, serving mainly the interests of other wealthy citizens and corporations. Additionally, political parties make decisions about who should run for office based on who is likely to raise the most money, and members of Congress are required by their leadership to prioritize fund raising rather than their constitutionally assigned tasks. The legislative process is further corrupted by extensive lobbying campaigns that attempt to influence every legislative act.

Nor has the US judiciary escaped commodification. State judges in the US are mainly elected to their positions, as are state prosecutors. The election of state judges is in the interests of democracy to the extent that, as public officials with a great deal of authority over the lives of the governed and the enforcement of laws and punishments, they should be answerable to the electorate. As with legislative campaigns, however, political contributions influence judicial selection, often in favour of judges who will be tough on petty crime but easy on corporate fraud. Additionally, moneyed interests may find it relatively easy to escape harsh enforcement of laws they may have violated, while those who are without money can find themselves being harshly punished. Whereas laws are supposed to be equally and non-arbitrarily enforced, a judiciary biased by moneyed interests cannot guarantee this element of democracy.

Widespread commodification threatens not only access to the goods people need to flourish, but the stability and integrity of democratic institutions themselves. When the rule of law is threatened by the (direct or indirect) purchase of votes, political speech, public office, or judicial elections, commodification threatens the institutions of democracy. And since these institutions form the very foundations of a democratic society, the commodification of democratic goods themselves is arguably the most pernicious instance of money's overreach.

IV

The question about what should and shouldn't be for sale in a market economy is a pressing one and also a puzzling one. If we endorse a market economy, why should we limit its reach? My argument is that we should do so to the extent that we wish to preserve our democratic institutions and the democratic values they express, including the promotion of human flourishing. Not all market exchanges threaten these institutions or values. But those that do must be curtailed. Democratic goods are those that are essential to the flourishing of a democracy itself. These must remain free of market exchange or monetary influence in order to retain their integrity and value. These democratic goods, and the institutions and caretakers which protect them, not only enable the flourishing of a democracy itself, but also allow for the proper distribution of the goods necessary for citizens themselves to flourish. The necessary goods that citizens require for flourishing must be subject to the rule of law, rather than to the rule of the market.

The question of what money cannot buy is an old one, yet one that seems to become more pressing everyday as more social institutions which protect democracy and human flourishing come under the threat of moneyed interests and unequal market distribution. Renewed and continued attention to the question of how to stem the tide of commodification is essential. This recognition is precisely what motivated this volume, and what makes it so valuable. The contributors come from different continents, different fields of research, and different methodological traditions. But they are asking the same questions and trying to solve the same problem. I am thrilled to see that the question that has motivated my own writing for many years continues to motivate others, that the answers I proposed are informing the work of others, and that the trenchant and urgent issues the editors here define as belonging to a unique field of research they call Commodification Studies will continue to be debated, and hopefully advanced. Our political institutions and our public lives would gain much from it.

ACKNOWLEDGEMENTS

We would like to thank Andy Humphries at Routledge UK for approaching us to edit this handbook, and Holly Martin for seeing it through production. We are also very grateful to Peggy Radin for her excellent preface, written with great style under arduous circumstances.

All of our contributors accepted our comments and endless demands with diligence and efficiency, and we thank them for that, and for their encouragement throughout this process. Many of them also kindly accepted the additional task of serving as referees for other chapter(s), which we greatly appreciated. We extend our thanks to Maxime Menuet from University of Orléans (France) who also refereed one of the chapters, and to Ben Young for his help in preparing final versions of several chapters.

We are grateful to all of the participants at the "Contested Markets: Theories and Controversies" conference held at the Sorbonne in June 2022. This was a lively, interdisciplinary, and international event at which our contributors shared their work in progress, and which felt like the meeting of a true scholarly association – following on the heels of a 2018 conference at the Sorbonne ("The limits of the market: commodification of body and environment") which may turn out to have been the inaugural meeting of what we hope will become the Society for Commodification Studies.

We could not have organized the 2022 conference without the assistance of Pierre Januard, Marina Krivitsky, and Cléo Salion-Girault, or without the support or our sponsors, including University Paris 1 Panthéon-Sorbonne, CNRS, LabeX Dynamite, and the Social Sciences and Humanities Research Council of Canada.

I (Vida Panitch) would like to thank Elodie Bertrand for bringing me into this incredible project, for the multiple invitations to Paris, and for her tirelessness and commitment to the book.

I (Elodie Bertrand) would like to thank Vida Panitch for jumping in this boat with style and a smile. Her enthusiasm and intelligence were greatly appreciated.

More than that, each of us is grateful for the friendship we have built through this process that will long outlast it and is truly priceless.

Many challenging events took place globally, and in our own lives, during the preparation of this book (which began in June 2020). We are forever changed. We are forever connected with one another and our authors, as many of them are with one another. We shared a network, a forward looking project, and a great time in Paris just as the world seemed to be breathing a sigh of relief.

INTRODUCTION

Contested markets and commodification studies

Vida Panitch and Elodie Bertrand

Why a handbook on commodification studies?

Some goods are freely traded as commodities without question or controversy. For other goods, their commodification – their being made available in exchange for money, or their being subject to market valuation and exchange – is hotly contested. "Contested" commodities range from labour and land, to votes, healthcare, and education, to human organs, gametes, and intimate services, to parks and emissions. But in the context of a market economy, what distinguishes these goods as non-commodifiable, or what defines them as contestable commodities? And why should their status as such justify restricting the market choices of rationally consenting parties to otherwise voluntary exchanges?

Although the question of what should and shouldn't be for sale is one that is increasingly captivating to many contemporary theorists, it is not new. Whether certain goods should be exempted from market valuation and exchange has been the subject of argumentation and inquiry for centuries, and the reasons given for such exemptions have been sundry, conflicting, and controversial, as indeed they remain today. Contemporary theorists who take up this question owe a debt to the arguments of Aristotle, Immanuel Kant, Karl Marx, Georg Simmel, and Karl Polanyi who asked at different periods and for different reasons why voluntary exchanges might nonetheless be inappropriate, impermissible, or even unjust due to the nature of the item being sold or to the context in which their sale takes place.

Contemporary theorists who examine this question do so from across the disciplinary spectrum, and ground their answers in diverse scholarly literature and divergent methodological approaches. They are philosophers, economists, jurists, political scientists, sociologists, policy-analysts, feminist theorists, and ecologists, among others. However, scholars addressing questions about the legitimate scope of markets have tended to self-isolate within their respective fields. And this has perhaps been aggravated by further divisions in regionalities and their associated scholarly traditions: analytic, continental, post-colonial, etc. But despite their different disciplinary perspectives and scholarly traditions, what unites these theorists is a shared inquiry into the question of whether or not particular exchanges within a market economy are cause for alarm, if not sanction. In asking the same question, these theorists are participants in and contributors to a unique field of research we refer to as commodification studies. The term "commodification

DOI: 10.4324/9781003188742-1

studies" is not widely in use – as of yet – but we think it ought to be. Important work is being done across the disciplines and this work would benefit from being in a more direct dialogue. This book endeavours to start that dialogue in earnest.

This volume does so by drawing together wide-ranging, interdisciplinary research on the legitimate scope of markets and the kinds of goods that should be exempt therefrom. In bringing diverse answers to this question together for the first time, it aims to finally identify commodification studies as a unique field of scholarly research in its own right. In so doing, it will foster interdisciplinary dialogue, advance scholarship, and enhance education in this controversial, important, and growing field of research. The authors in this volume take diverse and divergent positions on the benefits of markets in general and on the possible harms of specific contested markets in particular. While some favour free markets and others regulation or prohibition, and while some engage in more normative and others in more empirical analysis, our contributors all advance nuanced and thoughtful arguments that engage deeply with the complex set of moral and empirical questions at the heart of commodification studies. This volume collects their new and provocative work together for the first time; work that we hope will come to define the very field of commodification studies.

In this introduction, we specify the central question of commodification studies, and then offer a theoretical overview of its origins. From there we make our case for having organized a volume on commodification studies according to the types of goods and markets that are most widely contested (political goods, physical goods, and environmental goods) and present in brief the arguments of our contributors. We conclude by identifying challenges for future research.

What questions does commodification studies ask?

Commodification studies ultimately aims to answer one question: "why some things should not be for sale" (Satz, 2010) within a market economy? Markets have long been defended and promoted on the grounds that they protect freedom and private property, develop private virtues and social relationships, and promote economic efficiency. While commodification studies asks after the legitimate scope of the market, its central aim is not to mount a case against markets in general, or the market economy as such. Rather what makes the aim of commodification theorists unique is that they focus on the defensibility or permissibility of specific markets that pose distinctive ethical, social, economic, or political problems. The vocabulary used by commodification theorists to describe these particular markets varies. They are said to be "contested" (Radin, 1987), "taboo" (Fiske and Tetlock, 1997), "obnoxious" (Kanbur, 2004), "repugnant" (Roth, 2007), "noxious" (Satz, 2010), "controversial" (Elias, Lacetera and Macis, 2019), and "immoral" (Sandel, 2012).

To explain why some things should not be for sale, commodification theorists must perform several tasks. First, they must determine what *counts* as a "contested commodity" or a "noxious market," even before explaining *why* it is contested or noxious. This is no small task. It is simple to eliminate goods that it is wrongful to possess (slaves, hard drugs, child pornography). It is also simple to eliminate goods that cannot be given away at all, often but not always because they are wrong to possess (Brennan and Jaworski, 2016). Goods that are wrong to give away will inevitably be wrong to sell; and in that sense their sale is not "contestable" but straight up wrong. Slavery is wrong because it is wrong to possess a slave, and you can neither sell nor gift a slave for this reason. Citizenship, however, is something you can possess and renounce, but it is not something you can alienate to another by gift or by sale.

For all remaining goods, commodification theorists must identify which goods can be gifted but not sold. In some cases this is easy: love and friendship can be gifted but not sold, because in the very act of sale they become something else altogether. If you pay someone to be your friend, they become an employee instead, so in that very straightforward sense you cannot sell friendship. Such goods are not contested commodities, therefore, because their sale changes their very nature: what you're paying for isn't what you're getting. True contested commodities are those that can be alienated but not sold, even though their sale would not fundamentally change the good that is thereby acquired. Organs are the quintessential example: they can be gifted and they can be sold without becoming something else altogether, yet they can't be sold without serious concern. Commodification theorists must identify the goods that meet these criteria, and account for the relevant concerns that make their sale contestable.

A second task of commodification studies is to define what commodification actually consists in, because otherwise we could not hope to determine what, if anything, makes it harmful. What commodification is, and what the relevant market principles, norms, processes, or mechanisms involved are, will vary according to authors, in part depending on their particular disciplinary approach. There is, however, meaningful consensus among the authors in this volume that what characterizes a market involves the selling and buying of goods or services, with the use of money, in a context involving multiple participants and where prices are more or less freely set. The term commodification can thus refer to true markets in this sense, or to the purest form of financial markets, but it may also refer to markets in theory or in discourse, or to various degrees of monetization and marketization, such as monetary valuation, enhanced choice, non-monetary exchanges, monetary compensation, taxation, or end-user payment. Different understandings of what makes something a market and what qualifies as commodification is part of the richness of commodification studies. But one of our hopes in putting diverse arguments and methodologies into direct dialogue is to promote greater consensus and shared understandings, and thus to remove barriers to more fruitful developments within the field.

These precisions being made, we can return to the main question of commodification studies: why should some things not be for sale? Answering this question requires both empirical and normative analysis. The empirical part of the project consists in identifying which markets are or were once contested, and which mechanisms have been put in place to contain or address their contestation. This part of the project also consists in identifying markets that would be contested if not highly regulated, such as those in land and labour. To the extent that the question of commodification studies is empirical, the term "commodification" as such is not pejorative; the identification of a "contested market" can be a simple observation of fact, not a normative claim about its immorality.

The normative part of the project consists in identifying markets that should be contested, or in defending the moral appropriateness of existing contestations. For many commodification theorists who engage with the normative component of the project, it also involves determining what should be done about said markets, from banning them, to simply ignoring their contestation, to redesigning the market mechanisms or social norms that underlie their contestation, to advocating for particular forms of state regulation. For some, the solution is simple: a bad market must mean no market. If a market poses problems, it should be forbidden. For these authors regulation alone can't solve the real problem, which is the penetration of markets into areas of social life where they simply don't belong (Walzer, 1983; Sandel, 2012). However, while prohibition may allow us to express our consternation through law, it often just turns white markets black, meaning that the same sales still occur while leaving vendors more vulnerable than ever. For other theorists, regulation rather than prohibition may solve some (or all) of the relevant problems with the markets they identify as noxious. But these theorists must determine what kind of regulation is required. And as with prohibition, we must still ask whether regulations endanger or empower those in the relevant trades. Radin (1996) famously called this the problem of the "double bind."

The origins of commodification studies

The commodifying tendencies of capitalism were made plain by Marx in *Capital*, where he argued that an object's use-value is defined by its own physical properties and the human needs it can be used to satisfy, while its exchange value is defined solely by what it can be traded for. For Marx, "[t]he exchange relation of commodities is characterized precisely by abstraction from their use values." ([1867] 1990, p. 127) The estimation of an object of use-value solely in terms of its exchange value – what can be acquired from it or for it – is an intrinsic element of capitalism. So, therefore, is the exploitation and alienation that arise when human labour and the relations to which it gives rise are themselves estimated solely as tokens of exchange.

Marx famously drew from Aristotle who worried centuries earlier that all exchanges involving goods with incommensurate values would inevitably degrade the goods themselves and produce an injustice between buyer and seller (1996, Bk.V). But it was Immanuel Kant who best articulated the moral conflict engendered by commodification, specifically of personhood itself, to which our labour power, for Marx, is inextricably tied. According to Kant to estimate a bearer of human dignity, or even her powers and parts, as mere instruments of use, is to degrade her moral worth. He stated that "what has a price can be replaced by something else as its equivalence; what on the other hand is raised above all price and therefore admits of no equivalent has a dignity." ([1785] 1996, n4:434) To treat an agent with inherent value as a mere object of instrumental use constitutes the highest order of moral wrong. To the extent that commodification involves assigning price values to the priceless it is inherently wrongful.

In *The Philosophy of Money*, sociologist Georg Simmel articulated a deep concern with precisely the ways in which money had become a stand in for all estimations of value in the modern period. Simmel argued that the tendency of modern capitalism is "to derive from the surface level of economic affairs a guideline that leads to the ultimate values and things of importance in all that is human." ([1900] 1978, p. 361) In this way he issued an early warning with respect to cost-benefit estimations (advocated and popularized by the Utilitarian tradition) by drawing from Kant and Marx. He shared with Marx a worry about the alienation of workers as both their labour and the products thereof become valuable as mere objects of exchange, and with Kant the concern that if the worth of all human relations and objects of value are estimated in monetary terms, everything and *everyone* thereby becomes consumable.

Drawing from each of these insights, Karl Polanyi, in *The Great Transformation* (1944), offered his now classic argument according to which the expansion of capitalism depended entirely on the commodification of labour, land, and money in the eighteenth century. In his view, these three goods are not commodities per se, in the sense that they are not *produced*, or not produced *for sale*, but are nonetheless treated as commodities. The transformation of these goods into commodities involved force and violence (enclosures, abolition of the Poor Laws, end of the gold standard), and was ultimately brought about by the destruction of the social links essential to human relations and life itself. As a result, "instead of the economy being embedded in social relations, social relations [have become] embedded in the economic system." (Polanyi, [1944] 1971, p. 57)

Contemporary commodification debates were renewed in the twentieth century largely by the publication in 1970 of Richard Titmuss' *The Gift Relationship,* in which he presented his comparative research on paid versus unpaid blood donation and concluded that unpaid donation produced both higher quality blood and higher quality social behaviour. These conclusions aroused a debate between economist Kenneth Arrow (1972) and moral philosopher Peter Singer (1973) as to whether paid donation in fact expands freedom and preference satisfaction or limits them by reducing opportunities for altruism. Similar commodification questions have also been ignited in the last few decades by increased evidence of blackmarket organ sales, largely between vendors from developing countries and buyers in wealthy countries. Notable reactions have been offered by ethicists decrying the tendencies of markets to prey on vulnerable persons (Hughes, 2009; Rippon, 2014), and by economists who helpfully sought to examine how market mechanisms could both reduce organ shortages and decrease reliance on persons in desperate circumstances (see Becker and Elias, 2007; Roth, 2007).

In their infamous paper, "The Economics of the Baby Shortage" Elizabeth Landes and Richard Posner (1978) applied a similar line of thinking to argue that market principles could in fact help lessen the "baby shortage" in adoption. But not long after, the infamous Baby M surrogacy case arose in New Jersey (1986) sparking an international outcry in which the parallels between paid pregnancy and child-selling were brought to the fore. This, in conjunction with the Landes and Posner argument, lit a fire for many theorists who had yet to enter the commodification studies fray but who were now determined to argue that efficiency as a norm should govern neither the allocation of children nor many important social goods besides. For many such theorists the worry was that, while markets can yield more efficient outcomes, they do so by pushing out the moral and social norms essential to maintaining meaningful personal relationships and even human flourishing (Anderson, 1993).

Margaret Jane Radin was among those most famously spurred into commodification studies by the Landes and Posner proposal. And writing in the thick of the Baby M case, she argued in her paper "Market-Inalienability" (1987) that certain market exchanges are problematic not because some goods are inalienable (even children, who can be adopted but not sold), but because the mode of market exchange does not always accord the appropriate value to the object of transfer. Many goods can be transferred or alienated by gift or contract, but should not be sold for money. For Radin, these goods should be deemed market-inalienable, to indicate that they lie "outside the marketplace but not outside the realm of social intercourse." (Radin, 1996, p. 18) Radin popularized the use of the term "commodification" to refer "to the social process by which something comes to be apprehended as a commodity, as well as to the state of affairs once the process has taken place." (Radin, 1996, p. xi) She also popularized the term "contested commodities" in her 1996 book of that name, to refer to goods whose monetary valuation regularly occurs but which should nonetheless be protected from unfettered exchange on the grounds of their importance to human flourishing. Radin's work has explicitly and implicitly informed the work of many scholars from across a multitude of disciplines; work that today constitutes the very core of commodification studies.

We leave it to our various contributors to take it from here. They will elaborate further on many of these historical ideas, and will demonstrate the development and expansion of commodification studies within (and beyond) their respective disciplines, and professional and intellectual traditions. In the chapters to come, our contributors elucidate and draw upon the work of many key participants in the commodification studies debates taking place within philosophy (Walzer, 1983; Anderson, 1993; Satz, 2010; Sandel, 2012), political science (Phillips, 2013), cultural studies (Appadurai, 1986), sociology (Zelizer, 1994), law (Radin, 1996; Trebilcock, 1993), and economics (Roth, 2015). Our contributors will draw on the work of these theorists, and many more besides, in application to the broad array of contested commodities that are considered throughout.

The organization of the book

This handbook is organized not by methodology, argument, or discipline, but by category of contestation. We began by asking what goods are typically the subject of commodification debates, and set out to solicit papers from experts on the relevant types of markets. We opted to focus on three types of goods with which commodification studies largely concerns itself, namely political goods (Part 3), bodily goods and services (Part 4), and non-human nature (Part 5). We made this choice precisely so as to weave together the work of diverse scholars from different fields who are nonetheless concerned that the same kinds of goods warrant contestation or even market exemption. In this organizational regard, the volume differs from the other important recent collections that we think helped to shape the field of commodification studies (Ertman and Williams, 2005; Steiner and Trespeuch, 2015; Bertrand and Catto, 2020).

Moreover, the organization of the book according to category of contestation highlights that the justification required for the regulation or prohibition of these individual markets may vary considerably, and arguably *should* vary. Commodification studies can exhibit a tendency towards generalism, or the presumption that one line of reasoning or argumentation can serve as suitable grounds for all market exceptionalism, and can be applied to all categories of contested commodities. Call this the generalist fallacy of commodification studies (Panitch, 2020). But it is a mistake to think that the same arguments that might explain and/or justify the contested status of contract sex, for example, should also be able to explain and justify market exceptions for such goods as animal meat or health care. Each distinct good that is the subject of contestation deserves its own analysis and argumentation (and hence chapter), and that was certainly a significant consideration in the organization of the volume.

We could not set off on this particular organizational endeavour, however, or ask our contributors and readers to accept this approach, without first laying out the relevant background to and theoretical foundations of commodification studies. The volume thus begins by placing commodification studies in a theoretical context, opening with an examination of the traditional arguments that serve as the foundations of the field (Part 1). The first part of the book includes a presentation of traditional pro and anti-market arguments, followed by discussions of the reigning economic, philosophical, and sociological arguments in commodification studies for and against certain markets.

After laying out the theoretical foundations of commodification studies, the book moves on to historicize the field (Part 2). This is essential because a good deal of commodities accepted today as uncontroversial were once deeply contested. A narrow focus on presently contested markets can involve a kind of taking for granted of the acceptability of markets that were once themselves thought to be deeply noxious; along with a failure to appreciate that goods whose commodity status is now contested were once also contested but for different reasons, such as land and certain forms of labour. Part 2 of the book on the history of contested commodities deals with not only land, money, and labour, but also with sacraments and risk, including insurance and gambling.

The remaining three sections of the book, devoted to contested markets in a contemporary context, are organized according to markets in goods we identify as political (Part 3), physical (Part 4), and environmental (Part 5). The goods discussed by contributors to these sections of the book are the site of much fascinating contemporary debate and each chapter helpfully lays out the substance of those debates and advances them with new and original insights and argumentation. We begin with political goods, or goods whose contested status seems directly correlated to some failure not necessarily on the part of the market but on the part of the state. Or rather, goods that are related to and perhaps even integral to our status as citizens, such that their allocation by non-market mechanisms may be required to effectuate our equal political status. The goods addressed in this part of the book include votes, health care, education, prisons, culture, and care work.

We move from there to the category of goods and services that have been central to commodification studies (at least arguably since Titmuss), those relating to the human body. The question of why the gift exchange of such goods is so highly praised, while their sales are so widely impugned, is a fascinating one, but also an urgent one in light of the ever changing sea of prohibitions and regulations that affect so many people's lives. Here our contributors examine the sale of body parts (kidneys) and products (plasma and gametes) as well as the sale of intimate services (commercial surrogacy and contract sex). We have included a chapter on adoption here because it often faces similar objections to surrogacy with respect to the supposed commodification of children.

In the fifth and final part of the book we turn to the commodification of non-human nature. Not only essential to our lives, and necessary to our sustenance and our continued existence, the natural world has an inherent value that is being increasingly acknowledged, even within a Western tradition that has for so long celebrated the widespread exploitation of the earth and its non-human inhabitants. The chapters in this part of the volume address important topics pertaining to non-human nature, be it tangible – parks and forests, water, animals, and seeds – or intangible – natural capital and biodiversity, ecosystem services, and licenses to pollute.

The chapters in the volume address what we take to be the most contested of commodities and were solicited and selected for this reason. The goods that have been deemed most contestable, historically, include above all land, labour, and money loans. Goods that are deemed contestable by more contemporary theorists pertain primarily to the state, and the body; and somewhat less but problematically so, the environment. We have therefore organized the book according to category of contestation as a reflection of the current state of the research in commodification studies. But also because these strike us as the categories of contestation that most urgently require attention. Campaign finance, education, health care, prisons, kidneys, blood, sex, gestation, ova, animals, parks, grains, and water are goods whose sales raise the most pressing questions, restrictions on which require urgent consideration but equally careful justification.

Contested commodities: Theory and controversy

The first part of this book presents the theoretical foundations of commodification studies: the central authors, arguments, questions, and debates that animate the contributions that follow. The first chapter highlights the typical arguments offered in favour of the extension of markets – consent, efficiency, social cohesion – arguments that are often questioned by anti-commodification theorists. This very questioning is then undertaken in the three following chapters. Chapter 2 analyzes traditional arguments against markets by focusing on Polanyi's theory, which undermines the social cohesion plea for markets by illuminating how capitalist markets in labour, land, and money threatened society itself by transforming its very substance into commodities. The two following chapters evaluate contemporary arguments against contested markets, and take up the more normative question of which markets should be contested and why. Chapter 3 deals with the economic externality objection, and Chapter 4 with philosophical corruption and inequality objections to contested markets. These two chapters expose the limits of various classical pro-market arguments, but also make a plea for more sophisticated arguments against unfettered markets, which must be grounded in a conception of justice. Chapter 5 presents the sociological approach to contested markets taken by classical and contemporary economic sociologists, and offers a valuable heuristic device for undertaking empirical analysis of moral contestation and for understanding institutional responses to it.

In Chapter 1, Marie Daou and Alain Marciano present the main arguments in favour of markets. The first one is that market exchange is voluntary, and hence respects freedom of consent. It is this consent that gives market transactions their legitimacy. Such transactions also respect individual private property rights, and thus, again, guarantee a form of individual freedom. The second type of argument in favour of markets is moral, and is here detailed in three respects: markets drive individual self-interest towards public interest; they transform individuals so that they are more virtuous; they make compatible various individual desires and thereby contribute to social order. The third argument in favour of markets is efficiency, and Daou and Marciano examine two traditional accounts thereof: the Walrasian and the Austrian.

In Chapter 2, Nicolas Postel and Richard Sobel explore classical anti-commodification arguments. They offer a plea for commodification studies to stop misusing the concept of fictitious commodities, and focus on the intensification of market norms rather than on the extension of markets. Reconstructing Polanyi's institutionalist thought, they stress that his concept of fictitious commodities applies only to land, labour and money, that are not commodities but *have to be* treated as commodities so that capitalism may function. Polanyi would not have described capitalism as an unlimited extension of markets, but rather as requiring from its very origin the commodification of what are not commodities, namely its three factors of production. However, since land is the place of living, labour is human life, and money is the social cement of economic and social relationships, these fictitious commodities form the substance of society. Their commodification is necessary but socially unbearable: it thus leads to the disembeddedness of the economic sphere and to social and economic disaster. The development of capitalism (between the end of the eighteenth century and the inter-war period) caused the destruction of society, for Polanyi. Postel and Sobel invite us to think about commodification not so much in the form of the extension of markets, but rather as a deepening of market logic.

Chapter 3 by Elodie Bertrand focuses on the economic argument for identifying contested markets, namely negative externalities. Commodification studies often appeals to the externalities argument, taken from standard welfare economics, according to which some market exchanges produce negative effects on third parties that are not taken into account by participants, leading to inefficient results. This argument aims to undermine the efficiency thesis in favour of markets. In commodification studies, these externalities justify banning, or regulating certain markets, such as those that cause pollution. Some authors include *pecuniary* externalities, i.e. changes in prices, or in conditions of choice, which is a version of the inequality argument against markets – this is typically the case with markets for organs. Other authors focus on *moral* externalities, i.e. offence, that is the "repugnance" argument against markets – typically applied to contract sex or paid surrogacy. The externality argument for market-inalienability chooses to evaluate markets relative to their efficiency, and makes moral and political presuppositions on the legitimacy of public intervention. In this chapter, Bertrand argues that while the concept of negative externalities remains useful in analyzing the unintended consequences of certain markets, what is needed is in fact a theory of justice to enable us to determine which externalities are indeed troubling enough to warrant limits to commodification.

Chapter 4 by Vida Panitch presents and critically evaluates the central contributions of philosophical anti-commodification (PAC) theory. PAC theorists have in the main offered two kinds of arguments against the commodification of certain important goods. Theorists who offer corruption arguments hold that the sale of certain goods for money, or their exchange via market mechanisms, erodes something of significant value, be it the inherent meaning of the good itself, the value of important social norms, or the value of human flourishing. Theorists who offer equality arguments hold that the sale of certain goods for money, or their exchange via market mechanisms, erodes important relations of equality in which we ought to stand with one another, be they relations of equality in resource shares, in moral dignity, or in democratic status. Panitch argues that corruption-based PAC arguments depend on claims either empirically or morally unsound and that equality-based views cannot tell us which goods to withhold from sale without appealing to corruption claims of their own. She goes on to offer a brief defence of an alternative justice-based argument according to which the goods that should be exempt from sale are those whose market valuation and exchange would impede the satisfaction of the principles of justice appropriate to a liberal society.

Chapter 5 by Philippe Steiner presents the sociological account of market contestation, highlighting the specificity of the sociological approach to commodification studies, which takes morals (people's ideas about the right and the wrong) as a social fact. Classical economic sociology examined the relationships between morals and markets from various angles: from Durkheim's emphasis on how public opinion regulates markets (by its perception and judgment of inequalities, for example) to Weber's tensions between market economies and moral values. The author's own empirical approach to the contemporary sociological analysis of contested markets identifies two types of vulnerable people – those endangered by the existence of certain markets and those endangered by their absence – as well as the "cooling" institutional devices that offer protection to those endangered by the existence of said markets.

Contested commodities of the past

After having presented the theoretical foundations of commodification studies, it was important to historicize contested markets. Most of the markets we today take for granted were once contested. Recall, for example, that opera singers in the seventeenth century were not paid for their performances, and canonical medieval law forbade professors from selling their knowledge (Davis, 2000). The historical journey in this part of the book illustrates how some moral contestations led to the banning of certain markets (slavery as a case in point), or to regulations that transformed their contested status (labour above all else). It also illustrates many of the social, conceptual, and legal processes that were necessary to transform certain things into commodities. We solicited chapters on land, labour, and money loans; and we chose to complete the historical picture with chapters on insurance and gambling since their commodification reflects the longstanding contestation of the monetization of risk. We present these historically contested markets in the order of the periods that are examined, from the Middle-Age (money loans and sacraments) to the most recent decade (internet gambling).

These ancient theoretical debates raise many issues that are still controversial today in commodification studies. Chapter 8 on labour alludes to contemporary debates on body parts and intimate services in asking similar questions as to what constitutes (physical) labour and where the moral limitations of a labour contract should lie. Chapter 6 on land foreshadows contemporary debates on markets involving non-human nature and the role of the commons. In Chapter 7, we see the emergence of the view of money loans and sacraments as political goods in the sense that they have to be distributed so as to protect the status of persons, and specifically the poor. Chapter 10 on insurance also raises questions about the commodification of persons and the kinds of protections they are owed by states, and in this regard serves as an effective transition from the historical analysis of the volume to its discussion of political goods.

Chapter 6 by Pierre Crétois explores the historical commodification of land. He begins in Ancient Rome, where land possession determined the status of citizen, and where market transfers thereof were impermissible. In the Feudal period, Crétois continues, land was owned only by masters, was mainly transferred by war, and peasants had a common right to usage of land. This period was followed by the advent of the famous enclosure movement, which itself was intimately connected to the development of the modern conception of private property as absolute. The violence of land enclosures exemplified the advent of property as we understand it today, and represented the commodification of land, provoking rural exodus and poverty that fed the burgeoning labour market in urban centres. The ownership of land was central to early debates about the efficiency and political importance of commons. Crétois concludes that land is still not a commodity like others, and should not be regarded as such, as demonstrated by the ecological crises and increasing movements in favour of preserving the commons.

Chapter 7 by Pierre Januard and André Lapidus examines money and sacraments whose sales were considered sins (of usury and simony) in Christian theology and hence as socially reprehensible practices during the Middle-Age. The authors turn to the work of Thomas Aquinas to explore the reprehensibility of these monetized practices in his time. On his view, they demonstrate, the commodification of money itself was impossible for ontological reasons (since money is destroyed in its use). Besides, a price for some sacraments (like ordination) would be too high – or indeed impossible – since no amount of material wealth could ever be rendered equivalent to spiritual wealth. While for other sacraments (like mass), compensation would have been a permissible and common practice (so that the priest could survive), but would not have been perceived as having a price. The debates examined in this chapter prefigure contemporary discussions about the differences between tariffs, compensation, and market prices.

Chapter 8 by François Vatin explores the commodification of labour. Vatin highlights the liberal criticism of contract labour according to which, because it is sold for a long period of time and its requirements can be indeterminate, it is too akin to slavery to be permissible. He argues that this criticism was only put to rest with the development of the conception of limited servitude (limited both in time and in content), and that this in turn made the development of the modern labour market possible. Moreover, Vatin demonstrates, the apparent limitation of servitude was said to preserve the (formal) freedom of the labourer, thus further dispelling the liberal objection that labour could not be distinguished from indentured servitude. This means that, paradoxically, labour was taken out from ordinary commodities (whose sale generally implies freedom of use) to become a full one.

Chapter 9 by Marie Trespeuch focuses on gambling, and specifically on wagering games in France as an example of a contested market that was (almost) banned until the nineteenth century. The first step in the commodification of gambling was the creation of state monopolies, serving "general interest" (tourism through casinos, horse breeding through horse races). The market then developed most significantly in the 1980s, with diversification leading to competition between monopolies. In the new millennium, internet gambling developed, which the European Commission deregulated despite France's appeal to worries about social disorder and individual vulnerability, and the market is now open to international competition. Trespeuch examines, on the one hand, the transformation of moral contestation to gambling (from public disorder and protecting the poor to the medicalization of addiction) and, on the other, the processes put in place to address this contestation, with the aims of protecting populations viewed as vulnerable (poor, children, excessive gamblers), through everything from entrance fees in casinos, to restrictions on access to apps in individualized devices and internet channels.

Chapter 10 by Emily Nacol explores the question of whether insurance counts as a commodity, and a contestable one at that. The central premise of the chapter is that the commodification of insurance entailed other processes of commodification, mainly of risk and of human life. Drawing on examples from Britain between 1500–1800, Nacol argues that insurance is best understood as a group of technologies, practices, and institutions that have offered individuals and groups security and support in the face of an unknown future. As insurance developed, it contributed to the contestable commodification of other important goods. First, insurance practitioners commodified risk by making it the object of the insurance settlement. As insurers became keen to hedge against risk, they also devised ways of making human beings more insurable. Second, insurance – especially life insurance – blurred the line between property and people, making human beings subject to commodification and speculation in ways that violated their freedom and moral status as persons. Nacol concludes that insurance has an ambiguous legacy that continues to warrant our critical attention because of the troubling commodifying tendencies to which it gave rise and continues to contribute.

Contested commodities of the present

The remaining three sections of the book, devoted to contested markets in a contemporary context, are organized according to markets in goods we identify as political, physical, and environmental. We will introduce each of the three following sections with an account of what the contested commodities in that section of the book have in common. But it is worth noting here that goods belonging to each of the three different categories may have more in common than our taxonomy could seem to suggest. To the extent that political goods include certain of the necessary goods we need to survive (such as health), we might well have included bodily goods such as organs, and environmental goods such as water under this same mantle as well. And to the extent that bodily goods refer to our physical bodies, we might well have included animals here, while under intimate services, we might well have included care. Our taxonomy itself is thus open to debate, which we welcome.

Political goods

We begin our presentation of contemporary commodification debates with a series of chapters exploring the contested commodification of political goods, which include both civic goods (votes, prisons, culture) and necessary goods (health, education, care). These goods are integral to our status as citizens. And as a number of contributors to this section of the volume argue, this necessitates their allocation by non-market mechanisms to preserve and effectuate our equal political status. For other contributors to this section, however, the fact that these goods may be integral to our equal political status has no bearing – or at least less bearing than we might expect – on whether these goods can or should be commodified.

That these goods are political seems to necessarily implicate the state in their provision, or at least in their guaranteed accessibility. If their distribution via principles others than ability to pay is required, then a failure to meet the appropriate allocation of these goods is squarely a reflection of some failure on the part of the state. While it may be the state's responsibility to regulate or prohibit other markets found genuinely noxious, the state's failure to involve itself in the regulated distribution of political goods seems almost definitionally troubling in light of the very nature of the goods themselves. This position, however, is not taken as given by all the contributors to this section of the book, and the connective tissue that runs through the chapters in this section is the question of whether or not state allocation is indeed necessary to the just distribution of political goods; if not, why not, and if so, how?

Chapter 11 by Jason Brennan and Christopher Freiman examines the contentious topic of vote selling. For many this is the most important of political goods, that can neither be alienated for free nor for money. This is a view that the authors challenge. They argue against what they take to be the most substantial objection to commodifying votes, which holds that the commodification of votes would corrupt democracy by preventing states from implementing policies which best serve citizens' interests or which best reflect their preferences. The authors challenge this argument by showing, first, that paying people to vote is morally superior to compulsory voting, second, that certain forms of vote commodification do not run afoul of this objection, and third, that the objections to vote commodification turn out to apply also to many uncommodified votes.

Chapter 12 by L. Chad Horne addresses the question of commodified health care. Horne asks whether health care is, or should be, a commodity, on the understanding that a commodity is a good the production, distribution, and consumption of which is properly governed by the norms of the marketplace. He argues that one perspective from which health care should clearly *not* be a commodity is the perspective of standard welfare economics. Markets for health care and health insurance suffer many sources of inefficiency, and, for Horne, this explains at least in part why no developed country leaves the provision of care to the unregulated market. Although philosophers have sought a deeper and perhaps more moralized rationale for the refusal to treat health care as a commodity, grounded in concerns of distributive justice or of the preservation of important social values like community or solidarity, Horne examines these supposedly deeper arguments and finds them all inconclusive. Only the appeal to efficiency, he concludes, can in fact provide a complete and appropriately nuanced account of the imperative to decommodify health care.

Chapter 13 by Harry Brighouse addresses the topic of education. Primary and secondary level schooling are often thought of as the least commodified of public services: they are typically funded, regulated, and provided by the government, and are often compulsory. But some recent "market" reforms appear to commodify education – the advent of the charter school system in the US primarily, which promises to increase parental choice through the use of market mechanisms. But, Brighouse argues, once it is understood that even in traditional models, markets played a very large role in schooling provision, it is not clear that these reforms really increase, as opposed to just make more transparent, the extent of commodification in primary and secondary education. Brighouse argues that concerns about commodification should not guide educational decision-makers: what should guide them is the related question of what educational goods a system produces and how that system can best distribute those goods. Provided those goods are distributed in the right way, it should not matter whether or not market mechanisms are involved.

Chapter 14 by Jonathan Peterson addresses questions about commodification in the sphere of security and prisons. A broad range of institutions and practices, including policing, punitive incarceration, and immigration detention, raise commodification concerns in this sphere. In this chapter, Peterson surveys forms of commodification in the carceral system specifically and evaluates arguments according to which commodification in the context of punitive incarceration (private prisons and the sale of inmates' labour) is morally wrong or unjust. He agrees that some current practices of carceral commodification are seriously harmful, but leaves open whether this conclusion calls for reform or an end to commodification in the carceral system altogether. However, he offers compelling argumentation according to which commodification of prisons and prisoners' labour should strike us as especially objectionable in the context of a history of race-based oppression. In such contexts, the commodification of incarceration continues a pattern of racial subordination and carries a symbolic message of unequal status.

Chapter 15 by Michael Joel Kessler advances a novel objection to markets in cultural goods, according to which they can, in certain contexts, lead to and entrench objectionable forms of cultural appropriation. In this way, the commodification of cultural goods (Indigenous art work and customs, for example) is wrong to the extent that it intensifies a deeper wrong. While the connection between cultural commodification and cultural appropriation is contingent rather than necessary, the connection can be quite strong, and mutually re-enforcing, according to Kessler. He argues that as with many contested commodities, while money can exacerbate the issue, money is not the main problem when thinking about markets in cultural goods. Rather, the key issue is power: when the goods of one's own culture are under the control of another culture, there are strong moral reasons to doubt that their commodification, or acquisition by the dominant group, can be legitimate. As such, Kessler concludes that to the extent that there is a reasonable worry about cultural appropriation, there is a justifiable worry about the existence of markets in cultural goods.

Chapter 16 by Jennifer Nedelsky examines the commodification of care. Care is routinely provided both as a commodity (paid care) and as unpaid care, usually by women. All care is treated as of low value and care givers, paid and unpaid, are seen as being of low status. This devaluing of care and those who do it infects all forms of care, making care a major component of social hierarchy and inequality. Since commodified care rests on and maintains economic, racial and gendered inequalities, the solution is not more commodification (like wages for housework), according to Nedelsky, but a norm of universal, unpaid care-giving, according to which everyone, regardless of the "importance" of their work, would contribute about 22 hours a week of unpaid care to family. This would, she argues, redress four pressing problems: the failure to recognize the value of care; how care structures inequalities; family stress from incompatible demands of work and care; and the ignorance of policymakers about the care that life requires. These solutions rest on the revaluing of care that would arise when everyone understands themselves as both a caregiver and a care receiver.

Commodification and the body

We turn at this juncture to debates around the commodification of the body, including body parts and products, and intimate services. The assignment of price values to the body, the transfer of cash to providers of bodily goods and services in the form of payment or even compensation, and the decriminalization or deregulation of commodified bodily services have been the subject of much consternation and controversy among activists, academics, jurists, politicians and policy makers alike. That cash or even cash valuation degrades the providers of such a good or the social norms (like altruism) that are thought appropriate to their exchange is a tough case to mount, and yet is equally tough to combat. For the most part, contributors to this section of book argue that regulation can address the most pressing concerns with bodily commodification. That leading theorists who evaluate the commodification of physical goods now largely endorse regulation over prohibition is a fairly new phenomenon, and is certainly representative of significant developments in the field in recent years.

The body as site of contested commodification is both old and new. Debates have raged over sex work for centuries, grounded largely in religious consternation and only relatively recently based on feminist concerns. Debates raged a century ago over the purchase of cadavers by medical schools and of skeletons by medical offices (although much of this had to do with how those cadavers and skeletons were come by) (Carney, 2011). Debates were spurred in the 1970s over payment to blood donors by the publication of *The Gift Relationship* (Titmuss, 1970). Debates raged over surrogacy in the 1980s in the wake of the Baby M trial. Debates about payments for ova were sparked in the 1990s when erotic photographer Ron Harris infamously used his website to auction off the eggs of his models. Some of these debates have intensified with advances in medical technology. This has made debates about the body's permissible commodification all the more urgent, because, while vendors in body sales are often vulnerable, buyers themselves are often desperate.

Chapter 17 by James Stacey Taylor takes up the question of the moral permissibility of markets in human organs (particularly kidneys), which are often rejected based on worries about the authenticity of consent on the part of desperate sellers (calling into question the consent argument in favour of markets presented in Chapter 1). Taylor, however, takes the position that a moral concern for human well-being – in particular the well-being of those who desperately need an organ transplant – supports the position that a market in human organs is morally permissible. To defend his position, Taylor argues that if such markets were to exist, persons would consent to participate in them as organ buyers and organ sellers, and that we can infer from said consent that they believe this would make them better off. He considers two serious challenges to this, however; first that the consent of some of the sellers will not be genuine, and second, that we cannot infer from a person's participation in a market that she would prefer for that market to exist. The first of these objections is unsound, Taylor argues, but the second is sound. Rather than merely asking if a person would consent to transact in a market if it existed, we should also ask if she would consent to that market being allowed to exist in the first place. Only if the answer to both of these questions is affirmative, Taylor contends, can we infer that she believes that she would be made better off by participating in the market. He concludes that this could support allowing markets in some human organs.

Chapter 18 by Peter M. Jaworski explores the commercial model of plasma collection. He demonstrates that compensation has a record of generating plasma collection surpluses, while non-commercial models operate at plasma collection deficits. The non-commercial model exposes patients who rely on plasma and plasma products to foreseeable and avoidable risk. One set of arguments typically offered in support of payment prohibitions appeal to donor altruism and community solidarity (which were Titmuss' main concerns), and another set appeal to a variety of possible harms to donors, including donor health, donor dignity, and wrongful exploitation concerns. Jaworski explores each of these arguments but finds them inadequate to support bans on paid plasma provision given the impacts that deficits therein have on patient health and well-being, especially given that the proper regulation of the commercial model can address most if not all of these concerns.

Chapter 19 by Kimberly D. Krawiec explores commodification debates in the gamete market. She employs the payment guidelines laid out by the American Society for Reproductive Medicine (ASRM) as a lens through which to understand the controversy around oocyte commodification as compared to sperm commodification. Although the physically invasive nature of egg donation likely contributes to the significant difference in moral controversy generated by these two practices, researchers have argued that presumptions regarding the differing (altruistic vs pecuniary) motivations of women and men engaged in reproductive activity on behalf of others significantly shapes ethical debates about gamete commodification as well. Krawiec also examines the arguments raised (and rejected) in the *Kamakahi* litigation, in which oocyte donors in the US brought an anti-trust lawsuit against the ASRM for price-capping practices. According to Krawiec, this case should be of interest to all observers and researchers of contested markets because the arguments raised in defence of price-capping in the oocyte market are the very corruption, undue influence, exploitation, and equality of access arguments that permeate commodification debates more generally.

Chapter 20 by Laurie J. Shrage takes up one of the most infamous contested commodities – contract sex. She notes that there is a growing consensus among human rights activists, feminists, health organizations, and progressive democratic governments that soliciting or accepting payment for sex should not be a crime. Criminalizing the activities of service providers does little to protect them from harm and, instead, makes their livelihood much less safe by pushing it underground, generally without deterring markets in sexual services. Moreover, whatever concerns we may have with the commodification of sex are not allayed by simply turning the white market for sex black. Shrage points out, however, there is much less consensus among social reformers about the conditions under which payment for sex should be permissible or impermissible (when it becomes unacceptably exploitative or manipulative, for example). While debates about sex work remain stuck on the question of criminalization, Shrage argues it is high time the debate turn to issues of legalization – where the relevant question is about how governments should regulate sex as an economic activity in order to serve and protect sellers of contract sex. Shrage draws examples from cannabis regulation in the US to generate helpful conclusions regarding the legalization, as opposed to criminalization, of markets in sexual services.

Chapter 21 by Stephen Wilkinson makes a meaningful contribution to ongoing debates about the ethics of paid surrogacy by explaining, reconstructing, and subjecting to scrutiny many of the numerous ethical, philosophical, and policy arguments directed against this practice. He evaluates three main types of arguments against paid surrogacy, first, that paid surrogacy is a form of baby-selling, second, that it is exploitative and depends on impoverished consent, and third that it is degrading and instrumentalizing of surrogates and/or their children by treating them as objects of use rather than persons worthy of respect and consideration. Wilkinson engages deeply and meaningfully with each of these objections but ultimately finds them unpersuasive. Although he concedes the seriousness of the second set of worries, he offers an insightful and compelling proposal for reform. He argues for what he calls fair trade surrogacy, to alleviate exploitation and coercion concerns in the context of global commercial surrogacy arrangements in particular.

Chapter 22 by Martha M. Ertman discusses the well-known dangers of commodification in adoption, but also highlights the positive role of payments in adoption processes. These include payments to legal, medical, and social work professionals and to birth parents for expenses such as psychotherapy, maternity clothes and living expenses, along with state subsidies that enable people to adopt children out of foster care. The chapter argues that adoption contracts can be either exploitative or welfare-enhancing, but that neither aligns perfectly with the presence or absence of payment. Ertman proposes a "Mosaic" view as an alternative to the extreme options of understanding adoption as either market-inalienable or completely commodifiable, as there are elements of each in all adoption contracts. And she argues that it offers a more nuanced focus on who controls and benefits from financial contracts in adoption. Ertman concludes that a "Mosaic" theory of commodification in adoption supports bans on outright baby-selling but also allows courts to enforce welfare-enhancing adoption contracts.

Commodification and the environment

While debates over environmental commodification began as early as the 1960s, the contemporary philosophical and legal anti-commodification literature has largely centered on civic and bodily goods, and did not significantly address environmental questions. This section of the volume aims to rectify this oversight. The first three chapters in this section examine successively three market-oriented instruments recently invented to deal with environmental problems: offset markets (in the 1970s), negotiable permits markets (in the 1980s), and payments for ecosystem services (in the 2000s), and thus focus on three main threats to non-human nature: erosion of biodiversity, emissions, and the destruction of ecosystems. The three subsequent chapters examine the commodification of human sources of sustenance: water, animal products, and seeds. As sustenance related goods, these may rightly qualify as necessary goods and hence political goods, proper access to which may not be satisfiable through market distribution. The last chapter of this section, on parks and forests, brings us full circle back to the question of land commodification which was the very first of the contested commodities explored in this volume.

This section of the book is illustrative of several trends in commodification practice, and in debates among commodification theorists. First, the commodification of emissions and ecosystems is an example of a type of commodification that first only existed in economic theory, and was then translated into practice – and their contested status transitioned from theoretical objection to empirical concern. Environmental issues more generally offer us a window into the domino effect (Radin, 1996) that can occur when the mere conceptualization of a good in monetary terms leads to its total commodification. Second, the goods examined in this section illustrate numerous degrees of commodification (from monetary valuation to financial markets through end-user payment, in-kind compensation, monetary compensation, etc.), demonstrating just how the examination of non-human nature as a problem for commodification studies can help us sharpen our very understanding of what commodification consists in.

These chapters also illustrate that while various regulation mechanisms proposed by contributors to the previous section may be adequate to resolve moral contestation in the realm of the body, opposition to the commodification of environmental goods remains stringent in the face of proposed market regulation. Contributors to the section on the body more or less universally reject prohibitions, and offer myriad regulatory proposals for mitigating the harms of body markets that would avoid creating the even greater harms involved in banning them. Many contributors to the section on the environment, however, are more sympathetic to decommodification. For example, although a rejection of the ownership relation with the body has been proposed as a solution to the contested commodification of physical goods (Radin, 1996; Phillips, 2013), in this volume we find little uptake of this idea when it comes to the body, but a good deal when it comes to the natural world. Contributors to the section on the environment are more adamant that a radical reconceptualization of the value of the non-human world is in order, as is the relationship between humans and non-human nature.

Chapter 23 by John O'Neill explores the topics of natural capital and biodiversity. O'Neill argues that while environmental problems are often thought to come from market failures, they come instead from commodification itself. He defines commodification both as the process of market exchange and as the conceptualization of a good as marketable. The notion of natural capital may encompass ecosystem services, compensation, substitutability, monetization, and markets. With respect to offset markets, in particular, commodification first and foremost favours growth and hence environmental destruction. It also means that an ecosystem is valued according to certain use-related features only and is assumed to be substitutable with any other ecosystem characterized by the same features, whereas ecosystem value is and must be seen to be multidimensional and non-substitutable. Finally, he argues, offset markets face distributional objections, among which is the concern that they measure value according to willingness to pay. Set against wealth inequality this has the problematic outcomes that the rich can be seen to value the natural world more than the poor.

Chapter 24 by Nathalie Berta focuses on emissions trading, both in terms of how these markets are defended in economic theory and in political debates, and in terms of how they function in practice. The idea of markets in emission emerged in the 1960s in economic theory, but it was isolated: economists were at that time promoting taxes, which were widely rejected by US Congress. Monetizing pollution was highly contested, and a tax on outputs was viewed as an "immoral license to pollute." This contestation progressively faded away, Berta demonstrates, and the conceptualization of pollution as an externality became more widely accepted. Moral contestation diminished when the resistance of industry to regulations became organized and brought with it the idea that direct control would carry regulatory and compliance costs. From the 1980s, the idea and practice of "cap-and-trade" quickly expanded for both sulfur dioxide, and carbon dioxide. At this stage, markets were viewed as preferable to taxes because equilibrium was assumed to be achievable at no cost, which, as Berta shows, is highly questionable.

Chapter 25 by Julia Martin-Ortega and her co-authors examines how the very concept of ecosystem services both contributed to and reflects the commodification of non-human nature. The widespread use of the concept was encouraged by the United Nations, and allows for monetary valuation of the natural world, which has become dominant in both policy and industry decision-making. The conceptualization was, ironically, first developed to help protect nature by insisting that its value be taken into account. But estimating the value of nature in terms of its value *for* humans, and monetizing ecosystems in accordance with the services they can provide or that can be provided from them, paved the way for widespread commodification of the natural world. Once monetized, ecosystem services avail themselves to exchanges and thus to the conceptualization of ecosystems as interchangeable objects of use. Building on O'Neill's insights, Ortega et al. argue that the commodification of non-human nature through its conceptualization in terms of the services it can provide is both reductivist and inequitable.

Chapter 26 by Adrian Walsh identifies numerous problems posed by the commodification of water. He considers but sets aside the arguments according to which assigning price values to water could violate certain expressive norms and run counter to the understanding of nature as having an intrinsic value, either in environmental terms or in spiritual terms. He focuses instead on the distributive effects of the commodification of water, and in particular on the risks of making water available on the basis of ability to pay. This, he argues, is not inevitably wrong, provided everyone's basic need for water is sufficiently satisfied. Water is a basic need. But since it is possible for this need to be satisfied to a sufficient degree without curtailing all water commodification, the relevant responsibility falls on states to ensure sufficiency. Following Panitch's sufficientarian approach (see Chapter 4), Walsh argues that the commodification of water is possible when basic needs are met. To the extent that markets impede the satisfaction of this basic need, they should be blocked. But provided this need is being satisfied, markets need not be blocked altogether. In this sense, water is here treated as a political good.

Chapter 27 by Aksel Braanen Sterri concerns farm animals, and starts from the position that animals have interests that matter, interests in many ways equivalent to those of humans. Markets for farm animals create harms, or negative externalities, for animals themselves, namely their pain and untimely death. But complete decommodification would prevent animals from being brought into existence at all and thus from living lives that are ultimately worth living. As such, Sterri argues that the commodification of animals is ultimately in their best interest, provided that we can ensure their lives are indeed worth living, even if they are ended for the purposes of human consumption. We can do this, on his view, not by decommodifying meat, but by commodifying animal welfare through markets or taxation (i.e. by imposing a cost on the production of the relevant externality). Sterri argues for a commodified solution to a market problem, and he favours a tax on animal suffering and death. Sterri's proposal to commodify animal welfare aims to mitigate the harm done to animals themselves, by commodifying the externalities created by the market for meat on humans who are pained by animal suffering.

Chapter 28 by Fabien Girard, Christine Frison and Christine Noiville focuses on seeds, understood as physical grains and genetic resources. The market for seeds is an extended market, related to modern agriculture, that has always been contested at its margins, but whose contestation has now grown steadily for over a decade. The authors begin by examining the historical drivers of seed commodification, mainly the biotech revolution and the advent of intellectual property rights, which gave birth to agricultural oligopolies and a phenomenon they describe as "new enclosures." The authors go on to analyze various experiments in the decommodification of seeds (understanding them as common property, or reestablishing local sovereignty), as a means of exploring what is gained and what is lost by markets in seed. The authors conclude that the existence of these attempts at decommodification raises questions about the potential for coexistence between a market and a non-market conceptualization and allocation of seeds.

Chapter 29 by Catherine Larrère concludes this book by taking up the first commodity examined in it, namely land. Her contribution deals with specific forms of land (de)commodification, namely national parks and forests. As we saw in some of the previous chapters, ecological movements endorse the idea of returning to common property to oppose private property and commodification. Larrère argues, however, that commoning must be understood as distinct from state appropriation. For her, the central question is, to the extent that parks and forests cannot be private, must they necessarily be public? She says no, because there is also a third option, that is the commons (understood as a community who rules the use of a free access resource); and the commons stand not only in opposition to the private realm, but also to the public. Larrère examines two historical episodes in which this is well demonstrated. First, when the nineteenth-century French engineers of forests appealed to the state to save mountain forests against the deforestation due to the communal traditional uses. And second, when US national parks were created by destroying commons, and delimiting new enclosures (with the exclusion of traditional inhabitants). The author concludes that the state cannot fully protect against commodification (indeed, it can contribute to it by enclosures and economic valuation); so it is necessary that the state protects commons in the form of parks and forests.

Concluding remarks: Alternative markets and market alternatives

The chapters included in this volume are illustrative of the richness and diversity of commodification studies. But the variety of approaches, methodologies, and proposed solutions offered by our contributors should not obscure the strong commonalities and points of agreement among them. The authors share the view that commodification – whether this refers to mere exchange, monetary exchange, monetary valuation, efficiency norms, etc. – is not a neutral mechanism and has to be questioned, on both theoretical and empirical grounds. As is typical in a collection, but perhaps all the more so here given the diversity of views presented, we as editors do not endorse all the arguments offered, although we find them all to serve as instructive, illuminating, and provocative contributions to the field.

Rare are the chapters that conclude in favour of complete decommodification. But equally rare are chapters that defend free markets as a response to contested commodification. The majority of contributors conclude in favour of some type of regulation that could address the commodification concerns they identify as most pressing. Some authors argue for partial decommodification that might involve the blocking of markets only to the extent that they interfere with the satisfaction of basic needs. Some invoke appeals to equality and propose redistributive solutions that could render certain markets unlikely, harmless, or unnecessary. Others offer proposals for market expansion or the introduction of new markets as a strategy of addressing externalities generated by those they contest. Others still endorse a total reconceptualization of the very ideas of property and ownership.

An interesting commonality among the chapters is a rejection of the kind of binatristic thinking popular among certain commodification theorists. One such binarism is entailed in the widespread view that the state and the market are inevitable distributive opponents, such that the allocation of a good via one entails non-allocation of that good via the other. This binaristic assumption is problematic for a number of reasons identified by various contributors. The state may be an alternative to markets in some sense, but it is not only an alternative, nor the only alternative. Often the state participates in the creation of markets, not only by defining and enforcing property rights (this is crucial for seeds, for example, see Chapter 28) or by acting as a supplier (see Chapter 9 on gambling), but also by enforcing regulations and offering social protection, thereby potentially resolving the very sources of a market's contested status (see Chapter 8 on labour). Moreover, when the state's role is to provide an alternative to markets, it can often do as poorly as markets, as may be the case with schooling (see Chapter 13). And, as suggested in Chapter 2, the state can itself infuse market norms in supposedly non-market spheres of human activity, thereby participating in the intensification of markets (as is the case, for example, with new public management).

There is also a great deal of *moral* binarism in anti-commodification arguments (Bertrand, 2019). For critics of commodification, gift-giving is often regarded as altruistic and market-exchange as self-interested, while the latter mode of exchange is viewed as antagonistic to the former. These kinds of arguments depend on what Panitch in Chapter 4 identifies as an empirical claim (markets crowd out altruism) and a moral claim (self-interest is always bad and altruism is always good). Many authors in this volume take issue with this binarism and reject it for a variety of reasons. For one, it simply isn't true that the introduction of a market in a particular good eclipses its altruistic exchange (see Chapter 19 on plasma, for example). For another, commodified and non-commodified versions of the same good can coexist (sex, as a prime example) such that the market exchange of one should not be thought to destroy or denigrate the gift exchange of the other. Moreover, there is altruism present along with trust in almost any market exchange (Macauley, 1963; Rose, 1992; Zelizer, 1994), while gift-giving can itself be an act of self-interest to the extent that the giver is seeking social approval or symbolic capital (Bourdieu, 1977; Lordon, 2006; Steiner, 2016). Ertman (in Chapter 22) invites us to use a "mosaic" framework for thinking about commodification in the context of adoption, and this may be a useful framing for other authors keen to upend binaristic thinking about many other markets as well. Indeed, the rejection of binarism might well represent a new feature of commodification studies itself.

Before inviting our contributors to take over the discussion we would like to address – or at least acknowledge – two potential challenges that our conceptualization of commodification studies may face, and along with it, our organization of the volume and the rationale we have offered for it. As we outlined earlier, we had good reason to organize this book according to discrete contested commodities, or at least according to the categories of contestation to which we think they belong. But there is of course a downside to this, which is that treating contested commodification discretely, or individualized by commodity, may be to miss the broader themes and concerns that connect the contestation of these goods, and the larger questions their shared contested status should perhaps have us asking. If we focus narrowly on discrete goods, do we miss broader threats to social norms, practices, and relationships that the increased expansion of markets may carry?

Thankfully our contributors have solved this problem for us. We have asked them to focus on a singular commodity and they have done just that, but so much more besides. The historical chapters remind us of the radical and deleterious social shifts that occurred due to the imposition of forced commodification. The chapters on political goods ask us what it means to be a citizen, what kinds of obligations and entitlements this carries, and whether markets enhance or impede the satisfaction thereof. The chapters on bodily goods ask us to think anew about what constitutes labour, what vulnerability and coercion consist in, what exploitation looks like, and whether feminist empowerment lies within the market or beyond it. The environmental chapters ask us what it means to relate in proprietary terms to the goods we commodify, and what this entails for the inherent worth of the goods themselves, the essential social links they sustain, and the very sustainability of life on this planet. Each chapter, while addressing a discrete commodity, nonetheless invites the reader to consider how market relations impact social relations and how changing even a discrete market can be fundamentally related to impactful social change.

The final challenge we want to consider before concluding is that, in having organized both our presentation of commodification studies as devoted to inquiring about the noxiousness of discrete markets, and our book according to these individual markets, we may have landed commodification theorists in hot water (ourselves included). This book explores dozens of markets, all of which face contestation, albeit it to varying degrees at this particular point in time. And we identified as the first key feature of commodification studies that it asks after the permissible regulation or prohibition of discrete markets within a market economy, rather than asking after the permissibility of the market economy itself. But then the very simple question presents itself: if *so many* discrete markets are contestable within a market economy, perhaps the problem is "the market" after all. If it cannot be contained, should it be retained? If the domino effects of the market are inevitable, to what end should we be scrutinizing individual markets, rather than mandating revolution?

References

Anderson, E. (1993) *Value in Ethics and Economics*. Cambridge, MA: Harvard University Press.

Appadurai, A. (ed.) (1986) *The Social Life of Things: Commodities in Cultural Perspective*. London: Cambridge University Press.

Aristotle (1996) *The Politics and the Constitution of Athens*. Everson, S. (ed.) Cambridge: Cambridge University Press.

Arrow, K.J. (1972) "Gifts and exchanges", *Philosophy & Public Affairs*, 1(4), pp. 343–62.

Becker, G.S. and Elías, J.J. (2007) "Introducing incentives in the market for live and cadaveric organ donations", *Journal of Economic Perspectives*, 21(3), pp. 3–24.

Bertrand, E. (2019) "Don ou marchandise: les deux fictions de la GPA", in M.-X. Catto and K. Martin-Chenut (eds), *Procréation Assistée et Filiation, AMP et GPA au Prisme du Droit, des Sciences Sociales et de la Philosophie*. Paris: Mare & Martin, pp. 213–44.

Bertrand, E. and Catto, M.-X. (eds) (2020) *Les Limites du Marché: La Marchandisation de la Nature et du Corps / The Limits of the Market: Commodification of Nature and Body*. Paris: Mare & Martin.

Bourdieu, P. (1977) *Outline of a Theory of Practice*. London: Cambridge University Press.

Brennan, J. and Jaworski, P.M. (2016) *Markets Without Limits. Moral Virtues and Commercial Interests*. New York: Routledge.

Carney, S. (2011) *The Red Market: On the Trail of the World's Organ Brokers, Bone Thieves, Blood Farmers, and Child Traffickers*. New York: William Morrow.

Davis, N.Z. (2000) *The Gift in Sixteenth-Century France*. Madison: University of Wisconsin Press.

Elias, J.J., Lacetera, N. and Macis, M. (2019) "Paying for kidneys? A randomized survey and choice experiment", *American Economic Review*, 109(8), pp. 2855–8.

Ertman, M.M. and Williams, J.C. (eds) (2005) *Rethinking Commodification. Cases and Readings in Law and Culture*. New York: New York University Press.

Fiske, A.P. and Tetlock, P.E. (1997) "Taboo trade-offs: Reactions to transactions that transgress the spheres of justice", *Political Psychology*, 18(2), pp. 255–97.
Hughes, P.M. (2009) "Constraint, consent, and well being in human kidney sales", *Journal of Medicine and Philosophy,* 34(6), pp. 606–31.
Kanbur, R. (2004) "On obnoxious markets", in Cullenberg, S. and Pattanaik, P. (eds), *Globalization, Culture and the Limits of the Market: Essays in Economics and Philosophy*, New Delhi: Oxford University Press, pp. 39–61.
Kant, I. ([1785] 1996) "Groundwork of the metaphysics of morals," in Guyer, P. and Woods, A.W. (eds) *Kant's Practical Philosophy,* Cambridge: Cambridge University Press, pp. 37–108.
Landes, E.M. and Posner, R.A. (1978) "The economics of the baby shortage", *Journal of Legal Studies*, 7(2), pp. 323–48.
Lordon, F. (2006) *L'intérêt Souverain. Essai d'Anthropologie Économique Spinoziste*. Paris: La Découverte.
Macaulay, S. (1963) "Non-contractual relations in business: A preliminary study", *American Sociological Review*, 28(1), pp. 55–67.
Marx, K. ([1867] 1990) *Capital: Critique of Political Economy*. New York: Penguin.
Panitch, V. (2020) "Liberalism, commodification, and justice", *Politics, Philosophy, and Economics,* 19(1), pp. 62–82.
Phillips, A. 2013, *Our Bodies, Whose Property?* Princeton: Princeton University Press.
Polanyi, K. ([1944] 1971) *The Great Transformation. The Political and Economic Origins of our Time*. Boston: Beacon Press.
Radin, M.J. (1987) "Market-inalienability", *Harvard Law Review*, 100, pp. 1849–937.
Radin, M.J. (1996) *Contested Commodities.* Cambridge, MA: Harvard University Press.
Rippon, S. (2014) "Imposing options on people in poverty: the harm of a live donor organ market", *Journal of Medical Ethics,* 40(3), pp. 145–50.
Rose, C.M. (1992) "Giving, trading, thieving, and trusting. How and why gifts become exchanges, and (more importantly) vice versa", *Florida Law Review*, 44(3), 295–317.
Roth, A.E. (2007) "Repugnance as a constraint on markets", *Journal of Economic Perspectives*, 21(3), pp. 37–58.
Roth, A.E. (2015) *Who Gets What — and Why: The New Economics of Matchmaking and Market*. Boston, Mariner Books.
Sandel, M. (2012) *What Money Can't Buy: The Moral Limits of Markets*. New York: Farrar, Straus and Giroux.
Satz, D. (2010) *Why Some Things Should Not Be For Sale. The Moral Limits of Markets*. Oxford: Oxford University Press.
Simmel, G. ([1900] 1978) *The Philosophy of Money*. London: Routledge & Kegan Paul.
Singer, P. (1973), "Altruism and commerce: a defense of Titmuss against Arrow", *Philosophy & Public Affairs*, 2(3), pp. 312–20.
Steiner, P. (2016) *Donner... Une Histoire de l'Altruisme*. Paris: Presses Universitaires de France.
Steiner, P. and Trespeuch, M. (eds) (2015) *Marchés Contestés. Quand le Marché Rencontre la Morale*. Toulouse: Presses Universitaires de Toulouse.
Titmuss, R.M. (1970) *The Gift Relationship. From Human Blood to Social Policy*. London: Allen and Unwin.
Trebilcock, M.J. (1993) *The Limits of Freedom of Contract*. Cambridge, MA: Harvard University Press.
Walzer, M. (1983) *Spheres of Justice: A Defense of Pluralism and Equality.* New York: Basic Books.
Zelizer, V.A. (1994) *The Social Meaning of Money: Pin Money, Paychecks, Poor Relief, and Other Currencies*. New York: Basic Books.

PART 1

Commodification studies

Past and present

1

COMMODIFICATION

The traditional pro-market arguments[1]

Marie Daou and Alain Marciano

Introduction

Commodification has been proposed and defended because the market as an institution is said to have some virtues and advantages. Which are they? This is the question we try to answer in this chapter. We will not review all pro-market arguments, but rather focus on the arguments that are important in the debates on commodification and to which anti-commodification theorists respond. Our chapter is divided in three sections. The first two arguments relate to the moral and ethical dimensions of markets—on the one hand, markets protect individual liberty and, on the other, they teach individuals moral principles and make them virtuous. The last and third argument is that of efficiency, which is said to be a major advantage of markets as compared to other forms of organizing economic or societal interactions.

Liberty, consent, and property rights

Let us thus start with a first argument in favour of markets, namely the defense of liberty. A market system leaves people "free to choose", to use Milton and Rose Friedman's words (1980). Markets respect individual economic freedom and guarantee that individuals consent to or, to put it differently, do not force or coerce them into the transactions they engage in. This was how Buchanan (1954, p. 340) characterized liberty—"somewhat narrowly as the absence of coercion". With this definition, he was drawing the Chicago tradition of his mentor Frank Knight—who indeed also defined freedom "as the opposite of coercion" (1941, p. 91)—and passed along to the next generation of Chicago economists. More precisely:

> the central feature of the market organization of economic activity is that it prevents one person from interfering with another in respect of most of his activities. The consumer is protected from coercion by the seller because of the presence of other sellers with whom he can deal. The seller is protected from coercion by the consumer because of other consumers to whom he can sell. The employee is protected from coercion by the employer because of other employers for whom he can work, and so on.
>
> (Friedman, 1962, pp. 14–15)

DOI: 10.4324/9781003188742-3

For instance, as some pro-market scholars note, including Adam Smith himself, the birth of a labour market, that is the commodification of labour, has made it possible to substitute an imposed master-servant relationship for a voluntary and free transaction. The argument was then more broadly also used by the partisans of an extended use of the market beyond its traditional limits about some potentially contested commodities such as blood (see, e.g., Cooper and Culyer, 1973; Reuben Kessel, 1974), organs (Brams, 1977) or babies (Landes and Posner, 1978; Posner, 1986 [1973], pp. 141–142; 1979, pp. 138–139; 1987; also, among many others, Pritchard, 1984). To these thinkers, markets are valuable, and market transactions legitimate, because the moment the individual engages in a market transaction, he or she can be taken to have consented to it.

One can justify consent as Posner did, in terms of "ex ante compensation" (1980, p. 492). This means that, when they engage in a transaction, individuals are supposed to have discounted and capitalized the future possible losses; these losses are included in the prices individuals accept to pay; in other words, if they engage in a transaction, individuals are already compensated for these losses because the price they agree to pay includes them. Whatever the outcome of the transaction (even in the event of an accident or loss), individuals have thus consented to. Besides, consent can be justified by the fact that, as Debra Satz (2010, p. 25) notes, (competitive) markets are by definition characterized by the "possibility of exit". Individuals can thus leave the market whenever they want. Thus, again, those who accept a transaction stay on the market and therefore agree to what is happening to them.

Thus, no one is or can be coerced when engaging into market transactions, since she or he has consented to it. Put differently, coerced market transactions are, by definition, impossible.[2] Thanks to the market, the individual satisfies his or her needs while preserving his or her freedom, and the freedom of others.[3]

That individuals necessarily consent to the transactions they engage in—and therefore that markets promote freedom—depends on a particular conception of property rights.[4] The relationship between markets and property rights works in two ways. First, individual property rights have to exist to allow uncoerced transactions—free markets cannot function without property rights. This means that consent on the marketplace presupposes property rights—for consent to be meaningful, individuals need to have ownership in the goods they trade. Reciprocally, because it is assumed or claimed that markets guarantee voluntary transactions, it can be said that a market transaction also guarantees individual property rights. Indeed, if people have a right to their property prior to a market exchange, and people consent to all transactions, the new allocation of property will reflect what people rightfully own. Consequently, when a market transaction takes place, the parties' property rights are respected.

In the liberal economic tradition, freedom is closely associated with these two institutions, namely the market and individual (private) property rights. For some economists of this tradition, liberty consists in the unhindered use of one's property. This is how property rights give to people the right to do whatever they want with what they own, including trading it on a market. Therefore, to prohibit, to limit or to undermine market transactions in one way or another prevents individuals from using their property rights and accordingly reduces their liberty.

This brings us to the specific case of self-ownership. Indeed, if individuals have rights, then "there are things no person or group may do to them (without violating their rights)" (Nozick, 1974, p. ix). Furthermore, if markets are based on consent, no transaction can take place to which an individual has not consented (and any transaction to which he or she has consented is admissible). Finally, if consent cannot exist without being in possession of the property of oneself, then having property or ownership rights over oneself should also be a necessary condition for the existence and functioning of a system of free markets. Indeed, self-ownership is defined by the fact "that there are things that may not be done to a person without their consent, but which may be done with consent" (Van der Vossen, 2019). Therefore, market participants are self-owners. Or, put differently, markets (and consent) *without* self-ownership are impossible. The absence of self-ownership empties consent and voluntarism of any meaning.

There is a certain circularity around the self-ownership argument: property supposes self-ownership as a necessary condition to (freely) engage in transactions and at the same time that self-ownership is also used as necessary to justify property. But it is an extremely complex and difficult concept to grasp. From an ontological perspective, it could be argued that individuals may well have property rights on objects but no right over themselves because only a non-human, superior to human beings, entity can claim an ownership right over human beings. For example, in the Christian religion, self-ownership does not exist: "the Lord owns the earth and all it contains, the world and all who live in it" (in the Bible Psalm 24 of David). From a philosophical perspective, another difficulty comes from the nature of what is owned. Cartesian dualism—or any form of dualism, for that matter—between the owner (the subject) and ownership (the object/body), makes self-ownership inconsistent. Since, from this perspective, the two entities cannot be brought together to form a whole, they are by nature perceived as dual. Thus, owning objects and owning a human being cannot be put on the same footing. This is what Emmanuel Kant, for instance, explained when he wrote:

> Man cannot dispose over himself, because he is not a thing. He is not his own property—that would be a contradiction; for so far as he is a person, he is a subject, who can have ownership of other things [...] it is impossible, of course, to be at once a thing and a person, a proprietor and a property at the same time.
>
> (1997, p. 157)

In view of the limits previously presented, self-ownership therefore appears to be both a necessary but debatable perquisite of the defence of markets. However, if one leaves aside the difficulties about the notion of self-ownership and admits that human beings can own objects and themselves at the same time, then one question becomes important from the perspective of a discussion on commodification. Can we alienate ourselves as we would our property? In other words, can a market transaction—to which the parties have consented—allow individuals to sell and therefore abandon self-ownership? Can human beings be sold on a market? In other words, is slavery, or voluntary enslavement, possible?[5]

At first sight, liberty/consent and self-ownership seem to be complementary, rather than rival: property involves consent and the freedom to dispose of his property, and by extension the freedom to dispose his own body and his labour. However, it seems there is a case where liberty and property are in competition when the ownership right of some legitimizes the deprivation of freedom of others or, more specifically, when slavery exists. Thus, the materialist vision of slavery manifests itself in the denial of the right to freedom. In this specific case, property takes precedence over freedom and that is why Locke rejected the slavery.[6] Actually, Locke put forward a twofold reason to oppose slavery. First, he insisted that "every man has a property in his own person" (1824 [1690], p. 116), and consequently, no one can thus be deprived from the property of oneself. Second, he also noted that a human being does "not hav[e] the power of his own life" and therefore "cannot by compact or his own consent enslave himself to anyone, nor put himself under the absolute, arbitrary power of another to take away his life when he pleases" (1824 [1690], p. 143).

Other pro-market scholars also oppose the selling of oneself into slavery. From this perspective, one of the most interesting positions is Murray Rothbard's. A libertarian, Rothbard developed an inalienability theory on self-ownership upon which rests his strong opposition to slavery—"slavery, and even "voluntary slavery", as we have seen, cannot be enforced on the free market because of the inalienability of personal will" (2004 [1962], p. 348). His point helps to clarify a pro-market argument about commodification. To Rothbard (1998 [1982], pp. 40–41), "[t]he concept of 'voluntary slavery' is an oxymoron", a contradictory one. Indeed,

> so long as a laborer remains totally subservient to his master's will voluntarily, he is not yet a slave since his submission is voluntary; whereas, if he later changed his mind and the master enforced his slavery by violence, the slavery would not then be voluntary.
>
> That slavery cannot be voluntary means that it can result only from violence. Rothbard again:
>
> The interpersonal relation under slavery is [...] one of command and obedience, the commands being enforced by threats of violence. Thus, slavery [...] is defined as a system in which one must labor under the orders of another under the threat of violence.
>
> (2004 [1962], p. 82)

Thus, from this perspective, property rights over oneself are inalienable. Harold Demsetz made this point when discussing the importance of property rights, and that he made a connection with "slave labor":

> A law which establishes the right of a person to his freedom would necessitate a payment on the part of a firm or of the taxpayer sufficient to cover the cost of using that person's labor if his services are to be obtained.
>
> (1967, p. 349)[7]

On the contrary, Nozick's position on this particular matter was anti-Lockean. For instance, Nozick asked "whether a free system will allow [an individual] to sell himself into slavery", he replied, "I believe that it would" (1974, p. 331). Even if he specified that the individuals were not forced to accept the transaction; the decision to enslave oneself would have to be voluntary. And to Nozick, individuals are not coerced if they are led to choose an option that improves their situation. Thus, for instance, an individual could sell his lifetime labour to avoid starving and live a little longer.

A similar argument to Nozick's is offered by Walter Block (2003) who questions the idea of inalienable right in one's own person and supports the possibility that "everything should be legally alienable or commodifiable" (p. 41), thus the "claim is that if I really own my liberty, then I should be free to dispose of it as I please, even if, by so doing, I end up no longer owning it" (p. 44). From such a perspective, self-ownership does not impose any limits on commodification but consent, including the consent to abandon a further right to consent.

Markets, morality, and social cohesion

That markets—and market-based societies—could be vicious or virtuous has largely been emphasized by those who believe that *not* everything should be for sale, as Debra Satz put it (2010; see also Anderson, 1998; Sandel, 2012, 2013). For instance, Michael Sandel insisted that "some market transactions are objectionable" because of "the tendency of market practices to corrupt or crowd out nonmarket values worth caring about ... nonmarket norms of moral importance" (2013, p. 123), such as love, or "attentiveness and thoughtfulness" (p. 124) (see Vida Panitch's chapter in this volume—Chapter 4).

Although central to the contemporary debate about commodification, such statements are not new. "There is a long tradition" Ian Maitland pointed out, that "go[es] back to Aristotle" and that consists in "viewing commerce as hostile to the virtues" (1997, p. 17) and in believing that "the market frees individual acquisitiveness from moral, social and/or religious constraints" (p. 18). The very fact that markets lead individuals to focus narrowly on their own interests supposedly works to the detriment of their social obligations and moral duties. Consequently, markets are said to not only undermine the moral foundations of the good society, but also the moral foundations of market itself. Thus, wrote Fred Hirsch (1976, p. 122, 124), "the full permeation of an individualistic calculus", that characterizes a free-market economy, weakens the social morality that is necessary to guarantee an efficient functioning of markets. Markets do not only work against morality. By promoting self-interest and immoral behaviours, they are also working against themselves.

Against such arguments, pro-market scholars have developed different analyses that do not always complement each other but that all contribute to defending the thesis that markets do not destroy virtue and moral values.

A first line of defence can be found in the famous *Fable of the Bees* (1714) of Bernard de Mandeville. Self-interest—vices, in his words—are certainly not detrimental to the common good—or "public benefits"—still in Mandeville's words. Much to the contrary. The pursuit of self-interest, and the adoption of vicious behaviors, contribute to generate a wealthy and prosperous society:

> The root of evil, avarice, that damned ill-natured baneful vice, was slave to prodigality, that noble sin; whilst luxury employed a million of the poor, and odious pride a million more: envy it-self, and vanity, were ministers of Industry; their darling folly, fickleness, in diet, furniture and dress, that strange ridiculous vice, was made the very wheel that turned the trade. [...].
>
> [However] vice nursed ingenuity, which joined with time and industry, had carried life's conveniences [...] Pleasures, comforts, ease, [...] nothing could be added more.
>
> (Mandeville, 1924 [1714], pp. 24–26)

Thus, to Mandeville, markets encourage immoral individuals to behave morally, and work for the common good. Markets do not, however, transform individuals, do not improve their morality. Individuals remain self-interested, greedy, and vain. They put their "vices" at the service of the society.

A more ambitious pro-market argument consists in arguing that markets transform individuals in positive ways. The thesis could already be found in the works of Montesquieu's doctrine of the "doux commerce". The following quotation perfectly illustrates what the doctrine means:

> Commerce cures destructive prejudices, and it is an almost general rule that everywhere there are gentle mores, there is commerce and that everywhere there is commerce, there are gentle mores [...] Commerce [...] polishes and softens barbaric ways.
>
> (1989 [1748], pp. 338)

Here, one understands the difference with Mandeville's view: commerce, or put differently market exchange, changes individuals for the better; it is not only a matter of inciting them to behave morally but to become morally virtuous individuals. Here, market exchange is defended on explicitly moral grounds.

This view was further developed by the enlightenment philosophers and classical political economists (see Hirschman, 1977; Maitland, 1997; for a recent and complete analysis, see Storr and Choi, 2020).[8] Markets "encourage" (Storr and Choi, 2020, p. 54) and "support moral development" (p. 57). They do this in two ways. First, the market is supposed to limit or prevent immoral behaviours. Thus, Adam Smith (1976 [1776]), for example, believed that markets rest on mechanisms that lead economic agents to moderate the intensity of their passions (Paganelli, 2010), and temper the importance of their self-love (Walraevens, 2010). As Walraevens (2014) noted about Smith's analysis of markets: "the competitive market is a place of education in impartiality and self-control through the moderation of personal interest that it demands. No one can permanently impose their will on it" (p. 426). Second, markets encourage moral behaviours by teaching individuals how "to be better people" (Storr and Choi, 2020, p. 43). The idea here is that markets teach individuals virtues such as honesty, tolerance, generosity, industriousness, frugality, probity, hospitality (Montesquieu, 1989 [1748]). Virgil Storr and Vini Choi (2020, p. 53) quote Smith's *Lectures on Jurisprudence* (1982 [1763]) where one can read that market exchange (commerce) promote virtues such as "probity and punctuality".[9]

Crucial in this process is the role of "sympathy". According to Smith, even if sympathy is lacking, repeated contracts can generate minimal levels of courtesy: "The market promotes civility because commercial success depends on the courteous treatment of people who have the option of taking their business elsewhere" (Brozen, 1978, p. 15). Moreover, market participation develops and strengthens the ability to share the feelings or emotions of others. Indeed, in the economic system described by Smith, the division of labor makes the subsistence means of economic agents dependent on the successful satisfaction of the needs of others. In other words, the interdependence between economic agents increases with the division of labour. Meanwhile, sympathy helps us anticipate the needs of others and combined with market exchange, contributes to economic success. Indeed, by allowing perspectives to be compared and the adoption of an impartial point of view through mutual concessions until a reciprocal agreement is obtained, the market participates in the expression of sympathy, by supporting cooperation and positive social and economic relations.

A third type of defence of markets on moral grounds consists in arguing that "[m]arkets… are *socializing* spaces" (Storr and Choi, 2019, p. 134, italics in original). This thesis was defended by economists as different as Léon Walras and Friedrich Hayek. But they saw the market as virtuous for the same reason, as contributing to the promotion of social cohesion.[10] This is thus how John Hicks (1934) interpreted Walras's general equilibrium theory, for having the merit of demonstrating the unity of economic life, with the idea that individual ends are made compatible by the market mechanism:

> One is the realization of the unity of economic life which emerges so forcefully from his pages. Other economists had had a sense of this unity, but none before had shown it so well. For the unity which Walras demonstrated is not a unity of resources being allotted among a single system of ends—the only unity which really appears in Menger [1985]—it is a unity of diverse individual ends reconciled through the mechanism of the market.
>
> (Hicks, 1934, p. 347)

In this sense, markets bring isolated and independent individuals together, link them to other individuals and therefore contribute to the stability of social relationships.

In the same vein, economists from the Austrian school and the ordoliberals[11] also support the idea that the market is not simply a place where goods are traded. These economists are convinced that the market order is more than a term used to characterize a commercial society. It is a genuinely social institution that allows individuals to interact peacefully with one another to achieve ends that are not purely economic. One could also refer to Jacques Rueff, a French liberal thinker sympathetic to ordoliberals and Hayek's notion of social order, who argued that far from being a mere institution of transaction, the market is the most appropriate societal organization to achieve "collective ends",[12] for it is the only form of economic order which enables us to maintain human freedom and social harmony:

> [M]arket [...] is, in our political structures, the fundamental change which will unite tomorrow, in a common civilization, all individuals and people who want freedom without disorder, and welfare without servitude, while reducing, as far as is humanly possible, inequality and injustice.
>
> (Rueff, 1958, pp. 9–10)

Markets and efficiency

Markets are supposed to guarantee that individuals consent to the transaction, and therefore that their freedom and sovereignty are respected. As a corollary, markets guarantee that those who want or need to buy or sell a commodity (contested or otherwise) can indeed complete the transaction as they wish. This points to another major argument in favour of extending the use of markets: efficiency. Markets are often viewed as the most efficient way to deal with scarce resources.[13] A society in which market transactions take place is supposed or claimed to be *wealthier* than it would be without such markets. To understand the argument requires a clarification as to what efficiency means and, as a corollary, as to how markets are defined—and even as to how economics itself is described. Here, two perspectives exist: the static vs the dynamic definitions of efficiency and markets, which corresponds to the standard or mainstream vs the heterodox definitions.

Efficiency in what is now the standard, mainstream, neoclassical and static sense of the word finds its origins in the works of Walras (1874) and Wilfredo Pareto (1906). Walras introduced a general equilibrium approach, according to which, if competitive conditions prevail, and consumers maximize their utility and producers maximize their profits, a situation of general equilibrium can be reached. Put differently, there always exists a system of price that guarantees that all markets simultaneously are in equilibrium. A few years later, Pareto (1906) went further than Walras. He defined what would be the best possible situation that can be reached in an economy—Pareto optimality—and also gave the first formulations of what would be known as the two fundamental theorems of welfare economics. These theorems, that would be formally demonstrated by Kenneth Arrow in the 1950s, establish a twofold correspondence between competition and Pareto optimality. The first theorem says that, under certain conditions (given technology, given resources, stable and given preferences, perfect information, perfect competition), the allocation of resources resulting from the equilibrium system of prices is Pareto efficient. In other words, any competitive equilibrium leads to a Pareto efficient allocation of resources. The second theorem states that, with a given endowments of resources, any Pareto optimal allocation can be achieved through a competitive, decentralized market mechanism. In other words, markets lead to social optimality. All the potential gains from trade are exhausted (see Chapter 3 by Bertrand in this volume).

Such views on general equilibrium and markets, are very specific. Efficiency can be reached if very strong and restrictive conditions are satisfied. So strong and restrictive that it seems difficult to defend market efficiency on this ground. Such perfect models are not problematic in themselves, that is as long as they remain used for what they are—modeling—and are not compared to real-world markets. Unfortunately, this not the case and the "perfectly competitive equilibrium" has become used as "a normative benchmark to assess real-world markets" (Boettke et al., 2018, p. 126). Indeed, some pro-market economists did assume that the "static perfection" of competitive general equilibrium and Pareto efficiency "must (somehow) be attainable" and that "real markets" were "breathtakingly close to approximating the efficiency properties of general competitive equilibrium" (Boettke, 1997, p. 23). The model is then conflated with the reality. Accordingly, some aspects of that reality are missed: that information is not perfect, that individuals have limited cognitive capacities, that human activities are dynamic, that institutions matter. These are the dimensions that are captured essentially by heterodox (especially the Austrian) views on efficiency.

Such an approach on efficiency of markets was already captured by the classics who defined markets in terms of processes, as the process of adjustment towards equilibrium: "the classical understanding of the market process was a dynamic process of adjustment, in which factor prices serve as guides to exchange and production" (Boettke et al, 2018, pp. 127–128).[14] From this perspective, a market is not efficient because it produces an equilibrium but because it allows individuals to learn, and to adapt themselves to what others do by coordinating their actions with other individuals; that is, by allowing them to discover what others plan to do. The market is not only an anonymous and inter-temporal place which brings together buyers and suppliers, and where goods and services are exchanged, but a process during which information is created, disseminated, and adjusted for. From this perspective, a market economy cannot be affected by ongoing crises. Because any disequilibrium is a means of allowing the individuals to learn what is wrong and how to avoid such a crisis in the first place.

This approach is later deepened and refined by the Austrian school of economics. The importance of markets as a means of transmitting information to economic agents is central to Austrian tradition. Hayek and Israel Kirzner are certainly the most prominent among the many economists who contributed to developing this perspective. Both insisted on "the unavoidable imperfection of man's knowledge" (Hayek, 1945, p. 91; see also 1937), and the need to learn and thus for the "need for a process by which knowledge is constantly communicated and acquired" (1945, p. 91). This is a key role markets play. Indeed, as Kirzner (1979) wrote, the market "emerges as the necessary implication of the circumstances that people act, and that in their actions they err, discover their errors, and tend to revise their actions in a direction likely to be less erroneous than before" (p. 30). For his part, Hayek argued that, in an institutional environment of private property rights, the market price system uses dispersed knowledge in order to align production and supply with consumption and demand. And, indeed, for both Hayek and Kirzner, prices are crucial in this dynamic learning process. They convey information about the changing conditions, giving individuals the possibility to adjust their behaviour accordingly. And they also allow the market participants to evaluate the relevance of their past market decisions and thus to correct possible mistakes. *Ex post*, prices reveal the ultimate (un)profitability of economic decision. Efficiency remains a major advantage of markets and of a market system.

Conclusion

Without trying to be exhaustive, we reviewed the main arguments that are used to legitimate an expansion of markets without limits. These are the arguments that can be opposed to the anti-commodification theorists concerned with contested markets.

We have thus insisted on the notion of consent and property rights because, to pro-market thinkers, the market is a place in which individuals consent to the transactions they engage in. But the argument is circular: the market rests on consent and property rights which themselves presuppose the consent then necessary to engage in a transaction. Obviously, this works because property rights protect individuals. When this is the case, the claim is that no one can be forced to trade anything on a market—by contrast, the regulation of the trade of a commodity introduces coercion because individuals can no longer buy and sell the commodity as they want to. Thus, markets for new commodities—those commodities that are not usually traded on markets—guarantee that those who want or need to buy or sell a contested commodity can indeed complete the transaction as they wish. This is all the more profitable because, though market processes, individuals learn how to behave morally and virtuously, as the argument goes.[15] Such markets should not be dismissed out of hand.

These points were repeatedly made by the advocates of an extension of markets to any kind of good. For them, without a free market, there exists a gap between supply and demand that cannot be closed; using a price mechanism would eliminate it.[16] Therefore, the individuals who are on a waiting list—due to lack of organ—could acquire a "good" they would not have the possibility to "buy" otherwise. Complementarily, those who would be ready to sell organs or body parts are not forced against their will not to engage in transactions. Here, as one realizes, efficiency can be viewed in a narrow and static sense or in the broader and dynamic meaning of the concept, that is either as allowing a better allocation of resources or an improvement in the information individuals have.

Notes

1 A first version of this chapter was presented at the conference "Contested Markets: Theories and Controversies", Paris, 3–4 June 2022. We thank Élodie Bertrand, Vida Panitch and Aksel Sterri for extremely useful comments.

2 Some authors question the voluntary nature of consent. This is the case, for example, of Michel Walzer (1984) who considers that formally voluntary consent is called into question in the case of the sale of organs. To Walzer, individuals are necessarily constrained by poverty. Fabienne Peter (2004) makes a similar point, arguing that individuals may be free to choose within a set of given alternatives, but are not free to choose the set itself.

3 This definition is arguably narrow and specific (Dworkin, 1980; Westen, 2004a, 2004b).

4 Brennan's and Jaworski's with their "Principle of Wrongful Possession" questions not only the existence of property rights but also their alienability—"If it is inherently morally wrong for someone to possess (do, use) X, then (normally) it is morally wrong for that person to buy or sell X" (2016, p. 11). They introduce the moral factor in the definition of property rights, which inevitably impacts what can be commodified and what cannot.

5 The case of body parts is probably of a different nature. It indeed seems that we do not abandon self-ownership when we sell a part of our self, but that we only sell our self-ownership if we sell our self permanently into slavery (thanks to Vida Panitch for having stressed this point).

6 Mentioning Locke does not mean, obviously, that he was the only one to oppose slavery. He was not. Among the important philosophers who were, one finds Immanuel Kant, for instance, who was even more vehement than Locke, and developed a different argument, namely the existence of a dualism according to which the individual cannot be the owner and the thing possessed at the same time.

7 Another way of putting the argument would be by saying that it is not the selling of one object that is problematic but the conditions in which the object is sold. Which is exactly the point Debra Satz (1992; 2010) made in her discussion of surrogacy.

8 These economists are, among others, Adam Smith, David Ricardo, Robert Torrens or John Ramsey McCulloch and John Stuart Mill.

9

> Whenever commerce is introduced into any country, probity and punctuality always accompany it. [...] Of all the nations in Europe, the Dutch, the most commercial, are the most faithful to their word. The English are more so than the Scotch, but much inferior to the Dutch [...]. This is not at all to be imputed to national character, as some pretend. There is no natural reason why an Englishman or a Scotchman should not be as punctual at performing agreements as a Dutchman. It is far more reduceable to self-interest, that principle which regulates the actions of every man, and which leads men to act in a certain manner from views of advantage [...]. A dealer is afraid of losing his character, and is scrupulous in observing every engagement.
>
> (Smith, 1982 [1763], p. 458)

10 For alternative views, see Postel and Sobel's Chapter 2 in this volume, on Polanyi.

11 Ordoliberalism is a liberal doctrine which gives the State the economic mission to create and maintain a framework allowing free competition on the markets.

12 Rueff did not define exactly the term "collective ends". We know only that they are not simply the sovereign functions (police, justice, and army) since they are already ensured by the protection of property rights in Rueff's thinking.

13 This does not however mean that other ways of allocating resources would not create wealth too. The argument is not put in absolute but in relative terms.

14 Classical refers to Smith and Classical Political Economy.

15 The defence of markets is made *ceteris paribus*, so to speak. Since the market is an "institution", one assumes that the virtues of advantages of the existing markets can be replicated to the new markets that are created.

16 This reasoning has even been applied to babies (Landes and Posner, 1978) and to organs (Posner, 1979; Hansmann, 1989; Erin and Harris, 1994; Becker and Elias, 2007; Elias, Lacetera and Macis, 2015).

References

Anderson, E. 1998. *Value in Ethics and Economics.* Cambridge: Harvard University Press.

Becker, G.S. and J.J. Elias. 2007. "Introducing Incentives in the Market for Live and Cadaveric Organ Donations", *Journal of Economic Perspectives*, 21(3), 3–24.

Block, W. 2003. "Toward a Libertarian Theory of Inalienability: A Critique of Rothbard, Barnett, Smith, Kinsella, Gordon, and Epstein", *Journal of Libertarian Studies*, 17(2), 39–85.

Boettke P.J. 1997. "Where Did Economics Go Wrong? Modern Economics as a Flight from Reality", *Critical Review*, 11(1), 11–64.

Boettke P., C. Rosolino and K. Woltz. 2018. "Is the Market Wage the Just Wage? A Reassessment of Factor Pricing and Distributive Justice", *Erasmus Journal for Philosophy and Economics*, 11(2), 124–143.

Brams, M. 1977. "Transplantable Human Organs: Should Their Sale Be Authorized by State Statutes?", *American Journal of Law & Medicine*, 3(2), 183–195.

Brennan, J. and P.M. Jaworski. 2016. *Markets without Limits. Moral Virtues and Commercial Interests*, New York/Oxon, Routledge.

Brozen, Y. 1978. *Can the Market Sustain an Ethic?*, in Y. Brozen, E.W. Johnson, Charles W., Chicago: University of Chicago.

Buchanan, J.M. 1954. "Individual Choice in Voting and the Market", *Journal of Political Economy*, 62(4), 334–343.

Cooper, M.H. and Culyer A.J. 1973. "The Economics of Giving and Selling Blood". In Alchian A., Allen W. (eds) *The Economics of Charity. Essays on the Comparative Economics and Ethics of Giving and Selling, with Applications to Blood*, pp. 109–123. London: Institute of Economic Affairs.

Demsetz, H. 1967. "Toward a Theory of Property Rights", *American Economic Review*, 57(2), 347–359.

Dworkin, R. 1980. "Why Efficiency?–A Response to Professors Calabresi and Posner", *Hofstra Law Review*, 8(3), 563–590.

Elias, J.J., N. Lacetera and M. Macis. 2015. "Sacred values? The effect of information on attitudes toward payments for human organs". *Working paper, National Bureau of Economic Research,* www.nber.org/system/files/working_papers/w20866/w20866.pdf
Erin, C.A. and J. Harris. 1994. "A Monopsonistic Market: Or How to Buy and Sell Human Organs, Tissues and Cells Ethically". In *Life and Death under High Technology Medicine,* pp. 134–153. Manchester: Manchester University Press.
Friedman, Milton. 1962. *Capitalism and Freedom.* Chicago: University of Chicago Press.
Friedman, M. and R. Friedman. 1980. *Free to Choose.* San Diego: Harcourt.
Hansmann, H. 1989. "The Economics and Ethics of Markets for Human Organs", *Journal of Health Politics, Policy and Law,* 14(1), 57–85.
Hayek, F. 1937. "Economics and Knowledge", *Economica,* 4(13), 33–54.
Hayek, F. 1945. "The use of Knowledge", *American Economic Review,* 35(4), 519–530.
Hicks, J.R. 1934. "Léon Walras", *Econometrica,* 2(4), 338–348.
Hirsch, F. 1976. *Social Limits to Growth.* Cambridge: Harvard University Press.
Hirschmann, A.O. 1977. *The Passion and the Interests. Political Arguments for Capitalism before its Triumph.* Princeton: Princeton University Press.
Kant, I. 1997. *Lectures on Ethics.* Cambridge: Cambridge University Press.
Kessel, R.A. 1974. "Transfused Blood, Serum Hepatitis, and the Coase Theorem", *Journal of Law and Economics,* 17(2), 265–289.
Kirzner, I. 1979 *Perception, Opportunity and Profit.* Chicago: University of Chicago Press.
Knight, F.H. 1941. "The Meaning of Freedom. Review of Freedom: Its Meaning by Ruth Anshen", *Ethics,* 52(1), 86–109.
Landes, E. and Posner, R.A. 1978. "The Economics of the Baby Shortage", *Journal of Legal Studies,* 7(2), 323–348.
Locke, J. 1824. *Two Treatises of Government,* New-York: Barnes and Noble Publishing (first edition, 1690).
Mandeville, B. de. 1924. *The Fable of the Bees: or, Private Vices, Publick Benefits.* Oxford: Clarendon Press. (first edition, 1714, London: J. Roberts).
Maitland, I. 1997. "Virtuous Markets: The Markets as School of the Virtues", *Business Ethics Quaterly,* 7(1), 17–31.
Menger, C. 1985. *Investigations into the Method of the Social Sciences: with special reference to economics.* New York and London: New York University Press.
Montesquieu, C. 1989. *The Spirit of the Laws.* Cambridge: Cambridge University Press (first edition, 1748).
Nozick, R. 1974. *Anarchy, State and Utopia,* New York: Basic Books.
Paganelli, M.P. 2010. "The Moralizing Role of Distance in Adam Smith. *The Theory of Moral Sentiments* as Possible Praise of Commerce", *History of Political Economy,* 42 (3), 425–441.
Pareto, V. 1906. *Manuale d'economia politica,* Milano: Società editrice libraria.
Peter, F. 2004. *Public Helath, Ethics, and Equity.* Oxford: Oxford University Press.
Posner, R.A. 1979. "Utilitarianism, Economics, and Legal Theory", *Journal of Legal Studies,* 8(1), 103–140.
Posner, R.A. 1980. "The Ethical and Political Basis of the Efficiency Norm in Common Law Adjudication", *Hofstra Law Review.* 8(3), 487–507.
Posner, R.A. 1986. *Economic Analysis of Law,* New York, Little Brown & co (first edition, 1973).
Posner, R.A. 1987. "The Regulation of the Market in Adoptions", *Boston University Law Review,* 67, 59–72.
Prichard, J.R.S. 1984. "A Market for Babies?" *University of Toronto Law Journal,* 34(3), 341–357.
Rothbard, M. 1998. *The Ethics of Liberty.* New York: New York University Press (first edition, 1982).
Rothbard, M. 2004. *Man, Market and the State. A Treatise on Economic Principles,* Auburn, Ludwig von Mises Institute (first edition, 1962).
Rueff, J. 1958. "Le marché institutionnel des communautés européennes", *Revue d'économie politique,* 68(1–6), 1–10.
Sandel, M.J. 2012. *What Money Can't Buy: The Moral Limits of Markets.* New York: Farrar, Straus and Giroux.
Sandel, M.J. 2013. "Market Reasoning as Moral Reasoning: Why Economists Should Re-Engage With Political Philosophy", *Journal of Economic Perspectives,* 27, 121–140.
Satz, D. 1992. "Markets in Women's Reproductive Labor", *Philosophy & Public Affairs,* 21(2), 107–131.
Satz, D. 2010. *Why Some Things Should Not Be For Sale. The Moral Limits of Markets.* Oxford: Oxford University Press.

Smith, A. 1982. *Lectures on Jurisprudence*. Glasgow: Glasgow Edition (first edition, 1763).
Smith, A. 1976. *Inquiry into the nature and causes of the wealth of nations*, R.H. Campbell and A.S. Skinner (eds), textual editor W.B. Todd. Oxford: Oxford University Press (first edition, 1776).
Storr, V.H. and G.S. Choi. 2019. *Do Markets Corrupt Our Morals?* New York, NY: Palgrave MacMillan.
Storr, V.H. and G.S. Choi. 2020. "Measuring Markets and Morality", *Erasmus Journal for Economics and Philosophy*, 13 (1), 42–60.
Van der Vossen, B. 2019. Libertarianism, *Stanford Encyclopedia of Philosophy*.
Walraevens, B. 2010. "Adam Smith's Economics and the Lectures on Rhetoric and belles lettres: The Language of Commerce", *History of Economic Ideas*, 18(1), 11–32.
Walraevens, B. 2014. "Vertus et justice du marché chez Adam Smith", *Revue économique*, 2(65), 419–438.
Walras, L. 1874. *Éléments d'économie politique pure*. Lausanne: Corbaz, Paris.
Walzer, M. 1984. *Spheres of Justice*. New York: Basic Book.
Westen, Peter, 2004a. "Some Common Confusions About Consent in Rape Cases", *Ohio State Journal of Criminal Law*, 2, 333–359.
Westen, P. 2004b. *The Logic of Consent. The Diversity and Deceptiveness of Consent as a Defense to Criminal Conduct*. London: Routledge.

2

CLASSICAL ANTI-COMMODIFICATION ARGUMENTS

Commodification and fictitious commodities – Polanyi's decisive contribution

Nicolas Postel and Richard Sobel

Introduction

For commentators and actors who think about the spread of market rationale in contemporary society (especially the neoliberal turn of the 1980s),[1] Karl Polanyi is rightly viewed as an essential figure when it comes to addressing the ecological and social effects of commodification. This is the case for several commodification scholars with a justified claim to a Polanyian pedigree. The question of commodification goes to the heart of Polanyi's analysis of capitalism[2] as a mode of production that emerged in the late eighteenth century – particularly in England – and has now spread worldwide. Polanyi provides essential conceptual and analytical resources for dealing with the many current-day questions about what seems to be the limitless extension of market rationale and the social and environmental damage it causes. This extension takes two separate but interrelated forms: financialization of economies (and therefore the primacy of financial markets that extend its grasp) and inclusion within the market of things that were previously excluded from it (law, knowledge, seeds, etc.) causing an extension of market logic. It is this second aspect that is examined more particularly in commodification studies. This new stage of capitalism has given new currency to Polanyi's arguments that relate to a first period of financialization/commodification in the inter-war years. The current period bears many similarities in socio-economic terms with the period Polanyi characterized as the "great transformation".[3]

This "posterity" of Polanyi's work entails a degree of confusion. The most common confusion is to take the view that Polanyi analyzes the dangers of an unlimited and continuous extension of the market. This chapter argues that Polanyi does not so much deal with "the extension of the market" as a gradual process that lays hold of anything that can be turned to a profit by adopting what would ultimately be a perspective akin to ordo-liberalism (Foucault, 2008); but it argues instead that Polanyi defends the analysis of capitalism as requiring *from the outset* that things be treated as commodities that cannot be treated in that way: the three factors of production – land, labour, and money – that Polanyi claims are also three pillars of social life. It is these three fictitious

DOI: 10.4324/9781003188742-4

commodities – and these three only – that form the kernel of Polanyi's argument, emphasizing a dual characteristic of this fictitious commodification: it is both "indispensable" to the capitalist mode of production and it is also "impossible" to bear socially. This for Polanyi is a prime contradiction, a fundamental dialectic that is inherent in what he characterizes as the "self-regulating market system" (the term he uses for the capitalist mode of production). This contradiction entails a structural transformation, new to human history, in the form of an attempt to disembed economics and further still an attempt by the economic sphere to prevail over the social sphere and the biosphere. It is this attempt at disembedding that, Polanyi claims, led in the 1930s to social collapse and to fascism and its abominations. It is therefore on these three fictitious commodities – labour, land, and money – that the question hinges of the construction of the regulatory institutions of capitalism that Polanyi believes he sees emerging in the aftermath of the Second World War.

Polanyi's argument is therefore separate from – and probably complementary to – the argument of "contested markets": it bears not on any particular market or commodity but on the principle, which is both necessary and impossible, of the commodification of land, labour, and money in the capitalist mode of production. To clarify this point, we propose to unravel Polanyi's analytical thread: (1) by setting out his institutionalist framework of analysis; (2) by showing that the "self-regulating market system" is characterized by reversing the relationship between environment, economics, and society; (3) by emphasizing that this reversal operates around the fictitious commodification of land, labour, and money; and (4) by suggesting a potential contribution from his analysis to the analysis made by commodification studies.

Polanyian institutionalism

Polanyi offers a famous definition of economics: "an instituted process of interaction between man and his environment, which results in a continuous supply of want satisfying material means" (Polanyi, 1957, p. 248). This definition prompts two observations. First it is noteworthy that Polanyi emphasizes the "instituted", that is, the socialized and collective dimension of any economic process devised for creating and distributing material wealth. This means there cannot be any economic process that fails to take on a particular social form for supporting economic organization institutionally. But Polanyi specifies, too, that this institutionalized process, in some sense, governs the relationship that people maintain with nature: "The substantive meaning of economics derives from man's dependence for his living upon nature and his fellows. It refers to the interchange with his natural and social environment" (*ibid*, p. 243). Accordingly, the institutional form that economic organization takes on derives from the prime necessity for human societies to ensure their development is ecologically sustainable. There is therefore a double meaning embedded in this definition: the economy is shaped by the social (institutional) organization; but social institutions are themselves shaped by the necessity for collective life to be adapted to the living environment (on Polanyi's core contribution to institutionalism, we fully concur with the analysis by Stanfield, 1980).

There is a degree of diversity among economic forms related to the period of time and the geographical location of human groups confronted with the economic question of subsistence. But beyond that diversity, Polanyi ([1944] 2001, pp. 53–58) identifies three forms that co-exist and are complementary (to varying extents) in the history that precedes our modern times: "Broadly, the proposition holds that all economic systems known to us up to the end of feudalism in Western Europe were organized either on the principle of reciprocity or redistribution, or householding, or some combination of the three" (*ibid.*, p. 57). Each of these forms is part of a specific social organization. Accordingly, economics is determined by the social sphere. Reciprocity, the archetypal form of which is the gift/counter-gift system analyzed particularly by Mauss ([1925] 1990), refers to a symmetrical organization of society that enfolds all individuals in a movement of complete social inclusion. Redistribution, with the social state (Ramaux, 2012) as its recent archetype (the Soviet mode of production might also be cited; Polanyi, for his part, takes potlatch as an example), assumes the existence of a society with a central authority that takes decisions and coordinates the pooling and redistribution of goods and services produced. The domestic model – typically found in autarkic models based on self-sufficiency in foodstuffs – rests on organization around a nuclear family presupposing fundamental structures that are small in scope and relatively isolated from each other (Servet, 2007). Trade takes place during this period and is sometimes organized as markets that are often non-competing. However, these markets, whether local or long-distance, remain on the margins[4] of society: "never before our own time were markets more than accessories of economic life" (Polanyi, [1944] 2001, p. 71). Commercial exchange is underpinned by a principle of exchange that may involve the existence of a monetary equivalent, with or without competition, based on participants enjoying some degree of autonomy from each other and relative to the social framework. This is why this economic form long remained marginal, traditionally designed not to meet the population's basic needs but to satisfy its desire for diversity (especially in its diet).

These four economic forms (we should probably say the three main forms plus this marginal form) are alternative but not exclusive organizations: they combine and complete each other within one and the same human group, thereby responding to a degree of diversity of social structures. These economic forms are "inserted" in the social organization, which is itself related to the geophysical characteristics of the space occupied by that society (one can readily imagine that centrality/redistribution is easier to organize in a continuous space than, say, in an archipelago and that this centrality runs up against physical barriers when the space is discontinuous (mountains, seas, etc.).

The emergence in the late eighteenth century of the self-regulating market system as a form of economic organization upsets this arrangement for the first time in human history. It is the great break that Polanyi identified at "the origins of our time". It corresponds to the emergence of an economy organized around the invisible hand of markets. Accordingly, whereas until then, "[t]he economic system was submerged in general social relations [...] The economic system was absorbed in the social system" (Polanyi, [1944] 2001, p. 70–71), the self-regulating market system reverses the relationship between the economy and society (and, hence, with the biosphere):

> The market pattern [...] is capable of creating a specific institution, namely, the market. Ultimately, that is why the control of the economic system by the market is of overwhelming consequence to the whole organization of society: it means no less than the running of society as an adjunct to the market. Instead of the economy being embedded in social relations, social relations are embedded in the economic system.
>
> (Polanyi, [1944] 2001, p. 60)

This unprecedented phenomenon, Polanyi claims, lies at the origins of all our contemporary history: that history is characterized both by the pressure exerted by this systemic logic of the self-regulating market and by social resistance to this tendency of disembedding; resistance that ends in the atrocious morbid convulsion of the fascist regimes of the 1930s.

It should be observed here that Polanyi makes a very clear distinction between commercial exchange relations (that date from the origins of humankind), a competitive price-making market (a modern form that was long "contained" by legal and social embedding), and finally the emergence in the late eighteenth century of "one big market", in point of fact of a single market "system" joining up all markets and forming a supposedly self-regulating mechanism. The existence of trade and of local markets had not until then challenged the pre-eminence of the social sphere over the economic sphere:[5]

> Where markets were most highly developed, as under the mercantile system, they throve under the control of a centralized administration which fostered autarchy both in the household of the peasantry and in respect to national life. Regulation and markets, in effect, grew up together. The self-regulating market was unknown.
>
> (Polanyi, [1944] 2001, p. 71)

Conversely the market system creates this outgoing, overarching character of the market, which tends to impose its own law on society (and on the biosphere). It is a mythical aim: neither in theory[6] nor in practice is the system self-regulating and it cannot become independent of social rules … but this myth effectively pervades contemporary society, in the nineteenth century and the first half of the twentieth century … and has pervaded it once again since the neoliberal turn of the 1980s.

The self-regulating market system tends to impose uniformity on the social body by bending it to its own rules, crushing the historical and contingent substance of the social sphere at the risk of dissolving it. Polanyi identifies this dramatic pressure with regard to the problematic status that is taken on by land, labour, and money. On the one hand, for Polanyi, the living environment (land), human life (labour), and social ties (money) form three fundamental pillars of society. This is why it is impossible to commodify them. On the other hand, it is precisely these three production factors (land, labour, and capital) that capitalism (the market system) requires be treated as commodities. This makes their commodification indispensable. Impossible and yet indispensable – such are the phenomena that punctuate the rise and then the collapse of the myth of the self-regulating market system.

The three fictitious commodities

> The crucial point is this: labor, land, and money are essential elements of industry; they also must be organized in markets; in fact, these markets form an absolutely vital part of the economic system. But labor, land, and money are obviously *not* commodities; the postulate that anything that is bought and sold *must have been produced for sale* is emphatically untrue in their regard. In other words, according to the empirical definition of a commodity they are not commodities. […] [But] *no society could stand the effects of such a system of crude fictions even for the shortest stretch of time unless its human and natural substance as well as its business organization was protected* against the ravages of this satanic mill.
>
> (Polanyi, [1944] 2001, pp. 75–77, emphasis added)

The idea of fictitious commodities, exclusively referring to land, labour, and money for Polanyi, forms the crux of his analyses for two reasons: first, because it is through these three commodities that the relationship of the economic and social spheres is reversed (or tends to be reversed); and second, because it is also on these three commodities that the question of the institutionalization of the self-regulating market system (of capitalism) turns.

Let us begin with the first term of Polanyi's line of argument: the postulate that land, labour, and money are "produced for sale" is "emphatically untrue".

To demonstrate his point, Polanyi states in the quotation above that a commodity is defined as something "produced for sale". This definition implies two criteria: a criterion of production (the commodity is created by humans) and a criterion of the purpose behind that production, which from the outset of the production process, presupposes that selling is the objective and the justification of production.[7] This definition of commodities, which is consistent with David Ricardo's, avoids the confusion of considering that anything that circulates on the market or is the subject of a market exchange is a commodity. For Polanyi, ahead of (and beyond) the *circulation* of goods and services on a market – which is part and parcel of their distribution – it is the nature and purpose of the decision about their *production* that defines their commodity status: their existence is only legitimized by the purpose of being sold in a competitive market. This definition obviously denies *a priori* commodity status to land, labour, and money.

Land – understood as our planet or "living environment" – was not created to be sold. Indeed, it was not created by humans. It is not a resource for people but their living environment; it is not something people live off but the place where they live.[8] It is precisely this natural embedding, as emphasized, that raises the problem of subsistence and forms the fundamental economic question. That resources from nature should be extracted to be sold is obvious. That there has been trade (generally non-market exchange in the ancient world) in this type of resources from the dawn of humanity is something Polanyi would not dream of denying. But these resources cannot be *re*-produced because they are not produced. In this sense, the point that they are the object of trade or even that they circulate on a market does not make commodities of them. Polanyi ([1944] 2001, pp. 36–41), anxious to trace the way the market system treated nature as if it were a commodity, describes the enclosure movement (in sixteenth – and seventeenth-century England) and the resistance to it (especially by the Tudor aristocracy) as a decisive stage (a conviction he shares with Marx), allowing the artificial creation of "a property right" over nature. In this way the illusion arises of ownership of land and from that of the possibility – for anyone who owns a piece of it – to trade in natural resources as if they were commodities (see Chapter 6 by Crétois).

Labour, Polanyi says, is "no other than the human beings themselves of which every society consists [... it] is only another name for a human activity which goes with life itself" (Polanyi, [1944] 2001, p. 75). It is incontrovertibly created, since human life is not the result of some spontaneous generation but a more or less conscious human decision. However, that decision does not follow any principle of market validation. The existence of a labour force, of human population, is not the effect of any collective decision, nor even a series of individual decisions having as its characteristic to "produce" humans "for sale" (or for hire). Yet human life, when justified by the necessity of productive accumulation is thought of as a commodity. It is this fiction that still today worries the social body over the debate stigmatizing living on benefits or stigmatizing those people who are fit for work but unable to find any work as "useless to the world" (Castel, 2003). Polanyi reviews in his book the Speenhamland Law and more generally the Poor Laws enacted in England from 1795 to 1834 and that were fiercely criticized, notably by Thomas Robert Malthus. Malthus criticizes those laws that discourage effort, that go against the message of Paul the Apostle in his Second Epistle to the Thessalonians ("He who does not work, neither shall he eat") and that remove the goad necessary to toil. As Dale (2010) points out, Polanyi takes up this criticism in his book, emphasizing that these Poor Laws form a final illusory rampart against the pressure to completely commodify labour. Speenhamland, based on control of the poor by the Church as part of a reactionary process that creates an unbearable dependence is analyzed as "an automaton for demolishing the standards on which any kind of society could be based" (Polanyi, [1944] 2001, p. 103) and ultimately makes ready for the reign of the labour market imposing its laws. Polanyi thus describes how the utopia of labour "perceived" as a commodity can be gradually imposed on traditional societies (see Chapter 8 by Vatin in this volume).

Money, for its part, is obviously produced for an explicit purpose. But that purpose is not and cannot be its sale. Money forms the cement of a society's economic relations, which it binds and organizes. As a fundamental and founding institution of market economies (Servet, 1993), a "total social fact" (as Marcel Mauss put it), or "sovereign" for Aglietta and Orléan (1998), money arises from a power of creation dedicated to an overarching authority whose behaviour has to ensure trust in the value of money. Money cannot arise from autonomous production and does not really arise from monetary validation since the money market is a "quasi-market" arising from the straightforward interrelation of the volume produced and the decision of the monetary authorities in terms of creation of money, the outcome of which is price (which, from a classical perspective, the monetary authorities have to try to stabilize so as not to artificially mask variations in real output). It is this role of supervision that European nations confer on the collective system of the gold standard, and Polanyi points out its importance for the course of the nineteenth century. He sees in it, as with the resistance to enclosure for land or the enactment of the Poor Laws for labour, a way for traditional societies to resist the self-regulating power of the market. He sees in its crisis and its failure a decisive feature of the crisis of the 1930s and of the collapse of the myth of the self-regulating market.[9]

The second point of Polanyi's argument is that, despite everything, land, labour, and money "must be organized in markets". This necessity is related to the mode of market production based on the accumulation of means of production that must be permanently supplied with natural resources, labour, and credit money (enabling investment). Polanyi characterizes the industrial phenomenon as a "satanic mill" in reference to William Blake's famous poem, *Jerusalem*, published in 1804.[10] Blake, the romantic poet, expresses the confusion of imagining a mythical and eternal Jerusalem – symbol of a Garden of Eden – buried beneath the industrial factories in early nineteenth-century England. Polanyi draws on this reference to emphasize the extraordinary artificiality and violence that the self-regulating market system creates, the most visible aspect of which is formed in the nineteenth century by the great industrial concentrations. This system, based on the accumulation of means of production with a view to producing commodities in keeping with the rules of efficiency, creates an enjoinder to be efficient with respect to all of society and the biosphere.

"What 'satanic mill' ground men into masses?" (Polanyi, [1944] 2001, p. 35). It was the consequence of the need to continually stoke the productive capital accumulated with the means of production (natural resources, human life, credit facilities):

> Since elaborate machines are expensive, they do not pay unless large amounts of goods are produced. [...] They can be worked without a loss only if the vent of the goods is reasonably assured and if production need not be interrupted for want of the primary goods necessary to feed the machines. For the merchant this means that all factors involved must be for sale, that is, they must be available in the needed quantities to anybody who is prepared to pay for them. [...] But what he buys is raw materials and labour – nature and man. Machine production in a commercial society involves, in effect, no less a transformation than that of the natural and human substance of society into commodities.
>
> (Polanyi, [1944] 2001, pp. 43–44)

Should the continuous inflow of any of these production factors dry up, the entire system is endangered.

The shortage of labour or the refusal to work during social unrest in the nineteenth century; recurrent financial crises threatening the system with credit crunches; or – and nowadays obviously – the sudden restriction of raw materials (notably energy sources): whether separately or collectively, these three evils are a permanent threat to the working of the self-regulating market and a permanent watch must be mounted to ensure that the "myth" of the three fictitious commodities works. That, in some sense, is the reverse side of the apparent fluidity of the market, continuously adapting to the conditions of supply and demand via flexible prices: for it to operate, the living environment, the social bond of money, and human life must also be made flexible. The capitalist undertaking is the nexus of this fiction, the space from where pressure is exerted by the market system on society as a whole so that, through this fictitious commodification, it becomes an "adjunct of the market" (Polanyi, [1944] 2001, p. 60).[11]

The necessity of institutions

The self-regulating market system was deployed, Polanyi claims, for 150 years between the late eighteenth century and the years between the two world wars. This deployment gave rise to a double movement: on the one side pressure was exerted by the system so that market logic could spread and prevail; while, on the other side, social resistance to that pressure also built up (Block, 2008). The failure of the social backfires ignited to counter the primacy of the economic sphere propagated by the self-regulating market system is reflected in the collapse of the system itself. As explained, the status of fictitious commodities requires an institutional construction that both supports the myth and protects society. Disregard for the fictitious character of these three commodities and the collapse of the institutions that made the market system viable by limiting its extension therefore also sign its demise.[12] It is this collapse that Polanyi identifies in the fascist movement of the 1930s and more generally in the totalitarianism of the inter-war years … and the terrible war that ensued. Polanyi pithily emphasizes: "The Vitalist's vision of a life sapped and destroyed by impersonal entities of the Mind-world is not entirely fictitious: it is that condition of things in a market-society which is seen in Totalitarianism" (Polanyi, 1935, p. 382).

This Polanyian analysis is, in some sense, the antithesis of the connection traditionally made between the extension of market logic and the pacification of human relations (see Chapter 1 by Daou and Marciano in this volume). Smith's logic of the invisible hand is often associated (rightly or wrongly) in this respect with Montesquieu's famous remarks on sweet commerce:[13] the extension of market logic seems to be a vehicle for a form of spontaneous order based on autonomy and the best interests of those involved. Fragile as it is theoretically and epistemologically, this fable of pacification via the market is still deeply rooted today in our shared representation of geopolitical issues (e.g. the way the European Union has been built, first by the construction of a Common Market). Polanyi's approach is a powerful denial of this.

Polanyi associates this collapse with the disappearance of a social space where practical reason can be exercised (Dale, 2010, pp. 89–136 develops this point). For Polanyi the self-regulating market system is reflected by pressure exerted on individuals eliciting the primacy of an instrumental calculation over any other social consideration: "The commodity fiction handed over the fate of man and nature to the play of an automaton running in its own grooves and governed by its own laws" (Polanyi, 1947, p. 110); and further on:

> Hence man was believed to consist of two components, one more akin to hunger and gain, the other to honor and power. The one was "material", the other "ideal"; the one "economic",

> the other "non-economic"; the one "rational", the other "non-rational". The Utilitarians went so far as to identify the two sets of terms, thus endowing the "economic" side of man's character with the aura of rationality. He who would have refused to imagine that he was acting for gain alone was thus considered not only immoral, but also mad.
>
> (*ibid.*, p. 113)

This primacy of instrumental rationality crushes the social capacity of individuals, their capacity to debate, to act – a capacity that may be designated by the concept of "practical reason" from an Aristotelean perspective. This disappearance of the space of practical reason creates a difficulty in "forming a society" and leads to fascism. Society, exhausted by the market system and anomic, can no longer hold its members together; it comes together again in forms of gregarious totalitarianism that do not extend as far as practical reason: race, ethnic community, convergence behind a providential leader. Totalitarianism appears to Polanyi as the ultimate possibility of forming a society when there is no space left for practical reason – the ultimate, ailing and malfunctioning form caused by what a market society is "in reality".[14]

For Polanyi, this collapse ends the ill-fated experience aimed at putting in place a self-regulating market system and requires thought be given to how to avoid a new collapse by transforming (one is tempted to say "once again") the relations between the economy and society:

> Within the nations we are witnessing a development under which the economic system ceases to lay down the law to society and the primacy of society over that system is secured […] the market system will no longer be self-regulating, even in principle, since it will not comprise labor, land, and money.
>
> (Polanyi, [1944] 2001, p. 259)

Polanyi thinks therefore, in the aftermath of the Second World War, that the matter is understood and the liberal interlude ended (which is obviously a mistake as underscored quite rightly by Blythe (2002). Polanyi describes in the final chapter of his book this de-commodification at work, not settling the question of whether or not it will go so far as to abolish private property and asserting that it is fully compatible with the continuation of multiple markets – other than in land, labour, and money.[15] He also marks out philosophically what a policy must be that is aware of the reality of society (versus the liberal illusion) and preserving the principle of freedom (versus fascist ideology): this "freedom in a complex society" requires that institutions be built to "manage" the status of fictitious commodities. The "great transformation" that Polanyi believes he sees at work was not to be reflected by an escape from capitalism but by the state taking control of the ambiguous status of labour, land, and money.

Things are comparatively clear and documented for the de-commodification of labour and money during the years of the Fordist social compromise (from 1945 to the late 1970s). The Bretton Woods agreements initiated a Keynesian phase of management of money via an international monetary system (anchored to the dollar) and by direct financing of the economy by Western nation-states. Financial markets were to take a back seat during the thirty years following the war, the financial system was made to serve growth, and demands from capital holders were left aside until the 1970s and the crisis of the international monetary system. Likewise, the Declaration of Philadelphia (Supiot, 2010) and in France the work of the National Resistance Council opened up a phase of de-commodification of labour. It was characterized by the establishment of a specific labour law framing the particular private agreement of the employment contract (permanent contract, wage-setting rules, social protection, etc.). It continued by the construction in Western countries of social protection of employees (unemployment benefits, retirement pensions, sickness benefits) that Robert Castel terms "social ownership" (Castel, 2003) and Gotha Esping Andersen (1990, especially pp. 51–74) refers to as a de-commodification of labour. During this period, the price of labour was no longer determined by the market (it was the subject of rules and collective bargaining agreements) and the employee was covered when out-of-work and escaped the vicissitudes of the market. This double de-commodification took place within a broader institutional dynamic: it was the whole of the education and training and preservation of the labour force that was taken in charge by the state: knowledge production, education and training, the public health system, supervision by law, production of public infrastructures (for transport, power, and telecommunications), cultural services, and so on, were kept away from the market and taken in charge by states that were concerned with maintaining the social compromise. There was therefore not just an ebbing in the process of commodification of labour and money but also a shrinkage in the market for a whole series of goods and services "associated" with labour and employees (to which we shall return).

As regards land, its exploitation continued on the contrary and intensified without it really being possible to pinpoint any change in the predation stage characterizing the take-off of industrial capitalism. To take up Polanyi's terms, the "natural substance" was continually squeezed by western productive needs … although this enjoinder to feed the productive machinery did not take the form of a properly organized market. Where the exploitation of natural resources was concerned, it was states that were behind operations and imposed a form of plunder of resources in the name of productive necessities (Ost, 1994 and 1995; de Bonneuil and Fressoz, [2013] 2017). This phase of de-commodification emphasized the complex status of fictitious commodities: their designation related at least as much to the purpose of their production (for sale) as to their mode of distribution. For this reason the de-commodification that went on in the thirty years following the war was only partial (which Polanyi could not perceive in 1944 (2001): if the status of labour, money, and land (albeit differently for land) were largely changed and de-commodified, state direction of them (especially in Europe) was still designed to feed the productive machinery in a way that was uninterrupted and adapted to these needs (one thinks, for example, of the connection between the huge effort in education and training and the corresponding needs of industry). The state stood in for the market in part by ensuring the right balance between the need for a continuous flow of resources feeding market growth and the need to preserve the social foundations of communal life. The state constructed the possible conditions ahead of and after the production activity, so productive accumulation could be a collective project accepted by and desirable for the actors of this compromise.[16] The consensus built around GDP was in a way the archetype of this period, linking growth in market output and well-being thanks to (internationally coordinated) national policies of redistribution and the re-embedding of labour. That was the decisive role of the institutions of capitalism.

The crisis that hit Fordism and the transition to a new stage of "financialized" capitalism (Aglietta and Reberioux, 2004) overturned this institutionalization of fictitious commodities. The "re-commodification" of money further to the IMS crisis and then the emergence of shareholder governance progressively undid the Fordist social compromise and led to a very clear retreat in the public authorities' control over the employment regime leading to a "re-commodification" of labour.[17] We therefore witness a clear return of the principle of the self-regulating market again exerting tremendous pressure and with the same effect on societies and especially western societies (Blythe, 2002).

Re-commodification and market extension

Beyond the more or less prominent return to market management of money and labour, financialized capitalism involves the formation of new markets. First, the "commodification" of nature is undergoing a phase of institutionalization with the formation of markets or quasi-markets for natural resources (see Part 5 of this volume). The development of environmental law and the process of decolonization both mean that arrangements must be made for Western and Asian firms to have access to remote natural resources (Ost, 1995). Second, the process of re-commodification of money and even more so of labour is opening up a new market domain. The reduction of public control over these two resources opens up a new space of value-enhancement for this re-commodification. The extension of market rationale with respect to education and training, for instance, is closely bound up with the mechanisms for the re-commodification of labour. It is probably partly a consequence thereof. Likewise, the pressure exerted on the patentability of seeds (of the living world in general) is probably a consequence of the commodification of nature. Polanyi's analysis sheds useful light in this sense on the extension/retreat of the market sphere in our economies, by inviting us to focus on the form that production factors take on. The multiplication of contested markets is in part related to a change in the stage of capitalism that can be understood in terms of re-commodification (as Polanyi defined it). That multiplication is reflected by pressure being extended to productive efficiency – which is impelled by the self-regulating market system – deep within our relationship with nature, human life, and money.[18]

In this sense, it is in our interest to think as Polanyi did about the commodification process not as an extension of what "circulates" in markets but as the pressure market competition exerts on our societies through the productive sphere. It is this pressure, that he identifies in the expression of disembedding of the economy from society, that imperils societies subjected to the self-regulating market system. The distancing of this pressure by institutional and public mechanisms for the institutionalization of fictitious commodities makes this pressure more bearable, whereas the weakening of those mechanisms revives this tension that is in part socially unbearable. The "commodification of the world" understood in this way is not attributable primarily to the fact that ever more trade and social exchanges take a market form that they did not have before; it is due instead to them being paced, framed, and pervaded by productive efficiency as a market necessity, including when formal exchanges no longer take the form of markets in a classical sense. It is the systemic enjoinder for the formation of a market that Polanyi analyses, more than its actual manifestation in the form of a multitude of markets. Through his concept of commodification, he focuses not so much on whether or not there is a market,[19] as on the interrelating and networking of everything that contributes to productive efficiency in the form of "one big market". The pillars of this are the market management of production factors (land, labour, and money) which imposes a (more or less modulated or regulated) instrumental economic logic on society.

So with Polanyi we have a global and systemic analytical picture of "commodification" that often appears diffuse and sparse. We also and above all have an analysis that clearly posits the distinction between "market logic" and "self-regulating market system logic", between "economy comprising markets" and "capitalism". This analysis does not claim to be able to serve as a backdrop to any analysis of contested markets. That would be presumptuous and probably mistaken. Some markets derive their dynamic from segments that have been excluded from the market on moral or ethical grounds (e.g. trade in organ transplants studied by Philippe Steiner, 2010) and for which the connection with productive dynamics is not at all self-evident and in any event is very indirect.[20] But that dynamic may be, we believe, a useful supplement to commodification studies. Polanyi's idea of commodification, precisely by trying to develop an analysis of the global process of extension (and we might say of retreat, which opens up a dynamic perspective) of the self-regulating market system may help in situating these analyses and interweaving them with more general thinking about more or less prominent stages of liberalization of capitalism.

Our own contribution to the necessary and prolific thinking about the many forms that commodification takes on when interpreted through the extension of the market attempts to propose a distinction between what is at the heart of capitalism – in the sense that there cannot be any capitalism without the (even partial) fictitious commodification of land, labour, and money – and what counts as an extension of this capitalism to new terrains. This extension – on our analysis – is often connected with the institutional form that fictitious commodities take on. The concept of fictitious commodity can be used to grasp the idea that commodification serves above all as a general enjoinder to be efficient dictated by the market system to society as a whole (more than by the mere presence of a market or by the fact that some goods and services are marketable in a way they were not previously). The institutions that control the problematic market status of land, labour, and money underpin and maintain the fiction of commodification on which capitalism stands. The form these institutions take, the greater or lesser degree of the framing/protection of these pillars of society that these institutions impel, can be used to identify specific stages and forms of capitalism. These institutions are, we believe, the core of society. And an awareness of the development of these fundamental institutions may well be a useful key for analysing with precision the dynamics of any particular contested market.

Notes

1 Stiglitz (2001) emphasizes the contemporary interest of Polanyi's work:

> Because the transformation of European civilization is analogous to the transformation confronting developing countries around the world today, it often seems as if Polanyi is speaking directly to present-day issues. [...] The most recent global financial crisis reminded the current generation of the lessons that their grandparents had learned in the Great Depression: the self-regulating economy does not always work as well as its proponents would like us to believe.
> (Foreword, pp. vii–ix)

The present-day interest of Polanyi's arguments is examined further in Block and Somers (2016).

2 Polanyi only uses the term capitalism residually, preferring the expression "self-regulating market system". However, it is important to understand that these two different expressions designate one and the same mode of producing and distributing wealth: the one we currently live under and is usually referred to as capitalism. In this chapter, we opt for Polanyi's term of "self-regulating market system". For a critique of the use of capitalism inspired by Polanyi, see Block (2012).

3 Polanyi begins his book by stating that "Nineteenth-century civilization has collapsed. This book is concerned with the political and economic origins of this event, as well as with the great transformation which it ushered in" (Polanyi, [1944] 2001, p. 3). The term "Great Transformation" therefore designates – if taken literally – the transformation of western economies and societies in the aftermath of their collapse before and during the Second World War. The book deals, however, very largely with the "origins" of this collapse and of this great transformation (and practically not with what happens next) to the point that it often creates confusion among readers – and probably for Polanyi too (Block, 2003) – because of the feeling that what is described as a transformation is the necessary and impossible transition from feudal society to "market society". In his introduction to the French edition of Polanyi's book in 1983, Louis Dumont returns (p. II) to the term suggesting that "great transformation (*grande transformation*)" should be read rather as "great turnaround or reversal (*grand retournement*)", which seems judicious. It seems

to us that the term "great transformation" refers to a process rather than a date: in any event, Polanyi's argument bears on all of the social convulsion caused by the self-regulating market from its birth (in the late eighteenth century) to what he (wrongly) views as its collapse in the 1930s. The essential point is therefore to emphasize that it is the self-regulating market regime and its social effects that form the core of his analysis (on this point, see McRobbie and Polanyi-Levitt, 2005).

4 The term market, associated when first used with forms of non-competitive trade, derives, Alain Guery (2017, p. 437) reminds us, from the term "march" meaning the "margins" of the empire, the areas of non-law where exchange escaped from the dominant form of social control.

5 Three factors should be distinguished: the existence (from Antiquity) of forms of trade not related to the market, the existence (from the Middle Ages) of competitive local markets, and the existence (from the late eighteenth century) of a self-regulating market system. The distinction between trade and market is a central point in Polanyi's analyses and is at the centre of the reference work in economic anthropology that he initiated (Polanyi, Arensberg, and Pearson, [1957] 2017). There have been and there can be forms of trade that are not part of market exchange. For Guery (2017) this distinction is important but may lead to a difficulty if it overlaps the other essential difference between the existence of "local markets" and a "market system" that is more important for us here. Guery emphasizes that a "first transformation" occurred in the Middle Ages with the appearance of markets that were not interconnected but did produce prices independently of outside rules (which is what the Mercantilists discover).

> Markets did indeed remain embedded in the rest of civilization to the point of being in symbiosis with it, but that enabled them to disseminate new simpler and more general rules that led to a first, longer-lasting great transformation that Polanyi had not thought of, being more attentive to more geographically remote societies.
>
> (Guery, 2017, p. 457)

Polanyi's subject matter, and that of our chapter here, is the transition in the late eighteenth century and throughout the nineteenth century, from a host of markets "embedded" in society to a self-regulating market system extricating itself from the social control of marketplaces and imposing its own law.

6 The economic theory of general equilibrium has failed to demonstrate the existence of a systematic process of equilibrium price formation (Sonnenschein, 1972) that could have provided a demonstration of a general law of supply and demand. In this sense, the law of supply and demand does not exist (Postel, 2011) (see Chapter 3 by Bertrand in this volume).

7 Postel and Sobel (2010) examine this process in depth, emphasizing that the second criterion – that of the market purpose of production – actually rests on two different levels: the possibility of market "validation" of what is produced but also the existence of a market pre-existing what is produced. These two aspects are very clear in the standard economic theory of the "producer" who, as a price-taker, calculates the volume of output depending on what is observed as the existing price of the type of good they are making ready to produce. However, it seems to us that this distinction is not essential to our argument in this chapter.

8 This reflection by Polanyi resonates loudly today with the way philosopher Bruno Latour analyses the transition from the question of *development* to that of *envelopment*: "Economics focused on the mobilization of resources for production, but is there an economics that can turn its attention to maintaining the conditions for the world to be inhabitable? This is the challenge facing the new ecological class" (Latour and Schultz, 2022, p. 24).

9 It was John Maynard Keynes who most clearly showed the importance of money and its non-market regulation for the socially bearable operation of the self-regulating market system.

10 "And did the Countenance Divine, / Shine forth upon our clouded hills? / And was Jerusalem builded here, / Among these dark Satanic Mills?"

11 It is noteworthy, but not the crux of this chapter, that this centrality of the production phenomenon that places the firm as the locus of revelation of the market pressure exerted on society should be at the heart of the three major criticisms of capitalism in institutional economics. Marx is of course the philosopher of labour as a commodity. Keynes highlights the specific status of money as a commodity. Ricardo and then later the proponents of ecological economics point out the problematic character of land as a commodity.

12 If readers will allow us to venture a rugby metaphor here, the logic of this double movement is that of a "scrum" that collapses when one of the props collapses. In religious architecture, it is the logic of two arches resting against one another without a keystone (in early Romanesque architecture).

13 The origins of a defence of liberalism has often been read into Montesquieu's argument especially since Hirschman's analysis (1982) of it. We fall in behind the analysis of Catherine Larrère (2014) who points out it is more a defence of political liberalism.

14 There is no room here to bring out other than intuitively the strange and significant proximity in the conclusion of Polanyi (on it being impossible to have a society founded solely on a market system) and of K.J. Arrow (1967) in his impossibility theorem (individuals under instrumental rationality cannot agree on a social choice other than by dictatorship or imposed norms) (Postel and Lengaigne, 2004).

15

> That for an infinite variety of products competitive markets continue to function need not interfere with the constitution of society any more than the fixing of prices outside the market for labor, land, and money interferes with the costing-function of prices in respect to the various products.
>
> (Polanyi, [1944] 2001, p. 260)

16 Postel and Sobel (2019) provide an analysis of the regulation of capitalism based on this special status of the Fordist compromise (and of its connection with the emergence of corporate social responsibility (CSR) in the transition to financialized capitalism). It should be emphasized for example that the aspect of commodification of labour by way of the homogeneity of the content of labour (not of the status of workers) continues throughout the twentieth century in particular by way of the extension of Taylorism. Coutrot (2018) points out that true de-commodification would also have raised questions about the "content of labour" and aimed to release it from market and productive pressure.

17 In parallel, the end of colonization and the growing importance of environmental issues (exhaustion of resources and pollution problems) have compelled the authorities to organize a market for natural resources by further framing the distribution of property rights over natural areas (considered as clear of any rights in the Fordist accumulation mode). Here again, there is indeed an extension of commodification (even if this is not a retreat/predation period that characterizes Fordism).

18 The whole debate about the patentability of living organisms, seeds, and GMOs, is tied up with the commodification of nature. The pressure for labour competitiveness generates numerous new markets: the market for education and training but also markets for domestic services or for health products that can boost performance. Financialization is reflected by almost unlimited creativity in producing financial market instruments that are the subject matter of new markets in banking, insurance, consultancy services, etc.

19 The changing academic landscape in France and Europe, although it cannot be claimed that universities have been commodified, or that research is no longer supported by the public sector, is indeed liable to be analysed as being increasingly subject to the rules and necessity of market competition.

20 Polanyi's insistence on explaining that the process of establishing a self-regulating market system changes actors' behaviour by confining them to instrumental rationality means it can be imagined that the re-commodification of land, labour, and money entails a surge in the instrumental motive in behaviour, which may lead to extending the market relation to areas that were heretofore unaffected by it.

References

Aglietta M. and Orléan A. (eds) (1998) *La Monnaie Souveraine*, Paris: Odile Jacob.

Aglietta M. and Rebérioux A. (2004) *Dérives du capitalisme financier*, Paris: Albin Michel.

Arrow, K.J. (1967) "Values and collective decision making", in Laslett and Ruciman (eds), *Philosophy, Politics and Society*, Oxford: Basil Blackwell. Republished in *The Collected Papers*, vol. 1, pp. 59–77.

Blake, W. [1804] "Jérusalem", *"Milton a Poem, copy B object 2". The William Blake Archive. Ed. Morris Eaves, Robert N. Essick, and Joseph Viscomi. Retrieved 8 June 2019.*

Block, F. (2003) "Karl Polanyi and the writing of *The Great Transformation*", *Theory and Society*, 32, pp. 275–306.

Block, F. (2008) "Polanyi's double movement and the reconstruction of critical theory", *Revue Interventions économiques*, 38, http://journals.openedition.org/interventionseconomiques/274; https://doi.org/10.4000/interventionseconomiques.274

Block, F. (2012) "Varieties of what? Should we still be Using the Concept of Capitalism?", in *Political Power and Social Theory*, 23, pp. 269–291.
Block, F. and Somers, M.R. (2016) *The Power of Market Fundamentalism. Karl Polanyi's Critique*. Cambridge, MA: Harvard University Press.
Blythe, M. (2002) *Great Transformations, Economic Ideas and Institutional Change in the Twentieth Century*. Cambridge, MA: Cambridge University Press.
Bonneuil C. and Fressoz, J.-B [2013] (2017) *The Shock of the Anthropocene*. London: New York: Verso, transl. D. Fernbach.
Castel, R. (2003) *From Manual Workers to Wage Laborers Transformation of the Social Question*, Routledge.
Coutrot A. (2018) *Libérer le travail.* Paris: Seuil.
Dale, G. (2010) *Karl Polanyi: The Limits of the Markets*. Cambridge: Polity Press.
Dumont L. (1983) "Preface" in Polanyi K. *La grande transformation*. Paris: Gallimard.
Esping-Andersen, G. (1990) *The Three Worlds of Welfare Capitalism*. Princeton, New Jersey: Princeton University Press.
Foucault, M. (2008) *The Birth of Biopolitics Lectures at the Collège de France, 1978–1979*, London: Palgrave Macmillan.
Guery, A. (2017) "Des marchés au marché d'une transformation à l'autre", in Polanyi, Arensberg, Pearson, *Commerce et marché dans les premiers empires: sur la diversité des économies*. Paris, éditions du bord de l'eau, pp. 435–459.
Hirschman, A.O. (1982), *Shifting Involvements: Private Interest and Public Action*, Princeton, NJ: Princeton University Press.
Larrère, C. (2014) "Montesquieu et le 'doux commerce': un paradigme du libéralisme", *Cahiers d'histoire. Revue d'histoire critique*, 123, pp. 21–38.
Latour, B. and Schultz, N. (2022) *Mémo sur la nouvelle classe écologique*. Paris: La Découverte.
Mauss, M. [1925] (1990), *The Gift: variations on the theme of solidarity*, London: Routledge.
McRobbie, K. and Polanyi-Levitt, K. (2005) *The Contemporary Significance of The Great Transformation*, 2nd edition, Critical Perspectives on Historic Issues, Montreal: Black Rose Books.
Ost, F. (1994) *Legal System Between Order and Disorder*. Oxford: Oxford University Press.
Ost, F. (1995) *La nature hors la loi, l'écologie à l'épreuve du droit*. Paris: La Découverte.
Polanyi, K. (1935) "The essence of fascism" in K. Lewis, K. Polanyi, D.K. Kitchin (eds), *Christianity and the Social Revolution*. London: Gollancz, pp. 359–394.
Polanyi, K. [1944] (2001) *The Great Transformation: The Political and Economic Origins of Our Time*, 2nd ed., Boston: Beacon Press.
Polanyi, K. (1947) "Our obsolete market economy. Civilization must find a new thought pattern", *Commentary*, 3, pp. 109–117.
Polanyi, K., Arensberg C.M., Pearson H.W. (eds) (1957) *Trade and Market in the Early Empires. Economies in History and Theory.* Glencoe: The Free Press.
Polanyi, K. (1957) "The Economy as Instituted Process" in Polanyi, K., Arensberg C.M., Pearson H.W. (eds), *Trade and Market in the Early Empires. Economies in History and Theory.* Glencoe: The Free Press. pp. 243–270.
Postel, N. (2011) "From the search for natural laws to the discovery of contingent rules in economics", *Journal of Philosophical Economics*, V1(1), pp. 35–61.
Postel, N. and Lengaigne, B. (2004) "Arrow et l'impossibilité: une démonstration par l'absurde", *Revue du MAUSS*, 24(2), pp. 388–410.
Postel, N. and Sobel, R. (2010) "La notion de 'marchandises fictives' pierre angulaire de l'institutionnalisme polanyien", *Revue de Philosophie Economique*, 11(2), pp. 3–36.
Postel, N. and Sobel, R. (2019), "Corporate social responsibility (CSR): An institutionalist Polanyian analysis", *Society and Business Review*, 14(4), pp. 381–400.
Ramaux, C. (2012) *L'Etat Social*. Paris: Fayard.
Servet, J.M. (1993) "L'institution monétaire de la société selon Karl Polanyi", *Revue économique*, 44(6), pp. 1127–1150.
Servet, J.M. (2007) "Le principe de réciprocité chez Karl Polanyi, contribution à une définition de l'économie solidaire", *Revue Tiers Monde* 190(2), pp. 255–273.
Sonnenschein, H. (1972) "Market excess demand functions", *Econometrica*, 40(3), pp. 549–563.

Stanfield, D. (1980) "The institutional economics of Karl Polanyi", *Journal of Economics Issues*, 14(3), pp. 593–614.

Steiner, P. (2010) *La transplantation d'organe. Un commerce nouveau entre les êtres humains*. Paris: Gallimard.

Supiot, A. (2010) *L'Esprit de Philadelphie, la justice sociale face au marché total*. Paris: Seuil.

Stiglitz, J. (2001) "Preface" to Polanyi, K. *The Great Transformation: The Political and Economic Origins of Our Time*, 2nd ed., Boston: Beacon Press.

3

CONTEMPORARY ANTI-COMMODIFICATION ARGUMENTS

Market failures – Identifying contested markets without morals? An analysis of the externality argument for inalienability

Elodie Bertrand

Introduction

The arguments employed in commodification studies to justify the limitation of certain markets come in four typical forms, appealing respectively to the degradation of social norms, repugnance, inequalities, and externalities; it is with the fourth of these that the present chapter is concerned. The interdisciplinary study of contested commodification borrows the externality argument from standard welfare economics, where appeal is made to externalities in order to justify the regulation, or the outright banning, of some markets. In a typical example, consider a factory that emits fumes (the externality) that are polluting a nearby laundry: the factory's production cost does not take into account the cost it imposes on the laundry, and since the result is hence inefficient, the market (for the commodity produced by the factory) should be regulated or even forbidden. In this chapter I will be concerned with the structure of the externality argument for banning certain markets as it appears in economic theory, and with what happens when it is used to water the soil of commodification studies: what transformations does it undergo along the way, and what presuppositions does it carry with it?

The concept of externality has traditionally faced two main difficulties, the one concerning the extent of its application, and the other the solutions that might be offered; and these difficulties are carried over, in a magnified form, when the concept is applied to commodification. First, within economics the concept of externality has traditionally been limited to effects that are physical and unpriced (typically pollution); but this reasoning has subsequently been applied by commodification studies to all sorts of externalities, including moral effects – such as the offence felt by some people about the very existence of certain kinds of sales (the repugnance argument) –, and pecuniary effects – such as the effects of certain kinds of sales on income inequalities (one version of the inequality argument). Second, regarding the solutions, economic theory advises

 DOI: 10.4324/9781003188742-5

the banning or regulation of the markets that cause externalities. This, then, becomes the standard economic reason why some goods should not be commodified, or at least not traded as freely as other goods. But externalities are two-faced: they legitimate the restriction of some markets for efficiency reasons, but they also legitimate the *extension* of markets – for the same reasons of efficiency. The economists' chain of reasoning indeed did not stop at proposals for bans and regulation: they also advocated for the creation of new markets for externalities themselves, in which case, from having been the problem, the market now also becomes the solution. It is on this basis that markets are developed for emissions credits and other forms of commodification of pollution. Externalities can therefore be a justification for both the limitation and the extension of markets. Hence, we are led to ask, why, or under which conditions, can this argument nevertheless be used *against* commodification?

Both these theoretical difficulties, of extent and solution, arise because the concept of externality is "thick" in Williams's (1985) sense: it is both descriptive and evaluative, externalities being a cause of inefficiency and then furnishing the basis for public intervention. And questions regarding extent and solutions are not independent, since we need to be able to draw a line between legitimate and illegitimate public intervention in order to mark the frontier between externalities and other effects: for example, pollution will generally appear as a more legitimate reason for intervention than the offense caused by the existence of contracts for sex. This implies that the externality argument for market-inalienability is not as value-neutral as it pretends to be: it not only evaluates markets relative to their efficiency, but it also takes a position on the extent of and the solution to externalities, and, in so doing, makes moral and political presuppositions about the legitimacy of public intervention. What happens when these presuppositions are transferred from economics to commodification studies?

The first section analyzes how economic theory frames and defines the concept of externality, and how solutions are selected in terms of market bans or extensions. I will give some preliminary hints at the normative choices that are made at each step. Faced with the potentially extensive public intervention that may be justified by reference to externalities, economists have adopted two strategies: restrict the extent of the concept (i.e., to physical externalities), and limit the bans and regulations. The second section argues that some trends in commodification studies have adopted the reverse strategy: they retained the idea that externalities may justify market-inalienability, they enlarged the notion beyond economic activities, and included pecuniary and moral externalities. The third section then explores some reasons why the externality justification of market-inalienability becomes insufficient or inconsistent when it stands on its own. Commodification studies has not paid enough attention to the philosophical and theoretical background in which the concept is embedded, and which it imported when it began to deploy the concept for its own ends. I conclude, briefly, that while the concept of externality (in the welfarist context) is an inappropriate tool to account for many of the problems posed by certain markets, it nevertheless remains useful as a way of analyzing some of them, provided that it is complemented by a theory of justice that can rationalize its extent and ground its solution. Although markets cannot be studied only from the angle of their external effects, this angle is still necessary; but it needs to be clarified by combining insights from economics and philosophy. Commodification studies seems to be a good place to undertake this task.

The economic account of market-inalienability by externalities

General Equilibrium Theory, axiomatized in the 1950s, formalized the intuition that coordination can exist in a decentralized economy through prices, and that this coordination is better than any other system (Pignol, 2017). This is an abstract, fictional, and ahistorical model of markets conceived as a theory of prices (Satz, 2010, ch. 2; Bourdieu, 2017, pp. 164–165), and it forms the core of standard economic theory. It is also the only theoretical framework in which the concept of externalities is technically meaningful: the introduction of externalities disrupts efficiency and hence – potentially – justifies bans on some markets.

The so-called efficiency of markets without externalities

The general equilibrium model assumes two types of agents, consumers and producers, characterized by a preference relation and a positive revenue for the former, and a production function for the latter. They maximize respectively their utility and profit, taking prices as given (i.e., out of their control), which results in supply and demand on each market. Some technical assumptions are necessary so that these maxima exist, and the supply and demand functions have the desired shape. The model does not have any descriptive aim, and the assumptions are made just for the sake of obtaining the desirable result (an optimal equilibrium) – among them, the famous assumption of perfect competition means there is one price per commodity (or complete system of markets) and that prices are given. There is therefore a third type of agent, the auctioneer, whose role is to give prices and to modify them until the equilibrium is reached.

In terms of results, the existence of an equilibrium can be proven mathematically (Arrow and Debreu, 1954) but, due to the interdependencies between markets, we cannot prove that prices will converge towards an equilibrium (Sonnenshein, 1973; Mantel, 1974; Debreu, 1974) – in other words, there is no reason why the auctioneer should find the equilibrium price except by chance. It remains that the equilibrium is blessed with the feature the model was built for: it allows an efficient allocation – and this is the first theorem of welfare economics (Arrow, 1951; Arrow and Debreu, 1954). In this theorem, and hence in all the discourses that implicitly rely on this demonstration of the efficiency of markets, efficiency means Pareto optimality. An allocation is Pareto-optimal if it is impossible to improve the situation of one agent without damaging the situation of at least one other, and it is thus obtained when all the mutually beneficial exchanges have taken place. The existence and optimality theorems together establish the conditions of validity at the core of economic liberalism, namely that prices permit the best "decentralized" coordination.[1]

It is this model that justifies the claim that markets are efficient, and this belief, as Pierre Bourdieu observed, flows down the hierarchy from the Arrow-Debreu model to the academic economist, to the media economist, and hence to the journalist (2017, pp. 145–146). And this is despite the fact that the model retains no link with the real world. This efficiency is not value neutral: the framework is welfarist (Sen, 1979), where welfare is defined as satisfaction of subjective preferences, and Pareto optimality is indifferent to the justice of distribution.

However, by setting out the assumptions necessary for optimality, the model also identifies the reasons why an equilibrium may not be optimal: and all such gaps between the model and the real world are labelled market failures, seen as legitimating public intervention. Standardly, economists identify three main conditions under which the optimality conditions may not be met: (i) natural monopolies (bridges, network infrastructures), where it is more efficient that there should be only one producer; (ii) public goods, which may be enjoyed without having paid for them and/or may be enjoyed even when others have already enjoyed them (commons, lighthouses); and (iii) externalities, where there is an effect that has not been priced, or an incomplete system of markets.

Restraining the extent of externalities

At root, externalities (or external effects, side effects, spillovers) are defined as the involuntary effects of *A*'s activity (the factory) on agent *C* (the laundry) with whom *A* has no contractual relation (the factory sells its products to *B*); since *A* doesn't take this external cost into account, *A* produces too much compared to what is socially optimal.[2] After their identification by welfare economist Arthur Cecil Pigou (1932), the economic discussion on externalities took off in the 1950s and focused on the disparity between general equilibrium and Pareto-optimum, to which externalities give rise (Medema, 2020a; Berta, 2017). Note that economists at first considered this concept to just be an esoteric and theoretical source of suboptimality, before realizing that it had a real – and significant – counterpart, namely pollution. The history of the concept from the 1950s to the 1970s is thus a story of restriction, under a dual constraint. On the one hand, the concept was increasingly associated with a specific phenomenon, that of pollution. On the other, since the concept was associated with sub-optimality, and could formally encompass almost every interaction and so justify extensive public regulation, it was imperative to circumscribe it (Berta, 2017).[3] As already remarked, it is because the issue of externalities is so entangled with that of public intervention that "philosophical pre-suppositions are at work within [this] economic categor[y] of market failure" (Claassen, 2016, p. 542). According to a general consensus among economists, the relevant externalities should be limited to physical and unpriced third-party effects. This consensus came with three main restrictions of the concept, of which two are problematic – and would be rejected by certain commodification theorists.

First, as stated in the above definition, the concept was limited to effects without prices, that is to *technological* externalities, by opposition to *pecuniary* externalities, which were excluded. Pecuniary externalities arise through prices and are therefore not an obstacle to optimality, but rather are the symptom of the "good" functioning of markets; they hence do not legitimate public intervention – not for reasons of efficiency, at least. Technological externalities, on the contrary, those that matter for economists, have no price; they are missing markets and provoke suboptimalities (Arrow, 1969). They are therefore formalized as interdependencies between production and/or utility functions, but this may lead to a confusion with two other concepts.

Second, it was then necessary to exclude malevolence, and to this end the phenomenological definition must add a second feature, namely that externalities are involuntary. Economist Ezra Mishan clearly notes:

> What the notation alone does not succeed in conveying, however, is that the essential feature of the concept of an external effect is that the effect produced is not a deliberate creation but an unintended or incidental by-product of some otherwise legitimate activity.
>
> (1971b, p. 2)

The externality is involuntary in the sense that the external effect – e.g., pollution – is not the primary aim of the action that caused it. The tort may be caused knowingly, but the action does not aim at this tort and the action would be undertaken even if it did not result in it (see Chauvier, 2013; Hausman, 1992).

Finally, the formal definition also does not convey that economists generally focus on *technological* externalities exclusively in the sense of physical externalities. This aims at excluding from the domain of relevant externalities other forms of utility interdependencies, or what economists call other-regarding preferences (or external preferences) – like envy or homophobia.

This exclusion first mainly concerned envy, which, along with other Veblen effects (positional externalities), were excluded from the analysis, even while the formal definition encompassed them.[4] For example, Mishan argues that it is by a social consensus "drawn on basic values that are apparently widely acceptable in the Western communities" that "tangible" externalities (like noise and smoke) are recognized as counting in welfare, and hence as legitimating public intervention (1965, p. 8). On the contrary, he goes on, the same consensus excludes that envy could legitimate public intervention, i.e., could count in the evaluation of welfare:

> If [...] a man were bold enough to complain that the mere fact of others becoming better off saddened him considerably, [...] it is hardly likely that practical measures would be contemplated which were calculated to impoverish others in the hope of restoring his spirits.
>
> (*ibid.*)

Welfare economists de facto excluded other types of other-regarding preferences which create moral externalities, like embarrassment or discomfort, such as when some persons are offended as a result of others' behaviour. This exclusion came about in the same vein as the exclusion of envy and by the same argument. In Mishan's view, the exclusion by social consensus also applies to moral externalities: "If the mere sight of a person, or the mere knowledge of his existence or behaviour, offends me, it is not likely that society would support my claim to damage" (1971a, p. 119, fn. 1).

The exclusion, first, of pecuniary and, second, of moral externalities poses some problems, and it is necessary to examine them, since precisely these kinds of effects appear regularly in the debate about commodification. First, while they do not pose a problem of efficiency, pecuniary externalities do pose a problem of distribution and hence of justice. It is impossible not to worry about negative pecuniary externalities that can lead people to starve, or to flee from their homes and countries, and we must be able to morally evaluate activities that have such consequences (Hausman, 1992). This argument is all the more important since these externalities are more serious when the goods are not substitutable (like basic commodities – food, health care, housing), and when the good's consumption represents a large share of the consumer's income (this will more often be the case with people on lower incomes) (Stark, 2020, p. 186).

Second, the exclusion of other-regarding preferences from the domain of relevant externalities is not consistent with the economists' so-called neutrality towards preferences, and hence involves an additional evaluative choice about which preferences are to count. As Satz noted, "[w]hat counts as an inefficiency [...] involves prior ethical judgements" (2010, p. 34). Moral externalities in particular cannot be quickly brushed aside: just as with physical externalities, some person's utility is diminished, and their preferences are affected. If economists stuck resolutely to their view of welfare as satisfaction of all preferences, there would be no way of distinguishing between moral and physical externalities, since in both cases *C*'s utility is unintentionally diminished by *A*'s behaviour. Guido Calabresi, one of the founders of the new law-and-economics movement, holds that moral external effects are "no less real and costly" (2016, p. 27). Therefore, "[t]o ignore or treat as nonexistent some tastes and values – some things that are in individuals' utility functions, and the costs that result from their being there – constitutes a taking of a position – *sub silentio* – on tastes and values" (*ibid.*, pp. 150–151).

Welfare economists, however, focus on physical external effects, those that are suboptimal according to a socially acceptable welfare criterion, which sets some preferences apart from the evaluation of welfare – i.e., such a stance combines welfarism with normative presuppositions about which preferences are to count.

From market-inalienability to commodification as solutions to externalities

The initial reaction to externalities among economists consisted in limiting the markets that cause them. Traditionally, the first solution to technological externalities was the prohibition of the externality, through the market-inalienability of the good whose production or consumption created that externality (i.e., the market of the good exchanged between *A* and *B*). In this case, the good is not produced. Pigou (1932, p. 186), for example, justified the ban of the (production and) sale of intoxicants by the higher level of crime they provoke, causing extra cost in policemen and prisons (concerning pollution, see, e.g., Mishan, 1971b).

The second solution is to propose regulation of the market for the good in question, which may take different forms: either economic (bounties, taxations) or administrative (quotas, standards, zoning) (Pigou, 1932, pp. 192–195). In Margaret Jane Radin's words, this kind of regulation can be classified as "incomplete commodification", in the sense that the good that provokes externalities is still commodified, but not as freely as other goods, for its exchanges are submitted to various constraints. Still using her typology, commodification is here incomplete in a "weak sense", since regulation of the market is justified by only market failures (Radin, 1996, p. 116).[5] With taxation, in addition, the external effect itself is partially commodified: typically, in the case of an emissions tax, it suffices to pay to be allowed to emit – without that being a real market since there is no proper exchange.

However, this would be too simple a story. Economists could not countenance that such an immense territory should potentially render any market illegitimate. Hence, after that initial reaction, a new line of response was developed such that, since externalities are a problem of missing markets, the solution would be to create new markets for the externalities themselves. Because the problem comes from their absence of price, or of market-alienability, commodification of the externalities of markets was to be considered as a possible solution.[6] It was Ronald Coase (1960) who first suggested that commodification of the right to create externalities could restore efficiency, assuming that by negotiating their rights to emit externalities or to be protected from them, the two parties would reach an efficient result. This idea came to be known as the famous "Coase theorem" (see, e.g., Bertrand, 2019; Medema, 2020b). This line of thought justified the idea that private property rights serve to control externalities, even that they are the best means to this end and that this is why they originally developed (Demsetz, 1964; 1967). From then on, the economic debate on the commodification of externalities took off in two main directions, depending on how we conceive of the exchange mechanism.

The first direction is through the model of a perfect competition market between polluters. Dales (1968) suggested a system of exchange of property rights that became the basis for emissions trading schemes, or what is now called cap (the objective of maximum permitted pollution) and trade (of individual quotas between emitters) (see Berta, 2020). In theory, the exchange between polluters gives an equilibrium price, and allows the cap to be achieved at the least abatement cost.[7] The idea of markets for emission quotas took a long time to become accepted. Taxes at that time were considered as already too much of a step in the direction of commodification, but the debate later evolved into an opposition between (centralized) tax versus (decentralized) cap-and-trade. Besides its theoretical problems, cap-and-trade encountered practical problems, including unjust grandfathering, high volatility of prices, and bigger public intervention than expected (see Berta's Chapter 24 in this volume).

The second line of thought envisages exchange as Coase did: as bilateral bargaining. This is the theoretical basis of the idea of payments for environmental or ecosystem services (see contribution by Martin Ortega et al. in this volume (Chapter 25)), and also justifies proposals for the commodification of the moral externalities of commodification (see Buchanan and Tullock, 1962, 3.18.10–12 about sex work, and Lusk, 2011 about animal welfare – see Chapter 27 by Sterri in this volume). The main theoretical difficulty is that Coase's result has not been proven; it is at best circular, since it rests on the assumption that all the mutually beneficial agreements are struck (Bertrand, 2019). But Coase's original 1960 article in fact focused on another problem, that the commodification of externalities encounters an obstacle in the form of transaction costs, namely the costs of information, negotiation, and enforcement. Because of these costs, he was not arguing for a generalized commodification of externalities, but for a case-by-case analysis that would compare the benefits and costs of each solution: market with allocation of property rights to the polluter or to the polluted, taxation, standards, or status quo. For example, if the market transaction costs exceed the benefits expected from this solution, the market will not be chosen (see Demsetz, 1967). Therefore, externalities may indeed still justify market bans, but the argument is refined by introducing the relative costs of external effects and of transactions.

The generalization of the Coasean framework in the economic analysis of law issued in what Radin has called the "transaction cost model of inalienability" (Radin, 1996, p. 22), in which tradition she includes Calabresi and Melamed (1972), Epstein (1985), and Rose-Ackerman (1985). These authors apply the Coasean framework to explaining why the transfers of some property rights may have to be limited, and why some property rights should still be market-inalienable: specifically, when the costs of transacting externalities are greater than the benefits. Depending on the amounts of the transaction costs and external costs, a solution will be chosen on a scale ranging from market inalienability to commodification, via incomplete commodification.

Let's see, for example, how Calabresi and Melamed's seminal 1972 paper applied this framework to moral externalities, which they call "moralisms". Their famous illustration is the following:

> If Taney is allowed to sell himself into slavery, or to take undue risks of becoming penniless, or to sell a kidney, Marshall may be harmed, simply because Marshall is a sensitive man who is made unhappy by seeing slaves, paupers, or persons who die because they have sold a kidney.
>
> (1972, p. 1112)

The commodification would mean that "Marshall could pay Taney not to sell his freedom to Chase the slaveowner", but the Marshalls, however, are numerous (which implies high transaction costs), and "the external cost to Marshall does not lend itself to an acceptable objective measurement" (*ibid.*). Because the commodification of liberty is therefore too costly (even if we cannot measure this cost), the solution is to make freedom inalienable.[8]

As this example illustrates, despite the fact that externalities may justify an extension of markets (for externalities), two reasons explain why they still imply the banning of some markets (at the source of externalities): (1) when commodifying them is too costly; (2) when commodifying them is socially unacceptable. Calabresi and Melamed, as we see in the passages quoted above, conflate both reasons by interpreting the social norms of morality in terms of costs (or by conflating tastes and values). In fact, and as I identified above, there is a third, theoretical, reason for a potential ban: even if transaction costs were zero, we do not have any satisfactory model of the efficient commodification of externalities. On the one hand, the assumptions of perfect competition are heroic (and even more so for externalities); on the other, bilateral bargaining has not been proven to be efficient. Commodification is therefore not a solution, and not only because of transaction costs, but also due to other theoretical and practical difficulties.

How commodification studies makes use of the externality argument

Commodification studies has retained the idea that externalities may justify market-inalienability (sometimes in a more refined way compared to considerations of the transaction costs of the market), and has enlarged the concept to ensure that technological externalities are not related only to economic activities, and that externalities also include pecuniary and moral ones. But in so doing it forgot the theoretical framework in which the concept was originally embedded and from which it derived meaning (with its restricted assumptions of perfect competition, and specific definition of efficiency).

How commodification studies makes use of the technological externality argument

Not surprisingly, Radin's pioneering work was first seized upon by the law-and-economics movement, and it was Michael Trebilcock (1993), a lawyer, who sought to formalize her intuitions more systematically, mainly in terms of externalities.[9] He generally argues, however, in favour of regulation rather than bans. Since his aim is to extend rather than limit the domain of contracts, his guiding question concerns not so much market-inalienability per se as which type of regulation should be used.

Of course, the economists' participation in the debate also explicitly introduced externalities. Alvin Roth invoked technological externalities to explain the ban on the commerce of some products, the most evident being sex work (by the effects on the neighbourhood) and alcohol (by the effects on crime) (Roth, 2007, p. 40 and 41). Ravi Kanbur (2004) includes impacts on third parties as one source of the "weakness of agency" that accounts for a market being "obnoxious", citing those for arms or hard drugs, which may cause crime and addiction. This source of weak agency refers to the kind of technological externalities welfare economists are familiar with, when a transaction has negative consequences for a party that is not involved in the transaction. Kanbur, however, adds a feature that was absent from the economists' discussion: the lesser the control, the greater the offence. He notes for example that the traditional analysis overlooks the outrage felt when someone is confronted by the arms trade: those who exchange arms are not the civilians who are hurt, killed, or see their houses or villages destroyed by those arms.

This framework also permeated the associated philosophical literature. Since Satz's (2010) own criteria for identifying noxious markets are inspired by Kanbur's (2004) (and Trebilcock, 1993), we again find technological externalities, at least at first glance, in her criteria of "very weak or asymmetric agency" (e.g., for future generations, p. 96) and of "extremely harmful outcome[s] for individuals" – the last referring to the gravity and seriousness of the results on not only contracting but also not-contracting parties (e.g., when a market causes serious effects on natural resources, p. 94).

Explaining market-inalienability by reference to technological externalities, however, faces some limits: most of the time, it cannot account for the specific problems posed by commodification. Arms, drugs, and alcohol are goods whose consumption creates negative external effects in and by itself (whether they are sold, given, or self-produced); contested commodities (sex, pregnancy, organs), meanwhile, are goods whose *sale* poses problems, but whose other modes of transfers (like gift) would not – at least, this is how the question is framed by commodification studies, even if some confusion sometimes arises in this regard (Brennan and Jaworski, 2016; and the introduction to this volume). Now, more often than not, it is consumption and production that provokes externalities, not sale and exchange (see, e.g., Mildenberger, 2018, p. 1211, who asserts that the exchange that seems to cause externalities is not in itself unjust). This is to say that while a commodification ban appears to be a solution to some externalities, the mere fact that the existence of a market changes the extent of the problem does not imply that the problem stems from commodification itself. Nevertheless, the other types of externalities (pecuniary and moral) are caused by this specific mode of transfer, i.e., sale, and this may justify a ban.

How commodification studies makes use of the pecuniary externality argument

I begin with how pecuniary externalities may explain the resistance to the commodification of some goods. As a first illustration we may take Kanbur's (2004) inequality criterion, which in fact refers to this kind of externality. He argues, for example, that the increased mobility of capital lowers the labour price, and more generally that globalization has deleterious effects on the price of labour, resources, and assets such as land and livestock. This is why he classifies short-term capital flows, which may provoke crises and increase poverty, as "obnoxious markets".

The concept of pecuniary externalities also lies behind some forms of the coercion (or inequality) argument against commodification. For example, Kaushik Basu's 2007 article is known for suggesting an economic rationale for placing limits on contracts based on coercion, but this is for welfarist reasons that are neither paternalistic nor moralistic. His model shows how coercion can appear in a setting of free exchange. Suppose one person agrees to be sexually harassed in exchange for a higher wage: this exchange is mutually advantageous and has no effect on anyone else. But if a large number of people accept this type of contract, then the wage for labour contracts with no sexual harassment decreases. Those who refuse will be worse-off: "many workers accepting such contracts may have a negative welfare impact on *other* workers" (Basu, 2007, p. 575, his emphasis). And this effect must be prevented. Basu's argument for limiting the possibilities of contracts rests therefore on pecuniary externalities (lower wages) which lead to coercion.[10] Conversely, he adds, it is true that forbidding *one* child to work impoverishes her family, but forbidding *all* children to work raises all the adults' wages (*ibid.*, p. 576), again a pecuniary externality.

Since pecuniary externalities are pervasive, Satz's argument aims at identifying those that matter. She uses the concept of pecuniary externalities when discussing markets for organs and for child labour. In her words, the problem may appear when "the terms of trade [are worsened] for those who do not want to participate in such markets", and who therefore "will have less effective choices" (2010, p. 203). This pecuniary externality, which is common in markets, may matter in certain cases and justify bans. Were a market for kidneys to exist, for example, kidneys might be used as collateral for loans, and hence people who cannot or do not want to sell them would not find reasonable loan rates.

> [T]his is where the argument from pecuniary externalities becomes relevant. Allowing the desperately poor to sell their organs as a social practice will have an effect on the choices that are open to those who do not want to participate in such a market. Some may think that it is inappropriate to make people pay a cost for exercising their choice not to sell their kidney. (*ibid.*)

We see here that we need something to discriminate between the pecuniary externalities that matter from those that do not, otherwise almost every market would be problematic regarding this issue.

How commodification studies makes use of the moral externality argument

Finally, commodification may be banned for its moral external effects. The moral externality argument against markets has to be distinguished from the thesis of degradation or corruption (on which see Panitch's Chapter 4 in this volume). With the former, the proposal to ban the market is legitimated by the offense caused to many people, irrespective of the analyst's judgment; with the latter, the analyst judges that the societal change caused by the market is condemnable, and hence proposes to ban it.[11]

Moral externalities are actually the first reason picked out by Roth to explain why certain markets are considered "repugnant":

> Why can't you eat horse or dog meat in a restaurant in California, a state with a population that hails from all over the world, including some places where such meals are appreciated? The answer is that many Californians not only don't wish to eat horses or dogs themselves, but *find it repugnant that anyone else should do so*, and they enacted this repugnance into California law by referendum in 1998.
>
> (2007, p. 37, my emphasis)[12]

But the problem with this specific case is the same as with technological externalities: it is not the sale of horse meat itself that creates these external effects, but its consumption.

Calabresi provides a more convincing argument. He is arguably one of the authors with the longest record (since the 1970s) of supporting the restriction of markets because of the moral externalities linked to the sale of certain goods. He has long insisted on the prevalence of moral externalities, in contrast to economists' tendencies to overlook them: "Many people are upset, 'do not like it,' if prices are put on life and on body parts. [...] And yet this kind of moral externality is too often treated as non-existent in economic models", which would prevent them from understanding the widespread reluctance towards the commodification of certain things (Calabresi, 2014, p. 321). He has recently extended the argument. Moral externalities justify the inalienability of what he calls "merit goods",[13] of which he distinguishes two types: first, those, like life, "whose pricing, in and of itself, causes a diminution in utility for a significant group of people" (2016, p. 26); second, those, like organs, that, if commodified, cause a decrease in utility due, not to their pricing itself, but to their unequal distribution: "the pain I suffer if I see the rich buying body parts that pretty much only the poor sell" (*ibid.*, p. 28). In other words, the inequalities created by commodification cause "significant external moral costs" (*ibid.*, p. 43). Calabresi's move here consists in transforming a problem of justice into a problem of efficiency, which in his view justifies the legislator's interest.[14] He provides the examples of the draft, body parts and products, elections, education, health, and the environment. In his view, many of the legal structures concerning merit goods (of both types) become understandable when we realize that the moral externalities caused by their commodification are not negotiable.

One of the difficulties with this kind of argument, as with the pecuniary externality argument, is that nothing helps us discriminate between the relevant and the irrelevant moral externalities, yet moral externalities are ubiquitous. And this is one of the reasons why we have to think differently about externalities if we want to build a strong anti-commodification argument along these lines.

Why the externality argument for inalienability is insufficient or inconsistent

I will now explore several reasons why the argument for market-inalienability structured in terms of externalities, originating from economics but imported into commodification studies, is to be deemed insufficient or inconsistent.[15] One of the main problems with this argument is that it pretends to be objective and value-neutral even while it carries normative presuppositions that are implicit, and which indeed may even be in contradiction with one another. That the economists' concept of externality is not independent of normative presuppositions – the criterion of efficiency being the first and not the only one – is not new. But the difficulty increases when the concept is imported abstracted from its theoretical background, which at least lent it some consistency. On the one hand, some of these presuppositions are imported without any analysis of their compatibility with the new framework. On the other hand, this importation without the theoretical background aggravates the fuzziness of the definition of an externality, and calls for additional presuppositions. But what are these presuppositions?

First, the choice of the criterion of efficiency is not value-neutral; behind its apparent objectivity, it depoliticizes social relations and hides conflicts of interests (Fourcade and Healy, 2007). Efficiency itself has become a moral rule, and this is why the discourse of economics, which has real-world consequences, is so important (*ibid.*). Specifically, the Pareto criterion defines welfare as satisfaction of preferences (rather than in terms of rights, for example), where these preferences may be manipulated or antisocial, and may contradict themselves or contradict needs; furthermore, the Pareto criterion is not neutral in terms of distribution, since extremely unequal distributions may be deemed "optimal" (e.g., Macleod, 2008).[16] And, regarding the issue that interests us here, how could we judge a market without any consideration of its unequal results (Sen, 1985)?

Second, the concept of externality is normative because an externality is judged as such relative to an ideal (the optimum); hence it depends on the definition of this ideal and on the ease with which the gap is thought to be resolvable. On the first count, and this is linked to my previous point, "[t]his implies that the notion of externality is not purely factual but always partly normative, and therefore subject to ethical controversy" (Fleurbaey et al. 2021, p. 197). On the second count, since the externality lies in the deviation from the norm, our perception of its extent depends also on our perception of the market's ability to attain this norm. Carl Dahlman, with a flash of lucidity about his own view, thus remarked:

> What is involved is a value judgment: if you believe that markets internalize everything, you will believe that externalities do not exist; on the other hand, if you believe that markets do not internalize side effects, you will believe in the persistence of externalities as deviations from an attainable optimum. This is not science; it is metaphysics: value judgments and political goals will enter into the determination of whether externalities occur in our world. [...] It is thus doubtful whether the term "externality" has any meaningful interpretation, except as an indicator of the political beliefs and value judgments of the person who uses (or avoids using) the term.
>
> (1979, p. 156)

This applies to commodification studies: some authors will tend to avoid using the concept (e.g., Brennan and Jaworski), while some use it extensively (e.g., Calabresi), and others use it but with circumspection (e.g., Trebilcock, Epstein).

Third, both as a consequence and an explanation of Dahlman's assertion, the evaluation of external and transactional costs cannot be simply a technical matter. The economic reasons for inalienability are allegedly technical (the size of external costs and transaction costs), but they cannot hide the social dimensions of these valuations in the absence of prices for externalities and for transactions.[17] The problem is aggravated in the case of the measurement of moral externalities (Krawiec, 2022, p. 9). Calabresi and Melamed illustrate this problem when they write that we cannot, by definition, objectively measure moral external costs, yet go on to identify cases where they may nevertheless be significant (1972, pp. 1111–1112).

I will focus, lastly, on these moral externalities, beginning with Satz, who takes aim directly at Calabresi and Melamed (1972) when she says:

> The sale of certain goods seems to many people simply unthinkable; it may be possible to justify prohibitions on slavery by appeals to costs and benefits, but the problem is that such justification makes contingent an outcome (no slavery) that we do not hold contingently. It makes little sense, phenomenologically, to describe the moral repugnance people feel toward slavery as "just a cost". Even if we are interested in tracking third party costs, [...] externalities (especially if we count moralisms [in the sense of moral externalities] as externalities) are nearly universal in practice. If we view any market that generates disapproval as producing an externality that can justify intervention, then freedom of contract is on shaky ground. We need some way of marking which costs rise to the level of justifying interference and regulation and which do not. Nothing in economic analysis helps us to do this.
>
> (Satz, 2010, p. 140)

In my view, the externality argument against commodification leads to an aporia. Either the concept of externality includes moral ones and implies legal moralism; or it excludes them and is inconsistent. And all of this arises because, again, the concept of externality cannot be abstracted from questions of moral and political philosophy. Let me detail this aporia.

On the one hand, if the analysis of commodification *includes* moral externalities, then it is "contingent" as Satz says, and supports conventional morality. Identifying moral externalities rests indeed on social conventions of morality, those that are at the source of the offense felt. Invoking moral externalities of commodification then leads us to legislate according to these conventions. Recall the previous example: if the Marshalls were not harmed by seeing Taney selling himself into slavery, would he be forbidden from doing it? (Radin, 1996, p. 24). The authors who refer to moral externalities to justify inalienability take the offence of commodification as a given fact which lawmakers must make do with, and do not discuss its legitimacy (Roth, 2007; Calabresi, 2016). Invoking moral externalities of commodification is therefore open to the same criticisms as legal moralism (for a review, see Feinberg, 1988). John Stuart Mill (1859, IV) famously criticized this kind of "moral police": taking into account moral harms leads to legislation that reflects the rulers' morality, or the preferences of the majority or of the most powerful lobby, and this will eventually intrude into every domain of private life. This is the reason why moral externalities were excluded from traditional welfare analysis: putting moral and material externalities on the same level would open the door to intervention in both cases, and hence to Sen's paradox of the Paretian liberal (Sen, 1970).

On the other hand, however, when the analysis of commodification *excludes* moral externalities (but continues to frame the argument in terms of externalities), it implicitly adds in other value judgments. As I said before, the distinction that welfare economics makes between physical externalities, which should be taken into account, and moral externalities, which should not, cannot be justified within the framework of economic theory. When harm is defined as infringement of welfare and of preferences, there is no endogenous reason for excluding moral harm. Consequently, if including moral externalities in the analysis entails including the value judgments of the model's agents, excluding them imports the value judgments of the analyst. In pushing moral externalities out the door, back through the window comes the value judgment that the economist abstains from expressing, and more often than not without recognizing it.

> [T]he economist, if truly wedded to the notion that de gustibus non est disputandum, cannot speak *a priori* to whether these external moral costs are proper or not.[18] The economist cannot choose to treat them as improper or nonexistent and on that basis to decry the actions taken by the collectivity in response to them.
>
> (Calabresi, 2016, p. 143)

The problem here, as with externalities in general, is that a moral and political theory is required in order to complement the concept of externality, which would otherwise be too extensive: it is "empty of meaning without a prior conception of state legitimacy" (Brown, 1992, p. 17).

It will now be no surprise that the economists' desire to distinguish between moral and physical externalities, and exclude the first from the analysis – and from the domain of public intervention – implicitly rests on Mill's (1859) delineation of the harms to others that may justify interference with liberty. What Mishan called a social or "ethical consensus" is in fact the Millian liberal consensus that excludes moral harms from among the harms that legitimate public interference (see Herzog, 2000, pp. 912–914; Satz, 2010, p. 32; Bertrand, 2018). The same is true in some parts of commodification studies: for example, although he constructs his argument in terms of externalities, Trebilcock 1993 (ch. 3) refuses to take into account moral ones in the name of Mill's delimitation of the harm principle, and as part of his stance against legal moralism.[19] Consequently, excluding moral externalities from the analysis rests on specific conventions, which should be made explicit and rationalized by reference to a moral and political theory. As Satz noted,

> the economic argument for identifying inefficiencies in the case of only certain externalities – pollution but not intolerance of religious diversity – feeds off moral theory done elsewhere. That's not necessarily a problem, as long as we attend to the moral theory and make it explicit in our understanding of inefficiency.
>
> (2010, p. 32)

In the parts of commodification studies that refer to physical externalities but not to moral ones – since their argument is drawn mainly from economics and law-and-economics – the exclusion of moral effects is equally rarely made explicit, and even less often rationalized – Trebilcock and Epstein look like exceptions in this respect. Besides, even when explicit, the application of the harm principle is indeterminate, hence this exclusion is based on a conventional definition of the "private sphere", whereas in fact the delimitation between private and public is the object of ongoing reconfigurations of social forces.

This aporia returns me to my first point: what counts as an externality involves value judgments concerning which subjective preferences are legitimate and do matter. Again Satz: "any plausible measure of the costs of various activities presupposes a substantive conception of what is important to human welfare, of which subjectively felt harms count as costs. Efficiency turns out to have a moral dimension after all" (2010, p. 34). And indeed we can read her book as an attempt to build an argument for market-inalienability that is not economistic, and as a rebuttal of the efficiency criterion and therefore of the concept of externality itself. She argues, in the tradition of classical political economy (particularly Smith and Marx), that exchanges and markets influence the people we become, and give rise to dominance and subordination, vulnerability and dependence; markets thus shape individuals (their capacities and preferences) and hence society. Consequently, efficiency cannot be the only criterion to assess them, which is why she refuses to use the economic concept of externality.[20] As I said above, she nevertheless refers to the concept of (technological and pecuniary) externality to identify noxious markets. But she also adds that pecuniary externalities have to matter in terms of justice to account for market-inalienability: they do not justify bans in and by themselves. And although Satz mentions technological externalities in detailing her criteria of weak agency and individual harmful outcome, this is not related only to a welfare criterion, since she includes in this outcome the "undermining of basic interests" in welfare and autonomy (in Sen's sense, *ibid.*, p. 95). This is why interpreting some of Satz's arguments in terms of externalities, i.e., in the welfarist framework (as I did in Bertrand, 2020), misses what is unique about her approach, which is to add a discussion of political philosophy to the economic framework used to evaluate markets (Satz, 2010, p. 99). She "offer[s] a particular way of thinking about harmful outcomes and externalities that is tied to a theory of equality" (*ibid.*, p. 220, fn. 7). While Kanbur's criteria of "extreme outcomes and inequality are characterized in terms of welfare economics" (*ibid.*, p. 219, fn. 6), she ultimately evaluates the legitimacy of markets in relation to their effects on the relative standings of the parties.[21] This is why the solution may not be to add some new market, or regulate the existing one, but to abandon it altogether (*ibid.*, p. 94).

Satz's reasoning illustrates the idea that the concept of externality is flawed, but nevertheless needed in commodification studies: why is it needed? And how could we base it on a theory of justice in order to solidly ground an externality argument for market-inalienability?

Conclusion: The need to build a stronger argument against commodification by founding the concept of externalities on a theory of justice

The concept of externality in its utilitarian welfarist framework is flawed as an argument to justify market-inalienability because it implies that no pecuniary externality should matter, but that all moral externalities should; whereas, in fact, we may want to reintroduce pecuniary externalities (Hausman, 1992; Claassen, 2016; Endörfer, 2022) and discriminate between them (Satz, 2010), and we still require a rational criterion with which to discriminate between moral externalities (Claassen, 2016) or to exclude them (Trebilcock, 1993; Satz, 2010). But first, we may ask, why should we retain the concept of externality at all? The answer is because it remains useful, including for non-economists. It captures something of the reality of markets. Let's return to the phenomenological definition of externality. It specifically designates an *involuntary* harm to *third-parties*, for which there is no equivalent in philosophy.[22] Its study cannot, however, be limited to a welfarist analysis. Externalities cannot be thought of only in terms of efficiency because they are non-consented to by victims, whose moral status as victim is neutralized by calling them third-parties: "Economists' definitions of externalities do not focus on this feature, and none seems entirely suitable for an inquiry into the justice of market outcomes" (Hausman, 1992, p. 95).[23] So even if the concept is coloured by its welfarist and economistic origins, it is still relevant because it insists on the involuntary and unconsented dimensions of this harm.[24] Hausman therefore defines externalities as obstacles to justice, and includes among them all the unintentional effects of our actions on non-consenting parties, irrespective of whether these actions are economic, or these effects technological or pecuniary, and he also includes the effects on our preferences, for example, of the fact that our personal relationships are mediated by the market (in other words, one form of the degradation thesis). That being said, we need to discriminate between these external effects, which are pervasive, by defining what the obstacles to justice are.

The concept of externality therefore needs to be grounded upon a preliminary discussion carried out within the domain of moral philosophy. If externality is no longer seen as a narrow economic concept but rather as a philosophical one, it will no longer be an error of economic reductionism to use it as a lens through which to analyze phenomena pertaining to the moral sphere. Since externalities are regularly discussed in relation to Mill's harm principle, we may wish to start anew from the philosophical discussion of this principle (as does Claassen, 2016). Holtug (2002), for example, asserted that a welfare understanding of the harm principle (like Feinberg's) cannot exclude moral harms (of IVF or homosexuality, for example), and that only a moral understanding of harm and, beyond that, an underlying theory of justice (like that of Raz, 1986) can. This reasoning confirms that we cannot content ourselves with a welfarist view of externalities. We have to accept a moral view of external effects as wrongful violations of rights – of what people are entitled to; and this is why the concept of externalities depends upon a prior theory of justice. Drawing on Holtug, Claassen (2016) remarks that Feinberg's and Raz's definitions of harms are actually structurally identical: they are harms to basic interests, and this is why in his view externalities should be defined as such. Defining basic interests is still a matter of dispute in philosophical and democratic theory, but this is where the externality theory should begin. The argument that uses externalities to justify the market-inalienability of some goods has therefore to be based on an explicit theory of justice. Satz makes the first steps in this direction when she defines rights that should not be violated in a relational equality perspective, as access to specific goods like education, health care, and employment, but she does not give this list a rational grounding in a theory of justice (why these goods and not others?), and does not detail which type of equality is required for each item (Claassen, 2012; Chapter 4). A theory of justice is needed to form a base for explicit and rationalized value judgments which would allow us to discriminate between relevant and irrelevant technological, pecuniary, and moral externalities. Since, conversely, it may be useful to apply the economic logic of externalities to rights (as does Hammond, 1998), it is not a matter of abandoning the economic logic, but rather of combining multiple logics in the analysis of markets. This is a task that commodification studies can broach, thanks to its interdisciplinarity – the task of defining and identifying the externalities that justify limits to market-alienability.

Notes

I thank Nathalie Berta, Vida Panitch, and participants at the 2022 Sorbonne Conference "Contested Markets: Theories and Controversies" for useful comments; and Ben Young for his help preparing the final version of the manuscript.

1 The mechanism is actually *centralized*, which is translated into its personification by the fictitious character of the auctioneer (cf. e.g., Pignol, 2017, pp. 88–89; Inoua and Smith, 2022).

2 Externalities may be positive or negative. Only negative effects may justify market bans, which is why this chapter refers to negative externalities only.

3 The general equilibrium model was built to eliminate any interdependency between individual agents other than through prices, hence the concept potentially makes reference to just about everything that had previously been eliminated (e.g., Vatn and Bromley, 1997).

4 On envy as an externality, see Hammond, 1987b; see also Claassen, 2016, pp. 549–550 and references therein. On the same lines, altruism can be seen as a positive externality (Hammond, 1987a), usually classified with social preferences (along with fairness and reciprocity).

5 If market regulation recognizes the "plural meanings" of the good, commodification is said to be incomplete in a stronger sense. Radin (1996, ch. 7 and 8) proposes several definitions of incomplete commodification.

6 The phrase "commodification of externalities" is an oxymoron. When externalities are commodified, or have a price, they are, strictly speaking, no longer externalities.

7 Dales's model was rigorously formalized by Montgomery (1972), in the line of Arrow (1969). Crocker (1966) is also credited for the idea, but the mechanism he suggests is actually different (Berta, 2021).

8 They conclude more ambiguously:

> Here, though we are not certain of how a cost-benefit analysis would come out, liability rules are inappropriate because any monetization is, by hypothesis, out of the question. The state must, therefore, either ignore the external costs to Marshall, or if it judges them great enough, forbid the transaction that gave rise to them by making Taney's freedom inalienable.
>
> (Calabresi and Melamed, 1972, p. 1112)

9 Trebilcock's theoretical framework also contains other contractual problems like coercion and information default, but the corresponding chapters do not evoke contested markets.

10 Basu does not give any solution for the underlying problem of inequality, which is not helped by a ban. This was popularized by Radin as the "double bind problem": "[I]f we sometimes cannot respect personhood either by permitting sales or by banning sales, justice requires that we consider changing the circumstances that create the dilemma" (Radin, 1996, p. 124).

11 It is true that effects on society like degradation or corruption may also be interpreted in terms of externalities (Bertrand, 2020; Krawiec, 2022). For example, Epstein calls "soft externalities" of surrogacy the "negative impact on the social status and psychological self-definition of women as a class" (1995, p. 2323), which he deems irrelevant. In the same line, it was noted by Besley that Sandel's (2012) "arguments could be characterized as a particular kind of externality that arises if market transactions affect motivation, preferences, and norms in a way that is not properly priced in the market transaction" (2013, p. 485).

12 In the remainder of his article, Roth seems confused about how he defines repugnance (or revulsion) and repugnant transactions (or inappropriate, distasteful, unfair, undignified, unprofessional). He first tries to distinguish repugnance from externalities proper: repugnance is assimilated in one place to Fiske and Tetlock's 1997 taboo trade-offs, in another to the social reluctance towards monetary payments (Roth, 2007, p. 40 and 44). But when he studies an empirical case "in which little else besides repugnance seems at work", he interprets it in terms of externalities: "Thus the UN committee, like the French Council of State, essentially concluded that dwarf tossing was so repugnant that it imposed a negative externality by diminishing human dignity, a public good" (*ibid.*, p. 42). See also Khalil and Marciano 2018 on Roth's confusion.

13 The term "merit goods" obviously refers to Musgrave 1959. On the proximity, and differences, between the two concepts, see Desmarais-Tremblay 2019.

14 Calabresi and Melamed (1972, p. 1115, fn. 51) already had an intuition of this idea.

15 For other criticisms of the relevance of the concept of externality itself, see, e.g., Coase, 1960; Kapp, [1950] 1971; Brown, 1992; Vatn and Bromley, 1997; Zerbe and McCurdy, 1999; Barnett and Yandle, 2009.

16 Other criteria have been proposed, like the Kaldor-Hicks potential Pareto improvement, which is the basis of cost-benefit analysis and is widely used (for example for environmental decisions) despite its being entirely rejected by normative economics. See Hausman, McPherson, and Satz 2016 for a discussion of the implicit philosophy of welfare criteria.

17 For a sociological view on the social construction of actual externalities, see Callon 1998.

18 "De gustibus non est disputandum" refers to the title of a famous article by Nobel Prize winners George Stigler and Gary Becker (1977).

19 Epstein's transaction cost model of inalienability is explicit in rejecting "soft externalities" (degradation of moral values), mainly because in his view they cannot be included in the Millian harm principle:

> John Stuart Mill's classic statement that the sole justification for restricting individual liberty is the prevention of harm to others is wholly gutted if the conception of harm is given a meaning as broad as that supposed in this context.
>
> (Epstein, 1995, p. 2325)

20 She writes:

> Efficiency is clearly not the only value relevant to assessing markets: we have to think about the effects of markets on social justice, on who we are, how we relate to each other, and what kind of society we can have.
>
> (Satz, 2010, p. 4)

21 In other words:

> A market exchange based in desperation, humiliation, or begging or whose terms of remediation involve bondage or servitude is not an exchange between equals. On my view, lurking behind many, if not all, noxious markets are problems relating to the *standing* of the parties before, during, and after the process of exchange.
>
> (Satz, 2010, p. 93, her emphasis)

22 The involuntary character of externalities is called into question by Kapp [1950] 1971 (see Chapter 23 by O'Neill in this volume):

> [A] system of decision-making operating in accordance with the principle of investment for profit cannot be expected to proceed in any way other than by trying to reduce its costs whenever possible and by ignoring those losses that can be shifted to third persons or to society at large.
>
> (Kapp, [1950] 1971, p. xiii, cited in Vatn and Bromley, 1997, p. 147)

The cost-shifting may be intended, but what is important, I think, is that the action of production or consumption which causes external effects would be undertaken even if it would not have this effect.

23 Coase (1960) also did a lot to negate the status of victims by insisting on the reciprocity of the parties in causing the harm, from the standpoint of efficiency.

24 Hausman continues:

> I suggest that the properties of what economists have called "externalities" that are relevant to questions about the justice of the outcomes of voluntary transactions are that they involve an *unintended* (side) effect of A on B to which A or B have not consented. Although it may be misleading to think of this as a definition of the term, "externality", which might be better left as a concept with which to address questions of efficiency, I think it is worth doing so. For most of what economists have called externalities are unintended effects of A on B to which A and B have not both consented.
>
> (1992, p. 95, his emphasis)

References

Arrow, K.J. (1951) "An extension of the basic theorems of classical welfare economics", in Neyman, J. (ed.), *Proceedings of the Second Berkeley Symposium on Mathematical Statistics and Probability*, Berkeley: University of California Press, pp. 507–532.

Arrow, K.J. (1969) "The organization of economic activity: Issues pertinent to the choice of market versus non market allocation", in Joint Economic Committee (ed.), *The Analysis and Evaluation of Public Expenditures: The PPB System*, vol. 1, Washington, DC: Government Printing Office, pp. 47–64. Repr. in *Collected Papers of Kenneth J. Arrow, vol. 2: General Equilibrium*, Oxford: Basil Blackwell, 1983, pp. 133–155.

Arrow, K.J. and Debreu, G. (1954) "Existence of an equilibrium for a competitive economy", *Econometrica*, 22, pp. 265–290.

Barnett, A.H. and Yandle, B. (2009) "The end of the externality revolution", *Social Philosophy and Policy*, 26(2), pp. 130–150.

Basu, K. (2007) "Coercion, contract and the limits of the market", *Social Choice and Welfare*, 29(4), pp. 559–579.

Berta, N. (2017) "On the definition of externality as a missing market", *European Journal of the History of Economic Thought*, 24(2), pp. 287–318.

Berta, N. (2020) "Efficiency without optimality: Environmental policies and pollution pricing in the late 1960s", *Journal of the History of Economic Thought*, 42(4), pp. 539–562.

Berta, N. (2021) "A note on John Dales and the early history of permits market", *Cahiers d'Économie Politique / Political Economy Papers*, 79, pp. 61–84.

Bertrand, E. (2018) "John Stuart Mill and the concept of externality: What counts as a harm", mimeo.

Bertrand, E. (2019) "Much ado about nothing? The controversy over the validity of the Coase theorem", *The European Journal of the History of Economic Thought*, 26(3), pp. 502–536.

Bertrand, E. (2020) "Les effets externes des marchés contestés", in Bertrand, E. and Catto, M.-X. (eds), *Les Limites du Marché: La Marchandisation de la Nature et du Corps / The Limits of the Market: Commodification of Nature and Body*, Paris: Mare & Martin, pp. 21–42.
Besley, T. (2013) "What's the good of the market? An essay on Michael Sandel's 'What Money Can't Buy'", *Journal of Economic Literature*, 51(2), pp. 478–495.
Bourdieu, P. (2017) *Anthropologie Économique. Cours au Collège de France 1992–1993*, ed. by P. Champagne and J. Duval, Paris: Seuil.
Brennan, J. and Jaworski, P.M. (2016) *Markets Without Limits. Moral Virtues and Commercial Interests*, New York: Routledge.
Brown, P.G. (1992) "The failure of market failures", *The Journal of Socio-Economics*, 21(1), pp. 1–24.
Buchanan, J.M. and Tullock, G. (1962) *The Calculus of Consent: Logical Foundations for Constitutional Democracy*, Michigan: The University of Michigan Press.
Calabresi, G. (2014) "Of tastes and values", *American Law and Economics Review*, 16(2), pp. 313–332.
Calabresi, G. (2016) *The Future of Law and Economics*, New Haven and London: Yale University Press.
Calabresi, G.A. and Melamed, D. (1972) "Property rules, liability rules, and inalienability: One view of the cathedral", *Harvard Law Review*, 85(6), pp. 1089–1128.
Callon, M. (1998) "An essay on framing and overflowing: Economic externalities revisited by sociology", *The Sociological Review*, 46(1), pp. 244–269.
Chauvier, S. (2013) *Ethique Sans Visage*, Paris: Seuil.
Claassen, R. (2012) "Review of *Why Some Things Should Not Be For Sale: The Moral Limits of Markets*, by Debra Satz", *Business Ethics Quarterly*, 22(3), pp. 585–597.
Claassen, R. (2016) "Externalities as a basis for regulation: A philosophical view", *Journal of Institutional Economics*, 12(3), pp. 541–563.
Coase, R.H. (1960) "The problem of social cost", *Journal of Law and Economics*, 3, pp. 1–44.
Crocker, T.D. (1966) "The structuring of atmospheric pollution control systems", in Wolozin, H. (ed.), *The Economics of Air Pollution*, New York: W.W. Norton & Co, pp. 61–86.
Dahlman, C.J. (1979) "The problem of externality", *Journal of Law and Economics*, 22(1), pp. 141–162.
Dales, J.H. (1968) *Pollution, Property and Prices*, Toronto: University of Toronto Press.
Debreu, G. (1974) "Excess demand functions", *Journal of Mathematical Economics*, 1(1), pp. 15–21.
Demsetz, H. (1964) "The exchange and enforcement of property rights", *The Journal of Law and Economics*, 7, pp. 11–26.
Demsetz, H. (1967) "Toward a theory of property rights", *The American Economic Review*, 57(2), pp. 347–359.
Desmarais-Tremblay, M. (2019) "The normative problem of merit goods in perspective", *Forum for Social Economics*, 48(3), pp. 219–247.
Endörfer, R. (2022) "Should market harms be an exception to the Harm Principle?", *Economics and Philosophy*, 38(2), pp. 221–241.
Epstein, R.A. (1985) "Why restrain alienation?", *Columbia Law Review*, 85, pp. 970–990.
Epstein, R.A. (1995) "Surrogacy: The case for full contractual enforcement", *Virginia Law Review*, 81, pp. 2305–2341.
Feinberg, J. (1988) *The Moral Limits of the Criminal Law. Vol. 4: Harmless Wrong-Doing*, New York: Oxford University Press.
Fiske, A.P. and Tetlock, P.E. (1997) "Taboo trade-offs: Reactions to transactions that transgress the spheres of justice", *Political Psychology*, 18(2), pp. 255–297.
Fleurbaey, M., Kanbur, R. and Viney, B. (2021) "Social externalities and economic analysis", *Social Research: An International Quarterly*, 88(1), pp. 171–202.
Fourcade, M. and Healy, K. (2007) "Moral views of market society", *Annual Review of Sociology*, 33, 14.1–14.27.
Hammond, P.J. (1987a) "Altruism", in Eatwell, J.M., Milgate M. and Newman, P. (eds), *The New Palgrave Dictionary of Economics*, online.
Hammond, P.J. (1987b) "Envy", in Eatwell, J.M., Milgate M. and Newman, P. (eds), *The New Palgrave Dictionary of Economics*, online.
Hammond, P.J. (1998) "Rights, free exchange, and widespread externalities", in Laslier, J.-F., Fleurbaey, M., Gravel, N. and Trannoy, A. (eds), *Freedom in Economics: New Perspectives in Normative Analysis*, London: Routledge, pp. 139–157.

Hausman, D.M. (1992) "When Jack and Jill make a deal", *Social Philosophy and Policy*, 9(1), pp. 95–113.
Hausman, D.M., McPherson, M.S. and Satz, D. (2016) *Economic Analysis, Moral Philosophy, and Public Policy*, Cambridge: Cambridge University Press.
Herzog, D. (2000) "Externalities and other parasites", *University of Chicago Law Review*, 67(3), pp. 895–923.
Holtug, N. (2002) "The harm principle", *Ethical Theory and Moral Practice*, 5(4), pp. 357–389.
Inoua, S. and Smith, V.L. (2022) "Neoclassical supply and demand, experiments, and the classical theory of price formation", *History of Political Economy*, 54(1), pp. 37–73.
Kanbur, R. (2004) "On obnoxious markets", in Cullenberg, S. and Pattanaik, P. (eds), *Globalization, Culture and the Limits of the Market: Essays in Economics and Philosophy*, New Delhi: Oxford University Press, pp. 39–61.
Kapp, K.W. ([1950]1971) *The Social Costs of Private Enterprise*, New York: Schoken Books.
Khalil, E.L. and Marciano, A. (2018) "A theory of tasteful and distasteful transactions", *Kyklos* 71(1), pp. 110–131.
Krawiec, K. (2022) "Markets, repugnance, and externalities", *Journal of Institutional Economics*, advanced online publication pp. 1–12. doi:10.1017/S1744137422000157
Lusk, J.L. (2011) "The market for animal welfare", *Agriculture and Human Values*, 28(4), pp. 561–575.
Macleod, C.M. (2008) "Market failure, justice, and preferences", *Ethics and Economics*, 6(1), pp. 1–7.
Mantel, R. (1974) "On the characterization of aggregate excess demand", *Journal of Economic Theory*, 7(3), pp. 348–353.
Medema, S.G. (2020a) "'Exceptional and unimportant'? The rise, fall, and rebirth of externalities in economic analysis", *History of Political Economy*, 52(1), pp. 135–170.
Medema, S.G. (2020b) "The Coase Theorem at sixty", *Journal of Economic Literature*, 58(4), pp. 1045–1128.
Mildenberger, C.D. (2018) "A liberal theory of externalities?", *Philosophical Studies*, 175(9), pp. 2105–2123.
Mill, J.S. (1859) *On Liberty*, London: J.W. Parker and Son.
Mishan, E.J. (1965) "Reflections on recent developments in the concept of external effects", *The Canadian Journal of Economics and Political Science*, 31(1), pp. 3–34.
Mishan, E.J. (1971a) "Pangloss on pollution", *Swedish Journal of Economics*, 73(1), pp. 113–120.
Mishan, E.J. (1971b) "The postwar literature on externalities: An interpretative essay", *Journal of Economic Literature*, 9(1), pp. 1–28.
Montgomery, W.E. (1972) "Markets in licenses and efficient pollution control programs", *Journal of Economic Theory*, 5(3), pp. 395–418.
Musgrave, R.A. (1959) *The Theory of Public Finance: A Study in Public Economy*, New York: McGraw-Hill.
Pignol, C. (2017) *La Théorie de l'Équilibre Général*, Villeneuve d'Ascq: Presses Universitaires du Septentrion.
Pigou, A.C. (1932) *The Economics of Welfare*, 4th ed., London: Macmillan, 1948.
Radin, M.J. (1996) *Contested Commodities*, Cambridge, MA: Harvard University Press.
Raz, J. (1986) *The Morality of Freedom*, Oxford: Clarendon Press.
Rose-Ackerman, S. (1985) "Inalienability and the theory of property rights", *Columbia Law Review*, 85, pp. 931–969.
Roth, A.E. (2007) "Repugnance as a constraint on markets", *Journal of Economic Perspectives*, 21(3), pp. 37–58.
Sandel, M. (2012) *What Money Can't Buy: The Moral Limits of Markets*, New York: Farrar, Straus and Giroux.
Satz, D. (2010) *Why Some Things Should Not Be For Sale. The Moral Limits of Markets*, Oxford: Oxford University Press.
Sen, A. (1970) "The impossibility of a Paretian liberal", *Journal of Political Economy*, 78(1), pp. 152–157.
Sen, A. (1979) "Utilitarianism and welfarism", *Journal of Philosophy*, 76(9), 463–489.
Sen, A. (1985) "The moral standing of the market", *Social Philosophy and Policy*, 2(2), pp. 1–19.
Sonnenschein, H. (1973) "Do Walras' identity and continuity characterize the class of community excess demand functions?", *Journal of Economic Theory*, 6(4), pp. 345–354.
Stark, A. (2020) "Value, externalities, and the boundaries of the market", *Journal of Social Philosophy*, 51(2), pp. 180–204.
Stigler, G.J. and Becker, G.S. (1977) "De gustibus non est disputandum", *The American Economic Review*, 67(2), pp. 76–90.

Trebilcock, M.J. (1993) *The Limits of Freedom of Contract*, Cambridge, MA: Harvard University Press.
Vatn, A. and Bromley, D.W. (1997) "Externalities – A market model failure", *Environmental and Resource Economics*, 9, pp. 135–151.
Williams, B. (1985) *Ethics and the Limits of Philosophy*, London: Fontana Press.
Zerbe, R.O., Jr. and McCurdy, H.E. (1999) "The failure of market failure", *Journal of Policy Analysis and Management*, 18(4), pp. 558–578.

4

CONTEMPORARY ANTI-COMMODIFICATION ARGUMENTS

Corruption, inequality, and justice[1]

Vida Panitch

Introduction: Philosophical anti-commodification theory

Are there some things that money can't, or shouldn't buy, even in a market economy? Are there some things that should never be assigned price values or traded as market goods? Many contemporary political and moral philosophers have been concerned with these questions. Although the answers that have been offered by philosophers such as Michael Sandel (2012; 2000), Margaret Jane Radin (1996), Elizabeth Anderson (1993; 1990a; 1990b), Michael Walzer (1984), Anne Phillips (2011), and Debra Satz (2010), among others, vary in analytical and normative content, they share several unifying features that constitute jointly the core of a theory that might be termed *philosophical anti-commodificationism* (PAC).

One key feature of PAC is the claim that some "capitalist acts among consenting adults" (Nozick, 1974, p. 163) should be restricted, but not others. Only some goods are wrong to commodify, according to PAC theorists, by which they mean wrong to value in monetary terms and/or wrong to distribute in accordance with market principles such as instrumental value, ability-to-pay, or skill at bargaining.[2] A second but closely related feature of PAC is that it takes aim at distinct markets, not at "the market" as such. The capitalist mode of production is not the problem, nor even the liberal market economy. Despite worries about the domino effects of commodification (Radin, 1996), or the commodification creep found in capitalist and neo-liberal market economies (Phillips, 2008), it is particularly noxious markets – those that trade in uniquely contestable commodities – that are of primary concern to PAC theorists.

A third feature of PAC is a fundamental concern to explain which goods should not be for sale, rather than to merely identify the processes by which, or the conditions under which goods in general should not be sold. Particular markets are noxious not (or not only) due to transactional defects that cause or reflect a failure of autonomy on the part of one of the parties to the exchange (Walzer, 1984). Rather, they are noxious in light of the specific type of good being exchanged. PAC theorists do not deny that fraudulent, coercive, or exploitative transactions are wrong, but tend to find these kinds of transactional accounts inadequate at best (Sandel, 2012, p. 9). Protections against coercion and fraud, and even wealth redistribution to correct for bargaining asymmetries,

DOI: 10.4324/9781003188742-6

are insufficient because they serve to bolster the market by improving bargaining and purchasing power, rather than limiting the market's reach into areas of human life where it doesn't belong (Anderson, 1993; Walzer, 1984).

For some PAC theorists, their aim is to cast moral aspersions on troubling markets, and for others it is to take the additional step of offering grounds for the criminalization thereof. In some sense, the PAC project implores us as moral agents to refrain from engaging in certain market transactions; in another, it implores the state to prohibit citizens from engaging in such transactions. But legal "oughts" do not inevitably follow from moral "oughts". Raising reasonable concerns with markets in sex, for example, does not pull the trick of grounding its criminalization, in light of the many harms such laws can have. Some PAC theorists make entirely reasonable moral claims that may simply not be adequate to justifying legal limits on the markets they identify as noxious, while those who aim at legal prohibitions often concede that ultimately more overall harm might be done by criminalizing certain markets than by allowing them (Satz, 2010; Radin, 1996).

Ultimately, the PAC project is one of explaining the wrongness of specific markets that involve the sale of goods for money which they believe should be traded and valued exclusively on non-commodified terms. Philosophers who take up this project must do two things: identify which goods should be exempt from market exchange and offer a coherent account of why these particular goods should be so exempt. In this chapter, I do not call into question the importance of the PAC project, nor its underlying aims and features, which I take to be both reasonable and compelling.[3] Nor will I query the list of items that PAC theorists have argued should be exempt from market exchange. What I will do is explain and critically evaluate the arguments they have supplied by way of justifying these market exemptions.

The goods that have been identified as contested commodities by PAC theorists can be classified as belonging to one of five categories: **social goods** (love, friendship, kinship); **honourific goods** (prizes, awards, offices); **civic goods** (votes, speech, citizenship); **necessary goods** (education, health care, housing); and **physical goods** (body parts, and intimate labour including sex work and surrogacy) (Panitch, 2020, p. 63). PAC theorists have spent less time thinking about environmental goods as contested commodities, which is something contributors to Part 5 of this volume aim to correct. Many PAC theorists take issue with the commodification of goods belonging to only one or two of these categories, while others have raised the alarm with respect to goods belonging to all five. An argument against the sale of the goods belonging to one category, however, does not often work to justify restricting markets in goods belonging to another category. When a PAC theorist offers the same argument against the sale of each one, they can make the mistake of misplaced generality (Panitch, 2020, p. 66).[4]

PAC theorists have in the main offered two kinds of arguments against the commodification of these goods.[5] Theorists who offer **corruption arguments** hold that the sale of such goods for money, or their exchange via market mechanisms, erodes something of significant value, be it the inherent meaning of the good itself (*ontological corruption*), important social norms (*normative corruption*), or human flourishing (*teleological corruption*) (Anderson 1993, 1990a, 1990b; Radin, 1996, 1987; Sandel, 2010, 2000; Walzer, 1984). Theorists who offer **equality arguments** hold that the sale of certain goods for money, or their exchange via markets, erodes important relations of equality in which we ought to stand with one another, be they relations of equality in resource shares (*simple/complex equality*), moral dignity (*moral equality*) or democratic status (*democratic equality*) (Phillips, 2011; Sample, 2003; Satz, 2010, Walzer, 1984).

In the first part of this chapter, I will explain and critically evaluate each of the main variants of corruption-based PAC arguments. I will show that each variant faces unique challenges, but that on the whole, corruption arguments depend on claims that are either perfectionist or morally conservative, which is problematic when corruption claims are offered as a basis upon which to ground criminal legislation in a pluralist society. In the second part of this chapter, I will turn to examining equality-based PAC arguments and the main variants thereof. I will show that although this approach to answering the fundamental questions of anti-commodification theory is more promising, equality arguments cannot tell us *which* goods should not be sold (as opposed to merely telling us *how* goods in general should not be sold) without appealing to corruption claims of their own.

I will go on to offer a brief defence of a third kind of anti-commodification view – one that honours the underlying commitments of PAC theory and shares in its unifying features – but that promises to avoid the troubles facing corruption and equality arguments. I will refer to the view as a justice-based PAC argument. According to this view, the goods that are wrong to commodify are those whose sale would be precluded by the principles of justice that would be endorsed by free and equal citizens committed to diverse and incompatible conceptions of the good (Panitch, 2020). It thereby offers an account of commodification theory consistent with the commitments of a liberal democratic state. Although I will not be able to fully develop the view here, I do hope to sketch the parameters of a justice-based PAC argument and highlight the theoretical and practical promise thereof.

Corruption arguments

Corruption-based anti-commodification theory "point[s] to the *degrading effect* of market valuation and exchange on certain goods and practices" (Sandel, 2000, p. 94). As Michael Sandel (2012) explains it, "putting a price on the good things in life can corrupt them … because markets don't only allocate goods; they also express and promote certain attitudes toward the good being exchanged" (p. 9). These claims pack a lot of rhetorical punch and can be difficult to unpack in part because there are many distinct corruption claims contained within them. To point to the 'degrading effect of market valuation and exchange', is in one sense to claim that cash erodes the very meaning of the goods it acquires (call this *ontological corruption*). It also expresses a concern that the norms of the marketplace can corrupt the motives in accordance with which certain goods should be exchanged (call this *normative corruption*). It also highlights a third, albeit closely connected worry, that by corrupting the value of certain goods and the norms in accordance with which they should be exchanged, commodification inhibits the attainment of human flourishing (call this *teleological corruption*). Let's examine each in turn.

Ontological corruption

According to the first version of the corruption argument, we alter the very meaning of a good by selling it, and thereby degrade what is valuable to us about having it. Michael Sandel (2012) argues that money can never capture the inherent value of important goods, and that in assigning an economic value to such goods we thereby degrade their true or inherent value (p. 7). On the ontological view, it is the effect of monetary exchange on a good whose inherent meaning is not collapsible to its exchange value that renders commodification morally troubling. Sandel is drawing from Aristotle here, according to whom each good has an inherent meaning, value, or purpose, that makes it unique and unlike every other thing in existence (NE 2014, Bk I, s1.). But as Aristotle observed, if no two goods are identical in value, all exchanges are of incommensurable goods, rendering exchanges unjust to both buyer and seller, and degrading of the goods themselves. Money can't solve this problem, because its true value lies in its fungibility, unlike any other good (PC 1996, Bk V). For Aristotle, no amount of money can ever be morally equivalent to a good whose inherent values lies in something other than its exchangeability. Sandel is very much drawing from this tradition when he argues that money degrades the inherent value of the goods he identifies as contested commodities.

According to Michael Walzer (1984), it is the social meaning of goods, rather than their inherent value, that is threatened by market exchange. Walzer argues that goods do not come into the world with meanings already embedded in them. Rather, we bring goods into the world so that they might hold certain meanings, serve certain functions, occupy certain roles, and define certain relationships (Walzer, 1984, p. 17). Here he is drawing from Marx's critique of (Aristotelian) commodity fetishism. For Marx, goods do not have inherent values around which we should organize our social practices; rather, we create goods to hold meanings that sustain our social practices (Marx, [1867]1990, p. 163). Walzer argues in this vein that the socially dominant meanings of goods must be preserved to sustain the social practices they define (1984, p. 13). Where the socially dominant meanings of goods would be altered and corrupted by market exchange, such exchanges should be prevented. Allocating needed or meritorious goods based on ability to pay, for example, would fundamentally degrade their social meanings and the social relationships those meanings sustain (1984, pp. 18–21).

The force of the ontological argument is best appreciated when we consider its application to the case of social goods. If you pay someone to be your friend, they become something else by definition: a lackey. So too with love; if you have to pay someone to love you, they don't. What you acquire at the end of these financial transactions is altogether different than the thing you sought to attain; the market changes the very meaning of friendship and love and thus what we find valuable about having them in our lives. The same can certainly be said of honourific or meritorious goods. Awards and honours retain their value only when they reflect merit not payment. If awards could be bought, anyone with a Purple Heart could be signaling her success in an online auction rather than the nation's recognition of her bravery in wartime, and anyone with a Nobel Prize could be a brilliant physicist or just a wealthy collector of memorabilia. A bought honour, like a bought friend, becomes something else by definition, something with a different meaning, and of inferior value.

But as it turns out, market regulation, or even moral reprobation, isn't required to protect social and honourific goods from ontological corruption. Because no one seems to want to buy them. People have deduced for themselves that a bought friend or a bought award is actually not at all what they wanted to acquire. As such, these goods hardly warrant the moniker of "contested" commodity (Panitch, 2020, p. 66). Meanwhile, the ontological argument isn't able to explain what's wrong with buying other kinds of contested commodities. The very meaning of needed goods, like an education or health care, is not corrupted through the assignment of price values. The meaning of an education remains the same whether it is provided publicly or privately, as long as an education of equal quality is available to all. And the value of a surgical operation doesn't change whether it's paid for by the state or by a wealthy benefactor. The value of physical goods also remains unchanged by purchase; a kidney doesn't become something else of lesser value when paid for, nor does plasma, or even a baby. When assigned prices, these goods retain their ontological meaning and fundamental value. Corruption theorists should therefore be able to supply alternative justifications for the restriction of markets in these kinds of goods.

Normative corruption

A second type of corruption argument holds that what is degraded by commodification are the norms in accordance with which certain goods should be properly exchanged. This version of the argument has roots in the work of sociologist Richard Titmuss (1997), who concluded from his multi-decade study of paid versus unpaid blood donation that the introduction of markets into something as intimate as the body "represses the expression of altruism … and erodes the sense of community" (p. 314). His concern was that the offer of payment creates a self-interested motive where there would otherwise be an altruistic one, and thereby deprives individuals of an opportunity to act for the sake of others and their community. Titmuss echoed Marx's ([1844]1988) worry about the alienation that occurs when individuals are forced to relate more and more as competitive market actors and are thereby deprived of the chance to stand in relationships of mutual concern (pp. 69–84).

Elizabeth Anderson (1990a) articulates this worry when she asserts that the "worth of goods depend on the motives that people have in providing them" (p. 183). For her, the norms of self-interest, competition, greed, and individualism define market transactions. These norms and motives are inherent to the market and wholly appropriate in exchanges that involve goods with use value only. But they are inappropriate in the exchange of goods that possess something other than, or more than, mere use value. This is because market motives have a tendency to replace or crowd out the altruistic, cooperative, or beneficent motives that are essential to the proper appreciation of such goods (Anderson, 1990a, p. 186). Money introduces a desire for personal gain into spheres of human relations that should be governed instead by the desire to put other people's needs before our own. It distorts the norms of an exchange relation to ones of self-interest and individual gain, crowding out the other-regarding motives in accordance with which the value of certain goods can only be properly appreciated.

Other corruption theorists express a similar concern. Sandel (2012) provides myriad examples of other-regarding motives being disrupted by the introduction of cash incentives, in everything from child-care, to environmental protection, to culture and sport, to health insurance. His worry is that once financial motives are introduced into these (and many other) spheres of human activity, a concern for the well-being of others, or even for the proper appreciation of human excellence, is replaced by a concern only for personal gain (2012, p. 16). Similarly, for Walzer (1984), meeting the needs of others is an essential component of a healthy political community, which rampant self-interest and profit-seeking can threaten. Where self-interested motives are allowed to reign supreme, a concern for the needs of another wanes (p. 25). The introduction of a profit motive limits opportunities for altruism, which is deleterious to the individual, who either wants to act altruistically or who may be the beneficiary thereof, but also to the political community and its citizenry.

The normative corruption argument derives its conclusions from two problematic claims. The first is empirical (markets crowd out altruism) and the second is moral (self-interest is always bad and altruism is always good). Neither claim is wholly defensible. First, market relations are not exclusively self-interested. A person can sell something in order to make money without having self-serving motives in doing so. When we list our house on the market, we hope to get a good price for it, and maybe to even drum up a bidding war. But we might be downsizing to pay for our children's education or to support a meaningful charity. And if we work in medicine or education, we can still bargain with our employers for a higher wage while simultaneously doing work we value because it enables us to help others. As Margaret Radin (1996) puts it, "the spheres of justice are more porous than we think" (p. 112). When market norms invade supposedly non-market spheres of human relations, they do not erode non-market norms altogether; these norms can and do co-exist.

It is with respect to physical goods that normative corruption theorists most vehemently deny the possibility of such co-existence. The body, on their view, can only be exchanged altruistically or self-interestedly; never both. And since the body should only ever be exchanged altruistically, it should never be exchanged for money. When it comes to the human body, the relationships created and sustained by gift exchange are arguably the most meaningful relations in a human life. The sale of sex, organs, and gestation would insert self-interest into what are and should remain ultimate acts of gift-giving, and into relationships that must be defined by a concern for the needs and well-being of others (Anderson, 1990a, 1990b; Radin, 1996). If sex and gestation are assigned prices, and organs are sold rather than donated, acts of selflessness and gift-giving are under threat, but so too is a community that is sustained by regard for others rather than self. But once again, the empirical claim does not hold. Consider the father who sells his kidney to pay for his daughter's heart operation (Radcliffe-Richards, 1996, p. 376). Or consider that while the paid blood donors in Titmuss's study claimed to have done it for the money, we don't know whether they spent that money on their parents' rent or on their children's school fees. Commercial surrogates consistently articulate a profound satisfaction in knowing they helped others create a family, despite also negotiating the terms of the contract to better protect their interests (Busby and Vun, 2010). In the realm of the body, market and non-market norms can and do co-exist.

The moral claim on which the normative corruption argument also depends – according to which altruism is always to be preferred to self-interest – is even more troubling in the realm of physical goods. Normative corruption arguments, as applied to physical goods, impose the burden of preserving altruistic norms squarely on women. Sex work, surrogacy, and organ donation are all primarily undertaken by women. If these constitute ultimate acts of beneficence, the corruption of which would undermine relationships and communities that would otherwise be replete with altruism, it is women's bodies and the choices that women make about their bodies that must be regulated in the name of preserving other-regarding norms. But all exchanges technically present an opportunity for altruism – you always have the option to give rather than sell – so we should be wary of claims according to which its preservation depends mainly on the regulation of women's bodies. These claims may well reflect and entrench the patriarchal expectation of gendered altruism that has long governed women's sexual and reproductive lives (Panitch, forthcoming).

Even if normative corruption theorists were correct that markets inevitably do crowd out altruism, we still need to push back on the moral assumption that this is always a bad thing. Sometimes traditional norms are due to be crowded out when their sole defence is moral conservatism itself: consider, for example, the argument against marriage equality, according to which gay marriage was said to undermine the social value of marriage as a procreative union. And sometimes people putting their own needs first is a sign of moral progress, as was certainly the case as women began to have access to birth control that enabled them to make independent choices about their sexual and reproductive lives. All the better, frankly, that traditional norms governing sex and reproduction be supplanted by women making bodily choices in accordance with the supposedly market-driven norms of individuality and personal freedom (Panitch, 2020, p. 67). While we'd all rather live in a community replete with altruism, we must seriously ask whether its preservation is worth the policing of women's bodies, and whether an ideal political community is truly one that depends on and reaffirms a norm of gendered altruism.

Teleological corruption

A third type of corruption argument issues a warning with respect to human flourishing. On this account, when the value of important goods is degraded, or when the norms appropriate to their exchange are crowded out, the essential role these values and norms play in the attainment of the flourishing human life is corrupted. According to Margaret Jane Radin (1996), we should identify a commodity's "contested" status precisely by determining its importance to the attainment of a flourishing human life (p. 79). Since the market can drive out non-market alternatives to important social practices, then it is to the extent that certain non-market practices are essential to the good life that we have reason to want to regulate their marketization. Where the domino effect of commodification renders it such that we can no longer participate in non-monetized versions of important practices and relationships, we are unable to engage in the proper development of our true nature, and thus to flourish as the kinds of beings that we are (Radin, 1996, pp. 79–101).

The teleological corruption worry is closely tied to the previous two. Indeed, theorists who worry about normative and ontological corruption do so in large part because they worry that these will impede flourishing. For Sandel (2000), human flourishing is only attainable in a political community in which citizens are able to properly appreciate the inherent value of important goods and activities (pp. 105–109). For Anderson, relationships based on altruism, beneficence, and cooperation are essential to the flourishing life, and where markets encroach on them, the selfishness and competition they bring crowds out the other-regarding norms essential to the personal and political relationships without which we could not flourish (1990a, p. 193; 1990b, p. 73). The teleological argument also draws from Aristotle, according to whom our *telos* constitutes the ultimate end to which we should strive as the kinds of beings that we are (NE, Book I s.1), and from Marx ([1844]1988), for whom the development of our true nature as social beings is impaired by market practices that alienate us from one another (pp. 69–84).

The teleological view, like the normative view, rests on an empirical claim and a moral claim, both of which are once again problematic. First, we have to question the empirical claim that markets drive out non-market alternatives to various goods and activities. Sex work, after millennia, has yet to destroy what people find valuable about intimate partner sex. And paid surrogacy – following in a long tradition of handmaids, wet nurses and the like, as problematic as these were – has yet to cause us as a society to view gestation and motherhood in the same terms as baking or bus-driving. Sex and motherhood remain important to many people's conceptions of the good, regardless of the existence of their paid alternatives. Radin acknowledges this. But rather than attempt to settle it she raises the more important point that even if the empirical claim were true, we could not ground legislation upon it without finding ourselves in a double bind according to which the prohibition of certain markets would only turn them from white to black, thereby placing participants at greater risk without preventing sales that supposedly threaten our opportunities for flourishing (Radin, 1996, pp. 123–130).

This concession to the double bind is important. Radin is acknowledging that criminalization often requires a different rationale than moral condemnation. Her particular argument for this goes by way of harm mitigation (1996, p. 184). But there is another, more important reason that the teleological argument cannot supply grounds for criminal sanctions. This is because the moral claim on which it rests is fundamentally perfectionist in nature. Perfectionism is a philosophical view that starts with an account of the good or 'perfect' life for the type of being that we are, as determined by the kinds of activities and undertakings that are thought to be intrinsically valuable (Hurka, 1996). The aim is to be able to say what counts as a good life for a human being and to identify who is living a good life and who is not. But reasonable people disagree about what counts as a good life. Teleological PAC theorists presuppose that we understand and agree on what it means to flourish, but this is an even more inscrutable philosophical question than what to do about noxious markets.

Some people may be correct in their accounts of the good life, and others incorrect. But this should have no bearing on criminal legislation or even market regulation in a liberal society.

Arguably the most central tenet of liberal democracy is that, because it wouldn't be reasonable to agree to live under political institutions that impose on you what you take to be an unacceptable conception of the good, nor is it thereby rational to seek to use political institutions to impose your conception of the good on others (Rawls, 2001, pp. 18–28). Teleological arguments grounded in perfectionist moral claims about the good life therefore supply poor arguments for legislation and market regulation in a liberal state committed to remaining neutral on precisely this question (Kymlicka, 1989; Dworkin, 1985). Teleological PAC arguments may well supply grounds for the moral condemnation of various markets. But for PAC theorists who intend to offer more than mere moral condemnation, but also defensible grounds for regulation in our liberal state, they must appeal to something other than teleology. Certainly, there is ample debate as to the desirability no least the feasibility of liberal neutrality (Raz, 1986; Sandel, 1982). I cannot take on that debate here. But it should be reasonable enough to claim that if a view about contested markets can be mounted consistent with this commitment, it would provide a superior basis on which to restrict market choices in a liberal democracy than one which is not (Panitch, 2020, p. 67).

According to corruption-based PAC arguments, ascribing price values to goods and exchanging them in accordance with market principles is corruptive (and therefore wrongful) if doing so degrades the value of the goods themselves, the value of the norms proper to their exchange, and/or the attainment of a flourishing human life. As we have seen, each of these versions of the corruption argument encounters significant, if not insurmountable challenges, due either to their non-generalizability, their empirical unsustainability, and/or their conservatism and perfectionism. Let us turn now to the equality arguments offered by PAC theorists, which may appear at first blush to avoid these problems. What I hope to demonstrate in the next section is that this appearance is largely illusory.

Equality arguments

According to equality-based PAC arguments, the goods that should not be for sale are those whose market distribution and exchange threatens relations of equal standing. This type of account must first tell us which sorts of inequalities in standing are wrongful in order to then identify the kinds of goods that must be exempt from market exchange. We do not generally think of inequalities generated by markets in yachts as very problematic, but we do worry about inequalities generated by the market allocation of health care, for example. PAC theorists who offer equality arguments must identify which kinds of inequalities matter by way of explaining why the market exemption of some goods but not others is necessary in the name of protecting our equal standing. PAC theorists argue that contested markets depend on and/or entrench various kinds of inequalities, be they inequalities in bargaining power or diverse resources shares (call this *simple equality* and *complex equality* respectively), in moral status (call this *moral equality*), or in democratic status (call this *democratic equality*). Let's examine each in turn.

Simple equality/complex equality

According to the simple equality worry, markets are problematic when they involve unequally vulnerable bargainers. Market transactions are widely regarded as objectionable if one of the parties is explicitly coerced or misinformed, because the exchange is thereby non-consensual; but markets can also be problematic if one of the parties acts from a position of great vulnerability or desperation which can also threaten the autonomous nature of the exchange (Wertheimer, 1996). If one party sells something from a position of dire need this may not reflect a genuine choice on her part, and it puts her in a position from which her co-transactor can take wrongful advantage of her. On this account, noxious markets are those that operate against the background of inequalities that render some persons vulnerable to offers with respect to which they are poorly placed to bargain.[6] They are, in other words, desperate exchanges.

Desperate exchanges call out urgently for prevention and sanction. However, they are not strictly speaking a problem of commodification. What the simple equality view tells us is *how* a good should not be exchanged – namely, under conditions in which one party is desperate and unable to bargain. What is does not tell us is *which* goods should be exempt from market exchange. Simple equality does not identify some set of goods as those that shouldn't be sold, it only tells us how goods in general should not be sold (Panitch, 2020, p. 63). It is wrong that anyone should have to sell something they don't want to, and otherwise wouldn't sell but for their unfortunate circumstances. For some, it might be worse to part with a beloved heirloom than a kidney when they have no other choice. It's the lack of choice, and not the sale of the heirloom or the kidney as such, that renders the transaction desperate and thereby morally suspect. Under other conditions, were the vendor to have had myriad other options for acquiring what she needs or wants, the sale of the heirloom or the kidney, or of any other good she owns, would be unproblematic on this view. What the simple equality argument offers is thus not strictly speaking a PAC argument at all. The problem it identifies is one that attends to markets in general, not to markets in any particular goods, and one that could be addressed through the redistribution of wealth rather than through the blocking of specific markets.

For Michael Walzer (1984), an equality view needs to be "complex", rather than "simple" in order to qualify as a PAC argument (pp. 17–19). According to Walzer, complex equality requires not only that the material preconditions of desperate exchanges be addressed through the redistribution of wealth (which would satisfy the simple equality concern), but also that the market exchange of certain goods be blocked altogether. The redistribution of wealth does serve to lessen vulnerability and reduce desperate exchanges; but it also promotes and necessitates market interaction, requiring that we enter the market to satisfy even our most basic needs. There are certain goods to which we should all have equal access, for Walzer, without market interaction. Moreover, if instead of ensuring equal access to public education or health care, the state handed out extra cash, it could not guarantee that citizens would spend it on an education or health, or that those who could afford to wouldn't spend more to get more. Complex equality demands that we redistribute wealth to limit desperate exchanges, but that we also go further to block the sale of needed goods to prevent unequal holdings thereof (Walzer, 1984, pp. 97–103).

But, of course, the question remains: why block the market exchanges of some goods and not others? Why block markets in health care but not in yachts once some level of material sufficiency has been assured? Here, Walzer returns to his discussion of the social meanings of goods, and the importance of their social preservation. Yachts don't have a social meaning the preservation of which requires their equal distribution. Health care does. The social meaning of needed goods, like health and education, is corrupted by cash acquisition or market distribution. The goods whose market exchange must be blocked are those whose very social meaning depends on it (Walzer, 1984, pp. 21–16). If this sounds familiar, it should. Complex equality makes the egalitarian claim that certain goods should be accessible to all regardless of ability to pay. But it is only able to identify *which* goods these are by appeal to something that looks like an ontological corruption claim. As a view, complex equality progresses beyond simple equality by making a corruption argument for blocking the sale of certain specific goods. The appeal to corruptive ontology as a strategy of avoiding egalitarian simplicity is of course only a problem to the extent that I was able to mount a persuasive challenge to ontological corruption earlier in the chapter.

Moral equality

According to this type of view, the commodification of certain goods is wrong to the extent that their sale undermines the relations of moral equality in which we ought to stand with one another as members of humanity. This view is rooted in the Kantian ([1785]1999) dictum that "what has a price can be replaced by something else as its equivalence; what on the other hand is raised above all price and therefore admits of no equivalent has a dignity" (4:434). This argument is often taken to explain the moral impermissibility of slavery. It is wrong, even if it accords with the agent's own choice, that she be sold into slavery because her dignity precludes her having a price. Price values are appropriately assigned to goods that have instrumental value. But moral agents are not instruments of mere use. No one can assign a price value to another and still stand in a relation of moral equality to her, because in the very assignment of a price the agent's value is instrumentalized and the source of her human dignity is thus maligned.

Several theorists have taken up this line of argument. On Ruth Sample's (2003) account, human beings possess a value that exerts a powerful claim on us, and in commodifying goods essential to their humanity we fail to show them the respect this claim exerts. For Sample, this includes primarily but not only body parts and other physical goods. "We can fail to respect a person by commodifying or treating as a fungible object of market exchanges, an[y] aspect of that person's being that ought not be commodified" (2003, p. 57). We fail to demonstrate respect by commodifying a person's body parts or intimate capacities, on her view, because no one could in principle consent to having such essential aspects of their personhood treated as objects of mere use (2003, p. 69). We deny the fundamental moral worth and moral equality of persons in disrespecting them in this way.

For Anne Phillips (2011), the commodification of the body is also disrespectful in that it leads us to view other agents as beings of lesser moral worth. We all have bodies, Phillips argues, and none of us would choose to sell them except under conditions of dire need. This means that when we make financial offers to persons for their body parts or intimate services – offers we would never deign to accept ourselves – we regard those who do accept them as beings with less moral worth than we take ourselves to possess (pp. 740–744). For Phillips (2017), the relevant kind of equality that is threatened by noxious markets, and body markets in particular, is "the inequality that is at stake when one party to an arrangement treats the other as a being of lesser significance … It is not the level of payment … but what it asserts about our status as [moral] equals" (p. 110).

There are a number of concerns to raise in response to this line of argument. First of all, the idea that the body should be exempt from sale because it is too intimately tied to personhood runs counter to the philosophical conception of personhood on which it rests. We are beings possessed of dignity and deserving of respect, on the Kantian account, in virtue of our capacity to set ends for ourselves. It is our rational autonomy or our very capacity for choice-making that is definitive of our humanity, not our organs, gametes, plasma, or our intimate capacities. If our body parts and intimate capacities were truly essential to our personhood, we would not be able to alienate ourselves from them for money or for free (Panitch and Horne, 2018, p. 130). Organ donation would be just as wrong as organ sales; sex would be just as wrong as sex work. It is our capacity for autonomy and end-setting that determines our moral worth and moral equality, not our body parts.

The second problem is that although Sample and Phillips are explicitly concerned with moral equality, what they articulate is in fact a corruption argument of its own ilk. Returning to Kant's dictum that whatever is elevated above all price has a dignity, what troubles him is that an agent's inherent value may be esteemed in purely instrumental terms. When this occurs, an inequality in moral worth and moral standing can certainly follow. But the underlying problem is that the agent's value is degraded by being equivalated to something with a price. This is quite clearly a corruption concern, where the corruption in question is not of some good, nor of the norms in accordance with which a good should be exchanged, nor even of an agent's capacity to flourish; what's corrupted is the agent's dignity itself. Call this *deontic corruption* (Panitch and Horne, 2018, p. 129). Deontic corruption occurs when a moral agent is degraded by her estimation as an object of mere instrumental worth. It is wrong to view, and worse to treat an agent as an object of mere use. Moral equality arguments are, like complex equality arguments, corruption arguments in disguise.

And the trouble with deontic arguments is that they do not in fact point to a problem of commodification, but of instrumentalization. The two may overlap but need not. We often use people as a mere means without involving money. Nussbaum (1995) provides myriad examples of the degradation involved in objectifying persons independent of their commodification. And consider the moral consternation surrounding 'saviour siblings', born for the purpose of supplying spare parts to an older child. For Kant ([1775–1780]1997), premarital sex was just as bad as prostitution because of the instrumental use involved (p. 157). And what made slavery wrong for him is that a slave is forever relegated to the status of an object of mere use, which occurs regardless of whether the slave was bought or gifted. It's the instrumental use of a moral agent that degrades her dignity, and this can sometimes coincide with her commodification, but need not.

Moreover, the exchange of money is often what allows us to *avoid* making instrumental use of persons, our house staff, to take yet another Kantian example ([1797]1999, s.6:538). Sometimes – indeed often – we must engage in commodification so as to avoid instrumentalization. We pay workers a fair wage for their labour precisely so as to avoid treating them as slaves. And recall from our previous discussion that the withholding of payment for bodily goods and intimate capacities may well be grounded in the patriarchal expectation of gendered altruism. To deny women payment for the body parts or intimate capacities they make available to others is not necessarily a means by which to accord them the respect they are owed as moral agents (Panitch, forthcoming). Although I offer more nuance with respect to this point later, we should worry when some bodily efforts – ones performed primarily by women – are said to be accorded respect only through the withholding of payment, when payment is precisely what we generally use to demonstrate respect for the labours of others.

Moral equality is only incidentally a view about equality, but more precisely a view about corruption. Specifically, the deontic corruption of an agent's value when she is estimated in instrumental terms. However, deontic corruption is not an argument about commodification, but about instrumentalization. The two may coincide but need not. This line of argument can at best point to cases where we might have reason to worry about payment to agents for goods or services rendered, but it does not specify whether our worry should be with the provision or the withholding thereof.

Democratic equality

The most promising equality-based argument is one according to which the sale of contested commodities undermines equality in social status and democratic citizenship. Debra Satz (2010) argues that noxious markets interfere with the state's ability to guarantee "the conditions people need if they are to relate as equals" (p. 94). And to "participate competently and meaningfully in a democratic society" (p. 101). At least some of the goods essential to the exercise of equal and meaningful citizenship can be secured through the redistribution of wealth and income. Redistributing wealth would address the problem of weak agency which underlies a good many noxious markets, according to Satz. But, as we've seen, noxious markets are not a mere matter of desperate exchange. Certain markets undermine our democratic status, for Satz, and this is why the state must "block market exchanges altogether if citizens are to be equal" (p. 102). Satz argues that if all social relations were to become market relations, this would pose a threat to equal citizenship. In one sense, this is because market relations are so frequently desperate ones. But in another, it is because market norms corrode and displace the norm of equality itself.

Satz's view is compelling because it condemns markets that not only reflect asymmetric agency and vulnerability, but that perpetuate inegalitarian social relations. What's unclear, however, is whether equality functions for Satz as a political ideal or a distributive principle (Heath, 2011, p. 101). She argues that the market distribution of the goods essential to citizenship is only problematic if it frustrates our *equal status* (2010, p. 95). This implies that the state need only guarantee some fair distribution of certain goods to show all citizens an equal concern and respect. Yet she also suggests that the only way for the state to guarantee our equal status is to provide us with *equal shares* of the relevant goods. Satz offers the example of a ship with too few lifeboats, which fails to ensure the equal safety of its passengers (p. 100). Her heavy reliance on this example implies that the state only protects our equal status when it guarantees us a perfectly equal distribution of the goods essential to equal citizenship.

But is our equal democratic status really only assured by securing *equal shares* of relevant goods? The degree of market intervention required depends crucially on how this question is answered. The state treats citizens as equals, according to Satz, only if it guarantees the non-market distribution of goods essential to democratic citizenship – by which she has in mind primarily civic and necessary goods (2010, pp. 94–100), and in some cases physical goods, such as organs (p. 204). The market cannot be relied on to produce a distribution of these goods that preserves and affirms our equal status, she argues. Satz claims that some of these goods – namely votes – must be secured equally, and others – namely education – must be guaranteed to a sufficient degree (2010, p. 208). But she offers no robust account of how this determination was made, nor how we might assess which other civic and necessary goods require an equal and which a sufficient distribution. It is not clear that an appeal to the value of democratic equality as such allows us to make such an assessment.

We cannot be sure what distributive demands are issued by Satz's concern with the equal status of citizens. This is because the first half of her book is devoted to establishing equal status as grounds for interfering with noxious markets, and the second half of her book is devoted to examining markets in physical goods specifically. What is missing is an application of her argument to civic and necessary goods (this is a gap I aim to fill in the following section). This apparent oversight on Satz' part can best be made sense of if we infer that her primary interest lies not with extrapolating the distributive requirements thereof, but instead with making a case for the preservation of democratic norms themselves. In other words, it is likely not an oversight that Satz does not clarify what equality as a norm demands with respect to the distribution of specific civic and necessary goods. Because it is not an equitable distribution of these goods so much as the preservation of equality as a norm that is essential to her ideal of democratic citizenship (2010, pp. 101–102).

But if equality here functions as a valuable norm the preservation of which justifies the blocking of certain markets exchanges, we seem to be treading familiar ground. Here again, we seem to be engaging with a normative corruption argument operating under the guise of an equality argument, where the aim is to block the introduction of market principles into civic relationships in which they would erode or corrupt the norm of democratic equality. Granted, in my earlier discussion of corruption arguments, the focus was on the ways in which the market norm of self-interest threatened the social norm of altruism; but here a parallel case is being made according to which the market norms of self-interest, individualism, and ability to pay threaten the political norm of equality. This version of the corruption argument is less problematic both empirically and politically. However, it nonetheless rests its case on a similar appeal to the value of preserving a particular social norm that markets are said to threaten. And it is the preservation of the norm, rather than the distributive mandates it issues, or coherence with a broader conception of justice that might ground its value, that appears to be what's ultimately at stake.

According to equality-based PAC arguments, the goods that should not be for sale are those whose market distribution and exchange either depend on or produce inequalities in bargaining power, in moral status, or in democratic status. Unfortunately, simple equality can only tell us under what kinds of conditions goods shouldn't be sold, but not which goods shouldn't be sold. And complex, moral, and democratic equality only reach beyond the simple account, and thus can only explain why the sale of specific goods must be blocked, to the extent that they risk becoming corruption arguments by another name. Satz's democratic account is certainly the most promising, concerned as it is to both eradicate desperate exchanges and to block markets in goods whose sale threatens the equal standing of citizens. What remains unclear is whether the preservation of our equal democratic status requires a strictly equal distribution of civic and necessary goods, and thus the nature and degree of market intervention her view calls for. These are matters that cannot be settled by an appeal to the norm of democratic equality as such, nor to claims about the value of its preservation from the corruptive effects of markets.

My argument in what follows should be viewed as an addendum to rather than a rejection of Satz's approach. What I propose to do is to utilize her appeal to democratic equality as grounds for blocking noxious markets, but without overlooking the distributive requirements thereof nor resting the case on the value of preserving egalitarian norms from corruption. I will in effect attempt to ground Satz's account of democratic equality in a theory of political liberalism, as a means of unearthing more precise distributive requirements – of identifying which goods require an equal and which a sufficient distribution – and of grounding these distributive mandates in a broader account of state legitimacy from which the value of equal status itself must be derived. I will argue that we can and should appeal to democratic equality as grounds for blocking noxious markets, provided this appeal is grounded firmly in a politically liberal theory of distributive justice.

Justice arguments

The account I offer in the remainder of this chapter constitutes a justice-based PAC argument (Panitch, 2020). This approach takes as its starting point a commitment to two claims, one empirical and one normative. The empirical claim is that of pluralism, according to which our democratic society is marked by a plurality of reasonable yet irreconcilable conceptions of the good life. The normative claim is that of reciprocity, according to which no one is entitled to a larger share of the benefits of social cooperation than anyone else simply on the basis of the conception of the good they hold. If we take these two claims seriously then we are committed to a third regarding legitimacy, according to which citizens may exercise coercive authority over one another through the apparatus of the state only in accordance with principles they could all endorse. These three claims constitute what John Rawls (2001) calls the political conception of justice (p. 9).

On this conception, inequalities in the distribution of the benefits and burdens of social cooperation should be agreeable to anyone who subscribes to a reasonable conception of the good, and who rationally accepts that the only way to ensure non-domination of her own reasonable doctrine is to endorse principles of non-domination with respect to the doctrines of others (Rawls,

1996, pp. 18–28). In order that citizens might be expected to be reasonable and rational – or to possess what Rawls (2001) calls the two moral powers of citizenship – there are certain social conditions and all-purpose means that they must be guaranteed (pp. 18–19). The moral powers are the preconditions necessary for citizens to be capable of endorsing any principles as just (Scanlon, 2003). For Rawls (1996), citizens require a guaranteed sphere of social primary goods, including rights and liberties, along with opportunity, authority of office, income, and the social basis of self-respect in order to develop and exercise their two moral powers (pp. 308–310). But these primary goods cannot be expected to effectuate the two moral powers "unless the basic needs of citizens are equally met" (Rawls, 2001, p. 26). The principles of justice must ensure that the primary goods and the basic needs of all citizens are allocated in a manner that would promote the two moral powers and thus be agreeable to all reasonable and rational persons with diverse metaphysical commitments (2001, p. 15).

What I want to show in the remainder of this chapter is that the all-purpose means that citizens require by way of realizing and exercising the two moral powers of equal citizenship are precisely those belonging to the civic, necessary, and physical categories of contested commodities. And, moreover, that the distributive requirements mandated by Rawls' two principles of justice should determine the market's permissible role in allocating these goods. In other words, it is to the extent that markets frustrate the distributive guarantees mandated by the principles of justice appropriate to a liberal society, that they can and should be constrained (Panitch, 2020, p. 70).

Civic goods

According to the political conception of justice, the first principle thereof must guarantee the rights and liberties essential to free and equal citizenship. This principle demands that each citizen be guaranteed the same indefeasible claim to a fully adequate scheme of equal basic liberties consistent with the same scheme of liberties for all (Rawls, 2001, p. 17). Anyone denied the freedom to speak her own mind, to practice her beliefs, or to participate in government including through voting, could not be expected to engage reasonably with those to whom she is thereby subject. Nor could she devise for herself a conception of the good she regards as worthwhile if social and political opportunities are formally closed to her while open to others. These equal basic rights form the constitutional essentials to which all citizens must be equally entitled (2001, p. 28).

The basic rights and liberties are precisely the civic goods that PAC theorists are concerned to protect from sale. According to the justice-based argument I am offering, these goods are non-saleable because they are non-alienable (Freeman, 2007, p. 51). You cannot give away your civic and political rights because all citizens would recognize that, insofar as it would be irrational to accept a distribution in which they received an inferior share of rights and liberties, it would be unreasonable to ask others to accept an inferior share themselves (Rawls, 2001, p. 32). An equal distribution is the only one that would be agreeable to all free and equal citizens, and thus an unequal distribution of basic rights and liberties is an unjust distribution. It is precisely because you cannot give away the civic goods covered by the first principle of justice that you cannot sell them. And you cannot give them away because everyone having them (and keeping them) is a requirement of justice (Panitch, 2020, pp. 70–71).

Necessary goods

The second principle secures the social and material wherewithal required for citizens to develop and exercise the two moral powers. Both opportunity and income are necessary to this end.

Reasonable and rational persons would agree that these items should be distributed equally except where inequalities therein would be advantageous to the worst off (Rawls, 2001, p. 26). But they would also agree that the "basic needs of all citizens must be [equally] met … [because] below a certain level of material and social well-being … people simply cannot take part in society as citizens, much less as equal citizens" (Rawls, 1996, p. 166). The second principle thus presupposes a social minimum, which secures the fair value of the political liberties, and provides education and training, and a basic level of health care for all (2001, p. 176).

This principle gives us ample reason to worry about the sale of (at least) two necessary goods. Each citizen is entitled to a guaranteed minimum of education and health care, and this entitlement is no more saleable than an entitlement to an equal share of rights and liberties. Necessary goods are wrong to sell for the same reason as civic goods: we cannot sell them if doing so undermines the only principle of distribution (equality in civic goods, and sufficiency in necessary goods) that would be agreeable to all rational and reasonable persons. These goods must be guaranteed to a sufficient degree for all as background conditions to the two moral powers, and thus to equal citizenship; and this is why it would be neither reasonable nor rational for anyone to agree to anything less than a sufficient share thereof.

However, because necessary goods such as education and health care must only be met sufficiently, not equally, markets in these goods are perfectly defensible once the social minimum has been attained. On this account, health care and education are wrong to sell only to the extent they remain 'necessary'. The social minimum demands that these goods be guaranteed *up to the point* that they secure the ends of justice. The same goods, over and above this threshold, can be and indeed are commodities. Secondary education is regarded as necessary for adequate opportunity in many societies and is often (although not always, of course) provided universally at public expense. Post-secondary education is not, typically; and where it may be subsidized, it is usually made available at least partly at students' expense. Public health care, or health insurance, in many countries typically covers only what is 'medically necessary' and citizens are welcome to purchase additional insurance from private providers over and above the guaranteed minimum. A scheme of private education or health coverage should serve as an addendum rather than an alternative to a public system, however; parallel private systems can threaten the integrity of the public guarantee of sufficiency in necessary goods (Horne and Heath, 2022; Brighouse 2004).

What is wrong with the commodification of necessary goods is not that dollar values are ascribed to them, or even that they are distributed according to ability to pay, but only that their sufficient provision is not always guaranteed. But necessary goods are necessary only up to a point. Whether our institutions have got that point right is a legitimate matter of public debate. And different institutions have produced considerably different answers to the questions of what should be covered at public expense and to what extent. But this should not be mistaken for a debate about the non-commodifiability of these goods themselves. Unlike civic goods, whose distribution must be perfectly equal to be just, necessary goods need only be sufficiently guaranteed to satisfy the political conception of justice. Beyond that they can be and routinely are commodified (Panitch, 2020, pp. 72–73).

Physical goods

The dilemma with physical goods – including kidneys, surrogacy, and sex – is that, while we laud their gift exchange, we often decry their commercialization. It may seem that the justice-based argument I have been advancing would yield a simple equality answer to questions about the permissibility of markets in physical goods. Why should anyone be prevented from selling their body parts or intimate labours against the background of equal freedom and a sufficient social minimum? If these guarantees address the conditions of desperate exchange, what grounds are there to worry about body markets on a justice-based view? The grounds for worry are that the sale of physical goods may, in some instances, violate the principles of justice themselves (Panitch, 2020, pp. 73–79).

Some body sales violate the first principle of justice. Although contracts may be voluntary, they can still be coercive, and this is particularly troubling in the realm of body sales. Contracts may be entered into voluntarily and yet contain coercible terms of fulfillment. In making a contract, you make a promise to provide some good or service to another and agree to be held to the terms of your promise. This can be particularly troubling in the realm of the body. Consider how this might apply in the context of kidney markets. In regions where the practice of blackmarket kidney-selling is widespread, kidneys are increasingly seen as potential collateral for loans (Satz, 2010, p. 201). This is troubling because it constrains the options of the desperate who would prefer to obtain a loan without posting a body part as collateral and would prefer that kidney-selling not be allowed even though they may take advantage of the market where it exists (Rippon, 2014). But a worse problem is that when the debt is called up but cannot be repaid, holding the debtor to the terms of the contract would involve involuntary surgery and thus constitute a gross violation of his right to security of the person (Panitch, 2020, p. 74).

Markets that depend on violations of this right are clearly in tension with the guarantees laid out by the first principle of justice. The various rights and liberties this principle secures would be of little value were a right to bodily security not counted among them (Rawls, 1996, p. 7). And this is not something we can sell or promise to alienate later in exchange for present financing any more than we can alienate the other rights guaranteed by the first principle of justice. This argument does not only apply to kidneys. Commercial surrogates are routinely expected to agree at the outset of the arrangement to undergo fetal reduction or caesarian delivery at the behest of the intended parents. If a surrogate changes her mind before such a procedure, the enforcement of the contract would involve the violation of her right to refuse an invasive medical procedure. In the case of sex work, if a prostitute changes her mind between the street and the bedroom, the coercive enforcement of the contract is rape. When it comes to the body, consent must be ongoing. This means that what can never be for sale is an agent's fundamental right to retain control of her own bodily security. Any contract that denies this is invalid. And any market that repudiates it is unjust.

Body sales can also violate the second principle of justice. The kind of inequalities addressed by the provision of a social minimum may not address all social injustices, specifically those pertaining to race and gender. While racial and gender injustices are certainly correlated to wealth and opportunity, the unequal standing of certain groups to others in a racialized and patriarchal society is neither fully explicable nor eradicable by resource distribution. The guarantee of a decent social minimum should thus not be expected to provide an adequately just response to problems of gender and racial inequality (Fraser, 1997; Mills, 2017; Young, 1990). To the extent that body sales reflect and perpetuate racial and gender inequalities, some additional considerations of justice are required above the guarantee of formal rights and liberties and of a sufficient social minimum (Panitch, 2020, pp 75–79).

This is precisely why Rawls (1999) introduces the social bases of self-respect as a primary good unto itself (p. 67). Just as citizens could not be expected to be reasonable with others who denied them a fair share of the social product, neither could they be expected to rationally develop and pursue a worthwhile conception of the good just to see their ends denigrated, and their own worthiness denied in virtue of their membership in a particular social class (Rawls, 1999, p. 386). A fair share of liberties, opportunities, and income constitutes an essential affirmation of each citizens' worth. But this is not all that is required to ensure the development and exercise of the moral powers (Eyal, 2005). If certain social practices cause or reinforce denigrating social attitudes towards a particular class of citizens, its members may feel as though they are not worthy of participation in their political culture (Darwall, 1977; Doppelt, 2015).

While attitudes and beliefs fall beyond the reach of society's basic institutions, social practices that promulgate beliefs about the inferiority of others do not. Practices that undermine the social bases of self-respect are very much within the purview of society's basic institutions, principally the law. Our market choices can and should be legally restricted by considerations of justice, and on the political conception of justice, the social basis of self-respect is key among them. It is hard to have the sense of self-worth required to pursue our ends and effectuate our political standing if others deem our ends unworthy or us unworthy of their pursuit. A social practice that involves the commodification of goods whose sale contributes to beliefs about the inferior worth of members of some particular social group may therefore be restricted on grounds consistent with the political conception of justice (Doppelt, 2015, pp. 148–152).

Although there is not time to establish the case here, many theorists have argued that there is more than enough reason to think of intimate labour as just such a practice. That gendered intimate labour both trades on and reinforces women's inferior social status as objects of sexual and reproductive use has more or less substantiated the feminist critique of both practices from across the broadly liberal, radical, communitarian, and Marxist feminist spectrum (Jagger, 1999). There is a strong case that sex work trades on and confirms the view that women belong to an inferior social class, and that women themselves come to internalize this view (Satz, 2010, pp. 144–149; Shrage, 1989). A similar case has been made with respect to commercial surrogacy (Baylis, 2014; Phillips, 2011). As such, we might well conclude that these commercial practices threaten the social bases of women's self-respect.

Recall from our discussion of both normative corruption and moral equality, however, that bans on sex work and commercial surrogacy may in fact serve to bolster a patriarchal expectation of gendered altruism. Additional argumentation and empirical investigation are therefore needed to determine whether payment for intimate labour contributes more significantly to negative stereotyping and the internalization of a negative sense of self-worth and is thus more corrosive to the social bases of women's self-respect than bans on payment. Nonetheless, the requirement that a fair society must protect and promote the social bases of self-respect provides us with an important normative lens through which to consider the commodification of physical goods as a question of justice. And it offers a position from which to argue for reasonable regulations as required to constrain market practices that involve violations of bodily integrity or that promulgate beliefs which contribute to the marginalization and denigration of the members of any social group.

Conclusion

My aim in this chapter was to critically evaluate philosophical anti-commodification theory, while at the same time embracing the fundamental project thereof. I began by exploring corruption-based PAC arguments. I showed that corruption arguments depend on claims that are either empirically or morally suspect and are particularly problematic when perfectionist claims are offered as a basis upon which to ground criminal legislation in a pluralist society. In the second part of the chapter, I turned to examining equality-based PAC arguments. I argued that although this approach to answering the fundamental questions of anti-commodification theory is more promising, equality arguments cannot tell us *which* goods should not be sold (as opposed to merely telling us *how* goods in general should not be sold) without appealing to corruption claims of their own.

I went on to offer a brief defence of a third kind of anti-commodification view – one that honours the underlying commitments of PAC theory and shares in its unifying features – but that promises to avoid the troubles facing corruption and equality arguments. I referred to the view as a justice-based PAC argument, according to which the goods that are wrong to commodify are those whose sale is precluded by the principles of justice that would be endorsed by free and equal citizens committed to diverse and incompatible conceptions of the good. It thereby offers an argument against the commodification (to varying degrees) of civic, necessary, and physical goods that is consistent with both the underlying aims of philosophical anti-commodification theory and, importantly, with the commitments of a liberal democratic state.

Notes

1 I would like to thank Elodie Bertrand and Michael Kessler for their invaluable feedback, and to all the participants at the Contested Commodities conference at the Sorbonne in Paris, June 2022, and at the New Research in Practical Philosophy workshop at Universitat Pompeu Fabra in Barcelona, May 2023.

2 Philosophically, what it means to 'commodify' depends on the account that is given of its wrongfulness. As we will see, different theorists identify different problems – be it the assignment of a price, or distribution via ability to pay, etc. – and define commodification pejoratively by appeal to the processes they take to be most harmful. This is, to be sure, a frustrating way of proceeding. Yet, because commodification does avail itself to myriad definitions, that PAC theorists define it by appeal to its relevant wrong is to a certain extent helpful, even if somewhat question-begging.

3 My aim here is to engage critically with the PAC project but to do so in a way that takes seriously its central aims and insights. In this regard, although I share a critique of PAC arguments offered by Jason Brennan and Peter A. Jaworski (2015), I do not share their view that the PAC project is itself misguided. On their view, there aren't any goods that should be exempt from market exchange aside from goods you shouldn't have in the first place. They effectively disavow the project of anti-commodification theory with the statement "if you can do it, you can sell it" (2015, p. 11).

4 This generality is misplaced because it is unclear why we should expect the same argument that tells us why vote-selling is wrong to also be able to tell us why kidney-selling is wrong; or why we should think that the reason we offer against the sale of sex should also apply to the sale of honours or awards, for example (Panitch, 2020, p. 5). No single corruption or equality claim should be expected to do all the heavy lifting PAC theorists often assign to them. The justice argument I go on to offer can speak to the wrongfulness of the commodification of diverse goods, but only because it contains multiple principles with different distributive requirements.

5 PAC theorists do not explicitly cash out the harms they identify in terms of externalities, although many of these harms run parallel to those explored by Bertrand in Chapter 3 of this volume. And the arguments in this chapter, as with those in Chapter 3, have in common the aim of challenging the pro-market arguments presented in Chapter 1.

6 This view can certainly be applied to various contested commodities, but it is commonly voiced by PAC theorists (and non-PAC theorists alike) with respect to body sales (Baylis, 2014; Buyx, 2009; Hughes, 2009; Rippon, 2014; Shrage, 1989; Satz, 2010).

References

Anderson, E. (1990a) "Ethical limitations of the market" *Economics and Philosophy* 6(2), pp. 179–205.

Anderson, E. (1990b) "Is women's labor a commodity?" *Philosophy and Public Affairs* 19(1), pp. 71–92.

Anderson, E. (1993) *Value in Ethics and Economics*. Cambridge: Harvard University Press.

Aristotle (NE 2014) *Nichomachean Ethics*, Crisp, R (ed.) Cambridge: Cambridge University Press.

Aristotle (PC 1996) *The Politics and the Constitution of Athens*. S. Everson (ed.) Cambridge: Cambridge University Press.
Baylis, F. (2014) "Transnational commercial contract pregnancy in India," in F. Baylis and C. McLeod (eds.) *Family-Making: Contemporary Ethical Challenges*. New York: Oxford University Press, pp. 265–286.
Brennan, J. and Jaworski, P.M. (2015) *Markets Without Limits: Moral Virtues and Commercial Interests*. New York: Routledge.
Brighouse, H. (2004) "What's wrong with privatizing schools," *Journal of Philosophy of Education* 38(4), pp. 617–631.
Busby, K. and Vun, D. (2010) "Revisiting *The Handmaid's Tale*: Feminist theory meets empirical research on surrogate mothers," *Canadian Journal of Family Law* 26(1), pp. 13–93.
Buyx, A.M. (2009) "Blood donation, payment, and non-cash incentives," *Transfusion Medicine and Hemotherapy* 36(6), pp. 329–339.
Darwall, S. (1977) "Two kinds of respect," *Ethics* 88(1), pp. 36–49.
Doppelt, G. (2015) "The place of self-respect in *A Theory of Justice*," *Inquiry* 52(2), pp. 127–154.
Dworkin, R. (1985) "Liberalism," *A Matter of Principle*, Cambridge: Harvard University Press.
Eyal, N. (2005) "Perhaps the 'most important primary good': Self-respect and Rawls's principles of justice," *Politics, Philosophy & Economics* 4(2), pp. 195–219.
Fraser, N. (1997) *Justice Interruptus: Critical Reflections on the "Postsocialist" Condition*, New York: Routledge.
Freeman, S. (2007) *Rawls*, New York: Routledge.
Heath, J. (2011) "Review of Debra Satz' 'Why Some Things Should not be for Sale'," *Erasmus Journal for Philosophy and Economics* 4(1), pp. 99–107.
Horne, L.C. and Heath, J. (2022) "A market failures approach to justice in health," *Politics, Philosophy, and Economics* 21(2), pp. 165–189.
Hughes, P.M. (2009) "Constraint, consent, and well-being in human kidney sales," *Journal of Medicine* and Philosophy 34(6), pp. 606–631.
Hurka, T. (1996) *Perfectionism*. New York: Oxford University Press.
Jaggar, A. (1999) "Prostitution," in: M. Pearsall (ed.) *Women and Values: Readings in Recent Feminist Philosophy, 3rd ed.* Belmont: Wadsworth Publishing Company, pp. 168–182.
Kant, I. ([1797]1999) "The metaphysics of morals," in M.J. Gregor (ed.) *Practical Philosophy*. Cambridge, UK: Cambridge University Press, pp. 353–605.
Kant, I. ([1785]1999) "Groundwork of the metaphysics of morals," in M.J. Gregor (ed.) *Practical Philosophy*. Cambridge, UK: Cambridge University Press, pp. 37–109.
Kant, I. ([1775–1780)1997) *Lectures on Ethics*, in P. Heath, and J.B. Schneedwind (eds.) New York: Cambridge University Press.
Kymlicka, W. (1989) "Liberal individualism and liberal neutrality," *Ethics* 99(4), pp. 883–905.
Marx, K. ([1867]1990) *Capital: Critique of Political Economy*. New York: Penguin.
Marx, K. ([1844]1988) *Economic and Philosophical Manuscripts of 1844*. New York: Prometheus Books.
Mills, C.W. (2017) *Black Rights/White Wrongs: The Critique of Racial Liberalism*. New York: Oxford University Press.
Nozick, R. (1974) *Anarchy, State, and Utopia*. New York: Basic Books.
Nussbaum, M.C. (1995) "Objectification," *Philosophy and Public Affairs* 24(4), pp. 249–291.
Panitch, V. (forthcoming) "Decommodification as exploitation," in B. Ferguson and M. Zwolinski (eds.) *Exploitation: Perspectives from Politics, Philosophy, and Economics*. Oxford: Oxford University Press, ch. 12.
Panitch, V. (2020) "Liberalism, commodification, and justice," *Politics, Philosophy, and Economics* 19(1), pp. 62–82.
Panitch, V. and Horne, L.C. (2018) "Commodification, inequality, and kidney markets," *Social Theory and Practice* 44(1), pp. 121–143.
Phillips, A. (2017) "Exploitation, commodification, and inequality," in M. Deveaux and V. Panitch (eds.) *Exploitation from Practice to Theory*. London: Rowman & Littlefield, pp. 99–119.
Phillips, A. (2011) "It's my body and I'll do what I like with It: Bodies as objects and property," *Political Theory* 39(6), pp. 724–748.
Phillips, A. (2008) "Egalitarians and the market: Dangerous ideals," *Social Theory and Practice* 34(3), pp. 439–462.

Radcliffe-Richards, J. (1996) "Nephrarious goings on: Kidney sales and moral arguments," *Journal of Medicine and Philosophy* 21(4), pp. 375–416.
Radin, M.J. (1996) *Contested Commodities: The Trouble with Trade in Sex, Children, Body Parts, and Other Things*, Cambridge: Harvard University Press.
Radin, M.J. (1987) "Market inalienability," *Harvard Law Review* 10(8), pp. 1849–1937.
Rawls, J. (2001) *Justice as Fairness: A Restatement*. Cambridge: Harvard University Press.
Rawls, J. (1999) *A Theory of Justice, revised ed.* Cambridge: Harvard University Press.
Rawls, J. (1996) *Political Liberalism*. New York: Columbia University Press.
Raz, J. (1986) *The Morality of Freedom*. Oxford: Oxford University Press.
Rippon, S. (2014) "Imposing options on people in poverty: The harm of a live donor organ market," *Journal of Medical Ethics* 40(3), pp. 145–150.
Sample, R. (2003) *Exploitation: What it is and Why it's Wrong*. New York: Rowman & Littlefield.
Sandel, M.J. (2012) *What Money Can't Buy: The Moral Limits of Markets*. New York: Farrar, Strauss & Giroux.
Sandel, M.J. (2000) "What money can't buy: The moral limits of the market," in G.B. Peterson (ed.) *Tanner Lectures on Human Values, vol. 21*. Salt Lake City: University of Utah Press, pp. 87–122.
Sandel, M.J. (1982) *Liberalism and the Limits of Justice*. Cambridge: Cambridge University Press.
Satz, D. (2010) *Why Some Things Should Not Be for Sale: The Moral Limits of Markets*. Oxford: Oxford University Press.
Scanlon, T.M. (2003) "Rawls on justification," S. Freeman (ed.) *The Cambridge Companion to Rawls*. Cambridge: Cambridge University Press, pp. 139–167.
Shrage, L. (1989) "Should feminists oppose prostitution?' *Ethics* 99(2), pp. 347–361.
Titmuss, R.M. (1997) *The Gift Relationship: From Human Blood to Social Policy*. New York: New Press.
Waldron, J. (1986) "John Rawls and the social minimum," *Journal of Applied Philosophy* 3(1) pp. 21–33.
Walzer, M. (1984) *Spheres of Justice: A Defense of Pluralism and Equality*. New York: Basic Books.
Wertheimer, A. (1996) *Exploitation*. Princeton: Princeton University Press.
Young, I.M. (1990) *Justice and the Politics of Difference*. Princeton: Princeton University Press.

5

SOCIOLOGY OF MORAL CONTESTATION OF EXCHANGE INSTITUTIONS

Philippe Steiner

Introduction

This chapter aims at explaining how sociologists take into account the moral contestations of various forms of economic institutions. This means that the emphasis will be put on moral contestation of markets as an institution, but also on other economic institutions. After a brief review of the position held by economists, the chapter examines how Durkheim, Weber, and Simmel have dealt with moral issues within the market economy. Morality could take different meanings: the underpinnings of social life (Durkheim), the way people organize a coherent set of action (Weber), the way people derail from it (Simmel). However, for all of them morality was an important empirical fact to be studied for understanding the current social world. Then, the chapter considers the contributions of modern sociologists, which are mainly about the moral contestation of the market as an institution. Finally, the chapter brings to the fore the fact that moral contestation goes beyond the market. Accordingly, the last part of the chapter stresses the fact that moral contestations of alternative institutions for getting an access to resource – redistribution and reciprocity to use Polanyian categories – should also be considered carefully.

Political economy and classical sociology

In the beginning of the nineteenth century, the social sciences did not pay much attention to the use value of goods, or hence to their material nature. Classical political economists were focusing their attention on rules of exchange and growth whereas social scientists of that time raised moral question about the stability of the industrial social order, the moral consequences of the generalization of interested behaviours, and the commodification of social relations, as did Marx in his economic and philosophical manuscript in 1844, and Karl Polanyi in *The Great Transformation* (1944) a century later.

From Adam Smith to Léon Walras

Once the paradox of value had been considered, according to which utility and exchange value are often opposed, Smith limited himself to analyzing exchange value, measured by labour.[1] In the

DOI: 10.4324/9781003188742-7

Weberian language he was thus interested in the *formal* rules of exchange that could in principle be implemented with respect to any kind of goods. *Material* or moral considerations preventing the marketization of given products were of limited interest. Even if justice issues were of great value to him, Léon Walras ruled out the issue of morality or immorality from his theory of value and exchange.[2] William Stanley Jevons made utility a relation to pleasure and pain focusing his attention on the law of diminishing marginal utility, while Carl Menger paid attention to the knowledge that human beings need to have of materiality for being able to turn things into commodities.[3]

Marxism did not offer much by way of change. In *Das Capital*, Karl Marx examined the two faces of the commodity: use value and exchange value. The first is simple and transparent to market actors and economists since it is the commodity's utility function. On the contrary, exchange value is mysterious, and gives rise to a parallel with the religious world according to Marx[4]. Thus, with the exception of labour power, whose use value is to provide labour which is the foundation of value, use value plays no role in Marx's critique of political economy. A few decades later, moral issues became part of political economy with the German historical school, a school of thought that more closely aligned with the way sociologists were considering the role of the market in modern societies.

Émile Durkheim, Max Weber and Karl Polanyi

With Durkheim sociology is strongly linked to morality: one may say that social to him means moral; for example, crime is defined as an attack on social solidarity while punishment is the normal moral reaction to crime. However, Durkheim's sociology addressed more specifically moral issues related to the economic world notably with respect to the determination of wages and revenues. Durkheim referred to an ordinary form of judgment as the basis of fair remuneration: public opinion about the social value of different economic roles within the division of labour respectively should determine the remuneration that each should receive.

This ordinary judgment does not explain how remunerations are set, rather, it expresses the feeling of injustice, the "too much" or "too little" that is attached to particular professions and their associated incomes:

> The various functions stand as if they are ranked in a hierarchical order by public opinion and a certain coefficient of well-being is attributed to each one according to the place it occupies in the hierarchy [...] In vain, economists protest; it will always be a scandal for the public opinion that an individual can use too much wealth in absolutely superfluous consumption and it even seems that this intolerance is only relaxed during times of moral disturbances.
>
> (Durkheim, 1897, p. 276)

Public opinion does not tell the truth, but it expresses what is felt by citizens.[5] This moral assessment of remuneration is differential and fluctuating: the limits considered admissible depend on the profession considered, the state of the economy and moral rules that are not immutable. This moral evaluation is not opposed to the inequality produced by a market economy, it is often even associated with a form of fascination, but it does cause public opinion to be offended when "too strong" inequalities emerge.

Moreover, this moral evaluation makes people act. Social movements such as those of *Los Indignados* in Spain and *Occupy Wall Street* in the United States are well known contemporary examples. An outraged public opinion creates difficulties for market actors – who probably do not appreciate seeing their legitimacy challenged – and, above all, it is a threat to politicians who cannot allow such a situation to take root without seeking to respond to it at the risk of seeing indignation translated later in the ballot box. The strength of this opinion becomes considerable in times of economic crisis: this is what US President Barack Obama's formula describing Wall Street bonuses as obscene, in his "State of the Union Address" in January 2010, after the bailing out failing banks with public money.

In other words, according to Durkheim, there is a moral regulation of market exchange grounded in public intolerance for injustice. This moral regulation, while not governed by such precisely defined "laws" as the "laws of supply and demand", remains a social force that weighs heavily on economic functioning.

The argument may seem too marked by Durkheimian moralism, foreign to the approach of many other sociologists, Weber being the first. His position during the debate on the role of values in the social sciences shows that he rejected what was then called the "ethical approach" in the social sciences because he considered that a socio-economic understanding of societies was required to face unpleasant moral situations and that social scientists were not in a position to bring about a "more moral" world (Weber, 1917). But Weber's approach is in line with Durkheim's when he states that sociology takes "subjective assessments of human beings as the object of their research" (Weber, 1917, p. 12), that is to say morality was conceived as an empirical reality that sociologists must describe on the one hand, and understand in its consequences in the other. On this fundamental agreement, which distinguishes the sociologist's moral point of view from the consideration of the intrinsic normativity of the actors of social life. Beyond these considerations, Weber also opens new avenues at two important moments during which he examines the tensions between market economy and moral values.

First, in his sociology of religion, he examines the different tensions between the religious sphere and the family, political, military, economic, sexual and intellectual spheres. This is the so-called "war of gods", since there is a conflict between values insofar as they claim to rule over a given social sphere, the emergence of another value generates tensions, more or less strong depending on their degree of rationalization (Steiner, 2017). Second, the rationalization process brings about moral contestation because of the strong tension that may appear between formal and material rationalizations: the former deals only with logical coherence in a given sphere, while the latter takes into account external values that interfere with the functioning of that sphere. Regardless of the level at which the conflict of rationalizations occurs, contestation emerges. The classical example of this issue is given by the scholastic ban on interest as the price for lending money (see Chapter 7 by Januard and Lapidus in this volume): this material approach to this basic transaction was rejected by the formal approach of economists according to whom one can ask a rent when one lends a house, but not an interest when one lend the amount of money necessary to buy the house.

As an example, economists who endorse the formal rationalization of economic approach can be intolerant of others who seek to develop an approach based on competing principles. For example, Jean Tirole, when awarded the prize from the Bank of Sweden in honour of Alfred Nobel (in 2014), published a letter to the French Minister of Higher Education ready to create a new professional venue for heterodox economists – those relying on historical data and related social sciences, such as sociology or political science – to dissuade her from moving in this direction.

Georg Simmel's impressive book on money raised interesting issues (Simmel 1900). Firstly, money as an abstract and quantitative institution has a long history with the value of human beings, notably slaves, women, and more generally as a penalty for murder (*Wergild*) until the spreading of the incommensurable and absolute value of human beings by the Christian religion. Secondly, money has specific social properties as it intervenes in between a large set of human relations and is always at risk of creating an inversion of means and ends, because having money gives you access to so many things. Thus, the use of money on the market can create deviations from the rational economic behaviour (value – money as a mean – spending money – goods as a mean – the subjective end) which could, each of them (greed, avarice, extravagance, ascetic poverty, cynicism, and the blazé attitude), fall in the domain of moral failure. The last two pathological deviations singled out the modern world in which money can buy anything: in such a world, the cynic enjoys the devaluation of any final values whereas the blazé become indifferent to them.

Closer to our present time, the notion of contestation also emerges in Karl Polanyi's work. Beyond the embeddedness-disembeddedness issue, Polanyi's argument in the *Great Transformation* is driven by the so-called "double movement" thesis (Polanyi, 1944, p. 182, pp. 201–202).[6] According to this thesis, social dynamics comes from an opposition between social forces working to strengthen and extend the domination of the market system over society while others oppose it and seek to limit the expansion of the market economy through various forms of regulation. Polanyi illustrates this thesis when he points out that since the late 1830s the British Parliament has been legislating to regulate children's and women's labour, night work and men's working hours.

The double movement thesis has a solid empirical basis, a basis that has not been denied since, and indeed even further solidified by the work of others. For example, Gøsta Esping-Andersen highlights the changes in the balance of power between those in favour of the free labour market and those in favour of its regulation through the relationship between the share of wages that is directly linked to the labour force and that which is socialized, that is to say not dependent on the laws of supply and demand (Esping-Andersen, 1990, chap. 4). However, there is also a lesson to be learned from Polanyi's strong sociological thesis: "Interest, however, like intents remain platonic unless they are translated into politics by the means of some social institution" (Polanyi, 1944, p. 8).

What are these social forces capable of giving strength to the interests of those who hold opposing views on how to build the market-society relationship? It is the establishment of political organizations or social movements that make the social embedding of the market or, on the contrary, its disembodiment a major focus of their actions. In short, with Polanyi, moral contestation takes on a more explicit political dimension than that found in Durkheim or Weber. It will be emphasized below that Polanyi also makes a major contribution by conceptualizing economic action under three modalities supported by three economic institutions: market (market exchanges), the state (redistribution), close-knit groups (reciprocity).

Contemporary sociology

These conceptual considerations are still at work in contemporary sociology, but some new developments are addressing the issue of moral contestation in a different, but productive way. This is particularly true of pragmatic sociology.

Usually, the sociology of morality is "the sociological investigation of the nature, cause and consequences of people's ideas about the good and the right" (Abend, 2008, p. 87), but it is plagued with metatheoretical issues related to the notion of moral truth and value freedom (Abend, 2008, p. 88). A pragmatic approach offers the possibility of avoiding these two difficulties in stressing the social processes by which people deal with moral issues.

Pragmatic sociology: Critiques and compromises

The first trend comes with the pragmatic approach to the phenomenon of justification (Boltanski and Thévenot, 1992). Three proposals seem important to highlight. First, the two authors shift from the critical sociology of Bourdieu's school to the sociology of critique: in short, instead of seeking to understand and improve society through the study of social domination, they propose to study critique as a social process.

Secondly, the sociology of critique offers a generalization of this notion, by producing as a square matrix of the critiques between the six polities ("*cités*") in which they partition the social world. Moral and political critique is now only a subset of the whole set of critiques (grey line in Table 5.1) and counter-critique (grey column in Table 5.1) from the market polity to the five other polities – inspiration, domestic, opinion, civic and industrial – from which moral critique can emerge. This symmetry, as simple and trivial as it may seem, is of great importance. On the one hand, it prevents to think about the relationship between morality and the market in a unilateral way and, on the other hand, it extends the Polanyian idea of "double movement", since there are social and political forces pushing for greater market power against those who aim to limit it.

Thirdly, and this is a point of great importance, the sociology of critique highlights the moment of appeasement with the idea of compromise (see Table 5.2) thanks to which actors of the critique and the counter-critique agree to pacify their relations, endorsing temporarily a given mix of various moral values (Boltanski and Thévenot, 1992, p. 337). However, they rightly point out that compromise itself can become the basis for a new series of critique, precisely because it is a compromise, unacceptable to those pushing forward the critique in the name of a greater moral purity, the "virtuosi" of rationalization (Boltanski and Thévenot, 1992, pp. 343–344; Steiner, 2017). For example, in the 1930s French blood "donors" were paid, but after WWII, the French legislation decided to forbid the marketization of blood collection in the name of altruistic donation. Still, as

Table 5.1 Boltanski's and Thévenot's matrix of critiques

Polities	*Inspiration*	*Domestic*	*Opinion*	*Civic*	*Market*	*Industrial*
Inspiration		X	X	X	Cool blood in business	X
Domestic	X		X	X	Free from personal links	X
Opinion	X	X		X	Setbacks from speculation	X
Civic	X	X	X		Costs of justice	X
Market	Interested people	Money can't buy everything	Interested advertisement	Selfishness of the wealthy		Useless luxury goods
Industrial	X	X	X	X	Weak flexibility	

Lecture of table: (Domestic-column critique to the Market-line) Those who endorse the values belonging to the "Domestic polity" are critiquing the market polity on the ground that "Money can't buy everything" and leave some goods and services out of the reach of moneyed transaction. (Market-column critique to the domestic polity-line): those who endorse the values of the market polity will critique the domestic polity in saying that market relations free people from the limitations associated to personal links.

(*Source:* Boltanski and Thevenot, 1992)

Table 5.2 Compromises with the Market

Polities	*Market*
Inspiration	- Creative markets - A wonderful treat - Sublime is priceless
Domestic	- Inalienable property - Special services - Trust in business
Opinion	- Reputation
Civic	- Reducing income inequalities[7]
Industrial	- Product easy to marketize - Managing demand

(*Source:* Boltanski and Thevenot, 1992)

the altruistic blood collection was not enough for providing the patient the necessary amount of blood products – notably factor VIII given to hemophiliac patients – the compromise was then to prevent the commercialization and the buying of blood product from countries where commercialization was possible. This compromise is unstable (see Jaworski's Chapter 18 on plasma in this volume) and under the critique of those in favour of full commercialization in France.

Empirical research

Sociologists are interested in the *contested market* rather than the *contested commodity*. In other words, they focus on social institutions rather than on specific commodities. This shift moves from philosophical or legal discourse to empirical research on the functioning of markets where contestation occurs and gives flesh to broader considerations about the relations between morality and market societies (Fourcade and Healy, 2007).

Marie Trespeuch and I focused on various forms of contested markets (Steiner and Trespeuch, 2015; 2019). Indeed, there are many markets where contested goods are bought and sold, such as cannabis in some American states, kidneys in Iran, reproductive technologies in some European or Asian countries, etc. In addition, some markets are still in limbo as "paper markets", that is to say, as market that could in the future be created. Finally, there are many other cases where the contested goods have not been able to find their way to an effective market institution (children to adopt, human organs for transplantation, etc.). In order to explain this, we suggested considering the issue of contested markets in terms of two populations, one that is threatened by the emergence of the market, the other that is threatened by its absence. Beyond this clarification, our approach differs from that of Boltanski and Thévenot in that it specifies the place and modalities of the compromise: in our view, research should focus on "cooling devices" that introduce protections for populations morally and economically endangered by the creation of a market. For example, in the case of gambling, the creation of the market in France was associated to low rates of return to gamblers so as not to encourage a gambler to try to recoup his or her losses by prolonging the game, putting in jeopardy their economic resources, and medical treatment offered to those who feel under the influence of addiction (Trespeuch, 2015; and her Chapter 9 in this volume). When such cooling devices are lacking, the market cannot emerge as it is the case with human organ transplantation (Steiner 2010; 2015).[8]

Franck Cochoy proposed the concept of "concerned market" that he develops by following the pragmatic sociology of actor-network theory. Concerned market is way to escape the well-known opposition between the market theories of economists (or *interested market*) and the critique of market theories by sociologists (or *contested markets*), since according to actor-network theory the social – and consequently the moral – and the economic worlds are not disjointed, but are both necessary ingredients of the market economy. As a result, as is usual in this approach to sociology, there is no longer any distinction between the different markets; all are likely to be concerned. More interesting is the idea that marketing techniques are at work to make possible markets whose moral dimension is contested; these technologies would thus play the role of cooling devices of moral critiques and counter-critiques. This would be interesting to examine more closely, especially since it makes the link with the role of organizations, as the work of Philip Balsiger and Simone Schiller-Merkens (2019) invites us to do.

Cochoy's proposal brings us into what could be called "cold contestation", which Michel Callon (2017) also develops in his latest book on the markets that need to be understood in order to transform them. In contrast to market contestation, Callon's pragmatism (2017, pp. 476–477) leads to a cycle of market reconfiguration (design of a new framing – reframing – concern), disarming contestation by returning it as a tool for market reconfiguration, as Boltanski and Chiapello (1999) have shown. This approach leads to a form of acceptance of the market order, which could be described as Confucian, in the sense that it is a matter of adjusting to the world order, but not of changing it.

Another way of bypassing Bourdieu also emerges with the critical theory endorsed by Eva Illouz (2018) in her book on emotional commodities or *emodities*. In this case, it is not a question of taking an interest in the contestation of the emotional commodities market, nor in the compromises that make it possible to market them. The identification of these markets serves as a benchmark and empirical support for a post-normative critique of neo-liberal capitalism, avoiding a normativity that falls from the top of social science, to simply show that such situations are unnatural and socially constructed. This may be useful to activists, but it does not bring any new ideas to sociologists.

Decommodification and contested economies

Beyond these theoretical considerations, the moral contestation of markets has had the opportunity to develop in certain cases, two of which are worth recalling here. First, we must mention the abolition of slavery during the nineteenth century in England (1832), in France (1848), in the United States (1865), etc., until the late Brazilian abolition (1888). This "abolitionist revolution" to use Olivier Grenouilleau's (2017) formula, is a decommodification on a global scale of considerable importance. Second, closer to the present, the publication of Richard Titmuss' book in 1971 led the American legislator to ban the whole blood market – only plasmapheresis could be paid. Nevertheless, the relevance of moral contestation should not be limited to the market: there are as well moral critique addressed to reciprocity and redistribution, to take again Polanyi's analytical categories.

Contested reciprocity

The fact that the market institution may be contested does not constitute the end point of the economic sociology of contestation. Indeed, there is the possibility of carrying out transactions according to principles other than market exchange and the search for monetary gain. This is the case with donation. For example, the increasing number of organ transplants around the world shows that such transactions have multiplied; they are based on the principle of altruism, because the gain is received by someone other than the person who gives up the resource.

This position was defended very early on, in response to Dr. Harvey Jacobs' proposal to create a kidney import market to supply American hospitals. North American representatives reacted very quickly under Al Gore's leadership with the National Organ Transplant Act, which prohibited this type of transaction in 1984. This provision has been included in many legislations where it was not already included in the law – as has been the case in France since 1978. Since then, under the aegis of the WHO, the 2004 Istanbul Declaration has given this ban a global scope.

The first dimension of the contested gift comes from the fact that altruism does not cover the medical needs for organs to be transplanted, whereas it would be possible to open a market for dual organs (kidney, pulmonary lobe) or those that can reconstitute themselves (hepatic lobe). As the title of a book claims: Altruism is not enough! (Satel, 2008). The critique is therefore that altruism is not very effective, resulting in patients being at risk of remaining too long on waiting lists, and of receiving alternative care (dialysis) that is much more expensive than transplantation. This critique also has a moral dimension: is it moral to be ineffective when lives are at stake?

Beyond the argument of improving the lot of patients waiting for a transplant, proponents of an organ market are getting emboldened to the point of reversing the moral argument that has been used until now. On what moral grounds can access to kidneys be denied when other individuals would like to sell them a kidney and who, if they cannot do so, must accept jobs even more dangerous than a nephrectomy or who find themselves even worse off when they instead enter the black market in body parts?[9] What moral justifications can be given to imposing moral restrictions tinged with aristocratism – where gratuity and gift are valorized – in the face of those who are ready to implement market exchange, a trade historically valued for the equality and independence it provides? Why is the contractual freedom of individuals restricted in this way? Aren't the poor as rational as others? Are they not in a position to decide what is best for them? Proponents of the market for human body parts blame their opponents for imposing their own values on the rest of society and even of exploiting the poor:

> The rich and able-bodied by forbidding organ sales would be exploiting the poor to support their particular view of moral propriety, improper commodification, of human dignity, denying the poor this opportunity to choose freely on the basis of their own judgements regarding how best to advantage themselves. The out-come is robustly paternalistic.
>
> (Cherry, 2006, p. 98)

Against this moral paternalism, defenders of kidney markets argue for free choice based on the free disposition of one's body. Altruists could continue to give, but their moral values would not prevent others from selling and buying! This is the moral credo that is opposed to gift-giving.

This case of moral contestation of the gift may seem limited compared to the extent of the moral contestation of the market. I will however support the contrary opinion. Organ donation goes from the living to the living in only a limited number of cases, since mainly it goes from the dead to the living: organ donation is thus most often an intergenerational gift. This brings us to inheritance, an intergenerational gift, too often neglected. Organized in a political way (Steiner, 2016, Chapter 2) and not according to the "laws of the market", inheritance transfers wealth of such a considerable volume that Thomas Piketty estimates it as between 10 and 15% of the French national income for the coming decades (Piketty, 2013, Chapter 13). As these transfers of wealth generate a much greater inequality than that of incomes, the moral contestation of the gift cannot be neglected once we take into account the role of inheritance. The long series of critiques of inheritance (Steiner, 2008; Dockès, 2017) are facts that an economic sociology of moral contestation cannot neglect.

Contested redistribution

If the noble institution of reciprocity carried out by gifts and the rhetoric of altruism can be subjected to moral contestation, it is easy to imagine that the State and the principle of redistribution are also subject to political and moral contestations.

This contestation emerges with the economic role of the State when it levies taxes on market transactions and income, or erects customs barriers to protect certain actors (producers in the protected sector) at the expense of others (consumers of these products). This is referred to as the economic liberalism of the eighteenth and nineteenth centuries, an intellectual movement according to Polanyi, that, under the name of political economy opposed, among other things, the moral economy of the people around the marketing of basic food (wheat). The libertarian movement played the same role in the second half of the twentieth century when it came to the commercialization of human body parts and, now, in the twenty-first century, the commercialization of intimacy, emotions, particularly as regards nature – such as willingness to pay techniques for the assessment of environmental damage (Fourcade, 2011), carbon market to manage pollution and global warming (Tirole, 2016), etc.

The notion of contested tax does not refer mainly to political and parliamentary debates on the creation, implementation, mitigation or abolition of a particular tax, but rather to the practices of the actors. Recent research on tax evasion is useful for illustrating this phenomenon.

Economists working in the direction proposed by Thomas Piketty has shown the extent of this phenomenon, driven by the rise of the ultra-rich classes (or the now famous 1%). Gabriel Zucman (2013) estimates tax evasion at €5,800 billions, or 8% of households' financial wealth, resulting in a loss of €130 billions in tax revenue for governments and their "ordinary" citizens. The contested tax issue is no small matter, to say the least. The political and moral dimension of the contestation is a key point in Brooke Harrington's study of wealth managers (Harrington, 2016; see as well the recent work by Herlin-Giret, 2019).

Harrington shows that the role of family asset managers is not limited to developing legal arrangements to disconnect the owner from his property in order to avoid taxes, creditors or family requests. They are also lobbyists acting before members of the parliament and they design moral scripts justifying behaviours that respect the letter of the law but not its spirit. Harrington exemplifies with a manager protesting against the confiscatory nature of taxation against wealth creators:

> Social democracy is creating too big demands on the wealth creators. You can't get voted in now unless you support massive entitlement programs, because too many people receive them. With the result that governments now need an ever-increasing share of GDP from the producers to fulfill their promises. So naturally the wealth creators, like squirrels collecting their nuts, are scaling back; they are saying themselves that they don't want to collect as many nuts next year, because the government just take them away [...] it's nature, people

> don't like the fruits of their labor taken away so arbitrarily … This leads wealth creators to engage in the shadow economy and so forth.
>
> (quoted in Harrington, 2016, p. 228)

The argument is a direct echo of Hayek's (1976) political philosophy, pointing to the demands of the middle classes against the rich. In front of this moral point of view, NGOs, such as ATTAC in France, try to bring to the forefront of the public agenda the social and political problems posed by such practices.[10] However, they face a major difficulty in that it is difficult for them to isolate a specific population that would be directly affected by tax avoidance. To achieve its objective, ATTAC activists carry out a framing work (Schiller-Merkens, 2013) in order to construct tax evasion as a political and moral problem. This framing has two dimensions: the first concerns the quantification of the loss of tax revenue due to the combined effects of fraud and tax evasion, the second isolates the population threatened by these practices.

The quantification of uncollected taxes is a delicate matter. Between 1994 and 2018, the various figures (parliaments, public bodies, NGOs) oscillate in the range of 25–100 billion euros for France. The latter figure is the one used by ATTAC to launch the public debate on this issue. But who should be designated as the victim of this loss of income? The difficulty is all the greater as the tax evasion of the ultra-rich is compounded by the small-scale fraud of many people busy in poorly regulated professions. To solve this difficulty, ATTAC has chosen to associate this figure with the national debt and economic inequalities.

In other cases, tax contestation is easier to build insofar as it concerns the use of the tax collected. A good example of this situation is given in Wendy Espeland's research on dam construction on an Indian reserve northeast of Phoenix (Espeland, 1998). The opposing groups were of a classic design. On one side were the Indians who wanted to maintain their ancestral relationship with this land, as well as the defenders of the ecosystem that was about to disappear as a result of the construction of a dam, on the other side were farmers, water-using companies, property developers and representatives of many town halls who were seeking to stabilize their water supply. The two populations facing each other were well defined, and the balance of power was not favourable to the Indians. It is through an alliance between them and a new generation of engineers, in opposition to the methods of calculation used by the previous generation, that the balance of power was reversed and the contested use of taxes could be victorious.

Conclusion

The sociology of moral contestation of markets is well structured. Sociologist can join economists, philosophers, legal scientists and provide the public debates with insights about markets and commodification. In summary, a sociological approach underlines the usefulness of an empirical approach of morality issues; second, it stresses the importance of a symmetrical point of view, giving weight to the critique of the market but as well to the counter critique and the various forms of compromise that result; and, finally, it goes beyond the institution of the market and its critique since there are as well critiques of two other institution – redistribution based on taxes, and reciprocity through gifts and bequests –, from which people get or do not get access to resources

This chapter suggests that we have to look closely at how contestation affects all three of the Polanyian forms of economic institutions (market, reciprocity and redistribution), and how it contributes to the changing frontiers between the three institutions for determining the political arrangement in which a given collectivity wishes to live.

Notes

1 "What are the rules which men naturally observe in exchanging them either for money or for one another, I shall now proceed to examine. These rules determine what may be called their relative or exchangeable value of goods" (Smith, 1776, vol. 1, p. 44).

2 "Necessary, useful, pleasant or superfluous, all this for us means more or less useful. Moreover, the morality or immorality of the need to which the useful good answers and satisfies are not to be taken into account" (Walras, 1900, §3, pp. 45–46).

3

> If a thing is to become a good, or in other words, if it is to acquire a good-character, all four of the following prerequisites must be simultaneously present: 1. A human need; 2. Such properties as render the thing capable of being brought into a causal connection with the satisfaction of this need; 3. Human knowledge of this causal connection; 4. Command of the thing sufficient to direct it to the need.
>
> (Menger, 1871, p. 52)

4

> The mystical dimension of goods does not come from their use value [...] But value form and the value relations of the products of human labor have nothing to do with their physical nature. It is nothing but a determined social relation among human beings that takes for them the fantastic form of a relation between goods themselves.
>
> (Marx, 1867, pp. 84–85)

5 For example, the International Social Survey Program shows that in 1999, the French estimated the income of a CEO of a large company 16 times higher than that of a skilled worker, and whished that this ratio would not exceed 6, while the average income of a CAC 40 CEO was 177 times higher than that of an unskilled worker during the same period. This gap between what is estimated and what is happening in the reality of the contemporary economic world is not specific to the French, since the Americans thought that these incomes were in a ratio of 1 to 12, wished it in a ratio of 1 to 5, whereas the actual ratio was in the order of 1 to 300.

6 On the centrality of this thesis in Polanyi, see Gregory Baum (1996) and Gareth Dale (2010).

7 This is the kind of issues raised by Taylor's in his Chapter 17 on organs in this volume.

8 In the following paragraphs, I take the information about ATTAC's approach from the research done by Gaspard Richard (2019).

9 Boltanski and Thévenot (1992, p. 396) find no compromise in this case based on Durkheim's *Leçons de sociologie*. Sticking to this single book is too simplistic, as it would have been possible to build on the above-mentioned passage on remuneration of the study on suicide.

10 Since then, this approach has been applied to the catering market on tourist beaches in Brazil (Sartore, Pereira and Rodrigues, 2019), and to the creation of the pollution market (Valiergue, 2019).

References

Abend, G., 2008. "Two main problems in the sociology of morality", *Theoretical Sociology*, 37, pp. 87–125

Balsiger, P. and Schiller-Merkens, S. (eds.), 2019. *Moral Struggles in and out the Market*, Oxford, Emerald Publishing

Baum, G., 1996. *Karl Polanyi on Ethics and Economics*, Montréal, McGill-Queens University Press

Boltanski, L. and Chiapello, E., 1999 [2005]. *The New Spirit of Capitalism*, London, Verso

Boltanski, L. and Thévenot, L., 1992. *De la justification. Les économies de la grandeurs*, Paris, Gallimard. English translation *On Justification. Economies of Worth*, 2006, Princeton, Princeton University Press

Callon, M., 2017. *L'emprise des marchés. Comprendre leur fonctionnement pour pouvoir les changer*, Paris, La Découverte

Cherry, M., 2006. *Kidney for Sale by Owner, Human Organs, Transplantation and the Market*, Washington D.C., Georgetown University Press

Cochoy, F., 2014. "Concerned Markets, facing the future beyond 'interested' and 'contested markets'", in S. Geiger, D. Harrison, H. Kjellberg and A. Mallard (eds.), *Concerned Markets. Economic Ordering for Multiple Values*, Cheltenham, Edward Elgar, pp. 238–255

Dale, G., 2010. *Karl Polanyi, the Limits of the Market*, London, Polity

Dockès, E., 2017. *Voyage en misarchie*, Paris, éditions du détour

Durkheim, É., 1897 [1952]. *Suicide. A Study in sociology*, London, Routledge

Espeland, W., 1998. *The Struggle for Water. Politics, Rationality and Identity in the American Southwest*, Chicago, The University of Chicago Press

Esping-Andersen, G., 1990. *The Three Worlds of Welfare Capitalism*, Princeton, Princeton University Press

Fourcade, M., 2011. "Price and Prejudice: On Economics and the Enchantment (and Disenchantment) of Nature", in P. Aspers and J. Beckert (eds.) *The Worth of Goods. Valuation and Pricing in the Economy*, Oxford, Oxford University Press, pp. 41–62

Fourcade, M. and Healy, K., 2007. "Moral Views of Market Societies", *Annual Reviews of Sociology*, 33, pp. 285–311

Grenouilleau, O., 2017. *La révolution abolitionniste*, Paris, Gallimard

Harrington, B., 2016. *Capital Without Borders. Wealth Managers and the One Percent*, Cambridge Mass., Harvard university Press

Hayek, F., 1976 [1998]. *Law, Legislation and Liberty*, vol. 2, *The Mirage of Social Justice*, London, Routledge

Herlin-Giret, C., 2019. *Rester riche. Enquête sur les gestionnaires de fortune et leurs clients*, Lormont, Le Bord de l'eau

Illouz, E. (ed.), 2018. *Emotions as Commodities. Capitalism, Consumption and Authenticity*, London, Routledge

Marx, K. 1867 [1983] *Le Capital*, Paris: Les éditions sociales

Menger, C. 1871 [1976] *Principles of Economics*, New York: New York University Press

Phillips, A., 2013. *Our Body, Whose Property?*, Princeton, Princeton University Press

Polanyi, K., 1944 [2001]. *The Great Transformation. The Political and Economic Origins of Our Time*, Boston, Beacon Press

Richard, G., 2019. *Histoire d'une ressource en devenir. Enquête sur la mobilisation de deux associations contre l'évasion fiscale, 1998–2018*, Master thesis, Sorbonne Université

Sartore, M.S., Pereira, S.A. and Rodrigues, C., 2019. "Aracaju Beach Bars as Contested Market: Conflicts and overlaps between markets and nature", *Ocean and Costal Management*, 179, pp. 1–9

Satel, S., 2008. *When Altruism Isn't Enough. The Case for Compensating Kidney Donors*, Washington DC, The American Enterprise Institute Press

Schiller-Merkens, S., 2013. "Framing Moral Markets. The Cultural Legacy of Social Movements in an Emerging Market Category", Köln, Max Planck Institut Discussion Paper 13/8

Simmel, G., 1900 [2004]. *The Philosophy of Money*, London, Routledge

Smith A. 1776 [1981]. *An Inquiry into the Nature and Causes of the Wealth of Nations*, Indiana: Liberty Press

Steiner, P., 2008. "L'héritage en France au 19e siècle. Loi, intérêts de sentiment et intérêts économiques", *Revue économique*, 59 (1), pp. 75–97

Steiner, P., 2010. *La transplantation d'organes: un commerce nouveau entre les êtres humains*, Paris, Gallimard

Steiner, P., 2015. "Le don contesté", in P. Steiner and M. Trespeuch, (eds), 2015. *Marchés contestés. Quand le marché rencontre la morale*, Toulouse, Presses Universitaires de Toulouse, pp. 251–278

Steiner, P., 2016. *Donner.... Une histoire de l'altruisme*, Paris: Presses Universitaires de France.

Steiner, P., 2017. "Le concept de tension chez Max Weber", *L'Année sociologique*, 67 (1), pp. 163–188

Steiner, P. and Trespeuch, M. (eds), 2015. *Marchés contestés. Quand le marché rencontre la morale*, Toulouse, Presses Universitaires de Toulouse

Steiner, P. and Trespeuch, M., 2019. "Contested Markets: Morality, Market Devices and Vulnerable Populations", in P. Balsiger and S. Schiller-Merkens (eds.), *Moral Struggles in and out the Market*, Oxford, Emerald Publishing, pp. 33–48

Tirole, J., 2016 [2018]. *Economics for the Common Good*, Princeton, Princeton University Press

Titmuss, R., 1971 [1997]. *The Gift Relationship. From human blood to social policy*, London, London School of Economics Books

Trespeuch, M., 2015. "Moraliser le commerce des jeux d'argent. D'un marché contesté à un autre", in P. Steiner and M. Trespeuch, (eds), 2015. *Marchés contestés. Quand le marché rencontre la morale*, Toulouse, Presses Universitaires de Toulouse, pp. 184–218

Valiergue, A., 2019. "The Creation and Development of the Voluntary Carbon Market Through Moral Struggles", in P. Balsiger and S. Schiller-Merkens (eds.), *Moral Struggles in and out the Market*, Oxford, Emerald Publishing

Walras, L. 1900 [1988]. *Éléments d'économie politique pure, Œuvres économiques complètes,* Paris: Économica, vol. 8

Weber, M., 1917 [1965]. "Essai sur le sens de la 'neutralité axiologique' dans les sciences sociologiques et économiques", French translation in M. Weber *Essais sur la théorie de la science*, Paris, Plon, pp. 398–477

Zucman, G., 2013. *La richesse cachée des nations. Enquête sur les paradis fiscaux*, Paris, Seuil

PART 2

A history of contested commodities

6

LAND

Land as commodity—A history of a problem

Pierre Crétois

Introduction

It is customary to distinguish between personal property, that is the ownership of everyday objects such as clothes, tools, ornaments, etc., and the ownership of land. While evidence of the exchange of personal property dates to prehistory, the ownership of land, considered as a pure commodity with an exchange value, only comes much later, with the emergence of modern states (Polanyi, 2001 [1944]; Widerquist and McCall, 2021). Land ownership possesses specific features that distinguish it from the ownership of personal property, having been introduced rather recently in Western countries, and then internationally, under the pressure of the market economy, the international institutions, and a conviction that the extension of the scope of private property is likely to further the concordance of individual interests. This particular conception leads to an understanding of land as simply one commodity among others, allowing the creation of value through the emergence of new markets. As a consequence, markets for land have been created in developing countries, the main effect of which has been the disappearance of customary forms of ownership often linked to subsistence farming, while in Western countries there is also increasing speculation in agricultural and urban land. As the scarcity of land becomes more acute, the market for land is increasingly becoming a cardinal issue for the global economy. Yet land is not a commodity like any other; and the idea of the ownership of land raises political and anthropological issues concerning sovereignty that might cause perplexity concerning how land can be commodified at all. As Polanyi writes: "What we call land is an element of nature inextricably interwoven with man's institutions. To isolate it and form a market for it was perhaps the weirdest of all the undertakings of our ancestors" (2001 [1944], p. 187). Thus, despite the growing significance of land markets, certain parts of the land, which cannot be privately appropriated, are as yet excluded from the market, for example, the riversides, coastlines, and border areas which in France are still in the public domain.

The aim of this chapter is to sketch a historical and legal framework that enables us to understand how societies without a market for land have functioned, and how the ownership and commodification of land have gradually been able to impose themselves. Within the context of the economic analysis of institutions (Demsetz, 1967; Alchian and Demsetz, 1973), it is widely recognized that land ownership is a recent phenomenon and that its inception depended on specific

DOI: 10.4324/9781003188742-9

circumstances, such as a recognition of the negative externalities linked to the absence of ownership.[1] However, the adoption of a purely legal and economic framework for analysis in this area threatens to be reductive, in that it limits the explanation of the origin of the ownership of land to a utility calculation, albeit perhaps implicit, and treats land itself as a mere resource. Such an approach, which interprets long-term anthropological phenomena according to frameworks that do not fully capture the complexity of social realities, would be abstract and reductive, whereas in fact the commodification of land is a "total social fact" (Mauss, 1966 [1925], pp. 76–77; Blomley, 2016): it accompanies and reveals a global transformation of our societies and is related to what is commonly called "capitalist society". It is therefore appropriate to refer to broader historical, anthropological, and philosophical material in seeking to understand the introduction, over time, of the mercantile conception of land.

A history of the commodification of land could hardly be global or unified, since the forms of ownership of land will likely have varied from one society to another. I therefore propose to confine myself to insights centred mainly (but not exclusively) on European history and anthropology. The question of the commodification of land must be addressed in conjunction with that of the introduction and transformation of regimes of land ownership and, more generally, of the legal relationship to land. In order to be exchanged, land must first be conceived of as private property, i.e., as a commodity over which the owner has exclusive rights, in particular the right to transfer it to others in exchange for money. One should add that to be considered as a commodity, land must have a price: not only a compensation value for its loss, but a market price determined by supply and demand, which presupposes an institutionalization of its buying and selling. Such a type of relationship to land presupposes that the rights of ownership extend beyond the particular uses that may be made of it. Although this mercantile relationship to land has now become entrenched, its validity is far from self-evident; and land most recently has become the object not only of financial transactions but also of speculation.

For this reason it is essential to adopt a historical perspective in order to understand why only the contemporary period appears to present the conditions in which the commodification of land is possible; although in earlier periods land could be owned individually and indeed sold, this sale and ownership took a form that did not allow land to be viewed as a mere commodity, that is, as possessed solely of an exchange value that is established through a market transaction between buyers and sellers.

I propose to explore this through a broad historical review, focusing on the institutional conditions that rendered the commodification of land impossible before the modern period, and describing the changes to these conditions such that this commodification was subsequently made possible. After a review of ancient legal forms of the relationship to land, I argue that in ancient and medieval times, land had a political value that ruled out considering it as a commodity. With the development of the market society in the modern period, ownership of land appeared as desirable from the perspective of economic development, and attempts were made to turn land into a fenced and privately owned commodity. Finally, I look at the different types of objections that could be made to this process of commodification.

The traditional forms of land ownership in non-capitalist societies

For nomadic peoples, there was no requirement to commodify land. This does not mean that they did not recognize and enforce the distinction of territories; but these territories were not considered as a good that could be traded, but rather as places defended for the resources they contained or coveted for the ancestral links they encoded.

Traditionally, the forms of relationship to the land have been categorized in two ways: the nomadic life of hunter-gatherers, and the sedentary life introduced by the first forms of agriculture. A history of the ownership and commodification of land was first set out by Jean-Jacques Rousseau (2011 [1755]), and then by Lewis Henry Morgan (1877) and Friedrich Engels (1844). Nomadism implies the existence of a shared territory across which groups can range and from which the resources necessary for daily needs are drawn. Crucially, such a relationship to land implies that land has no value in itself. What is valuable are its uses, such as its capacity to link one place to another or to feed herds and people, and it is for this reason that conflicts over territory can arise. Classical authors thought that the sedentary life, especially agrarian life, implies the appropriation and defence of the land and an at least proto-legal relationship of ownership of the land. This new type of relationship to land is traditionally explained by the shift from hunter-gatherer nomadic to agrarian sedentary societies.

However, this categorization is itself reductive insofar as, on the one hand, there are many intermediate land appropriation regimes, and on the other because sedentarization and agriculture do not necessarily imply privative appropriation as we know it today (Widerquist and McCall, 2021). Privatization is the result of specific choices, namely of the decision to enclose the appropriated land, which is a quite recent phenomenon. This point may be demonstrated by looking at certain Native American peoples who were partly settled in territories: "what the Indians owned—or, more precisely, what their villages gave them a claim to—was not the land but the things that were on the land during the various seasons of the year" (Cronon, 1983, p. 65). Thus, sedentarization is fully compatible with the simple enjoyment of the uses of the land recognized in a customary manner and organized according to traditional considerations arbitrated by the village community itself.

Another oversimplification is to be avoided: the so-called original communalism of land. It has been thought that land was initially considered to be fundamentally common (Rousseau, 2011 [1755]; Morgan, 1877; Engels, 1844), an idea that emerged in the eighteenth and nineteenth centuries. Such a communalism would, in principle, make the commodification of land impossible. Indeed, if everything belongs to everyone, or if everything is distributed according to collective rules for allocation of cultivable areas to the families of the community, then a free-for-all exchange of land for money seems ruled out. This belief in an original communalism was fuelled by the historiography of Lewis Henry Morgan, as well as by Engels who takes up this thesis in *The Origin of the Family, Private Property, and the State*. However, this point is debatable, and Alain Testart (2003), for instance, has argued that this vision, too, is reductive. Even where land is supposed to be transmitted mainly through lineage, there are cases of individual appropriation and sale of land, particularly for individuals facing debt or foreclosure. Nevertheless, it remains that the existence of these rare cases of land alienation is not sufficient to create a land market or to make land into a commodity in the strict sense. Nor does it entail that there was a tacit or nascent belief in the private ownership and commodification of land, contrary to what the European settlers assumed when they tried to buy up Native Americans' land. As pointed out by William Cronon (1983), the Native Americans did indeed sometimes exchange land, but these exchanges were not commercial transactions (contrary to what the English colonists may have believed, who interpreted what they saw from their point of view). What was allocated was limited and circumscribed use of the land, very often for limited periods of time, contrary to what we now understand by land ownership. Although there were certainly cases of exchange, they were not essentially financial, and were less about the ownership of the land than the allocation of its use: "at least for the duration of the winter hunt, the kin group that inhabited a camp probably had a clear if informal usufruct right to the animals caught in its immediate area" (Cronon, 1983, p. 64).

As for the territories occupied by a social group, while they could indeed be exchanged, this was a diplomatic affair between tribal chiefs, which never ended in a sale strictly speaking, and again this should not be confused with the mercantile conception of property in the contemporary Western sense (Cronon, 1983, pp. 60–61). Once more, however, this model cannot be generalized insofar as it characterizes only certain Native American social groups.

It would therefore be wrong to assume that private ownership of land has always existed, and it is certain that, in its first forms, land as property did not receive the codification that characterizes its current form. Above all, it remained caught up in considerations of lineage, community organization, and religion.

The political value of land

It is widely accepted that the first forms of private appropriation of land emerged in Ancient Rome (Thomas, 2002; Widerquist and McCall, 2021), but legal relations to land, for the ancient Romans, were highly politicized, and not primarily economic. In predominantly agrarian societies, the legal relationship to land sealed the citizen's membership in the *Urbs* and ensured the permanence and legibility of the social order. Land, and the way it was carved up and distributed, had a political importance that made it almost sacred.

Indeed, the taking of land is the foundation of the political community, and partly constitutes the legal, political, and military power of the state (Widerquist and McCall, 2021). Carl Schmitt describes the visibility of land ownership as a "public sign of order":

> the solid ground of the earth is delineated by fences, enclosures, boundaries, walls, houses, and other constructs. Then, the orders and orientations of human social life become apparent. Then, obviously, families, clans, tribes, estates, forms of ownership and human proximity, also forms of power and domination, become visible.
>
> (Schmitt, 2003, pp. 42–43)

Because of its prominent political role, states are particularly sensitive to the protection of territory, and the stabilization of land ownership is essential to social stability, as well as to the stability of the state, especially in agrarian societies.

Schmitt's account gives a profoundly political dimension to the taking of land by the community. The mythological foundation of Athens echoes the Schmittian description. The myth of autochthony states that the first Athenian citizen was a son of the soil. The foundation of Rome by Romulus, as set down in ancient texts, also shows the politically foundational character of the taking of land: Romulus seized the land of Rome by delimiting the exterior and interior with a moat and thus founded the *Urbs*. The appropriation of land is thus linked to both the identity and the political-legal order of the social group, especially for predominantly rural societies. We can therefore understand the meaning of the ancient respect for land boundaries expressed by Plato:

> Let no one move the boundary markers or those of the property of a neighbouring citizen [...]. Everyone would rather undertake to move the largest of stones than a boundary stone, that small stone which fixes the limits between friendship and hatred, protected by oaths before the gods.
>
> (Plato, 1993, pp. 842e–843a)

This is why, throughout antiquity, a clear distinction was made between the movable and personal property that was the subject of daily exchange and the object of a regular trade, and the lands and real estate that were intended to constitute the patrimony of families, to be transmitted mainly by inheritance in a manner designed to maintain social stability. Thus, ancient Roman law distinguishes between *res mancipi* and *res nec mancipi* with regard to the property of its citizens (or "quirite" property). The *res mancipi*, which included land, slaves, and livestock, formed the patrimony of Roman citizens and was essential for defining their social status. Such property was the object of particular public attention and its transfer involved highly codified rituals and public acknowledgement called *in jure cessio* or *mancipatio* (a ceremony described in the *Institutes* of Gaius, Book I, §119). This property, reserved for Roman citizens, had been a constituent part of their patrimony since the reform introduced by King Servius Tullius (the legendary 6th king of Rome, who is said to have lived in the sixth century B.C.), and served as a basis for the establishment of the five classes of citizens, their military positions, and the calculation of the *cens*. A citizen didn't easily give up his slaves, his animals, or his land; such a transfer usually occurred because of debts or for other serious reasons. The division of the people into classes, according to wealth, is the basis of the system introduced by Servius Tullius through the *cens*. The distinction between *res mancipi* (containing the ownership of land) and *res nec mancipi* was essential to this system, and ensured the stability of social classes based on patrimony (Fresquet, 1857, p. 518). Land was thus not conceived of as a commodity but as the basis for the order and stability of society as a whole.

Beyond the fact that land was essential for resource production and the social order in agrarian societies, it was also a military issue linked intimately to questions of sovereignty. This is well illustrated by the European history of the Middle Ages. After the fall of the Roman Empire, and as a result of the barbarian invasions, land was not exchanged for money but was acquired by force of arms. The taking of land in this context had less of a legal and economic meaning than a military one: land was an issue of political power, as the lands together formed the territory of a lord.

This has implications for the nature of feudal law. In this context, land was not property that could be sold on the market; it was a domain over which the military power of the lord who took possession of it was exercised. The lord might give part of the domain, called a fief, to a vassal, following a ceremony in which the vassal who received the domain swore fealty and homage to his suzerain (the one who grants a portion of his territory), but the transaction was not monetary and did not release the vassal from any obligation, as it would had he become a full owner. In exchange for the fief he received, the vassal swore loyalty to the suzerain and became his "man", owing him certain duties such as military service or the payment of taxes (the *cens*). In addition, the suzerain retained a right over the domain he had transferred to his vassal. He was said to have the "direct domain" and his vassal had the "useful domain", which he could in turn grant in fief or lease out.

Moreover, the exploitation of the land was not the role of the lords, who did not work, but of the different types of land users, who had to give part of their production in exchange for the right to use a part of the domain. Thus, those who worked the land did not own it and therefore could not sell it, and even their production didn't entirely belong to them, one substantial part being due to the lord. Land labourers acquired the right to use the land on lease and were liable for the *cens*. No markets for land were therefore possible in such a legal framework. Although this system became more flexible over the centuries, the fact remained that the military dimension of the relationship to land implied that it could only be acquired by arms, not money.

In addition, in the medieval period, the rights of members of village communities over land were very strong, making it difficult or, in some regions, even impossible to fence off fields and therefore to sell or buy land. Indeed, the members of a village community might have had and exercised rights over land that was used and exploited by others. In France, for example, the right to graze (*vaine pâture*), the right to glean (*glanage*), the right to the "first grass" (*première herbe*), the right to the "second grass" (*deuxième herbe*), and the right to range (*parcours*) were all rights that were exercised in addition to the right of the person who properly speaking exploited the land. And these rights remained alive even in more recent times, as Longuet, a wealthy French landowner, could testify at the end of the eighteenth century (1794), evoking the persistence of the old agricultural practices of rural France. Longuet referred to the two main rights that had left the mark of collective functioning in land law and that were contested in the second half of the eighteenth century: the *droit de vaine pâture* and the *droit de parcours*. The former was the right of the members of the canton to graze their herds on the fields of the same canton according to certain rules and therefore to pass across a field that was being exploited by others (fields left fallow, or via the right to *deuxième herbe* or *regain*). The latter implied the possibility that the members of a village might move their herds onto the land of the neighbouring village.

The existence of the rights of members of the village community over the land attests to the fact that land was less the object of a trade between full owners than a place of cohabitation, where what was mine was intertwined with what was yours, and where questions of possession were connected less to the land itself than to the different uses made of it. The essential issue for rural communities was therefore not the commodification of land but rather the distribution of its uses: the allocation of rights to grazing and subsistence among the different users of the land (Thompson, 1963; Gauthier and Ikni, 2019).

Enclosure: The advent of land ownership and commodification

At the end of the Middle Ages, as a result of a series of complex factors, a conception of private property became progressively hegemonic that we would now see as distinctively modern. The weakening of feudalism and the application of the concept of private property to land accompanied the growing importance of modern forms of commerce. To sell something now implied that one has absolute control over it. Applied to land, this entails the right to exclude others—namely by enclosing it. From an economic perspective, Demsetz and Alchian explained the progressive proprietorship of land as a necessity based on the scarcity of resources, itself resulting from the development of trade (Alchian and Demsetz, 1973), which swept aside the old forms of common property (Blomley, 2016). And from the proprietorship of land to the creation of a market for it there is only a small step, because the proprietor, like a king in his castle (Singer, 2006), controls every aspect and every utility of what he owns, extending even to the right to order its destruction or sale (i.e., economic liberties). Thus, the enclosure of land and the trade in land are profoundly linked.

Land enclosure progressed in particular between the sixteenth and the nineteenth centuries, as a part of a process of transformation of agricultural activity and of the solidaristic relations of village life. In many regions of England and France there were communal fields as well as collective rights over the land which made it difficult to fence off fields. The land rights that, through various means, regulated social relations with regard to land, were therefore profoundly reshaped by the introduction of fences (Patault, 1989). The enclosure of fields led to a transformation of the landscape and of the ways in which the land was used (Pitte, 2003), as Thomas More testified in *Utopia*:

> when an insatiable wretch, who is a plague to his country, resolves to enclose many thousand acres of ground, the owners, as well as tenants, are turned out of their possessions by trick or by main force, or, being wearied out by ill usage, they are forced to sell them.
>
> (2006 [1516])

In 1689 John Locke offered a defence of property rights against the arbitrary exercise of political power: in Chapter 5 of his *Second Treatise of Government*, "On property" (1998 [1689]), he argued that property is a natural right and that one can be entitled to a good by one's own work or personal effort with respect to it. The jurist Blackstone, a few years later, defined property with the canonical expression "a sole and despotic dominion" (2016 [1766], p. 3). The keystone of Blackstone's approach was a utilitarian defence of property, which is founded on considerations of economic development and thus differs from natural law views like Locke's (Girard, 2021, p. 425): "Had not therefore a separate property in lands [...] been vested in some individuals the world must have continued a forest, and men have been mere animals of prey" (Blackstone, 2016 [1766], p. 5). This way of justifying property became dominant during the eighteenth century.

In France, the second half of the eighteenth century marked a tipping point in the history of enclosures. The operation was centralized and endorsed by the monarchy. Royal edicts were issued to modify customs so as to give landowners the freedom to fence. These edicts had been prepared by memoranda establishing the necessity and usefulness of fences in certain regions where collective practices were strongest. Under the ministry of the administrator Bertin, enquiries were commissioned in England to show the merits of repealing the *vaine-pâture*. Bertin drew up a draft edict, which was very cautious, and in 1766 sent it to the intendants and procurators-general for examination. A memorandum of 1763 (*Mémoire*, 1763) had already recommended granting landowners the freedom to enclose and, consequently, to abolish all collective rights that were likely to hinder this essential freedom of the landowner, such as fowl grazing and the right to roam.

It was this pattern, combining the affirmation of the freedom to enclose with the abolition of the old common property rights, that was repeated in the edicts. The administration of d'Ormesson, which followed that of Bertin, was much more radical and had a series of edicts published which from 1770 onwards allowed the enclosure of land. After the edicts of the early 1770s, the wind of reform died down, mainly because of the poor reception it received in the countryside (Bloch, 1999, p. 252), except in 1787 when the administration of Garnier Vergennes put the abolition of the right to range (*parcours*) back on the agenda with new investigations. All this was part of a vast project to 'rationalize' farms and modernize property law.

In parallel with the enclosure of fields, the commercial exploitation of their products developed under the influence of the Physiocrats, who decried the political restrictions placed on grain prices. In the eighteenth century, speculation (known as *accaparement*) led to rising wheat prices and in turn to shortages and famine. This may have contributed to the major peasant revolts of 1775, described as the "wheat war" (Gauthier and Ikni, 2019).

Revolutionary legislation made the abolition of collective rights and the affirmation of the freedom to enclose and dispose of land a matter of principle and a central instrument of individual emancipation. Thus, the decree of 28 September–6 October 1791 formally established the principle of the owner's complete freedom in the use of his property, both for legal reasons (the protection of individual freedom) and for agronomic and economic considerations (the maximization of agricultural production). With the expressions "free to vary [...] the cultivation [...] free to have [...] such quantity and such kind of herds [...] free to harvest [...] with any instrument and at the time that suits him", the decree guaranteed freedom via the affirmation of the right to enclose. This followed directly on from the principle stated in the 1763 memorandum:

> An inheritance enclosed by walls, palisades or hedges is the only true property. The master does with his land as he pleases, and often one sees in the same enclosed area all the productions of nature at the same time. Grains of all kinds, vegetables, fruit, hay, regains,

> hemp, etc., are all produced in the same field. It yields the owner three times more than the same quantity abandoned to seasonal cultivation and subject to *vaine pâture*. One chooses one's own time for harvesting, and is not subject to the ban. If this is to the advantage of an individual, it is also for the general good; for each individual cannot increase his harvest by a quarter, for example, each year, unless the general harvest is also increased by a quarter.
>
> (*Mémoire*, 1763, p. 11)

It was not only common land that was attacked, but all communal rights. In the enclosed fields, all old uses that were not motivated by necessity (for example, *droit de parcours*) were prohibited. *Parcours*, *vaine pâture*, *regain*, *glanage*, etc. were all abolished. The juxtaposition of individual and common ownership of land was thus definitively established in legal theory, while also becoming standard practice due to the authorizations and incentives to enclose that the decrees presented. The owner was recognized and defended as the absolute holder of a piece of land, with an absolute right prior to any commitment, which all others must respect. He was thus free to enclose and sell the land he owned.

The historian E.P. Thompson points out that enclosure contributed to breaking the traditional link between law and village customs (Thompson, 1963). He also shows that fences destroyed traditional forms of economy that sustained the poor. The installation of territorialized property, i.e., spatial exclusivity, "collided with habits of property that worked according to a different spatial logic" (Blomley, 2016, p. 604). Thompson insisted on the violence induced by the land enclosures and the brutal suppression of common and traditional forms of property, which could also be described as an expropriation and forced transformation of the peasant way of life. Against supporters of the enclosure system, who believed that it increased rental values and yields per acre, Thompson showed that the consequences of enclosure were devastating, having encouraged the concentration of land ownership while depriving landless peasants of their livelihoods. He detailed the forms of expropriation without compensation that poor farmers had to endure (Thompson, 1963). The enclosure movement profoundly affected the organization of village life, putting three classes of people at risk: small farmers, landless peasants (especially stockbreeders), and those who operated cottages. This phenomenon increased rural poverty, as villagers were driven off land and into cities with no livelihoods, and helped eliminate the small peasantry. It is undeniable that enclosures caused a rural exodus. Thus, even if enclosure allowed for an increase in production, which notably went to feed the non-rural population, it impoverished and transformed the living conditions of poor peasants, and did so in a particularly violent way.

Commodification of land in the contemporary period

During the twentieth century, the idea of a market in land was diffused in particular through international organizations such as the World Bank, while, at the same time, the developing world was the site of growing resistance to the social transformations wrought by the coercive policies issuing from these new international public agencies.

The promotion of property rights and commodification are rooted in the history of liberal democracies. As Rafe Blaufarb (2016) has shown, the French Revolution marked the advent of the modern idea of property. As Anne-Marie Patault notes:

> From the 18th century onwards, new economic conditions, an increasingly commercial society, the evolution of ideas towards individualism, and the active support of humanist

> jurists, made *abusus*, the free disposal of matter, the essential element of property [...]. The notion of *abusus*, the freedom to dispose of the corporeal thing and the freedom to choose the way in which one intends to enjoy it, would be the pivot around which the conception of property would slowly tilt, at the same time as the millenial social order. *Abusus*, which implies a single owner of the property, who is total master of the thing to the exclusion of all competing ownership, and free of all obligations to others, would be the spearhead of the idea of exclusive ownership.
>
> (1989, p. 136)

Among the absolute rights of the owner is the right to sell. From then on, there was no longer any obstacle to the commodification of enclosed land.

In reality, this process accompanied a profound transformation towards a more egalitarian democratic society. In this society, social positions are not destined to remain eternally stable. The function of land for social stabilization and the expression of hierarchy and power (as in agrarian or traditional military societies) was therefore progressively disappearing. The mobility of positions is reflected in the right to sell or buy land in order to escape one's rural heritage or to enrich oneself through work and individual initiative. This was Tocqueville's experience in America at the beginning of the nineteenth century. Tocqueville underlines the close relationship between democratization (i.e., the equalization of conditions), social instability, and the commodification of land (Tocqueville, 2002 [1835–1840]), noting that the acquisition of land rights through leases happened much faster in America than in Europe, where the enduring relationship to land enshrined the "immortality of families".

During the twentieth century, institutional economics promulgated the belief that the absence of land ownership would lead to tragedy (Ophuls, 1992). Garrett Hardin's influential 1968 article "The Tragedy of the Commons", published in *Science*, helped to diffuse the idea that private ownership of land could ensure the sustainability of resources (Hardin, 1968). Hardin used an example from the nineteenth-century economist William Forster Lloyd to argue that open access land would necessarily be over-exploited by the herders who used it to graze their animals (Lloyd, 1833). Thus, each agent tends to neglect the losses associated with overgrazing of the common field because this represents for him only a small part of the total shared by all; but at the same time each agent is inclined to add one more animal to his herd because of the gain it provides to himself. The result is the notorious tragedy of the commons. The only way to make farmers more responsible for the resource to which they have access is to divide the common land into individual private properties, so that they can take into account the losses incurred by adding an animal to their herd and adjust the number of animals in their herd to the capacity of their pasture. Thus, by making agents responsible for the use they make of them, private property would make it possible to sustain the resources so as to avoid the tragedy of open access goods (Falque, 2018). In addition, it was considered advisable to commodify land so as to create new markets and bolster economic growth in developing countries (Boisvert, Caron, Rodary, 2004). The school of economics known as 'new resource economics', based on the Austrian neo-liberalism of Mises and Hayek, stressed the importance of property rights and markets in the management of resources such as water or land (Anderson, 1982; Locher, 2013).[2]

On the same lines, Demsetz and Alchian derived an economic theory of property rights from the perspective of institutional economics (Desmarais-Tremblay and Stojanović, 2022, p. 15) by referring to the transformation of beaver hunting in Canada during the eighteenth century (Demsetz, 1968). They referred to the anthropological work of Eleanor Leacock to explain how it became economically justified for Native Americans to privatize their hunting territories with the development of the beaver trade (Leacock, 1954). But, as we know from Cronon's works (Cronon, 1983), to employ Western concepts such as private property rights to analyse Native American institutions risks serious error. Indeed, the influence of European settlers is of preeminent importance in explaining the shift in Native American institutions during this period. In fact, while hunting territory was indeed shared between families, it by no means became excludable as a private commodity.

Since the beginning of the 1980s, Elinor Ostrom and the Bloomington School of Political Economics have sought to show how land considered as a common good (i.e., as inadmissible for sale in the manner of a private commodity) could be economically efficient concerning the management of Common Pool Resources (Nagendra and Ostrom, 2008). Ostrom's idea, along with the jurist Edella Schlager, was to use the "bundle of rights" approach to theorize how Common Pool Resources are organized, with a rights structure which includes drawing rights, access rights, management rights, and even, in certain cases, but not necessarily, selling rights (Ostrom and Schlager, 1992; Orsi, 2014).[3] This approach allows us to understand how land considered as a common good can be efficiently exploited without the necessity to commodify it and treat it as private property. Nevertheless, this theory tends to reduce land to a mere resource and neglects its anthropological aspects. For, beyond questions of economics, land is also linked to "irrational" considerations (Nightingale, 2011, p. 120): it retains a symbolic dimension and is related to "socially embedded" arrangements (Warren and McCarthy, 2012, p. 20), i.e., institutions and relationships that sometimes "have little to do with resource management" (Nightingale, 2011, p. 120; Girard, 2021, p. 120). Land is also an environmental source and the site of life, both properties that cannot be entirely appropriated (Vanuxem, 2018). One might also think of the geographer Nicholas Blomley's view that land shapes relations between humans, between humans and non-humans, between the individual and society, and the between individual and nature (Blomley, 2016, p. 596). For all these reasons, land cannot be fully understood within the narrow confines of private property.

During second part of the twentieth century there was pressure from major international institutions such as World Bank for the private ownership and commodification of land in developing countries, where agriculture was still largely dependent on more traditional forms of appropriation. Land, which had become a market, thereby became the subject of intense speculation, whether this was for land in large cities, the price of which is constantly rising due to demographic pressure, or for agricultural land, which is an essential strategic issue in the access to food resources. These phenomena of commodification on an international scale led to predation and monopolization that tended to destroy subsistence agriculture, impoverishing small farmers while promoting intensive agriculture dedicated to export and international trade, with harmful environmental outcomes. It is worth mentioning that the FAO's recent "Technical Guide" on Land Governance of the Commons indicates that international organizations are indeed now interested in "land governance of the commons". Yet these "guidelines" are not hard law, and only offer advice on the question of "governing" land tenure:

> what interests the developers (international organizations, NGOs and states) to whom the guide is addressed is less what the land represents for the community than setting the institutional conditions to ensure productive and sustainable management of the land's resources.
>
> (Girard, 2021, pp. 429–430; FAO, 2016)

Another example showing that it is possible to avoid the total commodification of land is supplied by the Mexican institution Ejidos, which, after the 1910 revolution, succeeded in removing land from the commodity pool by making it impossible to sell. In this way, at the beginning of the twentieth century, the Mexican revolutionary government aimed to secure the means of subsistence for the rural population and to protect it from the speculative mechanisms of the market. But in the 1980s the indebtedness of some peasant families, and the pressure of the markets and from the IMF (following the 1982 crisis), caused the Mexican government to relax this rule, leading some families to sell their fields to repay their creditors, thus dispossessing them of their resources (Morett Sánchez, 2008).

Despite the increasing commodification of land and the speculative pressures that accompany it, land in all countries still has a specific status, associated with cumbersome public registration procedures on land registers and related taxation by notaries and the public administration. Irrespective of the particular public domain, whether state forests, riverbanks, roads, coastlines, or even the national territory and its borders, privatized land is, in reality, still embedded in land that is owned in common, and which is legally recognized as not being marketable in all respects.[4] From this point of view, despite market pressure, land remains a particular and, in many ways, ambiguous resource. Nevertheless, the mechanisms of public registration no longer stabilize social relationships to land and, in the absence of regulations aimed at limiting speculation, do not discourage investors or speculators.

Conclusion

Is land a commodity like any other? For a long time it was not: it was seen as the common ground for a political or village community, or as a domain of sovereignty defended by arms. Yet liberal democracies, with their core goal of economic growth, have made a world in which everything, including land, seems to be open to private ownership, exploitation, and sale. The hegemony of this idea has favoured the extension of the concept of marketable private property, including land, in the name of respect for human rights, freedom, and growth. This idea has been disseminated by most of the world's major development organizations, which see property rights as a way of escaping the arbitrariness and poverty allegedly associated with traditional forms of land ownership. Yet this type of public policy, by promoting intensive land use and monoculture to increase yields, has also profoundly disrupted livelihoods, destroyed traditional agriculture, and driven many expropriated people to urban centres. The ecological crisis, among many other phenomena, remind us that land is a place where a multitude of social and political relations intersect, and where multiple associated constraints exist, meaning that it is impossible to treat land as a commodity like any other. Land therefore deserves specific consideration, prohibiting its absolute appropriation, preserving the multiple interests that depend on it, and preventing it from being reduced to a pure object of commerce (Cotula, 2022).

Notes

1 See the chapter by Bertrand in this volume (Chapter 3).
2 On the Austrian view of market efficiency, see Chapter 1 by Daou and Marciano in this volume.
3 See Chapter 28 by Girard and al. in this volume.
4 On national parks and forests, see Chapter 29 by C. Larrère in this volume, which argues that national property is different from common property and may entail commodification.

References

Alchian, A. and Demsetz, H. (1973) "The Property Right Paradigm". *The Journal of Economic History*, 33(1).

Anderson, T.L. (1982) "The New Resource Economics: Old Ideas and New Applications". *The New Political Economy of Natural Resources*, 64–5, pp. 928–934 https://doi.org/10.2307/1240760

Blackstone (2016 [1766]) *Commentaries on the Laws of England.* Book II. Oxford: Oxford University Press
Blaufarb, R. (2016) *The Great Demarcation: The French Revolution and the Invention of Modern Property.* Oxford: Oxford University Press https://doi.org/10.1080/03612759.2017.1294950
Bloch, M. (1999) *La terre et le paysan.* Paris: Armand Colin
Blomley, N. (2016) "Territory of Property". *Progress in Human Geography*, 40(5), pp. 593–609 https://doi.org/10.1177/0309132515596380
Boisvert, V., Caron, A., and Rodary, E. (2004) "Privatiser pour conserver? Petits arrangements de la nouvelle économie des ressources avec la réalité". *Tiers-Monde*, 45, pp. 61–84 10.3406/tiers.2004.5448
Cotula, L. (2022) "Recalibrating rights, limitations and obligations in land governance". *Land Tenure Journal*, 1–22, FAO, Rome. www.fao.org/3/cb8933t/cb8933t.pdf
Cronon, W. (1983) "Bounding the Land". in *Changes in Land: Indians, Colonists and the Ecology of New England.* New York: Hill and Wang, pp. 54–81
Desmarais-Tremblay, M. and Stojanović, A. (2022) "Framing Institutional Choice, 1937–1973: New Institutional Economics and the Neglect of the Commons". *Review of Political Economy*, 34(4), pp. 665–691. https://doi.org/10.1080/09538259.2022.2096284
Demsetz, H. (1967) "Towards a Theory of Property Rights", *The American Economic Review*, 57(2), pp. 347–359 https://doi.org/10.1057/9780230523210_9
Engels, F. (1844) *Der Ursprung der Familie des Privateigenthums und des Staats.* Hottingen-Zürich: Verlag der Schweizerischen Volksbuchbandlung
Falque, M. (2018) "Approprier pour sauvegarder". *La Nouvelle Revue Foncière*, 22, pp. 26–30
FAO (2016) *Governing tenure rights to commons. Governance of tenure technical guide.* www.fao.org/3/a-i6381e.pdf
Fresquet, R. de (1857) "De l'origine politique et de l'importance de la distinction des 'res mancipi' et 'nec mancipi' dans l'ancien droit romain ». *Revue historique de droit français et étranger*, 3, pp. 509–524
Gauthier, F. and Ikni, R. (2019) *La guerre du blé au XVIII*[e] *siècle. La critique populaire de la liberté économique.* Paris: Kimé
Girard, F. (2021) "La terrestrialité des communs: justissima *tellus*. Bioculturalité et propriété collective". In Joye, J.-F., *Les "communaux" au XXI*[e] *siècle. Une propriété collective entre histoire et modernité.* Chambéry: Presses Universitaires Savoie Mont Blanc, pp. 415–447
Hardin, G. (1968) "The Tragedy of the Commons". *Science*, 162 DOI: 10.1126/science.162.3859.1243
Lloyd, W.F. (1833) *Two Lectures on the Checks to Population.* Oxford: S. Collingwood printer to the University
Leacock, E. (1954) "The Montagnais 'Hunting Territory' and the Fur Trade", *American Anthropologist*, 56(5), Part 2, Memoir n° 78
Locher, F. (2013) "Les pâturages de la Guerre froide: Garrett Hardin et la 'Tragédie des communs'". *Revue d'histoire moderne & contemporaine*, 60(1), pp. 7–36
Locke, J. (1998 [1689]) *Two Treatises on Government.* Cambridge: Cambridge University Press. https://doi.org/10.1017/CBO9780511810268
Longuet, C. (1794) *Clôture productive, qui ne porte aucun préjudice à la culture des terrains environnants, propre à contenir le bétail, et à le garantir des loups et des tous autres animaux, méthode imitée de l'anglais, pour l'éducation des bêtes à laine; ou moyens de tripler sur la plus grande partie du sol de la république, le nombre de ces animaux intéressants, en faisant moins de dépenses pour trois que pour un.* Paris: Imprimerie de l'Union
Mauss, M. (1966 [1925]) *The Gift. Forms and Functions of Exchange in Archaic Societies.* London: Cohen & West https://doi.org/10.4324/9780203407448
Mémoire concernant la clôture des héritages; le vain-pâturage; et le parcours, en Lorraine (1763). Nancy: chez Thomas père et fils.
More (2006 [1516]) *Utopia.* Cambridge: Cambridge University Press. https://doi.org/10.1017/9781316414972
Morett Sánchez, J.C. (2008) *Reforma agraria del latifundio al neoliberalismo.* Chapingo: Biblioteca Lui Gonzales, El Colegio de Michoacan
Morgan, L.H. (1877) *Ancient Society, or Researches in the Line of Human Progress from Savagery, through Barbarism to Civilization.* Londres: Macmillan and Co

Nagendra, H. and Ostrom, E. (2008) *Governing the Commons in the New Millennium: A Diversity of Institutions for Natural Resource Management*. Encyclopedia of the Earth. http://editors.eol.org/eoearth/wiki/Governing_the_commons_in_the_new_millennium:_A_diversity_of_institutions_for_natural_resource_management

Nightingale, A.J. (2011) "Beyond Design Principles: Subjectivity, Emotion, and the (Ir)Rational Commons". *Society & Natural Resources*, 24(2), pp. 119–132 https://doi.org/10.1080/08941920903278160

Ophuls, W. (1992) *Ecology and the Politics of Scarcity. The Unraveling of the American Dream*. New York: W.H. Freeman.

Orsi, F. (2104) "Réhabiliter la propriété comme *bundle of rights*: des origines à Elinor Ostrom et au-delà?". *Revue de droit économique*, 28 https://doi.org/10.3917/ride.283.0371

Ostrom, E. and Schlager, E. (1992) "Property-Rights Regimes and Natural Resources: A Conceptual Analysis". *Land Economics*, 68 https://doi.org/10.2307/3146375

Patault, A.-M. (1989) *Introduction historique au droit des biens*. Paris: PUF

Pitte, J.-R. (2003) *Histoire du paysage français*. Paris: Tallandier

Plato (1993) *Republic*. Oxford: Oxford University Press

Polanyi, K. (2001 [1944]) *The Great Transformation: The Political and Economic Origins of Our Time*. Boston (Mass.): Beacon Press

Rousseau, J.-J. (2011 [1755]) *Discours sur l'origine et les fondements de l'inégalité parmi les hommes*, Paris: GF

Schmitt, C. (2003) *The Nomos of the Earth in the International Law of Jus Publicum Europaeum*, New York: Telos Press

Singer, J.W. (2006) "The Ownership Society and Takings of Property: Castles, Investments, and Just Obligations". *Harvard Environmental Law Review*, 30, pp. 309–338

Testart, A. (2003) "Propriété et non-propriété de la Terre. L'illusion de la propriété collective archaïque (1re partie)". *Études rurales,* 1–2 (165–166), pp. 209–242 https://doi.org/10.4000/etudesrurales.8009

Thomas, Y. (2002) "La valeur des choses. Le droit romain hors la religion". *Annales. Histoire, Sciences Sociales,* 6 (57e année), pp. 1431–1462

Thompson, E.P. (1963) *The Making of the English Working Class*. London: Victor Gollancz Ltd.

Tocqueville, A. ([1835–1840] 2002) *Democracy in America*. Chicago: University of Chicago Press

Vanuxem, S. (2018) *La propriété de la terre*. Marseille: Wildproject

Warren, C. and McCarthy, J.-F. (2012) "Communities, Environments and Local Governance In Reform Era Indonesia". in Warren, C. and J.F. McCarthy (eds) *Community, Environment and Local Governance in Indonesia: Locating the commonweal.* Hoboken: Taylor and Francis, pp. 1–25 DOI:10.13140/2.1.1313.8560

Widerquist, K. and MacCall, G.S. (2021) *The Prehistory of Private Property: Implications for Modern Political Theory*. Edinburgh: Edinburgh University Press DOI:10.1515/9781474447447

Yelling, J.A. (1977) *Common Field and Enclosure in England, 1450-1850*. London: Archon Books. https://doi.org/10.1007/978-1-349-15797-6

Young, A. (1931) *Voyages en France en 1787, 1788 et 1789*. Paris: Armand Colin.

7
USURY AND SIMONY
Trading for no price – Thomas Aquinas on money loans, sacraments and exchange

Pierre Januard and André Lapidus

Introduction

Throughout the Middle Ages, the charging of interest on monetary loans, as well as the sale of sacraments, were generally considered to be special types of sins, respectively, *usury* and *simony*, and were strongly condemned by the ecclesiastical authorities. The repeated condemnations of interest loans and sales of sacraments, and the social disapproval that surrounded them, suggest to the contemporary reader that they might be viewed as prefigurations of *contested commodities*, insofar as their markets are "particular markets that may raise ethical, moral or social issues" (Bertrand and Catto, 2020, p. 13).

Money loans and sacraments were indeed not tradable goods that could be sold in a legally and socially accepted way, that is, according to a price, as it was for many other goods. Yet, despite the legal prohibition on interest-bearing loans and sale of sacraments, something was nevertheless given to the lender and to the priest. It is well known that sophisticated arrangements were conceived that allowed a lender to be paid without it being usury, and allowed giving a return for a sacrament without it being simony. In the first case, despite the prohibition on income received because of a loan, understood in the strict sense of a payment and an equal repayment, reasons other than the loan itself could be invoked to receive such income; and in the second case, although simony such as trafficking relics, lands, or consecrated vessels remained strictly forbidden, giving money for clerics' licit services, which are ostensibly the unilateral provision of a spiritual service, were to some extent tolerated or seen as unavoidable.

The interpretation of the practice of paying compensation to the lender or a stipend to the priest remains open: it can be regarded either as a gift, whereby the compensation is seen as something additional to the original service, or as an exchange, where this addition is seen as the counterpart of the opportunity cost of the loan or the sacrament, according to an exchange ratio.

In a gift-oriented approach, such arrangements point to the idea – supported, for instance, by Steiner (2015) – that some gifts are complex operations requiring the intervention of an organizational mechanism associated with market-like characteristics. Such a view could be supported for both money loans and transactions concerning sacraments, insofar as we interpret them as gifts to which would be added a supplement: a compensation for some opportunity costs suffered by the lender in the first case; a kind of tariff allowing the priest to live according to his condition in the

DOI: 10.4324/9781003188742-10

second. In the exchange-oriented approach, for the loan itself, the sum borrowed is simply paid back to the lender, but for the opportunity costs of the loan, a compensation can be received by the lender; in addition, the priest receives a stipend as a living allowance. These counterparts are paid within an exchange. Loans and sacraments could therefore hardly be viewed as commodities tradable according to a price, but they do enter an exchange relation and are in some sense traded against money. As such, they are a kind of commodity, although this commodification is not complete and remains contested.

In the following, we support this last interpretation, of an exchange-oriented approach that leads to an understanding of money loans and sacraments in terms of commodification. The reason for this lies in Aquinas's moral philosophy. From his point of view, it matters whether the transaction on money or sacraments is a gift (a one-way unilateral transfer, without any counterpart) or an exchange (implying a kind of counterpart). These two things are related to different virtues: a gift depends on charity, whereas an exchange depends on justice.

We will show that although it is always possible, for example, to transfer money through a gift, transfers whose object concerns money or sacraments were analyzed by Aquinas through the framework of *exchange*, not of *gift*: that is, in relation to a norm of justice in exchange – and not of charity. Since it is not the question of exchange that is challenged, we are therefore not concerned to point out some kind of medieval prefiguration of "market inalienability", in the words of Margaret Radin (1987), but rather the sharp, binary opposition between market and non-market situations (Bertrand and Catto, 2020, p. 14), for which the question of the nature and level of the exchange ratio is substituted.

Overcoming this binary opposition emerges as the outcome of a specific approach: relying on Aquinas's works, both early works like the *Commentary on the Sentences* and later works like the *Summa Theologiae* or the *Commentary on the Politics*, we show that money and sacraments, though exchanged, share this characteristic of being, in a sense, traded for no price. The result is the existence, in the framework of exchange, of various situations which might be ranked according to increasing commodification: first, an *absolute non-commodification* for the money loan, whose price is zero due to the prohibition of the payment of interest to the lender due to the loan itself, although an indemnity can be paid for other reasons and, from an economic viewpoint, appears as a counterpart for the opportunity cost of the loan. Then, two ways of expressing a kind of commodification in dealing with the sacraments: a *lexical commodification* in which sacraments do have a "price", as Aquinas mentioned, but one that is out of reach on this earth; and a *partial operational commodification*, again for sacraments (especially for the Eucharist through mass offerings), in which something like an exchange for sacraments takes place, not at an impossible price but according to a kind of tariff which allows the priest to live.

Prohibition of usury: The construction of a non-commodified exchanged object

The case of the prohibition of usury in the Middle Ages is a remarkable example of the construction of an object which, even though it enters into a process of exchange, by its very nature escapes commodification, i.e., sale on the market according to a price.

The basis of this development, to which Thomas Aquinas was to give the final touch, was the medieval understanding of money loans through a legal framework, a loan contract borrowed from Roman law called the *mutuum* (see *Digesta*, lib. 44, tit. 7.4). The *mutuum* was, according to the *Corpus Juris Civilis*, one of the ways a good could be transferred from one person to another and returned through a loan: From a more general point of view, the transfer might concern either use only or ownership, and could be made either for payment or for free – therefore giving birth to the *locatio*, the *commodatum*, the *foenus* and the *mutuum*. Whereas the *foenus*, for instance, was a loan contract in which ownership and use were transferred for payment, the *mutuum* was the same kind of contract, but for free. It is therefore obvious that if a money loan was made through a *mutuum*, the lender was not entitled to any payment on account of the loan contract itself. Robert of Courçon, for instance, in the first years of the thirteenth century, typified this approach to money loans by assuming the legal framework of the *mutuum* and relying on an alleged etymology of the word to explain why the lender should not receive any return for his loan:

> [T]he name of the *mutuum* comes, indeed, from that which was mine [*meum*] becomes yours [*tuum*] or inversely. As soon as the five shillings that you lent me become mine, ownership passes from you to me. It would then be an injustice if, for a good which is mine, you were to receive something; for you are not entitled to any return from that which is my possession.
>
> (*De Usura*, 15)

Thomas Aquinas's argument against usury might be viewed as a justification of the legal framework provided by the *mutuum*. As a consequence of this justification, the loan contract could no longer be perceived as the result of an arbitrary choice among the alternative possibilities offered by civil law. While the *mutuum*, that is a free contract transferring both property and use from the lender to the borrower, was acknowledged as the non-arbitrary legal framework for a money loan, it also gave a rigorous basis to the prohibition of usury, in the sense of the payment of an income by reason of the loan itself. Aquinas's classical argument, as presented in the *Summa Theologiae* (about the origin of the *mutuum* and Aquinas's position on usury in his early writings, see Januard 2021), might be considered a development of topics obviously arising from Roman law, from the Scriptures and from the teaching of the Church, but also from Canon law and from the Aristotelian tradition.

Changing the basis for a possible income of the lender

One of the sources of the pre-Thomist condemnation of usury was a palea (that is, an addition to Gratian's *Decretum*) from Canon Law, *Ejiciens*, falsely attributed to John Chrysostom. The author of *Ejiciens* aimed at identifying the types of goods whose transfer by a loan might give birth to an income to the benefit of the lender. He asked whether "the one who rents a field to receive its fruits or a house to receive an income is not similar to the one who lends money at usury" (*Decretum*, dist. 88, can. 11). The answer was negative for three reasons:

> First, because the only function of money is the payment of a purchase price. Then, because the farmer makes the earth fructify, the tenant takes advantage of inhabiting the house: in both cases, the owner seems to give use of his thing to receive money and, in a certain way, he exchanges gain for gain, whilst from money which is stored up, you make no use. At last, its use gradually exhausts the earth, deteriorates the house, whilst the money lent suffers neither diminishing nor ageing.
>
> (*ibid.*)

The two first reasons respectively referred to the Aristotelian argument about the sterility of money and to the prerequisite of a surplus, like that which comes from production. The third reason deserves special attention: it claimed that a good was a source of income from the moment it suffered a physical depreciation – the latter being the counterpart of the income generated. This might explain why the contract for lending a house was a *locatio* and why the contract for a money loan was not. But it is not absolutely clear that it required that the contract for this money loan was a *mutuum*. Aquinas took this final step by reversing *Ejiciens*' third reason (see Noonan, 1957, pp. 54–55), therefore giving an analytical foundation to its legal framework, the *mutuum*. His argument was expounded in *De Malo* (q. 13, a. 4, resp. et ad 4) around 1270 or shortly afterwards in one of the most frequently quoted passages from question 78 from the IIa–IIae of the *Summa Theologiae*:

> One must know that the use of certain things is identical with their consumption: thus we consume wine when we use it for drink and we consume wheat when we use it for food. In such [exchanges], one must not count the use of the thing apart from the thing itself but, as a result of conceding the use, the thing itself is conceded. And this is why, for such things, the loan transfers property. Thus, if someone wanted to sell wine on the one hand and the use of wine on the other hand, he would sell twice the same thing or sell what is not [...]. Conversely, there are things the use of which is not their consumption. So, the use of a house is to live in, not to destroy it. Therefore, one can concede separately use and property.
>
> (*Summa Theologiae*, IIa–IIae, q. 78, a. 1, resp.)

The conclusion is straightforward. Since for money, as for wine, it seems impossible to separate its ownership from its use, the loan contract could not be a *locatio* or, incidentally, a *commodatum*, in which only the use of the good was transferred to the borrower. It could not be a *foenus* either, since it would amount to selling to the borrower a use which he already owned along with the ownership of the money lent, during the time of the loan. This clearly constitutes a logical trap directed against the idea that a money loan might be something other than a *mutuum*. As a result, like in *Ejiciens* but for other reasons, a house or a field might be lent, for payment (a *locatio*) or for free (a *commodatum*); and money, like wine or bread, could only be lent for free, through a *mutuum*.

The ontological claim on the ownership and use of money

Aquinas's argument regarding the prohibition of usury is insightful, not only because it takes the opposite view of the usual position expressed in *Ejiciens*, but also because, differing from the Church Fathers, it does not rely primarily on the social effect of usury – the enslavement of the poor – but on the very nature of the transaction and of the good exchanged. Obviously, it can be argued that Aquinas's final issue was moral, but he did not address it directly as such; rather, it is implied by his ontological analysis.

This analysis rests on the crucial assumption, seemingly commonsense, that the ownership of money could not be separated from its use. Such would be the case if money was considered through what was called its "principal use", that is, in an Aristotelian way (see *Politicorum*, I, 7 and *Summa Theologiae*, IIa–IIae, q. 78, a. 1, resp.), as being an intermediary of exchange. As such, the money lent, once it is spent, is not, physically, the same object as the money paid back, so that the ownership of the lender has to be interrupted from the beginning of the loan till the moment it is paid back. This is confirmed by the case in which money would be desired in accordance to a "secondary use", such as the purposes of ostentation. When money was transferred through an ostentatious loan, the *mutuum ad pompam*, or *ad ostentationem*, the money lent and the money paid back could remain the same physical object, so that its use could be separated from its property. The lender could then maintain ownership of the money lent and only sell the use of it – thus justifying the charging of interest. As Aquinas wrote:

> [S]ilver money could have a secondary use: for instance, if money is conceded to somebody in order to make a display of it or to pawn it. And one can licitly sell such a use of money.
> (*Summa Theologiae*, IIa–IIae, q. 78, a. 1, ad 6)

The issue of the impossibility, for some goods including money, of separating property and use, could seem perturbing to contemporary economists (Chaplygina and Lapidus, 2016a, p. 33). One reason for this is that this impossibility does not rest on analytical grounds (say, a different theory), but on an ontological claim regarding the nature of money. This ontological claim was not unanimously supported in Aquinas's time either. For instance, in 1279, shortly after Aquinas's death, Pope Nicholas III promulgated an important bull, which was to be incorporated in Canon law (*Decretales*, Liber Sextus, V, tit. 11, c. 3, *Exiit qui seminat*). The purpose of the bull was to affirm the compatibility within the Franciscan order between the principle of poverty and the consumption of worldly goods – since, as Nicholas III saw it, their use through consumption might remain separate from their ownership; in this way, you can rightly argue that the wine you drink, or the fruit you eat, although consumed and therefore used by you, are not for this very reason in your ownership. But despite its different purpose, *Exiit qui seminat* could be potentially invoked to give an ontological basis to a non-Thomistic position, thus allowing that interest be paid on a money loan. However, accepting Aquinas's ontological claim about the impossibility, when money is concerned, of separating ownership and use, left no room for a payment to the lender.

Beyond a potentially disputable commonsense observation (like in *Summa*, IIa–IIae, q. 78, a. 1, resp.), the arguments in favour of Thomas Aquinas's ontological claim are to be found either, from around the time he wrote the question on usury in the *Summa*, in his commentaries on Aristotle's *Politics* and *Ethics*; or, earlier, in his commentaries on the *Sentences*.

When commenting on Aristotle's *Politics*, he stressed the conventional (in opposition to a metalist) nature of money,[1] which "is not invented by nature, but came about as a result of a certain experience and a certain art" (*Politicorum*, I, 7). Although this has no direct impact on the way the money loan has to be understood, for Aquinas this meant that it was a product of human reason, as the most complete form of exchange (*Politicorum*, I, 7). In this respect, he pointed out two functions of money, which he had already discussed when commenting on Peter Lombard's *Sentences*, but also on the *Politics* or on the *Ethics* and, of course, in the *Summa*.

The first function of money, a medium of exchange in the Aristotelian tradition, corresponds to its principal use, discussed above:

> But money, according to the Philosopher [Aristotle] in the *Ethics* (V, 5) and in the *Politics* (I, 3), was principally invented to facilitate exchanges: and so, the proper and principal use of money is to be consumed without diversion, because it is spent in exchanges.
> (*Summa Theologica*, IIa–IIae, q. 78, a. 1, resp.; see also *Politicorum*, I, 7, 6)

And hence a usurious loan would have the effect of distorting the nature of money (*Politicorum*, I, 8).

As for the second function of money, as a unit of account, from his earliest writings Thomas Aquinas also relied on Aristotle to conclude that a money loan could not give birth to an income which was to the benefit of the lender because of the loan itself:

> All other things have from themselves some utility: however, this is not the same for money. But it is the measure of the utility of other things, as it is clear from the Philosopher in the *Ethics* (V, 9). And therefore the use of money does not hold the measure of its utility from this money itself but from the things which are measured by money according to the various people who exchange money for goods. Hence, receiving more money for less seems nothing else than differentiating the measure in giving and receiving, which obviously brings inequity.
>
> (*Sententiarum*, III, d. 37, q. 1, a. 6, resp.)

The fidelity of this interpretation can be debated. Aristotle's original position, later acknowledged by Thomas Aquinas when commenting on the *Ethics*, was that "money itself is submitted to depreciations, for it has not always the same purchasing power" (*Ethicorum*, V, 5, 14). Nonetheless, the initial emphasis laid on money as a unit of account, and therefore free from either appreciations or depreciations, meant that it could not give rise to any supplementary income.[2]

The non-commodification of the money loan

The immediate consequence of the classical argument against usury should not be overestimated. Interest-bearing loans were rather frequent in the Middle Ages and the theological and legal rules evolved step by step after Aquinas. Moreover, even in Thomas Aquinas's own writings, it was already possible to identify arguments which might exculpate the payment of a supplement to the lender. On the one hand, obviously, Aquinas provided a firm analytical basis to the prohibition of usury. This means that if usury was "rightly blamed and loathed" (*Politicorum*, I, 8), such a feeling could be related to a fault against reason: the income received by the lender could not be explained by the loan granted to the borrower. But, on the other hand, the basis for this prohibition is narrow enough to allow alternative possibilities for explaining the lender receiving an income (see Chaplygina and Lapidus, 2016a, pp. 35–39; 2016b, pp. 62–74; 2022, pp. 98–101).

And this should not be regarded as an exception to the general case, given by the classical argument, but as an effect of the construction of this argument. The paradoxical possibility of an income being received by the lender, even though the monetary loan has been constructed in a way that seems to prohibit it, stems from an acknowledged propriety of the voluntary exchange in which the monetary loan took place. As an exchange in time, it was mutually beneficial for both the lender and the borrower (see, for instance, *Summa Theologiae* IIa–IIae, q. 77, a. 1, resp.), so that the situation of none of them could be made worse. An immediate effect of the implementation of the loan was then to give rise to a surplus resulting from the exchange. And whether the loan was usurious or licit depended on the allocation of this surplus between the lender and the borrower. Given that the loan contract, by nature, forbids any interest, the key to the allocation of the surplus ought to rest on other considerations. The latter were first expressed in terms of "extrinsic titles" – extrinsic to the loan contract and covering its opportunity cost – and Aquinas made their foundation clear:

> In his contract with the borrower, the lender may, without any sin, stipulate an indemnity to be paid for the prejudice he suffers while being deprived of what was his possession; this is not to sell the use of money, but to receive a compensation.
>
> (*Summa Theologiae*, IIa–IIae, q. 78, a. 2, ad 1)

The usual extrinsic titles, such as *poena conventionalis*, *damnum emergens* or *lucrum cessans*, gave, for each of them, reasons for the allocation to the lender of part of the surplus of exchange, but this was independently from the *mutuum* itself (see, among others, McLaughlin, 1939, pp. 125–147; Noonan, 1957, pp. 105–132; Lapidus, 1991, pp. 26–27; Langholm, 1998, pp. 74–76; Ege 2014, p. 403; Monsalve, 2014, pp. 231–232; Chaplygina and Lapidus, 2016a, pp. 35–37; 2016b, pp. 62–66; Januard 2021, pp. 607–608). Aquinas clearly accepted the principle of a compensation for the harm suffered in the event of delay (*De Malo* q. 13, a. 4, ad 14), that is, the *poena conventionalis*. He also accepted the *damnum emergens*, to compensate the harm suffered by the lender, in terms of opportunities for consumption, for going without in order to make his money available for lending (*Summa Theologiae*, IIa–IIae, q. 78, a. 2, ad 1). On the contrary, in the same passage he rejected the principle of the compensation for a prejudice consisting in the sacrifice of a possibility of profit by the lender, provided by the *lucrum cessans*. On the one hand, Aquinas did admit that the borrower might use the outcome from a profitable operation to compensate the harm suffered by the lender: "the loan may spare the borrower a greater loss than the one to which the lender is exposed. It is thus with his benefit that the first makes up the loss of the second" (*ibid.*). But, on the other hand, in the following lines of the same passage he also rejected not the *principle* of the compensation for a loss of profit, but the *opportunity* for it, because the profit expected from the transaction is uncertain:

> the lender cannot enter an agreement for compensation, through the fact that he makes no profit out of his money: because he must not sell that which he has not yet and may be prevented in many ways from having.
>
> (*ibid.*)

Along with the acceptance of some close substitutes to interest-bearing money loans, provided certain conditions related to property and risk are satisfied, the recognition of extrinsic titles provided a theoretical basis for the existence of an interest paid to the lender. Obviously, its practical incidence might always be disputed. Yet the counterpart is that, leaving aside the possibility of extrinsic titles or of close substitutes, the money loan in itself, understood through Thomas Aquinas's classical argument, displays unusual properties. Considered as a good, money transferred from the borrower to the lender and the other way around, it is obviously not a gift. But, since it has no price which would be figured into the supplement paid to the lender because of the loan itself, it is not a commodity properly speaking, either. Thus, the non-commodification at work in the classical argument nonetheless preserved the exchange dimension of the money loan, and even the possibility of interest being paid to the lender.

Simony: Intermediate cases of commodification

The sale of spiritual goods and sacred powers has been continuously prohibited since the Apostles (first century A.D.). This sin is called "simony" because of Simon the Magician. In the Acts of the Apostles, he offered money to the apostles in order to receive the power to communicate the Holy Spirit by the laying on of hands, to which the apostle Peter replied: "May your money perish with you, because you thought you could buy the gift of God with money!" (Acts 8:20). The prohibition is present in Gratian's *Decree* in 1140 (*Decretum*, II, causa 1, q. 1, c. 1–29) and in the *Sentences* of Peter Lombard in 1150 (*Sententiarum*, IV, d. 25, c. 2; 3; 5; 6). Simony is understood there in its original restricted sense of selling sacred powers. Thomas Aquinas took up the prohibition, but in the broader perspective of the sale of any spiritual good. This prohibition was based on the impossibility of certain goods being the object of a price, and thus of constituting a commodity that can be sold. However, we observe a twofold movement of commodification for the same kind of goods: a lexical commodification, with an expression of the impossibility of sale formulated in the later works in terms of unattainable price levels, and not only in terms of the impossibility of price; and a partial operational commodification, where the spiritual good is the object of an exchange, with an exchange ratio and counterpart, even if this exchange is not a sale according to a price.

A strong ontological prohibition of sale at a price

As early as his youthful work the *Commentary on the Sentences* (1254–1256), Aquinas addressed simony, which he defined as an "act of the will [...] to buy or sell [...] something spiritual or associated with something spiritual" (*Sententiarum*, IV, d. 25, q. 3, a. 1, qc. 1., resp.). At first sight, Aquinas affirms the ontological impossibility of trade, whatever the conditions. It is not simply a matter of respecting the regulation of trade practice that he had established earlier, such that trade is forbidden for clerics, and during feast days, and must be practiced without fraud and according to licit contract (*Sententiarum*, IV, d. 16, q. 4, a. 2, qc. 3). In the case of simony, any price would be unjust since the good could not be the object of a price. This impossibility was founded on the good itself. Aquinas wrote:

> If it is with respect to quantity [*in quantum*], then there is injustice, as when someone does not buy or sell at a just price; but if it is with respect to the object [*in quid*], as when he sells or buys what is not the object of a price, then it is the sin of the simoniac.
>
> (*Sententiarum*, IV, d. 25, q. 3, a. 1, qc. 1, resp.)

It was the very nature of the good that required its non-commodification, not the sellers' or the buyers' willingness to place themselves within the framework of the gift or the social context of the exchange, or the impact of the trade of the good on society. The expression "*in quid*", literally "according to what it is", expresses Aquinas's ontological approach: the possible seller or buyer is facing something which could not be viewed without reservation as a commodity with a price. A sacrament was a "cause of grace" of God (*Sententiarum*, IV, d. 25, q. 3, a. 1, qc. 1, ad 3), which, as such, by its very nature could not be viewed as having a price. Like in the case of a money loan, the qualities of the good exchanged pre-existed the exchange and were given to both the seller and the buyer.

Despite the strong affirmation of non-commodification, established not on the basis of a social judgement about the quality of the good which could be subject to change, but rather on an approach inherited from Aristotle concerned with the very being of the thing, its *quid*, a process of dual commodification can be observed in Aquinas's thought, one lexical, the other effective or operational.

A lexical commodification

Lexical commodification takes place in two stages. The first one seems paradoxical: whereas the good could not be priced, it was the notion of just price that ensured the full justice of a possible exchange of the spiritual good. Indeed, for other goods, the quantitative justice ensured by the just price had to be accompanied by a qualitative justice presented in the general framework of trade: conditions on the person and the date, the absence of fraud and the respect of the contract (*Sententiarum*, IV, d. 16, q. 4, a. 2, qc. 3). But in the case of simony, the conditions for qualitative justice focused on another element: the impossibility of a sacrament having a price. Thus, the entirety of justice, for all goods, including sacraments, concerning both its qualitative and quantitative aspects, is ensured solely by the price. Indeed, for sacraments, the quantitative aspect is ensured by its level (justice *in quantum*) and the qualitative by its impossibility (justice *in quid*). In practice, impossibility seems to render meaningless the question of the level, but it is important to keep these two aspects in the justice theoretical framework, because Aquinas went from one aspect to another. In early works, he justified the fact that the transaction was not made according to a price by considering that the sacrament has no price (impossibility). In mature works, he kept this, but he added another way of explanation: sacrament has a price, but this price is unattainable (level). There is no other criterion in Aquinas's treatment of the justice of spiritual exchange. In the *Commentary on the Sentences*, since the qualitative criterion requires that there is no price, the quantitative criterion is practically irrelevant (*Sententiarum*, IV, d. 25, q. 3, a. 1, qc. 1, resp.). So, justice is ensured by price as an effective qualitative criterion and a theoretical quantitative criterion. This is not the case at the second stage of the lexical commodification, in which there is a shift from the impossibility of a price to a specification of its level, i.e., from the qualitative to the quantitative criterion of justice. Justice is still ensured by the price, but price acts here as a quantitative criterion and remains implicitly as a qualitative criterion (theoretical possibility of a price).

The second stage of the lexical commodification is addressed by Aquinas years later, in the *Summa Theologiae* (around 1272). The separation between what is trade-related and what is not, still expressed *by nature* in the *Commentary on the Sentences* since the qualitative and quantitative criteria of justice are complementary and not substitutable, is now expressed in terms of *degree*. The non-possibility of the price was thus transformed into such a high price that it was out of reach. While Aquinas repeated that a spiritual good could not be estimated at a monetary price and motivated his prohibition of its sale by the description he gave of this good, two developments should be noted. On the one hand, the notion of justice with respect to the object (*in quid*), which was the major contribution concerning simony in the *Commentary on the Sentences* (*Sententiarum*, IV, d. 25, q. 3, a. 1, qc. 1), no longer appeared explicitly in the *Summa Theologiae* (IIa–IIae, q. 100). On the other hand, the twenty-two occurrences of the term "price" in *Summa Theologiae*, IIa–IIae, q. 100 took on a strong comparative tone:

> A spiritual thing cannot be compensated for by an earthly price [...] it is more precious than all riches [*cunctis opibus*].
>
> (*Summa Theologiae*, IIa–IIae, q. 100, a. 1, resp.)

or also

> the Gospel cannot be sold [...]. That would be selling a great thing for a very low price.
>
> (*Summa Theologiae*, IIa–IIae, q. 100, a. 3, ad 2)

If the sacrament has no price, this is because any earthly price would be lower than what it is truly worth. The just price is possible, but it is never attained, since it would implement commutative justice, ensuring an equality between things exchanged, as Aquinas explained in the *Summa Theologiae* (IIa–IIae, q. 77, a. 1, ad 3), and no amount of any material good can be made to be equal with a spiritual good. The just price that would enable the four functions highlighted by Hamouda and Price (1997, 200) (compensating for a loss, satisfying a need, providing a fair valuation and reducing abuses in exchange) is therefore inaccessible. Aquinas's formulation was even more explicit in the case of another non-tradable good, that of a free person: "The person of a free man surpasses all pecuniary estimation" (*Summa Theologiae*, IIa–IIae, q. 189, a. 6, ad 3). The non-commodification of the free man was no longer expressed by a qualitative non-substitutable criterion but by a price level, here again beyond reach.

Lexical commodification does not mean that the prohibition of the effective sale of spiritual goods might be in any way lightened, but it does mean that these goods were indeed thought of as commodities, albeit inaccessible since no price on earth could be high enough.

A partial operational commodification

In addition to a *lexical* commodification, which concerns all forms of spiritual goods, it is also possible to observe an *operational* commodification, in the sense that it is effectively implemented in transactions related to certain spiritual goods. The latter can be identified through a typology of simony, first contrasting *proprietary* simony (the trafficking in land, offices, relics and consecrated vessels), which is strictly forbidden, and *professional* simony (the payment for a cleric's professional service; see Ekelund, Hébert et al., 1996, p. 32). Proprietary simony is a personal enrichment through the sale of that which did not really belong to the seller and which came from God or was consecrated to God, whereas professional simony consists in charging for a legitimate professional service that should be free because it confers spiritual goods. Under the heading of professional simony, two situations can be distinguished, as the Fourth Lateran Council did in 1215. The purchase of sacred powers (consecration of bishops, blessing of abbots, ordination of priests) was harshly condemned (Fourth Lateran Council, *De simonia*, c. 63) because it was a matter of corruption, in the moral sense that still arises today in cases of bribing someone who works for an institution in order to obtain personal advantages. But another situation was regarded more positively: although the Council imposed limits on the amount of fees that could be charged and, furthermore, forbade priests to refuse services pending payment, clerics' remuneration for services was subject to progressive tacit approval and regulation, rather than condemnation (Fourth Lateran Council, *De idoneitate instituendorum in ecclesiis*, c. 30 and *Ut patroni compententem portionem dimittant clericis*, c. 32). And in return for such remuneration, priests were to render the required services and seek legal recourse in case of non-payment.

Commodification appeared with the payment of a sum in exchange for a service, but Aquinas distinguished between what would be "the price of a wage [*pretium mercedis*]", which is forbidden, and the legitimate "stipend of necessity [*stipendium necessitatis*]" (*Summa Theologiae*, IIa–IIae q. 100, a. 2, resp.) for the needs of the clergy. The priest

> may receive money [...] not as the price of the Mass, but as a means of subsistence [*quasi sustentamentum vitae*].
>
> (*Sententiarum*, IV, d. 25, q. 3, a. 2, qc. 1, ad 4; see also *Summa Theologiae*, IIa–IIae, q. 100, a. 2, ad 2)

At this stage, there is an exchange ratio and a counterpart. This is no longer a purely *lexical commodification*; indeed, the sacrament is now *effectively* exchanged. However, the exchange ratio is not a price (i.e., an exchange ratio that is only a ratio between values, without interference from other elements, and mainly (*principaliter*) a ratio of equal things (*aequalitas rei*), translated in terms of value, see *Summa Theologiae*, IIa–IIae q. 77, a. 1, ad 3). Here there is no equality between the sacrament and the amount of money given, and moreover the ratio is not a ratio between values: it is more a subsistence allowance which can be assimilated to a 'tariff', ensuring the financing of the good or service internal to the exchange (Steiner and Trespeuch, 2015).

It must be noted that Aquinas distinguishes the value of the professional service of transmission from the value of the content of the transmission, the infinite value of the grace of God. This distinction allows him to formally preserve the gratuity of the sacrament while introducing a counterpart on the service that consists in providing it: the sacrament "is repugnant to the fact that it is not given gratuitously" (*Summa Theologiae*, IIa–IIae q. 100, a. 2, resp.). In a way, God gives his grace, but the priest "sells" his service. However, the good and the service that consists in providing this good are not independent, for two reasons: on the one hand, there is a merging of values, the celebration of the sacrament (service) having a very high value coming from the sacrament itself (good); on the other hand, the nature of the good requires that the service of providing it is not remunerated according to its value but according to a subsistence allowance. In spite of the formal distinction made by Aquinas, we can therefore see the whole operation as a single economic transaction in which a good (the sacrament) is provided according to an exchange ratio that is not a price but a tariff in exchange for a counterpart which is a subsistence allowance. Thus, we can see this whole operation described by Aquinas as a partial operational commodification.

The equality of thing to thing, translated in terms of values, testifying that the price was just, was then out of scope for the two parties and so impossible to achieve. If it were a price, this price would never be just. However, clerical services are subject to an exchange involving an exchange ratio. They were not thought within the framework of a gift, but within an exchange framework where a counterpart was given. This partial commodification was not contradictory to the original prohibition of simony – the selling of a spiritual good, which could not be priced. The issue has moved from a question of a sale according to a price toward an exchange according to an offering. The plurality of ways to conceive exchange allowed Aquinas to conceive of certain goods as exchangeable, even though they could not be the object of a price and remained what we would continue to see as contested commodities.

Concluding remarks

This investigation shows that, at least in the mind of a major author of the Middle Ages, certain goods could not have been fully commodified, even though they were not gifts: a money loan was absolutely non-commodified, whereas a sacrament could be viewed successively as lexically commodified and partially commodified. In a way, this shows that a commodification grid might be helpful in order to account for such unfamiliar ways of dealing with what could still be seen today as contested commodities. But it also opens the path for two kinds of reflections on how to discuss commodification issues – let's say, two lessons that we can draw from Thomas Aquinas.

The first lesson is that if moral considerations do interfere with commodification, it is not necessarily by making the goods concerned non-exchangeable, so that they could be transferred only as gifts. The reason for this is that in Aquinas's moral philosophy, both gift and exchange are regulated by a moral virtue: charity in the first case, justice in the second. Transactions regarding both money loans and sacraments are submitted to considerations of justice, understood primarily not as a category from civil law but as a moral virtue. The consequence of this submission is that although for ontological, moral and legal reasons, neither the money lent nor the sacraments really have a price, they can yet be exchanged.

The second lesson follows from the first. It is that what we can learn from the simple recognition that a good is not fully commodified (i.e., is not traded with a price) is further supplemented by information about how such non-full-commodification occurs: in the case of a money loan, this concerns the external considerations which allow an independent reward for the lender, whereas the loan, as such, cannot give birth to interest; or, in the case of simony, it concerns the unattainability of a nevertheless existent price, or the absence of such a price even though a subsistence allowance is given to clerics in exchange for their services. We have seen that the money loan and the sacraments occupy intermediary positions between a gift and a commodity: they manifest different ways of not being a commodity (nor a gift). This suggests a porosity between what is commodified and what is not, so that instead of a hermetic border between them, we are faced with a diversity of cases, all of which fall within the scope of an assessment of commutative justice – that is, all belong in the realm of exchange.

Notes

1 The idea of an opposition between a "conventional" and a "metalist" approach to money is rooted in Aristotle's works on political and moral issues (see Lapidus, 1997, pp. 25–27). Insofar as Thomas Aquinas is concerned, the conventional approach was introduced in *Politicorum* (I, 7), where he explained, in his view after Aristotle, that the convention determining the value of money can be subject to discretionary change, to such an extent that a change in this convention among people (*transmutata dispositione hominum*) might lead to a zero value of money, if such was the intention of the king or of the community. This falls within a long-lasting tradition regarding the interpretation of Latin Aristotelianism, insofar as monetary matters were concerned. This tradition started with Emile Bridrey's book (1906), which came some decades after the rediscovery by Wilhelm Roscher of Nicole Oresme's fourteenth century treatise on money, where he tried to grasp what was specific to Oresme's account by contrasting a "sign theory" and a "commodity theory" of money (Bridrey 1906). The principle of a dual, but different, reading was supported later by Barry Gordon (1961) who rooted a "non-metalist" view in Aristotle's *Ethics* (and Plato's *Laws*) and a "metalist" view in Aristotle's *Politics*. A similar conception can be found more recently in Castiglione (2005) and Menuet (2018) who, though dealing with eighteenth-century monetary analysis, also stressed the difference between the positions expressed in the *Ethics* and in the *Politics*.

2 It could be argued that the *Politics*, unlike the *Ethics*, allowed Thomas Aquinas to introduce the store of value function of money. Such introduction is of special interest since it might be viewed as a first step in the transition between the two positions pointed out by Odd Langholm in his seminal book (1983, chap. 3): the first one in which money is conceived so as to prevent it from being stored for commercial purposes; the second, in which it allows the financing of economic activities – which we know, however, is not one of the points Aquinas most emphasized (Januard, 2022, pp. 31–44). But interestingly, the introduction of the store of value function of money influences the ontological argument neither through the nature of the approach to money, whether conventional or metalist, nor through the link between the property and the use of money. (i) The emphasis laid on the metal of which money is made does not mean that a metalist viewpoint is adopted; the latter would result from the existence of a determining link between the value of the metal and that of the coins which are made from it; now, despite some qualifications stemming from *Ethicorum* noted above, such a possibility is clearly dismissed, since Aquinas favoured the determining part played by men and reason. (ii) The seemingly intuitive idea that, unlike through the intermediate of exchanges function, property and use should be linked through the store of value function of money, is far from evident, and should be restricted to cases, illustrated by the example of the *mutuum ad ostentiationem* given above, in which money is considered through its secondary (and not main) use, so that it remains physically in the hands of the lender.

References

Bertrand Élodie and Catto Marie-Xavière. 2020. Introduction, in E. Bertrand and M.-X. Catto (eds), *Les Limites du Marché – The Limits of the Market*, Paris: Mare et Martin, pp. 13–18.

Bridrey Emile. 1906. *La Théorie de la Monnaie au XIVe siècle: Nicole Oresme*, Paris: Giard et Brière, (reprint Genova: Slatkine, 1978).

Castiglione Dario. 2005. Blood and Oil: Eighteenth-Century Monetary Anxieties, *Historical Reflections / Réflexions Historiques*, 31(1), [Money in the Enlightenment], pp. 27–48.

Chaplygina Irina and Lapidus André. 2016a. Economic Thought in Scholasticism, in G. Faccarello and H. Kurz (eds), *Handbook on the History of Economic Analysis*, Cheltenham (UK) / Northampton (USA): Edward Elgar, vol. 2, pp. 20–42.

Chaplygina Irina and Lapidus André. 2016b. Economic Thought in Medieval Europe [in Russian]. In A. Khudokormov and A. Lapidus (eds), *Economic Theory from an Historical Viewpoint* [in Russian], Moscow: Infra-M, pp. 32–86.6.

Chaplygina Irina and Lapidus André. 2022. Theorising Interest, How Did It All Begin?, in I. Amelung, B. Schefold (eds), *European and Chinese Histories of Economic Thought. Theories and Images of Good Governance*, Cheltenham (UK) / Northampton (USA): Routledge, pp. 93–105.

Decretales, in *Corpus Juris Canonici*, vol. 2, Leipzig: B. Tauchnitz, 1871–80.

Decretum, in *Corpus Juris Canonici*, vol. 1, Leipzig: B. Tauchnitz, 1871–80.

Digesta, in *Corpus Juris Civilis*, vol. 1, Dublin and Zurich, Weidmann, 1968.

Ege Ragip. 2014. La Question de l'Interdiction de l'Intérêt dans l'Histoire Européenne: Un Essai d'Analyse Institutionnelle, *Revue Economique*, 65(2), pp. 391–417.

Ekelund Robert B., Hébert Robert F. *et al.* 1996. *Sacred Trust: The Medieval Church as an Economic Firm*. New York/Oxford: Oxford University Press.

[Fourth Lateran Council in] *Conciliorum Oecumenicorum Decreta*. Fribourg: Herder, 1962.

Gordon Barry. 1961. Aristotle, Schumpeter, and the Metalist Tradition, *Quarterly Journal of Economics*, 75(4), pp. 608–614.

Hamouda Omar and Price Betsey. 1997. The Justice of the Just Price. *European Journal of the History of Economic Thought* 4 (2), pp. 191–216.

Januard Pierre. 2021. Analysis Risk and Commercial Risk: The First Treatment of Usury in Thomas Aquinas's *Commentary on the* Sentences, *European Journal of the History of Economic Thought*, 28(4), pp. 599–634.

Januard Pierre. 2022. *At the Risk of Exchange: Economic Activity in Thomas Aquinas's Early Works / Au Risque de l'Echange: L'Activité Economique dans les Œuvres de Jeunesse de Thomas d'Aquin*, PhD Dissertation, Paris: Phare, University Paris 1 Panthéon-Sorbonne.

Langholm Odd. 1983. *Wealth and Money in the Aristotelian Tradition: A Study in Scholastic Economic Sources*, Bergen: Universitetsforlaget.

Langholm Odd. 1998. *The Legacy of Scholasticism in Economic Thought*, Cambridge: Cambridge University Press.

Lapidus André. 1991. Information and Risk in the Medieval Doctrine of Usury during the Thirteenth Century, in W. Barber (ed.), *Perspectives in the History of Economic Thought*, vol. 5, Aldershot, UK and Brookfield, VT, USA: Edward Elgar, pp. 23–38.

Lapidus André. 1997. Metal, Money and the Prince: John Buridan and Nicholas Oresme after Thomas Aquinas, *History of Political Economy*, 29(1), pp. 21–53.

McLaughlin Terence P. 1939. The Teaching of the Canonists on Usury (1), *Mediaeval Studies*, 1, pp. 81–147.

Menuet Maxime. 2018. Les Nouvelles Ecclésiastiques (1728–1750) Face à leurs Opposants: Quelques Polémiques Autour du Prêt à Intérêt, *Œconomia*, 8(1), pp. 29–44.

Monsalve Fabio. 2014. Late Spanish Doctors on Usury, and the Evolving Scholastic Tradition, *Journal of the History of Economic Thought*, 36 (2), pp. 215–235.

Noonan John T. Jr. 1957. *The Scholastic Analysis of Usury*, Cambridge, MA: Harvard University Press.

Peter Lombard. *Libri IV Sententiarum*, t. 1 et 2. Claras Aquas: Typis Collegii S. Bonaventurae, Quaracchi, 1916.

Radin Margaret J. 1987. Market-Inalienability, *Harvard Law Review*, 100(8), pp. 1849–1937.

Robert of Courçon, *De Usura*, in G. Lefevre (ed), *Le Traité 'De Usura' de Robert de Courçon*, Travaux et Mémoires de l'Université de Lille, vol. 10, m. 30, Lille: University of Lille, 1902.

Steiner Philippe. 2015. Organisational Gifts, Gifts and Market exchange, in P. Aspers and N. Dodd (eds), *Re-Imagining Economic Sociology*, Oxford: Oxford University Press, pp. 275–298.

Steiner Philippe and Trespeuch Marie. 2015. Introduction, in P. Steiner and M. Trespeuch (eds), *Marchés contestés. Quand le marché rencontre la morale*, Toulouse: Presses Universitaires du Midi, pp. 7–27.

Thomas Aquinas. *Scriptum super Sententiis,* 4 t. Paris: P. Lethielleux, 1929–1947.

Thomas Aquinas. *Quaestiones disputatae De Malo*, edited by Commissio Leonina, n°22, Rome: Editori di San Tommaso, 1976.

Thomas Aquinas. *Sententia libri Ethicorum*, edited by Commissio Leonina, n°47, Rome: Commissio Leonina, 1969.

Thomas Aquinas. *Sententia libri Politicorum*, edited by Commisssio Leonina, n°48, Rome: Commissio Leonina, 1971.
Thomas Aquinas. *Summa Theologiae,* IIa-IIae, qq. 52–122, edited by Commissio Leonina, n°9. Rome: Typographia polyglotta S. C. de Propaganda Fide, 1897.
Thomas Aquinas. *Summa Theologiae,* IIa-IIae, qq. 123–189, edited by Commissio Leonina, n°10. Rome: Typographia polyglotta S. C. de Propaganda Fide, 1899.

8

LABOUR

From disguised servitude to limited servitude—A history of the social incorporation of the commodification of work

François Vatin

Introduction

This chapter aims to show how labour came to be an "acceptable" commodity through the institutionalization of salaried employment. For the liberal thinkers of the first half of the nineteenth century, the dependent nature of salaried labour rendered it unacceptable. In France, the legal framework resulting from the Napoleonic Civil Code indeed denied the very existence of wage dependence; and Kantian ethics, which forbids the reduction of subject to object, was called upon in support of the critique of the commodification of labour. This liberal denunciation of salaried work was inherited by Marx, who, by making the alienation of the worker a characteristic feature of the capitalist social order, was able, in contrast to the liberal economists, to create a conceptual framework in which to think about salaried employment; he stressed, however, that the form of subordination that is found in the context of wage employment does not assume the personal character that it has in slavery or serfdom. Certain "bourgeois" economists, such as Tocqueville and Courcelle-Seneuil, also reacted against the liberal *doxa*: in the spirit of institutionalism, they considered that wage dependence should rather be accepted as a positive social fact. For them, the challenge was to conceive a form of subordination that was limited in time as well as to the place of work, such as would finally be established in law at the beginning of the twentieth century.

I begin by examining the critique of the commodity theory of labour developed in 1840 by the little-known French economist Eugène Buret, and the reading of this author by the young Karl Marx. In the second part, I return to the Kantian sources to which this author appeals, and show that Kant admits the reduction of subject to object within the framework of an institution, be this marriage for sexual relations or patriarchy for labour relationships. Thirdly, I trace the institutionalization of the salary relationship as it developed in the case of France. This development rests on the invention of the notion of the "contract of employment", a notion that is distinct from the civil law contract in that it is based on "legal subordination", understood as something that must be impersonal and limited.

 DOI: 10.4324/9781003188742-11

The denunciation of the commodity theory of labour: Buret, Marx, and Polanyi

In 1840 the young French journalist Eugène Buret (1810–1842) wrote as follows about the economic theory proposed by Ricardo:

> The worker finds himself reduced by this doctrine to a thing insensible, to a machine from which we have the right to demand ever more precision, more labour and more productivity. The working population, selling its labour, is inevitably reduced to the weakest part of the product; we might almost say that it is declared to be exploitable at will, as was the enslaved and indentured class in feudal society. Is the commodity theory of labour anything other than a theory of servitude in disguise?
>
> (Buret, 1840, vol. 1, p. 43)

In the work cited, which was awarded a prize by the Academy of Moral and Political Sciences,[1] Buret develops a critique of the commodity theory of labour which foreshadows that formulated by Karl Polanyi a century later in *The Great Transformation* ([1944] 2001). Like Polanyi, Buret considered that labour could not be a commodity, because it cannot be separated from the person of the worker, or indeed from his own life:

> Work, in the case where the worker possesses no form of capital, such as day-labourers and factory workers, does not have the economic characteristics of a product; the wage does not have the character of a market; for the worker is in no way in the position of a free seller vis-à-vis the person who employs him. One might say that the Capitalist is always free to employ labour, and that the worker is always forced to sell it. The value of work is completely destroyed, if it is not sold at every moment. Labour, unlike a true commodity, has no capacity for accumulation, nor even of saving. Work is life, and if life is not exchanged daily for food, it soon suffers and perishes. If the life of man is to be a commodity, it is thus necessary to accept slavery.
>
> (Buret, 1840, vol. 1, pp. 49–50)

A Germanophile, Eugène Buret's source is probably the philosophy of law developed by Immanuel Kant, who wrote in his 1796 *Metaphysics of Morals*:

> It now seems, it is true, that one may bind himself to certain, according to the quality allowed, but according to the degree *undetermined*, services to another (for either hire, food, or protection), by a contract of *location conductio*, and thereby becomes a subject merely, but not a slave; however that is but a delusion. For, when his master is entitled to use at pleasure the powers and faculties of his subject, he may also exhaust them so as to occasion despair, or (as is the case with the negroes in the sugar-islands) even death, and the subject has actually given himself away to his master as a property; which is impossible.
>
> (Kant, [1796] 1799, vol. 1, p. 101)

Three years later, Karl Marx, then a young German journalist in exile in Paris, read Buret's work and noted down extensive passages in his notebooks, including those I have just quoted (Marx, [1844] 1959). While one could read Buret as a precursor of Marx, this would be only partially correct, for Buret was writing in direct contradiction to Ricardo, whose theory he considered "immoral". In contrast, Marx, who discovered Ricardo via Buret,[2] appreciated the "cynicism" of the British economist, who, according to him, spoke the truth about capitalist society:

> Thus M. Michel Chevalier[[3]] reproaches Ricardo with having ignored ethics. But Ricardo is allowing political economy to speak its own language, and if it does not speak ethically, this is not Ricardo's fault. M. Chevalier abstracts from political economy insofar as he moralizes, but he really and necessarily ignores ethics insofar as he practices political economy.
>
> (Marx, [1844] 1959, p. 52)

Two years later, Marx would affirm this position in his critique of Proudhon and, more generally, of the "humanitarian" spirit of French political economy of the time, which Buret embodied better than anyone:

> Doubtless, Ricardo's language is as cynical as can be. To put the cost of manufacture of hats and the cost of maintenance of men on the same plane is to turn men into hats. But do not make an outcry at the cynicism of it. The cynicism is in the facts and not in the words which express the facts. French writers like M.M. Droz, Blanqui, Rossi and others take an innocent satisfaction in proving their superiority over the English economists, by seeking to observe the etiquette of a "humanitarian" phraseology; if they reproach Ricardo and his school for their cynical language, it is because it annoys them to see economic relations exposed in all their crudity, to see the mysteries of the bourgeoisie unmasked.
>
> (Marx, [1847] 1955, p. 20)

Marx's engagement with Buret's legacy was not yet finished. For how, indeed, can one agree with Ricardo that labour is to be considered an ordinary commodity and still conclude with Buret that the worker is alienated and exploited in a market society? It took Marx more than twenty years to solve this problem, and so to start writing *Capital*.[4] We know his solution: labour is not a commodity; the commodity sold under the name of labour is "labour-power", that is to say, the capacity for labour. The capitalist, by buying labour-power, becomes the owner of the work done. The worker is "alienated", since he has sold himself; the worker is also "exploited", because the value of his labour-power is less than the value it can produce; and the surplus value, the motor of capitalist development, results from this difference.

By means of this skilful yet fragile theoretical construction, Marx tries to hold together Buret and Ricardo. It was precisely for this that Polanyi reproached him:

> From this time onward [the 19th century] naturalism haunted the science of man, and the reintegration of society into the human world became the persistently sought aim of social thought. Marxian economics—in this line of argument—was an essentially unsuccessful attempt to achieve that aim, a failure due to Marx's too close adherence to Ricardo and the traditions of liberal economics.
>
> (Polanyi, [1944] 2001, p. 131)

For Polanyi, the distinction between "labour" and "labour-power" is a useless rhetorical device. Dismissing this subtle distinction out of hand, he thus returns to Buret's point of view: work is only a "fictitious" commodity, much the same as land and money. It was upon these "fictions", and to the detriment of society, that capitalism was constructed (see Chapter 2 by Postel and Sobel in this volume).

And thus, paradoxically, the denunciation of commodified labour transpires to be less "socialist" than "liberal", following in the wake of the denunciation of slavery that exercised liberal thinkers throughout the eighteenth century. The liberal ideal, embodied in the doctrine of Adam Smith, is that of a society of small producers, where the labour market is not distinct from the market for produce. Pierre-Joseph Proudhon is the clearest advocate of such a doctrine: whereas Marx sought to show that capitalist exploitation rests on the institution of the market, which is expressed through the law of labour-value, Proudhon on the contrary considers that it is the non-respect of this law which causes inequity in capitalist society. His project for a labour bank aimed precisely at ensuring the equity of exchange between workers, which would, according to him, cause the disappearance of the capitalist system of rents. The problem for Proudhon's theory is therefore the wage system, that is to say the institutionalization of a market for labour that cannot be reduced to the market for products. This objection, on contrary, is at the heart of Marx's thinking. The liberal ideal which Proudhon did not renounce comes up against the development of large-scale industry, which is inseparable from wage labour.[5] It is at this point that we must return to Kant.

The ambivalence of the Kantian critique of wage subordination

The categorical Kantian prohibition against treating the other as an object has been debated in relation to prostitution, a contractual exchange in which the body itself becomes a commodity.[6] But every labour contract might in this sense be considered prostitution, since the worker puts his bodily power at the disposal of the employer, which amounts, according to Marx's famous formula, to bringing one's "own hide" to the market (Marx, [1867] 1976, p. 280);[7] and the Kantian argument was thus appropriated by some late nineteenth-century Marxists, such as Mikhail Tugan-Baranowsky (1865–1919) (Nenowsky, 2009). Kant might perhaps therefore have rejected the wage contract, which may be assimilated to prostitution, as Raymond Boudon wrote (1999, p. 69).

The question nevertheless becomes more complicated if we dwell on the details of Kant's doctrine. Boudon refers to the 1785 *Groundwork of the Metaphysics of Morals*; yet this text, however, contains nothing on this subject. One must refer to *The Metaphysics of Morals*, cited above, and more precisely to its first part, the Metaphysical Elements of the Doctrine of Law, to find an inquiry, on the one hand, about prostitution and concubinage as opposed to marriage and the family, and, on the other hand, about the multiple forms of subjection of labour (slavery, serfdom, farming, wage-earning). One finds here no explicit comparison between salaried labour and prostitution, but rather a discussion of the moral acceptability of the labour contract:

> He [the worker] therefore cannot hire himself but to work determined according to the quality and to the degree; either as a daylabourer, or a settled subject; in the latter case, that he, partly for the use of his master's land, which serves him, in lieu of wages, performs services upon the same land, partly for the proper enjoyment to the profits of it to pay determinate taxes (a rent) according to a lease, without thereby becoming a *bondman annected to the estate* (*glebae adscriptus*), whereby he would lose his personality, consequently may found a temporary or an hereditary farm.
>
> (Kant, [1796] 1799, vol. 1, pp. 101–102, italics in original)

The essential term in the first line, which I underline, is "determined". What Kant denounces in the exchange of labour is not that a man may, in general terms, put his strengths and talents at the service of another in return for payment, but rather that the object of the commitment can be indeterminate, which leads to a scenario of personal dependence (a stripping of individuality). Yet this is indeed what Marx also condemns as regards the market for "labour-power", which is a fundamentally indeterminate commodity. In salaried labour, in its pure form, the worker undertakes to place himself at the disposal of his employer without the terms of this commitment being precisely fixed.

What, however, does this have to do with prostitution? Kant mentions this theme only in an earlier paragraph on "conjugal law". For him, sexual possession is to a certain degree comparable to commercial possession, but the institution of marriage gives it a particular legal content:

> The natural commerce with the sex is either that according to the mere animal *nature* (*vaga libido, venus vulgivaga, fornicatio*), or according to the *law*.—The latter is *marriage* (*matrimonium*), *id est*, the conjunction of two persons of different sexes to a reciprocal possession of their properties of sex during life.
>
> (Kant, [1796] 1799, vol. 1, p. 38)[8]

It is then that Kant incidentally evokes prostitution, on the occasion of a condemnation of the contract of concubinage:

> That concubinage is as little susceptible of a stable contract, as the hiring of a person for a single enjoyment (*pactum fornicationis*), is a consequence of the foregoing grounds. For, as to the latter contract, every body will allow that the person, who has concluded it, cannot be convened to fulfil his promise, if he should repent of it; and thus drops the former likewise, namely, that of concubinage (as a *pactum turpe*), since it would be a contract of *hiring* (*locatio–conductio*), and indeed of hiring a member for the use of another, consequently, on account of the inseparable unity of the members of the person, this would be yielding one's self up as a thing to the arbitrement of another [...].
>
> (*Ibid.*, p. 40, italics in original)

In other words, paradoxically, what makes reciprocal possession permissible within marriage is its enduring, institutional character.[9] What Kant considers as prostitution is a contract of hire for persons or parts of persons in the absence of an institutional framework. Yet, to the contrary, he recognizes the legitimacy of the reciprocal possession of spouses in marriage, as well as the joint possession of children by the partners, and he also broadens this patriarchal conception to include servants: "The servants belong to the property of the master of the house, and indeed as to the form (*the state of possession*), as if according to a real right" (*ibid.*, p. 46); yet, he clarifies, "they are brought into his power but by contract". Kant thus comes to a conclusion that might be considered tenuous in light of the considerations concerning the labour market cited above:

> This contract, then, of the master and mistress of a house with the domestics, cannot be of such a quality, that the *use* made of them would be a *misuse*, the judgment whereof, however, belongs not only to the master of family, but to the servants too (which therefore can never be slavery) [...] .
>
> (Ibid.)

An equivalent restriction could be applied to any contract of employment, which would thence be legitimate as long as there is no abuse. What, then, for Kant, differentiates the conditions of domesticity from the conditions of ordinary waged labour? He returns to this problem in an appendix to a second edition of *The Metaphysics of Morals* in 1798, where he specifies what he calls the "personal right of a real kind", namely "the right which a man has to have another *person* than himself as *his*" (Kant, [1798] 1887, p. 237, italics in original). This is not, he writes, a case of property,

> for a man cannot even be the owner of himself, and much less of another person. It means only the right of Usufruct (*jus ustendi fruendi*) in immediate reference to this person, as if he were a thing, but without infringing on the right of his personality, even while using him as a means for my own ends.
>
> (*ibid.*, pp. 238–239)

For such an arrangement to be legitimate, it must be "morally necessary". This is the case with carnal relations in marriage, but also with the employment of domestic servants:

> In like manner, a relation of master and servant may be formed *outside of the family*, in accordance with a personal right of a real kind on the part of the master; and the domestics are acquired to the household by contract (*famulatus domesticus*). Such a contract is not a mere letting and hiring of work (*locatio conductio operae*); but it further includes the giving of the person of the domestic into the possession of the master, as a letting and hiring of the person (*locatio conductio personae*). The latter relation is distinguished from the former in that the domestic enters the contract on the understanding that he will be available for everything that is allowable in respect of the well-being of the household, and is not merely engaged for a certain assigned and specified piece of work.
>
> (Kant, [1798] 1887, p. 240, italics in original)

One might be surprised to find such casuistry in Kant, who seems to adapt his doctrine to the social realities of his time. We do not expect him to be so "counter-revolutionary". Yet by now the year 1793 had come and gone. Kant now admits the authority of the sovereign, rejects the right of sedition or rebellion of the people, and regards with horror the execution of Charles I and Louis XVI (Kant, [1796] 1799, pp. 86–91). He accepts the authority of the man over the woman, of the parents over their children, and, as an extension of the patriarchal schema, of the master over his servants (Kant [1796] 1799, pp. 45–47). Moreover, he grants no transcendence to human beings in their biological nature: he accepts the death penalty, and even, apparently, a form of slavery.[10] Furthermore, he rejects the legal personality of children born out of wedlock and thus outside civil law:[11]

> A bastard is born without the law, therefore without its protection. It is, so speak, slipped into the commonwealth, (like contraband goods), so that it may ignore its existence (since it should not have existed reasonably in this manner), consequently its destruction too [...].
>
> (Kant, [1796] 1799, p. 109)

What makes domesticity legitimate in Kant's eyes is therefore the special character of the contract, which is not reduced to "a mere market". In a decidedly "reactionary" spirit, he sees it as an "institution", an extension of the family, which is itself conceived in a patriarchal register. Reciprocally, one can conclude that it is this institutional character that is missing from the ordinary wage relationship, as it was originally considered. In other words, as Raymond Boudon writes, Kant could have accepted the wage relationship as it later developed: "If Kant had been able to imagine the evolution of labour relations, he would certainly not have proposed considering the wage relationship as a form of prostitution" (Boudon, 1999, p. 69).[12] It is this process of wage institutionalization, which is both ideological and material, and which is written into legal procedure and organizational practices, that I will now briefly describe, focusing on the case of France.

The genesis of salaried employment: Limited servitude

The term "salary" is ancient, deriving from the Latin *salarium*, the "salt ration" which designated the pay of soldiers in the Roman Empire. The first edition of the *Dictionnaire de l'Académie Française* (1694) gives this term the general meaning of "reward, payment for work, or for service". The term "salariat" is recent, introduced as a neologism in 1869 by Emile Littré in his *Dictionnaire* in the sense of "condition of a salaried person". The Académie Française defines it in the eighth edition of its *Dictionnaire* (1932–1935) as "an economic system in which the work of a factory worker is remunerated by a wage". In the same text, wages are always defined as "remuneration for work". This lexicographical tautology is symptomatic of a double problem: how can the salariat be a particular economic regime, if the salary is simply the remuneration for work? Why, moreover, should the term "salariat" apply only to the work of the "factory worker"?

At the origin of this question is an opposition, originating in Roman law and which remained relevant throughout the nineteenth century, between the "mechanical arts" and the "liberal arts" (from which derives our "liberal professions"). For the Romans, the former were characterized by the use of an instrument, unlike the latter which involved only the body. Only dance, theatre, oratory, or singing (but not instrumental music), are deemed worthy of a free man. For the jurists of the old regime and, for the most part, of the nineteenth century, the salary constitutes a remuneration only for the mechanical arts. In 1840 Raymond-Théodore Troplong asserted a radical distinction between the wages of labourers and the remuneration of physicians or lawyers (Troplong, 1840, § 787–811). The award of a wage to a worker leaves the parties equal, according to the principles of commutative justice (*do ut des*). In contrast, the fees offered to a doctor or lawyer cannot discharge the debt incurred in respect of their services. The distinction between wages and fees has not disappeared, but it is based no longer on the degree of honour associated with the task performed, rather on the nature of the legal relationship associated with the remuneration.

For this transmutation to have taken place, the notion of salary had had to shed its negative connotations, derived from that of the mechanical arts. According to the first edition of the *Dictionnaire de l'Académie Française*, "salary" "is also said of chastisement, or the punishment merited by a bad deed". The pejorative character of the expression is due to the concept's military origins: the wage earner has committed himself, has become "alienated", in just the way that Kant and Marx had denounced. Incidentally, it was for the same reasons that, in 1791, and then in 1795, the right to vote in France was refused to servants as well as to women. Women were considered to be subject to their fathers or husbands, and servants to their masters. This subservience debarred them from the free exercise of their civic rights. The term "salaried" has therefore long retained a negative connotation. It was thus that the industrialist and economist Louis Say (brother of

Jean-Baptiste) could write in 1836: "In French, the word 'salaire' is almost always taken in bad part. We say that someone receives a wage for a sinful deed; we speak of the wages of crime and not the wages of work" (Say, 1836, p. 81). And a century later, in 1932, the jurist Jean Lescudier would write: "There is a tendency which is more or less confirmed in ordinary society to consider the worker alone as a wage-earner, with all the pejorative connotations that this term may have among the masses" (Lescudier, 1932, p. 6).

These reminders help us to understand why an autonomous labour law, sanctioned in France by the constitution of a Labour Code in 1906, only so belatedly came into being. Until then, labour had been considered as a commodity like any other, the exchange of which was governed by the French Civil Code of 1804. The founding act of the liberal labour legislation in France was the Le Chapelier Law of 14 June 1791, which followed the Allarde Decrees of 2nd and 17th May. These documents, which abolished the guilds of the old regime and prohibited any form of workers' association, affirmed the principle of freedom of work, in the spirit of Turgot's edicts of 1776. For liberal thinkers, this presaged the founding of a community of free men, who were associated through commercial relations alone. The market rests on the legal principles of freedom and equality of the contracting parties, manifested in the contractual agreement. It also has a character of immediacy, so that the contracting parties can at any time part company with a clean slate. The difficulty lies in fitting labour relations, which develop over time, into such a scheme. This is the purpose of the "contract for work", "by which one of the parties undertakes to do something for the other, in return for a price agreed between them" (Article 1710 of the Civil Code). The engagement in the service of others takes the legal form of a lease. One does not "sell" one's body, of which one retains exclusive ownership, but one "hires" it out. In this way, Troplong emphasizes that "the leasing of work, the lifeblood of industry, considers labour as a capital capable of being traded and generating a revenue" (Troplong, 1840, vol. 1, p. 233).

Among those who lease their work, Troplong draws a distinction between servants and workers. The former are "those who are attached in a particular way to the person, the household, the house of the master" and whose condition is "within the free states, the one most reminiscent of slavery" (*ibid.*, vol. 3, pp. 76–78). Among the workers, he distinguishes between "day labourers", "who hire out their services for so much per day", and "those to whom work is agreed upon in return for a price", who for him are possessed of a higher status than the former. We can thus see at work a principle of social hierarchy based on the degree of commercial freedom: servants attached to the person, day labourers who sell their time, and genuine craftsmen who sell the product of their work. As Bernard Mottez has shown, the form of remuneration lies at the heart of the controversial genesis of the institution of the wage (Mottez, 1966). The model promoted by liberal thought is that of the worker as the "trader of his labour", according to the formula used in 1845 by the liberal economist Léon Faucher:

> Work according to the task is an advance on work by the day, just as work by the day had been an advance on work by engagement and by the year, which was itself an advance on servitude. [...] Finally, his independence became complete as soon as the work itself and not the person of the worker became the object of the market. The worker passed from servitude to domesticity, and from domesticity to the state of the day-labourer. When the day-labourer becomes a taskmaster (labourer according to the task) he becomes a vendor of his own labour, just as the manufacturer becomes a vendor of his products and the banker a vendor of his money. Labour is thus on the same footing as capital and intelligence.
>
> (Faucher, 1845, p. 29)

Nor is this a purely ideological matter, for the image of the worker as a "vendor of his own labour" does in effect correspond to the dominant form of social labour relations in nineteenth-century France. Whether we look at things from the perspective of lexicography, law, or statistics, the subject of debate is the same: how to seize the specific nature of the salarial form? The whole point of these debates is to distinguish between a commercial relationship, from entrepreneur to entrepreneur, and a wage relationship, from worker to entrepreneur. In order to achieve this, it was necessary to accept that the wage relationship falls outside the ordinary scope of civil law. This is the meaning of the notion of "contract of employment", which became a legal category at the very end of the nineteenth century. The rare uses of this expression which can be found in an earlier period concern configurations of forced labour, such as the long-term engagements that followed slavery in the sugar islands. Notwithstanding, this expression begins to appear in the mid nineteenth century in the works of authors such as Augustin-Charles Renouard in 1854 (pp. 161ff.), who deplored the "inadequacy of the Napoleonic Code" in terms of labour regulation. Following Renouard, it was mainly Jean-Gustave Courcelle-Seneuil who, from 1858 onwards, made significant use of this notion, leading to its dissemination among economists, and then among jurists (Courcelle-Seneuil, 1858, vol. 1, p. 133).

For these authors, the challenge is to break with the liberal mystique by admitting that the wage relationship includes a dimension of subordination, something which is alien to the philosophy of contractual relationships. However, the acknowledgment of this wage element must not lead to the repudiation of the ideological achievements of the French Revolution, which had founded the nation as a community of free men. How, in short, can we conceive a principle of limited subordination? In this regard, Courcelle-Seneuil draws inspiration from an evocative passage by Alexis de Tocqueville in *Democracy in America* (1839):

> At any moment a servant may become a master, and he aspires to rise to that condition: the servant is therefore not a different man from the master. Why then has the former a right to command, and what compels the latter to obey? —the free and temporary consent of both their wills. Neither of them is by nature inferior to the other; they only become so for a time by covenant. Within the terms of this covenant, the one is a servant, the other a master; beyond it they are two citizens of the commonwealth —two men.
>
> (Tocqueville, 1839/1840, p. 191)

Similarly, for Courcelle-Seneuil,

> in the most frequent cases, the contract for the provision of labour establishes relations of command on the one hand, and dependence on the other. This is what happens each time an individual commits himself to a time commitment for any service he may render during that time, such as the labourer by the day, the clerk by the month, the servant by the half-year or by the year, and these relations are all the more clear-cut as the services which are the subject of the contract are more personal and more indeterminate, such as those of the servant. However, even in this extreme case, the contract for the provision of work only establishes, between those who contribute to it, a dependence limited by custom and temporary, since at the end of the contract, each of them is free of obligation and civilly equal to one another.
>
> (Courcelle-Seneuil, 1858, vol. 2, p. 130)

Curiously, Courcelle-Seneuil's analysis converges with Marx's, despite starting out from opposing points of view. In Chapter 6 of *Capital*, Marx underlines the inadequacy of the "vulgar liberalism" which considers only the point-of-sale in the working relationship:

> When we leave this sphere of simple circulation or the exchange of commodities, which provides the "free-trader *vulgaris*" with his views, his concepts and the standard by which he judges the society of capital and wage-labour, a certain change takes place, or so it appears, in the physiognomy of our *dramatis personae*. He who was previously the money-owner now strides out in front as a capitalist; the possessor of labour-power follows as his worker. The one smirks self-importantly and is intent on business; the other is timid and holds back, like someone who has brought his own hide to market and now has nothing else to expect but—a tanning.
>
> (Marx, 1867/1976, p. 280)

In other words, for Marx, capitalist exploitation and wage alienation are hidden behind the liberal façade conveyed by the contract. For Marx, however, as for Courcelle-Seneuil, wage alienation is limited. He notes, in particular, that all European legislation stipulates a limit to the duration of the labour contract, in order to preserve the worker's freedom within the market (Marx, [1867] 1976, p. 271n3). As early as 1849 he had remarked on this feature of the wage system: "He does not belong to this or that capitalist, but to the capitalist class" (Marx, [1849] 2006, n.p.). It is in this sense that the establishment of wage-labour constitutes, for Marx, an emancipation in relation to the previous forms of subjection of workers, such as slavery or serfdom. Each in his own way, Marx and Courcelle-Seneuil seek to consider the complex combination of subjection and freedom that constitutes the institution of the wage.

Finally, acknowledging their debt to the economists, jurists at the beginning of the twentieth century invented the idea of the "contract of employment". As François Ewald (1985) has shown, following Jean Lescudier (1932), this legal innovation resulted from the French jurisprudence that followed the 1898 law on accidents at work. This law affirmed the principle of the civil liability of employers in the event of accidents, independently of any consideration of fault, which could be subject to a criminal trial. Its introduction led to the creation of compulsory social insurance, since employers had to cover themselves against the risk of accidents. However, in order to apply this law, it was also necessary to know when one was dealing with a relationship of employment and not a mere commercial relationship. The jurisprudence was based on the "principle of legal and technical subordination" of the employee to the employer. In this case, the contract falls outside the normal scope of civil law. The introduction of the Labour Code in 1906 affirmed this legal autonomy of labour law. And thus there was legal recognition of the wage factor, i.e., of the worker's relationship of dependence on his employer, who owes him "protection" in exchange for his submission to authority to which he consents on signing the employment contract.

The modern concept of salaried employment was born of the socialization of this protection system. The insurance principle was the instrument of the collectivization of risk. It led to the introduction of an "indirect wage": only part of the wage is paid directly to the employee; another part is made up of "social rights" which the worker can claim depending on the circumstances (accidents at work, illness, unemployment, retirement). The introduction in 1932 of the "family allowance" system, inspired by various local initiatives that had emerged at the end of the First World War, extended this partial collectivization of the wage. *In fine*, the wage link does not only bring employers and employees into association, but expands to encompass collective and even state institutions (Vatin, 2020).

Conclusion

The institution of the salary thus rendered the market for labour socially acceptable by imposing regulations upon it. For liberals, this entailed a reversal of roles. What was unacceptable to the liberals was the idea of work that could not be dissociated from the person of the worker. They could therefore only tolerate, to use an anachronistic expression, an extremely "precarious" labour market, tightly constrained in both content and temporality. Yet, at the same time, the institutionalization of this market made them fear a return to servitude. To overcome this ideological impasse, it was necessary, in the line of Tocqueville, to countenance the possibility of limited servitude. It was at the cost of institutionalizing the social relations of labour that the labour market could be rendered universal. But this posed a question that still remains open today, as shown by current debates on what is improperly called "Uberization", that is to say forms of de-institutionalization of labour relations in favour of a return to the direct market. It is thus clear that, contrary to common opinion, the institution of the salary is not a liberal category, and that it was only established at the cost of a partial renunciation of the ideal of a society entirely regulated by the market.

Notes

1 For this text in its historical context, see Vatin, 2001 and 2005.

2 All of Marx's quotations of Ricardo in the 1844 Manuscripts are in fact taken from Buret, reproducing his transcription errors. See Hattori, 1994.

3 Michel Chevalier (1806–1879), engineer, graduate of the École polytechnique, and follower of Saint-Simon, succeeded Pellegrino Rossi as chair of political economy at the Collège de France in 1841 and henceforth adopted a more liberal orientation.

4 It was in his 1865 lecture "Value, Price, and Profit" that Marx first clearly distinguished between labour and labour-power (Marx, [1865] 1969).

5 Proudhon's point of view, shared by many authors of his generation, is in this sense not irrelevant in the context, as large-scale industry remained quite marginal in nineteenth-century France. Marx's genius is thus to have understood the historical importance of a social form that was still emerging at the time. See Vatin, 2020.

6 On Kantian and contemporaneous accounts of the dignity argument against commodification, see Chapter 4 by Vida Panitch in this volume, as well as Nussbaum, 1995. My reading of Kant differs from these authors'.

7 See *infra* for the full quotation.

8 Kant does not, however, reduce sexuality to procreation, since, if one were to adopt this point of view, "marriage, when the begetting of children ceases, would naturally dissolve at the same time" (Kant, [1796] 1799, vol. 1, p. 38). For him, marriage aims to legalize the sexual trade, i.e., to take it out of the purely animal order.

9 Kant indeed supposes that it is the condition of reciprocity in the possession of the other that makes the sexual exchange possible (Kant, [1796] 1799, vol. 1, p. 39); but this is a necessary but not sufficient condition, since one could imagine this condition fulfilled in the case of concubinage, whereas he insists that it is only in the case of marriage that the condition is met (*ibid.*, pp. 39–40).

10 Kant countenances the possibility that a man "might have another *man* who had lost his civil personality and become enslaved as *his*" (Kant, [1798] 1887, p. 237, italics in original). However, he rejects that the state of slavery can be inherited from the parents by the child.

11 He therefore considers that maternal infanticide, under certain conditions, as well as homicide by duel, cannot be considered murder, as they are based on obligations of honour.

12 It was in response to this that he wrote to me in 2012, thanking me for sending him a book in which I addressed this question (Vatin, 2012): "I had always been intrigued by a statement by the great Immanuel Kant: that wage labour is a form of prostitution. Your historical analysis of wage-labour, the labour contract, etc. makes this transparent."

References

Académie Française (1932–1935) *Dictionnaire*, 8th edition.
Boudon, R. (1999) *Le sens des valeurs*, Paris: Puf.
Buret, E. (1840) *De la misère des classes laborieuses en France et en Angleterre*, Paris: Paulin.
Courcelle-Seneuil, J.-G. (1858) *Traité théorique et pratique d'économie politique*, Paris: Guillaumin.
Ewald, F. (1985) *L'Etat-Providence*, Paris: Grasset.
Faucher, L. (1845) "Coalition des ouvriers-charpentiers", *Journal des économistes* (August), pp. 25–33.
Hattori, F. (1994) "Marx und Buret", *MEGA-Studien*, no. 1, pp. 142–147.
Kant, I. (1785) *Groundwork of the Metaphysics of Morals*, Cambridge: Cambridge University Press.
Kant, I. ([1796] 1799) *The Metaphysic of Morals: Divided into Metaphysical Elements of Law and of Ethics [Die Metaphysik der Sitten]*, 2 vols., English translation, 1799, London. Edition cited available online in two volumes at www.google.com/books
Kant, I. ([1798] 1887) "Supplementary Explanations of the Principles of Right", in *The Philosophy of Law: An Exposition of the Fundamental Principles of Jurisprudence as The Science of Right*, Edinburgh: T. & T. Clark.
Lescudier, J. (1932) *Le salarié. Notion juridique*, Paris: Dalloz.
Littré, E. (1869) "Salariat", *Dictionnaire de la langue française*, vol. 2, pt. 2, Paris: Hachette.
Marx, K. ([1844] 1959) "Economic & Philosophic Manuscripts of 1844", trans. Martin Milligan, Moscow: Progress Publishers. Available online at www.marxists.org. www.marxists.org/archive/marx/works/download/pdf/Economic-Philosophic-Manuscripts-1844.pdf
Marx, K. ([1847] 1955) *The Poverty of Philosophy*, Moscow: Progress Publishers. Available online at https://marxistnkrumaistforum.wordpress.com/karl-marx-the-poverty-of-philosophy/344-2/
Marx, K. ([1849] 2006) "What are Wages? How are they Determined?" in *Wage Labour and Capital*, pamphlet first published in German in *Neue Rheinische Zeitung*, April 5–8 and 11, 1849, trans. F. Engels. Available online at www.marxists.org
Marx, K. ([1865] 1969) "Value, Price, and Profit", New York: International Co., Inc. Available online at www.marxists.org
Marx, K. ([1867] 1976) *Capital, Volume 1*, trans. Ben Fowkes, London: Penguin Classics.
Mottez, B. (1966) *Systèmes de salaire et politiques patronales. Essai sur l'évolution des pratiques et des idéologies patronales*, Paris: CNRS.
Nenovsky, N. (2009) "Place of Labor and Labor Theory in Tugan-Baranovsky's Theoretical System", *The Kyoto Economic Review*, 78(1), pp. 53–77.
Nussbaum, M.C. (1995) "Objectivation", *Philosophy & Public Affairs*, 24(4), pp. 249–291.
Polanyi, K. ([1944] 2001) *The Great Transformation*, 2nd ed. with a preface by Joseph Stiglitz, Boston, MA: Beacon Press, first published 1944.
Renouard, A.-C. (1854) "Mémoire sur le contrat de prestation de travail", in *Séances et travaux de l'Académie des sciences morales et politique*, no. 1, Paris: A. Durand, pp. 161ff.
Rossi, P. (1840–41) *Cours d'économie politique*, Paris: Joubert.
Say, L. (1836) *Etudes sur la richesse des nations et réfutation des principales erreurs en économie politique*, Paris: Librairie du commerce.
Tocqueville, A. de (1839/1840) *Democracy in America: Part the Second: The Social Influence of Democracy*, New York: J. & H. G Langley.
Troplong, R.-T. (1840) *Le droit civil expliqué suivant l'ordre des articles du Code: de l'échange et du louage, commentaire des titres VII et VIII du Livre III du Code civil*, 3 vols., Paris: Hingray.
Vatin, F. (2001) "Avant Marx et Polanyi, Eugène Buret: Le travail, la servitude et la vie", *Revue du Mauss*, 18, pp. 237–280.
Vatin, F. (2005) "Eugène Buret entre littérature et science sociale: Essai de biographie intellectuelle", in F. Vatin, *Trois essais sur la genèse de la pensée sociologique*, Paris: La Découverte, pp. 80–120.
Vatin, F. (2012) *L'Espérance-monde. Essai sur l'idée de progrès à l'heure de la mondialisation*, Paris: Albin Michel.
Vatin, F. (2020) "L'affirmation de la forme salariale", in F. Knittel, N. Mariotti, and P. Raggi (eds), *Le travail en Europe occidentale des années 1830 aux années 1930*, Paris: Ellipses, pp. 59–70.

9
GAMBLING
Using the market to regulate practices

Marie Trespeuch

Introduction

Gambling markets are now a well-established industry in many countries. Whether commodified by state monopolies (the most common case being lotteries), or distributed across a multiplicity of bookmakers (in the case of the sports betting), these games no longer seem to raise any serious objections and have become just another part of people's leisure activities. Historically, however, gambling games have been seen as "contested commodities" (Radin, 1996) because the organization of their market exchange means profiting from a passion which was deemed morally reprehensible and considered to have potentially devastating consequences. Regardless of the country, the expansion of gambling is traditionally associated with two main kinds of problems: crime (money laundering, theft, scams, organized crime) and addiction (Cosgrave and Klassen, 2001). Gambling "too much" can lead to serious financial problems, sometimes ruin, and can become an obsessive occupation to the point of the gambler being de-socialized. The problem of gambling addiction certainly originated with gambling itself (Belmas, 2006), but was not always thought of in medical terms. Until the end of the twentieth century, excessive gambling, like alcoholism in the post-war era (Freidson, 1973), was seen as a *moral* issue which disturbed the social and the public order, especially when poor people and children were concerned.

In France, since the sixteenth century, various laws have been passed to limit this plague. The most restrictive one was proclaimed in 1836, when all gambling in the country was banned. The slow construction of the French gambling market began, first, around certain monopolies which were established from the end of the nineteenth century, and developed during the twentieth century. The emergence of a market opened to competition dates from 2010, but only for online gambling. Today in France there are three main historical players on the market: the Pari Mutuel Urbain (PMU), which organizes bets on horse races (Tiercé, Quinté, etc.), the Française des jeux (FDJ), the historical public monopoly which operates principally lottery games (Loto, scratch cards, then sports betting and online poker), and a large oligopoly of 200 casinos, which organize table games (English Roulette, Black Jack, etc.) and make slot machines available to the public. In addition, for the past 10 years, there have been licensed online operators such as Betclic or Unibet, which are 'pureplayers' (they are not allowed to sell games in physical distribution outlets).

DOI: 10.4324/9781003188742-12

Does the rise of the gambling industry – through the growth in revenues and in the number of providers involved – reflect a normalization of the market? I will see that the successive transformations of the gambling market, towards more and more competition and growth, do not mean an abandonment of moral fears. I will underline how different devices have been imagined and highlighted over the years in order to legitimize the growth of the industry, and to regulate the potential public and social disorders caused by gambling practices. As such, I will show that the regulation of this market offers us a helpful perspective from which to understand the different forms of moral contestations specific to this industry. The gambling market therefore constitutes a "contested market" that is, a market where commodities considered morally sensitive may or may not be exchanged, thanks to devices (legal, fiscal frameworks, etc.), which make possible, suspend, or prohibit these transactions (Steiner and Trespeuch, 2014). In contested markets, the liberal theory that competition would lead to the best allocation of resources is contested in the name of other moral precepts such as the protection of "vulnerable populations". This chapter shows how the evolution of the structure of the gambling market has been the result of trade-offs between economic efficiency, budgetary and fiscal issues, and moral concerns.

First, I will describe the arguments that justified the general ban in 1836 and then the construction of monopolies. Second, I will show how the political context of the first decade of the new millennium, associated with the rise of addiction, was paradoxically conducive to the ending of monopolies on the internet. Finally, I employ the Foucaldian approach of governmentality to analyze the evolution of the different devices implemented to "cool-down" the contestations over gambling markets.

From prohibition to monopolies: Moral arguments and the general interest

Moral concerns

In France since the sixteenth century, games of chance and gambling have been prohibited and then authorized sparingly but in closed places (casinos, gaming circles, etc.) for moral reasons. The historian Elisabeth Belmas (Belmas, 2006) identifies two types of reprobation emanating from the religious and secular authorities in the Modern Age. Firstly, that invoking chance is inappropriate, especially for entertainment purposes, because it is a way of competing with the judgment of God. Moreover, that earning money by chance is also questionable, since social hierarchies based on heredity of rank – and then, with the third French Republic, on merit derived from work – would thereby potentially be undermined (Steiner and Trespeuch, 2013).

For as long as the practice of gambling was individual or constrained to a small collective, it has, over the centuries, been negatively judged but has not produced systematic coercive action from public or religious authorities. On the other hand, when it is done in public and taken over by an organizer who earns income from it, the situation becomes subject to sanctions. The metamorphosis of the private practice of gambling into an economic activity proper has meant creating a market where producers of games – the organizers or "operators" – meet consumers – the players – to sell a contested commodity – an expectation of gain determined by chance. This market is framed by legal rules, which condemn not so much the person who engages in gambling as the one who organizes it (Darracq, 2008), in accordance with the image of the vulnerable gambler who is a victim of his passions. In particular, the law seeks to keep "vulnerable populations" away from the market (Steiner and Trespeuch, 2019).

The definition of these targeted populations has changed over different periods with the changing conception of the problems of gambling themselves, although the problem was consistently seen primarily as a moral issue and not yet as a psychological condition. From the seventeenth to the beginning of the twentieth century, government policies were aimed especially at children (Belmas, 2006) and the poor (Darracq, 2008), both of whom were considered more vulnerable to the lure of easy money and, more importantly, also as unable to handle large gains (Collette, 1999). This recalls a point made by Viviana Zelizer in her study of American charitable organizations: in the late nineteenth century, cash given to the poor was considered a danger because their consumption choices were thought to be immoral, especially in the case of immigrants: "How could charity workers know how relief funds were spent; how, specifically, could they stop recipients from drinking or gambling their money away?" (Zelizer, 1994, p. 129).

Monopolies in the name of the general interest

The law adopted on May 21, 1836, under the French Second Empire, prohibited all lotteries, and more broadly games of chance and money, on the French territory. However, without this law ever being repealed, the gambling business has continued to develop in France since the nineteenth century, through exemptions, based on the idea, similar to the case of prostitution, of its being a "necessary evil" – in the sense of something impossible to ban. But this pragmatic argument did not lead simply to a massive opening up of the market. Each time a request for an exception to the 1836 law was made, there were tumultuous debates in parliament and in the press between those who favoured a firm ban and those who thought that a market should emerge, provided it was strongly regulated by the government, and justified in the name of the general interest.

What arguments were put forward to justify the commodification of certain games by a few selected operators? At the end of the nineteenth century the government regulated totalizator betting (*paris mutuels*) on horse racing, in order to strengthen horse-breeding activity, whose vitality was considered to be in the national interest; then casinos were allowed from 1907 to promote tourism in seaside resorts; and finally, the French National Lottery (*Loterie nationale*) was restored in 1933 to provide decent pensions for the victims of the Great War, and to aid widows and orphans in a context of economic crisis (Collette, 1999).

The operation of moral legitimization thus makes it possible to launder a contested activity by appeal to its virtuous ends: the gambling providers could exist as long as they proved the money they raised served good causes. This was accompanied by close control of the operators and their products by the public authorities: the Ministry of the Interior for casinos, and the Ministry of the Budget and Public Accounts for the Pari Mutuel Urbain (PMU) and the Loterie nationale (which would become the current Française des Jeux (FDJ)). Two positive effects of this monopolistic organization can be mentioned: first, the state found a simple way to control and limit the size of the market, since private interests were ruled out; secondly, the state could benefit from high amounts of taxes collected.

The 1980s–1990s: The rise of the gambling industry

The different instruments designed to channel gambling behaviours have evolved since the end of the nineteenth century, alongside the changes in the state's view of gambling as an economic sector. Indeed, the number of products as well as their accessibility increased sharply after the Second World War and even more so from the 1980s onwards. During and after the 1980s, the growth of the gambling sector accelerated, and each operator developed and diversified its offer under the benevolent eye of the public authorities (Trespeuch, 2019). Paradoxically, competitive tensions appeared between the operators who shared the gambling market, namely the two monopolies (FDJ, PMU) and the oligopoly constituted by the two hundred casinos. Thanks to innovations in gaming mechanics, the boundaries between the previously distinct offers were gradually becoming blurred. Previously, only casinos had games based on instantaneous play (English Roulette, Black Jack, etc., and later slot machines). But, this type of offer extended beyond the casinos facilities and developed strongly in the 1990s, with the arrival of instant lottery games (or "scratch cards"), which the Française des Jeux obtained authorization to operate in 1989. In addition, to imitating a mechanism that was close to table games and slot machines, the scratch games mushroomed by borrowing, both in their name and iconography, from the world of casino. This was the case with the release of "BlackJack" or "Vegas" in 2000. Then the game "Rapido" (a lottery broadcast in bars) ended this movement by offering draws every five minutes, bringing it dangerously close to the principle of slot machines. At the same time, the horse betting offer moved in exactly the opposite direction, with PMU products being more and more governed by the intervention of chance. In 1976 the "Quarté" appeared, followed by the "Quarté Plus" in 1986, and the "Quinté Plus" in 1989. It turns out that, even with a strong expertise in the world of racing, the ordering of five horses is difficult to establish with certainty. Finally, as far as casinos are concerned, a new regulation, which reformed their operation in 2007, allowed them to open Texas Hold'em poker rooms, thus calling into question the coherence of their former offer. Casinos were previously characterized by games of pure chance, like Black Jack or slot machines, where gamblers won at the expense, or lose for the benefit of the only casino. On the contrary, Texas Hold'em poker – as well as lotteries or horse betting – sets the players in opposition to each other, and the total amount of the prize money depends on their stakes. Futhermore, poker presupposes a knowledge of the elements of strategy if players hope to win.

In the first decade of the new millennium, therefore, it was difficult to identify a homogeneous offer according to the operator that provided it, since the perimeters of the products sold seemed to be intermingled. The monopoly on pure games of chance, the monopoly on horse betting, and the oligopoly formed by the casinos were, surprisingly, in hard competition with each other. As a result, these two decades were characterized by a huge growth in the sector's turnover, to the benefit of the operators, but also of the government, which collected substantial tax revenues.

The objective of governing gambling behaviours then faded away in favour of a more intense diversification of available products, the development of competition between operators and the accumulation of tax resources for the state. In addition, the arrival of foreign gaming operators on the Internet produced the need to develop on this channel: this is the case of the FDJ and PMU which exported part of their products via the web soon after the turn of the millennium.

Online gambling in the European regulatory context: New challenges for the contested market

It was thus also in the first decade of the new millennium that the possibility of gambling on the Internet changed the competitive balance. Firms based abroad, often in tax havens (Trespeuch, 2013), were illegally offering games to French Internet users. This offer placed new constraints on legal operators, particularly in the fixed odds betting segment, which represented a category of games that invested in the Internet very early on, as well as in poker (which French casinos were not allowed to offer online). The existing regulations, based on the sale of "material" games (a scratch card, a chip, a PMU ticket, etc.) and sold for the most part in physical distribution outlets, was deeply challenged by the advent of Internet gambling.

After receiving various complaints from bookmakers about European governments erecting barriers to entry in their market, the Directorate-General for the "internal market" of the European Commission launched various infringement actions in 2006 in order to stop what it considered to be the offences committed by 11 Member states in terms of gambling and betting. This procedure would mark the beginning of the deregulation process for the online gambling market, which eventually occurred in 2010.

Neil Fligstein (1996) conceptualized this kind of market transformation as a moment when the cards are reshuffled: as opportunities are up for grabs, those who wish to enter (the "*invaders*") come to challenge the positions of those who are already established (the "*incumbents*") by proposing alternative "conceptions of control", mobilizing repertoires of action that Fligstein refers to as those of social movements: "In stable markets, incumbent firms defend their positions against challengers and invaders. During periods of market transformation, invaders can reintroduce more fluid social movement-like conditions" (*ibid.*, 1996, p. 656). While the contestation had begun well before 2006 (since at this time the need to redefine the rules of the sector had already become apparent), after the announcement – still unofficial – of the liberalization, the stakes crystallized around the new rules that would be adopted and the need for the actors involved to have an influence on them. This greatly facilitated the public expression of the interests of actors who saw economic opportunities in liberalization.

Indeed, the European regulatory context of the period provided an ideal framework for the playing out of this debate. The letter of formal notice sent to the French government itself outlined three specific grievances and invited it to justify the compatibility of its legislation with the provisions of the European Treaty: (1) Betting certainly made a contribution to the overall budget and financing of the horse racing industry. But these two aspects had not been recognized by the courts as "general compelling reasons" and therefore they did not justify restrictions on competition. (2) In the fight against crime and fraud, there is no evidence that other jurisdictions (including those involving online gambling) are not just as fully able to prevent risks to public order. Moreover, unlike in France, other states have regulatory authorities for gambling that oversee and monitor operators. (3) Vulnerable populations such as children and addicts would not be protected but rather encouraged by the monopolies to engage in this dangerous activity.

Just like 11 other states that were being pursued by the European Commission at the time, the central argument in the French government's response was that there would be increased risk in the event of a multiplication of firms on the market. The French government, which specifically defended the FDJ monopoly, justified the growth of the gaming products and revenues by the need to maintain an attractive monopoly in relation to competing illegal online offers. In this it was re-deploying a rhetoric that went back to the governmental origins of monopolies, that is to their regulatory cogency, by using arguments which in the past had justified strong government intervention: prevention of the disorder associated with gambling. Thus, the answers given to the European Commission aimed to demonstrate that national restrictions were necessary, proportionate, and pursued systematically and consistently with regard to the general and compelling public interest reasons that underpinned them.

The European Commission was not convinced by these answers and invited France to make changes to its laws on gambling by opening the market to competition. This pressure, coupled with political will on the part of the French President from the autumn of 2007, then put the French market on the path towards the deregulation of gambling on the internet. Opening up the market to competition led to new thinking about the conditions for what could count as an acceptable trade in gambling.

Governing the gambling market by cooling-down devices

Once the opening of the French gambling market was officially declared, it renewed old debates and questions about the modalities of a market regulation that could be both efficient and virtuous. At the heart of the new legal arsenal of authorized gambling are various institutionalized devices for the "government of conducts" (Dubuisson-Quellier, 2016). From the beginning of the gambling monopolies, governments have sought to bring about "normal" practice by regulating the conditions under which they take place. First, it was a matter of not fanning the flames of gambling by limiting the opportunities to gamble, especially among certain populations. In addition to decrees prohibiting gambling by minors, the policies also included physical measures such as moving casinos away from cities, organizing a limited number of lottery draws, and setting an average payout rate for players. In addition, economic measures of demand selection were implemented, such as the introduction of entrance fees to casinos and gambling circles or high prices that aimed at turning less-well-off individuals away from gambling (Trespeuch, 2014).

In the framework of "governmentality" conceptualized by Michel Foucault, these instruments of market regulation can be interpreted as "apparatuses of security" (Foucault, 2004). Indeed, these devices are not conceived in a spirit of prohibition but are, on the contrary, means of controlling the population by defining the acceptable boundaries of its actions. Beyond the law, the establishment of an acceptable gambling norm has been achieved through the implementation of various instruments that tend to individualize the target of public action, and to lead individuals to exercise a liberal economic rationality through the transformation of the conditions for exercising their personal choices.

The period from 2006 to 2010 is crucial to understanding how the transformation of the former regulatory framework was initiated. The incipient reshaping gave the various actors concerned an opportunity to influence the process of writing the future law. This period can thus be likened to what Callon calls a "hot situation" where "everything becomes controversial: the identification of intermediaries and overflows, the distribution of source and target agents, the way effects are measured" (Callon, 1998, p. 260). The process of reframing an identified externality is long and costly, because it "assumes that the actions and their effects are known and measured" and that requires that a "space of calculability" be defined, which necessarily gives rise to controversies.[1]

Gambling addiction at stake: Reframing a new externality

In the first years of the new millennium, the challenge for the government had been reinforced by the growing awareness of a previously non-existent problem, one hardly even imagined until that time: "pathological gambling" (Mangel, 2009). Although excessive gambling behaviour is nothing new, the perception of the phenomenon as a disease or condition is a recent one and has had a lasting impact in changing representations of gambling. It is mainly through the influence of doctors and psychologists of addiction that the perspective has solidified. Their willingness to recognize problem gamblers as users of a "drug without a substance" (Valleur and Matysiak, 2006) has led to a strategy of challenging government to recognize gambling as a "disease" and to treat the resulting "patients". Addiction to gambling would henceforth be perceived as a strong market externality that needs to be channelled by the new rules of the liberalized market. The emphasis was on those people playing Rapido, or slot machines to excess, as these encouraged repetitive play leading to financial, family, work, or mental health problems. The rise in concern about gambling addiction can be interpreted as a modern and medicalized version of the old moral condemnation of gambling, especially in the lower classes (Fassin, 1996; Aïach and Delanoë, 1998), but the basis of criticism remains the same: faced with the unleashing of passions, the commercial business of gambling is considered unhealthy and its legitimacy is questioned.

The idea of "addiction" to gambling emerged as a new public health issue, giving rise to a new framing of the problem of "abnormal" gambling behaviour. This new framework was based in particular on an epistemological framework whose assumptions anchor the sources of disorders in individual psychology. The context of liberalization of the gambling market in 2010 provided an opportunity for the French government to rethink the methods of regulating the market by making companies more responsible, either directly – through taxation – or by modifying the conditions of choice offered to consumers through the use of online devices (Trespeuch, 2016).

Taxation and limitation of marketed products

When externalities appear in a market, taxation is a traditional economic lever used by governments to regulate the market (Pigou, 1948; Bertrand, 2020). Addiction is now considered as the main externality of the gaming industry and has been partially controlled by taxes on the stakes. The product in the gambling market is of a particular nature, since it consists of an expectation of winnings, which is driven by the notion of Return to Player (or RTP, i.e., the share of bets redistributed to players). For example, if each individual has a one in 19 million chance of winning the Loto jackpot, the FDJ ultimately returns half (RTP = 50.49%) of the bets to the players in the form of winnings on this game. The increase in the rate of redistribution of the stakes to the players, when it is possible, has a double effect: the players win more and it is therefore a relative loss for the company or the government, which share the remaining stakes. However, a game with a higher average win makes it more attractive: the winners play again and this increases the turnover of the game organizer.

The definition of these expectations is therefore at the heart of the functioning of the business models of the gambling operators, but also of the addictive potential of a product, putting the companies in the curious position of having to reduce the share of the players if they want to protect them from themselves. The RTP depends on the game formula, i.e., the way in which chance functions during the game, whether it functions alone or alongside a notion of expertise, as well as the method of taxation imposed by the government. In the case of the Loto, the average share redistributed to players depends on a law of probability, the organizational costs of the operator, and the share taken by the tax authorities. It is therefore impossible, without changing the rules of the game, to change its attractiveness. In the case of scratch cards or slot machines, on the other hand, the average payout is set by the operator. Setting a slot machine to "pay out" an average of 85% of the bets will ensure a higher frequency of play than a machine set to 60% of RTP.

During the preparatory period of the liberalization law (2008–2009), debates focused on the most risky games: the data were not yet established and the government had to take conflicting constraints into account (Trespeuch, 2011). Despite the alarm signals on poker sent by the association "*SOS Joueurs*" (SOS Players), for example, the government opened it to competition, as well as sports betting, because of their great popularity and the significant competition that existed on the Internet. The justification put forward was that the expertise required to play these games allowed for greater control – something which remains quite controversial. The objective of moderation is maintained through the cap on the RTP, which was set in the 2010 law at 85% of the stakes for online horse and sports betting.

Moreover, despite the reluctance of the candidate operators, the stake was first chosen as the basis for taxation, rather than the gross proceeds of the games (i.e., the revenue of the operators once the gains have been redistributed to players), because of technical constraints but also because of the regulatory objectives that the government had set for itself. The choice of this basis was openly justified on the grounds of prevention of excess: "It is the act of gambling or betting itself that is taxed, given the dangers of public order and social order associated with this activity", says J.-F. Lamour, rapporteur to the Finance Commission just before liberalization.

The power of online devices

The modality of the Internet calls for the implementation of very specific means to moderate gambling practices and avoid addiction problems. Even before the market was opened, some operators were quick to emphasize the need to offer players self-control options through weekly betting limits, indications of playing time, alerts in the event of repeated deposits, temporary or permanent self-exclusion processes from the gaming site (along the line of casino bans), etc. At the time, their objectives were to show that they were committed to protecting players from excessive practices, to gain legitimacy with the European authorities, and also to anticipate the strict rules that would inevitably be imposed subsequent to liberalization. Operators therefore voluntarily put in place a series of measures aimed at giving players greater control over their practices by activating parameters attached to their account. The promise was to give players the means to exercise effective self-control by stimulating their reflexivity (how they think about their own practices). Based upon the "governmentality" framework proposed by Foucault, we may see the government as producing devices for controlling behaviour (thanks to online account parameters) by organizing the conditions for players' freedom of action.

In terms of taking care of gamblers who ask for help, a mechanism has also been proposed, notably through the Adictel company, which provides help to Internet users via a telephone center that certain casino and online gaming companies finance to receive calls for help from gamblers in distress. In terms of technical instruments for "combating excessive or pathological gambling" itself, the law has been described as restrictive, in order to prevent risks. For example, according to Senator Trucy's report, it is based on "co-responsibility between operators, gamblers and the structures responsible for assessing the measures put in place to combat addiction" (Trucy, 2011, p. 260). This means that operators must set up gambling moderators, that players themselves can set them up, and that the Autorité de régulation des jeux en ligne (ARJEL) – the new authority created to regulate the market – must evaluate the prevention efforts made by operators to limit risks. Thus, it is planned – on the model of the former FDJ–COJER relationship[2] – that a report be submitted annually by licensed operators, taking stock of the means put in place to prevent pathological gambling and promote "responsible gambling" to the regulatory authority, which can then make recommendations to improve the measures put in place by the operator.

The exclusion and self-limitation measures that must be offered by gambling sites to their customers include the terms and conditions for opening an account: each player must set his or her account funding limit and betting commitment limit. To help them set their own limits, the sites sometimes suggest that players "test" themselves, to evaluate their profile, for example by answering questions about their gambling habits, as proposed by the FDJ site inspired by the Canadian excessive gambling index, or the "*SOS joueurs*" (SOS Players) website (to which a large number of operators automatically redirect players). After ten or so questions, it is possible to make recommendations or even to direct players to a help structure if they answer "yes" to more than five out of ten questions. According to Foucault, the origins of governmentality are based on the Christian pastorship (Foucault, 2004): the pastor does not constrain the flock of sheep but guides it along a path, leaving it room for freedom. All of the online devices we have just described stimulate the players' reflexivity in order to guide them in a good way, rather than compelling them. They are obviously free to play, but inside the limits operators have built for them. By doing so, the online gambling market should have become virtuous "by design".

In order to encourage players to moderate their gambling practices, the operator must also communicate their account balance each time they visit the site. Finally, at any time, the user must be able to ask to be excluded temporarily (at least seven days) or permanently, which would result in the closing of his account. In practice, the degree of constraint produced by these measures differs from one site to another, producing vast disparities in the betting limits depending on the website. As François Trucy points out, "another solution could have consisted of an imperative and transversal limitation of player accounts" but this would not have "constituted an effective instrument" because the problem of excessive gambling is based more on the frequency of betting than on the amount of bets, and moreover "an adequate level of capping of bets is delicate to define: according to the level of income of the player, the same maximum amount of stake will prove to be either symbolic or considerable" (Trucy, 2011, p. 161). Certainly, the borderline case of the very wealthy player who must be able to bet 100,000 euros on a team if he wishes, has often been mobilized as an argument by online operators applying for a license. With this type of reasoning, they tend to suggest that the root requirement is to make sure every player faces up to their own responsibilities: the individual alone knows his or her level of resources and must act with full knowledge of the facts so as not to exceed his own limits.

These technologies are therefore as coercive as they are reflexive: the player's freedom stops where the machine's rationality begins. The internet user is constantly informed of the state of his account during his gaming sessions, possibly discouraging him from voluntarily prolonging the game or doubling his bets; but, in the absence of self-control, the system will simply block access to the account for a few days.

Ten years after: Privatization and wider opening?

Ten years after the opening, the French gambling market has evolved again. From 2019, the tax base is no longer the stake but the Gross Gaming Revenue of the online operators (i.e., the difference between the amount of money players wager minus the amount that they win). The ANJ (the new name of the former regulation authority ARJEL) justified this measure by economic arguments:

> Until 2019, the gambling sector has been subject to a specific tax system, based essentially on stakes, with a wide variety of rates and types of levies depending on the gambling segment. For sports betting in particular, the tax base based on stakes has proven to be very uneconomic for the market, since it does not take into account the sums paid out by operators to players in the form of winnings.[3]

Highlighting the attractiveness and efficiency of the market contrasts with old arguments based on moral protection and limitation of deviant behaviours.

Moreover, the opening of the capital of the Française des Jeux (FDJ) in the fall of 2019 reminds us of the long process of the state distancing itself from the gambling operators themselves. This economic history is emblematic of the market transformations at work more globally in France and Europe since the 1980s. Very few former state monopolies have escaped the opening up to competition, itself accompanied by partial privatizations (Post Office, Telecoms, electricity sector, railway industry, etc.). Until this very recent development, the gaming operator had retained the status of a majority-state-owned monopoly, in the name of protecting social order (limiting excessive gambling and gambling by minors) and public order (combating money laundering and the illegal gambling trade). Now, the capital is shared between the French state (around 22%), the *Union des blessés de la face* (Union of facial injuries) (around 15%)[4] and other stakeholders which possess more than 51% of the capital.

Another deep change is already being planned: the online gaming sector alone accounts for barely 10% of all games of chance sold in France. Since this market, which is open to competition, has managed to stabilize itself and to be effectively regulated, we can imagine that the shape of the market will evolve further in the future: why would foreign operators, especially bookmakers with experience in physical distribution outlets, be satisfied with online gaming alone? It is likely that the "opening up" of 2010 has acted as a trial balloon in prospect of a wider competition for the gambling activities sold in physical outlets. The opening of the FDJ's capital would then be a new preparatory stage for the competition of its activities, and the mark of a normalization of gambling in the French economic landscape (Trespeuch, 2019).

Conclusion

Contested markets are largely characterized by the implementation of devices capable of "cooling down" the moral challenges that develop around the marketization of contested goods (Steiner and Trespeuch, 2014). The examination of the French gambling market has shown that the contours of some populations affected by the existence of the market, such as children and excessive gamblers play a central role. Nevertheless, the way the government reconciles moral concerns and fiscal appetites has evolved over time. It seems that the discipline of supply has left place for more individual devices to channel the gamblers' behaviours.

The new instruments implemented after the liberalization in 2010 ultimately make the player "responsible" for his or her own actions by proposing that the player limit himself or herself, and delegate to the platform the task of making it impossible to exceed the limits. At the same time, this relieves the operators of any responsibility for excessive behaviour. A real process of successive delegation of the government of conduct has thus taken place since the first accusations were made in the early 2000s: the public authorities, accused of playing both sides of the fence (those of regulation and taxation), first supported their action concerning the conduct of operators through closer monitoring of their commercial actions and the encouragement of voluntary policies of information and moderation of customers. Liberalization offered the opportunity to transpose these instruments into a policy aimed more at the player's reflexivity and his control by the machinery. Finally, by means of a law stipulating the new rules of the market, the government has clarified its intentions in terms of governing conduct, not only that of the players, but also and above all that of the operators whose appetites, in this context of liberalization, have been tamed in the name of preventing excessive gambling.

However, the recent transformations I underlined at the end of the chapter now suggest two scenarios for the future: the first, optimistic, suggests that the protests have now cooled down and that a normalization of the market has taken place, promising to make the concept of a contested market for the gambling industry obsolete in the foreseeable future. Another interpretation points to new excesses in the future and the need to invent new safeguards to reframe the disorders associated with excessive gambling. Time will tell.

Notes

1 On the normativity of the concept of externality, see Chapter 3 by Elodie Bertrand in this volume.
2 In order to respond to European criticism of the "Etat croupier" (which could also be translated as "card dealer"), a decree was issued in early 2006 creating an independent authority, the *Comité consultatif pour l'encadrement des jeux et du "jeu responsable"* (COJER) (Advisory Committee for Gaming Control and Responsible Gaming), to prove that the state was aware of the problems of addiction and was putting in place measures to curb them. Charged with advising the Ministry of the Budget and guiding it in its decisions concerning the FDJ's offer, the COJER was expressly created to fight against excessive gambling and, to a lesser extent, against money laundering.
3 https://anj.fr/offre-de-jeu-et-marche/le-marche
4 The presence of this union refers to the history of the French national lottery, which was restored in 1933 to help widows, orphans and the wounded of the First World War (the "*Gueules cassées*").

References

Aïach, P. and Delanoë, D. (1998) *L'ère de la médicalisation. Ecce Homo Sanitas*. Paris: Economica.
Belmas, É. (2006) *Jouer autrefois: essai sur le jeu dans la France moderne (XVIe–XVIIIe siècle)*. Seyssel: Champ Vallon (Époques).
Bertrand, É. (2020) "Les effets externes des marchés contestés", in E. Bertrand, M.-X. Catto (eds) *Les limites du marché. The Limits of the Market. La marchandisation de la nature et du corps. Commodification of Nature and Body*. Paris: Mare & martin, pp. 21–42.
Callon, M. (1998) "An Essay on Framing and Overflowing: Economic Externalities Revisited by Sociology", *The Sociological Review*, 46(1), pp. 244–269.
Collette, S. (1999) *De la Loterie nationale à la Française des jeux (1933–1998): contribution à une sociologie de l'Etat moderne*. Thèse de doctorat en science politique, University Paris X–Nanterre.
Cosgrave, J. and Klassen, T.R. (2001) "Gambling against the State:The state and the Legitimation of Gambling", *Current Sociology*, 49(5), pp. 1–15. Available at: https://doi.org/10.1177/0011392101495002
Darracq, J.-B. (2008) *L'État et le jeu: étude de droit français*. Aix-en-Provence: Presses universitaires d'Aix-Marseille.
Dubuisson-Quellier, S. (2016) *Gouverner les conduites*. Paris: Sciences po-les Presses.
Fassin, D. (1996) *L'Espace politique de la santé. Essai de généalogie*. Paris: Presses universitaires de France.
Fligstein, N. (1996) "Markets as politics: a political-cultural approach to market institutions", *American sociological review*, 61, pp. 656–673.
Foucault, M. (2004) *Sécurité, territoire, population. Cours au Collège de France, 1977–1978*. Paris: Gallimard-Seuil.
Freidson, E. (1973) *Profession of Medicine. A Study of the Sociology of Applied Knowledge*. New York: Dodd, Mead and Co.
Mangel, A.-C. (2009) *Analyse de la construction sociale de la notion de "jeu pathologique" et de ses effets sur les représentations et pratiques des joueurs de la Française des jeux*. Ph. D. thesis, University Paris-Descartes.
Pigou, A.C. (1948) *The Economics of Welfare*. 4th edition. London: Macmillan.
Radin, M.J. (1996) *Contested Commodities. The Trouble with Trade in Sex, Children, Body Parts and Other Things*. Cambridge Mass.: Harvard University Press.
Steiner, P. and Trespeuch, M. (2013) "Managing Passions and Constructing Interest. Online Gambling, Human Body Parts and the Market", *Revue française de sociologie*, 54(1), pp. 155–180. https://doi.org/10.3917/rfs.541.0155
Steiner, P. and Trespeuch, M. (2014) *Marchés contestés. Quand le marché rencontre la morale*. Toulouse: Presses universitaires du Mirail.
Steiner, P. and Trespeuch, M. (2019) "Contested markets: morality, market devices and vulnerable populations", in S. Schiller-Merkens and P. Balsiger (eds) *The Contested Moralities of markets*. Oxford: Emerald Publishing, pp. 33–48.
Trespeuch, M. (2011) *Le secteur des jeux d'argent à l'heure numérique: émergence et transformation d'un marché contesté*. PhD. thesis, ENS Cachan.
Trespeuch, M. (2013) "Lîle de la tentation: Malte ou les ressorts de la construction d'un district européen des jeux d'argent en ligne", *Réseaux,* 180, pp. 126–153.

Trespeuch, M. (2014) "Moraliser le commerce des jeux d'argent. D'un marché contesté à l'autre", in P. Steiner and M. Trespeuch (eds) *Marchés contestés. Quand le marché rencontre la morale*. Toulouse: Presses universitaires du Mirail.

Trespeuch, M. (2016) "Gagner moins pour rejouer moins? Les ressorts de la modération des pratiques de jeux d'argent dans un contexte de libéralisation du marché", in S. Dubuisson-Quellier (ed.) *Gouverner les conduites économiques*. Paris: Presses de Sciences Po.

Trespeuch, M. (2019) "Le marché des jeux d'argent: une concurrence sous contrôle", *Regards Croisés sur l'économie*, 25, pp. 115–125. https://doi.org/10.3917/rce.025.0115dubui

Trucy, F. (2011) *Rapport d'information du Sénat fait au nom de la commission des finances sur l'évaluation de la loi no 2010-476 du 12 mai 2010 relative à l'ouverture à la concurrence et à la régulation du secteur des jeux d'argent et de hasard en ligne*. Sénat.

Valleur, M. and Matysiak, J.-C. (2006) *Les pathologies de l'excès*. Paris: JC Lattès.

Zelizer, V. (1994) *The Social Meaning of Money. Pin money, paychecks, poor relief, and other currencies*. New York: Basic Books.

10
INSURANCE

Emily C. Nacol

Introduction

As with other objects of inquiry in this volume, insurance's status as a commodity appears somewhat unclear at first glance. Insurance certainly displays at least some of the features of a commodity. Private insurance is packaged as a policy that can be bought and sold for a price on a market or an exchange by interested consumers. Yet, these policies are, at bottom, contracts for future services rendered in the case of a broad range of contingent events like car accidents, house fires or floods, medical treatments, or deaths. Insurance policies are not material inputs or products, nor are they interchangeable. In fact, they are often tailored to particular consumers by insurance brokers. On the face of it, then, insurance cannot really be classified as a commodity proper, although it bears a family resemblance.[1]

This chapter thus departs from a straightforward treatment of the commodification of insurance. Instead, it takes up how insurance—understood as a technology and a practice with corresponding institutions—has played a critical part of the story of other contested commodities. In other words, the question at the heart of this chapter is one of how insurance operates as a *commodifier*. I concentrate especially on its role in two overlapping phenomena: the commodification of risk, and the commodification of human lives. In so doing, I highlight some of the severe moral and political consequences of these commodification processes and show how historical scholarship on insurance—especially life insurance—has laid bare these effects. As Dan Bouk (2015, p. xx) aptly writes in his study of life insurance and the statistical sciences in modern America, "the making of risks from human lives and the events of human lives" bore a strong resemblance to other key processes of commodification in the story of the US's economic development in the nineteenth and twentieth centuries. This chapter shows that Bouk's claim applies to other chronological and cultural settings, too. Wherever insurance developed, so did these processes of commodification.

This chapter looks primarily at episodes in the rise of insurance in early modern Britain, ca. 1500–1800. It focuses especially on life insurance, which is the industry in which concerns about the commodification of risk and the commodification of human life meet. Life insurance, perhaps more than any other form, calls to mind the contours of debates about contested commodities. As this chapter will show, its history has been shaped by arguments about whether life (and death) should be assigned a monetary value in the form of an insurance policy, and whether and what

DOI: 10.4324/9781003188742-13

kind of people should be allowed to purchase such a policy for themselves or others. Furthermore, even as life insurance has become part of the portfolio of a financially responsible person's life, questions about its moral and political ramifications persist, firmly rooted in its history. As Margaret Jane Radin (1996, p. 7) notes, anxieties about contested commodification do not take a pure form but are steeped in other social and political problems that concern us. Studying insurance, and life insurance in particular, points to at least two of these: the human desire for security in the face of an unknown future, and the human desire for freedom and self-ownership. Insurance has always been animated by the friction between these two, and thus it deserves our critical attention.

The core premise of this chapter, then, is that scholars interested in the ethical and political conundrums and contestations that accompany commodification would do well to look to insurance as a critical case study. I have chosen to look most closely at the development of insurance in early modern Britain, because it embraced life insurance much earlier than anywhere else. The case shows how moral frictions and problems characterized the development of markets for life insurance arose from its inception. While some of these have been laid to rest, others will be familiar to us as contemporary readers (and potential consumers of life insurance policies ourselves).

This chapter will proceed in three parts. The first section provides a brief conceptual overview of insurance as a constellation of technologies and practices and suggests that this capacious understanding of insurance allows us to home in on its role in commodification processes. In the second section of this chapter, I look more closely at the rise of different forms of insurance in early modern Britain: friendly societies of mutual aid and insurance, life insurance, and the intersection of marine and life insurance. These different forms of insurance played instrumental roles in the troubling commodification of both knowledge and persons. In the chapter's concluding section, I elaborate on how the logic of insurance has permeated modern life and left us with inheritances both salutary and concerning.

What is insurance?

By the time Samuel Johnson compiled his *Dictionary of the English Language* in 1755, insurance had a precise meaning in the Anglophone world. At this particular historical moment, insurance was, as Lorraine Daston (1987, p. 244) has aptly put it, wholly in vogue as a practice and a business and thus worthy of attention. It has only gained in momentum since. Johnson (1785, p. 701), compiling his dictionary within this context of vibrant activity, defines insurance as a kind of aleatory contract, an "exemption from hazard, obtained by the payment of a certain sum".[2] Johnson's entry shows that, some four centuries after insurance practices began to take hold in Britain, insurance was commonly understood as a contractual agreement intended to provide security against probable material loss in the future.[3] His definition makes room for two models of insurance that were in play by the mid-eighteenth century and that persist in our own time: risk exchange and risk pooling. On the exchange model, the insured paid sums in the present to an insurance firm, with the understanding that the insurer would reimburse or compensate them in the event of a loss or damage in the future. On the other side of this relationship, insurers stood to profit if the expected loss and subsequent payout never transpired. Perhaps the exchange model comes closest to helping us see why insurance might be treated as a kind of commodity. In the risk-pooling model, which assumed more symmetrical relationships among participants, groups of people with similar risk profiles paid premiums into a shared fund, on the assumption that they could later draw on it for support in the event of loss or damage.[4] Both of these models—each intended to make life more predictable and secure for people vulnerable to the unknown—will appear in more concrete form in the next section of this chapter.

But for now, Johnson's definition usefully highlights for us the transactional and contingent character of insurance contracts. It is also, however, important to take a step back from his account in favor of more conceptual renderings both of what insurance is *intended* to help people do and what it has *actually done*. One of the major contentions of this chapter is that thinking more broadly about insurance illuminates how it has contributed to commodification processes in ways both purposeful and unexpected. To open this line of inquiry, I turn to some conceptual treatments of insurance from the turn of the twenty-first century.

Two of the most succinct, but theoretically rich, accounts of insurance come from Carol Heimer and François Ewald. Each of them emphasizes—in broad strokes—that insurance is really a "constellation of technologies, institutions and practices that developed to help measure, predict, and control an unknown future" (Nacol, 2020, p. 79). They also stress that the insurance perspective is one that prioritizes the possibility of loss—a point embedded in Johnson's dictionary entry and one that seems obvious to us now. It was not always so, however; in the early modern period, insurance was often hard to tell apart from gambling in practice, as "it was possible to take insurance against a much broader range of events than any modern insurer would contemplate" (James, 2013, p. 6). The early days of insurance witnessed all kind of schemes and projects that were turned to profit-making, many of which were highly unstable and subsequently failed. Lorraine Daston (1988), has emphasized the shift to a loss-based perspective in her work on the science of probability, showing that insurance companies worked hard to link perceptions of the future tightly with fears of looming loss and threat, while simultaneously delinking insurance from gambling (pp. 185–197).[5] Over time, then, insurers themselves produced a loss-oriented idea of the future, and they did so to make their own industry viable and profitable.

From this varied history, Heimer's work usefully strips common understandings of insurance to their bare bones, explaining that "at its most basic, insurance is a social arrangement to reduce the effects of losses by employing the resources of the group to cushion individuals" (2003, p. 288). Her account thus captures one key logic of insurance—risk pooling—and its complex moral and political valence. Heimer emphasizes here that insurance depends on cooperation or, more strongly, on a commitment to mutual aid among individuals seeking to protect themselves against loss. It is, at its root, an enterprise in building social solidarity in anticipation of an unknown future—one that contains at least the *possibility* of loss or damage to valuable goods or persons.

Ewald (1998) makes this point about social solidarity even more robustly when he compares insurance to the social contract, a theoretical device that gripped the political imagination in the seventeenth and eighteenth centuries, also a critical period for the development of insurance. Insurance is, he explains, "a mode of association which allows participants to agree on the rules of justice they will subscribe to" (p. 207). This normative dimension of insurance frequently gets lost in the weeds of the complexity of states, insurance firms, contracts, and exchanges. And this is no accident, as Rachel Friedman (2020) reminds us in *Probable Justice*, her study of risk, insurance, and the rise of the modern welfare state. There she notes astutely that "it is part of the character of insurance to elide any clear separation between the logic of commercial exchange and that of cooperative mutual aid", making it sometimes difficult to keep sight of the latter as a fundamental principle of the enterprise (p. 19). This elision between speculation and protection has, she argues, always shaped the practice of insurance (p. 25). It may also heighten the temptation to treat insurance as a commodity.

Ewald also considers in greater depth how insurance—understood as a set of technologies—has left another kind of linguistic and conceptual imprint on human beings, our relationships to each other, and our orientation to the future. He asserts that "insurance can be defined as a technology of risk", and then boldly observes that "the term 'risk' which one finds being used nowadays apropos of everything has no precise meaning other than as a category of this technology" (Ewald, 1998, p. 198).[6] Here Ewald explores how insurance has shaped how human beings in particular contexts have confronted the future. For those of us who live in these contexts, he rightly suggests that a return to the fundamental features of insurance can help us refine how we conceive and communicate about what lies ahead. Namely, it offers us the opportunity for more precision in how we understand the future as a terrain of risk:

> In everyday language the term 'risk' is understood as a synonym for danger or peril, for some unhappy event which may happen to someone; it designates an objective threat. In insurance, the term designates neither an event nor a general kind of event occurring in reality (the unfortunate kind), but a *specific mode of treatment* of certain events capable of happening to a group of individuals.
>
> (Ewald, 1998, p. 199. Emphasis added.)[7]

In this brief reflection, Ewald emphasizes that insurance is both a way of probabilistically *calculating* unknown future events that affect collectives and their capital and a means of *organizing* in anticipation of their arrival. Put another way, insurance has given us the very concept of risk itself, a tool we use to make sense of a future that has not happened yet. Over time, we have untethered our understanding of risk from insurance as a "specific mode of treatment" of events that might happen, linking it instead to danger of unwanted harms. One could argue that this notable shift in risk's meaning was overdetermined from the start, given that the history of insurance is a story about developing and refining responses to catastrophic events, either on an individual or a collective scale. Further, as Daston has shown, insurers themselves worked diligently to emphasize that the future was a place of loss, as this assumption was the bedrock of their business. Ewald's work, in response, calls for a return to a more precise, historically situated understanding of risk, one that revisits the role of insurance in the development of our ability to use the tools of probability to envision the future and what awaits us there.

This brief accounting of how some scholars have defined and conceptualized insurance in the early modern and modern periods draws out three related points to keep in mind when considering the question of whether insurance is itself a commodity or bears some other relationship to commodification. First, although insurance is best understood not as a commodity but as a set of technologies, institutions, and practices, it has contained elements of exchange and even speculation since its inception. Second, insurance has, over time, attuned us to the future as a place of loss. As an outgrowth of a human—and arguably humane—urge to make the future a more predictable, safe place for human beings, their communities, and their capital, insurance has socialized us to keep an eye out for the dangerous and the catastrophic. Third, the contractual nature of insurance has historically compelled us to think in terms of "objects of settlement" and their value in monetary terms, an impulse that may butt up against some of the more humane and solidaristic impulses that motivate insurance. We can see these points about exchange, loss, and objectification come together in Giovanni Ceccarelli's (2016, p. 118) claim that "insurance is the first known contract in which risk becomes the specific object of the settlement". Ceccarelli's historical reminder invites us to take up hard questions about how we assign value to both risk itself and that which we risk, a series of considerations that allow us to think more capaciously about insurance's role in commodification processes. The next section of this chapter turns to insurance and commodification, with a particular focus on life insurance.

Insurance and commodification

Building on the previous section's consideration of how to properly define and conceive of insurance, I turn to two lines of inquiry about insurance and commodification. First, how has insurance—understood as a set of technologies, practices, and institutions—shaped our relationship to the future, and has it encouraged the commodification of our provisional knowledge of what lies there? What effects has this had on moral psychology and behavior? Second, how has insurance supported unacceptable practices of commodification, particularly the possibility of holding property in other people? These are complex questions that animate the historical literature on life insurance in particular (and, at points, its intersection with marine insurance).

As already noted in this chapter, from ca.1500–1800 in Britain, insurance became an entrenched feature of commercial and social life, and even, as Daston diagnoses it, something of a passion. A number of developments are worth noting. First, the period witnessed the piecemeal establishment of marine insurance, in which underwriters worked out individual contracts to protect sea merchants' commodities and goods against loss. Over time these small-scale, individualized efforts evolved into more corporate forms of marine insurance, supported by government-backed joint-stock companies. Second, home property insurance begins to take root in this period, with the development of fire insurance companies (and adjacent firefighting brigades) in the wake of the Great Fire of London in 1666, which destroyed more than 10000 homes. Third, early modern Britons participated in the formation and growth of smaller insurance collectives known as friendly societies. Spurred by ordinary people who clubbed together and pooled their resources to protect themselves and their families in the event of injury or death, friendly societies were social projects that were both highly solidaristic and at times quite disciplinary. Lastly, and unique to Britain in the context of Europe, life insurance became something of a mania, one which lent itself to speculating and gambling on the lives of others.

Taken together, these four developments display the distinct but at points overlapping features of insurance as detailed in the previous section of this chapter. In these different forms of insurance, we can see both the exchange and pooling models at work, sometimes in hybrid form. Insurers began to develop technologies and institutions—aleatory contracts, new corporations, mutual aid organizations—to manage these efforts to exchange or pool risk. New forms of knowledge production emerged, with the aim of compiling information about the lives and habits of those who sought insurance, including everyone from sea merchants to homeowners to labouring families one disaster away from poverty. The variety of forms of insurance unfolding in early modern Britain thus reflects the dramatic contours of human confrontation with an unknown future: the pursuit of reliable probabilistic knowledge about what might lie ahead; growing efforts to band together in solidarity with others for explicit protection against the unpredictable events of the natural and social world; and even quests to exploit the risk of future loss and turn it into a handsome profit. The rise of insurance is, when viewed from this perspective, strongly emblematic of the "Projecting Age" that Daniel Defoe ([1697] 1887) memorably captured in his reflections on Britain as a place of schemes and projects for improvement, security, adventure, and profit.

With these developments came the advent of certain commodification processes, beginning with the commodification of risk.[8] At first glance, this move is perhaps obscured by the recognition that insurance was initially devised to protect against the loss of particular, defined entities: a ship hauling wheat to trade, a wooden or brick home, or the life or limb of the primary breadwinner for a middle-class or poor family. But as Ceccarelli (2016) and Daston (1987) remind us, the insurance contract itself has always been centered on risk, and risk is its true object of settlement. As Daston notes, in the early modern period "risk became the defining characteristic for a distinct class of legal agreements, the aleatory contract", a contract that exchanged "certain for uncertain goods" (1987, p. 240). That is, risk became the thing to be measured, gauged, quantified, and valued. Daston goes on to note that these contracts—so closely associated with insurance—effectively brought two kinds of risk-oriented activities under the same umbrella. That is, she argues, they blurred the line between insurance and gambling, making it difficult to parse these two ways of approaching a future populated by probable, but not certain, events. Other scholars of insurance, such as Geoffrey Clark (1999) configure this relationship even more tightly, suggesting that at bottom insurance is really no more than "wagering on contingent events" (p. 35). This elision of the insurance contract and the wager was nowhere more evident than in the case of life insurance in Britain, which until the middle of the eighteenth century saw people taking out policies on everyone from the monarch to their neighbours, in hopes of turning a profit in the event of the person's death.[9] Clark and others have drawn on such cases to show how gambling and insurance were nearly indistinguishable in cases like these, wherein people explicitly treated insurance policies as wagers and bets rather than as sources of protection and security.

These speculative acts of "betting on lives", to use Clark's (1999) phrase, highlight most clearly how life insurance commodified risk, but it is important to recognize that this was true of all forms of insurance. Those seeking insurance always purchased policies or paid premiums in anticipation of some risk materializing—a storm, a fire, an injury, or a death. In turn, insurance providers seeking to maintain a profit made their calculations based on the likelihood that the risk would *not* materialize and trigger a payout to the other party in the relationship. In the interest of protecting their own financial stability and future profits, insurers began to develop techniques for hedging their bets, too. They searched for and compiled patterns of events and behaviors, so that they would have more refined probabilistic knowledge to guide their decisions about which ventures and which people to insure.[10] Zachman (2014) expresses this nicely: "In order to get the calculations right, risk takers wished to learn new methods of forecasting the future course of events beyond traditional practices of divination, the belief in the wisdom of gods, and resignation to an unknowable fate" (p. 16). Here, risk takers include not only those who seek insurance, but those who do the insuring. Their efforts in particular underscore that risk was the precious commodity animating the technologies, practices, and institutions comprising insurance.

Bouk (2015) catalogues this process of knowledge production in *How Our Days Became Numbered*, his excellent study of life insurance as a practice of risk making in the modern United States. Bouk focuses on how insurers teamed with a range of experts—actuaries, doctors, and other knowledge creators—to smooth out the risks to insurers by making individuals seeking insurance more "knowable" through systems of calculation and surveillance. Bouk traces a complex system of statistical knowledge production, but it is worth noting that this drive for knowledge and protection among insurers was also present among early insurance collectives that were working with simpler forms of probabilistic thinking. The friendly societies offer a clear example of this quest.

As I (2020) have written elsewhere, friendly societies were early modern mutual aid organizations, to which members voluntarily paid dues or subscriptions.[11] In return, in cases of injury, illness, disability, or death, members or their families were able to draw on the pool of accumulated funds to support themselves. The friendlies were most closely associated with what we might call life or disability insurance, but their explicitly solidaristic character also offered other forms of support and safety for their members: employment networks, friendship and neighbourly care, and social rituals and activities (Cordery, 2003). They were seen as good not only for individual members, but as sources of improvement for society at large—bulwarks against widespread isolation, poverty, and suffering (Ansell, 1835, p. 1, Defoe, [1697] 1887).

For the purposes of this chapter, however, what is most interesting were the systems of governance and surveillance friendly societies developed as a means of hedging against the risks posed by their members. Put simply, to keep from collapsing, these societies had to maintain their funds, taking care not to pay out too much too often. Some danger of this was built into the structure of the friendlies themselves; in periods of widespread illness or in the face of an aging membership, the society's pool of funds would naturally become more strained. But there is ample evidence that these societies also thought carefully about how risk and responsibility were distributed. For example, by recognizing that some lines of work were much more dangerous than others, they often organized society membership by professional affiliation. This way, people in exceptionally risky professions would not draw too heavily on the funds generated by others who worked in more secure environments (and who thus might have relatively little need for support). Here we see an early form of the classificatory impulses that would later animate the work of modern life insurance firms.

More disquieting, however, was the strong moralizing tone of the rules and regulations of membership in many of these societies. Those who joined friendly societies could expect to be closely watched for risky or imprudent behaviour, including profligate spending, deception, and even adultery. The rationale here was that those who did not behave soberly and cautiously were more likely to encounter harm, and thus to draw more heavily on the fund at the expense of their more prudent fellow members. But furthermore, these rules and regulations were often animated by the belief that those who behaved immorally were likely to shoulder punishment in the form of sickness, injury, or death. Hence profligate members were viewed as a genuine moral and financial risk to the rest of the membership (Cordery, 2003, p. 26). Whether governed by a hierarchical or more democratic structure, as Charles Ansell (1835) reflected,

> one of the chief guarantees for the good management of Friendly Societies is the constant care and watchfulness exercised by all the members over the conduct of each; and such watchfulness can never efficiently exist without all possessing a competent and clear knowledge of the institution.
>
> (p. 26)

This explicit reliance on the surveillance and evaluation of conduct should again direct our attention to the ways that even the most solidaristic of early modern insurance schemes worked to gauge, value, and commodify risk. It was, in fact, the only way they could stay afloat as an enterprise, even as some of the techniques they used introduced troubling processes of moralization and coercion that could be levied against members, leading to their exclusion and expulsion from these networks of care and community. The tools that served the measurement and commodification of risk would only grow in precision and sophistication over time and under the auspices of burgeoning insurance industries, and we can see evidence of them at work here in early form.

Although I have thus far focused on how insurance has commodified risk, the brief discussions of life insurance (both as a type of insurance policy and as a service offered by friendly societies) point to another critical role insurance has played in commodification. The insurance industry has, without question, also participated in the commodification of human life, by configuring it as a form of property that can be assigned monetary value. To return to this chapter's earlier reference to life insurance *qua* gambling, until the latter part of the eighteenth century, life insurance policies were frequently treated as a bet between insurers and policy holders on the life of a third person, which gave both parties a vested, "proprietary interest another person's life"—perhaps someone they did not even know (Clark, 1999, p. 53). This is an unusually stark example but worries about commodifying the loss of another person also hounded life insurance more broadly, as scholars have shown. Even if we set to one side the extreme cases of "betting on lives" in the analysis of life insurance, it still came with moral anxieties and costs.

Even in the British context, where life insurance was legally permitted, discussions about its moral ambiguities persisted for decades if not centuries. On the one hand, procuring a life insurance policy could be seen as a praiseworthy act of prudential foresight and caring responsibility for others, in the event that one's death would mean financial devastation for one's dependents. On the other hand, this salutary ethical framing had to compete with meaningful moral qualms about what it meant to assign monetary value to a loss that was "emotional and psychological" (Clark, 1999, p. 26).[12] In her study of the development of life insurance in the modern United States of America, Viviana Zelizer (1979) beautifully highlights this moral friction and its consequences. She offers a cultural account of how life insurers navigated prevalent mixed feelings about the relationship between money and death and shows how they leveraged widespread desire for control over life and death to establish their businesses. This process produced meaningful consequences for social attitudes towards both life and death. As she writes of the American case,

> Life insurance did more than simply respond and adjust to prevailing values regarding death. It influenced those values by introducing economic overtones into many traditional concepts. For instance, life insurance assumed the role of a secular ritual and introduced new notions of immortality that emphasized remembrance through money. A "good death" was no longer defined only on moral grounds; the inclusion of a life policy made financial foresight another prerequisite. Finally, *life insurance redefined death as an economic episode and life as an economic asset.*
>
> (Zelizer, 1979, p. 79. Emphasis added.)

Here Zelizer makes the case for analysing life insurance as a commodified good, through the lens of contested markets. The approach of this chapter is somewhat different, as I have been arguing that while insurance itself is *not* a commodity, attention to its development lets us see how it has commodified other things, in this case, human life. Zelizer ably shows, however, how insurers drew on prevailing moral sentiments about a good life and a good death, and also how they produced new sentiments and attitudes that would serve their business interests. She also documents carefully how insurers altered the social meaning of death in a significant way, placing an accent on its economic consequences instead of on its emotional fallout. Finally, insurers—in treating "death as an economic episode"—commodified human life as an asset that could be quantified in terms of monetary value, perhaps hollowing out some of its ineffable value. It is on this final point that Zelizer's work and the analysis of this chapter converge. The processes that Zelizer traces are specific to the American case, but her account resonates with what transpired in other historical settings, too. Even in the British context, where life insurance was legally permitted and widely embraced earlier than anywhere else, similar discussions about its ethical legacy persisted for decades if not centuries. These anxieties about the consequences of life insurance are likely traceable to the darkest part of life insurance's origin story.

The mingling of marine and life insurance in the early modern period also threw the dangers of the commodification of human life into even sharper relief. As Geoffrey Clark (1999) and Lorraine Daston (1987) have explored, life insurance may in fact have found a point of origin in early modern marine insurance, as it was permitted by insurance law for marine policies to cover the cargo of transatlantic voyages. This cargo also frequently comprised both material goods and people, including sometimes free passengers but, more importantly for our purposes, human beings being trafficked by slavers during the centuries of the global slave trade. As Clark (1999, p. 17) comments, "the insurance of slave cargoes was one of the oldest and most important constituents of the life insurance business as a whole", and perhaps another reason why it was held in some moral suspicion across Europe well into the eighteenth century. While not wholly responsible for the slave trade, insurers were, at minimum, complicit in its operation. Well beyond the question of whether life insurance policies commodified human life, then, insurers supported the business of markets in enslaved people, the starkest means of treating people as property with monetary value.

At least in Britain, the role marine insurers played in the commodification of the lives of enslaved people might have gone relatively unnoticed by the general public, were it not for the now-famous *Zong* massacre (1781), the ensuing insurance cases in British courts in the early 1780s, and the efforts by abolitionists to draw attention to the massacre to shift public opinion on whether the British slave trade should be ended. In brief, the *Zong,* a slave ship registered to a syndicate of Liverpool businessmen, was on its way from Africa to Jamaica when it apparently missed its final stop and began to run out of water, at least according to reports from the crew. The ship's captain then made the decision to address the water shortage by murdering 132 of the African men, women, and children aboard the ship, so that the remaining enslaved people on the boat might survive long enough to be sold at market. The crew killed them in three rounds by throwing them overboard. As James Walvin (2011) comments, "the atrocity might have passed virtually unnoticed but for one extraordinary fact: the syndicate [...] who owned the *Zong* took their insurers to court to secure payment for the loss of the dead Africans" (p. 2). Walvin shows in detail how the subsequent insurance litigation and public writing about it opened up fierce debates about what it meant for the syndicate to claim insurance on the lives of enslaved people who were killed by the *Zong* ship's crew—in effect, to profit from murder by drawing on an insurance contract. It was common practice in long marine voyages to jettison cargo to preserve a ship and other cargo, and marine insurance agreements often factored in compensation in case crews needed to throw goods overboard. Moreover, enslaved passengers were insured as cargo and covered as such, except in the cases of their natural deaths or murder in the event of a suppressed slave insurrection on board. But the people murdered on the *Zong* were not rebelling against their captors, nor did they die of natural causes, so whether their lives and deaths were to be compensated by insurers became a matter for the courts to settle. Importantly for our purposes, as Walvin puts it, the case showed the "links between the staid world of insurance and the violent world of slave ships" (p. 116). It exposed how insurance agreements perpetuated and codified the commodification of people as insurable property. The public airing of the details of the *Zong* insurance case also spurred public deliberations about the slave trade, debates that focused on what it meant to commodify people as property to be bought and sold on a market and that ultimately led to the end of the trade in Britain.

These different examples, recounted briefly in this section, show the troubled legacy of insurance, particularly life insurance—a practice that would eventually take hold in many countries beyond Britain. They show that while insurance was devised as a means of helping people cope with the risks of an unknown future, it also reshaped common life in ways that have warranted moral and political scrutiny and criticism. In commodifying risk, and seeking to know more about people as risk-takers, insurers and their technologies and practices have effectively reshaped human beings into risky subjects deserving of surveillance and governance. Further still, the history of insurance is, without question, entwined with the history of the commodification of people, whether we look to the history of life insurance policies and organizations or to the history of marine insurance and its role in the slave trade.

Conclusion

This chapter has considered how the development of insurance has entailed other processes of commodification and the commodification of other things, and in so doing, has attended largely to the dark underside of this "staid world of insurance". By way of conclusion, I would like to suggest that close study of insurance shows that this world is not staid at all, but a complex place of security, predictability, and community on the one hand, and profit, misadventure, and violence on the other. These two sides of insurance are inseparable in its history, and we see traces of each today in our own encounters with the technologies, practices, and institutions that make up insurance.

To be sure, insurance has nearly always been claimed as a humane enterprise, one that makes the world safer and more predictable for people who may be only one adverse event away from catastrophic ruin. It is an exercise in social solidarity, as we can see from the formation and endurance of friendly societies all the way to the development of the social welfare state and the assurances its policies can offer the ordinary people who live under its auspices. Insurance surely is protection against the risks posed by the natural and the human-made worlds we inhabit.

But, if we approach insurance with questions about commodification in mind, we immediately see the other side of the story. Insurance has produced a novel way of thinking about the future—risk—one that favours data collection, calculation, and prediction about human psychology and behaviour, largely spurred by insurers and the teams of experts they assemble. Such a form of knowledge production has advanced the project of commodifying risk and turning it into profit, largely to be claimed by insurers and their firms and corporations. This drive to acquire knowledge of risk and to hedge against it has long encouraged insurers to govern the insured, by linking access to the benefits of insurance to certain kinds of prudent behaviors and choices. It thus turns us into insurable subjects—"good bets" for the industry. The history of insurance also reveals how people themselves become commodified through various insurance agreements—gambled on as the object of a wager or figured as material property with monetary value. Thus, while insurance itself resists classification as a commodity, the history of insurance is a story about how commodification has, in ways subtle and by means overtly violent, narrowed the scope of human freedom and self-determination, even as it has made the world safer for people, too. It thus belongs in ongoing conversations about contested commodities, because scrutinizing insurance helps us look more deeply at the conflicts between human desires for both security and freedom and the conflicts between these sometimes-competing values.

Notes

1 Since the 1990s, insurance-linked securities have available for investors on global capital markets to sell and trade, but again, this does not warrant classifying them as commodities *per se*.

2 Johnson's term is *ensurance*, which was used interchangeably with *insurance* in eighteenth-century English usage.

3 It is difficult to know precisely when insurance took hold as a practice in Britain. The first known insurance agreement or contract was formed ca. 1350 CE for a cargo of wheat shipping from Sicily to Tunis (Lewin, 2003, p. 86). Scholars think that English merchants probably learned about insurance from their Italian trading partners, and they went on to develop their own marine insurance market by ca. 1500 (Lewin, 2003, p. 91; Rossi, 2016, pp. 131–132). From there, the insurance business diversified, branching into life and fire insurance, as well as other protective schemes (Zachman, 2014, p. 7).

4 As Rachel Friedman (2020) points out, while distinct in theory, these two models of insurance are not cleanly separable in practice. Both have been treated as forms of exchange, and elements of each have been incorporated into different insurance schemes over time (p. 29).

5 On the autonomization of gambling as commodity, see Trespeuch's chapter in this volume.
6 Ewald's (1998) account expands well beyond this, as he begins his essay with the insight that *insurance* is an "equivocal" term; in his essay, he explores it as "institution," "abstract technology," form," and even "imaginary" (pp. 197–198).
7 Mary Douglas (1992) offers a similar observation, noting that the meaning of risk has been wrested loose from its relationship to probabilistic thinking about the likelihood of future events (and ensuing gains and losses) and has instead become "a decorative flourish on the word 'danger'" (p. 40). Although she does not call for a return to risk's roots in insurance technologies, she does call for a recovery of its precise meaning. And as Ewald notes, this recovery should take us back to the multi-century history of insurance, which may well account for how we have come to elide risk and danger conceptually. As noted above, Daston's (1987) work traces this process very carefully.
8 Bouk (2015) makes this connection directly in his excellent study of how life insurers in the modern US produced risk through their work. In the preface he writes,

> Societies have always had ways of thinking about the hazards and dangers that face them and their constituents—we sometimes talk about those dangers as risks. But with the spread of insurance, risk took on a more specific definition: a risk became a kind of commodity.
>
> (p. xx)

9 This kind of speculation came under fire in the second half of the eighteenth century, and the Gambling Act of 1744 addressed it directly through legislation. It decreed that anyone taking out a life insurance policy on another person had to prove that they held a "legitimate financial interest" in that person's survival (Clark, 1999, p. 53).
10 It is worth noting that this was learned behavior that took time to develop, and the early days of insurance witnessed the rise and nearly immediate fall of many small insurance firms and schemes (Zachman, 2014, p. 7; Clark, 1999, p. 3).
11 These organizations had their heyday in the sixteenth to nineteenth centuries, but many still exist and operate today.
12 Viviana Zelizer traces out these debates about life insurance in the context of the United States in the nineteenth and twentieth centuries, noting how critics argued that life insurance monetized something sacred; the life (and death) of a husband or father was assigned a monetary value that was then paid out to widows and orphans (1979, pp. 49–50).

References

Ansell, C. (1835) *A Treatise on Friendly Societies: In Which the Doctrine of Interest of Money and the* Doctrine *of Probability are Practically Applied to the Affairs of such Societies*. London: Baldwin and Craddock.

Bouk, D. (2015) *How Our Days Became Numbered: Risk and the Rise of the Statistical Individual*. Chicago: University of Chicago Press.

Ceccarelli, G. (2016) "Coping with unknown risks in Renaissance Florence: Insurers, friars, and Abacus Teachers," in C. Zweirlein (ed.) *The Dark Side of Knowledge: Histories of Ignorance, 1400–1800*. Leiden: Brill, pp. 118–138.

Clark, G. (1999) *Betting on Lives: The Culture of Life Insurance in England, 1695–1775*. Manchester: Manchester University Press.

Cordery, S. (2003) *British Friendly Societies, 1750–1914*. London: Routledge.

Daston, L. (1988) "The domestication of risk: Mathematical probability and insurance 1650–1830," in L. Krüger et al. (eds.) *The Probabilistic Revolution, Volume I: Ideas in History*. Cambridge: MIT Press, pp. 237–360.

Daston, L. (1995) *Classical Probability in the Enlightenment*. Princeton: Princeton University Press.

Defoe, D. ([1697]1887) *An Essay Upon Projects*. London: Cassell & Company, Ltd.

Douglas, M. (1992) *Risk and Blame*. New York: Routledge.

Ewald, F. (1998) 'Insurance and risk,' in G. Burchell et al. (eds.) *The Foucault Effect: Studies in Governmentality*. Chicago: University of Chicago Press, pp. 197–210.

Friedman, R. (2020) *Probable Justice: Risk, Insurance, and the Welfare State*. Chicago: University of Chicago Press.

Heimer, C. (2003) "Insurers as moral actors," in R.V. Ericson and A. Doyle (eds.) *Risk and Morality.* Toronto: University of Toronto Press, pp. 284–316.

James, H. (2013) "Introduction: The insuring instinct," in H. James, P. Borscheid, et al. (eds.) *The Value of Risk: Swiss Re and the History of Reinsurance*. Oxford: Oxford University Press, pp. 1–20.

Johnson, S. (1785) *A Dictionary of the English Language in Which the Words are Deduced from their Originals, and Illustrated in their Different Significations by Examples from the Best Writers: To which are Prefixed, a History of the Language, and an English Grammar,* 6th edn. London: J. F. And C. Rivington.

Lewin, C.G. (2003) *Pensions and Insurance Before 1800: A Social History*. East Linton: Tuckwell Press.

Nacol, E. (2020) "The entanglement of profit and loss: Risk and the language of insurance in Early Modern political thought," in B. Ghosh and B. Sarkhar (eds.) *The Routledge Companion to Media and Risk.* London: Routledge, pp. 79–90.

Radin, M.J. (1996) *Contested Commodities.* Cambridge: Harvard University Press.

Rossi, G. (2016) "England 1523–1601: The beginnings of marine insurance," in A.B. Leonard (ed.) *Marine Insurance: Origins and Institutions, 1300–1850*. London: Palgrave: pp. 131–150.

Walvin, J. (2011) *The Zong: A Massacre, the Law, the End of Slavery*. New Haven: Yale University Press.

Zachman, K. (2014) "Risk in historical perspective: Concepts, contexts, and conjunctions," in C. Klüppelberg, D. Straub, and I.M. Welpe (eds.) *Risk–A Multidisciplinary Introduction*. New York: Springer, pp. 3–35.

Zelizer, V.A.R. [(1979) 2018] *Morals and Markets: The Development of Life Insurance in the United States*. New York: Columbia University Press.

PART 3

Contested commodities and the state

11
VOTE BUYING AND CAMPAIGN FINANCE

Jason Brennan and Christopher Freiman

Introduction

"Commodification" is a term referring to the process of placing something for sale that was not previously the kind of thing people would buy and sell (Brennan and Jaworski, 2015; Brennan and Jaworski, 2016). A "contested commodity" or "taboo market" involves the sale of something that many people think ought not to be commodified. Perhaps *votes* are the most contested commodity of all. Generally, most people believe that people ought not to be paid to vote, period, and certainly not paid to vote *a particular way*. You may vote as you please for free, but not vote for money. Relatedly, people generally oppose anything that they regard as the commodification of political power. For this reason, many oppose private donations to campaign finance, or at least private donations by certain groups or above certain sizes, because they worry that this will lead to improper exercises of power.

There are a wide range of objections that different theorists and laypeople could and have raised to vote buying and selling. These include:

1. Rights violations: Perhaps buying and selling votes or power violates others' political rights, as it amounts to a loss of equal political liberty.
2. Harm to others: Perhaps when voters sell their votes, this causes improper harm to third parties.
3. Harm to self: Perhaps voters selling their votes causes improper harm to themselves.
4. Exploitation: Perhaps buying and selling votes takes pernicious advantage of disadvantaged voters' misfortune; they sell votes because they are desperate.
5. Misallocation: Perhaps buying and selling votes, or certain campaign finance practices, cause power to be misallocated in unfair and unjust ways.
6. Corruption: Perhaps buying and selling votes or power corrupts the motivations of those with power, causing them to develop improper or immoral preferences.
7. Semiotic: Perhaps buying and selling votes or power expresses disrespect for democracy or for others; it communicates the idea that the exercise of power is not different from buying apples (Brennan and Jaworski, 2015, pp. 1054–1056.)

DOI: 10.4324/9781003188742-15

In the academic literature, one can find all sorts of variations of arguments against vote buying and selling which adopt arguments like these. Reviewing all the variations in depth would take more space than we have here (for an overview, see Freiman, 2014).

In this chapter, we focus primarily on the most important and widespread kind of argument against commodifying votes or power. We will refer to this as the "Big Objection to Commodifying Power". It goes as follows:

> *The Big Objection to Commodifying Power*
> Introducing money into politics in certain ways, such as by buying votes or allowing high campaign donations, tends to induce elected representatives or other government agents to implement policies which advance the interests of buyers or donors at the expense of others. Therefore, such commodification is wrong. Keeping democracy safe from money is essential to making it function correctly.

This is the most significant argument against vote buying and against excessive private funding in campaign finance. The best way to understand this argument is to see how well it withstands challenges. In this chapter, we will meet those challenges by introducing a range of arguments *in favour* of vote buying and private campaign finance.

Compulsory voting versus paid voting

Electoral turnout rates vary around the world and by election type. For instance, local Swiss elections enjoy higher turnout than national referenda, while the US has higher turnout for presidential elections than for local. Many democratic theorists believe low turnout is bad or unjust and advocate compulsory voting as a remedy. Some of the arguments for compulsory voting include:

1. In voluntary voting regimes, the advantaged (high income, educated, employed, etc.) turn out at higher rates than the disadvantaged. This can lead to democracy disproportionately representing the advantaged better than the disadvantaged. Compulsory voting is an effective means to ensure the disadvantaged vote at the right rates (Brennan and Hill, 2014.)
2. Voters fail to vote because they face an assurance problem. They know that what matters is not their individual votes, which make no difference, but whether enough people like them and with similar interests also vote. However, they have no effective mechanism to ensure others with shared interests do vote, so they abstain. Compulsory voting penalizes non-voting and thus creates assurance that others will vote.
3. Voting is a duty. Therefore, those who violate this duty ought to be punished by law. (This argument is complicated by noting that many moral duties are not enforceable by law, and so here one needs to explain why *this* particular duty is.)

If you find any of these arguments for compulsory voting plausible, then it's worth asking whether authorizing the state to pay people to vote is a better alternative than coercing them.

Consider argument 1, that voluntary voting leads to higher rates of participation among the advantaged. The mechanism is supposed to be that the disadvantaged face impediments to voting, for instance, by not being able to take time off from work or having childcare issues. Coercing them into voting does not remove these underlying impediments; it instead tries to get them to vote by making abstention even more burdensome. One might think here that governments should use carrots instead of sticks. Perhaps everyone who votes could receive a three-hundred-euro tax credit. Or consider argument 2, which says compulsion overcomes an assurance problem. Again, one might think using carrots is better than sticks. Instead of harming those who fail to vote, we could pay people to vote.

In both these cases, we are imagining a government paying citizens to vote, but not paying them to vote any particular way. They are not paid to vote Liberal over Green or Conservative over Labour. They are paid to cast a vote according to their conscience instead of being penalized for failing to do so. In general, there is a presumption against government coercion; government should coerce people to do something only if a non-coercive alternative is not available. If one favours compulsory voting for these two reasons, one should presumptively favour paying voters to vote instead of compulsion.

The third argument may not have this implication. We do not pay people not to murder each other but we punish them for murder. Still, one might think that even here, if payment works better or as well as compulsion, that's a reason to pay for voting rather than compel it. For instance, suppose paying people an annual "don't murder anyone" fee were both A) less costly than traditional law-enforcement and B) more effective at preventing murder. We would regard this as a strong argument in favour of such a fee.

Paying people to vote the way they would vote anyway

The Big Objection holds that commodifying votes would induce voters to vote in favour of the interests of the rich, or at least in favour of whatever special interest groups were able to buy votes. On this argument, a vote contains information about what voters want and care about. Votes are a mechanism by which the will of the voters is transformed into power. If we allow vote buying and selling, interest groups will buy votes to ensure they get their way. Government will represent the buyers rather than the voters.

There are other objections to commodification, but here we are focusing on objections concerning whether vote buying will lead to unfair representation or unjust outcomes. But, as the previous discussion of compulsory voting showed, this objection is too facile. After all, we can imagine governments paying all citizens to vote their conscience as a means of generating increased and more representative voter turnout. This mechanism might enhance rather than undermine democracy. Indeed, we might reply that if you oppose commodifying votes this way, you must not care much about fair representation, or must fetishize using sticks over carrots.

But this kind of example seems to generalize. If the government could permissibly pay people to vote this way, why not others? Imagine that, say, Bill Gates or Jeff Bezos become concerned with underrepresentation, and started offering $100 vouchers to anyone who votes, regardless of how they vote. Whatever merits or demerits this might have, at least it escapes the objection we are now discussing. Here, Gates is not inducing voters to vote for Big Tech; he is simply inducing them to vote, period.

Or, consider a micro-example. Our friend Loren Lomasky never votes because he considers it a waste of time. After all, he has published extensively on the low probability that a vote will be decisive and has argued there is no duty to vote per se (Lomasky and Brennan, 2000, Brennan and Lomasky, 2003). He instead focuses his altruistic behaviour on more effective endeavors. But Lomasky is also a careful, cautious, and open-minded thinker. Suppose that we, the authors, offer to pay Lomasky to vote his conscience because, *pace* Lomasky, we think his individual vote does matter, and we want to do the world a favour by getting a good person like him to the polls. Here, again, it's far from clear that the Big Objection applies to us or Lomasky in this example. Instead of spoiling the ballot in favour of special interests, we are ever so slightly raising the epistemic quality of the electorate by inducing a lifelong abstainer to cast a careful, smart vote.

One might object here that this is wrong because votes are inalienable. An alienable right is one that people cannot freely give up. For instance, Jason has many guitars, but he is free to give them away and thus alienate his right to property in those guitars. However, we might think a citizen may not alienate their right to vote. However, this objection misunderstands what is happening in the examples so far. When we pay Lomasky to vote, or Bezos or the government pay everyone to vote, no one loses their right. Rather, they are simply being paid to exercise it. In much the same way, when we are paid to give talks on this or that, we commodify the exercise of our right to free speech to some extent, but we do not thereby lose or alienate the right. The universities that pay for our speech do not acquire our rights of free speech; they merely pay us to perform certain speeches. (And, even then, only within limits. They pay us to say what we think, not to say what they think.)

These considerations are starting to point toward a candidate principle for the ethics of commodifying votes. Consider the following:

> *If it's morally permissible for a person to vote X for free, then it is morally permissible for others to pay that person to vote X.*

In other words, this thesis claims that money does not introduce wrongness where there was not any to begin with. Money might indeed motivate people to vote in bad or unjust ways, and so money can surely induce bad behaviour. But, according to this thesis, if it is morally permissible for a person to vote in a particular way for free, then voting that same way after being paid does not transform the otherwise permissible action into something wrongful (Brennan and Jaworski 2016).

We have not proven this thesis yet. More cases and objections remain. Still, it is worth pausing to ask whether many objections to paid voting are not about the payment per se, but about *how* people might vote after being paid. If they are about the latter, then it seems people should be opposed to those modes of voting even if done for free. Consider two cases:

1. Jeff Bezos pays a majority of Americans to vote in favour of candidates who will promote Amazon's interests over everyone else's.
2. A majority of Americans decide to vote in favour of candidates who will promote Amazon's interests over everyone else's. They do so for free.

In case 1, critics of vote selling regard the case as wrongful because the payment leads to unfair or improper representation; it leads to the government making bad choices. In case 2, though, the exact same outcome occurs, but this time it occurs without payment. If your concern in case 1 is the *bad outcome of the election*—i.e., that the democracy will represent the interests of the few over the many or produce unjust policies—then you should also think that voters act wrongfully in case 2 as well. In case 1, money induces voters to vote badly, but the fundamental problem is the bad voting, not the money. You might still oppose money in politics because you think it makes bad voting more common, but you should also oppose the root problem: bad voting.

One way to test this is to consider what we should think if people instead paid citizens to vote *for justice*. We consider that next.

Paying someone to vote the objectively right way

Imagine that in the late 1940s USA, a progressive-thinking billionaire has had enough of Jim Crow. The billionaire funds information campaigns with the goal of educating citizens to care about equal civil rights for all. Alas, the campaigns fail, and most voters continue to support these unjust rules. Imagine, however, a ballot referendum is held over whether to retain Jim Crow. Since arguments failed to persuade, the billionaire bribes many voters to vote against the racist laws. As a result, Jim Crow laws are overturned and Black Americans enjoy better civil rights.

Or, imagine that an election will soon be held between a genuinely good candidate and a terrible candidate. Again, suppose information fails to persuade, but a billionaire bribes voters to support the genuinely good candidate. As a result, the good candidate wins, thus preventing the government from implementing various evil and unjust policies. For instance, imagine that in late 1932 Germany, a billionaire bribed voters not to vote for the Nazis or Nationalists.

What should we say about these actions? We, the authors, think the hypothetical billionaire is a hero and his actions are right. We do not accept the view that democracies have the authority to commit evil simply because they make evil decisions democratically. If the collective earnestly votes for evil, that does not render evil good, but renders the collective blameworthy. Just as Schindler was right to sabotage munitions production, so the billionaire is right to sabotage the democratic process here.

You might disagree for any number of reasons. In this chapter, though, we are limiting ourselves to considering the Big Objection to Commodifying Democracy. Note that the Big Objection does not seem to apply to this case though. The Big Objection holds that the problem with buying votes or power is that this will lead to democracy representing the interests of the rich and powerful over the many. Here, though, the billionaire is not bribing people to support his own self-interest. Rather, he is bribing them to support justice.

The unwelcome implications

So far, we have considered cases where the government or others pay people to vote their conscience, and then a case where a heroic billionaire pays people to vote for what is in fact just, instead of supporting what is in fact unjust. So far, none of these cases run afoul of the Big Objection. Accordingly, the Big Objection, even if sound, does not show that *all* instances of vote buying are wrong. In this section, though, we make more trouble for the Big Objection and for additional objections to commodification.[1] We worry that these objections have unnoticed implications which the objectors are unwilling to endorse.

To begin, consider an objection from economist Greg Mankiw, who argues that vote selling can harm third parties:

> Suppose three voters are deciding whether to provide a public good that costs \$9, which would be financed by a \$3 tax on each voter. Andy values the public good at \$8, while Ben and Carl do not value it at all. Under majority voting, Ben and Carl vote against, and the public good does not get provided, which is the efficient outcome. Suppose, however, that Andy could buy Ben's vote for \$4. He could then ensure the project gets passed. Andy is better off by \$1 (the \$8 benefit minus the \$3 tax and the \$4 price of the vote), Ben is better off by \$1 (the \$4 price of the vote minus the \$3 tax), and Carl is worse off by \$3 (the \$3 tax). The Andy–Ben vote deal has negative externalities on Carl.
>
> (Mankiw, 2007)

Mankiw is surely correct that vote selling can create negative externalities. But this conclusion is insufficient to establish that vote selling is wrong or ought to be prohibited. Consider that Andy may write a persuasive op-ed that convinces Ben to vote for the public good. The op-ed would thus make Carl worse off, but it seems neither morally nor legally impermissible for Andy to write it. Mankiw has not identified a principled difference between externalities caused by op-eds and vote buying.

Perhaps the bigger worry concerns *widespread* vote buying. If Andy buys one vote, the impact is minimal. However, if many buyers purchase votes, the social costs could be significant. Here again, though, this conclusion doesn't establish that vote sales ought to be prohibited. After all, widespread biased or uninformed voting may produce significant social costs, but democrats believe that uninformed voting ought not to be prohibited. An unusually persuasive op-ed, book, or comedy routine might produce significance social costs, but democrats believe political speech should be protected.

A further objection, raised by theorists including Michael Sandel and Debra Satz, alleges that vote markets inappropriately turn votes into commodities that are used to advance citizens' self-interest rather than the common good (Sandel, 2012; Satz, 2010.) But using one's vote to advance one's self-interest, while perhaps morally suspect, is not criminal.[2] For instance, a sugar grower is at liberty to vote for sugar subsidies on the grounds that these subsidies will work to her material benefit.

A related concern is that buying and selling votes sends the wrong message about the value of a vote. In this spirit, Sandel writes, "We believe that civic duties should not be regarded as private property but should be viewed instead as public responsibilities. To outsource them is to demean them, to value them in the wrong way" (Sandel, 2012, p. 10). Let us first note that valuing something in the wrong way, while possibly objectionable, is far from criminal. (Freiman 2019, p. 128.) To treat your family portrait as nothing more than a giant tissue is to value it in the wrong way, but it's not prohibited. Similarly, even if we grant that treating your vote as a commodity misvalues your vote, that doesn't make it a crime. Indeed, we suspect Sandel would argue that casting a write-in vote for Santa Claus demeans the vote, but that's not illegal.

Moreover, it's far from clear that "outsourcing" your responsibilities is objectionable in the first place. Consider that you have a responsibility to ensure that your children get vaccinated. But it is perfectly fine, and likely obligatory, to outsource the act of vaccinating your child to a doctor who is better suited for the task than you are. Many of us should outsource our children's education to experts rather than doing it ourselves. Similarly, then, perhaps you may fulfill your public responsibilities by outsourcing your vote to someone who you justifiably believe has greater political experience than you do. Indeed, we'll note that deferring to experts is often recommended as a strategy for voters to overcome their own political ignorance and biases. But there's little meaningful difference between simply voting for your favourite think tank's preferred candidate and transferring it to them to cast the vote for you. Indeed, the latter might be regarded as a more effective form of using heuristics, because it reduces the chance of error.

Finally, we doubt that citizens who sell their vote out of ambivalence demean the vote. Such a sale simply transfers the vote from someone who values it less to someone who values it more. It doesn't demean the Vermeer you unearthed in your attic to sell it to an art collector because you value it less than she does. And if anything, the buyer expresses how *highly* she values it by her willingness to pay the price.[3] If someone is genuinely concerned about people demeaning the vote, then rather than complaining about selling votes, they should complain about ignorant, irrational, or apathetic voters.

Institutionalizing vote markets

A number of additional objections to vote markets concern what Jason Brennan and Peter Jaworski call the market *architecture.* (Brennan and Jaworski, 2015, p. 35) That is, they concern *how* something is sold rather than *what* is sold. For example, some egalitarians object to sub-minimum wage labour contracts on the grounds that they exploit workers. However, this objection doesn't show the impermissibility of buying and selling labour as such—rather, it would only show the impermissibility of buying and selling labour in certain ways or under certain conditions.

Similarly, we may interpret the Big Objection partly as a concern about the architecture of a vote market rather than a concern about the sale of votes as such (Freiman, 2014; Taylor, 2017). For instance, Satz writes, "A market in votes would have the predictable consequence of giving the rich disproportionate power over others since the poor would be far more likely than the rich to sell their political power" (Satz 2010, p. 102). Even if we grant Satz's prediction, it wouldn't establish the impermissibility of vote markets as such. Rather, it would only establish the impermissibility of *unregulated* vote markets, or perhaps only to markets that have this problem. To accommodate the Big Objection, states could cap the amount that people may spend on vote purchases or the total number of votes they may purchase. Or the rich could voluntarily choose not to act this way.

Furthermore, one might worry that a functional vote market is incompatible with a secret ballot. Presumably Alice pays Bob to vote because she wants him to vote in a particular way. But if Bob's vote is secret, she has no way of knowing who he voted for. Thus, very few, if any, vote sales would actually occur. The secrecy problem is simple enough to solve with the right market architecture, though. Sellers could simply transfer their vote to buyers, who in turn gain that extra vote to use as they please. Think of it as Venmo for voting. In this way, the buyers are able to ensure that the purchased vote is cast for their preferred candidate without compromising the secrecy of the vote itself.

Campaign finance: Much ado about nothing?

It is dogma among many democratic theorists that private campaign finance spoils democracy and thus ought to be prohibited or greatly restricted. For instance, John Rawls argues that citizens ought to be guaranteed the fair value of their political liberties, which he understands as requiring that every citizen have roughly equal chance to influence political outcomes. He then announces that this may require public financing of elections (Rawls 1999, p. 198).

While the absence of any sort of empirical inquiry into campaign finance in Rawls's work seems objectionable at first blush, he would assert that no such inquiry is needed. After all, Rawls is theorizing for *ideal* conditions—that is, he is considering which institutional structures are appropriate for a fully just society where everyone is motivated to do what's right so long as others do the same (Rawls, 2001). Thus, he can safely assume that public financing of elections will not have any corrupting effects and will work precisely as intended.

However, Rawls fails to notice an inconsistency in his argument: in ideal conditions where all are motivated to do what's right, presumably no one will be tempted to buy up unfair sums of political power by hypothesis—and therefore public financing of elections will be unnecessary.[4] It is only when we assume that some people are motivated to seize political power for their own purposes that public financing of elections would have a point. But then we must inquire into the effects of public financing on less than perfectly just people such as those that occupy the actual world. In what follows, we briefly review the debate in political science and economics, which shows not quite that Rawls's claims are false, but instead that they are at least not well-supported.

Let's begin by noting some puzzling features of American (and other) elections which are hard to square with the claim that money buys power. These include:[5]

- The incumbent candidate usually wins.
- The person with the views closer to the median voter usually wins.
- During midterms, the party opposite of the president usually gains seats.
- If there has been a recession in the last six months, the incumbent usually loses, regardless of blame.
- If personal income is growing, incumbents usually win.
- The better-looking candidate usually wins.
- There are very few swing voters; most people vote the same way every time, and most citizens either always vote or never vote.

If money were simply buying elections, we would not expect to see such results year after year.

Gordon Tullock famously identified a puzzle which sounds absurd to many philosophical readers, though familiar to empirical social scientists: why is there so little money in politics? Many would regard this question as absurd, but that's because they haven't given the issue much thought. US GDP in 2021 was about $23 trillion. The total size of the US government, including local and state branches, is over $7 trillion (more than twice the size of Canada's GDP). In 2020 and 2021, thanks to spending sprees, it was higher than that. There is tremendous power and wealth out there to capture. But when we look at the actual amounts of money being spent on campaign marketing, donations, or direct lobbying, they are tiny compared to the amount of power and wealth that could be captured through politics.

For instance, the total amount of money spent on all US campaigns in 2020 is only about three times what Nike alone spends on marketing, with Nike's goal of capturing as much value as it can in a $181 billion sports apparel industry. Overall, campaign finance expenditures are about two orders of magnitude smaller than we would expect them to be if they were like any other form of marketing. Marketing costs in most industries are about 8% of total revenue, but in US campaigns, they are closer to a tenth of a percent of actual government revenue and an even smaller fraction of possible revenue. So, there is indeed a puzzle of why there is so little money in US politics.

One might conclude that, aha!, this must mean that campaign marketing and financing has unusually high returns and is unusually effective. But this objection faces two problems. For one, it's self-defeating. If campaign finance were so effective, we would expect selfish and greedy special interests to therefore spend more than they do, because by hypothesis they would see exceptionally high returns on such spending. This objection claims that greedy corporations and special interests use money to buy elections, but then the fact there is so little money in politics with such high returns implies they are leaving trillion-dollar bills on the floor. Usually, when X has high returns, selfish and greedy individuals and corporations chase X until diminishing returns puts X back to the normal rate of profit. Second, it doesn't square with the findings mentioned above, such as that incumbents tend to win or that fundamentals such as the economy's performance tend to determine winners.

In a famous paper, Stephen Ansolabehere and his co-authors (2003) review forty major studies in elite political science journals which use sophisticated regression techniques to measure the impact of campaign donations on which candidate wins or how elected officials later vote. The results were clear: overall, there is no statistically significant impact on either. Yasmin Dawood's (2015) review of the related literature gets the same result.

In another related paper, Ansolabehere et al., (2004) examines natural experiments in campaign finance laws. At various times, the US Supreme Court, US Congress, or various state legislatures and courts have allowed or forbidden different kinds or amounts of corporate donations and lobbying. If these donations are influencing legislators and others to support corporate interests, then what we should expect to see is that when donations are restricted, donating firms' gross revenue or rate or profit fall, while when they are permitted or expanded, their revenue and profits increase. We should expect to see corporations have better returns in US states where they can "buy power" than in those they cannot. But, on the contrary, there are no significant changes in companies' bottom lines before or after changes that restrict or permit expansions in their spending.

In Hans Noel's (2010) famous paper "Ten Things Political Scientists Know That You Don't", he lists as item #10 that political scientists don't know many of the things that laypeople assume they know. He then gives a list of things laypeople think political scientists have proven but which they have, after extensive study, been unable to demonstrate. His top two are the money buys the votes of the public or votes of legislators.

The claim that money corrupts democracy has been heavily tested and the tests do not come out the right way. In fact, there is very little money in US politics, let alone other advanced democracies' political systems, and the outcomes of US politics are far more strongly influenced by other factors, such as those we listed above. The Big Objection to Commodifying Power presumes facts that are most likely false.

Democratic realism vs anti-commodificationism

In this section, we note that the Big Objection rests upon other likely-to-be-false empirical assumptions. According to the Big Objection, money is bad because it spoils democracy. Normally, what happens in a democracy is something like this: Voters know their own interests. They learn how the world works and thus form an ideology, where an ideology is a set of political beliefs which hold that certain policies or political behaviours will produce certain values. Voters then vote for candidates and parties that best match their ideology, or at least are a good enough match and have a good chance of winning. Politicians, in turn, run platforms that they expect to match voters' policy preferences, because that is what it takes to win. The winning candidates thus tend to reflect the will of the majority or at least plurality of their constituents. They then try to implement this political will. If they fail, they will lose power next election. So, the story goes, democracy tends to ensure that those in power serve citizens' interests. But, supposedly, introducing money corrupts this system by causing politicians to instead serve donor interests.

We saw above that we have very little evidence that money in fact has this corrupting effect. But it gets worse. The other problem with this objection is voters themselves do not behave as described. Money doesn't spoil democracy because democracy does not work the way the Big Objection implicitly assumes. Any theory of commodification needs to deal with the following facts:

First, most voters are extremely ignorant of basic political information. They generally do not know who their elected representatives are, which party controls their legislature, what major bills have been passed, or even what the party platforms are. (Campbell et al., 1960; Delli-Carpini and Keeter,1996; Converse, 1964; Friedman, 2006; Caplan, 2007; Somin, 2013; Brennan, 2016). They do not merely lack the social scientific expertise needed to assess these facts, but lack the facts themselves.

Second, many voters are not merely ignorant, but systematically misinformed.[6] For instance, during the Brexit vote, UK citizens vastly overestimated the number of EU immigrants in the UK, overestimated Chinese foreign investment, dramatically underestimated EU investment in the UK, and vastly overestimated how much the UK sends to the EU in terms of various welfare payments. (Ipsos Mori, 2016)

Third, the majority of voters are innocent of ideology. They have few political policy preferences. If surveyed, they may offer an "opinion" on the spot because survey respondents in general hate saying, "I don't know", but if surveyed again, they will usually offer a different opinion and will not even know they "changed their minds". Only around 15% of voters genuinely vote on the basis of ideology. There are few "single-issue" voters (Converse, 1964; Barnes, 1971; Inglehart and Klingemann, 1976; Arian and Shamir, 1983; Converse and Pierce, 1986; Zaller, 1992; McCann, 1997; Zechmeister, 2006; Muddle, 2007; Achen and Bartels, 2016; Kinder and Kalmoe, 2017; Mason, 2018). In fact, rather than voters supporting a party because they share its ideology, it is more common that voters share the party's ideology or policy preferences *because* they vote for it. That is, they do not choose parties on the basis of policy, but instead choose a party for other reasons, and then adopt whatever platform it happens to push (Achen and Bartels, 2016).

Fourth, voters are generally irrational or biased in how they process political information. They do not seek truth, but instead try to maintain whatever beliefs they currently have or instead conform their beliefs to whatever their peer group thinks (Kahneman, Slovic and Tversky, 1982; Rasinki, 1989; Bartels, 2003; Kelly, 2012; Chong, 2013; Erison, Lodge, and Tabor, 2014).

Fifth, for most voters, political affiliation is about signaling one's identity rather than expressing policy preferences. Citizens vote on the basis of partisan loyalties grounded in their identities, and these loyalties do not track ideology, sincere policy preferences, or their interests. Political affiliation is largely a costly signal that one is a bona fide member of a particular identity group (Achen and Bartels, 2016; Simler and Hanson, 2018; Mason, 2018). Just as, say, giving out expensive engagement rings to prove one is genuinely interested in getting married, voting Republican and parroting Republican talking points helps prove to fellow evangelical southerners that one is a really one of the group.

This is a quick summary of a massive deal of empirical work on voter knowledge, psychology, belief formation, information processing, and party affiliation. We would hope that readers who specialize in political philosophy or democratic theory would be familiar with it, but we know from experience that many democratic theorists pay little attention to the relevant empirical political science, often because it is uncomfortable for them.

We invoke all this here because it complicates the Big Objection. According to the Big Objection, money in politics messes up politics. Democracies *would* serve the public interest—or at least would serve the interests of many voters, if only it stayed clean. But money sways politicians away from voters' interests to the interests of buyers. The previous section explained that the evidence for this thesis is very poor, because money seems to have little effect. But it's worse than that, because we have little reason to think voting succeeds in making politicians serve voters' interests all that much either. Instead, as Achen and Bartels say, elections "… turn out to be largely random events" (Achen and Bartels, 2016, p. 2). Far from being crucial junctures at which the will of the people is expressed, they are largely expensive ceremonies in which people express their fidelity to randomly allocated political tribes that have little to do with ideology, beliefs, or interests.

To conclude, the Big Objection alleges that introducing money into politics via vote sales or large campaign contributions will incentivize representatives to favour policies that advance the interests of buyers or contributors at the expense of the public. We have argued that this objection is unsuccessful and that the case for allowing money in politics is stronger than commonly believed.

Notes

1 The arguments in this section draw on Freiman, 2014.
2 For an argument against self-interested voting, see Brennan, 2011.
3 See Freiman, 2015.
4 On this point see Freiman, 2012, Freiman, 2017a, and Freiman, 2017b. On Rawls's problematic idealizing assumptions more generally, see Brennan, 2014.
5 For a discussion of some of these features, see Noel, 2010.
6 See Brennan, 2016; Somin, 2013, and Caplan, 2007 for a review.

References

Achen, C., and Bartels, L. (2016) *Democracy for Realists: Why Elections Do Not Produce Responsive Government*, Princeton: Princeton University Press.
Ansolabehere, S., De Figueiredo, J.M. and Snyder Jr., J.M. (2003) "Why is there so little money in US politics?" *Journal of Economic Perspectives* 17, pp. 105–130.
Ansolabehere, S., Snyder Jr, J.M. and Ueda, M. (2004) "Did firms benefit from soft money," *Election Law Journal* 3, pp. 193–198.
Arian, A., and Schamir, M. (1983) "The primarily political functions of the left-right continuum," *Comparative Politics* 15, pp. 139–158.
Barnes, S.H. 1971. "Left, right, and the Italian voter," *Comparative Political Studies* 4, pp. 157–175.
Bartels, L. (2003) "Democracy with attitudes," in ed. G. Rabinowitz and M.B. MacKeun (eds.) *Electoral Democracy,* New York: Oxford University Press.
Brennan, G. and Lomasky, L. (2003) *Democracy and Decision*. New York: Cambridge University Press.
Brennan, J. (2011) *The Ethics of Voting*. Princeton: Princeton University Press.
Brennan, J. (2014) *Why Not Capitalism*? New York: Routledge.
Brennan, J. (2016) *Against Democracy*. Princeton: Princeton University Press.
Brennan, J, and Hill, L. (2014) *Compulsory Voting: For and Against*. New York: Cambridge University Press.
Brennan, J, and Jaworski, P. (2015) "Markets without symbolic limits," *Ethics* 125, pp. 1053–1077.
Brennan, J. and Jaworski, P. (2016) *Markets Without Limits*. New York: Routledge.
Campbell, A., Converse, P.E., Miller, W.E., and Stokes, D.E. (1960) *The American Voter*. New York: John Wiley.
Caplan, B. (2007) *The Myth of the Rational Voter*. Princeton: Princeton University Press.
Chong, D. (2013) "Degrees of rationality in politics," in D.O. Sears and J.S. Levy (eds.) *The Oxford Handbook of Political Psychology*, New York: Oxford University Press, pp. 96–129.
Converse, P. (1964) "The nature of belief systems in mass publics," *Critical Review* 18(1–3), p. 1–74.
Converse, P. and Pierce, R. (1986) *Political Representation in France*. Cambridge MA: Harvard University Press.
Dawood, Y. (2015) "Campaign finance and American democracy," *Annual Review of Political Science* 18, pp. 329–348.
Delli-Carpini, M.X. and Keeter, S. (1996) *What Americans Know about Politics and Why It Matters*. New Haven: Yale University Press.
Erison, C., Lodge, M., and Taber, C.S. (2014) "Affective contagion in effortful political thinking," *Political Psychology* 35, pp. 187–206.
Friedman, J. (2006) "Democratic competence in normative and positive theory: Neglected implications of 'The Nature of Belief Systems in Mass Publics'," *Critical Review* 18, pp. i–xliii.
Freiman, C. (2012) "Equal political liberties," *Pacific Philosophical Quarterly* 93, pp. 158–174.
Freiman, C. (2014) "Vote markets," *Australasian Journal of Philosophy* 92, pp. 759–774.
Freiman, C. (2015) "Cost-benefit analysis and the value of environmental goods," *Georgetown Journal of Law and Public Policy* 13, pp. 337–348.
Freiman, C (2017a) "Ideal theory," in J. Brennan, D. Schmidtz, and B. van der Vossen (eds.) *The Routledge Handbook of Libertarianism*. New York: Routledge, pp. 301–311.
Freiman, C. (2017b) *Unequivocal Justice*. New York: Routledge.
Freiman, C. (2019) "The case for markets in citizenship," *Journal of Applied Philosophy* 36, pp. 124–136.
Inglehart, R., and Klingemann, H. (1976) "Party identification, ideological preference, and the left-right dimension among Western mass publics," in I. Budge, I. Crewe, and D. Fairlie (eds.) *Party Identification and Beyond*. London: Wiley, pp. 243–273.

Ipsos Mori (2016) "The Perils of Perception and the EU." www.ipsos-mori.com/researchpublications/researcharchive/3742/The-Perils-of-Perception-and-the-EU.aspx
Kahneman, D., Slovic, P., and Tversky, A., eds. (1982) *Judgment under Uncertainty: Heuristics and Biases*. New York: Cambridge University Press.
Kelly, J.T. (2012) *Framing Democracy*. Princeton: Princeton University Press.
Kinder, D. and Kalmoe, N. (2017) *Neither Liberal nor Conservative: Ideological Innocence in the American Public*. Chicago: University of Chicago Press.
Loren L. and Brennan, G. (2000) "Is there a duty to vote?" *Social Philosophy and Policy* 17, pp. 62–86.
Mankiw, G. (2007) "On selling votes," [Online] Available at: http://gregmankiw.blogspot.com/2007/11/on-selling-votes.html. 2007.
Mason, L. (2018) "Ideologues without issues: The polarizing consequences of ideological identities," *Public Opinion Quarterly* 82, pp. 280–301.
McCann, J.A. (1997) "Electoral choices and core value change: The 1992 presidential campaign," *American Journal of Political Science* 41, pp. 564–583.
Muddle, C. (2007) "The single-issue party thesis: Extreme right parties and the immigration issue," *West European Politics* 22, pp. 182–197.
Noel, H. (2010) "10 Things political scientists know that you don't," *The Forum* 8(3), article 12.
Rasinki, K.A. (1989) "The effect on question wording on public support for government spending," *Public Opinion Quarterly* 53, pp. 388–394.
Rawls, J. (1999) *A Theory of Justice*, revised ed. Cambridge, MA: Belknap Press of Harvard University Press.
Rawls, J. (2001) *Justice as Fairness: A Restatement*, ed. Erin Kelly. Cambridge: Harvard University Press.
Sandel, M.J. (2012) *What Money Can't Buy*, New York: Farrar, Straus, and Giroux.
Satz, D. (2010) *Why Some Things Should Not Be for Sale*. New York: Oxford University Press.
Simler, K., and Hanson, R. (2018) *The Elephant in the Brain*. Oxford: Oxford University Press.
Somin, I. (2013) *Democracy and Political Ignorance*. Stanford: Stanford University Press.
Taylor, J.S. (2017) "Markets in votes and the tyranny of Wealth," *Res Publica* 23, pp. 313–328.
Zachmeister, E. (2006) "What's left and who's right? A Q-method study of individual and contextual influences on the meaning of ideological labels," *Political Behavior* 28, pp. 151–173.
Zaller, J. (1992) *The Nature and Origins of Mass Opinion*. New York: Cambridge University Press.

12
HEALTH CARE

L. Chad Horne

Introduction

Say that a commodity is an ordinary market good; in other words, say that a commodity is a good the production, distribution, and consumption of which is properly governed by the norms of the marketplace. This definition is vague; in particular, what it means for something to be "properly" governed by the norms of the marketplace needs to be specified. But let this definition stand as a first pass. Is health care a commodity in this sense?

One important perspective from which health care clearly is *not* a commodity is the perspective of standard welfare economics. Free markets in health care and health care insurance are subject to multiple sources of market failure. Indeed, all of the major sources of market inefficiency – incomplete and asymmetrical information, imperfect competition, and incomplete property rights – are present in health care and health care insurance, often in overlapping and compounding ways. As a result, there are significant efficiency gains to be realized by erecting institutions that can correct these market failures, including social insurance programs (Arrow, 1963; Barr, 1989; Horne and Heath, 2022). This must be at least part of the reason why no developed country on earth treats health care as an ordinary market good.

However, many philosophers hold that there must be a deeper and perhaps more moralized rationale behind the imperative to decommodify health care. For some, this deeper rationale amounts to a distributive justice concern; health care, they say, is not a commodity, but a right (e.g. Brock, 2007). For others, this deeper rationale is best expressed as a concern about the corrupting influence of market norms or the profit motive on the provision of care; in particular, the provision of health care through the market has been alleged to corrupt both the way health care is properly valued and the quality of care that is provided (e.g. Walzer, 1983; Pellegrino, 1999).

The aim of this chapter is to argue that these supposedly deeper and more moralized arguments against treating health care as a commodity are all incomplete, in one way or another, without appeal to the fact that markets in health care and health care insurance are inefficient in the economist's sense. Considerations of distributive justice or corruption alone do not necessitate the decommodification of health care; only the appeal to efficiency offers a full and appropriately nuanced justification for the decommodification of health care.

DOI: 10.4324/9781003188742-16

After introducing some preliminary distinctions in the next section, the following two sections consider distributive justice arguments and corruption arguments, respectively. In both cases, I identify a gap in the argument; while these arguments point to valid moral concerns, it is not necessary to eliminate or constrain markets in health care in order to address them. The final section sketches the argument from efficiency for decommodifying health care. I argue there that Pareto-efficiency provides a more complete justification for the many departures from the normal operation of the market that we see in health and health care.

Some preliminary distinctions

Philosophical discussions sometimes treat the commodification of health care as if it were a simple yes or no proposition: either health care is treated as a commodity, or it is not. This is far too simple. Even among countries that have achieved universal health care coverage, there are significant differences in the role allowed to the market. A brief sketch of health care systems around the developed world will reveal a few key distinctions that any discussion of the commodification of health care should keep in view.

Perhaps the most fully "decommodified" model of health care provision is the "Beveridge model," exemplified by Britain's National Health Services, and named for the British economist and politician William Beveridge for his role in their creation. On the Beveridge model, health care is treated as a basic public service, much like primary education or police protection; thus, hospitals and doctors' offices are state-owned enterprises, doctors and nurses are salaried employees of the state, and health care is largely free at the point of use to any resident who needs it. This is a system of fully socialized medicine, taking practically all aspects of health care provision out of the market and placing them in the hands of the state. But while this model is appealing to philosophers – Walzer sometimes speaks as though this model is a requirement of basic justice (1983, pp. 86–91) – it is not often found outside of the British Isles and Scandinavia.

Countries like Canada and Taiwan provide not socialized *medicine* but rather socialized *insurance*. This is sometimes called the "Douglas Model," after Canadian politician Tommy Douglas, who established Canada's first universal health insurance program while Premier of Saskatchewan. On this model, the state provides health insurance directly to residents, but most health care providers are private practitioners and most hospitals are privately owned. Thus, on this model, we might say that health care *insurance* has been fully decommodified, but health *care* has not (Heath, 2003). A typical doctor's office in Canada, for instance, is essentially a small for-profit business, with physicians responsible for providing their own office space, hiring their own staff, purchasing their own equipment, and billing the public insurer on a fee-for-service basis.

Unified single payer systems like Medicare in Canada or the NHS in England may dominate the philosophical imagination, but in practice they are not that common around the world. More common are multi-payer systems of one kind or another, with many differences among them. Germany, for instance, relies on a mix of public and private insurance funds paid for out of payroll tax receipts; this is sometimes called the "Bismarck model." Other countries, like Switzerland and the Netherlands, rely on mandatory private insurance to finance health care. In all of these multi-payer systems, doctors and hospitals are mostly private, although private hospitals and private insurers are typically organized as non-profit rather than for-profit enterprises.

Just this brief sketch of health care systems around the world reveals a couple of important distinctions that any normative analysis of the commodification of health care ought to keep in view. First, and most obviously, we should not conflate the issue of *universal coverage* with the issue of *commodification*. As we have just seen, there are many paths to universal coverage worldwide, and different paths rely on the market in different ways and to different degrees. Insofar as questions of commodification are questions about the proper role and limits of the market, anyone interested in the commodification of health care ought to pay some attention to the differences among these paths.

Second, a normative analysis of commodification should be wary of the distinction between health *care* and health care *insurance*: are we concerned about the commodification of one or the other, or perhaps both? As we have seen, most universal health care systems around the world are in fact universal health care *insurance* systems, while health care providers in these systems remain market actors in important respects. On the other hand, the complete decommodification of health *care*, in the form of fully socialized medicine, is relatively rare.

If concerns about commodification are primarily concerns about securing universal coverage and equality of access, particularly for the poor and vulnerable, then it makes sense that commodification concerns would focus not on health care but rather on how people *pay* for health care – i.e. on health care *insurance*. Because people's health care needs are both unpredictable and often quite expensive, individuals will want insurance for their future health needs, and there are a variety of ethical concerns with the market provision of health insurance, as we shall see. But there may be reason to worry about the commodification of health *care* as well, perhaps related to the impact of the "profit motive" on physicians' decisions about what or how many treatments to provide (Gawande, 2009, 2015).

Finally, there is a third distinction that a normative analysis of commodification should attend to: we should be wary of conflating *decommodification* with *state provision*. Some philosophers seem to suppose that the alternative to treating health care as a market good is for health care or health care insurance to be provided directly by the state; however, there may be ways of decommodifying care through various non-governmental organizations as well. For example, if there are concerns related to the influence of the profit motive on health organizations like insurance companies or hospitals, it is possible to address those concerns by structuring those organizations as private non-profits rather than as fully public, state-owned enterprises.

Thinking along these lines, it is helpful to think of commodification, not as a simple yes or no proposition, but as occurring along a spectrum. At one extreme would be a completely unregulated market, with the allocation of health care resources fully determined by the "invisible hand" of the price system; at the other extreme would be the fully socialized medicine of Britain's NHS, with health care resources directed entirely by the "visible hand" of lawmakers and bureaucrats.[1] But there are many intermediate positions, involving various forms of market regulation, alternative governance structures (e.g. non-profits, cooperatives), and perhaps other institutional innovations besides. And once again, all of this can be said of both health *care* and health care *insurance*. Any normative analysis of the commodification of health care must attend to all these complexities.

Anti-commodification arguments I: Distributive justice

There is a vast literature on the problems of distributive justice in health care.[2] Questions of distributive justice in health care are, in the first instance, questions about what kinds of distributive *outcomes* are just – whether all citizens are owed access to a package of basic health care services as a matter of justice, for example, and if so, what particular services belong in that package.

The issue of the commodification of health care is somewhat different, at least at first glance. Questions about the commodification of health care are questions primarily about the suitability of a particular institution or economic system – namely, the market – for the delivery of health care or health care insurance. In other words, concerns about commodification are in the first instance concerns about distributive *mechanisms* or *processes* rather than distributive *outcomes*.

But of course, concerns about the market as a distributive *mechanism* may ultimately stem from concerns about the market's ability to reliably produce just distributive *outcomes*. In this way, many arguments against the commodification of health care invoke distributive justice concerns. Typically, these arguments appeal to egalitarian or sufficientarian considerations (see Segall, 2018). For instance, the market distributes goods and services according to willingness and ability to pay. For this reason, it is sometimes alleged that treating health care as an ordinary market good would be unjust because it would leave some unable to afford, and hence unable to obtain, the care they need and are entitled to (e.g. Brock, 2007, p. 126; Daniels, 2008, pp. 19–20). This is clearly a distributive justice concern. And even those who oppose the commodification of health care primarily on other grounds, such as the corruption arguments canvased in the next section, will sometimes mention the prospect of some being denied essential care due to inability to pay as further evidence of the problems with markets in health care (e.g. Walzer, 1983, pp. 89–90).

The first thing to notice about this line of reasoning is that it is incomplete, at least as stated. It is possible to believe *both* that individuals are entitled to certain specific goods (as a matter of distributive outcome), *and* that such goods ought to be provided by the market rather than the state (as a matter of distributive mechanism). Indeed, such a set of beliefs is not merely logically possible; together, they describe the default arrangement around the world for the provision of most justice-affecting goods, including most basic needs like food, clothing, and shelter. Individuals have claims of distributive justice to access these goods, but they go to the market to obtain them, and those who are unable to afford the goods they need receive assistance in the form of cash transfers or vouchers that they take to private sellers. The question is why an arrangement like this would be unsatisfactory when it comes to the provision of health care.

Thus, there is a logical gap in arguments that would derive anti-commodification conclusions directly from distributive justice premises. The mere fact that individuals have valid claims of justice to access a specific good like health care is not by itself a decisive argument against the market provision of that good. There would need to be some further reason, perhaps specific to the good in question, why market provision of that good would fail to produce just distributive outcomes.

In the case of health care, special complications arise because health care needs are both expensive and unpredictable. For this reason, the suggestion that individuals might go to the market to meet their health care needs, in the same way that they go to the market to meet their other basic needs, might seem fanciful. Even relatively well-off people simply cannot afford to pay for a significant health care expense out of pocket, and the kinds of redistributive programs that provide predictable monthly income or nutritional support to citizens would hardly be adequate to close that gap.

But what the unpredictability of health expenditure shows above all is the need for health care *insurance*. Insurance allows individuals to convert a risky gamble with a certain expected value into a stable monthly payment (called a premium) approximately equal to that expected value. Insurance does this by pooling the risks of many similarly situated individuals together, taking advantage of the law of large numbers to bring the *average* costs of the group in line with the *expected* cost (Heath, 2006, pp. 322–324). People tend to prefer the stability that insurance provides over the uncertainty that comes from bearing risk alone.

The introduction of health *insurance* changes the distribution of health care in significant ways. It is arguably the very function of health insurance to distribute health care "according to need" and to ensure that individuals are not denied needed care due to inability to pay (Horne, 2016). Thus, we might say that health insurance decommodifies health care in important ways, and decommodification of this sort may well be required in the name of distributive justice. But this only pushes the question of commodification back a step. We must now ask what would be wrong with the commodification of health care *insurance*. There is private insurance, after all! If concerns about the commodification of health care boil down to a distributive justice concern that individuals should be unable to afford unexpected, costly care, it would seem those concerns could be addressed simply by making sure individuals are able to afford adequate market-based health insurance.

Thus, we return to the same logical gap we encountered before. It is possible to believe *both* that individuals have claims of justice to an adequate health insurance policy *and* that such a policy ought to be provided by the market rather than the state. It is still not clear, from the point of view of distributive justice, what would be wrong with private insurance coupled with subsidies for those individuals unable to afford an adequate insurance policy.

Having said all of that, there is one distributive justice argument that, if successful, would indeed necessitate significant decommodification of health care. The argument I have in mind would be one to the effect that individuals are owed access to health care that is not just *adequate* or *decent* but perfectly *equal* (e.g. Hughes, 2020). The idea would be, not just that is some basic level of coverage that should be guaranteed to all, but also that wealthier or more health-conscious individuals should be prohibited from purchasing additional coverage beyond that basic level. To achieve this, it would indeed be necessary to seriously constrain the market in the name of distributive justice, by banning the purchase of additional health care or health care insurance outside of the basic system.

That said, there are compelling reasons related to liberty and human welfare (or efficiency) to reject such a position. To say that individuals may use their personal wealth to buy fancy vacations or expensive jewelry but not to purchase necessary health care, especially necessary care that would not otherwise be available to them, would be a serious infringement on individual liberty, and it would have potentially devastating costs for individual well-being.[3] It would amount to achieving equality through "leveling down," or in other words, achieving equality by worsening the situation of those better-off rather than improving that of the worse-off. For reasons like these, even egalitarian theorists tend to oppose banning various forms of two-tiered medicine (e.g. Daniels, 2009, p. 369ff.), and as far as I am aware, no country actually prohibits the purchase of supplementary private care.[4]

In sum, arguments for the decommodification of health care on distributive justice grounds are generally inconclusive (except for arguments that entail strictly equal access to care, though I think we have strong independent reasons to reject such arguments). It is not normally necessary to constrain or supplant the market to secure a distributive outcome where everyone has access to specific justice-affecting goods like health care or health care insurance. Indeed, the usual arrangement is to rely on the market to provide justice-affecting goods, while offering income support or vouchers to those who need assistance. If there is a reason to think that an arrangement like this would be unsatisfactory when it comes to the provision of health care, I argue it is not a reason of distributive justice.

Anti-commodification arguments II: Corruption

A different set of anti-commodification arguments appeals to the idea that the market provision of health care would be unjust, or otherwise morally wrong, because it would corrupt the good of health care in some way. As Michael Sandel has claimed, "certain moral and civic goods are diminished or corrupted if bought and sold for money" (1998, p. 94). On this view, health care must be provided by the state or the community rather than the market, not to achieve a more just distributive outcome, but rather because the communal provision of health care expresses or preserves something important about the good of health care or how that good is properly valued.

It is worth distinguishing broadly between two different kinds of corruption arguments. According to *normative* corruption arguments, the market provision of health care represents a kind of *normative* or *moral* corruption, in that it amounts to a collective failure to value the good of health care in the right way.[5] On the other hand, according to *quality* corruption arguments, the market provision of care corrupts the quality of care itself rather than the moral value of such care. (Though of course these arguments are not mutually exclusive: it is possible to believe that the market provision of health care corrupts *both* the quality of care *and* the spirit in which such care ought to be provided.)

To begin with normative corruption arguments, the intuitive idea here is that moving the provision of needed goods from the community to the market turns an expression of communal care and mutual support into one of mere self-interestedness. This is in much the same way that an act of helping another is diminished if it is done for personal gain rather than from a sense of altruism or moral obligation. This intuition, that it is not enough that our fellow citizens' needs be met, but that they must also be met *in the right way* or *for the right reasons*, is generalized to provide an account of the grounds of the welfare state and the moral limits of the market.

Thus Michael Walzer, in *Spheres of Justice* (1983, pp. 64–94), argues that the communal provision of necessary goods is in some sense constitutive of community itself. Each community comes to its own understanding of its citizens' needs, but once this understanding is established, the community incurs an obligation to distribute necessary goods *according to need* rather than ability to pay. As Walzer says, "Needed goods are not commodities" and should not be treated as such (1983, p. 90). Similarly, in "Ethical Limitations of the Market" (1990), Elizabeth Anderson argues that the communal provision of certain needed goods expresses valuable ideals of fraternity and social democratic freedom. Anderson sees value "in collectively taking a stand on what goods the community regards as so important that it would be a disgrace to let any of its members fall short in them" (1990, p. 198). Note that Anderson is explicitly ascribing value here to the act of *collectively taking a stand* on this matter, and not simply to the distributive outcome whereby no members fall short in the goods that are deemed important.

One thing to note about this family of views is that they seem to rely on a conception of need that is too broad to serve as the basis for drawing the line between market and state. Nothing is a need *simpliciter*; things are needed only *for* this or that purpose. Walzer and Anderson seem to understand needs in terms of what citizens need *for* full and equal participation in community or civic life. But such an expansive notion of need could be understood to require the public provision of practically everything: food, clothing, housing, transportation, and more. Of course, Walzer and Anderson sometimes speak as though their view is not that *all* needed goods must be provided by the state rather than the market, but merely that *some* needed goods must be so provided – but this latter interpretation is clearly inconclusive as an argument for the public provision of health care in particular.[6]

Be that as it may, the normative corruption arguments of Walzer and Anderson exhibit much the same logical gap we saw in distributive justice arguments. If the idea is merely that the community must provide certain needed goods for one reason or another, then this alone does not show the need to circumvent the market at all. The communal provision of needed goods can easily be accomplished *via the market*, with cash transfers or vouchers for those who need assistance; again, this is the default arrangement around the world for the provision of necessary goods. Anderson herself seems to acknowledge this possibility when she notes that citizens' needs can be met "through community guarantees or outright provision" (1990, p. 193); the nod to "community guarantees" as something distinct from outright provision seems to be in explicit recognition of the fact that it is not essential for the community to actually produce or deliver the goods in question in every case. Thus, we encounter the same logical gap as in distributive justice arguments; it is possible for the community to provide necessary goods without supplanting the market at all.

It may be possible to fill this logical gap in one way or another. Anderson argues, for instance, that public provision of needed goods is superior to market provision with vouchers because public provision requires that citizens deliberate together to come to a shared, reasoned understanding of people's needs as citizen. To her, this not only honours the intuitively important distinction between needs and mere wants, but it also expresses important ideals of democratic citizenship (Anderson, 1990, pp. 199–200). But not only does this argument give no reason to think that *health care in particular* is one of the needs that citizens must provide for in this way (as opposed to any other basic need); it also seems to totally discount the possibility that the use of vouchers could be constrained in various ways to correspond to the public's "reasoned understanding" of individuals' needs. For example, you could imagine a voucher that could only be used to purchase a health care package that meets certain minimum standards set out by the community.

I turn now to quality corruption arguments. On these arguments, the problem with the market provision of health care is not (or anyway not *only*) that it tends to corrupt important values; the problem is that market provision tends to corrupt the quality of health care itself. The idea is that the introduction of monetary incentives may "crowd out" moral motivation, causing people to act more strategically or self-interestedly than they otherwise would – and thus leading to worse outcomes overall.[7] This is certainly a real phenomenon, but as an argument for decommodification, it needs to be formulated quite carefully.

To see what I mean, consider the risks of quality corruption lurking in the "fee-for-service" model of medicine, where providers bill insurers for each individual service they provide. This model clearly incentives overtreatment, which is problematic not only from the point of view of system-wide costs but also from the point of view of patient welfare; overtreatment creates significant health risks of its own (Gawande, 2009, 2015). A system of socialized medicine like the NHS in England addresses this problem by paying physicians a fixed salary rather than compensating them for each service performed; private managed care organizations (often called health maintenance organizations or HMO's) achieve cost savings in the exact same way. This can be seen as a form of decommodification: by eliminating the profit motive as an input to physician decision-making, we also eliminate the incentive to overtreat, freeing physicians to focus on providing the best care to patients.

Interestingly, however, in a 1999 special issue of the *Journal of Medicine and Philosophy* on commodification in health care, rather than celebrating these benefits of managed care, several authors rail against them. To them, managed care represents commodification, not decommodification, because managed care involves the imposition of strict rules around the approval of care for the sake of increasing HMO profits (Pellegrino, 1999, p. 245f.; Callahan, 1999, p. 231; Kaveny, 1999, p. 207). Managed care is said to constrain the professional judgment of the physician; the physician is no longer able to order any test or procedure she deems appropriate, but must instead follow bureaucratic guidelines around best practices. In this way, as Pellegrino notes revealingly, HMO cost-cutting measures put "substantial portions of the physician's income at risk" (1999, p. 245).

Does managed care represent beneficial cost savings and patient protection, or does it represent nefarious penny-pinching for the sake of HMO profit? To some extent, these are simply different ways of describing the same underlying tradeoff between institutionalizing best practices for cost-effective care while still leaving appropriate space for the professional judgment of the physician. It is not clear what is gained by dismissing one or the other of these alternatives as commodification, especially when neither of these alternatives can be equated with the market in any straightforward way. (Notice that the problem arises in the first place only because a third party, the insurer or HMO, is paying for the patient's care.) Ideally, one would like a more systematic account of when market incentives tend toward quality corruption, or when they tend toward bad outcomes more generally – a question I return to in the next section.

But first, I would close this section by emphasizing that existing corruption arguments exhibit much the same logical gap that we saw in distributive justice arguments. With normative corruption arguments, if the goal is to ensure that needed goods are provided in the right spirit or for the right reasons, it is not necessary to supplant or constrain the market to do this. Quality corruption arguments exhibit this same gap: although there may be cases where market incentives lead to bad outcomes, there may be ways to address these incentives through private sector initiatives rather than full-blown public provision (for example through private HMO's rather than full-blown socialized medicine on the Beveridge model). Thus, again, if we are looking for reasons to constrain or eliminate markets in health care, we should look elsewhere.

Anti-commodification arguments III: Efficiency

There is more than a grain of truth to concerns about quality corruption. It is easy to find situations where the introduction of financial incentives creates collective action problems where none existed before (Heath, 2003). A collective action problem describes a situation where the outcome of individual rational choice is worse for some and better for none, by their own lights, compared to some other available alternative. The problem of overtreatment discussed above is a clear example: when the cost of treatment is spread over the whole insurance pool, patients may pursue more treatment or testing than they otherwise would. This can make all patients worse off than they would be if health care resources were rationed more judiciously, not only in terms of overall health expenditure (and hence their own insurance premiums), but in many cases in terms of health outcomes, too.

Another way to define a collective action problem is to say that a collective action problem is a situation where the outcome of individual rational choice is *inefficient* in the sense of Pareto. A state of affairs is Pareto-inefficient when it is possible to make at least one person better off without making at least one other person worse off; conversely, a situation is Pareto-efficient or Pareto-optimal when it is *not* possible to raise any one person's welfare without lowering the welfare of someone else. It is important not to confuse Pareto-efficiency with efficiency in its merely technical sense. Technical efficiency involves minimizing the quantity of inputs necessary to produce a given level of some output. Pareto-efficiency, by contrast, has to do with optimizing the amount of human welfare in society. Pareto-inefficient situations are those where some are worse off in ways that are not necessary to benefit anyone else; in that sense, as Joseph Heath has put it, the pursuit of Pareto-efficiency involves the elimination of "gratuitous suffering" (2011, p. 24).

From this point of view, the significance of the market as an institution is that it is normally quite good at realizing efficiency gains. However, there are certain circumstances that can generate collective action problems in the market and hence that can impede Pareto-improving transactions from occurring: these circumstances include when market participants lack full information, when property rights are incomplete, and when competition is imperfect. When these circumstances are present, the market will fail to realize all possible Pareto-improvements. Of course, if the standard is perfect efficiency, then the market always fails, as these circumstances are always present to some degree. Significantly, however, sometimes the market will fail *so egregiously* that it will be possible to achieve a more efficient outcome – it will be possible to raise everyone's welfare – by constraining or supplanting the market in one way or another. This might mean imposing regulations on market transactions, or it might mean circumventing the market altogether and organizing cooperation hierarchically instead.

These methods of circumventing the market need not always involve the public sector; private organizations can perform some of these functions, too. For instance, Arrow (1963) invites us to see the ethical code of the physician as a kind of private regulation, aimed at mitigating some of the problems stemming from the serious asymmetries of information that obtain between professional and client. By certifying physicians' qualifications and setting and enforcing a code of conduct, the professional organization mitigates a trust problem between physician and patient, and it thereby allows mutually beneficial transactions to occur where they otherwise might not. Similarly, Williamson (1985), following Coase (1937), suggests that we can see the private firm or the corporation as a response to certain collective action problems that emerge in market cooperation; due to various costs of market contracting, it can sometimes be more efficient to organize production hierarchically instead. The distinctive role for the state in all this stems from the state's power to coerce, and hence its power to solve particularly stubborn collective action problems that cannot easily be addressed through these private (and thus voluntary) means (Heath 2011, pp. 24–26).[8]

In applying this framework to health care, much could be said. There are multiple sources of market failure in health care and health care insurance, including not only the asymmetries of information between physician and patient just mentioned, but also the imperfect competition between health care providers and the many positive externalities associated with health care and public health measures. As a result, many unusual institutional arrangements both public and private have emerged to mitigate these failures (see Horne and Heath, 2022, pp. 69–174). However, if our aim is to understand the efficiency rationale for universal health care provision as a component of the welfare state, as has been our focus in this chapter, then market failure in the provision of health care *insurance* is the key.

As we have seen, because of the unpredictability of individuals' future health care needs, individuals will typically want health care insurance to see to those needs more effectively. But serious asymmetries of information obtain between patient and insurer, which can lead to problems of adverse selection. These problems in turn tend to undermine and even destroy voluntary market-based insurance programs.

The way adverse selection unfolds is like this. For obvious reasons, patients who know that they will have more expensive future health needs are more likely to purchase voluntary health insurance compared to patients who do not have such expensive needs; health insurance is simply a more attractive deal for high-cost patients. At the same time, insurance companies have a hard time identifying and excluding high-cost patients, because the relevant information is typically possessed only by the patients themselves. As a result, voluntary insurance pools will typically contain an "adverse selection" of patients, patients with relatively high expected health care costs. Eventually, the insurer will have to raise prices to cover these higher costs. As prices rise, more and more low-cost patients will tend to drop out of the insurance pool, as health insurance becomes a less beneficial arrangement for them. This drives up average costs and thus prices even further for those remaining. In extreme cases, this dynamic of rising costs and rising prices can accelerate into a "death spiral," where the plan becomes so expensive that it prices itself out of existence, destroying a significant source of collective benefit (Akerlof, 1970; Cutler and Zeckhauser, 1998).

There are a variety of market-based strategies for controlling adverse selection, including things like mandatory health screenings to identify costly patients and lifetime spending caps and waiting periods to discourage them from signing up. But these have costs of their own, and they raise the price of care for all (Woolhandler et al., 2003).

The way that universal health care systems worldwide address this problem is by using the state's coercive power to make the purchase of health insurance mandatory in one way or another; this ensures that the insurance pool does not contain a preponderance of high-cost persons, and in that way it stops the dynamic of adverse selection from taking hold. Some countries do this by mandating the purchase of private insurance, as in Switzerland or briefly in the US as part of the Affordable Care Act. Other countries have the state itself provide insurance to all citizens directly, as in Canada. Still others provide their citizens with an indirect form of insurance, in the form of mandatory participation in a nationwide HMO, as in England under the NHS; there, the same risk-pooling effect is achieved simply by having so many patients in the system, with high-cost patients balanced out by low costs ones, without the need for a separate insurance program. All of these can be understood as alternative ways of preventing a collective action problem from undermining the viability of health insurance programs and hence as promoting Pareto-efficiency (Horne and Heath, 2022, p. 177).

The aim of this chapter is to assess the merits of alternative arguments for the decommodification of health care. With that in mind, it is notable that what universal health care systems worldwide have in common is not the direct public provision of health care or health care insurance, as distributive justice or normative corruption arguments seem to imply. Rather, what they have in common is some form or another of *mandatory purchase* of health coverage, whether public or private, and whether in the form of health insurance or a managed care plan. Mandatory purchase is a significant departure from the normal operation of the market, but as I have argued, it is a departure that fits naturally within an efficiency framework. On the other hand, it is hard to see how mandatory purchase could be said to promote distributive justice or prevent normative corruption – at least, apart from the market failure that mandatory purchase corrects. We would not force an individual to submit to unwanted medical treatment in the name of distributive justice or community solidarity, so why would we force them to purchase unwanted health insurance for those reasons? The answer suggested here is that mandatory purchase is instrumental to the efficient functioning of the health insurance system, as it prevents a serious collective action problem from undermining or even destroying that system. In this way, efficiency arguments do better at making sense of exactly *where* and *how* the market needs to be constrained compared to the alternatives.

When individuals have health care insurance, new collective action problems may emerge. One such problem, as we have seen, is that with insurance, patients are less likely to concern themselves about cost and more likely to consume low-value care, simply because someone else is paying; physicians, too, have their own reasons for overtreatment, including not only the obvious reasons of personal pecuniary advantage but also a strong professional ethos which demands the maximum level of care for each patient. These are problems of moral hazard, and they are among the drivers of rising health care spending.

The discussion at the end of the previous section focused on one strategy for addressing these problems: eliminating the fee-for-service model of payment entirely and bringing the physician "inside" the insurance company, paying them a fixed salary or by capitation, as in a private HMO or in a system of socialized medicine; this eliminates the incentive to overtreatment on the physicians' side, at least. But of course other strategies are available. Typically, insurers, whether public or private, will attach some form of cost-sharing (a co-pay or deductible) to the use of medical care, as a way of partially "internalizing the externality" involved in spending funds from the insurance pool. Health care systems organized on a fee-for-service model also rely to some extent on physicians and other providers to play a gatekeeping role, to be responsible stewards of health care resources and to provide covered interventions only to those patients who truly need them; here again the ethical code of physicians acts as a kind of private self-regulation. And more broadly, the use of cost-effectiveness analysis to decide what kinds of treatments should be covered is a common cost-control strategy. Just as we saw with the problem of adverse selection, there are multiple strategies available for addressing this particular collective action problems, and it is unlikely the choice among them can be made *a priori*; there are costs and benefits to each, and these costs may vary from place to place. However, some such strategy is necessary to prevent moral hazard from driving health spending up to a level that makes everyone worse off.

Much more could be said here.[9] There is a complex set of interlocking problems surrounding the market provision of health care, and a variety of different institutional responses that have been developed to address them. These responses include things like professionalization and non-profit provision, mandatory participation in an insurance or managed care plan, as well as cost-effectiveness analysis and other forms of cost control. One might add the public funding of biomedical research and education (Callahan, 1999), as well as the provision of various public health measures (Horne, 2019); these are goods that involve significant positive externalities, and thus their provision fits naturally within an efficiency framework. All of these represent deviations from the normal operation of the market, and all can be understood in terms of efficiency.

I argued in previous sections that, as grounds for decommodification, distributive justice and normative corruption arguments exhibit a logical gap: the goals they identify are worthy, but they are also goals that can be achieved *via the market*, with subsidies or vouchers for those who need assistance. It is not clear why we must constrain or supplant the market to express important social values or to achieve a more equal distribution of health care resources. On that score, the efficiency arguments canvassed in this section fare better. While normally the market is quite effective at facilitating mutually beneficial transactions, sometimes certain such transactions will fail to occur due to the presence of various collective action problems; sometimes the outcome of individually rational market choices will be Pareto-inefficient. When that happens, it may be possible to achieve a more efficient outcome by regulating the market or by circumventing it altogether; in other words, it may be possible to achieve a more efficient outcome through decommodification.

Conclusion

I noted earlier that many anti-commodification arguments seem to treat the issue of commodification as an either-or proposition: either health care is treated as a commodity, or it is not. One of the aims of this chapter has been to show that we ought to think about commodification instead as a matter of degree and as occurring along a number of different dimensions. Which parts of the health care and health care insurance sectors need to be taken out of the market, and which parts do not? When is it appropriate to constrain the market through professional codes or non-profit provision, and when is it appropriate to circumvent the market entirely through the public sector?

It is hardly an exaggeration to say that distributive justice and corruption arguments provide no guidance in answering these questions. Indeed, if these arguments exhibit the logical gap that I have claimed they do, then they imply no need to interfere with the market at all. But even if I am wrong about that, distributive justice and corruption arguments tell us practically nothing about where, why, and how the invisible hand of the market needs to be constrained by the visible hand of the state. There is a complex set of problems of institutional design to be solved in health care, and these accounts offer little guidance in how to do it.

Efficiency arguments, by contrast, offer a more nuanced account of the problems with the market provision of health care, as well as a more detailed picture of the policies and institutions available for addressing those problems. On this view, cooperation in the market is sometimes vulnerable to serious collective action problems that make everyone worse off, and it can sometimes be possible to raise everyone's welfare by constraining or circumventing the market in one way or another. Of course, just because a market failure exists, that does not necessarily mean that state intervention can improve upon it; interventions in the market invite collective action problems of their own, and the resulting costs will sometimes be higher than the costs of the market failure they were meant to correct. Addressing these issues in practice thus invokes complex questions of public choice. My aim in this chapter has been to lay out the theoretical case for such efficiency-promoting interventions, and to show the merits of that case compared to alternatives based in distributive justice or corruption.

Acknowledgments

Earlier versions of this chapter were presented at the Philosophy, Politics, and Economics Society Annual Meeting in New Orleans in February 2022, at the New Research in Practical Philosophy Workshop at Northwestern University in May 2022, and at the *Contested Markets: Theories and Controversies* conference at the Sorbonne in June 2022. I am grateful to my audiences there for their helpful comments and questions. I would also like to thank Douglas MacKay, Vida Panitch, Elodie Bertrand, and Jason Brennan for their generous and insightful comments on earlier drafts.

Notes

1 The term "visible hand" is from Alfred Chandler (1977).
2 For an overview of the recent literature, see Segall (2018).
3 Hughes (2020) finds a system of two-tiered medicine objectionable because it makes poor individuals dependent on discretionary private charity for access to health care that is not included in the basic package. He argues that this amounts to an objectionable form of private domination. Strangely, he seems unconcerned about the *public* domination that would be involved in refusing to allow people to purchase necessary, potentially life-saving medical care they would not otherwise receive.
4 Canada famously bans private coverage of procedures that are already covered by the public insurance system; in other words, Canada bans *duplicative* private insurance, or insurance that would compete with the public system. However, Canada does not ban *supplementary* coverage, or coverage for procedures that are *not* covered by the public system.
5 See Panitch's contribution to this volume (Chapter 4) for a more detailed discussion of normative corruption worries.
6 As I mentioned in the previous section, it is a natural feature of health care *insurance* that it distributes health care "according to need." If we are drawn to the idea that health care should be distributed according to need, while the distribution of other necessary goods like food and clothing can be left to the market, plausibly this is because we are drawn to the idea that people should have health care *insurance*, due to the unpredictable nature of health needs (Horne, 2017, pp. 578–580; Horne and Heath, 2022, p. 176).
7 The classic source here is Titmuss (1970). See the chapter by Peter Jaworski in this volume.
8 For an introduction to Pareto-efficiency and market failures, see Bertrand's contribution to this volume.
9 For a longer discussion, see Horne and Heath (2022).

References

Akerlof, G.A. (1970) "The market for lemons," *Quarterly Journal of Economics* 84(3), pp. 488–500.
Anderson, E. (1990) "The ethical limitations of the market," *Economics and Philosophy* 6, pp. 179–205.
Arrow, K.J. (1963) "Uncertainty and the welfare economics of medical care," *American Economic Review* 53(5), pp. 941–973.
Barr, N. (1989) "Social insurance as efficiency device," *Journal of Public Policy* 9, pp. 59–82.
Brock, D.W. (2007) "Health care resource prioritization and rationing: Why is it so difficult?," *Social Research* 74(1), pp. 125–148.
Callahan, D. (1999) "Medicine and the market: A research agenda," *Journal of Medicine and Philosophy* 24(3), pp. 224–242.
Chandler, Jr., A.D. (1977) *The Visible Hand: The Managerial Revolution in Modern Business.* Cambridge, MA: Belknap.
Coase, R.H. (1937) "The nature of the firm," *Economica* 4(16), pp. 386–405.
Cutler, D.M. and Zeckhauser, R.J. (1998) "Adverse selection in health insurance," in A. Garber (ed.) *Frontiers in Health Policy Research*, vol. 7. Cambridge, MA: MIT Press, pp. 1–31.
Daniels, N. (2008) *Just Health: Meeting Health Needs Fairly*. New York: Cambridge University Press.
Daniels, N. (2009) "Is there a right to health care and, if so, what does it encompass?" in H. Kuhse and P. Singer (eds.) *A Companion to Bioethics*, second edition. Malden, MA: Wiley-Blackwell, pp. 362–372.
Gawande, A. (2009) "The cost conundrum," *New Yorker* May 25. Online at: www.newyorker.com/magazine/2009/06/01/the-cost-conundrum
Gawande, A. (2015) "Overkill," *New Yorker* May 11. Online at: www.newyorker.com/magazine/2015/05/11/overkill-atul-gawande
Heath, J. (2003) "Les soins de santé comme marchandises," *Ethique Publique* 5(1), pp. 84–90.
Heath, J. (2006) "The benefits of cooperation," *Philosophy & Public Affairs* 34(4), pp. 313–351.
Heath, J. (2011) "Three normative models of the welfare state," *Public Reason* 3(1), pp. 13–43.
Horne, L.C. (2016) "Medical need, equality, and uncertainty," *Bioethics* 30(8), pp. 588–596.
Horne, L.C. (2017) "What makes health care special?: An argument for health care insurance," *Kennedy Institute of Ethics Journal* 27(4), pp. 561–587.
Horne, L.C. (2019) "Public health, public goods, and market failure," *Public Health Ethics* 12(3), pp. 287–292.
Horne, L.C. and Heath, J. (2022) "A market failures approach to justice in health care," *Politics, Philosophy, and Economics* 21(2), pp. 165–189.
Hughes, R.C. (2020) "Egalitarian provision of necessary medical treatment," *Journal of Ethics* 24(1), pp. 55–78.
Kaveny, M.C. (1999) "Commodifying the polyvalent good of health care," *Journal of Medicine and Philosophy* 24(3), pp. 207–223.
Pellegrino, E.D. (1999) "The commodification of medical and health care: The moral consequences of a paradigm shift from a professional to a market ethic," *Journal of Medicine and Philosophy* 24(3), pp. 243–266.
Sandel, M. (1998) "What Money Can't Buy: The Moral Limits of Markets," in G.B. Peterson (ed.) *The Tanner Lectures on Human Values*, Vol. 21. Salt Lake City: University of Utah Press, pp. 89–122.
Satz, D. (2010) *Why Some Things Should Not Be for Sale*. Oxford: Oxford University Press.
Segall, S. (2018) "Health," in: S. Olsaretti (ed.) *The Oxford Handbook of Distributive Justice.* Oxford: Oxford University Press, pp. 460–478.
Titmuss, R.M. (1970) *The Gift Relationship: From Human Blood to Social Policy*. London: Allen & Unwin.
Walzer, M. (1983) *Spheres of Justice.* New York: Basic Books.
Williamson, O. (1985) *The Economic Institutions of Capitalism*. New York: Free Press.
Woolhandler, S., Campbell, T. and Himmelstein, D.U. (2003) "Costs of health care administration in the United States and Canada," *New England Journal of Medicine* 349(8), pp. 768–775.

13
EDUCATION
Commodification and schools[1]

Harry Brighouse

Introduction

For much of the twentieth century, the way schooling was organized in most wealth liberal democracies was widely regarded as non- or de-commodified. Although there were plenty of deviations at the margins, the model was roughly this: most schools were provided, paid for, and regulated by the government, attendance at *some* school was mandatory, usually on the basis of geographical catchment areas. Reforms introduced starting in the 1980s, and accelerating after the turn of the new century eroded this model, introducing parental choice and other transparent market mechanisms. This process has widely been labelled by sceptics as 'commodification'.

My purpose in this chapter is to put the accusation of commodification in its place. Section 2 expands on the background tersely described in the previous paragraph. Section 3 provides a working definition of commodification, understanding it as the involvement of market processes in the creation and allocation of schooling. Understood that way commodification is a matter of degree, but that section also provides an account of *complete commodification*, the likely results of which I subsequently explore. I interpret the reasonable concerns that theorists have expressed about commodification of schooling as concerning the possible underproduction and possible maldistribution of the educational goods produced by schooling. Section 4 argues that complete commodification would indeed result in the underproduction of educational goods, and section 5 that it would also result in the maldistribution of educational goods, showing how those two results would come about. But section 6 argues that the market reforms pursued since the 1980s fall far short of complete commodification and shows that market processes, already present in the traditional, supposedly non-commodified, model, negatively influenced both the production and distribution of educational goods. Some of the market reforms simply make transparent, and some can actually counteract, this malign influence. Section 7 draws attention to the risks inherent in a completely non-commodified schooling system by observing that many of the most serious factors undermining the production of, and maldistributing, educational goods have been straightforward government policies (like housing and school segregation by race and socio-economic class, indoctrinatory political education, and unjust allocation of funding). The upshot is that when evaluating the methods of school governance we should go directly to what specific mechanisms

DOI: 10.4324/9781003188742-17

affect production and distribution, rather than more generally condemning or lauding commodified or non-commodified forms.

Background

The idea that most of the population should receive formal education past the age of 7 or 8 took hold in industrialized countries in the latter half of the nineteenth century. By the middle of the twentieth century almost all children in industrialized countries were educated to the age of 14, many to the age of 16, and a substantial number beyond that age. By the beginning of the twenty-first century, most were educated to age 18.

This remarkable progress was a response to dramatic changes in industrial economies, and specifically in the kinds of skills demanded by labour markets. It was widely assumed that more technologically complex economies required increasingly educated workforces: but employers, despite demanding new skills, did not solve the problem by creating and supplying them. Mass schooling, ensured by the government, was a natural solution. By the beginning of the twenty-first century, in most substantially developed countries, governments *mandated* education to the age of 16 or beyond, *funded* schools so that they would be free at the point of delivery, and imposed sector-specific *regulations* on schools. In almost (though not quite) all of these countries governments also *provided* the schools they funded.[2]

The model that emerged made schooling an exceptional institutional design in capitalist economies.[3] Even publicly owned utilities with monopoly status typically *charged* customers for units of use. Even roads, provided by the government and, normally, free at the point of delivery, were merely a convenience: nobody was (or is) *required* to use them. In a few capitalist countries the government provided healthcare fully free at the point of delivery, but, again, using it is optional for adults.

So the standard model of schooling in capitalist countries was (and still is, though I'll say more about this later) in some sense, highly non-commodified. Most countries have a fully private sector that is used be a small part of the population, but for the most part schools, and school places, are not directly bought and sold on a market, despite being used by nearly everybody. Governments normally mandate, fund, regulate and even provide schools.

Since the early 1980s though, market-like reforms spread the idea that schools should compete with one another, and that parents should have more power to select what school their child should attend. The 1981 Education Act for England and Wales established that local authorities must take account of parental preference when allocating children to schools; after the 1988 Education Reform Act a full-blown school choice system started to emerge. Now, all parents must rank order several schools, and those preferences play a substantial role in determining where children attend. From the 1970s many large US cities have had magnet schools which harness parental choice usually to promote racial integration. In the early 1990s, though, two major reforms were introduced. Wisconsin established a *voucher school* system in Milwaukee, through which low-income parents could opt out of traditional public schools and the State would pay for their children to attend chosen, and eligible, private schools, which are independent of the government and largely free of education-specific regulation. Minnesota and California passed *charter school* legislation, establishing schools which, though licensed by the state and disallowed from charging tuition or selecting their students, are less strictly regulated than traditional public schools, and which children attend on the basis of choice (when the schools have more applicants than they have room for, they must select by lottery). As of 2022 voucher programs were operating in several cities. Around 45 States and the District of Columbia had charter school legislation, and charter schools enrolled about 7.5% of all public school children (about 3.7 million).

The intellectual case for market-based reform was made forcefully by the classical liberal economist Milton Friedman as early as 1955 (Friedman, 1955; Friedman, 1962). He thought that defenders of government provision of schooling conflated three functions: funding, regulation, and provision. He argued that there was a strong case, grounded in the public interest in education, for the government to ensure some amount of funding for every child to attend school; but that this case has no bearing on how the government should *regulate* schooling or whether it should *provide* schooling. He argued that government provision was unresponsive to the interests of parents: if your child effectively has to attend a particular school, and that school will receive funds for the child whatever you do, then the school has no incentive to listen to any complaints or suggestions you might have. If, on the other hand, schools were run by independent firms that had to compete for students (and the financial resources that accompany them), they would be more responsive.

Although the intellectual case for market reforms in general came from the political right, the specific idea of charter schools was developed on the political left. Friedman imagined the government completely withdrawing from the provision of schooling, and adopting a regulatory framework that had no special curricular aspects; the government would provide a voucher for each child, and private providers would compete on an open market. But Albert Shanker, the long-time leader of the American Federation of Teachers, made a different proposal (Shanker, 1988; Kahlenberg, 2007). Most of the school system should stay more-or-less as it was, but groups of parents or teachers, or members of the community could establish small schools of choice, funded by the government, but operating under much looser regulations than the traditional schools with which they would coexist. This would enable the system to harness the efforts of teachers and parents whose talents and inclinations are not efficiently used in the heavily bureaucratic traditional system. Shanker envisioned charters as crucibles of innovation and experimentation, potentially developing better ideas and better practices that could be emulated throughout the system.

Voucher programs in the US have, very partially, implemented Friedman's vision; in some States charter schools are used roughly as Shanker envisioned, whereas in others they resemble Friedman's vision. But both innovations, in most places in the US, operate alongside more traditional arrangements. In England, by contrast, the whole system now resembles a kind of compromise between the two visions: central government specifies a national curriculum and payscale, but decision-making is otherwise mostly at the school level.

What is commodification and why should anybody care about it?

What exactly is commodification? A narrow definition is suggested by the titles of books like *What Money Can't Buy* (Sandel, 2012) and *Why Some Things Should Not Be For Sale* (Satz, 2010). Simply speaking, something is commodified when it is bought and sold for cash. The developments I've described above, though, have not increased the direct influence of cash in schooling: in almost all the parental choice systems that have been introduced, including the largest of the voucher systems in the US, schooling remains free at the point of delivery for all families. And yet, social theorists routinely describe these changes under the rubric of commodification (Apple, 2001; Ball, 2003). The two books above, though, share a subtitle, *The Moral Limits of Markets*, which suggests that they are not just about cash sales, but market mechanisms more broadly. I'm going to use the broader understanding here, because it fits best with the actual complaints theorists and activists make about the market-like reforms I have described. Critics complain that schooling is being commodified by the reforms, because they move the private choices of parents to the centre of both financing and the process through which children are allocated to schools, even though none of those I have described involve cash payments at the point of delivery.

Few critics of commodification believe that it is bad for *all* goods and services. Most people regard markets in oil, consumer durables, food, clothing, services like those provided by restaurants, or dry cleaners or landscapers as innocent enough. Vida Panitch offers a taxonomy of the kinds of goods which anti-commodification theorists generally think should not be bought and sold on markets: Social Goods (love, friendship, kinship); Honorific Goods (prizes, awards, offices); Civic Goods (votes, citizenship, speech); Necessary Goods (education, health care, shelter); and Physical Goods (sex, gestation, body parts) (Panitch, 2020, p. 63; see also Chapter 4 in this volume).

Opposition to markets in different kinds of goods is underwritten by different concerns. Michael Sandel distinguishes two distinct reasons for objecting to market mechanisms for specific goods.

> One is about inequality; the other one is about corruption. Consider inequality. In a society where everything is for sale, life is harder for those with modest means. The more money can buy, the more affluence (or lack of it) matters … The second reason … [is about] … the corrosive tendency of markets. Putting a price on the good things in life can corrupt them. That's because markets don't only allocate goods; they also express and promote certain attitudes toward the good being exchanged.
>
> (Sandel, 2012, pp. 8–9)

He offers baby-selling as a paradigm case of the latter kind of reason: "having babies in order to sell them for profit is a corruption of parenthood, because it treats children as things to be used rather than as beings to be loved" (Sandel, 2012, p. 46).

Debra Satz distinguishes approaches to commodification differently. Regarding the commercial selling of sexual services, she says that "The *economic* approach attributes the wrongness of prostitution to its consequences for efficiency: the fact that it generates externalities … its treatment of sex [is] as a morally indifferent matter". By contrast, "The *essentialist* approach stresses that sales of sexual labour are wrong because they are inherently alienating or damaging to human happiness". Her own, egalitarian, approach specifically to the selling of sexual services emphasizes "the role of commercialized sex in sustaining a social world in which women form a subordinated social group" (Satz, 2010, p. 135). She also invokes, in relation to evaluating some market transactions, including education, T.H. Marshall's suggestion that "some goods function as prerequisites for *full inclusion* in society, for counting as an equal member" (Satz, 2010, p. 102).

Opponents of market-like reforms in schooling do not always make the distinctions that we've seen from Satz, Sandel, and Panitch. Sometimes they take it for granted that commodification is bad without specifying why. Some emphasize the distributive effects of commodification; others evince something like Panitch's category of necessary goods, still others take some variant of the essentialist approach identified by Satz.[4] Is the problem that education is corrupted, or underproduced, by the commodification of schooling, or is it that it will be maldistributed? Or is there no problem at all?

By 'corruption' Sandel seems to have two things in mind that for my purposes I want to distinguish. Neither of the examples of markets encroaching on education involves the way that children are allocated to schools, and he only claims of one that it is corrupting:

> Even if corporate sponsors supplied objective teaching tools of impeccable quality, commercial advertising would still be a pernicious presence in the classroom because it is at odds with the purpose of schools. Advertising encourages people to want things and satisfy their

> desires. Education encourages people to reflect critically on their desires, to restrain or elevate them. The purpose of advertising is to recruit consumers; the purpose of public schools is to cultivate citizens.
>
> (Sandel 2012, p. 200)[5]

The example concerns an experience that students might have in school which might, in turn, undermine their achievement of an educational goal we have reason to seek for them (citizenship). Jeopardizing the desired outcome is bad, but Sandel also seems to think that the experience is bad (corrupting) independently of its long-term outcomes.

Many readers will (rightly) be sympathetic to Sandel's concern with the experience itself. But to simplify matters, the analysis I will pursue here is entirely consequentialist. I shall focus exclusively on the (likely) effects of commodification on i) what educational goods children end up being equipped when they finish school and ii) how those educational goods are distributed. In doing so I do not mean to imply that we should not be concerned with anything else (such as the daily lived experience of school for children), indeed I think we should be. But I hope the reader will tolerate my attempt to keep the analysis manageable.

I'll explain why we have reason to believe that *complete commodification* of schooling might result in what I will call *underproduction* (rather than corruption) of the goods of education, and might have unjust consequences for distribution of education. Before we explore the likely consequences of complete commodification, I want to define it, stipulatively, as follows:

Schooling is *completely commodified* when it operates within a pure market system in which:

- schools are run by private entities, and succeed or fail entirely in response to market forces.
- the government refrains entirely from paying for schooling so that families are reliant only on their own resources and private philanthropy,

and

- the government also refrains from any education-specific regulation. Schools are regulated just like other businesses, but it is entirely up to the market whether teachers are licensed, what curriculums schools adhere to, and how students are allocated to schools.

No schooling system in the developed world comes close to being completely commodified, and, in fact, very few people openly advocate it.[6] The purpose of considering complete commodification is to help us get a handle on the particular ways that specific aspects of commodification might be troubling.

Would complete commodification underproduce educational goods?

We can't evaluate whether commodification would lead to the underproduction of the goods of schooling without an account of what those goods should be. Consider Sandel's a limiting case: honours. Suppose that Nobel Prizes, or Victoria Crosses, were purchasable. The goods that the Nobel Prize and the Victoria Cross confer are the goods of expressing honour for particular achievements. Somebody who bought either one, at however high a price, could not, thereby, attain the good which they confer: the success of honours in conferring honour depends on them not having been purchased. Indeed, if they were purchasable, and widely purchased, pretty quickly they would lose some of their capacity to confer honour for particular achievements even for those who did not purchase them.

Since we understand what goods the Nobel Prizes and Victoria Crosses are supposed to produce, we can see how commodification would underproduce (or, in Sandel's parlance, corrupt) – indeed, eventually, eviscerate – them when they are purchasable on the market. For some other markets, what goods are associated with what is purchased is more contested. Consider sex: some think that paying someone else to engage in sexual acts with you corrupts the goods associated with sexual acts because those goods depend on the sexual acts being voluntarily gifted (Anderson, 1990, pp. 179–205). Sexual acts are valued, at least somewhat, as expressions of love, or affection, or of attraction, which are much more likely to be present if the sexual acts are not responses to a financial incentive than if they are. But that is not necessarily the right way of thinking about sex. Whereas a Victoria Cross is *just* an honour for extreme valour in the presence of the enemy, sexual intercourse has many dimensions, including, simply, sexual pleasure. Someone who enjoys sexual pleasure from another person engaging in sexual intercourse with them for cash is not missing the point of the transaction. Whether markets in sexual services corrupt the goods associated with sexual intercourse depends on what goods we ought to associate with sexual intercourse and how those goods interact with one another.

So whether commodification leads to the underproduction of the goods associated with schooling depends on what those goods are. As with sexual services, this is a contested matter. I'm going to offer a specific account of what goods we should associate with schooling. I've defended this account elsewhere, so will not do so in great detail here (Brighouse et al., 2018). I request the reader to accept it provisionally, for the sake of testing the underproduction claim.

I'll call this the Educational Goods account. The goods we should principally associate with schooling are the development of specific capacities which underwrite the ability of people to flourish and to contribute to the flourishing of others. The capacities are: the capacity to contribute to the economy broadly conceived (economic productivity); the capacity to make and act on one's own independent judgments (personal autonomy); the capacity to participate responsibly and effectively in collective decision-making (democratic competence); the capacity to participate in healthy emotional relationships with other people (personal relationships), and the capacity to pursue projects that, while they may or may not be contributions to the economy broadly conceived are meaningful and satisfying (personal fulfilment).[7]

It's easy to think of ways in which the market-based allocation of children to schools combined with the lack of curricular regulation might affect what goods are produced. Let's start with the most obvious. Personal autonomy – the capacity to make independent judgements about how to live, and act on those judgments – is an educational good. But if parents are inclined, as many undoubtedly are, to shape their children's values to be like their own, then they may be inclined to seek out schools which reflect their own values. At the limit this could be disastrous for their children's prospective autonomy. Imagine a child whose parents are left-wing, atheistic, and anti-militarist. They can seek a school for their child that embodies left-wing, atheistic, and anti-militarist values; and if sufficient diversity and choice prevails in the local schooling market, most of the other children in that school will have similar values. Where will the child meet teachers who challenge them to reflect on their parents' values? Where will she encounter children raised as Muslims or Christians who will give her a more realistic understanding of the nature of the religious life than her parents (and the mainstream culture) may have presented? Where will she encounter children from military families whose parents she might come to know and appreciate, lending nuance to her understanding of the motives and character of members of the military. In the absence of curriculum regulation, allocation of students through parental choice is a recipe for the reinforcement of the parents' values, not for the development of autonomy.

Of course, this might *not* happen. If the local market contains sufficient diversity of political and religious commitments and is sufficiently small that no monocultural school would be viable, or if a (probably large) critical mass of parents are strongly committed to fostering their children's independence and autonomy, there would be no problem. Restriction of children's prospective autonomy is not an *inevitable* consequence of complete commodification; but it is a consequence to which a completely commodified system is always vulnerable.

Now consider the prospects of our child of left-wing atheist anti-militaristic parents for developing the knowledge, skills, dispositions and habits that characterize democratic competence. To become a competent democratic citizen, she must come to understand the values of her religious, and her conservative, fellow citizens, both so that she can argue with them, and so that she can offer reasons for public action that *they* can understand and appreciate. A school that is designed to reflect and reinforce her parents' views, and where she does not meet students with different values, is unlikely to facilitate that understanding. And, of course, a rival school down the street catering to the children of conservative religious parents which, again, lacks any regulatory obligation to implement a curriculum fostering the kind of understanding needed for those children to become competent democratic citizens will, similarly, tend to produce incompetent citizens. Just as with autonomy this outcome is not inevitable: fortuitous market conditions might not allow for the economies of scale that would produce ideologically segregated schools, or a critical mass of parents, despite their deep personal commitments, might be sufficiently enlightened to prioritize competent citizenship when choosing among schools (thus shaping what schools do). But complete commodification puts democratic competence *at risk*.

Something similar can be said, albeit to a much lesser extent, about the capacities for economic productivity and healthy personal relationships. So-called "soft" skills, including interpersonal communication skills, are highly valued in modern developed economies, and they are valued because of their effect on productivity. And maintaining healthy personal relationships probably depend to a considerable extent on the ability to disagree respectfully across difference which, in turn, probably requires, or is at least enhanced by, the experience of doing so in school. *Complete* commodification probably jeopardizes, *to some extent*, the development of these capacities.

Of course, a curriculum well-designed to produce democratic competence or personal autonomy might have some success even in the absence of a heterogenous student body; and it might be possible to compensate for a curriculum that pays little or no attention to democratic competence or personal autonomy by having schools which have students of many different faiths and outlooks, and from different cultural and socio-economic backgrounds. So regulation of the curriculum could mitigate the effects of market-allocation of children to schools, and vice versa. These two aspects of commodification operating together probably intensify the problems, but eliminating the problem requires attention to both.

Would complete commodification maldistribute schooling?

Just as we can't assess whether complete commodification would corrupt educational goods without knowing what they ought to be, we can't establish whether it has negative effects on their distribution without knowing how they should be distributed. For the purposes of this discussion I want to posit two different principles of distribution: Equality of educational goods, and prioritizing benefit to the less advantaged.

Equality of educational goods – that is, an outcome in which everyone arrived at adulthood with knowledge, skills, attitudes and dispositions that were equally valuable for the exercise of the capacities I have listed, in their environment – would ensure equal opportunity to compete for positions in the labour market, to contribute to society, and to flourish in their lives. The reasons for endorsing this principle are, then, just the reasons we have for wanting equality of opportunity: nobody deserves a worse, or a better, chance to flourish than anyone else, and equalizing educational goods would level the playing field as it were. Of course, there are reasons *not* to do some of those things that would be needed to achieve equality of educational goods; *fully* achieving that, if it were possible at all, would probably require undermining the family, and perhaps also medical interference to level down the abilities of the most talented children. Such means would conflict with other, more important, values. But that does not mean that we should reject the principle of equality of educational goods; just that other principles are more important.[8]

One of the reasons not to do everything that would be needed to achieve equality of educational goods is that it might harm the less advantaged people in society. Educational goods benefit those who have them in competitions with others, but the productivity they facilitate can *benefit* others. Levelling down educational goods would be bad not only because sometimes the means involved would violate the physical and psychological integrity of the person, but could also reduce the pool of developed talent available to society as whole which can be harnessed to benefit the less advantaged. The thought here is not that enhancing the educational goods of some can result in greater educational goods for those who have less, but that it can enhance the prospects for flourishing of those whose prospects are worst. Consider, most obviously, the case of the cognitively impaired, whose opportunities for flourishing may not be greatly influenced by their possession of educational goods beyond some threshold. To make their lives go better, we might plausibly subordinate their level of educational goods to whatever distribution of educational goods will produce the technological and medical developments most conducive to their well-being (Schouten, 2012).

I think it is obvious that under *complete* commodification, at least in a society with a fair amount of background economic inequality, it would be very unusual for either of these principles to be realized – indeed it is unlikely that systems would even come close to approximating them. Remember: under complete commodification school places are bought and sold at the price the market will bear. Parents are often motivated to a large extent by consideration of their own children's future advantage, and considerably less motivated by consideration of the advantage of others. More affluent parents will go to some trouble and expense to secure positions for their children in schools where their peer group will challenge and support them, and which teachers find it appealing to teach in (and such schools will have a better chance of hiring and retaining high quality teachers).

Families with more cultural capital, more money, and/or more time will be better able to navigate the market. And schools have incentives to attract students who will be less expensive to teach, have more support at home, and will be less likely to disrupt the classroom. Given that parental choice would be accompanied by selection on the part of schools, more socially advantaged children would be liable to cluster together in schools where they have more favourable educational environments, while socially disadvantaged students concentrate in other schools. And unregulated pricing would lead almost inevitably to the clustering together of students from wealthy background into schools with high tuition prices and the resources those prices make available, while students from lower, and low, income backgrounds cluster in schools with low tuition prices and limited resources. It's hard to imagine anything other than a highly segmented schooling system dividing the more and the less affluent, and it is hard to imagine such a system coming anywhere close to meeting either of the distributive goals I've described.

Markets and commodification in the real world

I've concentrated on the likely effects of complete commodification. I've implicitly contrasted that with the vision many people have of a less or non-commodified system of provision. Now, though, let's think more realistically. The market reforms wrought since the late-1980s have not represented anything like complete commodification, even in those jurisdictions where they have been most pervasively implemented. And the system into which they were introduced (and which, roughly, still prevails in much of the United States, for example) was already considerably more commodified than opponents of market reform sometimes imply. In fact, as I will show, it might be a mistake to think of some of these reforms as increasing the level of commodification at all.

Let's start with the market reforms. It is worth noting that the reforms I've described have, so far, been limited in various ways. In the US, it is still the case that, outside of large cities, a substantial majority of students are allocated to schools based on residence. In England, New Zealand, and Australia, by contrast, most secondary school, and many primary schools, students attend on the basis of a formal system of parental choice. Even so, none of the schools are allowed to charge fees.[9] In England, New Zealand, the Netherlands, and Australia, indeed (and in contrast with the US system which has less formal parental choice), the government spends considerably more per-students in schools with higher concentrations of disadvantaged students. In England the gradual introduction of formal parental choice mechanisms was accompanied by a similarly gradual introduction of constraining, and detailed, curricular standards, thus constraining considerably the ability of schools to differentiate themselves from one another in terms of academic offerings. All charter schools and most voucher schools in the US are prohibited from selecting students (lotteries are used); even in England, most primary schools give priority to students who live nearby, and although secondary schools can select students, their ability to do so is highly regulated.

The market reforms, then, do not come close to implementing complete commodification. And traditional arrangements with which they are often contrasted already gave very considerable place to market mechanisms, including two different variants of a price mechanism. Let's start with the most obvious fact: in all developed countries private schools are legal and so at least the more affluent parents have a market-based option: if they don't like the public schools that are readily available in their locale, they can choose to exit the public system for the private system, albeit at a cost. In the UK about 7% of children of school age attend private schools; in the US the figure is roughly 12%. In many countries – and especially in the US – parents with the relevant resources can also home-school their children. And, again for more affluent parents, even if their child attends a public school, they can supplement with additional lessons, or compensate for low quality instruction, by purchasing tutors and other kinds of educational support in the supplementary educational services market.

Also obvious is the fact that, again more affluent parents, can exercise choice over their children's schooling without ever resorting to exit from the public school system, through decisions about where to live. In the very common jurisdictions in the US and UK in which most children attend their neighbourhood schools, realtors and estate agents normally include 'school quality' as a major selling point for houses. Less affluent parents typically have less choice; they have fewer resources to spend on housing and, if they are in the private rental market and especially if they have insecure employment they may have to move mid-year and have very limited choices that do not afford them giving much if any weight to school quality (Desmond, 2017). The housing market, then, has long been a mechanism through which the affluent exercise choice on behalf of their children, and indirectly pay a premium for getting their child into the desired school.

Markets are also involved even in the public education system in less visible and perhaps less obvious ways. Governments must either contract with developers to build schools or build them themselves using workers hired in the labour market and materials purchased from the private sector. Books, desks, chairs, computers, white boards, curtains, power, and all other resources used in the buildings are, ultimately, purchased in the marketplace. But, at least for now, the single most important input into education is *labour*; the developed and embodied skills of teachers, administrators, advisors, secretarial and custodial staff, counsellors, psychologists, and social workers. The labour market thus has a profound effect on the cost, and distribution, of quality education. Let's just consider teachers. If salaries in comparable professions increase faster than salaries in teaching, we should expect talented people who might otherwise enter teaching to prefer those other professions – to train as nurses, doctors, lawyers, or engineers for example. And as salaries and working conditions in more affluent school districts improve we should expect it to become more difficult for less affluent districts to attract and/or retain skilled teachers. Unless society decides to conscript teaching labour in the way that some societies conscript into the military in times of war or insecurity, the labour market influences the quality and the distribution of educational opportunities.

These particular market mechanisms, which are embedded in the traditional system, are almost certainly implicated in the fact that educational goods are not distributed either equally or optimally to the overall benefit of the less advantaged (for a comprehensive account of the US case see Duncan and Murnane, 2011). Affluent families can always exert market discipline on schools to favour their children through the housing market and the private option. If schools do not respond, they can use their ability to pay (for private schools, or for housing close to more desirable schools, and the ability of those schools to hire from a better pool of teaching labour) to ensure that their children get better education.

Taking these price mechanisms out of schooling isn't impossible, exactly. But it would come at a very high cost. The government could prohibit private schools. It could (in principle, if not in practice) heavily regulate the freedom to choose where to live. And it could conscript teaching labour, requiring potentially excellent teachers to work in teaching rather than in the law or medicine, or the tech sector, and allocating the better teachers to schools with more disadvantaged students. Left wing parties in contemporary democracies sometimes propose the first of those measures, but never propose the other two, and for good reason. We have good reason to value the freedom to choose where to reside. Conscripting teachers could certainly radically reduce the cost of education in general, and especially educating the less advantaged, because society could require young people with great potential as teachers to train as teachers, and then allocate more skilled teachers to more disadvantaged students, without having to bear the costs of financial incentives. But we generally resist the conscription of labour except in times of potential catastrophe for two reasons. People should be free to choose among potential career opportunities. And the real costs of social enterprises such as educating the next generation should be distributed fairly among all of us, rather than an excessive proportion of those costs being borne by those whose talents happen to suit them particularly well to socially urgent labour.

Of course, one systemic way of reducing the impact of these markets mechanisms on distribution would be to reduce inequalities of income and wealth. This wouldn't alter the extent of commodification, but would alter the stakes, by making the private option, and housing, more equally available to all, and would reduce the stakes. And in the absence of reductions of inequality of income and wealth reformers (including left wing reformers) have generally proposed *harnessing* market mechanisms, specifically through funding schools which serve disadvantaged students better and even allowing them to pay teachers more, so they can compete more effectively for teaching labour.

In fact, some of the mechanisms introduced during marketization may be thought of as counteracting, or at least attempting to counteract, commodified aspects of the status quo. Most obviously: parental choice systems, especially when, as in the case of charter schools in the US, they require oversubscribed schools to select by lottery, and as long as they are not accompanied by allowing schools to charge tuition, make it harder for more affluent families to *guarantee* their children's presence in a desired (non-private) school through the operation of the housing market. Charter school reforms make transparent the role of parental choice which is made opaque by the combination of neighbourhood schooling and housing markets; and they reduce the inequality of market power between affluent and low-income families that is entrenched in the more traditional arrangement.

Schooling was, then, always partly commodified. The 'market' reforms won't fully commodify schooling; indeed it is not clear whether they even extend, as opposed to merely make more transparent, commodification. Some 'market' reforms may even improve the level of educational goods produced, and improve the fairness of their distribution. For example, the use of lotteries for admissions in charter schools reduces the inequality of market power between parents that are entrenched by a system in which governments decide who attends which school on the basis of housing. And, as we'll see in the next section, the case for complete non-commodification turns on unrealistic assumptions about how governments actually act.

The risks of complete non-commodification

Suppose it were possible completely to decommodify schooling: that is, to provide it in a way that didn't allow parents any choice, through private schooling or housing market, and in which teaching and other key labour inputs were conscripted. Would that guarantee justice in the distribution of educational goods, and ensure that educational goods were not undersupplied?

It would make it *possible*, assuming that the government was sufficiently committed to distributing resources to ensure that the best teachers work with the most disadvantaged students, and if the government had just the right conception of educational goods, and had the capacity and will to hold schools appropriately accountable.

But I think it is obvious that a wholly non-commodified system wouldn't come close to *guaranteeing* distributive justice or the optimal production of educational goods. For example, the government might choose to spend more on educating affluent students than on less affluent students. Indeed, immediately prior to market reforms spreading in the 1990s, this was the main complaint against the government in the US.[10] Or the government might decide to teach students from different racial backgrounds in separate schools, leading to the undersupply of the good of democratic competence, and, if it expended fewer resources on students from some racial background than on others, unjust distribution of educational goods. Indeed, racially segregated schooling in the US, which persisted as a policy well into the 1970s, was a consequence of deliberate government decisions, both over schooling and over housing, not a side effect of parental choice.[11] The government might decide to require that history be taught in ways that distort the facts, and misrepresent the intentions and achievements of that country's political system, thus leading to the undersupply of democratic competence. Again, this kind of history teaching in the US and the UK (and presumably elsewhere) has not been due to the market but due to the political culture. A government might consign 70%-80% of 11-year-olds to a pathway that all but guaranteed they would not attend higher education, on the basis of a crude test: again, the practice of academic selection at age 11 in the UK from 1944 till the late 1970s was a government decision, not the result of market choices.

It was the Federal Government in the US that developed the accountability system embodied in No Child Left Behind. NCLB required States to hold schools accountable using student performance reading and mathematics tests and nothing else. And State governments, not the market, interpreted that as a mandate (initially) to hold schools accountable simply for raw test scores rather than for test score growth. Establishing the Common Core State Standards or some something similar in most States in the US has been a valuable resource for teachers and school systems but little movement has been made on accountability measures in other subjects. Sex education remains lamentably bad in US schools, despite a universal policy of allowing parents to opt their children out, which should, in theory, allow schools to adopt high quality curricula and pedagogy for those students who remain. In this case, a market-like mechanism (opt out) facilitates good policy, but good policy is nevertheless not forthcoming, because governments either make bad decisions or lack the competence to enact good ones. Non-commodification might do better than complete commodification with respect to the goals we have reason to value, but only if the government is both well-willed and highly competent. An induction on the history of government provided and funded schooling does not give us reason for boundless optimism.

Concluding comments

I've presented a deflationary story about commodification of schooling. It is true that complete commodification would mis-serve many of those goals. So, quite probably, would complete non-commodification in most circumstances, even if it were possible. But provision of schooling *inevitably* involves markets in several ways, at least in a society that allows free choice of occupation and has a housing market. The difference between the traditional, *apparently* close-to-completely non-commodified, system of schooling and recent market-like reforms is not so much in the extent of markets as the different specific mechanisms at work and how transparently they are involved: opaquely in the traditional system, transparently in the reforms. We should evaluate the arrangements for schooling provision according to whether they produce the right kinds of educational outcomes, how justly they distribute those outcomes, and how efficiently they achieve those two goals, not by looking at how commodified the systems are or appear to be.

Notes

1 I'm grateful to the editors, an anonymous reader and as always these days to Gina Schouten and David O'Brien for detailed comments on and in the latter case discussions of previous drafts, and to Maddy Aaronson for research and editorial assistance.
2 One notable exception is the Netherlands, where the vast majority of schools are privately-run entities. The first robust more-or-less universal public schooling systems were established in some of the States within the United States, where not only economic efficiency, but also nation-building (and, specifically, the integration of immigrant populations who were not Protestant Christians) was a central justification. See Kaestle (1983).
3 Policing and fire services and military forces are similar.
4 Ball (2003) emphasizes the distributive dimension; Apple (2001) tends toward the essential goods approach. For what seems like an essentialist approach see McMurtry (1991), Silbaugh (2011). https://openscholarship.wustl.edu/law_journal_law_policy/vol35/iss1/15. All three dimensions surface in Molnar (2001).
5 See also Soroko (2020); Brighouse (2005).
6 Tooley (1996); Friedman & Friedman (1990).

7 Brighouse, Ladd, Loeb, & Swift (2018).
8 Jenks, (1988); Brighouse & Swift (2008); Brighouse & Swift (2014).
9 A number of students in publicly funded voucher systems in the US attend schools that are allowed to charge a small fee on top of the voucher provided by the state.
10 See, eg, Kozol (1991). The complaint has lost some of its force during the period in which market reforms have taken hold in the US Federal Government spending on schools (which is, by design, highly equalizing in effect) has increased considerably.
11 On housing see Rothstein (2017). Schooling is still segregated to a considerable, but much lesser, extent; some of that extent is now the result of market processes, and some of it is the result of past, and continuing, government decisions about housing and other goods.

References

Anderson, E. (1990) "Ethical limitations of the marker," *Economics and Philosophy* 6(2), pp. 179–205.

Apple, M. (2001) *Educating the "Right" Way: Markets, Standards, God and Inequality*. New York: Routledge.

Ball, S. (2003) *Class Strategies and the Education Market*. New York: Routledge.

Brighouse, H. (2005) "Channel One, the anti-commercial principle, and the discontinuous ethos," *Educational Policy* 19(3), pp. 528–549.

Brighouse, H., & Swift, A. (2008) "Putting educational equality in its place," *Education Finance and Policy* 3(4), pp. 444–466.

Brighouse, H., & Swift, A. (2014) "The place of educational equality in educational justice," in K. Meyer (ed.) *Education, Justice and The Human Good*. London: Routledge, pp. 14–33.

Brighouse, H., Ladd, H.F., Loed, S., & Swift, A. (2018) *Educational Goods Values, Evidence, and Decision-Making*. Chicago: University of Chicago Press.

Desmond, M. (2017) *Evicted: Poverty and Profit in the American City*. New York: Crown.

Duncan, G, and Murane, R. eds. (2011) *Whither Opportunity: Rising Inequality, Schools, and Children's Life Chances*. Russell Sage Foundation and Spencer Foundation.

Friedman, M. (1955) "The role of government in education," in R. Solo (ed.) *Economics and The Public Interest*. Kirkwood: Vail-Ballou Press. pp. 124–144.

Friedman, M. (1962) *Capitalism and Freedom*. Chicago: University of Chicago Press.

Friedman, M., & Friedman, R. (1990) *Free to Choose: A Personal Statement*. Boston: Mariner Books.

Jenks, C. (1988) "Whom must we treat equally for educational opportunity to be equal? *Ethics* 98(3), pp. 518–533.

Kaestle, C. (1983) *Pillars of the Republic: Common Schools and American Society 1780–1860*. New York: Hill and Wang.

Kahlenberg, R.D. (2007) *Tough Liberal: Albert Shanker and the Battles Over Schools, Unions, Race, and Democracy*. New York: Columbia University Press.

Kozol, J. (1991) *Savage Inequalities: Children in America's Schools*. New York: Crown.

McMurtry, J. (1991) "Education and the market model," *Journal of Philosophy of Education* 25(2), pp. 209–217.

Molnar, A. (2001) *Giving Kids the Business: The Commercialization of America's Schools*. New York: Routledge.

Panitch, V. (2020) "Liberalism, commodification, and justice," *Politics, Philosophy & Economics* 19(1), pp. 62–82.

Rothstein, R. (2017) *The Color of Law: A Forgotten History of How Our Government Segregated America*. New York: Liveright.

Sandel, M. (2012) *What Money Can't Buy: The Moral Limits of Markets*. Cambridge: Cambridge University Press.

Satz, D. (2010) *Why Some Things Should Not Be for Sale: The Moral Limits of Markets*. Oxford: Oxford University Press.

Schouten, G. (2012) "Fair educational opportunity and the distribution of natural ability: Toward a prioritarian principle of educational justice," *Journal of Philosophy of Education* 46(3), pp. 472–491.

Shanker, A. (1988) National Press Club Speech [Speech]. Walter P. Reuther Library.

Silbaugh, K. (2011) "Testing as commodification," *Washington University Journal of Law & Policy*, 35(1), pp. 309–336.
Soroko, A. (2020) "Buying into dominant ideas about wealth and poverty: An examination of U.S. and Canadian financial literacy standards," *Teachers College Record* 22(3), pp. 1–50.
Tooley, J. (1996). *Education Without the State*. London: Institute of Economic Affairs.

14
SECURITY AND PRISONS

Jonathan Peterson

Introduction

This chapter addresses questions about commodification in the sphere of security and prisons. It surveys potential forms of commodification and considers arguments that aim to show that they are morally wrong or unjust. A broad range of institutions and practices, including policing, punitive incarceration, and immigration detention, raise commodification concerns in this sphere. This chapter will focus on commodification in the context of punitive incarceration. Although commodification is not the most important basis for objection to carceral institutions, I will argue that some current practices of carceral commodification are seriously harmful. I leave it an open question whether this conclusion calls for reform or an end to commodification altogether. However, I will suggest that commodification is especially objectionable in the context of a history of race-based oppression. In such cases, commodification may continue a pattern of racial subordination and carry a symbolic message of unequal status.

A background assumption of this chapter is that some forms of incarceration are sometimes morally permissible. If imprisonment cannot be morally justified, the commodification question would not arise in this domain. There are two caveats to be made to this point, however. First, prison abolitionists, who seek to eliminate and replace prisons with more supportive and restorative social institutions, might be concerned with commodification since any incremental approach to abolition must consider which strategies and goals to prioritize. Second, positions on the legitimacy of commodification depend on the correct theory of the justification of criminal punishment. For example, a general deterrence theory of punishment may support a different conclusion than a retributive or rehabilitation theory about the permissibility of commodification.

The structure of the chapter is as follows. In this introduction, I briefly characterize my understanding of commodification and distinguish commodification from privatization. I introduce several forms of commodification that are relevant to the sphere of incarceration and highlight the relevance of the racial dimension of mass incarceration to arguments about commodification. In the next part of the chapter, I consider commodification-based arguments against private prisons. I then turn to consider commodification-based arguments against prison labour. Finally, I explore the claim that commodification in the context of mass incarceration is especially wrongful. The arguments considered in this chapter might call for market reform, preventing commodification

DOI: 10.4324/9781003188742-18

by blocking the sale of some kinds of goods or services, or for complete de-commodification, i.e., ending currently permitted practices of exchange.

Commodification

Commodification, as commonly understood, is fundamentally connected to a market. I follow Brennan and Jaworski (2016, p. 4) in defining a market as "a relationship where the mode of interaction is consensual exchange." It should be noted that this is an idealized definition of a market. In considering prison labour, it will be necessary to consider non-ideal markets, especially ones with defects in consent or voluntariness. Given this understanding of a market, however, we can characterize treating something as a commodity as the act of offering it for sale or trade in a market. Commodification, then, will be understood to be the transformation of things, such as goods, services, ideas, etc., into objects of trade or exchange. The commodification question asks whether some goods and services should not be for sale.

Security and policing services involve numerous practices of commodification. Homeowners pay private agencies to monitor their home alarm systems and notify police of intrusions. Cities contract with private companies to reduce false alarms, handle accident reporting, or impose speeding fines using traffic cameras. Retail stores, clubs, and concert venues pay private companies for security services. In some American cities, private security districts charge residents fees for neighbourhood security patrols. Off-duty police officers often staff these patrols and aim to provide some of the security and deterrence customarily thought to be provided by police.

Questions of commodification also arise in immigration detention. In its current form in the United States, immigration detention raises many of the same issues that arise in punitive incarceration. In the United States, the state contracts with private companies to detain immigrants, including asylum seekers (Luan, 2018). As of this writing, 80% of immigrants in detention are held in private facilities (Cho, Cullen, and Long. 2020, p. 5). As noted above, this chapter focuses specifically on commodification in the context of punitive incarceration.

Commodification and privatization

Questions of commodification in prisons are typically discussed in relation to privatization. Before turning to practices that potentially involve commodification, we should distinguish commodification from privatization. Services may be privatized or privately delivered without being commodified. Examples of agencies that privately deliver non-commodified services could include volunteer fire departments, private adoption agencies, and private, non-profit juvenile detention centers. Moreover, some services can arguably be commodified without being privately delivered. For example, as we will see below, some states use paid inmate labour to provide community services such as firefighting or trash clean-up. The labour of the inmates is, arguably, commodified in this case, even though the inmates remain under the control of public carceral institutions.

Although privatization and commodification are distinct issues, much of the discussion about commodification in prisons centers around privatization. It will be helpful to provide some conceptual clarification about prison privatization. Robbins (2006) identifies three ways privatization might occur in this sphere. These are prison privatization, private industries in prisons, and services in prison facilities operated by private industries.

Private prisons are facilities owned or managed by private agents/corporations on behalf of a state. The private sector is involved extensively in incarceration worldwide (Byrne, Kras, and Marmolejo, 2019). In some countries, such as the United States and Australia, the state contracts with private firms to manage some of its incarceration needs. For example, Core Civic (formerly known as the Corrections Corporation of America or CCA) and the Geo Group are publicly traded American companies operating correctional and detention facilities, re-entry programs, and immigration detention for U.S. Immigration and Customs Enforcement (ICE). These companies provide an extensive and growing list of services involving the control of incarcerated persons and persons on probation and parole. Private companies may oversee a private prison's functions (as in the US) or only some delegated functions. In France, for example, the state retains the security role, while private firms are permitted to operate other aspects of prisons (Cretenót and Liaras, 2014).

The second form of privatization involves private industries in prison. Private industries use inmate labour for manufacturing tasks and the provision of services. Other private companies employ prisoners in work-release programs outside of prisons. It is important to note that not all organizations that use prison labour are run by private companies. Prison Enterprises is a division of the Louisiana Department of Public Safety and Corrections that employs inmates to manufacture goods such as office furniture, provide janitorial or groundskeeping services in communities, and perform agricultural work at Angola Penitentiary. The California Department of Corrections and Rehabilitation employs some inmates as firefighters (CDCR, 2023). Additionally, some prison labourers work for public works programs (ACLU, 2022).

A third form of privatization involves private industries' services in a prison facility (Robbins 2006; Worth Rises 2020). Private companies such as Corizen and Armor Correctional Health provide health services to inmates. Other private companies provide communications, personnel, and transportation services. Companies like Aramark and Sodexo provide kitchen and food services, including commissary and vending services. Other companies, such as Global Tel Link, offer telephone services to inmates for a fee.

Forms of commodification in the context of incarceration

As these forms of privatization suggest, there are several potential forms of commodification in incarceration, and the question of permissible commodification arises for each. First, there is the commodification of services. Firms compete to own, manage and operate prisons for the state. Here, the **service** of detention is commodified. Should such commodification be permitted?

A second form of commodification is the commodification of persons. It might be argued, for example, that **inmates** are commodified when prisons are run by private entities that profit from detention. A statement by the Catholic Bishops of the South associates privatization with this form of commodification. "Prisoners are persons with inherent God-given human dignity. When prisoners become units from which profit is derived, there is a tendency to see them as commodities rather than as children of God." (Catholic Bishops of the South, cited in Robbins 2006, p. 12). If inmates are turned into commodities when subjected to incarceration by private agents, is this a violation of human dignity?

Third, the **labour** of inmates might be commodified. When inmates labour (often non-voluntarily) to maintain and operate prisons, create goods that will be sold in the market, or provide services such as telemarketing or firefighting, their labour is, arguably, commodified. This type of commodification exists in both public and private prisons, and it raises moral questions. Should the state be permitted to offer prison labour to private companies seeking to profit from the resulting goods? Is it permissible to offer inmates the opportunity to sell their labour? May inmates be compelled to work and to work for private for-profit firms? Should inmates receive compensation and entitlement to workplace protections if they work or are forced to work? What wages are fair in the context of prison labour?

The relevance of the racial dimension of mass incarceration

The weight of concerns about commodification can be affected by the context and history of the systems in which these forms of commodification appear. Incarceration in the United States, for example, must be understood in the context of the history of white supremacy and the oppression of black, brown, and indigenous people. The history and current pattern of racial subjugation are important in the context of discussions of commodification. For example, the United States imprisons black and brown people at much higher rates per capita than white people (Carson, 2022, p. 13.). Even if there is no abstract reason to object to forced labour in a penal context, one might nevertheless find it morally objectionable if the pattern of labour replicates a pattern of historical injustice. Thus, when we assess markets in incarceration or prison labour, we need to consider their effects on historically marginalized and oppressed groups and how these markets may contribute to or exacerbate the continuing social, economic, and legal inequality of members of these groups.

Commodification arguments against private prisons

In this section, I consider anti-commodification arguments against private prisons. The two forms of commodification that figure primarily in this section are the commodification of services and of persons. The following section will consider the commodification of labour.

At least one prominent argument against private prisons does not rest on claims about commodification. This is the non-delegation argument in law and political philosophy. In its legal form, this argument draws its force from the non-delegation doctrine in U.S. law. According to this argument, the state is legally barred from delegating its punishment power to private agents (Field, 1987). In political philosophy, it has been argued that punishment is a non-delegable function of the state (Harel, 2014, p. 96). Non-delegation arguments apply to non-profit schemes as well as to for-profit ones. As such, they are not essentially about commodification. However, a widespread claim of opponents of private prisons is that the profit motive is inappropriate in the context of incarceration. This brings us squarely into the realm of anti-commodification arguments.

Anti-commodification arguments against private prisons can be divided into economic, legal, and moral arguments. Economic anti-commodification arguments against private prisons focus on efficiency concerns. The question is whether prisons run by private firms can offer better services and lower costs than those run by the state. Prisons can be compared on inmate safety and rehabilitation, recidivism rates, time spent in prison, harm to inmates or staff, and human rights violations. Private prisons might be thought to offer some advantages over public prisons. They may be easier to open to deal with overcrowding, and it may be easier to close them when they are no longer needed (Eisen, 2018a, p. 201). Cost savings might also come from innovation and increased competition among firms. However, recent scholars and government officials have argued that private prisons are less efficient than public institutions. Pratt (2019, p. 449) claims that "the results of cost-benefit analyses have not demonstrated any systematic advantage to private prisons." Likewise, according to Sally Yates, Deputy Attorney General of the Obama Administration, private prisons

> compare poorly to our own Bureau facilities. They simply do not provide the same level of correctional services, programs, and resources; they do not save substantially on costs; and … do not maintain the same level of safety and security (2016).

According to Eisen, there is little evidence of increased competition due to privatization and no evidence of increased innovation (Eisen, 2018a, p. 200). Mukherjee (2021) suggests that any cost savings of private prisons are partially offset by, on average longer sentences served by inmates in private prisons. Kim (2022, p. 28) emphasizes the limits of the data on the comparative costs of public and private prisons and notes that insufficient attention has been paid to cost-quality tradeoffs (Kim, 2022, p. 29).

In addition to the question of whether private prisons generate cost savings, there is also the possibility that privatization creates perverse incentives (Eisen, 2018a, p. 186; Subramanian, et al., 2022). Incarceration for profit may incentivize increases in the prison population and sentence length. It may also increase the risks to which inmates are exposed since cost savings typically come from reductions in programs and personnel (Eisen, 2018a, p. 204). Reduced staffing and compensation can lead to higher turnover and poorly trained staff. This can lead to worse outcomes for inmates.

Likewise, the fact that private prisons' profits often depend on the number of inmates they house means that there are incentives to advocate for policies that increase the prison population and to incarcerate inmates for more extended periods.

Pfaff has argued, however, that incentives to increase the prison population also exist in public institutions (Pfaff, 2017, p. 87). The success of the perverse incentives argument might depend on the structure of prison contracts. In the US, for example, a company might be paid per occupied bed, which incentivizes retaining more prisoners and may contribute to mass incarceration. According to Eisen (2018b), some contracts in Australia are structured using performance metrics rather than occupancy rates. These contracts include bonuses for non-recidivism and financial penalties for some types of bad outcomes. However, there are issues of transparency and oversight here as well. It needs to be made clear whether the prisons are audited in ways that prevent these kinds of problems from arising. Moreover, more transparency about the content of private prison contracts is needed.

In addition to economic arguments, legal anti-commodification arguments against privatization are based on the concept of dignity in international human rights law. In 2009, for example, the Supreme Court of Israel ruled that private prisons violated a right to human dignity (Henry, 2019). If private incarceration deprives or tends to deprive human beings of dignity, that may count as a human rights violation. One way that inmates might be deprived of dignity is by being commodified. If inmates of private prisons are commodified, it follows that private prisons would be illegal under international law because they violate human rights (Robbins, 2006, Henry, 2019).

One response to this argument is to deny that inmates are commodified by companies that own or manage private prisons. Inmates in private prisons are treated as a means of generating profit for shareholders. It is even plausible to say that they are treated as mere means because the mode of profit generation is coercive and non-consensual. However, even if they are treated as mere means, it is a further step to say that they are commodified since they are not traded or offered for sale on the market. If the point about violations of dignity could be made merely by claiming that prisoners are treated as mere means, does the legal argument turn on concerns about commodification or instrumentalization? These can overlap but need not do so (see Chapter 4 in this volume).

However, Hallett (2006, p. 4) points out that prisoners' value for firms and shareholders is in the revenue they generate in the form of payments from the state. This itself might be regarded as a form of commodification in which persons are used as a mere means to generate value for shareholders. If we understand commodification as including profit generation, then it makes sense to say that inmates themselves are commodified in private prisons.

However, this is also true in the case of public prisons. Some jurisdictions rent empty beds to other states (Subramanian, et al., 2022). Louisiana sheriffs engage in prisoner transfers between parishes to maintain state payments for occupancy (Chang, 2012). Thus, prisoners held in public prisons are also used as a means of generating payments and profit for prison institutions and the communities in which they are incarcerated. For this argument to count against privatizing the service in incarceration, it would need to identify a commodification problem specific to private prisons. However, the fact that such commodification occurs in both public and private spaces does not rule out that it is seriously harmful and a violation of human dignity. Perhaps the solution is to adopt policies that preclude using inmates as a source of profit generation.

Finally, there are moral anti-commodification arguments against private prisons. These arguments might be divided into corruption arguments and equality arguments. Harel (2014) defends a version of the corruption argument. According to Harel, the good of punishment is the public condemnation of wrongdoing by the state on behalf of the community. He argues that private agents cannot achieve this good. When the state hands inmates over to the control of private prisons, they are subjected not to punishment but violence, which is morally impermissible and a corruption of the purpose of punishment. It is not clear that this corruption argument is successful because it depends on identifying a difference between state employees and the private individuals with whom the state contracts. It is difficult, however, to identify any salient difference between public and private prison officials or guards that would vindicate the corruption argument.

Equality arguments offer a different strategy for arguing against private prisons. Equality arguments focus on different ways in which commodification promotes inequality. Private prisons might be morally objectionable because they engage in unjust differential treatment or unjustly cause disparate outcomes between groups or because they subject some citizens to the dominating power of others. Commodified prisons may thus undermine the equal moral or citizenship status of inmates. In considering these arguments, we sometimes need to address factual questions. For example, to assess the disparate impact claim, we need to know whether commodified prisons contribute to racial disparities in incarceration. Although permitting private agents to exercise dominating power over others does appear to undermine the conditions of equal status, this argument is not fundamentally about commodification since it also applies to cases where power is exercised without profit or exchange.

Arguments against prison labour

Turn now to arguments regarding the commodification of inmate labour. Such arguments face an initial hurdle. The problem is that prison labour might not count as market activity. Brennan and Jaworski's (2016) definition of a market in terms of relationships of consensual exchange appears to exclude most prison labour. Prison labour is (often) forced rather than voluntary. If some forms of involuntariness invalidate consent, and if coercion, specifically, invalidates consent, then (most) prison labour is outside the bounds of the market. We would not say, for example, that protection payments to a mobster under extortion are market transactions. We might similarly hesitate to call it a market exchange when inmates receive a wage for forced labour. However, if prison labour does not count as market exchange, then it isn't clear that we can or should object to it on anti-commodification grounds.

Second, as Zatz (2009) points out, US courts have consistently viewed prison labour as a non-market activity. According to the courts, prison labour is an aspect of the punishment, so prisoners are not regarded as engaged in economic activity on the market. If this is correct, perhaps commodification is not the fundamental problem regarding prison labour.

There are several reasons to resist the claim that prison labour is not a market activity. First, it could be argued, in line with the above argument, that the state commodifies the labour of prisoners when it uses them to generate profit or makes their labour available to private firms. In other words, when the state permits private firms to hire prisoners and accepts payments for that labour, it is engaged in market activity. The state usually gets its cut by garnishing the wages of the prisoners or by receiving direct payments from private employers. Nevertheless, the state does derive a profit from inmate labour. Thus, the state exchanges inmates' labour for money, a form of commodification that arises in at least some prison labour.

Moreover, Brennan and Jaworski define an idealized market. In an ideal market, all exchanges are entirely voluntary. We must also consider non-ideal/real-world markets to assess claims about commodification. Engagement with markets is often on a continuum of voluntariness. Consider, for example, participants in certain kinds of public assistance programs. Persons in the United States who receive federal Supplemental Nutrition Assistance Program (SNAP) benefits are subject to work requirements. Participants are required to seek a job actively; if there is only one offer, they must take it. The choice here is between work and the ability to meet their basic needs. Intuitively, these persons are still engaged in market activity, even though not in an entirely voluntary way. It is not unreasonable to hold that the same is true of inmates who accept the option of forced labour rather than be sent to solitary confinement in a security housing unit. Although their labour is not voluntary, they are plausibly still engaged in market activity.

Finally, there is no reason to accept a sharp distinction between penal and economic activity as if the two were mutually exclusive (Leung, 2018, pp. 695–696). Courts likely conclude that inmate labour is a penal activity rather than a market activity to justify denying inmates job protections and minimum wage rights rather than because of some profound principled distinction between market activity and punishment (Zatz, 2009).

Several economic objections can be raised to prison labour. The first is that prison labour is a case of unfair competition. Because prison labourers are typically not paid even the minimum wage, they comprise a workforce that competes on terms that non-prison labourers cannot match. This has led to the objection that prison labour depresses wages or removes jobs from the free market. However, Derrick, Scott, and Hutson (2004) argue that prison labour (in the US) does not significantly impact the labour market.

A second concern about prison labour is that it may contribute to mass incarceration. Since prisons are a source of cheap labour, there will be incentives for firms to lobby for policies that increase the population in that workforce. However, less than 1 percent of prison labourers work for private companies (ACLU, 2022). Any incentives of this sort are likely unlikely to have a significant causal impact on mass incarceration.

There is a potential third problem. Prison labour reduces the public cost of incarceration by having prisoners labour to maintain the prison, cook food, launder uniforms, etc. If the state had to pay market rates for the labour involved in these tasks, the cost of incarceration would be much higher. The availability of free/coerced prison labour reduces the cost of mass incarceration, potentially making it more palatable to the public (ACLU, 2022).

As with arguments against private prisons, the most fundamental commodification concerns are not economic but moral or justice based. Some moral arguments in this domain focus on exploitation. On this view, the state exploits a vulnerability by forcing inmates to labour and permitting private firms to take unfair advantage of it. This may count as a form of exploited labour. And while exploitation need not necessarily involve commodification, this is a case where the two worries overlap.

Theorists of exploitation distinguish between harmful and mutually beneficial exploitation (Zwolinski, 2022). In many paradigm exploitation cases, the exploitative act or transaction harms the victim. If prisons force inmates to do dangerous work without pay, training, or adequate protective equipment, they are engaged in harmful exploitation. The inmates would be better off if they were not forced to work in these conditions. In many actual cases, the exploitation of prison labour is harmful; the inmates at Angola Penitentiary who are forced to work at hard labour in the Louisiana heat are probably not made better off (and at the very least, we should consult them about whether they are relative to a no-labour baseline).

However, in some cases, this exploitation may be mutually beneficial; in other words, the victim is not left worse off than they would be if there were no transaction (Zwolinski, 2022). A paradigm case of mutually beneficial exploitation is a rescue case. If I agree to pick you up from a sinking boat in the ocean only if you pay me a large sum, I may be exploiting you in a way that makes you better off than you would be if I had not come along. Some cases of prison labour might work like this. Where inmates have financial needs, as many do, the availability of paid work may allow them to earn a wage that permits them to meet at least some of their needs. To meet basic needs, inmates must purchase food and sanitary items such as tampons and pads from the commissary. It is also conceivable that labour could offer opportunities for skills training and productive use of one's time that could lead to increased well-being.

We need to know what baseline to use to evaluate these exploitation cases. We can distinguish between a no-transaction baseline and a baseline of a fair transaction (Zwolinski, 2022). Even if the inmates are made better off than they would be due to their wages, they are unlikely to be made better off relative to a baseline of what they reasonably ought to receive. When prisoners receive a wage at all, these wages are meager. One report found that the average minimum hourly wage for prisoners in non-industry jobs in the United States was thirteen cents per hour, while the average maximum wage was fifty-two cents per hour (ACLU, 2022, p. 55). In the UK, the average weekly income for working prisoners in 2010 was ten pounds a week (HM Inspectorate of Prisons, 2016). Prison labourers are often not provided basic workplace protections or compensation for workplace injuries, and, in the US, prison labour does not count towards social security (ACLU, 2022). So even if inmates use their wages to meet basic needs, it is unlikely that we should count most prison labour as mutually beneficial exploitation.

Of course, this requires a judgment about what inmates are entitled to as a matter of fairness. The issue here turns, in part, on views about what kinds of treatment are legitimate in punishment. Is it permissible to force someone to work as a response to wrongdoing? If so, who should benefit from this work? Do work and skills training help with rehabilitation? If so, how do work programs compare to other programs that aim to rehabilitate prisoners? One plausible moral view is that it is, at the very least, almost always unfair to force someone to work for nothing. Restitution cases may provide a counterexample to this claim, however. One might further argue that forcing someone to work even for a wage is unfair. If these views are borne out by argument, many prison labour practices will count as exploitative and morally wrong.

Although exploitation arguments have much power here, an argument can be made that the problem with prison labour is merely that it is coerced. However, the problem of prison labour can only partially be reduced to a question about coercion because some prison labour is or could be made voluntary. In this case, the issue of force does not arise, but the problem of exploitation does. Voluntary labour that does not receive the protections to which all workers are fairly entitled would still count as exploitation.

Mass incarceration and race

In this final section, I raise the question of the intersection of commodification and racial justice. How do prison privatization and prison labour relate to issues of racial justice? One position is that private prisons and prison labour, at least in the United States, are an aspect of the systemic commodification of people of colour. Prison privatization arose as a response to overcrowding in public prisons, a symptom of the prison population explosion (Eisen, 2018a, pp. 47–67; Kim, 2022, p. 25). Racist policies and patterns in policing, charging, and sentencing might thus drive the incentives to privatize (Hallett, 2006). Therefore, a critical framework for assessing privatization might see it as a new stage in the continued oppression of people of colour, or as a part of the carceral system that subjugates and marginalizes people of colour on behalf of white supremacy. According to one defender of this argument, the

> private prison industry is part of the mass incarceration era of the commodification of black bodies. It is the most modern attempt to commodify and profit from exploiting black bodies since slavery itself and the profiteering of the convict leasing system.
>
> (Hunt, 2020, p. 313)

Similar concerns can be raised about prison labour. Since people of colour are disproportionately incarcerated, one might discern a historical pattern from slavery to convict leasing to prison labour in its current forms. Leung (2018) provides one argument that prison labour policies are unjustly racist.

This analysis could support an abolitionist viewpoint. On this view, profit is the point of the private prison system. Systems of racist power provide the mechanisms by which profit is achieved. Thus, the system is not "accidentally" racist. The very point is the generation of profit by exploiting a population of marginalized persons who are disproportionally people of colour. From the abolitionist viewpoint, doing away with private prisons and prison labour would be necessary to liberate people of colour and overcome white supremacy. Unlike many of the standard objections to commodification, this abolitionist account tends to be more thoroughgoingly anti-capitalist.

This issue cannot be addressed fully in this chapter, but a few points can be made about the commodification of incarceration services. First, the claim that privatization is an opportunistic attempt to derive profit from a criminal justice system that disproportionately harms minority communities is plausible. However, it is also worth investigating whether privatization itself is a cause of that harm. One possible framework for considering this question is that of disparate impact discrimination. Disparate impact discrimination occurs when facially neutral or "colorblind" policies cause disparate harm to minorities. If commodification of the service of incarceration harmfully and disproportionally impacts Black or Brown communities, that provides one basis for a case that privatization is an unjustly racist policy.

People of colour are disproportionally represented in the prison system in the United States and suffer a disproportionate impact from the system of mass incarceration. Does privatization play a role in this disparate impact? To build the case, we might focus on several factors, including the contribution of privatization to mass incarceration and the role of prison placement in promoting this disparate impact. This leads to two questions. First, does the policy of privatization increase the total population of incarcerated persons, thereby contributing to the disproportionate impact of the system of mass incarceration on people of colour? Second, are people of colour more likely than white inmates to be incarcerated in private prisons?

An affirmative answer to the first question is a reasonable basis for a strong case that privatization policies involve disparate impact discrimination. If privatization is a contributing cause to systemic and disproportionate harm to individuals and communities of colour, then privatization counts as unjust discrimination. It is essential to emphasize the importance of the causal relationship in this analysis. Little is known about the effects of privatization on the number of persons incarcerated or the length of prison sentences (Kim, 2022), although a few studies have found minor effects on incarceration rates and sentence length (Dippel and Poyker, 2019; Galinato and Rohla, 2020).

What about whether people of colour are more likely than white people to be placed in private prisons? Do placement policies and decisions contribute to a disparate impact of incarceration on people of colour? This question is difficult to answer because of the lack of data. At the end of 2021, 96,700 persons were incarcerated in private prisons in the US, about 8% of the total number of prisoners. Little is known about the demographics of private prison inmates. Some research suggests, however, that white inmates are underrepresented in private prisons (Burkhardt, 2015, 2017; Montes and Mears, 2019). If people of colour are more likely to be held in private prisons and if the experiences, opportunities, and outcomes for inmates in private prisons are significantly worse on balance than in public prisons, then this could ground a case for the claim that prison placement policies and decisions unjustly impact people of colour. Again, more data is needed to assess the racial makeup of private prison populations and the comparative quality of private prisons (Kim, 2022).

Finally, however, a promising line of argument is that in a political system that has a long history of perpetuating ownership and exploitation of human beings along racial lines, there is a dignitary harm in allowing private custody and exploitation of labour as part of a system that disproportionally affects people of colour. In allowing this private control and exploitation, the state expresses a message about the value and dignity of inmates.

Incarceration raises important issues of commodification both in the domain of the provision of services and in the domain of the commodification of the body and its powers. Even if one thinks that private prisons or prison labour are morally permissible in the abstract, one can still find it objectionable when those institutions and practices replicate, entrench, and perpetuate historical patterns of injustice. When incarceration has a racial aspect, this increases the urgency of concerns about commodification because it engages concerns about equality more profoundly and sends a symbolic message about the value of those subjected to this system.

References

American Civil Liberties Union [ACLU]. (2022) *Captive Labor: Exploitation of Incarcerated Workers.* Available at: www.aclu.org/report/captive-labor-exploitation-incarcerated-workers

Brennan, J. and Jaworski, P. (2016) *Markets Without Limits: Moral Virtues and Commercial Interests.* New York: Routledge.

Burkhardt, B.C. (2015) "Where have all the (White and Hispanic) inmates gone: Comparing the racial composition of private and public adult correctional Facilities." *Race and Justice* 5(1), pp. 33–57.

Burkhardt, B.C. (2017) "Who is in private prisons? Demographic profiles of prisoners and workers in American private prisons," *International Journal of Law, Crime and Justice* 51, pp. 24–33.

Byrne, J., Kras, K.R. and Marmolejo, L.M. (2019) "International perspectives on the privatization of Corrections," *Criminology & Public Policy* 18(2), pp. 477–503.

Carson, A. (2022) *Prisoners in 2021: Statistical Tables*. U.S. Department of Justice, Office of Justice Programs. Available at https://bjs.ojp.gov/library/publications/prisoners-2021-statistical-tables

Chang, C. (May 13, 2012) *Louisiana is the world's prison capital*. [online] NOLA.com. Available at: www.nola.com/news/crime_police/louisiana-is-the-worlds-prison-capital/article_8feef59a-1196-5988-9128-1e8e7c9aefda.html

Cho, E.H., Cullen, T.T. and Long, C. (2020) *Justice-Free Zones: U.S. Immigration Detention Under the Trump Administration*. [online] Available at: www.aclu.org/report/justice-free-zones-us-immigration-detention-under-trump-administration

California Department of Corrections and Rehabilitation [CDCR]. (2023) *Conservation (Fire) Camps*. [online] Available at: www.cdcr.ca.gov/facility-locator/conservation-camps/

Crétenot, M. and Liaras, B. (2014) *Prison Observatory–Prison conditions in France*. [online] Available www.prisonobservatory.org/index.php?option=com_content&view=article&id=15&Itemid=119

Derrick, F.W., Scott, C.E and Hutson, C. (2004) "Prison Labor Effects on the Unskilled Labor Market." *The American Economist* 48(2). pp. 74–81.

Dippel, C. and Poyker, M. (2019) "Do private prisons affect criminal sentencing?" *NBER Working Paper No. w25715*. pp. 1–52. Available at: https://papers.ssrn.com/sol3/papers.cfm?abstract_id=3368005

Eisen, L.-B. (2018a) *Inside Private Prisons: An American Dilemma in the Age of Mass Incarceration*. New York: Columbia University Press.

Eisen, L.-B. (2018b) "Down under, more humane private prisons," *The New York Times*. [online] 14 Nov. 2018 Available at: www.nytimes.com/2018/11/14/opinion/private-prisons-australia-new-zealand.html

Field, J.E. (1987) "Making prisons private: An improper delegation of a governmental power," *Hofstra Law Review* 15(3), pp. 649–675.

Galinato, G.I. and Rohla, R. (2020) "Do privately-owned prisons increase incarceration rates?" Labour Economics 67(C), DOI 10.1016/j.labeco.2020.101908

Hallett, M.A. (2006) *Private Prisons in America: A Critical Race Perspective*. Urbana: University of Illinois Press.

Harel, A. (2014) *Why Law Matters*. Oxford: Oxford University Press.

HM Inspector of Prisons (2016) *Life in prison: Earning and spending money*. [online] Available at: www.justiceinspectorates.gov.uk/hmiprisons/inspections/life-in-prison-earning-and-spending-money/ [Accessed 6 March 2023].

Henry, B.F. (2019) "Private prisons and human rights: Examining Israel's ban on private prisons in a US context," *Concordia Law Review* 4(1), pp. 198–212.

Hunt II, C.J. (2020) "Feeding the machine: The commodification of black bodies from slavery to mass incarceration," the *University of Baltimore Law Review* 49(3), pp. 314–356.

Kim, D. (2022) "Prison privatization: An empirical literature review and path forward," *International Criminal Justice Review* 32(1), pp. 24–47.

Luan, R. (2018) "Profiting from enforcement: the role of private prisons in U.S. immigration detention." Migration Policy Institute. Available at: www.migrationpolicy.org/article/profiting-enforcement-role-private-prisons-us-immigration-detention

Leung, K.M. (2018) "Prison labor as a lawful form of race discrimination," *Harvard Civil Rights-Civil Liberties Law Review* 53, pp. 681–708.

Montes, A.N. and Mears, D.P. (2019) Privatized corrections in the 21st century: Reframing the privatization Debate," *Criminology and Public Policy* 18, pp. 217–239.

Mukherjee, A. (2021) "Impacts of private prison contracting on inmate time served and recidivism," *American Economic Journal: Economic Policy* 13(2), pp. 408–438.

Pfaff, J. (2017) *Locked In*. New York: Basic Books.

Pratt, T.C. (2019) "Cost-benefit analysis and privatized corrections," *Criminology & Public Policy* 18(2), pp. 447–456.

Robbins, I.P. (2006) "Privatization of corrections: A violation of U.S. domestic law, international human rights, and good sense," *Human Rights Brief* 13(3), pp. 12–16.

Simmons, W.P. and Hammer, L. (2017) "The human right to dignity and the commodification of prisoners: considering worldwide challenges to prison privatization," in M.A. Fineman, U. Andersson and T. Mattsson (eds.) *Privatization, Vulnerability, and Social Responsibility*. New York: Routledge, pp. 249–271.

Subramanian, R, Fielding, J. Eisen, L. Stroud, H., and King, T. (2022) "Revenue over public safety." *Brennan Center for Justice*. (online) Available at: www.brennancenter.org/our-work/research-reports/revenue-over-public-safety

Worth Rises. (2020) *The prison industry: mapping private sector players*. [online] Available at: https://worthrises.org/theprisonindustry2020

Zatz, N.D. (2009) "Prison labour and the paradox of paid nonmarket work." *Economic Sociology of Work*, 18, pp. 369–398.

Zwolinski, M., Ferguson, B., and Wertheimer, A. (2022) "Exploitation," *Stanford Encyclopedia of Philosophy*. Stanford University. https://plato.stanford.edu/entries/exploitation/

15
CULTURAL GOODS
Cultural commodification and cultural appropriation

Michael Joel Kessler

Introduction

This chapter will discuss markets in cultural goods. In commodification debates cultural goods tend to be identified with sculptures and paintings and other things that we put in museums and galleries. As I will argue, to capture the special *value* of cultural goods we need an account that includes artistic works, the spaces they fill, but also the reasons why we consider these to be part of culture in a distinctive way. With this account in place we can then see why these are contested commodities.

When a gallery sells an artist's painting, or when a patron pays a fee to access a museum, cultural goods are commodified. At first glance there are no major concerns about these transactions. They are not significantly different from buying a record or going to the movies. These are all instances of human creative effort, voluntarily brought to a market where there are willing buyers, often with the help of third parties. The problematic cases arise, I will argue, when cultural commodification involves cultural appropriation. In particular I will show that some markets in cultural goods *lead to (or entrench) objectionable forms* of cultural appropriation *that society has a pre-existing moral responsibility* to regulate and ultimately reverse. In this way, a market in cultural goods can intensify the distinct wrong of cultural appropriation. As such, to the extent that there is a legitimate worry about cultural appropriation, I will demonstrate that there is a corresponding worry about the existence of markets in cultural goods involving cultures that are subject to historical or ongoing oppression.

While the connection between appropriation and commodification is contingent rather than necessary, the connection can be quite strong. I will argue that, as with many contested commodities, while money can exacerbate problems, money is not the main problem when thinking about markets in cultural goods. Rather, the key issue is power: when the goods of one's own culture are under the control of another culture, there are strong moral reasons to doubt that the exchange from the weaker party to the stronger one can be justified. There is a similar observation with, for example, sex work. The power differential between the buyer and the seller can delegitimize what looks like a voluntary and uncoerced transaction. The main difference in the case of cultural commodification is that this is a market in which we all participate. As I will explain, culture is a shared good for all citizens, and so we are all implicated if our state engages in wrongful forms of cultural exchange.

DOI: 10.4324/9781003188742-19

There are well established literatures on both cultural appropriation and the legal protection of cultural heritage. One reason that states should pay special attention to the intersection of these two within their borders is that unrestricted commodification of culture can undermine the project of reconciliation. In countries with colonial histories there have been dedicated efforts to atone for the wrongs of colonialism. The focus of this process is on the wrongs done to individuals, families, tribes, and ancestral lands. My analysis here will be on the harms of colonialism as they pertain to culture and cultural goods. Many reconciliation programs look to make additional room for indigenous culture through subsidies and grants, as well as other forms of public support, like dedicated television stations and newspapers. The goal of these programs is to allow indigenous culture to compete in the cultural marketplace through a levelling-up of its presence. This is a good thing, in principle, from the point of view of reconciliation.

According to the argument I will make here the levelling-up strategy can, however, contribute to ongoing wrongful forms of cultural appropriation. More specifically, cultural appropriation involves taking something that is 'not yours' without permission. This kind of taking is wrong in virtue of violating conditions of meaningful consent. As I will show, within colonial societies, the historical lack of consent by indigenous cultures infects markets in indigenous cultural goods.[1] Since these cultural goods enter the market through corrupted means, their continued presence in the market – especially when subsidized by their colonizers – can be wrongful.

I begin in Part 1 of this chapter by offering an account of cultural goods and their political value. In Part 2 I unpack a widely shared worry about cultural appropriation and show that in order to make sense of this as a *wrong,* one needs an account of cultural goods as things that can rightfully be owned, and thereby misappropriated by others. To make this case I will devote Part 3 to offering an account of cultural ownership that can undergird a political charge of cultural appropriation. In Part 4 I explain the conditions under which, on this account of cultural ownership, restrictions on markets in cultural goods are necessary. I will argue that in the context of reconciliation some cultural goods require special protections. My argument will raise a number of questions as it proceeds to which I will not be able to attend in this brief discussion. The main aim here is to draw attention to the important connection between the wrong of cultural appropriation and the practice of cultural commodification, and to do so by way of providing an account of the rightful ownership and exchange of cultural goods. I conclude with some recommendations regarding reconciliation practices which must, on my view, involve restoring control over cultural goods to the groups from which they were taken.

What are cultural goods and why do they matter?

The main question of this chapter is whether some cultural goods should be prohibited from entering the commercial marketplace. In order to give some meaning to this question we need to do three things. First, we must explain what makes something a *cultural* good, as opposed to some other kind of good. Second, we need to know how cultural goods raise a matter of justice that would justify their commercial regulation by the state. Third, we need to distinguish between types of cultural goods, as issues of justice may differ across them.

As noted in the introduction, cultural goods 'live' in culturally meaningful spaces. The easiest examples are the works placed in museums and galleries. However, in order for these works and spaces to count as cultural ones we must already have some more abstract notion of what distinguishes culture from generic parts of human society. In this chapter I'll only be able to provide a sketch of how to draw this distinction. As a working definition let's call cultural goods those that have meaning to us collectively and individually as members of cultural groups. The groups in question can be geographic (my country, my hometown), ethnic, tribal, or racial (my people), historical (settlers, survivors, those who served), or spiritual (my faith). Naturally, these categories are not exclusive; people have intersecting cultural identities based on their geographic, ethnic, racial, historical, and spiritual connections. This intersectionality is compatible with an anthropological conception of culture as "the unique mix of beliefs, practices, values, and institutions shared by members of a society" (Brown, 2003, p. 4).

We can speak of cultural values at various levels of specificity, from national to local. For example, Canada has an official policy of respecting and promoting the multicultural heritage of all Canadians, which is enshrined in the Charter of Rights and Freedoms.[2] This value provides collective meaning to *all* Canadians as citizens, regardless of their other cultural identities. Yet, every country will also contain a multitude of sub-societies, and the values that emerge from these smaller units will have meaning *only* to members of these groups, as opposed to all citizens. So, while all Canadians could claim the cultural goods that emerge from the value of multiculturalism as 'theirs', there are specific cultural goods that only belong to Canadians who also belong to those groups. The point is that while there are some cultural goods that any citizen can count as 'theirs' in virtue of citizenship, there are other identifiable goods that emerge from, and thus belong to, specific cultural identities within a nation.

Spiritual identity can help illustrate the point of how cultural value implicates norms of ownership. Prayer cannot be claimed as the cultural invention of any given religion. However, many religions have specific rituals around prayer which help identify that religion's followers both to each other and to outsiders. While all religious people could take personal offense at someone mocking a prayer ritual, there is a specific offence that can only be felt by that religion's adherents. There is a difference between saying "faith is under attack" and "*my* faith is under attack". If one is not Muslim one can certainly take offence *on behalf of* Muslims, but not *as* a Muslim. What this example shows is that in order for a cultural good to count as 'mine' I need to be related to it in the right way, by belonging to the relevant group. The corresponding implication is that when someone is not part of the relevant group, the cultural goods produced by this group are not 'theirs'.

Next, let's consider why culture counts as a political value. According to a prominent strand of liberal thought, being able to access one's culture is essential to living an autonomous life within a multicultural society. For example, Kymlicka (1995) argues that

> societal cultures … [provide] members with meaningful ways of life across the full range of human activities, including social, educational, religious, recreational, and economic life, encompassing both public and private spheres […] [Societal cultures] involve not only shared memories or values, but also common institutions and practices.
>
> (p. 76)

We need to be careful how to understand this premise. The claim here is not that engaging with one's culture is a precondition on living a meaningful life. Whether one chooses to attach any importance to cultural identity is a personal decision and rejecting one's culture can also be part of an autonomous life. However, in order for that decision to be meaningful, one must make it from a position of being able to engage with people like ourselves, and with the values that people like us seek out (See also Dworkin, 1985, Taylor, 1992).

When a society erects obstacles to belonging to some cultural group, or shames those who choose to do so, then the authenticity of people's choice to abandon this identity can be called into question. Not being free to pursue one's preferred religion is a kind of personal invasion. This can be accomplished in formal ways, as when religious practice is forbidden, but also when society makes it harder for people to flourish in their chosen religion (Nussbaum, 2013). For example, by banning "burqinis" at public swimming pools France targets a distinctively Muslim religious observance while leaving other religious practices around modesty unfettered. This sets up an unnecessary conflict between a person's cultural identity and their standing as a full citizen, equal to all others.

Under a liberal account of justice, society must make room for a diversity of ways of life, allowing spiritual culture to thrive free from governmental restraint. In many cases, this simply means removing laws that single out certain religious practices. But governments must also adopt policies that are sensitive to the ways in which minority cultures can be choked, either intentionally or not, by dominant cultural groups. This leads in some cases to the adoption of subsidies for minority cultural practices so that they can continue to exist within society, for example, French language in Canada.

When combined, these two points show why culture counts as among the political goods related to *equal citizenship*. Culture is not a discretionary item or luxury taste, the costs of which can be left to the market to determine. Instead, access to one's culture is intimately related to the political autonomy of each person. As such, states must protect the fair value (Rawls, 1999) of everyone's liberty to seek out and identify with their culture.[3]

The argument so far is that culture establishes a connection between individuals and larger groups. The value of cultural *goods*, as distinct from other goods, comes from their resonance with something abstract and relational, like belonging, or identification, or appreciation. Non-cultural goods can have a similar value for individuals (e.g. my childhood home), but in order for something to be a cultural good it must have some broader connection that goes beyond the biography of one person or family. There is no definitive boundary between cultural and non-cultural goods, and reasonable people can disagree about whether some object has or lacks the relevant value. However, this should not undermine our belief in the existence of cultural goods and how culture is related to fundamental issues of justice.

Having discussed cultural goods and their political value we can now turn to examining the different forms this value can take. Despite the breadth of discussion about cultural goods in the literature there has been little attention to the ways they manifest in society. We can break them down into three rough categories: 1) works, 2) spaces, and 3) patrimony.

Cultural works include objects and performances that have group-based significance either based on their content or their style. In general, the arts and artistic expression are sources of cultural goods in the sense being discussed here. They tell the story of my people, our struggles, our triumphs, and where we came from. As with the example of faith, artistic expression doesn't belong to anyone, but some works of art are identifiable as the cultural expression of a given people. This can range from paintings, to tribal dances, to other characteristic expressive forms.

The second category is spaces, which can be further divided into two sub-categories. Spaces like parks and historical sites are cultural goods in the sense that they provide meaningful physical and emotional connections (Abercrombie, 2020). Parks enable access to nature, both in urban and rural settings. Historical sites connect citizens to important moments from a nation's past. The other sub-category within spaces can be grouped together as forums. Here we can include broadcast airwaves (radio and television), museums, galleries, and theatres. The reason these are cultural spaces is that they host cultural goods. This makes them different from shopping malls or sidewalks. We house our best art in galleries, we store our important historical items in museums, and we put musical performances on stage, and broadcast them on radio and television. Debates about ensuring public access to radio and television are familiar, but the same point applies to both subgroups more generally. These are all related to cultural goods as *points of access*. When people are denied the ability to enter these spaces, they lose the ability to disseminate their culture. This deprives both creators and audiences of something important. Thus, spaces – both literal and metaphorical – need to be considered in the analysis of cultural goods.

The final category is patrimony. This refers to a society's heritage, and more specifically the process through which culture is preserved and passed forward through time. Some of this is done intentionally, as for example when we choose to erect monuments to commemorate people and moments, or when we plan parades where our culture is on display. However, the transmission of patrimony can also be a more organic and informal process, based on oral traditions, story-telling and song, as well as customs related to clothing, language, naming, and food. I will focus mostly on patrimony in this discussion because it includes elements from the other categories. It is impossible to talk about heritage without mentioning the objects, works, and spaces that offer tangible insights into something fundamentally intangible.

Different societies will place different emphasis on these three categories. For some, nature will play a greater role than others. And in some cultures, the process of commemoration is done orally rather than through physical places like museums. When we recognize the political value of culture we must also make room for the variety of ways culture manifests itself. Put differently, there are many ways to express cultural value, and a just society must not merely acknowledge these differences but bear the costs of enabling equitable access to culture in the mode that is appropriate to each.

What is cultural appropriation and when is it wrong?

Having outlined why culture matters and how culture is expressed, we can now turn to the issue of the ways in which culture can be an object of interpersonal wrongs. The topic of cultural appropriation has received a lot of attention across a number of disciplines. There are difficult questions about how to identify appropriation of culture, as opposed to appropriation of something else, like property. In some cases, theft is just theft. In other cases, theft has a deeper meaning because it is also cultural theft. On some accounts, cultural appropriation is not about whether anything tangible is actually taken but rather about the modes of respect that are owed in cultural interactions (Young and Brunk, 2009). Accordingly, the issue has less to do with theft and more to do with attitudinal relations. Also, on any account, there must be some line between wrongful and permissible cultural exchange. Not all cultural interactions are problematic, and any plausible theory must leave room for the normal and healthy ways that cultures learn from each other.

To begin, consider the following question: what do we mean when we say that a culture is yours? There is a clear sense in which culture cannot belong to anyone. This is a conceptual point. Cultural value is relational: we connect to our culture, but do not thereby bring it under our control. It stands apart from us. A market in culture in this sense is impossible, because you can't transfer to someone what is not under your control in the first place. By contrast, specific cultural goods are obviously the property of their creators. In most contexts, creators are free to profit off their works, just as others are able to commodify their intellectual or physical talents. This pair of points is not especially puzzling, since the value of culture supervenes on the works and actions of individuals but is not reducible to them. I can own and sell *my* cultural works, without claiming ownership of the culture that imbues them with their distinctive cultural value.

There is however a puzzle when we consider how to reconcile the idea that no one owns culture with the idea that cultural appropriation is wrong. What can this charge amount to, if culture belongs to no one? Three necessary conditions stand out as grounding the charge of cultural appropriation, as a criticism of an action or policy. First, if cultural *appropriation* is wrong, then it must be possible for an agent to bring culture under one's control, in some sense. This means that one's actions must make use of some goods that are available. Accordingly, cultural appropriation has an active dimension – it involves *taking* from things outside of oneself. This leaves passive interaction with culture to one side. Merely appreciating or viewing another culture cannot count as appropriation, unless one violates privacy in order to do so.[4]

Second, this action must involve some kind of *wrongful* taking, or usurpation of control. Cultural appropriation only impugns the actions of outsiders; one can't be guilty of appropriating a culture that is one's own.[5] In order for a taking to count as a usurpation it must make use of something that is 'not yours'. If I don't stand in the right relationship to the goods in question, as a group member, then these goods aren't available to me in the way they are to in-group members. They are not mine to use.

And third, there must be some *unequal power dynamic* between the groups in question. When thriving cultures take from each other against a background of social equality, there is no claim that one is wrongfully appropriating from the other. Instead we tend to speak in terms of borrowing or inspiration. These terms imply a reciprocal, or least equally beneficial, relationship between the groups. By contrast, wrongful cultural appropriation describes interactions that rely on background inequalities, where one side lacks the power to exercise authority over what is theirs. As Matthes (2018) argues, "what makes cultural appropriation wrong, when it is wrongful, is the way it interacts with the oppression of certain cultural group members" (p. 1005).

This helps explain why, for example, a market in indigenous art by indigenous artists is unproblematic. People can claim ownership of culture, specifically their own. One doesn't need to do anything to acquire this claim other than belong to the relevant group. And once one has the relevant standing, then drawing from this culture in one's works is permissible. You are taking from what is already yours. At the same time, we can criticize artists from settler backgrounds who incorporate these styles, motifs, and experiences into their works. What they are taking is not theirs. Further, they are taking from a group that is already vulnerable *to them*. This is why group dynamics can't be eschewed by individual actors. Even if one has not personally created the historical circumstances of colonialism, one is still responsible for the choices one makes within those circumstances.

This picture of wrongful cultural appropriation supports the idea that, despite initial appearances, we can coherently talk about ownership over culture, and wrongs arising from violating the rights of others. But notice that this type of ownership has a peculiar quality: rather than being a general feature of culture, ownership rights do not obtain until other background conditions are met, particularly, a history of cultural oppression between groups. This means that the goods of some cultures come with restricted use conditions while the goods of other cultures are freely available to all.

This conception of cultural appropriation is, I believe, at odds with a competing value, and so comes at a theoretical cost. Socially we want important cultural ideas to be part of the public domain so that everyone can benefit from them. When we discover ancient skeletons, this is viewed as a triumph for humanity. These remains help us better understand where we come from as a species. According to one school within bio-anthropology, "ancient skeletons belong to everyone [as they are] the remnants of unduplicable evolutionary events which all living and future peoples have the right to know about and understand" (Thomas, 2002, pp. 209–210; Young and Brunk, 2009, p. 15). The same approach can be taken towards unearthed remnants of long-lost societies: our global culture is enriched by knowing how our ancestors lived. Accordingly, we resist attempts to privatize these discoveries, or to restrict scientists from studying them, because they are seen to be part of our shared heritage as human beings.

This point about common use is in tension with thinking of cultural appropriation along property-based lines, as the wrongful taking of something that belongs to someone else. The most famous North American piece of legislation about cultural ownership adopts this restrictive approach, attributing unearthed discoveries by current ancestry or historical territorial control. According to North American Graves Protection and Repatriation Act (NAGPRA) objects having "cultural patrimony" have the dual quality of belonging to some Native American groups but also being "inalienable" by and to anyone. This restrictive approach conceives of cultural heritage as both physical and intellectual property of groups, not as a belonging to everyone (Brown, 2003; Riley, 2004; Brown and Nicholas, 2012).

There is no answer to whether a restrictive or public approach is the right one except through a debate about values. The public approach has the appeal of making goods available to more people, which would in turn lead to wider appreciation. However, if we think cultural appropriation is wrong and further believe that it constitutes a violation of political equality, then states are under an obligation to enact measures to stop it. As such, I believe justice requires that we choose the restrictive approach, despite its attendant drawbacks to universal knowledge and cultural exchange. The public domain view, while attractive in theory, places unequal burdens on marginalized groups. Asking cultures to share their heritage, including allowing its free trade in the marketplace of cultural objects, negatively affects groups who value privacy (e.g. the Hopi Indians), those who treat cultural knowledge as a privilege of in-group members (e.g. the Pueblos), as well as those whose culture is more fragile and at risk of assimilation.

So far, we have an argument about the political importance of cultural identification, and the ways that cultural value manifests itself both materially and intangibly. We also have an argument that, as a good, culture can be misappropriated. When these two points are put together the result is that cultural appropriation raises a matter of justice. When dominant groups help themselves to the cultural goods of subordinated groups this reinforces substantive political inequalities (Brighouse, 2001). In the next section I'll propose an account of cultural *ownership* that allows subordinated groups to make a rights claim against appropriation of their culture by dominant groups.

Is cultural ownership possible?

According to the argument so far, when we use the phrase 'my culture' we imply three distinct propositions:

1) that something is 'mine' – I am a member of this group
2) that something is 'ours' – there is some distinctive group-based good we share
3) that something is 'not yours' – non-group members do not share this good

As I have suggested, cultural goods are relational in that they connect individuals to groups. This in turn gives individuals a moral claim to exclude others from accessing the relevant goods. The challenge now is to provide an account of how this moral claim could function as a legal claim within a system of rights. The claim is unusual in that culture is a kind of intangible good that only some people can rightfully commodify. This requires, as I'll show, some innovation in how we think about ownership.

Let's consider two different elements in how innovation in ownership happens. First, whether something can be mine is a social fact that reflects the technology available at a given point in time rather than something inherent in the nature of the good in question. Consider that digital currencies have only recently become commodities. Prior to the invention of blockchain technology there were few mechanisms for recognizing the labour of 'cryptomining', which is the process that discovers new digital coins. This is not significantly different from the labour of dredging the river for gold. Once technology advances enough the law can recognize both physical and digital resource mining. Second, social facts about what can and cannot be owned are not just about technology. They also reflect a society's values. The now widely utilized property type of condominium did not exist until the 1960s in the U.S. (Singer, 2001, p. 355). Prior to that time home ownership was limited to land and free-standing dwellings, and it was legally impossible to own property within a larger building. Apartment spaces could be rented, but not owned. The reason for creating the new property type of condominium is obvious, since it allows more people to enter the real estate market. But this requires some moral agreement that this outcome – greater access to home ownership – is valuable. The innovation here is moral, not technological. Condos are a solution to a problem rooted in a desire to see a more equitable society, where many individuals can own land that would otherwise belong to the very rich.

To sum up the point of these examples, there are forms of ownership that could exist but don't yet due to technical limitations. These can't be commodities because we haven't figured out how to make them 'mine', which in turn means they can't become 'yours' through transfer. There are also forms of ownership that are brought into existence because a moral consensus emerges. We want to live in a world where this type of thing can be 'mine' or 'yours'. These moral judgments become creatures of our legal institutions, shaping what we can and cannot own.

According to the argument of the previous section, there is a moral imperative to protect citizens belonging to historically subordinated groups from having their culture appropriated by dominant groups. In order to provide this protection, states should adopt a right to cultural ownership that reflects the tri-partite structure of cultural goods mentioned at the outset of this section: some cultural goods are, at the same time, 'mine, ours, and not yours'. We can derive a model for how to craft a right to culture from Kant's political theory. I will very briefly outline the elements of this account.

Kant argues that a variety of political rights grow out of the basic entitlement each of us has to exercise our humanity in a world we share with others. For Kant, it must be normatively possible to carry out plans and purposes, and to make a life for ourselves in a way that doesn't deprive others of doing the same. But in order to act in the world that we share with others I must know what I am allowed to do. A system in which each must secure the permission of every other before acting is incoherent. Accordingly, Kant argues there is a primitive sense of 'mine' that each of us acquires along with our humanity, which in turn licenses various kinds of actions. "That is rightfully mine with which I am so connected that another's use of it without my consent would wrong me" (Kant, 1999, p. 401/6:245). For Kant, rightful action is determined through authorization. The power to authorize comes from standing in the right relation – being "so connected" – to the things we want to use in the world.

Among the things to which we can be "so connected" as to acquire rights are: 1) objects, and 2) the choices of others, which we acquire via contracts. Objects can be mine, and once I have made them so, you cannot put them to rightful use without my consent. This is the familiar sense of property, where an object that belongs to me may only be rightfully used at my sole discretion. Specific things that you do can also be mine, like the labour you expend when I hire you to clear the snow from my steps. Notably, I cannot make your actions mine except by going through your will and entering into an agreement with you. That is, I can't take from you without your permission. In both cases I am able to appropriate something that is not yet mine and then count it among my legal holdings. There is reciprocity within the system of rights, since each of us can bind the other in the same ways.

In addition to objects and contracts Kant adds a nebulous category called "status rights" that includes spousal and parental rights.[6] For Kant, when people "stand in community with one another" in certain ways, they acquire a title that confers rights over that community that others must respect (Kant, 1999, p. 426/6:276). Spouses can speak on each other's behalf, and parents can represent their children. These are not property relations, but rather what Kant calls "rights to a person akin to rights to things". These rights exist when I am connected to others, not physically, but "as long as they exist somewhere or at some time" (Kant, 1999, p. 403/6:248). Notably, there is no reciprocity here. When I acquire a status right it is because of the special relation I stand in to the other people involved. Of course, you can stand in this relation to your own community, but in order to have the standing to speak for *this* community one must be connected in the right way to this particular group.

The category of status rights aims to bring together elements of both contracts (rights to persons) and property (rights to things). What is appealing about this model is that it establishes a form of rightful relation that connects groups across time and space. Importantly, one doesn't need anyone else's permission to acquire these rights, and once one has them, these rights restrict what others can do with respect to the community. When one is part of this community, what Kant calls "domestic society" one acquires rights to speak on behalf of that community, to manage its affairs, and to benefit from it. Importantly, one also acquires duties of stewardship to one's fellow community members. These prerogatives and responsibilities come along with the status of being part of the group.

What I will propose is that we can take this idea of a status right and extend the community in question beyond just the household, as Kant saw it, to the more intangible space of culture.[7] Cultural affiliation, like family relations, can authorize normative entitlements to others with whom we are "so connected" as to form a community. This provides a plausible way of understanding how culture can belong to someone in the sense of being able to block others from taking control of it – because they lack the relevant status – while at the same time licensing one's own ability to make use of it. According to this argument, the goods of a community can be mine, just as an object can be mine. Both cases share the feature that I am entitled to reject others' attempt use these things without my permission. This right to exclude is familiar in the case of property rights, but it is also applicable to the goods that belong to a given community. When culture is 'mine' in this sense, my rights over it extend to blocking what you can do, as if it were a thing that I own.

I have argued in this section that basic concepts like 'mine' and 'yours' rely on social institutions for their extensions. It is up to law and policy to establish what can be mine, and what I can do with that which is mine. This conventionalist approach helps dissolve some of the apparent confusion around what it would mean to give legal force to the charge of cultural appropriation. If we want to recognize this as a wrongful taking of something that is not yours, then we can establish a kind of ownership relation over culture that provides groups with the authority to block others from taking what is not theirs to take. Using the Kantian notion of a status right, we can conceive of a kind of ownership relation to culture that is like property in some ways. Cultural goods are a special kind of property: I can take from my culture because it is mine as a member of the community, and what I make by taking from this culture is also mine because it is the product of my own labour. As with any property, if something is mine then I can do things with it that others cannot, like sell it or give it away. And this is compatible with thinking that culture is also a collective good that is owned by the group. Cultural goods are not like other works we create through our labour because part of the value these goods carry comes from their connection to a community that is not itself anyone's exclusive property. Rather this good – heritage or patrimony – is held in common by group members, to the exclusion of others.

Cultural appropriation, commodification, and reconciliation

Finally, we can turn to thinking about how markets in cultural goods should be reformed in light of the argument that the wrong of cultural appropriation requires recognizing a legal right to culture for subordinated groups. In this section I will make some suggestions about how societies suffused with the legacy of colonialism can implement this right to culture for indigenous peoples in a way that moves beyond the "binary" of commodification versus decommodification (Radin, 1987, p. 1855; Sunder, 2003). Many of the wrongs of colonialism – like genocide, displacement, and internment – can be named without reference to culture. However, some colonial wrongs are distinctly related to the way that dominant groups wrongfully take from the culture of those who were there before. These distinctly cultural wrongs require distinctly cultural remedies.

Indigenous culture has been an object of both active and passive forms of oppression as a result of colonialism. Practices like Canada's residential schools program had the explicit goal of disconnecting Indigenous children from their culture and assimilating them into mainstream French and English Canadian society (TRC, 2015). One downstream effect of taking children from their homes is that they lose connection and contact with the spiritual and linguistic practices of their parents and grandparents. The cultural loss is profound: practices rely on practitioners. Without people to both receive and pass on these traditions, the culture itself faces extinction. "The self-identity of many Indigenous peoples hangs on the fragments of their culture that survive[.]" (Brunk & Young, 2009, p. 93)

As I have argued here, recognizing an ownership right to culture involves a value judgment about ongoing forms of oppression that we are committed to undoing. This supports a limited practice of recognizing ownership rights to "the tangible and intangible aspects of heritage" (Brown, 2003, p. 3). Many groups won't be able to stand on such claims. Rather, people whose culture has been suppressed through our political institutions have a special claim against these same institutions that they attempt to remedy historical wrongs. Public policy should be organized to address the forms of cultural appropriation that entrench the ongoing oppression of historical minorities. This means that ownership over culture, including symbols or other tribal identifiers, is not a general right. For any given society there will need to be a discussion around *which* groups have been historically oppressed and *which* aspects of their culture need protection from being used by others in ways that they have not licensed.

The legacy of colonialism infects each of the categories of cultural goods mentioned in Section I. Indigenous cultural works have been stolen by settlers, sometimes to be shipped back to their country of origin (Gerstenblith, 2019). Indigenous cultural spaces have been taken over or desecrated. And indigenous patrimony has been eroded and suppressed. One of the less visible wrongs of colonialism is the way that indigenous culture has been absorbed into settler culture only to be sold back to the wider public. In this way, indigenous culture is extracted from its traditional context and then packaged together with settler culture as if this were a joint venture. When people visit Hawaii, part of the authentic experience is soaking up indigenous culture (Stanley, 1998).

Visitors to Canadian national museums will see indigenous artifacts placed alongside French and English materials. Settlers gain the benefits of cultural tourism despite the fact that the culture in question is not theirs to share with the world (Comaroff & Comaroff, 2010). The fact that these benefits are packaged as public goods and housed in cultural institutions like museums does not detract from the wrongs associated with commodifying what is not yours (Harding, 2005).

States must provide mechanisms that allow historically wronged cultural minorities to block commodified use by others of their heritage. According to the argument here, there is no way to pull apart heritage from works and spaces. Heritage is promulgated through these. In order for patrimony to be a meaningful good, it must be undistorted. "*Self*-presentation is a central component of cultural identity" (Nicholas, 2005, p. 93). Thus, the promulgation of culture must be under the control of those whose culture this is, rather than under the "presumed stewardship" of colonial groups (Atalay, 2006, p. 271). Heritage that is corrupted or misrepresented is not what in-group members want passed forwards. In Australia, for example, Aboriginals have been concerned that their cultural rights protect physical materials but not the intangible aspects of their culture, such as "stories, songs, and dreaming tracks" (Janke, 1998; Nicholas, 2005, p. 97, Smith & Wobst, 2005). When these intangible items are packaged and presented to the wider world through museums and public performances, this carries the implication that what is being shared is done with consent.

The most recognizable form of commodified cultural appropriation is the theft of cultural goods by colonists, either for export back to their home countries or for use by settlers in their new homes. These cultural works became absorbed into the commodities markets of colonial society without compensation to either creators or owners. This problem affects other categories of cultural goods as well. Consider that many stolen works have made their way into collections of Indigenous art and artifacts that currently belong to public museums and galleries. Some of the pieces were bought by curators while others were donated by collectors who understood the mission of museums as being that of "harvesting the works of primitive peoples around the world" (Cole, 1995, p. 50).

All of this taints the spaces in which these works are *currently* collected, as well as the commercial transactions that link patrons to these collections. My argument here is specifically about the wrongfulness of allowing public institutions, rather than private ones, to be part of these transactions. Museums and galleries play a role in determining and shaping cultural patrimony. Part of how we learn about ourselves and others in society is through cultural spaces, and the content they make available. So the infection of these spaces by wrongs of colonialism means that the pictures they paint are at the very least incomplete, but more to the point, they omit willing participation from relevant voices. Within colonial societies, members of indigenous groups have a complaint when their conquerors absorb their distinctive culture and then distribute it back to the larger group as a shared cultural good in the form of national heritage. This is a form of cultural laundering: attempting to "wash" historical wrongs by placing them inside legitimate cultural institutions.

In the public sector, governments subsidize cultural institutions, like museums and galleries. This funding takes on a problematic character once we acknowledge that some components of cultural markets are the result of theft. Governments should not spend tax dollars supporting the display of stolen works. While this is simple enough to accept, this does not exhaust the wrong of commodified cultural appropriation. Where there exists ongoing oppression of some groups by dominant ones, this impugns cultural exchange between them. This is a familiar move from the commodification literature: background conditions of inequality matter when assessing seemingly voluntary transactions (Wilkinson, 2003; Satz, 2012). This is why the solution is not just a matter of returning what was stolen to those from whom it was taken. While a return of stolen objects can be one form of restitution, this will not restore what was lost through cultural erasure and suppression. Nor will this undo ongoing forms of oppression where dominant groups speak on behalf of subordinated ones.

This is a place where public funding can end up contributing to wrongful commodification of culture. Indigenous groups have a valid complaint when publicly funded museums and galleries display their historical works without consultation, or alongside colonial culture. This argument won't apply when the works in a collection are supplied by the artist themselves. But for historical collections, it makes sense to adopt the model provided by NAGPRA, where the default assumption is these items belong back with the groups whose culture is being represented. This follows the Kantian model of a status right: these cultural works are 'not yours', so displaying them is a kind of use that can only be rightful with permission from the relevant community.

Some institutions have taken steps towards decolonizing their collections voluntarily. However, this argument supports a stronger legal requirement, namely that any publicly funded forums and spaces turn over control of their indigenous collections to indigenous institutions. This would ensure that any *continued* participation in the market is done voluntarily by people who can speak on behalf of the group in question. Note, however, that continued participation in the market is not guaranteed. In some cases, items currently on display may be removed temporarily or permanently, if this is what the stewards choose. The same point applies to spaces. In some instances, currently public spaces may need to become restricted in order to be returned to those from whom they were taken. In many commodification debates, increasing public access is the solution. My argument here is that for some contested cultural commodities, privatization is in fact the correct policy approach.

Another policy approach that protects the cultural rights of subordinated groups is to recognize intellectual property rights over their own cultural practices. There is a tendency to treat ideas as part of the public domain but at the same time to protect the conjunction of these ideas with narration or images. What makes a culture distinctive, and worth protecting, will be a product of the specific clothing, rituals, stories, foods, and the like that constitute it. So, we have a model for recognizing intellectual property in abstract goods, insofar as they are made distinctive through their history. There are several recent examples of countries, including Australia, Canada, and the United States, granting intellectual property rights – including the right to censor – to images, research output, and other cultural products. This fits with an anti-commodification approach to indigenous knowledge precisely to block a "supermarket" model (Smith, 2000, p. 218) where dominant groups can help themselves to ideas that belong to one culture in the sense that they have not fully been able to consent to turning them over to the market.

As with historical works and culturally relevant spaces, the implication of recognizing intellectual property rights to indigenous culture – specifically as a *remedy* for wrongful cultural appropriation – is that those ideas may or may not remain part of the broader culture. On the one hand, some groups may find that financial compensation legitimizes the continued presence of their cultural goods in the marketplace. On the other, some groups may wish for their culture to be shielded from both public spaces as well as private markets altogether. A system of intellectual property rights grounded in this argument supports either an inclusive or exclusive approach. The scope of the legal recognition of culture – e.g. images, styles, fashion – can be as broad as needed to protect whatever dimension of the culture is most at risk of being controlled by non-groups members.

Finally, it is worth noting that the right to culture defended here may be temporary or permanent. Whether the wrongs of cultural appropriation in the colonial context can ever be righted is, in some sense, an empirical question. As Burrows (2017) argues, when social conditions are conducive, a nation's different cultures involve exchange and interdependence. This is and ought to be the goal within colonial societies: "Aboriginal tradition can thus support a notion of citizenship that encourages autonomy and at the same time unifies and connects us to one another, and to the lands we rely on" (150). So, if such conditions were to obtain then the case for exclusive control over one's own culture would be lessened. The exchange would no longer involve ongoing continuity with historical oppression.

However, it would be a mistake to think that increasing the amount of money going back to indigenous groups in the short and medium term will eventually obviate the long term need for the kind of exclusive status rights following from the Kantian view defended here. As noted by Sjorslev (2001), "Indigenous peoples' claim to self-determination should be regarded in this light: as a desire for *better protection of human rights than has so far been provided* by either states or the international community" (p. 60, emphasis added). It is precisely the historical failure to show adequate respect for the rights of indigenous people and their culture that has led to the need for the kinds of protection against cultural appropriation envisioned here. Accordingly, self-determination against this context may require permanent cultural rights that are asymmetric to those of dominant groups, as well as minorities who are not, to use Kymlicka's terminology, national minorities. This is because of the special role that public institutions play in promulgating a healthy national cultural identity while being honest about the role that these same institutions have played in appropriating the culture of those who were already here.

Notes

1 Most of what I say here applies to colonial societies where indigenous groups were already there, and then put under the rule of settlers, suffering setbacks to their culture as a result. My focus will be on what Kymlicka calls "national minorities" (Kymlicka, 1995) rather than immigrant minorities, that is, relations between the groups that make up the founding of a given country. It may be possible to extrapolate this argument to situations where a dominant group exercises control over a culture that is 'not theirs' but this is beyond the scope of the chapter.

2 See Section 27 https://laws-lois.justice.gc.ca/eng/const/page-12.html

3 There is a related but different debate about whether all citizens should be guaranteed access to "high culture" as opposed to just some culture or other, and whether there is something objectionably perfectionist about state subsidizing this. See Kessler (2021) and Ferdman (2021) for different answers to those questions.

4 This allows us to say, for example, that passing through tribal lands is permissible, while taking photographs of the local tribe would not be.

5 I don't mean to argue that wrongful forms of intra-group usurpation are impossible, only that cultural appropriation refers to inter-group dynamics. For a careful discussion of types of cultural appropriation see Nguyen, C.T., & Strohl, M. (2019).

6 Kant also includes servants in this category.

7 Thank you to Vida Panitch for suggesting this approach.

References

Abercrombie, N. (2020) *Commodification and its Discontents*. New York: Polity Press.

Atalay, S. (2006) "Guest editor's remarks: Decolonizing archeology," *American Indian Quarterly* 30(3/4), pp. 269–279.

Brighouse, H. (2001) "Democracy and inequality" in A. Carter and G. Stokes (eds.) *Democratic Theory Today*. New York: Polity Press, pp. 52–72.

Brown, D., & Nicholas, G. (2012) "Protecting indigenous cultural property in the age of digital democracy: Institutional and communal responses to Canadian First Nations and Māori heritage concerns," *Journal of Material Culture* 17(3), pp. 307–324.

Brown, F.M. (2003) *Who Owns Native Culture?* Cambridge, MA: Harvard University Press.
Brunk, C.G. & Young J.O. (2009) "The skin off our backs: Appropriation of religion," in C.G. Brunk and J.O. Young (eds.) *Ethics of Cultural Appropriation.* Sussex: Wiley-Blackwell, pp. 93–114.
Burrows, J. (2017) *Recovering Canada: The Resurgence of Indigenous Law*. Toronto: University of Toronto Press.
Cole, D. (1995) *Captured Heritage: The Scramble for Northwest Coast Artifacts*. Vancouver: University of British Columbia Press.
Comaroff, L.J., & Comaroff, J. (2010) *Ethnicity, Inc*. Chicago: University of Chicago Press.
Dworkin, R. (1985) *A Matter of Principle.* Cambridge, MA: Harvard University Press.
Ferdman, A. (2021) "Why the intrinsic value of public goods matters," in A. Ferdman and M. Kohn (eds.) *Solidarity and Public Goods.* New York: Routledge, ch. 9.
Gerstenblith, P. (2019) *Art, Cultural Heritage, and the Law: Cases and Materials* 4th ed. Durham: Carolina Academic Press.
Harding, S. (2005) "Commodifying intellectual and cultural property," in M.M. Ertman and C. J. Williams (eds.) *Rethinking Commodification: Cases and Readings in Law and Culture*. New York: New York University Press, pp. 137–154.
Janke, T. (1998) *Our Culture, Our Future: Report on Australian Indigenous Cultural and Intellectual Property*. Michael Frankel, Solicitors.
Kant, I. (1999) "Metaphysics of Morals," in M.J. Gregor (ed.) *Practical Philosophy.* Cambridge, UK: Cambridge University Press, pp. 353–605.
Kessler, M.J. (2021) "Engaging the reluctant taxpayer," in A. Ferdman and M. Kohn (eds.) *Solidarity and Public Goods.* New York: Routledge, ch 8, pp. 102–116.
Kymlicka, W. (1995) *Multicultural Citizenship: A Liberal Theory of Minority Rights*. Oxford: Clarendon Press.
Matthes, H.E. (2018) "Cultural appropriation and oppression," *Philosophical Studies* 176, pp. 1003–1013.
Nguyen, C.T., & Strohl, M. (2019) "Cultural appropriation and the intimacy of groups," *Philosophical Studies* 176, pp. 981–1002.
Nicholas, G.P. (2005) "The Persistence of memory; the politics of desire: archaeological impacts on Aboriginal peoples and their response" in C. Smith and H.M. Wobst (eds.) *Indigenous Archaeologies: Decolonizing Theory and Practice*. New York: Routledge, pp. 81–106.
Nussbaum, M. (2013) *The New Religious Intolerance*. Cambridge, MA: Harvard University Press.
Radin, M. (1987). "Market-Inalienability," *Harvard Law Review* 100(8), pp. 1849–1937.
Rawls, J. (1999) *A Theory of Justice, Revised Edition*. Cambridge, MA: Harvard University Press.
Riley, M. (ed.) (2004) *Indigenous Intellectual Property Rights: Legal Obstacles and Innovative Solutions*. London: Rowman & Littlefield Publishers.
Satz, D. (2012) *Why Some Things Should not be for Sale: The Moral Limits of Markets*. Oxford: Oxford University Press.
Singer, J.W. (2001) *Introduction to Property*. New York: Aspen Law & Business.
Sjorslev, I. (2001) "Copyrighting culture: Indigenous Peoples and intellectual rights," in K. Hastrup (ed.) *Legal Cultures and Human Rights: Vol.1 The Challenge of Diversity*. New York: Springer, pp. 43–65.
Smith, C., & Wobst. H.M. (eds.) (2005) *Indigenous Archaeologies: Decolonizing Theory and Practice*. New York: Routledge.
Smith, G.H. (2000) "Protecting and respecting Indigenous knowledge," in M. Battiste (ed.) *Reclaiming Indigenous Voice and Vision*. Vancouver: University of British Columbia Press, ch. 16, pp. 209–224.
Stanley, N. (1998) *Being Ourselves for You: The Global Display of Cultures*. Middlesex: Middlesex University Press.
Sunder, M. (2003) "Piercing the veil," *The Yale Law Journal* 112(6), 1399–1472.
Taylor, C. (1992) "The politics of recognition," in A. Gutmann (ed.) *Multiculturalism: Examining the Politics of Recognition*. Princeton: Princeton University Press, pp. 25–73.
Thomas, D.H. (2002) *Skull Wars: Kennewick Man, Archaeology, and the Battle for Native American Identity*. New York: Basic Books.
Truth and Reconciliation Commission of Canada (TRC) (2015) *Final Report of the Truth and Reconciliation Commission of Canada, Volume One: Summary: Honouring the Truth, Reconciling for the Future*. Toronto: James Lorimer & Company.
Wilkinson S. (2003) "The exploitation argument against commercial surrogacy," *Bioethics* 17(2), pp. 169–187.
Young, J.O., & Brunk, C.G. (eds.) (2009) *The Ethics of Cultural Appropriation*. Sussex: Wiley-Blackwell.

16

CARE WORK

Revaluing care through partial decommodification—In praise of unpaid care from all

Jennifer Nedelsky

Introduction

> One of the most important insights I got from having my children was the importance of routine physical caretaking for forming the basic bonds of connection… [that] initial insight… broadened into a belief that physical caretaking is part of what roots us in the world and permits us to feel a connection with the material foundations of life, from the care the earth requires to respect for the labor that permits us to live as we do.
>
> The dominant culture of North America treats virtually all forms of physical caretaking with contempt. Until there is a shift in this basic stance, those who do the caretaking will be treated with contempt: They will be paid little and defined as unsuccessful. If caretaking were actually valued, there would be a revolution in the structure of our society.
>
> (Nedelsky, 1999, pp. 320–321)

I wrote those sentences in 1998. Now, in *Part Time for All* (PTfA) Tom Malleson and I offer a path to that transformation through new norms of work and care. We argue that this restructuring of work and care could end the long-standing degradation of care and those who do it, as well as the policy distortions that flow from failing to recognize the value of care.[1] The core of what enables this revaluing of care is that everyone does it: everyone provides substantial unpaid care throughout their lives. Thus, the revaluing of care is enabled by removing a great deal of care from the market, a form of decommodifying care.

We advocate for new norms that could restructure people's lives so that *everyone* (no matter how "important" their work) experiences the joy and connection of care giving (both physical and emotional). The central norm would be that all who are able provide roughly 20–25 hours of unpaid care every week, an amount sufficient for them to acquire the knowledge and connection that care brings. The need to learn from care grounds our argument that everyone needs to do it. The time for this care would be made possible by the norm that no one does paid work for more than 30 hours a week.

We think these profound changes could have vitally important impacts. They could end the unsustainable stress on families and the gross inequality for those who provide care. The new

DOI: 10.4324/9781003188742-20

norms could also end what we call the care-policy divide: high level decision-makers who know nothing about care and care providers who are excluded from high level policy positions. In addition, the norms would transform the pervasive time scarcity that characterizes societies of the global North.

These norms have built into them new approaches to the commodification of care. Let me offer brief definitions of care and decommodification, and then turn to the links between care, commodification, and equality. A summary of the PTfA proposal follows, then a discussion of its main benefits and challenges. I conclude by highlighting the ways PTfA and the issues of commodification illuminate one another.

Definitions

A short version of what I mean by care comes from Glenn (2010, p. 5): "Caring can be defined most simply as the relationships and activities involved in maintaining people on a daily basis and intergenerationally." This includes direct caring for the person, maintaining the immediate physical surroundings/milieu in which people live, and fostering people's relationships and social connections.[2] For what counts as people's hours of unpaid care, I add the qualification that the care builds personal relationships, and I include the relationship with the earth and the care that reflects and sustains it. These hours also include care for oneself.

I rely on a common meaning of "commodification," but my use of "decommodification" is different from one that is widely used. I prefer the definition of commodification according to which: "the symbolic and institutional changes through which a good or service that was not previously meant for sale enters the sphere of money and market exchange" (Gómez-Baggethun, 2015, p. 67). A common usage of "decommodification," however, is *not* the return of such goods to a sphere of things not available for sale, but rather to a sphere of things where the state is the entity that purchases and provides goods and services, and then makes them available to members of society, sometimes universally, often on the basis of some kind of status (citizenship, permanent residence, community membership, poverty), but not by selling them. That is not what I mean by decommodification of care. I mean that significant care will not be part of market transactions, by either the state or individuals.

Care, commodification, and equality

PTfA argues that equality, the revaluation of care, and ending the care-policy divide requires a norm of unpaid care from everyone. This essential form of decommodification does not, however, require the end of all commodified care. Care has always been provided as both paid and unpaid labour, often in the same households. What matters is the norms around both, and most of the existing norms need changing. Almost all cultures have strong norms about what kind of care should be done by which kind of people (almost always with clear hierarchies), and whether it should be paid (almost always low paid) or seen as a labour of love (almost always by women), and thus free.

There are good arguments both for and against the commodification of care. I see the norm of unpaid care from everyone as so vital to the revaluing of care that I oppose relying on the commodification strategy of providing wages for housework, even in the interests of better support for female caregivers.[3] At the same time, it is hard to imagine all care being provided outside a market framework. The challenge is to make commodified care just and the norms around it consistent with the vital role of care in human flourishing.

In thinking about commodified care, it is important to recognize its scope. Much of what was once unpaid domestic labour has now taken complex forms of commodification outside the home—fast food outlets, prepared food in grocery stores, commercial laundry and dry cleaning, childcare centres, wrinkle free cotton dress shirts—as well as the more obvious paid domestic labour within the home. (Like the more traditional forms of paid care, these services usually involve bad jobs.) Commodified care also includes a great deal of health care and the many forms of "industrial care," like laundry in hospitals and the cleaning of office buildings. Given this scope, some commodification seems unavoidable. Yet (with some exceptions such as the professionalization of doctors, which long excluded women) commodification has not brought with it the (alleged) benefits of market competition for those who do paid care.

The low pay and low status of commodified care are sustained by a long-standing denigration of care. The mutually supporting devaluation of care and of those who do it keeps the price low. Without this devaluation and discrimination, the "forces of supply and demand" could not generate the consistent low pay for those whose skilled work provides this vital human need.

All forms of commodification disadvantage the poor, at least in the sense that they have fewer resources to acquire goods and services that are only available for sale on the market. But commodification of care distinctly disadvantages those who belong to the "lowly" categories thought suitable for caregiving: women and girls, immigrants, racialized people, people from low-income backgrounds. They will be funnelled into care jobs with low wages because of the combined force of the devaluation of the categories (e.g., race, gender) ascribed to them and the devaluation of care. Until both forms of devaluation are addressed, all forms of commodified care will participate in maintaining inequality. I believe that PTfA will foster a significant revaluation of care, thus undermining in part the mutual devaluation of care and those who do it that has for so long shaped the low status of (virtually) all care and the low pay for those who provide commodified care. In short, I think the role of universal unpaid care (the kind of decommodification I propose) will transform the value of all care so that commodified care can be used in an equitable way—although it will also require an ongoing effort to overcome deeply entrenched norms of hierarchy.

Under current arrangements, inequality (economic, racial, gendered) supports the devaluation of care and the low status of care cements inequality into place by keeping low status people tied to care, both paid and unpaid. This mutual reinforcement has been important for keeping those on top of the hierarchy both well provided with (free or cheap) care, and from ensuring that no one thinks they are the kind of people who should be asked to contribute care. The easy availability of *both* free and cheap care has been important. Even before the (incomplete) gender revolution, it was rarely possible for the powerful to insulate themselves from care responsibilities solely by relying on the unpaid care of women. The well-off have almost always combined paid care with unpaid female care (and management of care). And commodification of care, with its norms of low pay/low status, now supports hierarchy in new ways: professional women need to replace the unpaid care they no longer provide, and they want to pay less for that care than what they are being paid at work.

While PTfA is not an argument against all forms of commodified care, it highlights the complex layers of inequality that are built into our current forms of commodification. Care is a context in which a system of commodification can interfere with the relationships that care can foster—particularly when the norm is that successful people pay others to provide care for them and their families. Almost by definition, those who are providing the care are unsuccessful, and seen as deserving of their low pay and low status. This framework infects people's ability to recognize the value of the care they receive. Appreciation and *mutual* care for the well-being of those giving and receiving care are often missing. Nevertheless, I make no claim that constructive care relationships are impossible when the care is paid for. There are hundreds of compelling stories of the bonds of love and care that exist between nannies and children and between the elderly and their underpaid, but much appreciated caregivers. It is not the fact of commodification, but the devaluation of care and the carers that is the source of the problem. The argument for PTfA is that it can foster revaluation such that commodified care can be just and respected.

Rather than oppose all commodification, PTfA advocates a redistribution of paid and unpaid care—an increase of *paid* care in the formal sector (as publicly funded services, such as child and elder care, are better supported) and an increase in *unpaid* care in households, among friends, and in communities. Thus, commodified care would continue to exist in the public sector, but it would not be expected to replace unpaid care. Vastly increasing the scope of publicly funded care is urgently needed in many contexts, but PTfA argues that it is not a good alternative to the norm of unpaid care from all. State provided care may be better paid and better protected than many forms of domestic labour in private homes, but it cannot do the work of revaluing care that we think will follow when everyone is a care-giver (and knows they are a care receiver). It would be entirely compatible with the care policy divide and would not be tied to the highly desirable restructuring of work. And of course, public sector care cannot provide care from someone well known to the one needing care, which is often what they most want. Thus, commodified care would continue, and often increase, in the public sector and continue in private homes, but at a greatly reduced rate.[4] But both forms would be additional supports around the core norm of everyone providing unpaid care.

"Part Time for All": Restructuring work and care

Let me begin with two caveats. First, the very terms "work" and "care" are arbitrary. Care involves work and good work involves care. I expect this arbitrariness to become more and more obvious as people think about implementing the new norms. Right now, however, the distinction is necessary to describe the harms of current norms and to articulate a vision of radical transformation. Second, while I think a conversation about transforming the norms around work and care would be valuable all over the world, the solutions PTfA proposes are designed for high income countries.

There is a widely recognized crisis in care in all high-income countries. This became particularly obvious during the COVID pandemic with respect to care for the elderly, but most countries also have inadequate care for people with disabilities and for children. Of course, the rich can usually access good care, but especially in the Anglo countries (in varying degrees, U.S., Canada, UK, Australia and New Zealand) even the middle class often struggles with the costs of childcare and elder care—despite the low pay for the workers in these fields. The poor and people with precarious jobs often have to patch together unstable solutions for the care their families need. PTfA would make a great deal more unpaid care available to everyone, and the revaluation of care it would generate would foster greater public investment in care.

Even people who recognize a crisis in care do not always see that the structure of care is always intertwined with the structure of work. (Although the pandemic has highlighted the reality that people cannot get their work done unless someone is providing care for them and their families.) I see four interlocking failures of the prevailing system of work and care. The first is the pervasive failure to recognize the value of care and the second is care's fundamental role in structuring inequality. When a hierarchical society devalues care, it is unsurprising that care will be relegated to those low down in the hierarchy. The degradation of care and of those who do it become mutually reinforcing, making both seem "natural."[5] Hierarchies of inequality are then further cemented, perversely tied to what should be a core value, care. In such a context, the third problem, the care-policy divide, arises: some groups (historically white men) are the decision-makers and *different* groups (women, racialized people, and immigrants) provide the care, resulting in high-status, ignorant policymakers and subordinated care givers excluded from high-level decision-making. Fourth, contemporary high-income societies face the pressing problems of stressed families (as well as stressed workplaces) due to the incompatible demands of work and care—which ill-informed policymakers fail to respond to. Everyone faces chronic time scarcity.

A real solution must address all these problems. I think that the heart of the solution must be that *everyone* who is able is responsible for providing care. A society committed to equality, to respect for care, to good public policy, and to thriving families cannot assign care to only a subset of the population. Even if care givers were respected and well-compensated, if one group of people makes the policy (in corporations and government) and a *different* group does the care, we will continue to have dangerously ignorant policymakers. Under the new norms, high level policy makers, like everyone else, would contribute around 22 hours of unpaid care to family, friends, and community. Their experience would help them recognize all the areas of policy—such as transportation, housing, education, labour law—that intersect with care.

The basic rationale for the norm of universal care is that an equal, well-governed society, requires a population all of whom know about care from the experience of doing it. *Everyone is a care provider, just as everyone is a care receiver, and everyone identifies as both.* Everyone acquires the skills, disposition, and knowledge (Dalmiya, 2016) that come from doing sustained care giving. Everyone builds the relationships that care fosters and sustains. Everyone comes to recognize the care they receive.[6] Care givers are not looked down on because everyone is one, and individually and collectively everyone recognizes the real value of care. And everyone recognizes the full diversity of capacities to provide care as well as the huge range of needs for care. Everyone learns what they need to know about care to make good policy and, as community members, to assess that policy.

When the demands of friends and family are high (children are young, parents aging, or friends in need), most people would contribute their share of care within those intimate circles. When those immediate needs recede, people would provide care within their chosen "communities of care." They would form serious commitments to mutual care among people they know and care about—such as neighbours, faith communities, clubs, sports groups, or those they share a park with. People are not caring for strangers, but the communities of care are not primarily family or close friends. Thus, care responsibilities extend beyond family, and the solution to degradation and inequality is not paying for the care (e.g., wages for housework), but *everyone* offering unpaid, personally connected care. The objective is to recognize the forms of interconnection possible within the vast human diversity of talents, temperaments, and needs, and to encourage everyone to participate in ways suited to their particular needs and capacities. Care responsibility would start young (normally age 3 or 4) and last as long as people find creative ways to contribute. PTfA would foster such creativity so that very few people would come to see themselves (or be seen by others) as dependent recipients of care without some form of contribution to the care of others. When everyone knows they are a care recipient, care needs do not mark a person as excluded from social citizenship. When everyone is a care provider, everyone's (varied, shifting, and diverse) contribution is recognized. In their roles as both care recipients and care providers, everyone's voices are recognized as important. Under the norms of PTfA, equality takes on a daily, practical meaning that embraces diversity of need and capacity.

Mutual care within communities of care would, among its other benefits, disrupt the deep patterns of people of lower status providing care for those with more privilege (by gender, race, class, income, ethnicity and/or immigration status). Of course, there would still be a variety of challenges of continuing inequalities, oversight, training, and meeting the needs of the "hard to serve." But I argue that there is good reason to believe that in the presence of strong norms of equality and of contribution, the great diversity of capacities can be matched with the great range of needs. I expect the quality of care for most people will improve under these new norms.

In short, under PTfA care would reinforce equality rather than inequality.

To transform a structure of care so that everyone does it, will, of course, involve transforming the structure of work. If everyone is going to have time to provide care, most people will have to do less paid work. Work has to be restructured so that *good* part-time work becomes the norm. Everyone becomes a part-time paid worker and a part-time unpaid care giver. This would, of course, be a huge cultural shift affecting people's sense of identity, and the way care is connected to family, to the state, and to the market. It would also require a profound economic shift, redistributing significant resources to the bottom of the income distribution so that everyone is able to live well, with all their basic needs met, so as to be able to lead a comfortable, indeed a flourishing life, while working only part-time.

For PTfA to be feasible the central economic requirement is that everyone has access to good part-time jobs. By this I mean jobs that are *secure, flexible, and high quality* (in the sense that they provide rates of pay and benefits now common in good full-time work). Unfortunately, this is far from the case in many rich countries today, particularly the US, where part-time work is typically inferior, unattractive work. In many places, part-time work pays proportionally less than full-time work, provides fewer benefits, and offers fewer opportunities for career advancement.

More generally, a prerequisite for PTfA is economic security. This could be accomplished in various ways, through strong norms of a living wage (meaning a person and her child could live off 30 hours/week), through robust public services, an unconditional basic income, a job guarantee, or some combination thereof. In many parts of Europe, such security already exists.

In our proposal, paid work (between 10 and 30 hours per week) would continue to be a central way in which people contribute to society, and commitment to doing one's work well would be a respected value. But work would become just one among other important sources of identity and contribution. Transforming existing work to create good part time jobs would involve not only creatively restructuring jobs but challenging deeply held views about the nexus between long hours, success, and excellence. As paid work loses its central place in identity, income from work would also lose some of its significance. I expect that strong norms limiting hours of paid work would replace pride in high income and commitment manifested by long hours at work. People's contribution to care would become equally important as a source of pride and recognition. The link between work, money, and self-worth would shift significantly.

The new norms of work and care would be enforced not by state law, but (like most norms) by the complex power of social expectation and the socialization that happens in families, communities, workplaces, and schools—just as is now the case with the norms that women should provide care and men should "earn a living" and "support their families." One difference would be in levels of consciousness—and deliberation—around the norms. The norm around "supporting one's family" is so deeply internalized that most men do not think of their behavior as governed by a societal norm. By contrast, I would expect some level of ongoing deliberation in communities of care on the norms of PTfA. While the core value of everyone having a responsibility for care might become similarly deeply embedded, the many questions of how best to implement it would remain a subject of conscious reflection. Thus, democratic deliberation about norms, not just law and policy, would itself become part of the norms of PTfA.[7]

Finally, in the context of care, it is important not to underestimate the power of norms. Millions of hours of unpaid care are claimed from women around the world on the strength of gender norms.

Benefits and challenges of PTfA (and decommodified care)

Concerns, questions, and nuances

The most common concern I have heard is about "coercion."[8] Why does everybody, regardless of preference, temperament or talent have to contribute unpaid care? Of course, in the book we offer detailed answers. But the core is that everyone needs to learn what doing care can teach: the importance of care for the relationships that matter in life; the capacity to take the perspectives of others that is so important for good judgment; how hard care can be, how rewarding it can be. Making sure everyone has the benefits of learning from care, of being part of communities of care, is as important as a just distribution of the burdens of care. Among the benefits are the development of dispositions of care, which need to be nurtured throughout a lifetime.

A related concern is that if people feel they "have to" provide care, they will do a bad job of it. One important answer is that all over the world most of the women who provide most of the care are acting in accordance with strong norms that women should provide (free) care. If care compelled by norms were destined to be bad care, the human race would probably not have survived. (Even those who place great weight on female biological instinct should recognize the role of norms in governing the social arrangements of care.) And people who provide paid care are heavily driven by economic necessity to take care jobs when others are foreclosed by discrimination. In short, as Glenn (2010) so clearly demonstrates, the current structure of care relies on many forms of coercion. The norms of PTfA should not be compared to some vision of care offered free of norms or need. And, of course, I think the new norms would enhance the freedom and quality of life for all—including those whose privilege currently includes a cherished illusion of independence. That illusion would be dispelled as everyone came to understand care-based interdependence, but compensated by an expanded scope of options as paid work ceased to preclude so many other dimensions of life.

Another question is why does it have to be *unpaid* care? The short answer is that the transformations I expect to arise when everyone is a caregiver are unimaginable if the care were paid. It is one thing to persuade CEOs to contribute regular care to family, friends, and community so that they can become educated in the meaning of care and foster important relationships. To offer money—which would have to be much less than what they could earn for those hours in their jobs—would undermine the significance of their contribution. The nature of what they are offering and what they are receiving cannot be monetized (even though it is possible to assess fair rates of paid care). For example, both giving and receiving care build relationships that provide values such as security, trust, honour, self-confidence, and happiness. Providing care develops capacities for generosity, humility, attentiveness, perspective taking and judgment. I believe that the hope of ending the care policy divide lies in persuading people of the value of learning and bonding by offering unpaid care. I have confidence that the more people experience care (under good conditions), the more they will learn.

Any version of "wages for housework," including wages for our proposed 22 hours, would (at least in the beginning) be at such a low wage that it would do nothing to revalue care, could not shift the care-policy divide, and would undermine the plausibility of contributing care as something everyone should do. I think only the partial decommodification of care I propose can advance the kinds of transformations PTfA is aimed at.

Receiving much of one's care from people one knows can raise its own concerns. Sometimes people would prefer intimate care to be offered by someone with whom there is an arms-length relationship. At a public lecture I gave, someone offered the example that both she and her elderly mother preferred a paid care giver to help her with her toileting. This seems like the kind of preference that should be accommodated, but it also seems possible that some of the relationships within a community of care could be sufficiently distant to meet such needs. As people become accustomed to, and skilled at, such routine care, I think the need for professional paid care will decrease—but not disappear. What matters here is that an arms-length relationship need not be a paid one.

The employment relationship (commodified care) currently seems to stand in for distance, for control, and sometimes even for license (to be demanding or even rude to caregivers). As communities work out the details of the new norms, they will need to think through the kinds of distance, control, and predictable excesses (say from people in pain) that care relationships should tolerate, and what role paid care should play. Part of what matters here is that care is a relationship that should be characterized by mutual respect and generally a mutual concern for the well-being of the other. There has been such a long history of disregarding the preferences of the elderly and people with disabilities that the legitimate demand for autonomy in managing one's own care can sometimes spill over to a desire for control that seems to leave little space for a mutuality of caring respect between care giver and receiver. Perhaps at some point there will be help from robots that will remove this requirement. But until then, the new norms need to foster a careful attention to how to enact mutual care and respect in all the varied contexts of care, paid and unpaid.

Despite the special role I advocate for unpaid care, I expect that many people will continue to pay others to help them with care in the household. This would not be a violation of the norms of PTfA. But in addition to the need for mutual concern, I argue that people should avoid reinforcing long standing hierarchies of care. The new norms should support people in sharing all care responsibilities within households, so that "lowly" tasks of, say, cleaning are not allocated to "paid help," even for the purpose of providing more time for playing with children. This strategy, so widely used among my generation of professional women, should give way in the face of reduced time pressure, revaluing of all forms of care, and commitments to equality. Even commodified care should be governed by new norms, not hierarchies that have so long been inflected by race and class.

This objection to using "paid help" for "lowly" tasks has raised some opposition. I have heard suggestions that some material care is so mundane, so disconnected in its nature from who does it, that it makes no sense to treat it as part of the shared project of mutual care. For example, I have frequently heard the objection that cleaning toilets does not build relationships. I think this comment reveals several things. First, clean toilets can seem separated from the experience of care only if one can ignore how they got that way, or when that gift of care is treated as an (unconscious) entitlement by the recipient. Second, a person responsible for hiring someone else to do the cleaning (and thus not ignorant about how it gets done) may still experience the characteristic of care disappearing into an employment relationship: the clean toilet is the product of paid work, not an act of care. This may indeed characterize the experience of both the paid worker and the employer, while the rest of the family may be happily ignorant. So, I acknowledge that care can be transformed into paid work, changing its relational nature. But this transformation is not a necessary part of paying for care, although it might be very common if certain tasks, like cleaning toilets, are routinely delegated to paid (often marginalized) others.

What matters for PTfA is that clean toilets are part of what makes a home comfortable, and when everyone shares in those tasks and knows what they entail, the mundane task need not cease being part of care and its network of relationships. It is not the material requirements of a clean toilet that make it experienced as the result of care or as the result of a financial transaction. (Of course, in principle it is possible to be both. Paid care can be experienced as care by both those who do it and those who pay for it. It is a question of consciousness and of the nature and pattern of the relationships.) The point here is that mutual obligations of care within families are part of how the norms of care are learned. The knowledge that material, mundane care is an essential component of the experience of both being cared for and providing care is one of the most important things one can learn in the shared care of family or communal life. Of course, when women do most of the care (both intimate and material) and paid "help" does a lot of the "lowly" material work of cleaning, then instead of these lessons, children learn, and adults are confirmed in, beliefs about the low value of care (especially material care) and those who do it.

Benefits

In addition to the core benefits discussed in the sections above, I expect PTfA to foster a great deal more creativity in how people can contribute through both paid work and unpaid care. As noted, jobs will need to be creatively redesigned, and I hope that collaborative norms of workplace democracy will be part of that planning. In addition, I expect a great deal more creativity about how people with various kinds of limitations—such as the elderly and people displaying the full range of human cognitive and physical diversity—can offer care to one another and, indeed contribute to society more generally. Most people will find ways to contribute, and everyone will come to understand the mutual interdependence and diversity that characterizes human life.

I distinguish community participation and activism from what I mean by people's commitment to 22 hours of direct care. But I expect the collective encouragement of activism (at many scales) and community participation to be one of the benefits of the reduction of time scarcity and the demotion of work from the centre of identity.

I also expect a reduction in consumerism, with benefits to the environment as well as to broad cultural norms. As a lot of care is removed from the market, and paid work loses its centrality to identity, I think the new norms will foster a more general decentering of commodified material goods. Well off people will have less disposable income and more time for friends and family. I hope to see the reverse of what Hochschild (2001) found: people accumulating expensive toys in their garages with no time to use them. People will choose to "spend" their time rather than their money, pursuing less material interests. And as they have more time for leisure, there is more time to play with family and friends. For some, there might be greater uptake of local theatre and art shows, both as audience and participants (where people experience those terms as more apt than producer and consumer). As practices of care for the earth are encouraged, people will have more time to devote to enjoying nature as well as activities such as gardening, planting native species that attract pollinators, or propagating monarch butterflies. These overlapping practices of care and leisure can, in turn, foster larger scale activism to combat climate change.

All forms of care are time consuming, and in a culture dominated by "productive work" and consumption goods, the time for care can easily be seen as a "waste of time" or a form of self-indulgence. Care also has different rhythms of time, often slower and more variable than the clock time of "productive work." Part of the cultural shift of PTfA will be a revaluing of care that shifts our sense of how it makes sense not just to "spend" time, but to experience time. Perhaps in the wider shift away from a preoccupation with commodification and production as sources of identity and self-worth, the language of "spending" time will finally recede as time scarcity is no longer pervasive. One might say that the norms of PTfA could decommodify time: people would no longer feel compelled to "buy time" by paying someone else to provide care nor be anxious about "spending time" that was not "productive."

Part-Time for All is a proposal about part-time work and care. But it is important that its outcome would be *time* for all. As the pace and stress of life recedes, health, peace, and daily pleasures expand (Honig, 2014). There is time for reflection about what matters, fostering good judgment in both personal and collective life.

Finally, as PTfA generates new norms of work and care, it would not just enact existing norms of equality, justice, and democracy. Those norms would, through daily exercise, become strengthened, expanded, and more conscious.

Conclusion: Rethinking care and commodification in light of PTfA

PTfA highlights the depths of the connections between inequality and the commodification of care. And it offers a path out of this connection through the revaluing of care made possible by replacing a significant amount of paid care with unpaid care. At the same time, it challenges strategies of both commodification and (conventional) decommodification: neither the commodification strategy of "wages for housework" nor the conventional decommodification strategy of moving all responsibility for care to the state can provide the benefits and solutions of PTfA. In closing, I want to return to this issue of decommodification.

Some people have been suspicious of PTfA because they worry it strays from the focus on getting states to assume their responsibility for care. I don't think it does. That form of collective responsibility stands alongside the responsibilities of mutual care within families and communities and among friends. There are multiple benefits of having (virtually) everyone learn from care by providing it outside a market context to family, friends, and community. The new norms would reinforce the importance of intimate bonds of care, both within and beyond families—at the same time that it profoundly disrupts the deeply engrained gender norms around care.

I believe that decommodification as it is conventionally understood—transferring care responsibilities to the state—cannot alone redress the devaluation of care and of those who do it. Without a means to revalue care, this form of decommodification would mean that care jobs are poorly paid by the state rather than by individuals. Even with more equitable access to care and better labour protections than in households, state funded care is not an adequate solution (though under PTfA it would play a stronger role than is now common in Anglo countries).

Thus, I think issues of commodification are central to PTfA and PTfA helps illuminate those issues. But I also think it is helpful to highlight the ways in which PTfA asks us to transform all of the traditional relations of care—to the market, the state, and the family. Care responsibilities extend beyond the family, the state is not always the best source for care provision, and the role of the market in home care is reduced. Key to all of these transformations is the (virtually) universal contribution of unpaid care.

This is not a utopia. These transformations are possible within the parameters of the economic systems of the current Global North (Nedelsky and Malleson, 2023, ch. 3–4). And more and more people are experimenting with shortened work hours and expressing the kinds of desires PTfA is designed to meet.[9] PTfA will not solve all the problems of either stress or injustice, but we also do not have to wait for all those problems to be solved to bring about vast improvements in quality of life, greater equality, and better governance.

Notes

1 These opening paragraphs come from the preface to *Part Time for All: A Care Manifesto* (Nedelsky, J. and Malleson, T. (New York: Oxford University Press, 2023).

2 The full definition is:

> Caring labour involves three types of intertwined activities. First, there is direct caring for the person, which includes physical care (e.g., feeding, bathing, grooming), emotional care (e.g., listening, talking, offering reassurance), and services to help people meet their physical and emotional needs (e.g., shopping for food, driving to appointments, going on outings). The second type of caring labour is that of maintaining the immediate physical surroundings/milieu in which people live (e.g., changing bed linen, washing clothing, and vacuuming floors). The third is the work of fostering people's relationships and social connections, a form of caring labour that has been referred to as "kin work" or as "community mothering." An apt metaphor for this type of care labour is "weaving and reweaving the social fabric." All three types of caring labour are included to varying degrees in the job definitions of such occupations as nurses' aides, home care aides, and housekeepers or nannies. Each of these positions involves varying mixtures of the three elements of care, and, when done well, the work entails considerable (if unrecognized) physical, social, and emotional skills.
>
> (Glenn, 2010, p. 5)

3 For a discussion of wages for housework see K. Weeks, 2011.

4 There is an important advantage to decreasing "domestic labour," which is harder to regulate and protect and thus, in many contexts, a site of abuse.

5 For instance, see Adelle Blackett's work on the mutual reinforcement between degradation on the basis of race and degradation of domestic work. *Everyday Transgressions: Domestic Workers' Transnational Challenge to International Labor Law* (Ithaca, New York: Cornell University Press, 2019).

6 One might think this would be self-evident. There is, however, a lot of evidence that privileged men, in particular, take much of the care they receive—from intimate partners, staff assistants, and janitors—as entitlements and thus invisible to them (Prattes, 2020, pp. 25–45).

7 I offer as examples of recent deep norm beginning at grass roots level: the feminist transformations beginning in the 1970s, later taken up and advanced by legislation; norms around drinking and driving and around smoking; the acceptance of LGBTQ relationships. The interaction between social norms and governmental (including judicial) action varies.

8 These concerns have arisen in both public talks and private conversations. There is various talk on YouTube (search Nedelsky care).

9 Municipalities in Nova Scotia, Canada (Patil, 2020) and private companies in the United Kingdom (Dickson, 2022) have begun to pilot a four-day work week. Furthermore, record numbers of workers across the globe have resigned from their jobs since 2021, citing a need for greater work-life balance, in a movement now called the "Great Resignation" (Ellerbeck, 2022).

References

Dalmiya, V. (2016) *Caring to Know: Comparative Care Ethics, Feminist Epistemology, and the Mahabharata.* Oxford: Oxford University Press.

Dickson, C. (2022) "Interest grows in 4-day work week as employers consider impact on staff, retention, productivity," *CBC*, 11 June [online]. Available at: www.cbc.ca/news/canada/british-columbia/four-day-work-week-1.6482456

Ellerbeck, S. (2022) "The Great Resignation is not over: A fifth of workers plan to quit in 2022," *World Economic Forum*, 24 June [online]. Available at: www.weforum.org/agenda/2022/06/the-great-resignation-is-not-over

Glenn, E.N. (2010) *Forced to Care: Coercion and Caregiving in America.* Cambridge: Harvard University Press.

Gómez-Baggethun, E. (2015) "Commodification," in D'Alisa, G. et al.(eds) *Degrowth: A Vocabulary for a New Era*. London: Routledge, pp. 67–70.

Hochschild, A.R. (2001) *The Time Bind: When Work Becomes Home and Home Becomes Work.* New York: H. Holt.

Honig, B. (2014) "Three Models of Emergency Politics," *Boundary 2* 41(2), pp. 45–70.

Nedelsky, J. (1999) "Dilemmas of passion, privilege and isolation: Reflections on mothering in a white, middle class nuclear family," in Hanigsberg, J. and Ruddick, S. (eds.) *Mother Troubles: Rethinking Contemporary Maternal Dilemmas*. Boston: Beacon Press, pp. 320–321.

Nedelsky J., and Malleson, T. (2023) *Part Time for All: A Care Manifesto*. Oxford: Oxford University Press.

Patil, A. (2020) "This Nova Scotia municipality is trying out a 4-day work week," *CBC,* 12 June [online]. Available at: www.cbc.ca/news/canada/nova-scotia/municipalityguysborough-4-day-work-week-1.5609703

Prattes, R. (2020) "'I don't clean up after myself': Epistemic ignorance, responsibility and the politics of the outsourcing of domestic cleaning," *Feminist Theory* (21)1 pp. 25–45 doi: 10.1177/1464700119842560

Weeks, K. (2011) *The Problem with Work: Feminism, Marxism, Antiwork Politics, and Postwork Imaginaries* (a John Hope Franklin Center Book). Durham: Duke University Press.

PART 4

The body and intimacy as contested commodities

17
HUMAN ORGANS

James Stacey Taylor

Introduction

There are currently too few organs available for transplant given the medical need for them. As Vida Panitch and L. Chad Horne note, over 100,000 people in the United States alone are waiting to receive a transplant kidney. Over thirteen Americans die each day while waiting for a kidney transplant (2018, p. 121). There is thus a pressing need to increase the number of kidneys that are available for transplant, both in the United States and elsewhere. Various possible solutions to this shortage have been proposed, and some have been instituted. Several countries (e.g., Spain, Sweden, and Belgium) have, for example, instituted a system of posthumous organ procurement that presumes that persons have consented to have their organs removed for transplant unless they have expressly indicated otherwise (Matesanz and Doninguez-Gil, 2019). It has also been suggested that persons be required to indicate whether or not they choose to be organ donors (Cotter, 2011). But current systems of presumed consent have failed to secure enough organs to meet the demand for them (Matesanz and Doninguez-Gil, 2019). It is unlikely that systems of mandated choice will fare better.

The pressing need to increase the supply of organs available for transplantation together with the failure of the current methods of achieving this provides the impetus for the suggestion that human organs should be commodified. (In what follows I will focus on the commodification of kidneys, although my arguments generalize to the commodification of other organs.)[1] If persons were to be paid to donate, then the supply of organs would increase as the price offered for them rose. This simple economic observation provides the basis for the most common ethical argument offered in favour of the commodification of human organs. Based on the value of well-being, this argument begins with the observation that were a market in organs to exist, persons would participate in it as buyers and sellers. This, it is claimed, shows that some persons would (*ex ante*) consider themselves to be made better off by participating in this market. (If they did not believe that they would be made better off by either buying an organ or selling one, then they would not have consented to do so.) Hence, the proponents of this argument conclude, this market is supported by the moral concern for well-being.[2]

DOI: 10.4324/9781003188742-22

Coercion and consent

This initial argument in favour of commodifying organs is based on two inferences. The first is that we can infer that persons have consented to buy and sell their organs from the fact that persons would participate as buyers and sellers in a market for organs. The second is that we can infer that persons believe that they would be better off were they able to buy and sell organs in a market for them from the fact that they would buy and sell organs in such a market were it to be allowed. Both of these inferences are contestable.

The first inference (that we can infer that persons have consented to buy and sell their organs from the fact that persons would participate as buyers and sellers in a market for organs) is often challenged by opponents of markets in human organs. As Radcliffe-Richards has noted, many of those who oppose the sale of human kidneys claim that "there can be no genuine, free consent to the sale of organs," and hence that the prohibition of their sale would not wrongly infringe on the ability of persons to "control their own destinies as far as possible" (1996, p. 379). This claim was offered "not merely as the removal of a prima facie objection to prohibition, but as a positive reason for demanding it" (Radcliffe-Richards,1996, p. 379). Consent is required for any medical procedure, and so if persons cannot genuinely consent to a procedure (e.g., the removal of a kidney) then it should be forbidden.

A common objection to the first inference holds that some (perhaps even the typical) participants in a market for organs would have been coerced into (e.g.) selling a kidney by their economic situation: Given their economic situation, they had no choice but to sell. Such persons are held to be in a situation similar to that of a person who had been coerced into handing over her wallet to a robber who threatened her with harm if she did not comply. Just as the victim of a highwayman would hand over her wallet to avoid her situation getting worse, so too would some sell (e.g.) their kidneys only to avoid their situation from getting worse. And just as the victim of a highwayman would not be said to have given her free and genuine consent to transferring ownership of her wallet to him, to too would the (typical) kidney seller not give her free and genuine consent to the sale of her organ.

In response to this line of objection Radcliffe-Richards has argued that it was not true that persons' consent to sell their kidneys would be compromised as a result of their being coerced into selling.[3] Coercion, she argued, compromises a person's ability to consent to the proposals put to her owing to her coercer restricting the range of options that she had available. However, offering a person money for her kidney would not *decrease* the options that she had available but *increase* them. Such offers would thus not be coercive and so they would not compromise their recipients' ability to consent to sell their kidneys (Radcliffe-Richards, 1996, pp. 382–383). Radcliffe-Richards also argued that it is not true that the lure of cash for a kidney would constitute an "unrefusable offer" that would undermine the ability of the person to whom it was presented from being able to genuinely consent to its acceptance (1996, pp. 383–384). Such an offer does not reduce a person's options but (again) increases them. It thus cannot be a form of coercion.

Radcliffe-Richards' responses to the objection to the first inference on which the above pro-market argument rests are persuasive. But before turning to consider how the second inference on which the above pro-market argument is based can be challenged, an important clarification is in order. In holding that many of those who oppose organ sales "claim that there can be no genuine, free consent to the sale of organs" Radcliffe-Richards implicitly ascribes to them the view that organ sales are necessarily wrongful. But those whose arguments she addresses do not argue for this view. Instead, they offer arguments for the much weaker (and far more plausible) conclusion that such exchanges would typically be wrongful in certain social and economic circumstances. John B. Dossetor and

V. Manickavel, for example, argue that the exchange of kidneys for money would be wrongful in the West but not necessarily similarly wrongful in developing countries (1992, p. 65). Prospective kidney sellers in the West, they argue, would not need to sell their organs as their material needs would be met by the safety net of State welfare. Prospective kidney sellers in developing countries, however, would not have access to a similar safety net. Since this is so, they should be allowed to sell their organs to avoid poverty (Dossetor and Manickavel, 1992, p. 65). Similarly, R.A. Sells offers a consequentialist caution against the commercial procurement of kidneys (1991, p. 24). He does not argue that the commodification of human kidneys would always be wrongful.

This clarification is important to avoid attributing to those who oppose the commodification of organs the implausible view that while organs could be donated, they could never be sold. But it is also important as it emphasizes that debates over whether or not it is permissible to commodify human organs are concerned with whether organs should be commodified given the social and economic background against which this would occur. This observation (that the social and economic situation into which a market in kidneys would be introduced is relevant to the question of whether such a market *should* be introduced) can be drawn on to support the second objection to the above pro-market argument: That, *contra* that argument, we *cannot* infer that persons believe that they would be better off were they able to buy and sell organs in a market for them from the fact that they would buy and sell organs in such a market were it to be allowed.

Tiered consent and well-being

Radcliffe-Richards' defence of the above pro-market argument against the objection that the first inference on which it rests is illegitimate is sound. But she does not address the objection that the second inference on which it rests is illegitimate. She does not address this objection because (with many other defenders of markets) she does not recognize that this inference could be unsound.

Radcliffe-Richards' focus on establishing that a person could agree to a transaction in which she sold one of her organs is common among defenders of markets. In brief, the general approach they take is this: Establish that both parties to a transaction agreed to it. Then, from this, infer that since they agreed to the transaction then they each (*ex ante*) believed that engaging in it would make them better off when compared to the situation where they did not engage in it. Since this is so, a moral concern with well-being would support refraining from preventing them from engaging in this trade. Hence, if it could be assumed that persons would agree to engage in the buying and selling of (e.g.) organs were a market for them to be allowed then a moral concern for well-being would support allowing this market.

This is a compelling argument. But it is incomplete. It is possible for a person to agree to a transaction because she believes that *given the existence of the market* in the good or service that is the subject of the transaction then she would be made better off by so doing, while *also* believing that she would be *even better off* were the market in that good or service *not* to exist. In this case her preference ranking would be (No Market, No Transaction) > (Market, Transaction) > (Market, No Transaction). If the market in that good or service were to exist, then she would agree to transact in it. And she would do so because she would believe that she would thereby be made better off in comparison to her not transacting. But it would be mistaken to infer from this that she would be better off in a situation where this market existed in comparison to one in which it did not. Similarly, that she would agree to transact in this market were it to exist does not imply that she would agree to the introduction of this market into a situation where it was absent. Since she would not agree to the introduction of this market her agreement to any transactions that she performs within it were it to be introduced could not be taken to imply that she is a willing participant in the market. Her agreement to those transactions would thus be flawed and hence should not be taken to constitute morally authoritative consent (Taylor, 2017a, 2017b).

One might challenge the plausibility of the claim that a person could have the preference ranking outlined above. It might be thought that if a person agrees to a market transaction given the existence of that market because she believes that she would be made better off by so doing vis-à-vis the situation where she did not so transact then she *must* prefer the existence of the market to its non-existence. After all, one might think, a person who would prefer that a market in a certain good or service not exist could simply behave as though it did not exist by refusing to participate in it. Her participation in that market thus indicates that she prefers its existence to its non-existence. This is the line of thinking behind the second inference on which the above pro-market argument rests.

But the preference ranking outlined above is not merely a possible one. It would be one that would be rational for persons to hold in certain situations. Consider, for example, a hypothetical situation in which a market for votes is legalized. The political situation into which this market is introduced is one where there is a Rich Party and a Poor Party. Each party caters to their respective constituents. The Rich Party advocates for policies that aid the rich at the expense of the poor, and the Poor Party advocates for policies that aid the poor at the expense of the rich. The Rich Party is (of course!) rich, and the Poor Party is (predictably) poor. Eighty percent of the electorate are poor, while 20% are rich. The elections are run as "first past the post" elections, with a party needing to secure >50% of the vote to win.[4]

Prior to the introduction of a market for votes the Poor Party invariably won each election. With the introduction of a market for votes, however, things change. Given the size of the electorate no vote is likely to be pivotal. This leads to two consequences: Individual votes would be worth very little, and voters would come to realize that the outcome of the election would not be altered by the sale of their individual votes. Owing to the low value of each vote, rich voters are unlikely to be interested in selling their votes. But poor voters would be. Since votes are unlikely to be pivotal, poor voters would be indifferent as to whom they would sell. Since the Rich Party is rich and the Poor Party is poor the Rich Party would be able to outcompete the Poor Party in the (literal) market for votes. A market for votes would thus invariably lead to a Rich Party victory. The Rich Party passes policies that ensure that the costs of buying votes (i.e., the payments made to the poor) would be outweighed by the financial benefits that it can secure for its constituents. Since this is so, the result of allowing this vote market would be a net transfer of wealth from the poor to the rich.

The poor voters would thus be made worse off were this market to be allowed vis-à-vis a situation in which it was not allowed. Recognizing this, rational, self-interested poor voters would oppose the introduction of a market for votes. But were such a market to exist they would prefer to transact in it as sellers rather than refrain from participating at all. They would realize that given the existence of a market for votes the Rich Party would win. Their most favoured option (the sale of their vote followed by a Poor Party victory) would not be available to them. The only live options that they would be faced with would be to sell their vote and receive some compensation for it to defray the expenses that the Rich Party would impose upon them, or not sell their vote and thus lose the opportunity to defray those expenses. Given these options the poor voters would prefer to transact in the market for votes rather than stand apart from it—and they would do so even though they would prefer that that market not exist (Taylor, 2017a, Taylor, 2017b).

For a person to consent to a transaction such that her consent morally authorizes it in the view of someone who assesses the legitimacy of transactions against the test of whether they (*ex ante*) enhance or diminish the well-being of those party to them both the buyer and the seller must not only agree to the particular *token* transaction to which they are party. They must also agree that transactions of this *type* be available within their society. Only if both parties to the transaction consent both to the token transaction and also to its type being available to them can we infer that they believe that the ability to participate in the market will enhance their well-being.

That persons would sell their organs were a market for them to be allowed thus does not establish that those particular sales are morally permissible. It thus does not establish that a moral concern for well-being should lead one to support such a market. Consider a situation in a developing country where men tend to be wage-earners and women work in the home and where the economic value of wages is more obvious than that of home productivity. In this situation the loss of income that a male organ (e.g., kidney) vendor would suffer would be apparent while the adverse economic effect of a woman's time off work would be perceived to be lower (Prasad, 2018, p. 1002). In this situation were the option to sell a kidney to be made legally available women would typically serve as vendors. It is possible that out of the belief that they have a duty to supplement the family income many women would agree to sell a kidney. But it is also possible that some such vendors (perhaps even the *typical* vendor) would prefer that this option not have been made available to them. (That is, they would prefer that the market for kidneys not exist.) If so, then sales from the latter class of vendors would not (from the point of view of one concerned with the moral value of well-being) be morally permissible. And if it is the case that while the typical vendor would agree to sell given the presence of the option to do so she would prefer that this option be absent from her choice set, then a *prima facie* case could be made that the introduction of a legal market for kidneys into this situation would be morally impermissible.

Well-being and reasons for consent

On this two-tier approach to consent the potential parties to a transaction would need to answer two questions to determine if they genuinely consented to that transaction in a manner that would, from the perspective of someone concerned with the moral value of well-being, morally authorize it. The first is whether they prefer to engage or refrain from engaging in the token transaction they are considering. The second is whether they prefer that this type of transaction be available to persons in their society. In the examples above (vote sales and kidney sales) it was assumed that the answers to these questions would be based on the respondent's beliefs about the effects that pursuing (at the first-tier, token, level) or having (at the second-tier, type, level) these options to transact would have on her well-being. But they need not be.[5] A person might, for example, prefer not to (e.g.) sell her vote because she believes that vote-selling would be counter to the democratic purpose for which votes were created. For the same reason she might prefer that there be no markets in votes. Similarly, a person might prefer not to sell her kidney and also prefer that there be no markets in kidneys because she holds a neo-Kantian belief that a person's body parts should be market inalienable. Conversely, a person might prefer to sell his kidney as he believes that he has a moral duty to aid the less fortunate, even if he will be made worse off by so doing. He might similarly prefer that markets in kidneys exist to enable others to fulfill this moral duty in this way.

Recognizing that persons' preferences concerning both their own particular transactions and markets in the goods and services at issue might be based on beliefs *other* than those concerning their own well-being shows that the two-tier approach to evaluating the moral permissibility of transactions needs to be developed. This approach originated from the observation that the original inference concerning transactors' expected well-being drawn by the proponents of the above pro-market argument was mistaken. This approach corrected this inference by noting that it overlooked that a person might prefer that she lack the option to (e.g.) sell one of her kidneys (i.e., she preferred there be no market in kidneys) even though if it were to be available to her, then she would prefer to pursue it rather than refrain from pursuing it. But it did *not* challenge the claim that if persons *genuinely* consent to a transaction (i.e., they answer affirmatively at both the first, token, and second, type, tiers), then we can infer from this that they believe that it will make them better off. Rather than being a rejection of the original monoplane approach, then, the two-tier approach should be considered to be a modification of it.

This continued focus on well-being ignores the fact that persons could answer the questions about their preferences concerning both tokens and types of transactions by reference to reasons *other* than a concern for their own well-being. While the above two-tier account might thus be adequate as an account of when a person will genuinely consent to the transactions to which she is party the moral permissibility of those transactions will not necessarily be based on a moral concern for the value of the well-being of those party to them. Instead, it would be more accurate to view it as grounding the moral permissibility of those transactions to which persons consented on the moral requirement to respect persons' decisions—a requirement that would be based on the moral requirement to respect autonomy.[6] Moreover, recognizing that persons could genuinely consent to the transactions in which they engage *without* concern for their own well-being implies that there is nothing remarkable about the initial observation that led to the development of the two-tier approach: That one cannot infer from the fact that a person consents to a transaction that she believes that it will make her better off. The morally motivated kidney seller above, for example, could genuinely consent to the sale of his organ even though he believes that this will diminish his well-being.

The above observation that persons might have reasons other than their own well-being for engaging in transactions leads to an apparent counterexample to the two-tier approach. Consider a middle-class person who decides to sell one of her kidneys to pay for a luxury purchase. (Assume that this sale occurs in a legal, regulated market in the United States.) She prefers to engage in this transaction rather than not as she believes (correctly) that the sale of her kidney would enable her to achieve the ends she desires. However, although she desires to participate in the kidney market, she has a moral objection to it: She believes that it will exploit the poor. She accordingly opposes the existence of this market even though she believes that she will benefit from its presence. Since she would prefer that the type of transaction to which she has agreed (the sale of her kidney) not be available she would, on the two-tier approach to consent, be held not to have genuinely consented to the sale of her organ. But this conclusion is mistaken. That she desired that others whose situation differed from hers not be afforded the opportunity to sell their organs (and so she preferred that organ markets not exist) is not relevant to the question of whether she genuinely consented to the sale of her organ given her motive for sale. Since the two-tier approach is committed to the mistaken conclusion that this person did not genuinely consent to sell her kidney when it is clear that she did, it should be rejected.

This counterexample leads to the recognition that only *some* of the reasons that a person has for desiring to engage in or refrain from a particular transaction, or for desiring the presence or absence of the type of transaction of which it is a token, would be relevant to assessing whether her consent to the transaction in question was genuine. (In the above example the kidney seller's reason for desiring that others not be exploited in a kidney market is not relevant to the question of whether her consent to sell her kidney to enhance her own well-being is genuine.) To accommodate this recognition (and hence avoid counterexamples such as this) the two-tier approach must restrict the type of reasons that persons can invoke for endorsing or rejecting either the token transaction they are considering (e.g., the sale of their kidney) or the type of transaction of which this is a token (e.g., a general market for kidneys). Since the two-tier approach is intended to establish when a person would genuinely consent to a transaction no restrictions should be placed on the reasons for which she accepts or rejects a particular token transaction. Absent argument to the contrary there is no justification for holding that any reason for accepting a transaction could be identified *a priori* as necessarily precluding the person who invokes it from giving her genuine consent to the transaction in question. Any restrictions on the type of reasons that a person can draw on in making her decision must thus appear at the second tier of the two-tier approach (i.e., when the would-be transactor is deciding whether she desires the presence or absence of the type of transaction in question).

The above counterexample can also help determine where these restrictions should lie. In that example the would-be kidney seller was deciding whether or not to sell her organ on the basis of the effect that she expected that this would have on her well-being. Given this, her desires concerning the actions of others that would have no effect on her (i.e., the acts of the impoverished kidney sellers whose exploitation she was concerned about) were not relevant to her decision. Allowing these desires to govern her (second-tier) decision as to whether or not to endorse a kidney market thus generated a rejection of this market for reasons unconnected to those that governed her decision concerning the transaction she was considering. This irrelevant rejection of the market led, in turn, to the two-tier approach generating an intuitively false negative for the question of whether or not she genuinely consented to the sale of her kidney.

This analysis of how the unrestricted form of the two-tier approach fell prey to the above counterexample shows that the tiered approach to determining consent should restrict the reasons that it will recognize as being relevant to a person's decision at the second tier (i.e., concerning the type of transaction she is considering) to those that were relevant to her decision at the first tier (i.e., concerning the token transaction she is considering). In the above counterexample the would-be kidney vendor endorsed the sale of her kidney at the first tier on the grounds that she expected this to enhance her well-being. This reason for her endorsing the sale of her kidney would now, on the revised restricted version of the two-tier approach, *also* be that which should govern her assessment of whether she would endorse the buying and selling of kidneys in general. There would be no reason why others selling their kidneys would lead to her sale of her kidney resulting in the diminution of her well-being rather than its enhancement relative to its level prior to its sale.[7] Her concern for her own well-being would thus lead her to endorse this type of transaction. The restricted two-tier approach would thus hold that she would have genuinely consented to the sale of her kidney. And this evaluation is (as noted in the original counterexample) correct.

The move from the original unrestricted two-tier approach to determining whether a person genuinely consented to a transaction to which she was party to this restricted two-tier approach not only enables the tiered approach to avoid the above counterexample. It also reinforces the observation above: That this approach can be applied to assess whether a person has given her genuine consent to a transaction even if her reasons for transacting (or refraining from transacting) were not concerned with her own well-being.

This general applicability of the restricted two-tier approach raises an interesting question: Are there reasons other than a concern for her own well-being that could lead a person to endorse a token transaction but reject the type of transaction of which it was a token? It is clear that the converse is possible. A person might decide to refrain from a token transaction as he believes that engaging in it would violate a non-moral ideal that he holds, but also believe that this type of transaction should be generally available to himself and to others. (An example of such a person might be someone who had a snobbish antipathy towards "trade." He would not accept payment for his services, but he does not believe that others need similarly refrain. [Taylor, 2022, pp. 100–101].) But it is not clear that a person could assent to a particular transaction and yet reject the availability of such transactions in general if the reason for her original assent was something other than a concern for her own well-being. A person who assented to a transaction for moral reasons (e.g., she believed that trading this good or service with this partner would be an act of charity to him), for example, could not object to others engaging in similar trades. It might thus transpire that the only instances in which a person would endorse a token transaction (at the first tier) but reject this type of transaction (at the second tier) would be those where her initial endorsement was based on a concern for her own well-being. There is not space to pursue this question here. But if this is the case then the monoplane approach's initial focus on well-being as the primary guide to the permissibility or otherwise of markets in certain goods or services (such as organs) would appear to be vindicated.

Conclusion

In this chapter I have argued that a proper understanding of what is involved in a person consenting to a transaction (such as the sale of one of her organs) requires that she not only agree to the particular transaction in question but also agree to persons generally having the option of engaging in that type of transaction. This two-tiered approach to consent was initially motivated by the recognition that while a person's agreeing to a transaction might indicate that (given the situation that she is in) she would prefer to trade rather than not, it cannot be inferred from this that her possession of the option to engage in this transaction could be justified by appeal to its likely effect on her well-being. To make this latter inference one must address whether a person would also prefer to be in a situation where this type of option was available rather than be in one where it was not. But this tiered approach is not only applicable when a person consents to a transaction in an attempt to enhance her own well-being. It can be used to assess whether a person has genuinely consented to a transaction (and hence that that transaction is *prima facie* morally permissible) no matter what her reasons for trading were. When secured, a person's tiered consent to the sale of her organ will provide stronger evidence of the moral permissibility of this transaction than would her mere monoplane consent. However, adopting this two-tiered approach will reduce the number of sales of organs that would be considered morally permissible in comparison to the number of transactions that would be considered permissible were the monoplane approach to be retained. Finally, even if a person does give her tiered consent to the sale of her organ this will *not* establish that that sale is morally permissible. Securing a person's tiered consent to a transaction is a necessary, but not a sufficient, condition for its permissibility. The moral permissibility or otherwise of particular organ sales would have to be assessed against further moral questions—such as whether they were wrongly exploitative.[8]

Notes

1 Although care should be taken here, for markets in different body parts raise different moral issues (Taylor, 2022, pp. 161–165).

2 This pro-market argument is often offered in tandem with a second: That if persons consent to a trade of an organ for cash, then respect for their autonomy provides a *prima facie* moral reason to refrain from prohibiting this transaction (Taylor, 2005; Cherry, 2005, pp. 30–31). I focus here on the argument from well-being.

3 Radcliffe Richards also argued that if it was held that a person could not give her genuine consent to the sale of one of her kidneys as she was ignorant of the risks involved, then this deficiency should be remedied through education (1996, p. 380).

4 For further discussion of related issues see Jason Brennan and Christopher Freiman's entry in this volume (Chapter 11).

5 I thank Lucia Schwarz for pressing me on this point.

6 Although things become complex here. If autonomy is valuable both as a means to and part of well-being, then even on this account the fundamental moral ground for considering such authorized transactions to be morally permissible would still be a concern for the value of well-being (Taylor, 2009, Chapter 10).

7 Taking this to be the baseline ensures that a person will not oppose allowing a type of transaction on grounds that would subject her to market competition, and that this will make her worse off relative to a situation where she has a monopoly.

8 The question of exploitation is examined closely by Stephen Wilkinson in his chapter on surrogacy in this volume. I thank those who participated in the Zoom session on an earlier version of this chapter at the Commodification Workshop hosted by Carleton University in October 2021, and my audience at the Contested Markets Conference, Institut des Sciences juridque et philosophique de la Sorbonne, University Paris I, in June 2022. I especially thank Stephen Wilkinson, Adrian Walsh, and Philippe Steiner for their helpful comments on earlier versions of this chapter, and Vida Panitch and Elodie Bertrand for their extremely helpful written comments. I thank both Vida Panitch and Elodie Bertrand for organizing the Paris conference—and editing this volume!

References

Cherry, M. (2005) *Kidney for Sale by Owner: Human Organs, Transplantation, and the Market.* Washington D.C.: Georgetown University Press.

Cotter, H. (2011) "Increasing consent for organ donation: Mandated choice, individual autonomy, and informed consent," *Health Matrix* 21(2), pp. 599–626.

Dossetor, J.B. and Manickavel, V. (1992) "Commercialization: The buying or selling of kidneys," in: C.M. Kjellstrand and J.B. Dossetor (eds.) *Ethical Problems in Dialysis and Transplantation.* Dordrecht: Kluwer Academic Publishers, pp. 61–71.

Matesanz, M. and Dominguez-Gil, B. (2019) "Opt-out legislations: The mysterious viability of the false," *Kidney International* 95, pp. 1301–1303.

Panitch, V. and Horne, L.C. (2018) "Commodification, inequality, and kidney markets," *Social Theory and Practice* 44 (1), pp. 121–143.

Prasad, G.V.R. (2018) "Understanding the sex disparity in living kidney donation," *Journal of Evaluation in Clinical Practice* 24 (5), pp. 999–1004.

Radcliffe-Richards J. (1996) "Nephrarious goings on: Kidney sales and moral arguments," *Journal of Medicine and Philosophy* 21(4), pp. 375–416.

Sells, R.A. (1991) "Voluntarism of consent in both related and unrelated living organ donors," in W. Land and J.B. Dossetor (eds.) *Organ Replacement Therapy: Ethics, Justice, Commerce.* Dordrecht: Springer, pp. 18–24.

Taylor, J.S. (2005) *Stakes and Kidneys: Why Markets in Human Body Parts are Morally Imperative.* Aldershot: Ashgate.

Taylor, J.S. (2009) *Practical Autonomy and Bioethics.* New York: Routledge.

Taylor, J.S. (2017a) "How not to argue for markets, or, why the argument from mutually beneficial exchange fails," *Journal of Social Philosophy* 48(2), pp. 165–179.

Taylor, J.S. (2017b) "Autonomy, vote buying, and constraining options," *Journal of Applied Philosophy* 34(5), pp. 711–723.

Taylor, J.S. (2022) *Markets with Limits: How the Commodification of Academia Derails Debate.* New York: Routledge.

18

BLOOD AND PLASMA

Or, if you're such an altruist, why don't you sell your plasma?

Peter M. Jaworski

Introduction[1]

We collect blood and plasma for transfusion, but we also collect plasma to make plasma-derived medicinal therapies, or plasma therapies. These therapies include immunoglobulin, albumin, clotting factors, and others. These are used mostly for rare diseases and ailments, like primary and secondary immune deficiencies, a variety of bleeding disorders including von Willebrand disease and hemophilia, and a growing list of neurological ailments like multifocal motor neuropathy. Hardly any country, including the U.S., uses donor compensation when blood or plasma is used for transfusion. This is because as of yet we do not use pathogen inactivation and removal procedures for this purpose. But when we collect plasma in order to make therapies, we do use these procedures. These procedures make the therapies "inordinately safe", or "equally safe"[2] regardless of whether donors receive money for the donation or not.

Even though there are no safety or effectiveness concerns when it comes to therapies made with the plasma of compensated donors, most countries nevertheless have bans on commercial collections of plasma or ban donor compensation.[3] Every country with these bans has a plasma collection deficit for plasma therapies. To meet the needs of their patient communities, they import therapies from the commercial market. All of the therapies available on the commercial market are made using commercial compensated plasma collections in one of the handful of countries that allow it. Overwhelmingly, this plasma is collected in the United States, but some imports also come from Germany, Austria, Hungary, and the Czech Republic. These five countries are also the only countries with surplus plasma collections.

This chapter attempts to go some way in defending the view that a commercial model ought to be the default model for plasma collections used to make therapies. The commercial model preserves and promotes security of supply of therapies and so patient health, while non-commercial models put patient health at risk. The challenge to those who think banning commercial models is a good idea is to offer reasons that are important enough to justify the foreseeable risk to patient health. This chapter argues that the challenge has not been met, that bans on commercial models put patient health at risk without promoting, preserving, or protecting anything of even comparable moral weight.

 DOI: 10.4324/9781003188742-23

People have attempted to argue that the commercial models are objectionable enough to justify banning them. One set of objections have to do with donor altruism and community solidarity. They say that these values are undermined or threatened by commercial models, and so to preserve, promote, or protect these values, we have reason for a ban. Section II looks at these arguments and finds them wanting. Another set of objections have to do with how commercial models may harm or wrong donors. These include worries about donor health and donor dignity, as well as wrongful exploitation concerns. People argue that commercial models risk donor health because donors are incentivized to donate too frequently; that commercial models affront donor dignity by coercing the very poor to donate out of financial desperation; and that commercial models wrongfully exploit the poor and vulnerable for the sake of money and profits. Section III looks at these arguments and also finds them wanting.

When it comes to each of these arguments, we just don't have enough evidence to conclude that commercial models come at the expense of any of these values. But even if they did, they need not. We can redesign the models to avoid concerns about donor health and wrongful exploitation. We can revise the meaning of commercial collections and compensated donations in such a way that commercial practices will promote or preserve, rather than harm, donor dignity, altruism, and community solidarity. In each case, we should prefer the strategy of redesigning and revising over banning the models. In the case of altruism and community solidarity, even if you think these strategies can't or won't work, it doesn't really matter because these worries are not enough to outweigh the moral importance of patient health. When it comes to donor dignity, no current bans are justified on these grounds since they do not preserve nor protect donor dignity, but rather shift the affront to a different jurisdiction, or sometimes just shift how dignity is affronted within the jurisdiction.

Altruism and community solidarity

Many of the arguments in favour of banning commercial models were initially put forward by Richard Titmuss (1970). Titmuss argued that the UK model of non-commercial blood collections was better than the American system with its mix of commercial and non-commercial blood collections. It was better because on average and in general more blood was donated and had lower levels of "serum hepatitis" than in the US. He also argued that the UK system was morally better than the US system. The US relied on poorer and more vulnerable donors, raising concerns about wrongful exploitation. These differences between the UK and the US were a result of the UK's system being non-commercial, which made blood donation a special kind of "gift" relationship there, whereas in the US it was merely an exchange of commodities. When blood donation is seen as a special kind of gift, it expresses and reinforces altruism and promotes community solidarity. But when it is seen as just another market commodity, it represses altruism at the community level. So regarded, paid blood donations express, for example, the thought that people need to be paid to help their neighbours in need, and so undermines and corrodes our sense of community.[4]

The price of priceless plasma is patient health

Titmuss did not believe that there were trade-offs between the various values at stake and the quantity of blood or plasma collected by non-commercial models. He thought the non-commercial model was better in basically each and every way. But the evidence now suggests that we do confront a significant trade-off. We can collect sufficient quantities of plasma to manufacture plasma therapies and so promote and preserve patient health, or we can use non-commercial models.[5]

Around the world, commercial plasma collections account for more than four-fifths of the plasma used to manufacture plasma therapies, with the United States alone responsible for two-thirds to three-quarters of the world's supply (Jaworski, 2020). In 2014, New Zealand was the last and then only country to be self-sufficient, relying solely on non-commercial collections. Today, there is no country that is self-sufficient without use of the commercial model.

Commercial models attract more donors, and those donors give more frequently (Schneider and Kimber, 2017). The average commercial centre in the US collects between 50 to 60,000 litres, while non-commercial centres collect only around 20,000 litres (Jaworski, 2020, pp. 28–29). That translates to much higher per capita collections in countries with a commercial model, at a significantly lower cost. For example, in 2017, Germany, the Czech Republic, Austria, and the United States – each of which allow commercial compensated plasma collections – collected 36, 45, 75, and 113 litres per thousand, respectively. That same year, the Netherlands, France, and Italy, three of the best-performing European countries with a prohibition on commercial models, managed to collect only 19, 13, and 14 litres per thousand. Spain managed to collect just 8 litres per thousand (Jaworski, 2020, p. 27). These lower per capita collections come at a much higher price. A Health Canada Expert Panel concluded that "…the cost of collecting large volumes of source plasma utilizing volunteer donors is 2–4 times more expensive than the commercial plasma collection model" (Ballem et al., 2018, Part VIII).

Around the world, meanwhile, we have seen increases in demand for immunoglobulin of about 6–10% each year. The result of these increases in demand has been increasing plasma collection deficits, and so lower domestic self-sufficiency, for countries that ban commercial models, and increased global reliance on American plasma collections.[6]

To give an example, consider my home country of Canada. In 2012, two commercial plasma companies had plans to open 19 commercial plasma collection centres across Canada. In response, the province of Ontario banned commercial plasma collections through a law called the Voluntary Blood Donations Act in 2014. Alberta followed suit doing the same in 2016, and British Columbia did the same in 2018. Instead of the planned 19 commercial plasma collection centers in Canada, only three opened – one in Saskatchewan, one in New Brunswick, and one in Buffalo, New York.

Excluding Quebec, Canada needed 1.8 million litres of plasma to meet the immunoglobulin needs of patients in 2019. That year, Canada collected over 200,000 litres in recovered plasma from whole blood donations. If the three provinces mentioned above had not passed a ban, Canada would have collected about 1 million litres (approximately 740,000 litres from the 19 commercial centres). Today, Canada would likely be a net contributor to the global supply of plasma, rather than a drain on that supply. Could the non-commercial model have collected enough plasma? Not according to Canadian Blood Services. In their 2014 annual report, they wrote: "Given that self-sufficiency is not operationally or economically feasible in a volunteer, non-remunerated model, Canadian Blood Services strives to maintain a sufficiency of 30% for immunoglobulin (Ig)" (CBS, 2014).[7] Despite their striving, however, Canada dropped from 30% self-sufficiency when Ontario passed the ban, to around 13% by 2021 (CBS, 2020–2021, p. 22). The bans did not increase non-commercial plasma collections, they just resulted in more reliance on American commercial plasma collections.

It is possible that without the bans Canadian patients would not have had to suffer through a shortage of subcutaneous immunoglobulin in 2019. If other countries had not banned commercial models, the world would be in a better position to weather shocks like the current pandemic. As I write, Romania is entirely out of immunoglobulin, and is expected to be without it for 60–90 days. Spain is in an "emergency situation" (Tobalina, 2021) and England is "perilously short of supply" (Sandhu, 2021) with respect to the same therapy. Other countries are in similarly dire situations. There is nothing to be done for at least some patients, and so some will die. Over the years, many patients have died because of insufficient plasma collections.

Prior to the ban in Ontario, Graham Sher, the CEO of Canadian Blood Services, wrote an editorial entitled "Prohibiting pay-for-plasma would harm patients" for the *Toronto Star*. Sher (2013) argued that, "A prohibition on paying donors for plasma for commercial fractionation use would deny patients access to these products, both here in Canada and around the globe. When lives are at risk, that's simply not an option". Unfortunately, he was right that prohibitions deny patients access to these products.

Patient health matters more

Even if we grant for the sake of argument that donor altruism and community solidarity are promoted by non-commercial models and are undermined by commercial models, it is hard to see why these values are worth the risk of denying patients access to therapies. It is hard to see why a system of plasma collection should be more concerned with preserving the ability of donors to express their altruism, or to promote community solidarity over preserving and promoting patient health. But it is not hard to see that the primary point and purpose, and so the moral priority, of a system of plasma collection should be to collect enough plasma to ensure security of supply of therapies for patients. Altruism and community solidarity can be additional purposes, or relevant considerations, but only after and only if we are collecting enough plasma.

Suppose for a moment that we figured out a way to create plasma therapies without needing any human blood plasma. Maybe we make them in a lab or we find equally effective alternatives that cost just the same. If it were in our power to block this, so as to continue to have to rely on plasma collections, would we? It seems obvious that we would not. This would come at the expense of this way of expressing altruism, this space for altruism, and this way of promoting community solidarity, but that just wouldn't matter enough.[8] And even if it did matter enough, we can just express altruism and so promote community solidarity in some other way. Opportunities to express altruism are not rare. However, for many patients, there are no alternatives to immunoglobulin for their condition. So banning commercial models is likely to harm patient health, while only providing the benefit of yet another space for altruism, and yet one more way of promoting community solidarity amongst many others.

The altruistic paid donor

But the claim that donor compensation, an important element in all commercial models, is strictly incompatible with donor altruism seems independently controversial. For example, European courts have found no difficulty in thinking compensation to be compatible with altruistic "voluntary unpaid donations". For example, Grifols, one of the two largest commercial plasma collectors, used to collect plasma using donor compensation in their home country of Spain. In 1985, a Royal Decree was passed requiring altruistic donations, but Grifols continued to operate just as before. So, as far as Spanish law was concerned, there was no legal conflict between donor compensation and altruism. It wasn't until a separate Royal Decree passed in 1999 required all such collections to be done exclusively by non-commercial companies that Grifols shuttered their Spanish collection centres.

It's true that legal decisions do not settle the empirical or conceptual issues regarding the incompatibility of compensation and altruism, especially if we have independent evidence of the incompatibility. But we don't. There are very few studies regarding the motives of compensated donors, and those that we have do not support incompatibility. For example, I conducted a survey with my colleague William English of nearly 28,000 Americans. Just over 91.56% of both noncompensated blood donors and compensated plasma donors together listed "to help others" as amongst their motives for doing it. Disaggregating the data, 84.65% of exclusively compensated plasma donors indicated the same thing (English and Jaworski, unpublished manuscript). Relevant similar surveys, like a survey of compensated stool donors (McSweeney et al., 2020), and compensated kidney donors in Iran (Kelishomi and Sgroi, 2022), also reported altruistic motives.

It's true that these are just reports, and that social desirability bias may explain why donors say that helping others was important to them. For example, Lucie White (2015), summarizing the work of Wendy Espeland (1987), and Martin J. Kretzman (1992), explains that new compensated plasma donors attempt to describe their behaviour using altruistic language, but most donors "eventually admit to having economic motivations for selling their plasma" (p. 393). They "admit" this because they discover that the rest of us don't believe them, and don't grant them these motives. So when these donors indicate altruistic motives, this is seen as a mere "front" for their real motives, which are non-altruistic and driven by financial considerations. But why wouldn't social desirability bias also explain away the reports of non-compensated donors? There is some evidence to suggest that many blood donors give blood not for altruistic reasons, but based on other motives, like "image motivation" (Ariely, Bracha and Meier, 2009) or social pressure or guilt, or some of the "warm glow" reasons offered by James Andreoni (1990).

Whatever theory we want to use to help underwrite our scepticism of the possibility of what we might call an altruistic paid donor, the theory will not be grounded in some conceptual or other deep conflict between altruism and payment. Lots of people are paid to do something, but it doesn't follow that payment was their exclusive or even primary motive. For example, just about everyone, apart from the donor, is paid at non-commercial blood and plasma collection centres. The administrators get money to administer the system, phlebotomists are paid to stick donors, nurses and doctors collect a salary, and so on. These people are rarely volunteers, they are paid. But we don't think there's a deep incompatibility between altruism and payment in these cases. We think there are such things as altruistic paid nurses, altruistic paid administrators, altruistic paid phlebotomists, altruistic paid doctors, and so on. We are likely to think that a nurse was putting on an elaborate front if they told us they were in it just for the money.

The theory will also not be grounded in the fact that the money makes a big difference to donations. When compensation increases, we see more donors. When it decreases, we see fewer donors. If we were to stop paying donors, very few would give plasma, and we would have collection deficits, as is the case in every country that does not pay donors. But this is true of nurses as well. The number of nurses we have is responsive to the amount of money they are offered–the money makes a big difference. If we were to stop paying nurses, very few would volunteer, and we would have nursing shortages. If the latter doesn't prove paid nurses are lying when they report altruistic motives, then the former doesn't prove that paid donors are lying when they report altruistic motives.

The theory can't be grounded in the claim that it doesn't help other people. Selling plasma, like selling nursing labour, promotes patient health. Since it actually helps save the lives of patients, helping save the lives of patients is an available motive for doing it. So it is possible and conceivable for someone to choose to sell their plasma not because it is selling or a way to make money, but because it promotes patient health. More than that, we have some reason to think that selling plasma is preferable to giving it away if you want to do as much good as possible. Recall the data above showing that the cost of collecting a litre of plasma is much less (two-to-four times less) at compensated as compared with non-compensated plasma centres. It is possible that the marginal cost of your individual donation is less. If so, then you do more good giving plasma to commercial centres than non-commercial ones, even excluding the additional good you might do with the money you get for donating plasma.

In response, at least three things might be said. The first is to try to argue that the relative ineffectiveness and inefficiency of the non-commercial models might be partially explained by the presence of the commercial model, or to argue that the commercial model harms blood collections for transfusion. Banning commercial centres is a way of protecting blood collection and improving their plasma collection performance. The second is to accept that non-commercial models are poorer performers but to try to suggest that other values, like especially community solidarity, may be worth the poorer collection performance, and so tilt the balance in favour of bans. The third is to also accept the poorer performance of non-commercial plasma collections but to argue that there are harms to donors – including harm to their health or dignity, or their being wrongfully exploited – that count in favour of banning commercial models even if the ban harms patient health. Let's examine each in turn.

Encroachment

One criticism of Titmuss' view, summarized by David Archard (2002), had it that people just are "self-interested profit maximizers who will exchange their blood only for money, status, or some tangible reward" (p. 90). If people are like this, then we really should just compensate donors to make sure we have enough blood. But on behalf of Titmuss, Archard explains that "[f]ixed motives cannot be attributed to human beings to serve as free-standing measures by which practices and institutions may then be judged, for these very practices and institutions themselves 'encourage or discourage' the presence of certain motives" (p. 90).

Our practices and institutions influence how we are motivated. They do this partly through their social meaning. We think day traders on Wall Street in New York are interested in maximizing their profits. We think donors at non-commercial blood and plasma collection centres are interested in altruistically helping anonymous others. It is because non-commercial centers express altruistic motives that the norm of doing things for altruistic reasons is reinforced. Seeing people donate blood or plasma without getting money in return encourages others to do the same, sometimes perhaps out of gratitude.[9] And it is because commercial plasma centers express base, non-altruistic motives that the norm of doing things for altruistic reasons is discouraged. Around here, someone might think, people only help others if there's something in it for them.

How we talk about what we are doing may also play a role in encouraging or discouraging certain motives. Margaret Jane Radin (1987) tells us that "market rhetoric", the concepts prevalent in economic theory, can make us think and so behave in ways consistent with the model of human behaviour found in that theory. Concepts like "paid", "vending", "remuneration", "compensation", etc. can invoke norms that make us think that selfish, rational, and calculating motives are contextually appropriate.[10]

If we allow parallel operations of commercial and non-commercial collections, this might make the choice to give at a non-commercial centre difficult to comprehend (*"It is not rational to exchange P without remuneration when one could"* (Archard, 2002, p. 94)). The presence of the commercial option might also "contaminate" the meaning of giving at a non-commercial center and so lower giving at non-commercial centres (*"If blood is also a commodity, then all I have given to the recipient is the cash equivalent of the blood, not the gift of life itself"* (Anderson, 1990, p. 198)). Either way, having a commercial option may be enough to interfere with an acculturation process that would counterfactually make non-commercial plasma collections more effective and efficient.

While Archard is right that we don't have reason to hold motives fixed, the speculative arguments above are not supported by the empirical evidence for plasma. Countries with bans collect far less plasma than those with commercial collections. Countries that ban commercial plasma collections also do not collect more non-compensated blood. The countries that permit both models to operate have similar, if not sometimes better, rates of non-compensated donations.

To be sure, these kinds of comparisons are complicated, especially since different countries sometimes have very different histories, cultures, background institutions, and so on. But the burden of sorting through this data is on those who propose "domino effect" (Radin, 1987) arguments as grounds for banning the demonstrably better performing commercial models. The burden is not on those of us who are sceptical that compensating plasma donors will "contaminate the meaning" of giving blood, or make doing so without compensation incomprehensible.

Within-country comparisons appear to show the same thing. The Czech Republic saw the introduction of commercial plasma collection in late 2006. Plasma collections increased seven-fold over three years, taking the Czech Republic from a plasma collection deficit to a surplus. Not only did the introduction of the commercial model not decrease blood donations, we also saw an increase in non-commercial plasma collections (Jaworski, 2021). In Canada, the introduction of commercial models in Saskatoon, and Moncton in 2016 and 2017, and the expansion of plasma collections in Winnipeg from specialty plasma to all plasma in 2017 had a small, but positive effect on non-commercial blood collections in those cities. There was a smaller, but still positive, effect on non-commercial blood collections in three cities in the U.S. that saw the introduction of commercial plasma collections in the same time period. Meanwhile, the same study found that commercial plasma collectors had no impact on non-commercial blood collections in over 40 cities in the U.S. with long-term, parallel operations of the two models (Jaworski and English, 2020). It looks like different people are attracted to non-compensated as compared with compensated donations.

Again, this is a complicated empirical question, and we still need more evidence to conclude with any confidence that commercial plasma collections undermine or promote non-compensated blood collections. But the field evidence that we do have appears to run counter to the encroachment concerns, and the impact, whether positive or negative, appears to be very small anyways. Perhaps at one point in the past the burden was on those who were proposing to introduce compensated plasma collections, but it looks like now the burden is on those who speculate that such collections will negatively, and significantly, impact non-compensated collections for transfusion purposes.

Community solidarity

If the commercial models do not encroach on non-commercial blood (and plasma) collections, then we might be tempted to conclude that the commercial model has no impact on the level of altruism within the community. If so, then it should not negatively affect community solidarity either. But community solidarity may not be about donors' actual motives but, rather, about the social meaning of the practices, and so the presumed motives based on that meaning.

Titmuss' claim that "the commercialization of blood and donor relationships represses the expression of altruism" (Titmuss, 1970, p. 245), can be taken to refer to social meaning, rather than any actual motives. It is about how the *expression* of altruism "erodes the sense of community".[11] So long as commercial donations have a shared social meaning as being motivated by base, non-altruistic motives (regardless of the motivational facts), their presence can undermine community solidarity. Alternatively, as Archard suggests, they can contaminate the meaning of non-commercial donations so that these donors can no longer be understood as engaging in a pure gift relationship, and this might undermine community solidarity. If so, then we might wonder if the additional value of community solidarity can sometimes tip the scales in favour of bans, even if this comes at some cost to patient health.[12]

This way of understanding the argument – as expressive rather than indicative[13] – is important for the claim that non-commercial blood donations underwrite community solidarity as well. Suppose it turns out that most blood donors don't donate for altruistic reasons, but do it for "image motivation" reasons. This would not matter for the expressive argument. As long as we continue to (falsely) believe that what motivates blood donors is altruistic concern for others, it will help promote community solidarity. If we had an altruism detection device that accurately read motives, and if that device revealed to us that blood donors were not in fact altruistic, we would have norms-of-altruism and community-solidarity-promoting reasons to keep the results a secret, to stop using the device, or to lie about what it says.

But if the argument is expressive, then this opens it up to the same kind of "collapsing move" that all such arguments face.[14] Just as we don't have reason to hold motives fixed, we don't have reason to hold any meanings fixed either. The social meaning of commercial collections is a construction which in principle can be revised.[15] So we have at least two avenues to preserve and promote community solidarity. We can do the political work to try to ban commercial collections for the sake of community solidarity in deference to the social meaning of such donations, or we could do the cultural work of revising the social meaning of commercial donations so that they mean or express, for example, "*something an altruist does*" for the sake of community solidarity.[16] Since commercial plasma collections promote security of supply and patient health (and provide people with a beneficial financial opportunity) while non-commercial plasma collections do not, we should prefer the cultural work strategy over the political strategy of pushing for bans.[17]

Studies might reveal that commercial donors are not in fact altruistically motivated, but this would be as irrelevant to this argument as would be studies revealing that non-commercial donors are not in fact altruistically motivated. First, this instrumentalist solidarity argument depends on social meanings, which are about what motives are expressed or communicated and not what motives are actually possessed. Second, as Archard has pointed out and as is implicit in Radin's claims, the argument is forward-, not backward-looking. The institutions of non-commercial donation may, given what they now express, attract and make donors altruistic, encourage or discourage certain motives. Similarly, the institution of commercial donation, given what it could express or what rhetoric we use, may also attract and make commercial donors altruistic, encourage or discourage the presence of certain motives, just like commercial paid nurses. Third, our archetypes and cultural scripts are already often normative, rather than descriptive. Suppose it turns out that most nurses or most politicians are not motivated in the ways our archetypal nurse or public official suggests. We probably wouldn't change the archetype because its purpose is not to accurately describe the motives of a majority of instances of the type, but instead to specify what motives are appropriate or expected. We could have a similar normative archetype for all donors, regardless of whether they are compensated or not.

It might be said that the cultural strategy of changing social meanings might be very hard, or maybe infeasible altogether. But in the case of compensated blood and plasma donations, this difficulty is not as difficult as it may seem. One strategy might focus on insisting that the compensation is not for the blood or plasma itself, but for the time and effort involved in donating it. Consider that in Germany, where donors are compensated, many express this thought.[18] In those cases, the blood and plasma itself can be regarded as a "gift". Most commercial plasma companies say that they compensate donors for time, effort, inconvenience, and so on, not for the plasma itself. This conception of what the object of exchange is also reflected in court judgments in the United States. They have rejected the view that blood or plasma is property transferred via sale – for example, to patients in a hospital or to commercial plasma companies from donors – in favour of a service or time and effort conception of the object of exchange.[19]

That may be unpersuasive to you, but consider the danger posed to community solidarity by our current systems of non-compensated plasma collections. It does not seem far-fetched to suggest that our health care system's failure to ensure a sufficient quantity of plasma to meet the needs of patients from domestic plasma collections does more to erode our sense of community than commercial plasma collections do or might. The world's reliance on American plasma plausibly expresses or communicates the idea that we in countries that ban commercial collections don't care enough about our patient communities to roll up our sleeves and give plasma often enough. Permitting commercial plasma collections may be regarded by our community as an altruistic expression of concern for patients: "We allow commercial collections because they perform better, and around here we care more about preserving patient health than preserving spaces for altruism".

Bans on the commercial models come with theoretical benefits of altruism and community solidarity but demonstrated risks to patient health. Permitting commercial plasma collections, meanwhile, comes with theoretical risks to altruism and community solidarity but demonstrated benefits to patient health. Until what is theoretical is demonstrated, it seems to be a moral mistake to ban rather than permit commercial plasma collections for these sorts of reasons.

Donor health, donor dignity, and wrongful exploitation

Other reasons have been offered against the commercial models. The first are concerns about the safety of therapies made from commercial plasma as well as donor health concerns stemming from too-frequent plasma donations, and the second is a category of objections having to do with the way commercial donations may undermine the dignity of donors or to mistreat them, including possibly coercing and wrongfully exploiting donors. These kinds of objections, unlike space for altruism and community solidarity objections, are plausibly not easily outweighed by the value of patient health. For example, many believe that remuneration for kidney or liver donations would be an effective and efficient way of eliminating the waiting list for these organs. But some of these same people nevertheless believe that the risks to donor health and the affront to dignity is sufficiently severe such that it is all-things-considered permissible (indeed, preferable) to allow thousands of patients to die each year rather than permit remuneration.

Donor health

With respect to donor health, the commercial models have not yet been demonstrated to cause harm to donor health. This is so even at American and Canadian donation frequencies.[20] Health Canada's decision to recently change the rules to follow the higher frequencies in the US that accord with FDA rules lends at least some weight to the claim that this practice is not harmful. Although, importantly, there are studies that show frequent plasmapheresis donors have lower levels of certain proteins. These are still within what are considered acceptable ranges, although they do raise concerns.[21]

We may discover in future that these frequencies are too frequent, and are harmful to donor health. But if so, we can just redesign the model to lower donation frequencies. Canada and the

US could follow any of the commercial models in Europe. Austria allows once-per-five-days donations up to 65 times per year, Germany allows once-weekly donations up to 50 times per year, and the Czech Republic allows twice-weekly donations, but caps them at only 33 such donations per year. Despite the lower frequencies, all three of these countries collect surplus plasma, and all of these models are sustainable and more efficient than non-commercial models.

Donor dignity and wrongful exploitation

Some think commercial plasma donations and collections are degrading or exploitative. In general, they are stigmatized. This might be because of what they express, or because of what they indicate. If the stigma is merely a function of what these practices mean, then it will fall prey to the collapsing move we made earlier. We can imagine a culture where these practices are regarded as noble and dignified ways to help others. Since these practices have greater benefits than non-commercial donations and collections, we should, as Lucie White (2015) suggests, work to destigmatize and ennoble them. Doing so would not only promote patient health, but it would also thereby preserve (meaning-dependent) donor dignity.

The collapsing move will not apply if, instead of being merely expressive, the claim is that these commercial practices indicate facts or features that would make stigmatization appropriate or warranted. This would be so if, as some have argued, commercial plasma collections violate autonomy[22] (or are wrongfully exploitative). The claim would be that even if no one thought it undignified and the practice was not stigmatized, we would be wrong to fail to stigmatize it since it would in fact be undignified in virtue of violating autonomy sufficiently (or exploiting donors wrongfully).

Focusing on autonomy first: What we need is an account of how a commercial plasma donor's autonomy is sufficiently compromised to warrant stigmatization and prohibition without appealing to social stigma. However, as soon as we imagine a world where no stigma surrounds the practice of paid plasma donations, it becomes difficult to see how and why autonomy would be compromised to the extent necessary to underwrite not only stigma but prohibition. Alena Buyx (2009), for example, has raised doubts about whether or not we see sufficient desperation of this sort in high-income countries (p. 330). And once someone is above that level of desperation, then respect for bodily autonomy would counsel against prohibition with prohibition itself violating bodily autonomy, as Steve Weimer (2015) has pointed out.

Not only is the bar high, we also need a principled distinction between the practice of engaging in commercial plasma donation and other commercial activities we engage in on the basis of circumstances that are at least sometimes desperate. For example, we may sell our treasured Xbox or PlayStation, or pawn a meaningful item of jewelry when we fall on hard times, but we usually don't complain that this is a violation of our autonomy. Many jobs that people take, from working at fast food restaurants to delivering newspapers, are done from desperation. But this does not entail that we make non-autonomous decisions in the market. And even if it did, that would not support an argument in favour of prohibiting these commercial activities, or removing these people from being able to engage in these activities. Rather, a successful argument of this sort would count in favour of additional social insurance.[23]

There may be arguments that counsel in favour of removing certain choices from desperately poor people's choice sets, but why would anyone think paid plasma is a plausible candidate for choice-removal? Consider what Gerald Dworkin (1994) says in response to arguments like this when it comes to markets in kidneys. Arguments like these suggest that "poor people should not be allowed to enter the army", or "engage in hazardous occupations such as high-steel construction", or be Alaskan truck drivers, or fish crab, and so on. "But it seems to me paternalistic in the extreme … to deny poor people choices which they perceive as increasing their well-being" (p. 157). And this is especially so when we are talking about non-risky, non-hazardous, frankly no-big-deal plasma donations. Meanwhile, plasma donation is a practice that, unlike working at Arby's or pawning your jewellery, has the added benefit of saving and improving the lives of patients. If the potential for harm to the donor was greater, as in the case of kidney or liver donations or fishing crab or being a truck driver in Alaska, then a constrained-autonomy argument might work. But the claim that non-risky commercial plasma donations do this is too far-fetched.

Meanwhile, other incidental or contingent concerns can be addressed through redesigning the institutional rules commercial plasma centres operate under. We should prefer this if redesign avoids or eliminates our moral concerns while still producing greater net benefits or lower costs compared with prohibition. To illustrate, we could require donors to be either in the process of completing or having completed a college degree. College attendance correlates with wealth (and with lower levels of transfusion-transmissible infections), and so would predictably increase the wealth of the average donor. Perhaps a selection criterion could be introduced requiring donors to have secure employment. The specifics do not matter, these are just examples of possible policy changes that would predictably change donor demographics to one where concerns regarding undue inducement are less pressing.[24] Provided these rule changes do not undermine the net efficiency advantages of commercial collections, we should prefer these to prohibition.

If we think that donors are wrongfully exploited in the sense of receiving an unfair division of the benefits from trade,[25] then increasing how much donors are paid will fix this. In European jurisdictions, the donor fee is sometimes set by law, and not by market forces. Since the nature of this problem is not that people are paid but rather how much they are paid, then the problem is the legally-set fixed price or fee and not the commercial practice. We can change the law to raise the fee. In Canada and the U.S. where the fee is set by market forces, we can institute a price floor or minimum fee, like we do with wages through a minimum wage. As long as these changes do not undermine the efficiency advantages of commercial plasma collections, we should prefer this to prohibition.[26]

Bump in the rug

Even if we suppose that the above is unpersuasive, this wouldn't justify any current prohibitions in high-income countries. In practice, these countries have just met increasing demand by increasing reliance on commercial plasma. All they have done is pushed the dignity-affronting or wrongful exploitation bump in their rug over to someone else's rug (usually America's rug). This is not a moral improvement.

It might be said that countries and some subnational jurisdictions like provinces in Canada can only control what is done within their own jurisdiction, and so they are indirectly merely complicit in wrongfully exploiting or affronting donor dignity.[27] This argument might be plausible if the volume of plasma collected at commercial plasma centres in the US was independent of the choices of these jurisdictions. But it is not. The forward-looking contracts increase the number of commercial plasma collections directly, and so they are as morally responsible for the wrongful exploitation or any dignity thereby affronted in the US as they would be were they to permit the practice in their own jurisdiction.[28]

Prohibitions would have a chance of being justified on these grounds if prohibition was paired with sufficient increases in non-commercial plasma collections to avoid relying on imports. Some countries have tried to do this. However, they have all failed so far.[29]

However, since non-commercial collections are two-to-four times more costly, those additional resources spent on non-commercial collections will come at the expense of other priorities. In the case of public non-commercial plasma collections, the costs would come from the health care budget and so come at the expense of other health care priorities. Prohibition also results in at least some private investment capital being redirected from commercial plasma collections which are a public benefit, to other investments that may not have as much of a public benefit.

Prohibitions are no moral improvement, but they might be morally worse. This may be so for at least three reasons. First, it might be reasonable to suggest that we have greater negative obligations to non-residents (while we have greater positive obligations to fellow citizens). We can do certain things to "us" that we can't do to "them". If so, then it may be morally better to wrongfully exploit "us" or affront "our" dignity than it is to wrongfully exploit "them" or affront "their" dignity. Second, recalling what Alena Buyx (2009) pointed out, the background circumstances for the poor in the US may be worse than the background circumstances for the poor in places like Canada and the EU. If so, then to the extent the wrongful exploitation and affront to dignity is a function of financial desperation due to poor background circumstances, the exploitation or affront would be less (if at all)[30] in these jurisdictions than in the US.

The third way in which prohibition might be worse is if would-be plasma donors in our jurisdiction turn to equally or more exploitative or dignity-affronting practices after prohibition, something Margaret Jane Radin (1987) calls the "double bind" (p. 1911, fn. 226). This would be worse because not only are we exploiting or affronting the dignity of American donors through our imports, it would also not even come with the benefit of protecting against the exploitation, and preserving the dignity of would-be donors in our own jurisdiction. This, too, is a bump in the rug argument. Prohibition makes it impossible to sell plasma when financially desperate, but it doesn't make anyone less financially desperate, and so no less exploitable or coercable. As Radin (1987) writes, "If poverty can make some things nonsaleable because we must prophylactically presume such sales are coerced, we would add insult to injury if we then do not provide the would-be seller with the goods she needs or the money she would have received" (p. 1911).

This will be fine only if would-be donors either have or are likely to choose non-exploitative and non-dignity affronting options when financially desperate. It will not be fine if our removing the frying pan puts people into the fire. I'm aware of only one paper looking into this, which shows that the introduction of commercial plasma donations "reduces demand (inquiries) for payday and installment loans by 6.5% and 8.1%, respectively, with larger effects (13.1% and 15.7%, respectively) on younger borrowers" (Dooley and Gallagher, 2021). Alternatively, prohibition would be justified if it was paired with policies that improved the background circumstances that address people's being coercable or exploitable. But notice that if we instituted policies that address these latter issues, then prohibition would once again be unjustified.

Conclusion

Selling plasma is choiceworthy. It is a way of helping others. It is not risky, nor harmful. It is not unfair. It is an autonomy-affirming way of contributing to the health of others, and a financial opportunity as well. It is, since 2014, the only effective means of meeting the needs of patients, and is much more efficient, freeing up resources to do more good.

Selling plasma is plausibly more choice-worthy for altruists who wish to see more good done with their donation than giving it away. People may (wrongly) believe that you have the wrong motives, but it is an ersatz altruist that cares so much about her image reputation than she does about the good she can do.

If you're an altruist, selling your plasma should be on your list of things to consider doing (more) frequently.

Notes

1 For helpful comments on various arguments within this chapter, I would like to thank Leisha Colyn, David Faraci, Mark Herman, Mark Wells, Jason Brennan, students in my Senior Honors Thesis class at Georgetown, especially Elizabeth Collingsworth and Anthony Reznik, students in my "Blood Feud" class at UVA School of Law along with my co-professor Kimberly Krawiec, attendees at the conference in Paris on this handbook, as well as Vida Panitch and Elodie Bertrand.

2 These quotes are taken from a video produced by Canadian Blood Services featuring their CEO Dr. Graham Sher who says, "we don't believe that the existence of a paid plasma sector is a safety threat to product or to patients and I don't believe there is data or evidence to support that".

3 Spain allows compensation, but limits plasma collection to not-for-profit entities whether public or private. In Canada, the provinces of Ontario, Alberta, and British Columbia enacted the Voluntary Blood Donations Act in 2014, 2017, and 2018 which prohibits the use of either compensation or remuneration by commercial entities, but exempts Canadian Blood Services, the provincially-funded blood operator in every province outside of Quebec. In 2020, the province of Alberta repealed the prohibition and so now once again permits commercial collections.

4 Some of these arguments might be best understood as corruption arguments, which are discussed at greater length in Chapter 4 of this handbook.

5 Evidence from field and natural experiments, rather than survey- or lab-based studies, suggests that blood donations are not discouraged by financial compensation, but that they roughly track the relative price effect. See Lacetera, N., Macis, M., and Slonim, R. (2012).

6 For more recent trends, see Jaworski, 2021, p. 11.

7 The language was nearly identical in the 2013 annual report: "As self-sufficiency is not operationally or economically feasible in a volunteer, non-remunerated model, Canadian Blood Services strives to maintain a sufficiency of 30% for Ig" (CBS, 2013).

8 For this and other arguments about spaces for altruism, see Faraci and Jaworski (2021).

9 Recipients of blood or plasma may feel obligated to reciprocate the benefit they received. The fact that donors are anonymous may result in this sense of gratitude generalizing to the community, rather than to the specific person or persons whose blood or plasma they benefited from. So a fitting return for the benefit may be to do a similar act of anonymous or non-anonymous altruism.

10 For a detailed explanation of why Radin's (and also Elizabeth Anderson's (1990)) views require an empirical mechanism, and why that mechanism has to be the framing effect, see Gold (2020).

11 It should be noted that there is something incongruous or maybe self-effacing about this argument. The relevant altruism here is the desire to promote patient health, not the desire to promote community solidarity. If commercial collections are better with respect to patient health, then we are thwarting a part of the genuine altruist's objective for the sake of community solidarity via the appearance of altruism. This is like hijacking the vehicle they choose to attain their end for an end not of their choosing.

12 This argument does not suggest that the ability to express altruism and community solidarity have greater weight than patient health. To tip a scale, it may sometimes be enough for these values to have some weight, however little in comparison with patient health. This is especially so in contexts where one country has the option of purchasing finished therapies or raw plasma from a different country where compensation is allowed. We can preserve domestic expression of altruism and domestic community solidarity while ensuring patient health by relying on non-domestic commercial plasma collections.

13 For this distinction, see Jonker (2019). "Indication" in this sense is about pointing to a non-socially constructed fact (like, to use Jonker's example, smoke indicating fire) rather than pointing to a socially-constructed or conventional fact (like smoke indicating a call to war) which may be merely "expressed".

14 Julian Jonker (2019) calls it the "collapsing move". The "collapsing move" is in Brennan and Jaworski (2015, and 2016).

15 Just as the words that we use can be changed. If the use of market rhetoric to describe commercial plasma collections undermines altruism and community solidarity, but these kinds of collections are better with respect to promoting patient health than non-commercial plasma collections, then we should change the rhetoric we use, rather than ban commercial plasma collections. Considerations like this one are why I insist on using "compensated donation" rather than "plasma vending" or "paid plasma" or "selling". The latter comes with the potential danger of commodification, while the former seems less dangerous.

16 Lucie White (2015) notes the same possibility that non-commercial blood and plasma donations may not in fact be altruistic, recognizes the fact that only commercial plasma collections meet the needs of patients, but suggests a slightly different cultural work strategy: "reconceptualizing all types of blood and plasma donation as essentially the same rather than as fundamentally different; both involve benefits for the donor, and benefits for others. This could allow us to reframe paid plasma donation in a way that makes it easier for people to reconcile this activity with their self-conception and deeply held values, better allowing them to make a wholehearted, autonomous decision to engage in this practice" (pp. 397–398). If this reconceptualization also underwrites community solidarity, then this is an alternative meaning revision possibility to consider.

17 A variety of patient organizations mainly in the US, but also some in Canada and European Union, are currently engaged in attempting to construct an archetype of the paid plasma donor as a "hero", an archetype of paid plasma donation as a prosocial practice that an altruist should consider choosing. This effort, and others like it, may fail. It may be very difficult to change the cultural fact, the stereotype of the money-oriented plasma seller may be deep. But so might the legal status of commercial plasma centres, especially in the United States. It may be as difficult to try to change the meaning of commercial donation as it is to try to prohibit commercial plasma collections in the US. If this difficulty doesn't count against the argument for legal prohibition, then it shouldn't count against the argument for meaning revision.

18 For example, Stephan Dressler (1999) writes, "In general, there is no payment to whole-blood donors, but plasma donors may receive remuneration … as compensation for their time. Many in Germany do not consider this 'payment'" (p. 192).

19 Milot (2010) discusses several cases like, for example, the 1954 decision in *Perlmutter v. Beth David Hospital* that created a "sales/service" distinction. Martha Perlmutter had received a tainted blood transfusion, and so took the hospital to court. The argument was that she purchased blood, which was a product, and so was subject to strict liability under products liability law. The court rejected the argument by saying Perlmutter paid for a service, not for a product, and so products liability law did not apply. In 1970, Dorothy Garber was charged with tax evasion for failing to declare the significant payments she received for donating plasma. On appeal, she argued that she had sold property, and so was subject only to capital gains tax, but that the "basis" she had in her property was equal to the payment she received ($75,000–90,000 over several years), and so there was no gain on the capital to tax. The court rejected this argument, saying that she was not selling property but was selling services, or her time and effort.

20 In the US and Canada, the regulations permit twice weekly donations, with 48 hours in between, up to 104 times per year.

21 See, for example, Schreiber and Kimber (2017), which concluded that "frequent donation does not adversely impact iron stores". See also Laub et al. (2010), which found significant protein differences between frequent plasmapheresis donors and less-frequent donors but concluded that "Whether these significant differences have relevant health implications for the donors is questionable". They recommended further study.

22 See a discussion of this in Buyx (2009), White (2015), and Weimer (2015).

23 For similar arguments, see Chapter 21 by Stephen Wilkinson in this volume.

24 This way of addressing the autonomy and the related undue inducement concerns would also go some way in addressing Richard Titmuss' worry that paid systems will have the poor provide blood for the rich. But it doesn't apply anyways, since Canada and the European jurisdictions with commercial plasma collections have universal health care systems that provide therapies to rich and poor alike, while in the US therapies are covered by Medicare and Medicaid.

25 For responses to a wider variety of wrongful exploitation objections to commercial plasma collections, see Wells and Jaworski (forthcoming).

26 It is not clear that we need to redesign any of the commercial models. As it is, the compensation or remuneration for plasma seems like a fair deal. From one perspective, the amount is higher than the minimum wage in any of the jurisdictions where this practice is permitted. From a different perspective, donor compensation or remuneration is the highest cost for these companies, higher than employee,

infrastructure, marketing, and other costs. While we do not have access to the internal revenue and expense details, profit appears to be less than the amount given to donors per litre of plasma. Finally, as some have pointed out, including Panitch and Horne (2019, p. 4) specifically with respect to plasma, even if whatever amount is given to donors strikes you as unfair, any number is less unfair than the $ 0 given by non-commercial plasma collectors.

27 This argument will not apply to cases like that of the United Kingdom. When the UK shuttered domestic plasma collections in 1998 as a result of an outbreak of variant Creutzfeld-Jakob Disease, they did not indirectly rely on commercial plasma collections in the US. The UK government purchased and operated commercial plasma collections in the US for the benefit of UK patients. They sold all but a 30% interest in 2013, and fully divested in 2018. The French government, meanwhile, is the largest shareholder in LFB Plasma, a commercial plasma collector with three locations in Florida in the US.

28 Canadian Blood Services used to purchase recovered plasma from the American Red Cross, a non-commercial collector. However, this was abandoned probably because the volume was small and was likely more expensive than purchasing finished therapies from the commercial sector.

29 For example, New Zealand Blood Services has been trying to return to full self-sufficiency since they lost that status in 2014. These efforts have managed to increase domestic non-commercial plasma collections by around 5%, but demand increased by more than 5%, and so New Zealand's reliance on the US grew. Cases like New Zealand's are rare, with most countries simply increasing their dependence on US plasma without even trying to address their domestic plasma collection deficit.

30 White (2015), writing about Canada, makes a similar point:

> In a situation where the basic needs of the population are met in the vast majority of cases, where there are other opportunities to procure the income that could be gained through payment for plasma, and where the financial incentive is quite small, it is less clear that this option will prove irresistible, and thus coercive. (p. 391)

References

Anderson, E. (1990) "The ethical limitations of the market," *Economics & Philosophy* 6(2), pp. 179–205.

Andreoni, J. (1990) "Impure altruism and donations to public goods: A theory of warm-glow giving," *The Economic Journal* 100(401), pp. 464–477.

Archard, D. (2002) "Selling yourself: Titmuss's argument against a market in blood," *The Journal of Ethics* 6, pp. 87–102.

Ariely, D., Bracha, A., and Meier, S. (2009) "Doing good or doing well? Image motivation and monetary incentives in behaving prosocially," *The American Economic Review* 99(1), pp. 544–555.

Ballem, P., Decary, F., Sayers, M., and Robert P. (2018) "Protecting access to immune globulins for Canadians: Final report of the expert panel on immune globulin product supply and related impacts in Canada," *Health Canada*. Available at: https://donationethics.com/static/IGReport.pdf

Brennan, J. and Jaworski, P.M. (2015), "Markets without symbolic limits," *Ethics* 125(4), pp. 1053–1077.

Brennan, J., & Jaworski, P.M. (2016) *Markets Without Limits: Moral Virtues and Commercial Interests*. New York: Routledge.

Buyx, A.M. (2009) "Blood donation, payment, and non-cash incentives: Classical questions drawing renewed interest," *Transfusion Medicine and Hemotherapy* 36(5), pp. 329–339.

CBS Annual Report (2020–2021) "Changing Tomorrow," Canadian Blood Services.

CBS Annual Report (2013–2014). Canadian Blood Services.

CBS Annual Report (2012–2013). Canadian Blood Services.

Dooley, J., & Gallagher, E. (2021) *Blood Money: The Financial Implications of Plasma Sales for Individuals and Non-Bank Lenders*. Available at SSRN: https://ssrn.com/abstract=3940369 or http://dx.doi.org/10.2139/ssrn.3940369

Dressler, S. (1999) "Blood 'Scandal' and AIDS in Germany," In Feldman, E.A. and Ronald Bayer (eds.), *Blood Feuds*. Oxford: Oxford University Press.

Dworkin, G. (1994) "Markets and morals: The case for organ sales," In Dworkin, G. (ed.) *Morality, Harm, and the Law*. New York: Basic Books.

English, W. & P.M. Jaworski. Motives of paid and unpaid donors. Unpublished manuscript.

Espeland, W. (1987) "Blood and money: Exploiting the embodied self," in Fontana, A. and Joseph A. Kotarba (eds.) *The Existential Self in Society*. Chicago: University of Chicago Press, pp. 131–155.

Faraci, D., & Jaworski, P.M. (2021) "On leaving space for altruism," *Public Affairs Quarterly* 35(2), pp. 83–93.
Gold, N. (2020) "The limits of commodification arguments: Framing, motivation crowding, and shared valuations," *Politics, Philosophy & Economics* 18(2), pp. 165–192.
Jaworski, P.M. (2020) "Bloody well pay them: The case for voluntary remunerated plasma collections," *Adam Smith Institute & Niskanen Center*. Available at: https://static1.squarespace.com/static/56eddde762cd9413e151ac92/t/5ee543957ff72b39af3a76d6/1592083356837/Bloody+Well+Pay+Them+-+Peter+M.+Jaworski.pdf
Jaworski, P.M. (2021) "From deficit to contribution: the case for voluntary compensated plasma collections in Spain," *Institut Ostrom*. Available at: www.institutostrom.org/wp-content/uploads/2021/10/institut-ostrom-plasma-report-eng.pdf
Jaworski, P.M., & English, W. (2020) "The introduction of paid plasma in Canada and the U.S. has not decreased unpaid blood donations," SSRN. Available at: https://papers.ssrn.com/sol3/papers.cfm?abstract_id=3653432
Jonker, J. (2019) "The Meaning of a market and the meaning of 'meaning'," *Journal of Ethics & Social Philosophy* 15(2), pp. 1–10.
Kelishomi, A.M., & Sgroi, D. (2022) "A field study of donor behavior in the Iranian kidney market," *Institute of Labor Economics Discussion Paper Series*. Retrieved from https://docs.iza.org/dp15806.pdf
Kretzmann, M. (1992) "Bad blood: The moral stigmatization of paid plasma donors," *Journal of Contemporary Ethnography* 20(4), pp. 416–441.
Lacetera, N., Macis, M., & Slonim, R. (2012) "Will there be blood? Incentives and displacement effects in pro-social behavior," *American Economic Journal: Economic Policy* 4(1), pp. 186–223.
Laub, R., Baurin, S., Timmerman, D., Branckaert, T., & Strengers, P. (2010) "Specific protein content of pools of plasma for fractionation from different sources: impact of frequency of donations," *Vox Sanguinis* 99(3), pp. 220–231.
McSweeney, B., Allegretti, J.R., Fischer, M., Xu, H., Goodman, K.J., Monaghan, T., McLeod, C., Mullish, B.H., Petrof, E.O., Phelps, E.L. & Chis, R. (2020) "In search of stool donors: a multicenter study of prior knowledge, perceptions, motivators, and deterrents among potential donors for fecal microbiota transplantation," *Gut Microbes* 11(1), pp. 51–62.
Milot, L. (2010) "What are we–laborers, factories, or spare parts? The tax treatment of transfers of human body materials," *Washington and Lee Law Review* 67(3), pp. 1053–1108.
Panitch, V., & Horne, L.C. (2019) "Paying for plasma: Commodification, exploitation, and Canada's plasma shortage," *Canadian Journal of Bioethics* 2(2), 1–10.
Radin, M.J. (1987) "Market-Inalienability," *Harvard Law Review* 100(8), pp. 1849–1937.
Sandhu, S. (2021) "NHS calls for plasma donors as hospitals face 'perilously' short supply of drugs after 20-year donation ban," *iNews.co.uk*, August 6. Available at: https://inews.co.uk/news/uk/nhs-plasma-donors-hospitals-short-supply-donation-ban-covid-antibodies-1134925
Schreiber, G.B., & Kimber, M.C. (2017) "Source plasma donors: A snapshot," *Transfusion* 57(S3). DOI: 10.13140/RG.2.2.32748.87683
Schreiber, G.B., Brinser, R., Rosa-Bray, M., Zi-Fan, Y., & Simon, T. (2018) "Frequent source plasma donors are not at risk of iron depletion: the ferritin levels in plasma donor (FLIPD) study," *Transfusion*, 58(4), pp 951–959.
Sher, G. (2013) "Prohibiting pay-for-plasma would harm patients," *The Toronto Star*, March 13. Available at: www.thestar.com/opinion/commentary/2013/03/13/prohibiting_payforplasma_would_harm_patients.html
Titmuss, R. (1970) *The Gift Relationship: From Human Blood to Social Policy*. London: Allen and Unwin.
Tobalina, B. (2021). "La falta de stock oblige a racionar la inmunoglobulina," *La Razon*, April 7. Available at: www.larazon.es/salud/20210704/ycjv4vfzwfgjpbjjz4kvvqkeve.html
Weimer, S. (2015) "'I can't eat if I don't plass': Impoverished plasma donors, alternatives, and autonomy," *HEC Forum* 27, pp. 361–385.
Wells, M., and Jaworski, P.M. (forthcoming) "Exploitation does not justify prohibiting Canadian paid plasma," In Ferguson, B., and Zwolinski, M. (eds.). *Exploitation: Perspectives from Politics, Philosophy, and Economics*. Oxford: Oxford University Press.
White, L. (2015) "Does remuneration for plasma compromise autonomy?" *HEC forum* 27(4), pp. 387–400.

19

GAMETES

Commodification and the fertility industry

Kimberly D. Krawiec

Introduction

In August 2021, the Ethics Committee of the American Society for Reproductive Medicine (ASRM) published its most recent opinion on financial compensation of oocyte donors (hereafter, "egg donors"), replacing its earlier, 2016, guidance.[1] For those not steeped in the historical controversy surrounding payment to egg donors in the United States, the document is likely uneventful. Indeed, year after year much of the guidance has been a cut and paste job from prior years, dating back to the first such guidance, issued in 1994 (Ethics Committee, 1994). But for careful followers of this history, the tone and substance of the guidance arguably represent a sea change.

Most notably, the new guidelines remove the analogy to sperm donation for purposes of determining ethical egg donor compensation and abandon all attempts to quantify ethical payments to egg donors, fully removing all vestiges of the controversial, and likely illegal, limits on egg donor compensation that were the basis of an antitrust class action suit filed in 2012 (*Kamakahi v. ASRM*, 2012). In addition, by emphasizing that egg donors provide a valuable service and deserve compensation for their time and risk and by noting that commodification objections are rarely raised in connection with sperm donors, the guidelines represent a much more accepting, and less conflicted, view of compensated egg donation.

This chapter uses the development and eventual abandonment of these ASRM pricing guidelines over more than twenty-five years as a lens through which to understand commodification debates in the gamete market. In the United States, as in much of the world, oocyte commodification has generated far more controversy than sperm commodification.[2] Although the larger per transaction sums and physically invasive nature of egg donation likely contribute to this difference, researchers have argued that presumptions regarding the differing motivations of women and men engaged in reproductive activity on behalf of others significantly shapes ethical debates about gamete commodification as well. This chapter also pays special attention to the events giving rise to, the settlement of, and arguments raised (and rejected) in the *Kamakahi* litigation. Although the case settled after surviving a motion to dismiss, *Kamakahi* should be of great interest to all observers of contested markets because the defences raised by ASRM and the Society For Assisted Reproductive Technology (SART) in the suit are the same commodification, undue influence, exploitation, and access arguments that scholars have debated for decades.

DOI: 10.4324/9781003188742-24

Part I of this chapter discusses sperm markets. Part II turns to egg markets. Part III discusses the ASRM payment guidelines in detail, including the nationwide class action that ultimately prompted their abandonment. Part IV analyzes the commodification, undue influence, coercion, and exploitation defenses offered in defence of the guidelines, demonstrating that price caps are an especially poor (and self-interested) response to these concerns. Part V concludes.

Sperm markets

Artificial insemination, first developed and used in animals, gained popularity as a treatment for infertility in both Britain and the United States in the first half of the twentieth century (Haimes, 1993, Swanson, 2014). Sperm donation was not initially viewed as a commercial venture. Instead, sperm banking began as a step in the artificial insemination process for husbands otherwise unable to inseminate their wives. Only when banking by the husband was impossible would infertile couples turn to close friends or family members to provide sperm (Spar, 2006).

But some doctors and scientists recognized the benefits of relying on professional sperm donors. These pioneers faced a variety of hurdles, including the then low success rates of artificial insemination, medical beliefs that most childlessness was due to female infertility, and social and religious opposition to the use of non-husband sperm as adulterous and producing illegitimate offspring (Swanson, 2014). Nonetheless, some doctors provided artificial insemination using professional donors as a treatment for infertility and many patients sought such treatments. Unlike today's sperm industry which, like the egg industry, provides consumer choice over donors, U.S. doctors during this period exercised physician control over the donor selection process and resisted efforts at private collection that offered more consumer choice. Although the eugenics possibilities of such an approach were clear, this was considered a feature, rather than a bug, at least until eugenics discourse fell out of favour in the United States after World War II (Swanson, 2014).

For this reason, some trace the modern business of sperm donation to the Repository for Germinal Choice, started in the late 1970s by a retired optometrist and eugenicist, Robert Graham. Graham believed that, because humans had conquered their natural environment and implemented social welfare programs, natural selection could no longer be relied on to prevent "retrograde humans" from reproducing. Although Graham's initial plan was to collect sperm donations only from Nobel Prize winners, few were willing to associate with Graham's Repository and many were too old to have usable sperm. Eventually, Graham expanded to include sperm from scientists, former athletes, and business moguls, and advertised for mothers (who had to be well-educated and married to infertile men) in Mensa magazine. The Repository generated significant controversy in the 1980s, due to its avowed eugenics purpose and the involvement of William Shockley – a retired physicist whose views on race, genes, and intelligence had made him a national embarrassment – who was the only Nobel Laureate willing to publicly admit his donation to the Repository. The Repository closed in 1999, claiming to have produced 229 children (none of them fathered by Nobel winners) (Plotz, 2006).

Though Graham's Repository neither paid donors nor charged for sperm (beyond an application fee and shipping and storage costs), it helped set the stage for an active, modern sperm market by introducing the possibility of anonymous donation by men with particular, desired traits and characterized, not by the limited offerings at the doctor's office, but by customer choice from an array of catalogue listings. Today, the sperm business consists almost entirely of free-standing banking centers unconnected to any specific fertility clinic, serving customers that include, not only the infertile heterosexual couples for whom the market first developed, but single women and lesbian couples, among whom demand has surged in recent decades (Krawiec, 2009a).

Other than U.S. Food and Drug Administration (FDA) attempts to control the spread of infectious disease, there is little regulation of the sperm market in the United States. Unlike many other countries that impose limits on who may donate, who may purchase, how much will be paid, how many offspring can be born from any single donor, and whether anonymity is permitted, in the United States such matters have historically been left to the decisions of individual providers. Although ASRM promulgates donation guidelines – for example, their guidelines limit a single donor to 25 births per population of 800,000 – there is no enforcement mechanism, and such limits are often violated (Practice Committee, 2021; Zhang, 2021). As a result, the lack of regulation in the United States is increasingly met with criticism, including calls to regulate donor anonymity, the number of offspring (Cahn, 2009), and posthumous conception (Cohen, 2007; Simana, 2018).

Although some countries prohibit payment to sperm donors, in the United States, sperm donor compensation has largely proceeded without significant controversy. Instead, ethical debates about sperm markets historically centered on whether sperm donation is sinful or deviant (because it requires masturbation) or produces illegitimate offspring (Haimes, 1993, Swanson, 2014). Indeed, as discussed in more detail below, sperm commodification arguably performs a normalizing function, replacing unacceptable donor motives associated with sexual impulses or an egoistic belief in one's genetic superiority with a more acceptable profit motive (Haimes, 1993, Almeling, 2007, 2011).

Egg markets

In the egg market's early years, the term "donation" was a literal one – women unable to produce their own eggs would sometimes seek the help of a close friend or family member who bore genetic characteristics similar to their own. But so long as egg donation remained limited to altruistic transfers from known contributors, human eggs were fated to be undersupplied. Unlike sperm donation, egg donation is a complicated process with some health risks. Relatively few women are willing to undergo the process on behalf of a stranger in the absence of financial compensation. This is illustrated by the experiences of countries that have banned or severely limited compensation for egg donation, nearly all of which face egg shortages, generating a growing reproductive-tourism trade (Platts et al., 2021).

In contrast to sperm markets, egg markets have been a frequent target of commodification critics. Egg donor compensation has generated significant controversy, even in the United States where donor compensation is legal in every state but Louisiana. It was not obvious this would be the case, given that ASRM has publicly argued since at least 1994 that payments to egg donors are ethically justified, so long as they represent "reimbursement for expenses, time, risk, and inconvenience associated with the donation", rather than "compensation to donors for providing the oocyte itself" (Ethics Committee, 1994, p. 48S). Notably, in the ASRM Ethics Committee's 125-page first public statement on the ethics of assisted reproductive technologies, only two sentences address compensation to egg donors and the only concern or limitation mentioned regarding such compensation is that it should not represent direct payment for oocytes. It is wholly silent on the concerns that would come to dominate later discussions about egg donor compensation, such as commodification, price limits, exploitation, and undue inducement (Ethics Committee, 1994).

Very quickly, however, controversy about egg donor payments arose, first within particular geographic markets, and then nationally. From the start, some questioned whether such objections were really ethical concerns, as opposed to business concerns. For example, controversy erupted in

1998 when a New Jersey-based fertility clinic, the Saint Barnabas Medical Center, doubled its egg donor compensation rates, from $2500 to $5000, in apparent violation of a "community standard", prompting objections that such payment "potentially exploits or even coerces young women to participate" (Sauer, 1999a p. 7). In addition, some fertility specialists worried that:

> Inevitably, all of us will be forced to raise our compensation rates to meet this challenge. Most importantly, and most unfortunately, these expenses will have to be passed on directly to our patients, who are already spending considerable sums of money to seek this procedure.
>
> (Sauer, 1999a, p. 7)

The ensuing debate (during which many fertility doctors openly discussed fertility industry attempts to control egg prices) quickly garnered newspaper and other media attention, and generated arguments in major medical journals (Kolata, 1998, American Public Media). It also may have prompted ASRM to formally wade into the debate. One incensed fertility specialist, Dr. Mark Sauer, wrote letters to the current, past, and incoming presidents of ASRM and SART (The Society for Assisted Reproductive Technology), to prominent academics and medical journal editors, and to directors of fertility centres in the New York area (Sauer, 1999b). Dr. Paul Bergh of the Saint Barnabas Medical Center, the centre that started the controversy by first raising rates, responded that Dr. Sauer's concern was prompted more by business interests and his own center's physical proximity to Saint Barnabas than by a concern for egg donors. He also noted that many reputable centres across the country already paid similar rates to egg donors and that Dr. Sauer's clinic was one of the first in the New York metropolitan area to match the new, higher, Saint Barnabas compensation levels (Bergh, 1999).

The payment guidelines

Payment caps

In 2000, shortly after the events in New York described above, the ASRM Ethics Committee weighed in again on the ethics of egg donor compensation. After cataloging a litany of objections to paid egg donation, including undue inducement, exploitation, incentivizing a failure to disclose medical information, and commodification concerns – "the prevailing belief that gametes ought not to become products bought and sold in the marketplace" – the committee determined that egg donor compensation, within limits, was ethically warranted (ASRM Ethics Committee, 2000, p. 216). It analogized egg donation to sperm donation, noting that a study had concluded that sperm donors earned an hourly average of $60 to $75 in 2000. The same study estimated that egg donors spend fifty-six hours in a medical setting per donation cycle. If egg donors were paid the same hourly rate as sperm donors, then they should earn $3360 to $4200 per egg-donation cycle. However, because egg donation involves a time commitment, risk, and discomfort not associated with sperm donation, the committee determined that egg donors may deserve higher amounts, concluding:

> Although there is no consensus on the precise payment that oocyte donors should receive, at this time sums of $5,000 or more require justification and sums above $10,000 go beyond what is appropriate.
>
> (ASRM Ethics Committee, 2000, p. 219)

The Committee did not explain why sperm donor compensation was a relevant benchmark for calculating appropriate levels of egg donor compensation or why these amounts might represent a reasonable premium for the additional burdens faced by egg donors but not sperm donors. These guidelines were reiterated with only small changes in 2004 and 2007 (Ethics Committee, 2004, Ethics Committee, 2007).

Enforcement efforts

As already noted, ASRM has no independent enforcement abilities. Enforcement of the egg donor compensation guidelines thus largely occurred through The Society for Assisted Reproductive Technology (SART). In 2018, the most recent year for which membership is reported on the SART website, 86% of IVF clinics in the United States were members of SART, although at one time the percentage was as high as 90% (SART, 2021).

SART sets guidelines for best practices in the field of assisted reproductive technology as a requirement of membership. Among those requirements are the guidelines on the ethical compensation of egg donors promulgated by ASRM. Thus, at one time more than 90% of IVF clinics in the United States had entered into agreements to cap egg donor compensation.

It is unclear whether these enforcement efforts were effective, given the limited systematic data on egg donor compensation. Although the available evidence is consistent with some price suppression, that data is largely self-reported by ASRM-member fertility centres (that may have been reluctant to report pricing information that evidenced a violation of the compensation guidelines) or based on unverified price information gathered from websites, newspapers, and other venues (Krawiec, 2009b).

Lawsuit and aftermath

Against this backdrop, in April 2012, Lindsay Kamakahi and Justine Levy brought a class action on behalf of themselves and other egg donors against ASRM and SART, challenging the guidelines on the ethical compensation of egg donors as an illegal price-fixing agreement in violation of United States antitrust laws (*Kamakahi*, 2012). These laws prohibit business practices that unreasonably restrict competition and result in higher consumer prices for products and services. In March 2013, the court denied the defendants' motion to dismiss the case and on February 3, 2015, the judge certified the class of all egg donors who donated within the United States between April 12, 2007, and February 3, 2015 (*Kamakahi*, 2013, *Kamakahi*, 2015).

In August 2016, the final settlement was approved, awarding attorneys' fees and $20,000 in monetary damages to the named plaintiffs. As part of the settlement, ASRM also agreed to eliminate the challenged compensation guidelines and refrain from setting similar guidelines in the future.[3] SART further agreed that it would not require as a condition of membership in SART that any clinic adhere to limits on dollar amounts paid to egg donors (*Kamakahi*, 2016). Promptly thereafter, ASRM issued new guidance on the ethical compensation of egg donors, removing the offending sentence that "total payments to donors in excess of $5,000 require justification and sums above $10,000 are not appropriate", as required by the settlement agreement. It did, however, retain the analogy to sperm donor compensation rates, concluding that "this analysis … would justify a payment of $3,360–$4,200 to oocyte donors" (Ethics Committee, 2016, p. 18). In 2021, ASRM issued updated guidance on egg donor compensation, finally removing any comparison to sperm donation rates and any mention of acceptable payment amounts (Ethics Committee, 2021).

Analysis: Commodification, undue influence, coercion, and exploitation

The fact that the ASRM pricing guidelines went unchallenged for over a decade is itself a profound statement about American uneasiness with the egg market. An open agreement among competitors to control prices, such as the agreement among SART-member fertility clinics to follow the ASRM price caps, is referred to in antitrust law as a "naked price fixing agreement". Such agreements are traditionally presumed illegal for a simple reason – it has long been accepted that such restraints on competition are injurious to the public, with few or no offsetting benefits. This is true whether the agreement is one to keep output prices high or, like the egg donor pricing guidelines, to keep input prices low (Krawiec, 2016).

Although the case settled after surviving a motion to dismiss, *Kamakahi* should be of great interest to all observers of contested markets because the defences raised by ASRM and SART in the suit are the same commodification, undue influence, exploitation, and access arguments that scholars have debated for decades and that were foreshadowed by the late 1990s dispute among New York-area fertility clinics discussed above. I consider these objections to compensated egg donation at length elsewhere and find them lacking (Krawiec, 2009b, Krawiec, 2015, Krawiec, 2016). Here, I review some of those arguments, with a focus on two points: (1) price caps are an especially poor (not to mention, self-interested) response to these asserted concerns and (2) there is a disparity in the treatment of egg and sperm donor compensation, even when the ethical objection – most notably, the commodification objection – applies equally to the provision of both eggs and sperm.

Commodification

Since the first public controversy about egg donor compensation in the late 1990s erupted in New York, commodification has been a purported rationale for capping egg donor compensation. In particular, the commodification of particular genetic traits has been seen as especially troubling. A full critique of the commodification objection, as applied to gametes or more generally, is beyond the scope of this chapter, though I (and many others) have criticized this argument at length elsewhere (Krawiec, 2009b, 2016, Brennan and Jaworski, 2015, Wilkinson, 2004). Here, however, my lens is narrower, with the primary goal of highlighting the shortcomings of the ASRM guidelines as a safeguard against commodification concerns, particularly as those guidelines were operationalized and applied.

Although "commodification", as a moral critique, has no single meaning, the term is often associated with conceptions of improper valuation – of treating something or someone as a mere commodity, an instrument of profit and use, rather than noninstrumentally, as the subject of love, dignity, or respect. (Sandel, 2012, Anderson, 1995). As already noted, this argument has been critiqued at length in the literature, in part because market exchange is neither a necessary nor a sufficient condition for treating something or someone as a commodity (See Vida Panitch's contribution to this volume, discussing corruption arguments in detail). Using the example of pets, Brennan and Jaworski (2015), demonstrate that items bought and sold in the marketplace need not be conceived of as mere instruments of commerce. And Wilkinson (2004) argues that people can and do instrumentally value and treat gifts or other items acquired through non-market transactions as commodities. Finally, scholars have written at length about the extent to which market participants and interested third parties shape institutions and transactions specifically with the goal of reinforcing, rather than undermining, the non-instrumental elements of the exchange

(Rossman, 2014). This is particularly true in the oocyte market, as has been well-documented (Almeling, 2007, Almeling, 2011, Krawiec, 2022).

Whatever the merits of that debate, an anti-commodification defence of the ASRM guidelines faces an additional hurdle – whereas typical commodification arguments contend that money, or market valuation, is inappropriate to the item or relationship in question, an anticommodification defence of the ASRM guidelines must contend that payment amounts over, but not below, the guideline's threshold are inappropriately commodifying.[4] Nonetheless, there are a few possible arguments worth considering. Nearly all of these arguments boil down to a concern about commodifying particular genetic traits.

ASRM has put forward two related anticommodification defences of the price caps worth considering. The first is that price caps avoid commodification concerns by ensuring that donors are compensated for their time and inconvenience in donating, and not for the oocytes themselves. Second, and relatedly, this purportedly avoids a market in specific, desired traits. As stated in the ASRM Motion to Dismiss:

> [U]nfettered payment of oocyte donors "implies that [oocytes] are property or commodities, and thus devalues human life."…Such payments also "could be used to promote the birth of persons with traits deemed socially desirable, which is a form of positive eugenics." The challenged ethical guidelines are intended to allay these potential concerns that egg donation … is a form of "selective breeding" by striking a balance that compensates egg donors for their time and inconvenience instead of compensating them for either the oocytes themselves or any supposedly desirable traits of the donor of particular oocytes.
>
> (Motion to dismiss at 13–14 (quoting ASRM Ethics Committee Report, 2007 at 306))

Both claims, however, are undermined by studies of the egg market both before and after the lifting of the price caps. Studies undertaken while the price caps were in effect show that many customers sought donors with specific traits, including intelligence, athletic ability, musical talent, or a specific race or gender profile (Flores, et al., 2014, Holster, 2008). This is not particularly surprising. Parents have always shown a willingness to pay to procure for their offspring a possibility of future advantage – whether through elite school tuition, private tutors, music and art lessons, or a "better" egg donor. And price caps, after all, don't prohibit variations in payment so long as the amount remains below the price cap. In other words, one donor may earn $3000 and another $5000, while still complying with the maximum payment limits.

Moreover, both before and after the removal of price caps, systematic studies show that egg pricing is largely driven by geographic location and prior successful donation, with an additional premium for particularly in-demand demographic groups, such as east Asian and Jewish donors (Johnson, 2017, Sanders, 2022). Indeed, a recent study of compensation rates at 500 fertility clinics and egg agencies seeking to determine the effects of the *Kamakahi* settlement found that, although compensation rates for first-time donors had increased since the price cap removal, most continued to offer prices below the upper bounds of the prior ASRM guidelines, even in the most competitive marketplaces. Moreover, some clinics have not increased their compensation levels in over a decade, thus resulting in an inflation-adjusted decrease in compensation (Sanders, 2022).

Perhaps the most serious criticism of a commodification defence of the ASRM guidelines is that there has been no similar attempt to control sperm donor compensation, though sperm markets similarly commodify reproductive material and fertility customers also seek out specific genetic or other traits in sperm donors. Indeed, this dichotomy was explicitly recognized by ASRM in its most recent ethical guidelines:

> Another ethical concern is that compensation for oocytes could imply that gametes are property or commodities that can be bought and sold and thus could devalue their inherent linkage with human life. At the outset, *it is noteworthy that this critique is rarely, if ever, levied against the practice of sperm donation and appears uniquely in the realm of oocyte donation.*
>
> (ASRM, 2021, p. 321. My emphasis added)

The disproportionate focus on the commodification of genetic traits in egg donation, as compared to sperm donation, is particularly ironic given the eugenics history that has plagued sperm donation since its earliest days (Swanson, 2014).

Undue influence and exploitation

ASRM and SART defended the compensation guidelines by claiming they prevented the undue influence and exploitation of egg donors (*Kamakahi*, 2013). As demonstrated by Cohen (2014), however, undue influence and exploitation represent different, potentially contradictory, concerns. Exploitation is generally a worry that one party to a transaction has been treated unfairly or received an unequal share of the bargain. Although exploitation concerns are not limited to payment terms (and could include, for example, working conditions or safety issues), in the context of payment, exploitation would be a concern that one party is paid too little (Wilkinson, 2016). Undue inducement, in contrast, is a claim that one party is paid too much – that is, donors who otherwise would not donate may do so only for the money and may ignore health risks or other dangers in the process. Cohen argues that, although price caps may be a response to undue inducement, price floors are a more appropriate remedy for exploitation worries (Cohen, 2014).

More fundamentally, however, payment caps are simply an ill-fitting solution to undue influence worries, and an even worse fit for exploitation concerns. Many countries prohibit payments to egg donors (and a lesser number to sperm donors) at least in part due to such concerns. Leaving aside the debates about whether such policies are well-founded, the ASRM guidance is more problematic because it assumes that these ill effects appear only at amounts above $5000, without regard to the donor's socio-economic status. But women with debts and fewer income opportunities may be influenced by the possibility of $5,000 when a busy high-income professional would not. The most likely effect of payment restrictions of this sort is to drive from the market egg donors of higher socioeconomic status, who are likely to be better-educated and better able to evaluate the risks of egg donation against the monetary benefits – in other words, they should be less susceptible to the undue influence of money. This intuition is borne out by the experience of those countries that have severely restricted egg donor compensation. In addition to creating egg shortages, donors in such countries are from lower socio-economic groups (Thaldar, 2020).

As to exploitation, Vida Panitch argues that it is not payment for bodily services that creates the unfairness and disrespect that gives rise to exploitation, but the *lack of payment*. Writing about the ASRM price caps (after their removal), Panitch argues:

> Altruistic rhetoric served as a tool of deception used by ASRM members to increase their profit margin at the expense of the women upon whose contributions their industry depends.

> When the reasons given for not compensating providers of bodily goods and intimate services is that the body is not the kind of thing that should be commodified, while the very people who make these anti-commodification claims are profiting from its commercial exchange, we have a deception that can produce the unfairness and disrespect necessary for exploitation.
>
> (Panitch, forthcoming)

Finally, there are many other avenues for reducing the possibility of undue influence or exploitation that do not involve capping payments to egg donors. For example, ASRM or SART could mandate the use of egg-donor advocates; adopt comprehensive and standardized disclosure requirements; improve counselling and legal representation; or adopt other measures to promote the informed and voluntary nature of each donation. In addition, minimum earning or net asset requirements could be employed to identify donors who appear financially needy or who have not carefully weighed the risks of donation. But neither organization has required any of these measures, focusing their efforts instead on controlling egg donor compensation.

Access

ASRM and SART also defended the egg donor pricing guidelines with an access rationale that dates back to the dispute among New York-area fertility professionals in the 1990s – that higher egg donor prices would increase the total costs of fertility treatments using donated eggs, thus disadvantaging customers. (*Kamakahi*, 2013) This claim is highly suspect. The effects of collusive buyers' agreements are well known: product scarcity, which deprives fertility treatment patients of the full range and number of donor eggs that would be available to them in a free market. Although this affects all purchasers of donated eggs, it disproportionately affects minority providers and customers, who are most likely to command prices in the upper ranges. Moreover, the precise effect of monopsony (the ability of a firm or firms to set input prices) on final output price varies depending on a variety of market conditions and does not necessarily reduce the price paid by consumers for the final product and may increase it. (Krawiec, 2015).

Moreover, it is notable that neither ASRM nor SART member-clinics pursued other mechanisms for reducing the consumer costs of fertility services using donor eggs, such as offering discounts on fertility services to infertile patients using donor eggs or setting up an ASRM fund to pay for some of the costs associated with fertility services or donor eggs for patients unable to afford them. Instead, the pricing guidelines constrain prices in only one-half of the total bundle of goods and services that make up the costs of fertility services using donor eggs (payments to egg donors) but not the other (payments to fertility centres). If access to reproductive technologies were really a meaningful concern for fertility centres, then they adopted a particularly poor mechanism for addressing them.

Conclusion

Understood within this historical context, the most recent ASRM opinion on financial compensation of oocyte donors is arguably an important breakthrough in the conception of egg donation. First, and most importantly, the most recent guidelines contain no mention of acceptable or recommended compensation levels, nor do they analogize egg donation to sperm donation for purposes of payment comparison. Second, the guidelines explicitly acknowledge for the first time, after decades of emphasizing commodification concerns, that such objections are rarely applied to sperm donation. Finally, the guidelines emphasized that a failure to treat egg donors as adult women capable of making their own risk-return tradeoffs regarding their bodies and their livelihood would be demeaning and unfair:

> The existence of a system of fair recompense within the context of a professional relationship shows respect for women's autonomy and honors their capacity to make informed choices about their bodies and economic lives.
>
> (ASRM, 2021, p. 322)

Notes

1 Consistent with common usage, this chapter will refer to all gamete providers as "donors", despite the fact that in the United States nearly all gamete donors are paid.

2 For example, although sperm donation is permitted in nearly every European country, egg donation is prohibited in several, including Germany, Norway, Switzerland, and Turkey. (Calhaz-Jorge, 2020).

3 The settlement did not award monetary damages to any other class members, who retained the right to sue for damages.

4 Some scholars do advocate for price caps, or price setting, as a means of balancing exploitation and coercion concerns, a point to which I return below.

References

Almeling, R. (2007) "Selling genes, selling gender: Egg agencies, sperm banks, and the medical market in genetic material," *American Sociological Review* 72(3), pp. 319–340.

Almeling, R. (2011) *Sex Cells*. Berkeley: University of California Press.

American Public Media (radio broadcast), American RadioWorks: The Fertility Race (Part 10), *The decision to donate – assessing the risks* available at http://americanradioworks.publicradio.org/features/fertility_race/part10/section3.shtml

Anderson, E. (1995) *Value in Ethics and Economics*. Cambridge, MA: Harvard University Press.

Bergh, P.A. (1999) "Indecent proposal: $5,000 is not "reasonable compensation" for oocyte donors – a reply," *Fertility & Sterility* 71, pp. 9–10.

Brennan, J. and Jaworski, P.M. (2015) *Markets Without Limits: Moral Virtues and Commercial Interests*. New York: Routledge.

Cahn, N. (2009) "Accidental incest: Drawing the line-or the curtain-for reproductive technology," *Harvard Journal of Law & Gender* 32, p. 59.

Calhaz-Jorge, C., De Geyter, C.H., Kupka, M.S., Wyns, C., Mocanu, E., Motrenko, T., Scaravelli, G., Smeenk, J., Vidakovic, S. and Goossens, V. (2020) "Survey on ART and IUI: legislation, regulation, funding and registries in European countries: The European IVF-monitoring Consortium (EIM) for the European Society of Human Reproduction and Embryology (ESHRE). *Human Reproduction Open* 1, p. 44.

Cohen, I.G. (2007) "The right not to be a genetic parent," *Southern California Law Review* 81, p. 1115.

Cohen, I.G. (2014) "Regulating the organ market: Normative foundations for market regulation," *Law & Contemporary Problems* 77, p. 71.

Ethics Committee of the American Society for Reproductive Medicine (1994) "Ethical considerations of assisted reproductive technologies," *Fertility & Sterility (Supplement 1)*, 62, p. 47S.

Ethics Committee of the American Society for Reproductive Medicine (2000) "Financial incentives in recruitment of oocyte donors," *Fertility and Sterility* 74(2), pp. 216–220.

Ethics Committee of the American Society for Reproductive Medicine (2004) "Financial incentives in recruitment of oocyte donors," *Fertility and Sterility* 82, pp. S240-S244.

Ethics Committee of the American Society for Reproductive Medicine (2007) "Financial compensation of oocyte donors," *Fertility and sterility* 88(2), pp. 305–309.

Ethics Committee of the American Society for Reproductive Medicine (2016) "Financial compensation of oocyte donors: An ethics committee opinion," *Fertility and Sterility* 106(7), pp. e15–e19.

Ethics Committee of the American Society for Reproductive Medicine (2021) "Financial compensation of oocyte donors: an ethics committee opinion," *Fertility and Sterility*, 116(2), pp. 319–325.
Flores, H., Lee, J., Rodriguez-Purata, J., Witkin, G., Sandler, B. and Copperman, A.B. (2014) "Beauty, brains or health: trends in ovum recipient preferences," *Journal of Women's Health*, 23(10), pp. 830–833.
Haimes, E. (1993) "Issues of gender in gamete donation," *Social Science & Medicine*, 36(1), pp. 85–93.
Holster, K. (2008) "Making connections: egg donation, the internet, and the new reproductive technology marketplace," *Patients, Consumers and Civil Society* 10, pp. 53–73.
Johnson, K.M. (2017) "The price of an egg: oocyte donor compensation in the US fertility industry," *New Genetics and Society* 36(4), pp. 354–374.
Kolata, G. (1998) "Price of donor eggs soars, setting off a debate on ethics," New York Times, Feb. 25.
Krawiec, K.D. (2009a) "Altruism and intermediation in the market for babies," *Washington & Lee Law Review* 66, p. 203.
Krawiec, K.D. (2009b) "Sunny Samaritans and egomaniacs: price-fixing in the gamete market," *Law & Contemporary Problems* 72, p. 59.
Krawiec, K.D. (2015) "Markets, morals, and limits in the exchange of human eggs," *Georgetown Journal of Law and Public Policy* 13, p. 349.
Krawiec, K.D. (2016) "Lessons from law about incomplete commodification in the egg market," *Journal of Applied Philosophy* 33(2), pp. 160–177.
Krawiec, K.D. (2022) "Markets, repugnance, and externalities," *Journal of Institutional Economics*, pp. 1–12.
Lindsay Kamakahi v. American Society for Reproductive Medicine, et al. (2012) Consolidated Amended Class Action Complaint, United States District Court for The Northern District of California, Case No. 11-cv-01781-JCS (April 12).
Lindsay Kamakahi v. American Society for Reproductive Medicine, et al. (2013) Order Denying Motion to Dismiss, United States District Court for The Northern District of California, Case No. 11-cv-01781-JCS (March 29).
Lindsay Kamakahi v. American Society for Reproductive Medicine, et al. (2015) Order Regarding Motions to Exclude Expert Opinions and Motion for Class Certification, United States District Court for the Northern District of California, Case No. 11-cv-01781-JCS (Feb. 13).
Lindsay Kamakahi v. American Society for Reproductive Medicine, et al. (2016) Final Order and Judgment by Chief Magistrate Judge Joseph C. Spero granting 225 Motion for Settlement, United States District Court for The Northern District Of California, Case No. 11-cv-01781-JCS (Aug, 26).
Panitch, V. (Forthcoming) "Decommodification as exploitation," In Ferguson, B. and Zwolinski, M. (eds.), *Exploitation: Perspectives from Politics, Philosophy, and Economics*, Oxford: Oxford University Press, ch. 12.
Platts, S., Bracewell-Milnes, T., Saso, S., Jones, B., Parikh, R. and Thum, M.Y. (2021) "Investigating attitudes towards oocyte donation amongst potential donors and the general population: A systematic review," *Human Fertility* 24(3), pp. 169–181.
Plotz, D. (2006) *The Genius Factory: The Curious History of the Nobel Prize Sperm Bank*. New York, Random House.
Practice Committee of the American Society for Reproductive Medicine and the Practice Committee for the Society for Assisted Reproductive Technology (2021), "Guidance regarding gamete and embryo donation," *Fertility & Sterility* 115, p. 1395.
Rossman, G. (2014) "Obfuscatory relational work and disreputable exchange," *Sociological Theory* 32(1), pp. 43–63.
Sandel, M.J. (2012) *What Money Can't Buy: The Moral Limits of Markets*, New York: Farrar, Strauss & Giroux.
Sanders, B.K. (2022) "Setting the price of fertility: Egg donor compensation following Kamakahi V. American Society for Reproductive Medicine," *Houston Journal of Health Law & Policy* 22, pp. 231–271.
Sauer, M.V. (1999a) "Indecent proposal: $5000 is not "reasonable compensation" for oocyte donors," *Fertility & Sterility* 71, p. 7.
Sauer, M.V. (1999b) "Letters to the editor: The debate continues," *Fertility & Sterility* 72, p. 182.
Simana, S. (2018) "Creating life after death: should posthumous reproduction be legally permissible without the deceased's prior consent?" *Journal of Law and the Biosciences* 5(2), pp. 329–354.
Society for Assisted Reproductive Technology, What is SART?, accessed December 11, 2021, www.sart.org/patients/what-is-sart/

Spar, D.L. (2006) *The Baby Business: How Money, Science, and Politics Drive the Commerce of Conception.* Boston: Harvard Business School Press.

Swanson, K. (2014) *Banking on They Body: The Market in Blood, Milk, and Sperm in Modern America.* Cambridge, MA: Harvard University Press.

Thaldar, D. (2020) "Egg donors' motivations, experiences, and opinions: A survey of egg donors in South Africa," *PLOS ONE* 15(1), p. e0226603.

Wilkinson, S. (2004) *Bodies for Sale: Ethics and Exploitation in the Human Body Trade*. London: Routledge.

Wilkinson, S. (2016) "Exploitation in international paid surrogacy arrangements," *Journal of Applied Philosophy* 33(2), pp. 125–145.

Zhang, S. (2021) The children of sperm donors want to change the rules of conception," *The Atlantic*, October 15, *available at* www.theatlantic.com/science/archive/2021/10/do-we-have-right-know-our-biological-parents/620405/

20
CONTRACT SEX

Laurie J. Shrage

Introduction

Sex transformed into a commodified service typically involves a customer and one or more providers. There are many kinds of sex work, such as exotic dancing, escort work, phone/virtual sex, and pornography, which do not involve in-person, fee-for-service intimacy with a customer. In this chapter, I will focus on "prostitution," which is understood to involve the sale and purchase of non-virtual sexual acts and is generally more restricted. I will refer to the provision of in-person sexual services to an individual primarily for economic gain as "contract sex," rather than as "prostitution" or "sex work," as a means of distinguishing this kind of commerce from other ways of commodifying sex. "Contract sex," like "contract pregnancy," is a more neutral term than "prostitution." It is also more comprehensive than "sex work," which emphasizes the role of service providers, whereas "contract sex" encompasses the roles of workers, customers, and business owners. Contracts may be formal or informal, and they invite us to focus on how their terms are structured, negotiated, and enforced, and to what goods and services they may apply.

In jurisdictions where initiating and executing commercial contracts for sex constitute criminal acts, providers, customers and their business associates must conduct their activities in "underground" or clandestine markets. In such contexts, contract sex is typically organized through informal networks that are, by virtue of its legal status, criminal or law-breaking. Where contract sex is legally tolerated, it is usually heavily regulated in ways that include restrictions on business locations, advertising placement, street solicitation, as well as special business licensing, state registries, mandatory health checks, taxation rates, and minimum age rules for workers and customers.

There is a growing consensus among human rights activists, feminists,[1] health organizations, and progressive democratic governments that soliciting or accepting payment for sex should not be a crime. Criminalizing the activities of service providers does little to protect them from harm and, instead, makes their livelihood much less safe by pushing it underground, and generally without deterring markets in sexual services.[2] However, there is much less agreement among social reformers about when offering money for sex is unacceptably exploitative or manipulative, and what should be done to prevent or discourage coercing sex with money. Debates among human and gender rights activists about contract sex typically remain stuck on whether to decriminalize

 DOI: 10.4324/9781003188742-25

the activities of all parties (see for example, North, 2019; NSWP 2013; Mac, 2018)—i.e., full or partial decriminalization—and rarely focus on the forms of commerce that should be permissible following decriminalization. The latter issue, often referred to as "legalization," raises questions about how governments should regulate an economic activity in order to serve and protect the public good, whereas decriminalization raises questions about fundamental human rights and civil liberties.

The lack of attention to fair and efficient legalization schemes leaves the public in the dark about what to expect were contract sex to become "legal," that is, legally tolerated and regulated. By contrast, recent debates over the decriminalization of cannabis, in the U.S. and elsewhere, have focused on alternative legalization schemes: who will be licensed to provide the goods and services, who will have access to them, what sort of products can be marketed and how to ensure their use will be healthy and safe, potential tax revenues, and so on. As with cannabis, decriminalizing contract sex would remove a substantial barrier to the operation of various kinds of commercial enterprises, and there are many different models for regulating businesses offering personal sexual services. Yet productive debate over different models for regulating contract sex has remained stuck due to concerns about whether legalization is desirable at all.

Paradoxically, most sex worker rights groups that advocate for decriminalization oppose legalization, by which they mean special regulations devised for contract sex. Their opposition stems from experience with existing regulatory schemes that impose onerous requirements on sex workers, and that perpetuate their social and economic marginalization. Yet the failure to propose new comprehensive regulatory mechanisms for various kinds of market activities that could follow the decriminalization of contract sex may be impeding efforts to win public support for its decriminalization. In the remainder of this chapter, I will consider the need for regulatory mechanisms specifically tailored to contract sex, and whether there are legalization schemes that can address the concerns of sex workers as well as the communities in which they work.

Decriminalization without legalization[3]

For the purpose of distinguishing decriminalization and legalization, consider recent changes to state policies regarding markets in cannabis products. At the time of writing, 19 U.S. states and the District of Columbia (and two U.S. territories) have decriminalized and legalized recreational marijuana use and markets (for adults), while 27 states have decriminalized the possession and medical use of small amounts of marijuana (Hartman, 2021). Legalization permits regulated commercial markets in cannabis products, whereas mere decriminalization removes state criminal penalties for the use or transfer of small quantities without remuneration, and otherwise limits the distribution of this substance to state-regulated medical programs. Although many sex worker organizations are advocating for decriminalization without legalization of contract sex, they also want sex workers to be able to seek remuneration for their services, and not primarily through medical programs. The only way to make sense of the position taken by many advocates for sex worker rights is that they are demanding the removal of criminal penalties for the sale or purchase of sexual services, but they do not want governments to devise and impose legalization schemes specific to their industry.

Juno Mac (2018), for example, refers to legalization as "back-door criminalization". Mac points out that many regulatory schemes impose requirements that make it difficult for service providers to comply with them, and therefore many workers remain vulnerable to arrest (see also Weitzer, 2011, pp. 100–102). The political philosopher Peter de Marneffe (2013) distinguishes two types of criminal laws pertaining to contract sex: those prohibiting the exchange of money for sex informally among individuals, and those prohibiting the operation of organized sex businesses where people sell or purchase sexual services (p. 30). There is also a third type of criminal law: laws that regulate commerce in sexual services, where it is decriminalized and formally organized commercial enterprises are permitted. Mac and many sex worker organizations oppose all three types of laws. Their position is that contract sex should be decriminalized and regulated like other commercial enterprises (e.g., minimum wage standards, general occupational health and safety rules, protections for customer privacy, reporting requirements for income and profits, and so on), but there should be no special regulations imposed on this industry.

Where contract sex has been legalized, there are many poorly designed regulatory schemes that perpetuate the social stigmas attached to those who do this work. Regulations that mandate health exams for service providers (but not for customers) suggest that providers are a source of disease or contamination.[4] Requiring registration for sex workers by a governmental authority creates public records that render providers vulnerable to discrimination throughout their lives. Requiring sex workers to work at licensed brothels rather than as independent contractors or through self-organized collectives allows relatively wealthier and socially more powerful business operators to control the terms of their work. Some zoning restrictions force providers to work in areas where they have substantial safety and security concerns, while curfew restrictions often perpetuate the notion that those involved in this work are a public nuisance or threat.

Nevertheless, most industries require regulations unique to their enterprises to protect public health and safety and avoid becoming a nuisance, such as the cannabis industry, the restaurant industry, the health care industry, and so on. For example, regulating cannabis may include independent third-party testing of products, limits on concentrations of psychoactive chemicals, customer age minimums, use instructions and warnings on packaging, and licensing requirements for sellers and producers. There are at least three dimensions of contract sex that call for unique regulatory mechanisms for any commercial enterprise. First, regulations are needed to protect both providers and clients from STIs, which could involve mandatory condom use for those activities known to put one at risk for an STI, or some process of STI testing for both clients and service providers. Second, regulations are needed to prevent businesses from selling sexual services to minors, employing minors, or conducting their businesses in a way that would expose minors to these adult activities. Regulations are also needed to stipulate who is a minor relative to this industry, e.g., someone under 18 or 21? Third, regulations are necessary to ensure that all sexual services offered or purchased are consensual. At a minimum, this should involve the right of workers to refuse services to potential clients, and implementing safeguards to ensure that providers are mentally competent, are not being trafficked, and are reasonably informed about the nature and risks of their work. As with other industries, levels of regulatory oversight could be tailored to the size of the enterprise, on the assumption that smaller enterprises of say, two or three people, present less of a threat to public welfare, and are more able to self-regulate than large business operations.

Not every decriminalization movement opens avenues to new kinds of regulated markets and commodities. For example, the decriminalization of adultery and some forms of "sodomy" (e.g., private sexual acts between people of the same legal sex) in the U.S. did not lead to new types of businesses. People are able to engage in adultery or queer forms of intimacy without commercial establishments providing venues or paid partners for these activities. Of course, dating sites, such as Ashley Madison and ones that cater to LGBTQ2S adults, can operate without fear of government sanction once the activities they facilitate are decriminalized, yet the operation of such commercial enterprises is not integral to these activities. Similarly, the decriminalization of abortion services did not lead to the development of new forms of commerce (despite coinage of the phrase "the abortion industry" by opponents), instead these services are distributed only through state licensed medical providers and clinics.

By contrast, part of the purpose of removing anti-prostitution laws is to allow adults to purchase or be paid for sex. "Prostitution," by definition involves accepting remuneration for sex primarily for economic gain, and not as a gift between lovers or friends. If no form of payment is offered or received, the activity is not "prostitution" but simply sex. Moreover, where the distribution of paid sexual services is limited to therapeutic or medical purposes (sometimes called "sexual surrogacy"), such activity is not normally regarded as "prostitution." Commercial activity is integral to "prostitution" (sex for pay among strangers) in a way that it is not for other formerly banned activities. Consequently, legalization in some form (i.e., tolerating and regulating commerce in sexual services, even if only minimally) is inseparable from the decriminalization of contract sex. Below I will consider three legal schemes for restricting contract sex.

Full vs. partial decriminalization

Decriminalizing contract sex is an important human rights goal. The criminal legal status of this activity does little to discourage contract sex, while making it less safe. Criminalization not only makes it more difficult for sex workers to access health and legal services,[5] but operating under the fear of arrest renders providers more vulnerable to economic exploitation and sexual assault. Furthermore, criminal prosecution and detention is highly damaging to individuals—psychologically, physically, emotionally, economically—and this arguably does more harm to these adults and their families than their voluntary participation in contract sex. Contract sex among consenting adults, and in contexts where providers have substantial control over their working conditions, is generally a non-violent and relatively safe activity (Moen, 2014), and it is safer for all parties where it is legal. Laws proscribing contract sex are therefore ineffective, overly paternalistic, and counterproductive.

Moreover, the enforcement of anti-prostitution laws targets the most socially vulnerable people and, consequently, is discriminatory and unfair. In the U.S., arrests and incarceration for "prostitution," like cannabis use, serve to immiserate communities of color. Emily Bazelon (2016) reports that, in 2014 and 2015 in New York City, 84% of those arrested on prostitution-related offenses were women of color, and 93% of those arrested for patronizing a prostitute were men of color. During those years, people of color accounted for 56% of the city's population. Bazelon describes a prostitution sting operation located near a homeless shelter in which one shelter resident, with no previous arrests for prostitution, accepted a bribe for sex.[6] According to Bazelon, "low-income women, women of color and trans people are most likely to be arrested" (2016; Butler, 2015).

By contrast, law enforcement officials rarely arrest "sugar babies" who offer sex to "sugar daddies" in exchange for living expenses, college tuition, or expensive goods, especially if they are middle class white women.[7] Yet these adults are also engaging in contract sex, often using internet websites to solicit men for mutual advantage. The discriminatory enforcement of both drug and prostitution laws compounds the disadvantages faced by people of colour, trans individuals, and low-income adults, because having a record of arrests and convictions can lead to further social and economic marginalization. All adults who engage in contract sex should be treated equally, whether they are a middle-class white sugar baby, a rich sugar daddy, or someone from a socially and economically disadvantaged group. Criminalizing the act of accepting or offering money for sex (see ProCon.org, 2018; Findlaw, 2019), whether such arrangements take place informally or as part of an organized commercial activity, has led to the persecution of people deemed bad or unworthy because of their sexual activities, or their gender, race, or income status. For this reason, full decriminalization of contract sex is important for combatting invidious forms of discrimination and protecting the human rights and dignity of historically marginalized groups.

While many human rights and feminist groups support decriminalizing contract sex, most have been hesitant to propose or endorse any scheme of legalization. For example, Amnesty International's 2016 "Policy on state obligations to respect, protect and fulfil the human rights of sex workers" states:

> Amnesty International (AI) does not take a position on the exact form that regulation of sex work should take, or whether it is necessary for states to develop regulations specifically designed for sex work, which are separate from the general laws that broadly regulate other businesses or employment practices in a jurisdiction.
>
> (Amnesty International, 2016, p. 3)

The language here reflects the opposition of sex worker rights groups to special regulatory schemes for their industry. Yet, the statement as a whole emphasizes the obligations of governments to respect the rights of sex workers to healthy and safe working conditions, prevent trafficking and forced labour, prevent the exploitation of children, and end the discriminatory treatment of sex workers.

The AI policy clarifies the organization's general position as follows:

> This policy does not argue that there is a human right to buy sex or a human right to financially benefit from the sale of sex by another person. Rather, it calls for sex workers to be protected from individuals who seek to exploit and harm them and it recognizes that the criminalization of adult consensual sex work interferes with the realization of the human rights of sex workers.
>
> (Amnesty International, 2016, p. 3)

Peter de Marneffe argues that laws which prohibit an individual from accepting payment for sex violate our right to "self-sovereignty" or to control over the use of our minds and bodies. He writes

> engaging in prostitution is a way of expressing a distinctive attitude toward one's body, one's sexuality, one's genitals, and creates a distinctive relationship between oneself and one's body and sexuality. It expresses a distinctive view about the value of one's sexuality: that it is properly employed to make money.
>
> (2013, p. 34)

However, the purchase of sex does not represent a distinctive attitude toward sex or one's body, according to de Marneffe. Consequently, laws that prohibit someone from offering payment for sex do not violate one's right to self-sovereignty, and laws prohibiting people from owning or operating a brothel also do not violate their basic rights because they do not prohibit anyone from entering sex markets, they merely limit how they do so. In short, for de Marneffe, the choice to provide sexual services for payment should be protected by the basic guarantees in liberal democracies to the freedom of sexual expression, whereas the choice to pay someone for sexual services, or make profits from the sexual labour of others, is not protected by such basic guarantees.

De Marneffe's arguments are consistent with the partial decriminalization of contract sex. Under such policies, criminal penalties are removed for the act of accepting payment for sex, but not for offering payment for sex or operating a business that facilitates such commerce. Several countries have now adopted policies of this sort (known as the Swedish or Nordic Model) for somewhat more paternalistic reasons than de Marneffe's. Many feminists who support this model view service providers as victims, and they characterize customers and brothel owners as sex offenders or predators who violate the rights of those who are "prostituted" (Nordic Model Now!). For de Marneffe, people who exercise their right of self-sovereignty by selling sex typically are choosing to engage in activities known to be harmful, and governments are justified in imposing heightened restrictions on these activities, such as recreational drug use, and the consumption of alcohol and tobacco products (2013, pp. 37–38).

Unfortunately, under partial decriminalization, it is unclear how service providers would find clients without subjecting the latter to possible criminal prosecution. If the service provider communicates that she accepts payment for sexual services and the client agrees to pay, has the latter offered payment as an inducement for sex with that provider, and thereby committed a crime? Because partial decriminalization creates legal jeopardy for clients, sex workers and their organizations generally oppose it. Some argue that partial decriminalization forces service providers to work in ways that are unsafe (e.g., in remote areas, without police protection) in order to protect their clients. In this respect, governments that adopt partial decriminalization fail to promote safe and just working conditions, and subject workers themselves to arrest for activities related to their work. For example, sex workers may rent premises where they perform their work with other workers, share their income with friends and associates, and so on—all of which could be viewed as operating a brothel.

Under partial decriminalization, accepting payment for sex is permitted, but most of the related activities that allow sex workers to exercise their bodily autonomy and earn a living in a safe and dignified way remain illegal. This situation subjects the clients and coworkers of sex workers, and potentially the latter as well, to criminal prosecution. By contrast, legally permitting people to purchase sex or earn income from assisting service providers need not be justified by asserting a basic human right to such goods or services, but rather in terms of avoiding making contract sex risky and dangerous for those who choose to participate. Proponents of the Nordic Model view contract sex as inherently violent and victimizing, and aim to suppress the demand for it by criminalizing the activities of customers and pimps, but not the alleged victim. But the assumption that contract sex is an inevitably violent and victimizing activity, or that providers lack autonomy, is contested by sex workers and their labour organizations.

Some U.S. states have only partially decriminalized the use and distribution of cannabis products, and do not permit their recreational use or the commercial operations that would facilitate such consumption. These jurisdictions allow only for the medical production and distribution of marijuana. However, in many states, the requirements for medical access are loosely enforced, so that individuals who can afford to pay for a doctor's prescription can purchase cannabis products.[8] Consequently, limiting this industry to medical production and distribution does not effectively deter recreational use or "self-medication," but it makes obtaining legal cannabis products more time-consuming and expensive. Such supply and distribution channels disadvantage those with fewer financial resources, while providing relatively easy access for those who are well off. Moreover, the profits from medical marijuana go to doctors and wealthy pharmaceutical companies, rather than to less well off, or less socially powerful, entrepreneurs.

Partial decriminalization for contract sex would have a similar impact. Socially well-connected and savvy sex workers and their friends or partners with financial means would be able to pay for discreet ads, personal security, and other business services without facing criminal sanctions for "running a business." But sex workers who are more needy or less savvy would likely run afoul of laws suppressing business-type activities, such as public soliciting, or renting premises for the purpose of engaging in contract sex. In other words, people who are most dependent on contract sex for their survival would be least likely to find safe and economically feasible ways to do it. For these reasons, sex worker organizations generally oppose all laws that criminalize the activities and enterprises of sex workers and their associates.

Full decriminalization with legalization

Adrienne Davis (2015) claims that "in the arena of sex work, the feminist regulatory imagination remains stuck" (p. 1202). Feminists who want to abolish prostitution have won approval for partial decriminalization schemes, such as the Nordic model, while feminists who are advocating for full decriminalization have offered no new regulatory proposals.[9] Davis argues that pro-sex-work feminists need to move beyond the abolition/decriminalization debate and decide which legal markets should exist. Some sex workers may want to operate as independent contractors, similar to Uber drivers and Airbnb hosts, while others may want the benefits of hired employees. Some may want to work from home, or where their clients choose, or at an established and well-managed business location.

Davis develops "a sexual geography approach that parses sex work according to its institutional form and how that form affects worker risk" (2015, p. 1258). This approach distinguishes different kinds and levels of risk involved with different types of sex work (e.g., home-based, brothel, or outcall work), and proposes regulatory rules appropriate to each that can reduce these risks. For example, with some forms of contract sex, the risk of STI transmission may be negligible (e.g., BDSM). With other forms, this risk may be significantly higher, as well as the risk of economic exploitation (e.g., brothel work). The risks posed to one's personal safety can also vary (e.g., outcall vs. brothel work). Regulatory mechanisms can be tailored to minimize the risks in different kinds of settings.

Davis's approach recognizes that legalization schemes need to be feasible, in the sense that those whose activities they regulate are able to comply with them. Otherwise, as Mac points out, sex workers could be regularly subject to arrest and penalties for non-compliance. The sexual geography approach is also consistent with the 2016 AI policy, which commands governments to uphold the following principles in regulating sex work:

- "Respect and protect the right of sex workers to just and favourable conditions of work;
- Ensure that regulatory frameworks comply with international human rights law and that the safety and fulfilment of sex workers' human rights is the paramount objective for any such regulations;
- Ensure the meaningful participation of and consultation with sex workers, including those facing multiple forms of discrimination, in the development of any regulatory frameworks; and
- Recognize the rights of sex workers to associate and to form and/or join trade unions" (Amnesty International, 2016, p. 15).

I am suggesting that partial decriminalization without legalization does not fulfil these principles. First, countries that have adopted partial decriminalization have not ensured the meaningful participation of sex workers in the creation and implementation of these laws.[10] Partial decriminalization, for all the reasons given above, does not provide sex workers with "just and favourable conditions of work," or guarantee their safety and ongoing consent to engage in such work. Moreover, without legalization in some form, with designated venues or legal places of employment, the possibility for sex workers to form or join trade unions is significantly diminished.

Sex worker rights organizations, which understand best the sexual geography of their industry, together with their human rights allies and other public partners (health care experts, law enforcement, business leaders, community groups, and so on) need to work out the details of the regulatory structures that will apply to this industry in different jurisdictions. The evolution from criminalization with substantial penalties (including incarceration) to legal toleration is unlikely to occur without a detailed roadmap for how such commerce will be regulated in order to protect the interests of all parties. The movement to decriminalize contract sex should learn from other successful decriminalization movements, especially the recent successes of the cannabis industry as I've suggested above. In states that tolerate both its recreational use and the businesses that facilitate such activities, many cannabis-derived chemicals and products have been reclassified from the most restricted group of substances to much less restricted categories, similar to alcohol products or over-the-counter pharmaceuticals. This reclassification, with its potential for new forms of commerce to emerge, did not happen without detailed proposals from the industry and its supporters for some kind of special regulatory apparatus. Just taking one state, Colorado, as an example, the "legalization scheme" includes licensing for businesses and their employees, restrictions on public consumption, restrictions on cultivation and product design, third-party testing of products, a "marijuana enforcement division" to provide public oversight, and a community-driven process for developing and approving the rules for this new industry (Colorado Department of Revenue, 2021; Leafly, 2020).

The opposition by sex worker rights groups to special regulation for the sale and purchase of sex creates a substantial obstacle for the community-driven process of devising the industry rules. Sex workers and their organizational representatives need to be part of the rule-making process in order to ensure that their human rights and economic interests are protected. Demanding full decriminalization, without a detailed plan or process for creating and implementing regulations specific to the needs and challenges of this industry, is unlikely to win public support. Both cannabis consumption and sex work have been associated historically with numerous social ills, including addiction, broken families, immorality, and so on, and efforts to decriminalize these activities need to address such fears. The cannabis industry has been especially resourceful in assuring the public about the safety of their products, in part by accepting substantial restrictions on how they are produced and distributed. Sex workers need to debate the rules they will accept and that will assure the public that their businesses can operate in ways that protect the health and safety of all parties, including uninvolved third parties.

Toxic markets and special regulation

Debra Satz (2010) defends governmental interventions into markets that go beyond making them safe, efficient, and competitive. Satz has argued that liberal democratic governments should block or restrict markets that are toxic to shared moral values and basic human rights. Markets of this sort typically exploit and worsen the social vulnerabilities of people, depend upon the "weak agency" of participants, pose greater than normal risks to participants, or re-enforce the subordination of groups that have suffered historical discrimination (p. 98). Satz's criteria for identifying toxic or noxious markets are useful for thinking about general governmental constraints on markets in liberal democratic societies, but they are also helpful for thinking about how to configure some regulations specific to contract sex.

Liberal democratic societies need not tolerate markets that depend upon a supply of people who are desperate and destitute, for example, markets in babies (see Chapter 22 of this volume), and bodily organs (see Chapter 17 of this volume), and should instead aim to ameliorate the conditions that lead to such markets. Some markets in sexual services involve predatory practices and seek out participants who are young and inexperienced, have addiction or mental health problems, are socially isolated and economically needy, or are uneducated and lack access to the information needed to understand the consequences of their decisions. Vulnerable people may enter such markets voluntarily, but they are "weak agents" and some markets maintain or worsen their vulnerability. If all markets in sexual services were predatory in these ways, then there would be good justification for blocking them.[11] However, the existence of sex worker organizations across the globe that defend the dignity of their work, and call upon societies to recognize the basic civil and human rights of sex workers, suggests that not all sex workers are "weak agents" or extremely vulnerable people (NSWP, 2021; Beloso, 2012). In order to address the worries of those who believe that predatory practices are common and ineradicable in the sex industry, it would be helpful to have model regulatory rules that could reduce or eliminate the recruitment of highly vulnerable people for contract sex, as well as make their work safer. Some rules may be specific to the sex industry, such as age minimums for workers (perhaps 21 years old as for alcohol use in some countries (ProCon.org, 2016)), condom use for penetrative sex, treatment for workers with substance abuse problems, and mechanisms for screening out clients with histories of violence. In addition, businesses that facilitate contract sex could be required to offer their employees employment counseling, and access to affordable health care that included safe and effective contraception, STI prevention and treatment, and mental health care.[12]

Liberal democratic societies need not tolerate markets that pose abnormal levels of risk to the health and welfare of participants and others. Markets in highly dangerous or polluting products—e.g., some pesticides, medicines, and toys; chemical weapons; and coal—are examples of such markets. Also, markets that lead to or reinforce the subordination of socially stigmatized groups need not be tolerated—e.g., "freak shows" in which people with unusual body features are put on display for the amusement of others, conversion therapies, segregated private schools, and so on. If contract sex could not be done safely, or if it was inevitably traumatizing or degrading to service providers, then there would be good reason to restrict such markets. If contract sex reinforced the stigmatization of women, and promoted their social marginalization, then again there would be good reason to restrict such markets (Satz, 2010, p. 135). Employers could be fined for treating workers inequitably and for failing to prevent and address sexual harassment, as is done with other kinds of businesses. For example, brothels that refuse service to women customers or refuse to hire male providers could be penalized. In general, the methods for restricting markets should not render the people they aim to protect more vulnerable or subject to greater harm. Also, well designed regulations or restrictions need not aim to eradicate markets that can be transformed in ways that eliminate their toxicity. In short, criminalization and incarceration should be the tools of last resort in dealing with particularly problematic markets and commodities in general.

Some oppose fully decriminalizing contract sex because this move potentially opens the door to licensing large, industrial scale businesses that market sexual services (Jeffries, 2008). These opponents are right that repealing anti-prostitution laws removes a formidable barrier to many forms of legalization, but each scheme of legalization needs to be evaluated on its own merits. One could argue that decriminalizing the recreational use of marijuana could lead to a situation in which the existing big tobacco companies gain a monopoly on the production and sale of cannabis products. Many might worry (and with good reason) that these companies would promote the use of these products in the aggressive, socially irresponsible, and sometimes deceptive ways that they have promoted tobacco use and nicotine addiction. Such an outcome might trouble progressives who support the decriminalization of marijuana. However, governments need not allow existing tobacco companies to gain control of the market in marijuana products. In some places, there are efforts to offer retail licenses to people from communities that have suffered the most under decades of punitive marijuana laws. Similarly, while decriminalizing prostitution could open the door to industrial-scale, commercial trades in sexual services, there is no reason that any society would have to allow, say, existing large-scale pornography companies (now legal) to control future legal markets in sexual services. Instead, governments could establish policies that award commercial licenses to small-scale businesses, and to people and communities that have suffered harm from previous regimes of punitive laws.

Public policies regarding contract sex will need to devise criteria for determining when such activities should be categorized as a gift exchange or a market exchange. Regulatory restrictions specific to sex markets (legalization) would apply only to the latter, whereas restrictions imposed on gift-giving would apply to the former. Activities that fall under the category of gift-giving are typically self-organized and are less subject to outside interference, whereas market exchanges among strangers are usually subject to more governmental oversight. People who engage in contract sex among friends and acquaintances should be let alone to the same degree as others who engage in a gift exchange. But when their activities possess the attributes of market exchanges, then they should be subject to rules regulating similar market relationships. Some sexual service providers have ongoing and long-term social relationships with a relatively small number of clients, and their productive activities may have the attributes of a gift exchange rather than a market one. There is a complex web of rules and laws that determine when an exchange of goods or services falls outside the realm of "gift-giving" and possesses the characteristics of capitalist markets.

The attributes of a market exchange include the use of public venues for advertising one's services and attracting customers, the background understanding that the parties are each pursuing their individual interest or ends rather than celebrating or acknowledging an ongoing social tie, and the expectation that there can be financial or other penalties (e.g., loss of future opportunities) if the terms of the contract are not fulfilled. Importantly, in liberal democratic societies, these penalties cannot include forcing people to provide a service or labour even if they are under some kind of contract to do so. In societies that prohibit slavery, debt bondage, and trafficking, a person's body and labour capacities are inalienable, and only the services and goods a person creates with their body and labour can be offered voluntarily for exchange. Therefore, legalization schemes for contract sex in such contexts will not include the extraction of involuntary labour when contracts are breached, and they will need to incorporate other mechanisms for remedying the losses or inconveniences of broken contracts. The only contexts in which labour practices similar to slavery or debt bondage are permitted in contemporary liberal democratic societies are in some prison systems.[13] Consequently, policies that treat contract sex as a criminal offence, punishable by incarceration, are more likely to result in subjecting people to forced labour than decriminalizing and legalizing commerce in sexual services.

Conclusion

Decriminalizing contract sex and legalizing it raise different questions. When a society prosecutes and punishes adults for voluntarily participating in contract sex, especially when the activities are informally arranged among a small number of acquaintances (i.e., they are not operating an illegal commercial enterprise), it violates their rights to sexual autonomy and privacy. For this reason, all governments should decriminalize the act of accepting or offering payment for sex, informally arranged by adults in private. In addition, advocates for the full decriminalization of contract sex should develop schemes for its legalization. Developing effective and just regulatory mechanisms will allay many fears about the emergence of exploitative and damaging forms of commerce in sex, once anti-prostitution criminal statutes are repealed by legislatures or invalidated by courts. The offer of money for sex does not vitiate consent in all contexts, nor does it corrupt the activity for all actors. Sex can be enjoyed in both commodified and non-commodified forms, but we need different rules to govern these interactions.

Notes

1 To understand how sexual mores contribute to the subordination of women, feminist scholars and activists have researched the origins of prostitution (e.g., Rubin (1975), Lerner (1986)), its impact on society and women (e.g., Pateman (1988)), and schemes for restricting prostitution (e.g., Kempadoo and Doezema (1998), Nagle (1997)). Many feminists abhor the practice as well as punitive governmental responses to it, but have not, so far, coalesced around a common reform agenda regarding sex work or contract sex.

2 For a summary of anti-decriminalization and anti-commodification arguments, and some responses to them, see Shrage (2020), section 2.1 'Should Some Markets Be Prohibited?'.

3 This and subsequent sections draw from my previous work, especially my essay "Contract Sex: Decriminalization vs. Legalization."

4 The vast majority of sex workers I've interviewed oppose mandatory health exams for providers or clients. They argue that, when health care is affordable and accessible, people who work in or patronize sex businesses will take the needed steps to protect their health.

5 "Modelling studies indicate that decriminalising sex work could lead to a 46% reduction in new HIV infections in sex workers over 10 years; eliminating sexual violence against sex workers could lead to a 20% reduction in new HIV infections." *World Health Organization* (2021). Also see *Avert* (2019).

6 All women, but especially those who are already socially disempowered, can be harassed by police for being on the wrong street corner, or in some cases for carrying condoms in their purses. An adult woman who on a whim decides to accept an offer of cash from an acquaintance or friend to participate in a sexual act, but is otherwise not operating, or part of, an organized commercial sex business, commits an act of "prostitution," and can be subject to arrest and harsh punishment, including incarceration. Sidebar "How prostitution arrests target the most vulnerable women," Bazelon (2016).

7 You can do an Internet search for "sugar babies and sugar daddies" and find many news stories about this phenomenon, as well as websites that facilitate sex-for-pay among these self-described actors. Some of these relationships may be viewed as "gift exchanges" among friends, but many appear to be transitory commercial transactions among strangers for mutual gain, rather than for the purpose of cementing or celebrating a social tie.

8 The comedy team Key and Peele have a funny skit about this "The Worst Way to Get Medical Marijuana": www.youtube.com/watch?v=_8JtnUpkP0s

9 For a feminist defence of the Nordic model, see Watson (2019).

10 Private correspondence in the 1990s, and following decades, with sex worker organizations.

11 Of course, the mechanisms for blocking them should avoid creating even weaker agents: e.g., agents who cannot provide for their personal security due to fear of arrest, or are subject to arbitrary arrest and detention.

12 See Weitzer (2011) pp. 207–213, for a more expansive and detailed list of best practices for legalizing and regulating sex businesses. Weitzer develops his recommendations from his empirical studies of existing legal regimes, and they offer a starting point for discussion by community-based governing boards and agencies, which could be set up where contract sex is decriminalized. As I discuss above, advocates for decriminalizing cannabis use and commodity markets made significant progress by devising a process for legalization. E.g., see Canada's "Taskforce on Cannabis Legalization and Regulation": www.canada.ca/en/health-canada/services/drugs-medication/cannabis/laws-regulations/task-force-cannabis-legalization-regulation.html

13 For example, the 13th Amendment to the U.S. Constitution states: "Neither slavery nor involuntary servitude, except as a punishment for crime whereof the party shall have been duly convicted, shall exist within the United States, or any place subject to their jurisdiction" (Library of Congress Research Guides, 2018).

References

Amnesty International (AI) (26 May 2016) *Policy on State Obligations to Respect, Protect and Fulfil the Human Rights of Sex Workers,* pp. 1–17. Available at: www.amnesty.org/en/wp-content/uploads/2021/05/POL3040622016ENGLISH.pdf (Accessed: 22 November 2021)

Avert (2019) *Sex Workers, HIV, and AIDS* [online]. Available at: www.avert.org/professionals/hiv-social-issues/key-affected-populations/sex-workers (Accessed: 22 November 2021)

Bazelon, E. (5/5/2016) "Should prostitution be a crime," *The New York Times Magazine* [online]. Available at: www.nytimes.com/2016/05/08/magazine/should-prostitution-be-a-crime.html (Accessed: 22 November 2021)

Beloso, B.M. (2012) "Sex, work, and the feminist erasure of class," *Signs: Journal of Women in Culture, and Society* 38(1), pp. 47–70. https://doi.org/10.1086/665808

Butler, C.N. (2015) "A critical race feminist perspective on prostitution and sex trafficking in America," *Yale Journal of Law and Feminism* 27(1), pp. 95–139. Available at: https://digitalcommons.law.yale.edu/yjlf/vol27/iss1/3/

Colorado Department of Revenue (2021) *Marijuana Enforcement Division* [online]. Available at: https://sbg.colorado.gov/marijuanaenforcement (Accessed: 22 November 2021)

Davis, A.D. (2015) "Regulating sex work: Erotic assimilationism, erotic exceptionalism, and the challenge of intimate labor," *California Law Review* 103(5), pp. 1195–1275. Available at: www.californialawreview.org/print/03regulating_sex_work/

de Marneffe, P. (2013) "Vice laws and self-sovereignty," *Criminal Law and Philosophy* 7, pp. 29–41. https://doi.org/10.1007/s11572-012-9157-x

Findlaw (2019) *Federal and State Charges for Prostitution* [online]. Available at: www.findlaw.com/criminal/criminal-charges/prostitution.html (Accessed: 22 November 2021)

Hartman, M. (7/6/21) *National Conference of State Legislatures (NCSL) Cannabis Overview* [online]. Available at: www.ncsl.org/research/civil-and-criminal-justice/marijuana-overview.aspx (Accessed: 22 November 2021)

Jeffries, S. (2008) *The Industrial Vagina: The Political Economy of the Global Sex Trade*. New York: Routledge.

Kempadoo, K. and J. Doezema (eds.) (1998) *Global Sex Workers: Rights, Resistance, and Redefinition.* New York: Routledge.

Leafly (2/24/2020) *Cannabis Testing Regulations: a state-by-state guide* [online]. Available at: www.leafly.com/news/health/leaflys-state-by-state-guide-to-cannabis-testing-regulations (Accessed: 22 November 2021)

Lerner, G. (1986) *The Creation of Patriarchy*, New York: Oxford University Press.

Library of Congress Research Guides (2018) *13th Amendment to the U.S. Constitution* [online]. Available at: https://guides.loc.gov/13th-amendment (Accessed: 22 November 2021)

Mac, J. (2/23/2018) *National Public Radio (NPR) How Does Stigma Compromise the Safety of Sex Workers* [online]. Available at: www.npr.org/transcripts/587937751 (Accessed: 22 November 2021)

Moen, O.M. (2014) "Is prostitution harmful?" *Journal of Medical Ethics* 40(2), pp. 73–81. Available at: https://jme.bmj.com/content/40/2/73.info

Nagle, J. (1997) (ed.), *Whores and Other Feminists*, New York: Routledge. *Nordic Model Now! What is the Nordic Model?* Available at: https://nordicmodelnow.org/what-is-the-nordic-model/ (Accessed: 22 November 2021)

North, A. (8/2/2019) "The movement to decriminalize sex work, explained," *Vox* [online]. Available at: www.vox.com/2019/8/2/20692327/sex-work-decriminalization-prostitution-new-york-dc (Accessed: 22 November 2021)

NSWP, Global Network of Sex Work Projects (2021), *History of the NSWP and the Sex Worker Rights Movement* [online]. Available at: www.nswp.org/timeline (Accessed: 22 November 2021)

NSWP (12/16/2013) *Consensus Statement on Sex Work, Human Rights, and the Law* [online]. Available at: www.nswp.org/resource/nswp-publications/nswp-consensus-statement-sex-work-human-rights-and-the-law (Accessed: 22 November 2021)

Pateman, C. (1988) *The Sexual Contract*. Stanford: Stanford University Press.
ProCon.org (2018) *Countries and Their Prostitution Policies* [online]. Available at: https://prostitution.procon.org/countries-and-their-prostitution-policies/ (Accessed: 22 November 2021)
ProCon.org (2016) *Minimum Legal Drinking Age in Other Countries* [online]. Available at: https://drinkingage.procon.org/minimum-legal-drinking-age-in-other-countries/ (Accessed: 22 November 2021)
Rubin, G. (1975) "The traffic in women: Notes on the 'political economy' of sex," in *Toward an Anthropology of Women*, R. Reiter (ed.) New York: Monthly Review Press, pp. 157–210.
Satz, D. (2010) *Why Some Things Should Not Be for Sale: The Moral Limits of Markets*. Oxford: Oxford University Press.
Shrage, L.J. (2022) "Contract sex: Decriminalization vs. legalization," *Sexuality, Gender, and Policy* 5(1), pp. 8–25. https://doi.org/10.1002/sgp2.12041
Shrage, L.J. (2020) "Feminist perspectives on sex markets," *Stanford Encyclopedia of Philosophy*. Available at: https://plato.stanford.edu/entries/feminist-sex-markets/ (Accessed July 6, 2022)
Watson, L. (2019) "Philosophical debates about prostitution: State of the question," *The Southern Journal of Philosophy* 57(2), pp. 165–193. https://doi.org/10.1111/sjp.12320
Weitzer, R. (2011) *Legalizing Prostitution: From Illicit Vice to Lawful Business*, New York: NYU Press.
World Health Organization (WHO) (2021) *Global HIV, Hepatitis and STIs Programmes, Sex Workers* [online]. Available at: www.who.int/hiv/topics/sex_work/en/ (Accessed: 22 November 2021)

21

SURROGACY

The ethics of paid surrogacy

Stephen Wilkinson

Introduction

Writing in 2018, Bronwyn Parry observes:

> The desire for genetically related children is driving an exponential rise in assisted reproductive service provision worldwide, including the Global South ... This expansion has been accompanied by a similarly explosive growth in populist narratives that assert that one of the services offered by such clinics, commercial gestational surrogacy (CGS), is a form of labour that is so exceptional(ly) exploitative it should be banned. Provocative headlines proclaiming that surrogates are 'Renting their wombs' and 'Pimping their pregnancies' fuel such assertions, suggesting that surrogates become reduced to mere wombs, vessels for carrying the offspring of entitled and wealthy foreigners. Although superficially compelling, such arguments fail to withstand detailed interrogation.
>
> (Parry, 2018, p. 214)

This chapter contributes to ongoing debates about the ethics of paid surrogacy by explaining, reconstructing, and then (as Parry puts it) subjecting to 'detailed interrogation', some of the numerous ethical, philosophical, and policy arguments directed towards this practice. Its focus is on ethics and, in very general terms, on the normative question of which policy frameworks would be most defensible ethically; it does not address the specifics of surrogacy law and practice in particular states or countries.

Surrogacy is a practice wherein 'a woman carries and gives birth to a baby for another person or couple' (HFEA, 2022). There are two main kinds, described by the Human Fertilisation and Embryology Authority (the UK fertility treatment regulator) as follows:

> *Full surrogacy* (also known as *host or gestational surrogacy*) is when the eggs of the intended mother or a donor are used and there is therefore no genetic connection between the baby and the surrogate.
> *Partial surrogacy* (also known as *straight or traditional surrogacy*) involves the surrogate's egg being fertilised with the sperm of the intended father.
>
> (HFEA, 2022; emphasis added)

DOI: 10.4324/9781003188742-26

The term 'gestational carrier' is sometimes used instead of 'surrogate' to refer to full surrogacy, with the term 'surrogacy' then being reserved for traditional surrogacy (ASRM Ethics Committee, 2018).

This chapter focuses primarily on gestational surrogacy (cases where the gestational carrier is not also an egg provider) while continuing to use the term 'surrogacy'.[1] There are two reasons for this focus. First, gestational surrogacy is, in a sense, a purer and simpler case to discuss (because the genetic link may be thought to raise additional moral issues) and so it is easier to lay out the argumentative landscape clearly if we stick to gestational surrogacy. Second, gestational surrogacy is now the most prevalent version of surrogacy, since most intended social parents want to use their own gametes when they can, so that they can have genetic connections to the child. And even where the intended social parents can't directly provide the egg, they may still prefer to use a third-party egg donor, rather than relying on the surrogate; this option gives them more choice and avoids any real or perceived moral and social complications arising from the surrogate also being a genetic parent.

The most common scenario in which surrogacy services are used is when a 'commissioning' mother (the woman making use of the service) has health issues preventing conception or pregnancy or making pregnancy or childbirth too dangerous. Surrogacy can also be used by male same-sex couples or single men, using another woman's donor eggs (or the eggs of the surrogate). Another rarer scenario is 'social surrogacy' or 'convenience surrogacy', where a woman with no known infertility issues uses surrogacy for non-medical reasons: for example, because pregnancy is inconsistent with her career, or because she does not wish to experience childbirth and pregnancy.[2] Social surrogacy is often seen as particularly ethically problematic. The UK's *Warnock Report* for example, stated categorically that:

> … surrogacy for convenience alone … where a woman is physically capable of bearing a child but does not wish to undergo pregnancy, is totally ethically unacceptable.[3]

Some critics have serious reservations about surrogacy, whether it is paid or not: that is, even about 'altruistic' surrogacy. This makes it unlike many other contested bodily commodities such as blood (see chapter 18 by Jaworski in this volume) and organs (see chapter 17 by Taylor). Here are three examples of concerns or issues which can arise even in the case of purely altruistic surrogacy, all taken from the *Warnock Report*.

- That surrogacy introduces 'a third party into the process of procreation which should be confined to the loving partnership between two people'.
- That 'the relationship between mother and child is … distorted by surrogacy. For in such an arrangement a woman deliberately allows herself to become pregnant with the intention of giving up the child to which she will give birth, and this is the wrong way to approach pregnancy'.
- That surrogacy is 'potentially damaging to the child, whose bonds with the carrying mother, regardless of genetic connections, are held to be strong, and whose welfare must be considered to be of paramount importance' (DHSS, 1984).

Paid surrogacy is the focus of this chapter, however, in part because of its obvious connection with commodification, and in part because it is paid or 'commercial' surrogacy which provokes the most vehement opposition. All types of surrogacy listed above could be paid or unpaid. By 'paid surrogacy', I mean cases in which the surrogate receives remuneration over and above mere compensation for expenses, loss of earnings, or even for inconvenience or suffering: cases in which the payment is more akin to a fee for services or a wage – an incentive or reward. Drawing the line between compensation and fees or wages is not necessarily straightforward, and how best to do this is an interesting and important practical policy issue in some jurisdictions, like the UK, which distinguishes 'reasonable expenses' from the payment of fees for services.[4] Furthermore, it is acknowledged that even 'reasonable expenses' can amount to quite significant sums. A 2018 Surrogacy UK report, for example, tells of average payments to surrogates – *within* the 'reasonable expenses' framework – of over £10,000 for domestic arrangements and UK/India arrangements, and nearly £40,000 for UK/US arrangements. One UK/US case was reported to have involved an expenses payment of £96,000 (Surrogacy UK, 2018, p. 22). While it is an interesting topic, I will leave the distinction between fees and expenses to one side for the present purposes for if, as will be argued, fees and payments for surrogacy are morally permissible under certain conditions, then the same applies *a fortiori* to reasonable expenses.

In what follows, I will explain and subject to critical scrutiny three main types of argument against paid surrogacy. First, there is a claim that paid surrogacy is a form of baby selling. Second, there are concerns about paid surrogacy's being exploitative and about the quality of surrogates' consents. And finally there is a family of arguments which accuse paid surrogacy of degrading and instrumentalizing surrogates and/or their children, of treating them as objects of use rather than persons worthy of respect and consideration.

Baby selling and treating children as property

> … it is felt that a surrogacy agreement is degrading to the child who is to be the outcome of it, since, for all practical purposes, the child will have been bought for money.
>
> (DHSS, 1984, s.8.11)

This section looks at the claim that paid surrogacy would be tantamount to baby selling and/or would involve treating children as property, both of which (it is assumed) are serious wrongs. It addresses this by looking at three more specific questions.

- Would (or must) paid surrogacy involve treating children as mere property?
- Is paid surrogacy the same as allocating children to families on purely commercial or financial grounds?
- Is paid surrogacy more like a form of service provision (e.g. the selling of gestational services) or more like selling an item of property (in this case, a baby)?

Treating children as mere property

In practical terms, what it means to say that children are *not* mere property is that decisions about how they are raised and treated should be guided in large part by reference to their own interests and rights and, as they gradually become older and wiser, their aspirations and preferences – as opposed to being based just on the preferences of an 'owner', such as a parent. This is not to say that parents have *no* rights over their children, but such rights as there are probably best not conceived as *property* rights. Or at least if they *are* property rights then they are property rights of a special limited kind, ones allied with significant responsibilities and limitations. Such limited rights are analogous to people's property rights over animals, or buildings in conservation areas. Owning an animal does not (or should not) give one an unfettered right to be cruel to it, and the owners of buildings in protected conservation areas cannot substantially modify or destroy them, or at least not without authorization.

Some critics of paid surrogacy, such as Anderson (1990), have suggested that paid surrogacy requires us to think of parental rights as property rights:

> Commercial surrogacy … requires us to understand parental rights no longer as trusts but as things more like property rights – that is, rights of use and disposal over the things owned.
>
> (p. 76)

As Hanna (2010) argues however:

> … surrogacy contracts do not presuppose that parents have ownership rights over their children. In typical cases, to own something is to have nearly unfettered control over it. Parents have strong obligations to protect the interests of their children … and the commissioning couple acquires these obligations along with parental rights. The contract does not give them the right to treat the child in whatever way they please. The child is not sold, at least provided that all parties (and the legal system) recognize that parental rights are to be exercised for the child's good.
>
> (p. 342; see also McLachlan & Swales, 2000; Wilkinson, 2003)

This seems right. Children, including those created by surrogacy, are not literally owned by their parents and parental rights are restricted in numerous ways. For example, in many countries, parents are not allowed to abuse their children, are required to educate them, and are not allowed simply to sell their parental rights to the highest bidder, with adoption procedures being heavily regulated. Given this, the suggestion that 'commissioning' parents own their children (or that anyone owns, or should own, children) is false – and so it would be misleading to say that surrogates *sell* their babies when they relinquish control of them. Surrogacy, like most other routes to parenthood, does not (or need not) involve treating children as mere property.

The only sense in which 'property' *may* be involved here is if we want to think of parental rights as special property rights – analogous to the examples of owning animals and heritage buildings (above). But if that is the limited and special sense of 'selling' and of 'ownership' at issue then, it becomes unclear whether 'selling' and 'ownership' are ethically problematic in the first place (provided that any such special property rights are conceptualized in a way that gives children sufficient protection). I would not however recommend discussing the issue in these terms, even if it is technically coherent and defensible to do so, since the language of 'selling' and 'ownership' is potentially misleading in this case; it may encourage people mistakenly to think that children are (or worse, should be) treated as *ordinary* property, and may weaken or confuse our very proper commitment to the view that children should not be treated as mere commodities (as if they were ordinary property that can be exchanged or treated in whatever way the 'owner' wishes).

Allocating children to families on purely commercial or financial grounds

A second concern about 'baby selling' focuses less of the wrongness of children being owned *per se* and more on the allocation of children to families (see Chapter 22 of this volume by

Ertman). Allocating children to families on *purely* commercial or financial grounds could mean (for example) that a mother who wanted her child to be adopted could establish an auction and simply give the child to the highest bidder. This is generally thought wrong for a number of reasons. One is that the welfare of the child should take precedence over the size of the fee paid when deciding by whom the child will be raised; and at the very least a child should not be sold to the highest bidder if that family is liable to be abusive or cruel. A second is that such a system would be unfair to many prospective adoptive parents since the best parents and those in most need of a child are not necessarily the ones able to make the highest bid. A third (explored in detail in a later section) is that high fees may incentivize those who don't *really* want to relinquish their children to do so for the money, perhaps out of financial necessity. Finally, it is sometimes claimed that such a system could have psychological side-effects on adopted children who, as well as possibly thinking that they are not being raised by their 'real' parents, may accuse their parents of having 'bought' them; conversely, perhaps some adoptive parents will suffer from 'buyer's regret' if they pay a high fee and then are disappointed with how the child turns out. In short, financializing the parent-child relationship could be highly toxic to family relations.

While there are then some potentially powerful arguments against allocating children to families by means of an unfettered market, whether this is what paid surrogacy would (or must) amount to is far from clear – for there do seem to be important differences between paid surrogacy and a 'baby market'. Perhaps foremost amongst these is that, for most gestational surrogacy arrangements, while money does change hands, the child does not simply go to the highest bidder. Rather, it goes to one or more of its genetic parents. If the baby were simply auctioned, then that would be a different proposition altogether and not surrogacy (but rather something more akin to the commercial breeding of humans). Even where there is no genetic link between the commissioning parents and the child, the commissioning parents will usually have made a significant contribution to bringing the child into existence, by facilitating and resourcing gamete donation and IVF, and initiating the whole reproductive project. Thus, they have a stake in the child at birth based on the causal role of their intentions and actions prior to birth. So again, this scenario is far from an auction and, if it were that, then it would not be surrogacy.

Selling gestational services vs. selling a baby

> From the standpoint of contract, talk of baby selling reveals that surrogacy is misunderstood in exactly the same way that prostitution is misunderstood. A prostitute does not sell her body, she sells sexual services. In the surrogacy contract there is no question of a baby being sold, merely a service.
>
> (Pateman, 1988, p. 212)

A different way of distinguishing surrogacy from 'baby selling' is to argue that what is paid for in a surrogacy arrangement is not *the baby* but *gestational services*. At least in gestational surrogacy cases (where the surrogate does not provide an egg) these can be conceptualized as arrangements where the surrogate in effect looks after, grows, and nurtures an entity which, from the start, 'belongs' (in some sense) to the intended social parents. Thus, the baby, once it arrives, is not sold but merely, in a sense, returned having been the recipient of a developmental service.

One objection to this way of seeing things is that ultimately there must be an element of 'baby selling' in such arrangement because contracts typically do require the surrogate hand over the child or to pay a financial penalty – which is hardly surprising, given that having a baby is the whole point of the exercise for the commissioning parents. The UK's 1998 *Brazier Report* made the point as follows.

> 4.34 … It was argued by a number of the respondents to our questionnaire that surrogacy need not be equated with 'baby-selling', because any fee paid to the surrogate can be regarded as payment for the pregnancy, *ie* payment for her services, not the baby. We find it difficult to see how this distinction can be maintained, especially because any fully commercial transaction of this kind should be subject to the normal laws of contract. It is unimaginable that a commissioning couple should enter into a contract that required simply that the surrogate become pregnant and give birth. The contract would have to contain a requirement that in return for the fee the child was handed over to those contracting the pregnancy, with penalties for failure to fulfil this aspect of the agreement.
>
> (Brazier, Campbell, & Golombok, 1998)

An important first response to arguments of this kind is to note that the distinction between goods and services generally is not as straightforward as is sometimes assumed in discussions of surrogacy. In particular, it looks as if really there is a goods/services *continuum* rather than a clear and binary distinction. Rathmell, writing back in the 1960s, makes the point as follows.

> Economic products lie along a goods-service continuum, with pure goods at one extreme and pure services at the other, but with most of them falling between the two extremes … Most goods are a complex of goods and facilitating services; most services are a complex of services and facilitating goods.
>
> (Rathmell, 1966, p. 33)

Rathmell's examples of goods which are almost purely goods include food (unprepared food, not restaurants), tobacco, and clothing. At the other end, pure (or nearly pure) services include housing (rented housing), education, and religious and welfare activities.

Of particular relevance to surrogacy is this observation:

> This mixed nature of most economic products is well illustrated by the leasing transaction. If a product is purchased, it is a good; but if it is rented or leased, the rentee or lessee acquires a service. Yet for the service to have any meaning whatever, a goods component must also be present. Service would contribute time and place utility; the good would be the physical commodity made available and the service would be the act of making it available for a prescribed period of time as an alternative to outright purchase.
>
> (Rathmell, 1966, p. 34)

So perhaps what we should say is that, in gestational carrier surrogacy, the surrogate provides gestational services first and foremost but for the 'service to have any meaning whatever' the commissioning parents must end up with a child (or at least that is the *intended* endpoint as sadly not all pregnancies result in a live birth); the child is, so to speak, the 'goods component'. Traditional surrogacy, where the surrogate also provides the eggs, may be rather further towards the goods end of the goods-services continuum because the eggs are also in effect sold as part of the whole package.

What conclusions can we draw from this? The goods/services distinction (which is a more general version of the selling gestational services vs. selling babies distinction) probably will not help much in deciding on the ethics of paid surrogacy. The distinction is much less clear-cut than is sometimes suggested and the chances are that surrogacy will end up somewhere in the middle of that continuum, rather than being purely or clearly the sale of a good (a child) or a pure service (gestational labour).

Perhaps this does help us in a less direct way though by forcing us to refocus attention on what really does matter ethically and on what the fundamental concerns underlying the 'baby selling' objection are. There appear to be two. One is that surrogacy is morally the same as allocating babies in a purely commercial way, to the highest bidder. A second is that surrogacy may involve (mis)treating children as if they are mere property. For reasons discussed earlier, surrogacy is not – or at least needn't be – like this and so these concerns can be put to one side.

Exploitation and consent

Exploitation is arguably *the* principal ethical objection to paid surrogacy: the one which is both most prevalent in the literature and in discourses outside academia (see for example: Cattapan, 2014; Panitch, 2013; Wilkinson, 2016.) In addition, it is generally agreed that 'exploitativeness' is a morally negative feature of situations or transactions and thus to be avoided where possible.

Exploitation is a complex and contested concept but, in brief, the primary sense of 'exploitation', at least as it figures in applied ethics and policy debates, is as follows. A person (or organization) is exploited when another person (or organization) uses them in an attempt to gain advantage, does so unfairly (*unfair* advantage is taken), and makes use of some *vulnerability* in the exploited person's situation to do so. This latter feature of exploitation can normally be seen as a defect in consent. For example, if someone is underinformed or lacking mental capacity, they are vulnerable to exploitation because they may end up giving a defective consent, one which is insufficiently informed. Or a person may be vulnerable to exploitation if they are on the receiving end of manipulation or coercion, both of which can generate defective consents. So we can think of exploitation as, in the standard case at least, a combination of unfairness and defective consent (Wilkinson, 2003).

Pretty much any type of human interaction *could* therefore be exploitative. This includes *un*paid surrogacy. One possible example of unpaid surrogacy being exploitative would be a person who used 'emotional blackmail' to persuade their sister to act as a surrogate or took advantage of the sister's generous nature. Conversely, a woman who acts as a surrogate might exploit the prospective social parents in some way by 'guilt tripping' them during or after the pregnancy. The exploitation involved in cases like this generally relies on some degree of personal or situational vulnerability on the part of the exploited person.

So if exploitation can occur in non-commercial contexts, why is exploitation an issue specifically for paid surrogacy? This answer is that – in common with many other 'contested commodities' such as blood, gametes, organs for transplant, and sex – the possibility of remuneration means that particular kinds of vulnerability can be taken advantage of.

Foremost amongst these is *economic disadvantage or poverty*. The idea is that if surrogacy is paid it will become an attractive proposition for underprivileged women who will see it as a better option than alternative methods of earning a living, and certainly as preferable to not earning a living wage at all. This critique has been used against all types of paid surrogacy but is particularly prevalent in criticisms of international surrogacy, where the commissioning parents are often from relatively wealthy countries and the surrogates from economically disadvantaged countries (Panitch, 2013; Wilkinson, 2016). A slightly different argument focuses not so much on the surrogates' poverty but on the size of the payment. Here, the concern is that if surrogacy became generously rewarded then even non-impoverished women of childbearing age might find it a difficult thing to resist. Similar things have been said of paid egg donation, where donors with highly valued characteristics (e.g. educational success, athleticism) may attract high fees and thus be 'induced' to donate. (See Steinbock, 2004; Wilkinson, 2003; Wilkinson, 2013; and, in this volume, Krawiec's chapter, Chapter 19.)

As far as exploitation is concerned, the main argument or worry here is that paid surrogacy (transnational commercial surrogacy especially) may exploit women by virtue of the following features of the transaction:

- the surrogates' background poverty and lack of alternative means of earning a living;
- other (not directly financial) background conditions, such as surrogates' relative lack of education and information and/or oppressive family structures;
- unfairly low rates of pay for surrogates;
- the conditions in which surrogates are expected to live during pregnancy;
- that contracts are unfairly weighted in favour of the interests of the commissioning parent(s) (and/or other third parties, such as agents).

Undoubtedly, these are all factors that can render a transaction exploitative via the combination alluded to earlier of unfairness and defective consent. And certainly *some* – perhaps many – international surrogacy arrangements have been ethically problematic for these reasons. Where such exploitation exists, that is a morally bad feature of these situations and is to be avoided where possible – although it should be noted that exploitativeness is not the only moral concept in play and perhaps sometimes allowing a degree of exploitation to persist, in order to prevent other worse harms can be justifiable, all things considered.

Turning though to the more philosophical issue of whether paid surrogacy is inevitably exploitative, we need first to ask which of the features listed above are merely contingent features of actual practice (ones that in principle could be changed at a legislative or policy level) as opposed to being core elements of paid surrogacy. At least the bottom three items listed are contingent features of international surrogacy that could in principle be improved via legislative or policy actions, specifically by taking steps to avoid: underpayment; poor working conditions during pregnancy, and unduly onerous surrogacy contracts (from the perspective of the surrogate). Quite what constitutes under/over-payment, sufficient good working conditions, and a fair contract is not going to be easy to specify and there will not be space here to do that. There are however models and guidance that could serve as starting points. For example, a 2018 opinion by the Ethics Committee of the American Society for Reproductive Medicine makes plausible recommendations, such as:

- ensuring that 'gestational carriers are the sole source of consent regarding their medical care from embryo transfer through prenatal care, labor, delivery, and aftercare';
- making sure that they are 'fully informed of the risks of the gestational-carrier arrangement and of pregnancy';
- psychological evaluation of the surrogate before a commitment is entered into;
- independent legal representation for surrogates (ASRM Ethics Committee, 2018).

Similarly, Casey Humbyrd has proposed a Fairtrade model of international surrogacy. Humbyrd (2009) invokes three well-established Fairtrade standards: 'payment of a fair price, working conditions, and transparency and accountability'. On pay:

> Nominal wages may be less to surrogate mothers in developing countries compared to their counterparts in developed countries, but the real wages should be equivalent, and the surrogate mother should be fairly compensated relative to the total amount paid by the prospective parents to the surrogacy agency or broker. Additionally, surrogacy contracts would specify that payment is for the surrogate mother's time, risks, and labour … payment must be independent of pregnancy outcome (e.g. miscarriage, voluntary abortion, stillbirth, or disabled child) …
>
> (Humbryd, 2009, p. 117)

Surrogates must also have a 'safe and healthy working environment' (analogous to health and safety at work requirements) and:

> Transparency of financial transactions between surrogacy brokers, prospective parents and surrogate mothers will aid in the development of a market wage and help limit mutually advantageous exploitation …
>
> (Humbryd, 2009, p. 117)

Concerns about these contingent features of paid surrogacy arrangements, ones which are not directly generated by the nature of surrogacy itself, but rather by the *way* in which surrogacy is done, can largely be dealt with by advocating a Fairtrade approach. This would incorporate suggestions like those just mentioned and could be bolstered by regulation. For example, developed countries could regulate adoption, immigration, and/or the health and social welfare professions in ways that make Fairtrade surrogacy the only permitted kind, or at least in ways which encourage this approach, especially when dealing with international paid surrogacy arrangements.

So that is one important response to exploitation concerns – to *make surrogacy better* by making it as close as possible to the Fairtrade model. Of course, there are other debates to be had about the politics and practical feasibility of doing so but, as far as the *ethics* of surrogacy is concerned, invoking Fairtrade does seem a largely successful move. This however only deals with *some aspects* of the exploitation objection, and we are still left with worries about the fact that some surrogates come from economically disadvantaged countries with few other options, alongside other background issues such as a relative lack of education and/or oppressive family structures. In one way, implementing the Fairtrade model could exacerbate worries about women being 'coerced by poverty' because the model would make surrogacy even more attractive, but at least the Fairtrade approach increases the chances of any exploitation being *mutually beneficial* (with both surrogates and prospective social parents better off than they otherwise would be) as opposed to harmful for the surrogates (Bayliss, 2014). Also, these concerns – serious as they are – can be addressed and, in what follows, I examine some different ways of doing this. I start with another possible *policy* response and then move onto provide a more philosophical analysis.

One policy response would be to seek to exclude vulnerable populations, such as the economically disadvantaged, from the pool of potential surrogates. A model for this can be found in the debate about organ sale, Charles Erin and John Harris's 'ethical market in human organs', which they outline as follows:

> The market would be confined to a self-governing geopolitical area such as a nation state or indeed the European Union. Only citizens resident within the union or state could sell into the system and they and their families would be equally eligible to receive organs. Thus organ vendors would know they were contributing to a system which would benefit them

> and their families and friends since their chances of receiving an organ in case of need would be increased by the existence of the market. (If this were not the case the main justification for the market would be defeated.) There would be only one purchaser, an agency like the National Health Service (NHS), which would buy all organs and distribute according to some fair conception of medical priority. There would be no direct sales or purchases, no exploitation of low-income countries and their populations.
>
> (Erin & Harris, 2003, pp. 137–138; see also Erin & Harris, 1994)

I am not arguing here that we *should* adopt this model for surrogacy (although there may some mileage in the idea), but it does at least provide one answer, which is to seek to exclude the potential victims of exploitation from surrogacy altogether. Of course, one downside of this is that it would deprive some of the very people who stand to benefit most financially from this alternative source of income, but it could be argued that this is a price worth paying to avoid the exploitation. Erin and Harris's proposal applied to surrogacy would also have some other advantages, such as state funding and allocation – although those features may well not be attractive to some potential users of surrogacy services and may, like even the funding of IVF, be politically controversial.

Turning now to the philosophical analysis, I start by noting that the adverse economic circumstances of some surrogates are to be condemned and nothing said here is meant to be a defence of those. The issue at hand though is not so much the circumstances themselves but the effect that they are thought to have on the quality of prospective surrogates' consents and decision-making. In particular, the worry is that they are 'coerced by poverty' into surrogacy and that this could constitute exploitation.

The exploitation point can be dealt with by referring back to the Fairtrade model. If surrogates are fairly paid and fairly treated, then it seems not to make much sense to say that they are also exploited. Nonetheless, the point about coercion and consent can still stand on its own. It may be that, even in the case of Fairtrade surrogacy, there is an issue about coercion and consent. What could this be? Three specific claims often arise here. One is that the surrogates have a lack of acceptable alternatives; another is that paid surrogacy is too attractive to resist (even more so if it is Fairtrade); and a third is that at the conditions of background poverty are themselves a form of coercion. I shall consider each in turn. (See Wilkinson (2016) for additional detail and background).

While (when this occurs) a *lack of acceptable alternatives* is an unfortunate and regrettable feature of the surrogates' background conditions, this is not sufficient – or at least not on its own – to invalidate their consent. As I argued in an earlier paper:

> The decisive counter-example here is consent to essential life-saving medical treatment. If my surgeon says 'if I don't operate then I'm afraid you'll die within 24 hours', the starkness of that choice does not mean that I cannot validly consent. What is more, it would be more than a little odd to say that operations should not go ahead in such circumstances because of the irresistibility of the surgeon's offer to operate. For it is irresistible precisely because it is so good for me!
>
> (Wilkinson, 2016, pp. 133–134)

Similar considerations apply to the suggestion that paid surrogacy might be *too attractive to resist*. We must of course distinguish between surrogacy's real and merely apparent advantages and, as part of the consent process, ensure that prospective surrogates have a sound understanding of the risks and difficulties as well as the benefits, and of what they are signing up to contractually. This is why some of the Ethics Committee of the American Society for Reproductive Medicine recommendations are so important for valid consent: ensuring that gestational carriers are 'fully informed of the risks of the gestational-carrier arrangement and of pregnancy', that there is a psychological evaluation of the surrogate, and that surrogates have independent legal representation (ASRM Ethics Committee, 2018). But if, having passed these tests, and with sound understanding and mental capacity, a woman decides that paid surrogacy really is a very attractive option, then it would seem odd to rule this out as something she can consent to just in virtue of its extreme attractiveness.

So the first two claims can be dealt with relatively easily but that does still leave a more fundamental argument regarding coercion: *the suggestion that the conditions of background poverty are themselves coercive*. I have argued previously that there is an important distinction between situations in which a person's lack of options is caused by brute luck and ones in which it is caused by the coercive actions or omissions of others' and that 'only in the latter case can this (directly) invalidate consent' (Wilkinson, 2016, p. 135). Lack of options *per se* is not normally enough to invalidate consent, but where the person's option set is substantially constrained by the wrongful behaviour of third parties the quality of any consent given can be adversely affected. For example, as noted earlier, facing a stark choice between painful life-saving medical treatment and death is a situation with a lack of options but that fact alone does not prevent valid consent to the medical treatment from occurring. But consider a different situation. One in which someone threatens death if you refuse to donate a body part. The lack of options aspect of that situation is not dissimilar to the first case but ethically it seems very different and clearly the 'consent' in this case would lack validity. Similarly, if a husband were to keep his wife in dire poverty and insist that she enters into a surrogacy arrangement to make money for the family, her consent would be defective: not because of any wrongdoing or direct exploitation by the commissioning parents or any legal or medical professionals involved but because of the coercive action of a third party outside the surrogacy arrangements. (Of course, the commissioning parents and/or legal/medical professionals would have an obligation to check that this sort of thing was not happening, but that is a different issue.)

This sort of case gives us a way into seeing how the 'coercion by poverty' argument might work. If the poverty in question is a misfortune for which no one is morally responsible, then the argument won't be applicable. But if there are people or institutions who are responsible for it (either because they caused it or failed to alleviate it when they had an obligation to do so) then this could be a form of background coercion, one that could invalidate the consent of the surrogate. In some cases of international paid surrogacy, it is plausible to suppose that at least some of the background poverty is not morally neutral, that it is an instance of coercion – or at least structurally so similar to coercion that it has coercion's consent-invalidating characteristics. The form of the threat is that unless the woman accepts a low-quality job of one kind or another then she and her family will be faced with destitution. This is arguably coercive, rather than merely a case of brute luck because (let's assume) there are governments, corporations, or other transnational bodies, who are knowingly allowing the *threat of starvation* by failing to deliver on their obligations: failing to provide adequate welfare benefits for those not working perhaps, failing to pay adequate wages, or not implementing policies that would encourage the development of more and better jobs (Wilkinson, 2016, pp. 133–134). Additionally, the legacy of colonialism will be a factor in some cases. If the surrogates' countries' have been made worse-off by the past empire-building of the intended social parents' countries, this adds an historical injustice element to the argument for background conditions being not only unequal but unfair.

Exactly which institutions (e.g. nation states and their constitutive parts) are responsible for what would require a detailed consideration of each case and the chances are that numerous different actors and organisations will be involved. Still, the general point applies which is that the consent of surrogates can be defective when it is given against a backdrop of coercive poverty, by which I mean that her lack of acceptable options is caused by the wrongful actions or omissions of others.

While this is an important general point about justice and consent in international trade, it does not entail that we should adopt a negative or prohibitive stance towards paid surrogacy. There are three main reasons for this.

First, concerns about consent and coercion need to be weighed against the potentially negative welfare implications of not allowing paid surrogacy. These include negative effects on prospective surrogates (who would be deprived of a much-needed source of income), on intended social parents (who would need to find other reproductive options), and the non-existence of future persons who would otherwise have had worthwhile lives. (While the latter might not properly be a harm, the absence of future lives of value can, on some views at least, be a source of regret). This balancing argument is further supported by a point made by Janet Radcliffe Richards. She argues that there is something wrongheaded about preventing someone from accessing an option that would be hugely beneficial to them when the supposed justification for this is that the person's consent is defective. The fundamental rationale for having consent requirements is to protect the consenter's interest and rights and so preventing them from doing what they want to do when that thing is in their best interests is hard to reconcile with that (Richards, 2006, p. 290; Wilkinson, 2016).

Second, there is a strong practical argument for not prohibiting paid surrogacy, and on the contrary for having in place policies that facilitate surrogacy (paid or otherwise). For to do otherwise is liable to encourage people to go overseas and to encourage them to subvert whatever restrictions are in place. Surrogacy UK for example, in its 2018 report which criticizes many of the restrictions on surrogacy in the UK, suggests that if there were more 'transparency and openness about the procedures and costs involved [this] might encourage more IPs [intended social parents] to pursue surrogacy in the UK, rather than entering commercial arrangements overseas'. These overseas arrangements, it argues, tend to fall into one of two camps: those in more 'highly regulated' countries which 'cost incredible sums' and those which are 'cheaper but potentially raise ethical issues about the recruitment and treatment of women' (Surrogacy UK, 2018). So if our concern is with avoiding unethical practices, it would be better to have a facilitative surrogacy policy framework: one which allows surrogacy to happen, and to happen in people's home countries, in cases where that is what they want (which the majority presumably do, given that going overseas for surrogacy can be extremely difficult).

Finally, we need to consider *consistency*. The consent worry about adverse background conditions applies equally to *any* paid activities and hence to potential surrogates' alternative sources of income too (Wilkinson, 2003; Wilkinson, 2016). Therefore it seems inconsistent and unfair to attempt to prevent paid surrogacy, whilst still allowing many other forms of economic activity to continue. This is not to say that surrogacy is exactly like other types of labour in all respects but, as far as the background coercion argument is concerned, this does seem to apply to factory work and cleaning and even to more middle-class occupations just as much as it does to surrogacy. Hence, opponents of paid surrogacy will need to look elsewhere if what they seek is an argument against surrogacy, rather than against trade in general between citizens of richer and poorer nations.

Norms, motives, and degradation

To recap, my approach in the preceding discussion was to say that exploitation is a common type of wrongdoing, one that typically comprises transactional unfairness and defective consent; that surrogacy (like many other aspects of the world economy) very often *is* exploitative; but that it *could be* rendered non-exploitative (or less exploitative) by improving pay and conditions through facilitative regulation, and by improving consent practices. It was conceded that it may be very hard to solve *all* consent problems because of structural background coercion, but that that seems to be a general issue with world trade, not a criticism specifically of surrogacy.

Some scholars however (Anderson is a leading example) may think that this analysis fails to engage with some important deeper concerns: ones which cannot be assuaged just by improving pay and conditions. She states:

> When women's labor is treated as a commodity, the women who perform it are degraded. Furthermore, commercial surrogacy degrades children by reducing their status to that of commodities.
>
> (Anderson, 1990, p. 75)

These deeper concerns include the following:

- that paid surrogacy corrupts, distorts, or perverts people's motives, that they are caused to do things for money (becoming pregnant, giving birth, relinquishing a child) which they should only be doing for some other reasons (possibly altruism or love);
- that paid surrogacy involves treating people as mere means and not ends in themselves, that that which is intrinsically valuable is viewed as merely instrumentally valuable;
- that paid surrogacy involves valuing children (and women's 'gestational labour') by reference to inappropriate norms and values; that a price is assigned to something which should not be valued financially, perhaps because it is 'priceless' (the child, maternal-child relations).

Such claims raise complex and interesting questions and are embedded in a weighty body of literature which can't be dealt with in detail here.[5] Nonetheless, I will try to give an overview of what these concerns are and how we might think about and counter them. (Further discussion and evaluation of these arguments can be found in Chapter 4 of this volume by Vida Panitch.)

Let's start with the idea that there is something *degrading* about surrogacy. Anderson says that paid surrogacy is degrading to children because 'market norms' take over and displace more appropriate norms, in particular 'parental norms'. Love is central to the correct understanding of 'parental norms'. Children are 'to be loved and cherished by their parents, not to be used or manipulated by them for merely personal advantage'. Another 'parental norm' is understanding parental rights as 'trusts, which they must always exercise for the sake of the child'. Anderson's argument is that paid surrogacy is inconsistent with proper parental norms on at least two counts. First, it requires us to think of parental rights as 'more like property rights … rights of use and disposal over the things owned', as opposed to trusts. Second, when the surrogate relinquishes the child, she does so 'typically for her own sake (and possibly, if altruism is a motive, for the intended parents' sakes)', in contrast to (for example) cases of adoption where the child is relinquished for reasons connected to its own interests (e.g. if the birth mother does not have sufficient capacity to look after it properly (Anderson, 1990, pp. 75–76).

While Anderson's article is rhetorically powerful and raises important issues, it is far from clear how effective the critique is, especially if what's at issue is a judiciously regulated 'Fairtrade' version of surrogacy, rather than an unfettered market.

First, ethically speaking, we can't take for granted that the surrogate is the (only) parent, or at least it is not clear that surrogates' parental rights are any more important than those of the intended social parents, especially where one or both of the latter are also genetic parents. Hence, that surrogacy is a mother giving up *her* child cannot be just assumed.

Second, as was explained earlier on, even in paid surrogacy, parental rights should not be understood as property rights, or at least if children are property in a technical sense, they are a very special kind of property. Thus, Anderson's point about parental rights being treated as rights of use and disposal over the things owned is misdirected; surrogacy *shouldn't and needn't* involve such a construal of parental rights (as highlighted in the earlier discussion of baby selling).

Then there is the issue of a child being transferred from one parent to others for reasons not to do with *its* welfare but (for example) in order to secure financial remuneration for the surrogate or in order to satisfy the intended social parents' *desire* for a child. An initial practical response to this is that, very often, all parties will believe that allowing the intended social parents to raise the child is in the child's interests, in which case this critique won't apply. For example, a surrogate from the global South, who is relatively poor, has numerous children of her own, and is being a surrogate for financial reasons, may well think that this new child will do better with its rich European intended social parents, than if it were raised by her in difficult circumstances. But of course not *all* cases will be like that so what can we say about those cases where the motives are more purely self-interested? Two responses are worth noting. First, we might reiterate that perhaps the intended social parents have valid claims of their own to already be parents. Second, we should accept that while child welfare is of the highest importance in making allocation decisions about children, it is not the only thing that matters. Parents (and indeed those who wish to avoid being social parents) also have interests and preferences that carry some weight. If this were not the case then the strong default in favour of allowing biological parents to raise their own offspring would be a lot weaker and we might instead just allocate children to the best available parents with scant regard for the biological family, or for actual and prospective parents' wishes.

To broaden this out somewhat, an underlying concern is that children (and/or surrogates) are being treated as object of mere use, something that I have elsewhere discussed in more detail and termed *instrumentalization* (Wilkinson, 2003). Anderson makes the point as follows referencing Kant:

> Consider, for example, a standard Kantian argument against slavery, or the commodification of persons. Slaves are treated in accordance with the market norm that owners may use commodities to satisfy their own interests without regard for the interests of the commodities themselves. To treat a person without regard for her interests is to fail to respect her. But slaves are persons who may not be merely used in this fashion, since as rational beings they possess a dignity which commands respect. In Kantian theory, the problem with slavery is that it treats beings worthy of respect as if they were worthy merely of use. 'Respect' and 'use' in this context denote what we may call different modes of valuation.
>
> (Anderson, 1990, pp. 75–76)

So there is a concern here that paid surrogacy treats surrogates and/or their babies as mere objects of use, not as end-in-themselves, with their own interests, perspectives, and rights that need to be respected and considered.

Clearly if surrogates or their babies were treated merely as objects of use with no regard to their interests or wishes that would be wrong. If surrogacy ended up being like slavery, then it would be not merely wrong, but morally abhorrent. But again we come back to the point that what is (or should be) under discussion is whether surrogacy needs to be like slavery and the proposals above about Fairtrade surrogacy and facilitative regulation suggest that this is not the case. If surrogates were paid a fair wage, weren't subjected to unduly onerous contractual conditions, received appropriate and consensual healthcare *etc.*, then their position would look nothing much like slavery. Of course they should be treated with respect (as should their children), but this is best done not by preventing surrogacy altogether, but by ensuring that their autonomy is respected and there should be due regard for their wellbeing – expressed primarily in a high-quality consent process for surrogacy, and fair contractual conditions.

Finally, there is the suggestion that paid surrogacy involves valuing children and/or women's gestational labour by reference to inappropriate norms and values: that a price is assigned to something which is 'priceless' and should not be assigned a mere monetary value. There seem to be two worries here, or at least two interpretations of the worry. One is that assigning a monetary value to certain things (babies, or gestational services) is intrinsically wrong: they just ought not to be valued in that way. The second is that assigning a monetary value to certain things (whether intrinsically wrong or not) displaces other modes of valuation that ought to be operative – for example, if someone were to value a work of art primarily for its cash value that might lead to its aesthetic value being overlooked.

Asserting that assigning a monetary value to gestational services or the transfer of parental rights is intrinsically wrong is liable to be question-begging in the present context, since precisely what we are debating is whether or not it is wrong and why. A different sort of claim, that treating babies or surrogates as *merely* of monetary value is plausible (and at the heart of many seemingly reasonable critiques of capitalism in general) but then it is not clear that this critique would apply to the Fairtrade surrogacy system, one aim of which is to avoid treating the parties involved as merely means of extracting financial value.

The second interpretation is more interesting. If we assign monetary value, or more broadly use-value, to the providers of gestational services then are we at risk of overlooking their humanity, their personhood, their interests, their rights? There is certainly some risk of this. But situations in which we regard people are 'useful' and as having financial worth, *while at the same time* treating them with respect as persons and having due regard for their interests seem ubiquitous and often unproblematic. For example, teachers, bartenders, cleaners, lawyers etc. are all frequently valued for their utility and assigned a price. Of course there are alienated situations in which these workers are not treated as fully human, but that is just to say that things *can* and *do* go wrong in human relations – and that we must be vigilant about the potentially negative side-effects of money and markets. It does not however give grounds for thinking that there is something dubious about the professions themselves or provide an argument (for example) against paying teachers. The same goes for gestational services. We need to be careful not to allow the use-value of surrogates to displace other important modes of valuation but, at least with a Fairtrade system in place, there seem not to be any general grounds for thinking that this must happen, or that it would be any riskier in this respect than other established markets in human talents and labour (Wilkinson, 2003).

Conclusion

This chapter has reviewed the main ethical arguments against paid gestational surrogacy and found them to be deficient. The argument that paid surrogacy is a form of 'baby selling' was dismissed;

there are important differences between paid surrogacy and selling an existing child to the highest bidder. Similarly, it was concluded that paid surrogacy needn't be exploitative and that valid consent to surrogacy is possible, especially if what is proposed is a carefully regulated version of surrogacy that seeks to work in accordance with Fairtrade principles. Finally, concerns about commodification, degradation, and instrumentalization of surrogates (and children) were briefly examined and, for similar reasons, rejected. While, as critics of surrogacy point out, there are conceivable versions of surrogacy that share some such features with slavery (for example), versions that no reasonable person would want to defend, surrogacy need not be (and often is not) like this; hence, such criticisms are misdirected.

So, in principle at least, paid surrogacy can withstand the main arguments against it. It is however important to flag some challenges. In order to move from ethics to policy, a lot more work would need to be done to flesh out the specifics of what it takes for a surrogacy contract to be fair and what systems of regulation and international cooperation would be best placed to maximize fairness in surrogacy globally. In particular, there is the vexed question of how to manage situations in which one or more parties change their minds: e.g. scenarios in which the surrogate decides to keep the child, and ones in which the intended social parents no longer want the child. There has not been space to say anything much about these questions here but that should not be taken to imply they aren't important or can be easily answered. They are amongst the biggest challenges facing those seeking to manage or regulate surrogacy in an ethical way.

But while there are practical and political challenges, we must not forget that defining fairness in contracts and then trying to ensure that actual practice conforms to whatever definition of fairness we agree on is a massive challenge applying to trade and employment of all kinds. Most of these problems aren't specific to paid surrogacy and so do not constitute arguments against it.[6]

Notes

1 I am not wedded to the term 'surrogacy' and can see some advantages to moving to 'gestational carrier'. For the present however I continue to use it just for the pragmatic reason that it remains the established term and is one that is widely known and understood beyond academia.

2 Kleeman (2019) describes how this practice is becoming more common in California.

3 The United Kingdom government established a Committee of Inquiry into Human Fertilisation and Embryology in July 1982, chaired by Mary Warnock, 'to examine the social, ethical and legal implications of recent, and potential developments in the field of human assisted reproduction'. Its report, commonly known as the *Warnock Report*, played an important role in the shaping the Human Fertilisation and Embryology Act 1990 and the establishment of the Human Fertilisation and Embryology Authority, an 'arm's length' regulatory body. (Department of Health and Social Security, *Report of the Committee of Inquiry into Human Fertilization and Embryology*, London: Her Majesty's Stationery Office, July 1984 www.hfea.gov.uk/media/2608/warnock-report-of-the-committee-of-inquiry-into-human-fertilisation-and-embryology-1984.pdf)

4 Paying for surrogacy is not an offence *per se* but Section 54(8) of the Human Fertilisation and Embryology Act 2008 requires the court: 'To be satisfied that no money or other benefit (other than for expenses reasonably incurred) has been given or received by either of the applicants for or in consideration of – (a) the making of the order; (b) any agreement required by subsection (6); (c) the handing over of the child to the applicants; or (d) the making of arrangements with a view to the making of the order, unless authorized by the court'. In practice, this requirement is often disregarded due to the paramountcy of the welfare of the child: e.g. in cases where the child is already being cared for by the commissioning parents and all parties are satisfied with the arrangement (Horsey, 2015; Horsey, 2016).

5 Examples include: Arneson (1992), Capron & Radin (1988), Overall (2012), Pateman (1988), Phillips (2013), Radin (1994), Radin (1987), Satz (1992), and Wertheimer (1992).

6 I would like to thank Vida Panitch, Elodie Bertrand, and an anonymous referee for helpful comments on earlier versions as well as many of the participants at a workshop which took place at Université Panthéon-Sorbonne in June 2022.

References

Anderson, E. (1990) "Is women's labor a commodity?" *Philosophy and Public Affairs* 19(1), pp. 71–92.

Arneson, R.J. (1992) "Commodification and commercial surrogacy," *Philosophy & Public Affairs* 21(2), pp. 132–164.

ASRM Ethics Committee // Ethics Committee of the American Society for Reproductive Medicine (2018) "Consideration of the gestational carrier: An Ethics Committee opinion," *Fertility and Sterility* 110, pp. 1017–1021.

Baylis, F. (2014) "Transnational commercial contract pregnancy in India" in Baylis, F. and McLeod, C. (eds.) *Family-making: Contemporary Ethical Challenges*. Oxford: Oxford University Press, pp. 265–286.

Brazier, M., Campbell, A. and Golombok, S. (1998) "Surrogacy: Review for health ministers of current arrangements for payments and regulation – report of the review team, October 1998" Available at:https://webarchive.nationalarchives.gov.uk/ukgwa/20100408192620/http://www.dh.gov.uk/en/Publicationsandstatistics/Publications/PublicationsLegislation/DH_4009697 (Accessed 2 May 2023).

Capron, A.M. and Radin, M.J. (1988) "Choosing family law over contract law as a paradigm for surrogate motherhood," *Law, Medicine, and Healthcare* 16(1–2), pp. 34–43.

Cattapan, A. (2014) "Risky business: Surrogacy, egg donation, and the politics of exploitation," *Canadian Journal of Law and Society* 29(3), pp. 361–379.

DHSS // Department of Health and Social Security (1984) Report of the Committee of Inquiry into Human Fertilisation and Embryology, London: Her Majesty's Stationery Office. Available at: https://wellcomecollection.org/works/pxgeeqnf (Accessed 2 May 2023).

Erin, C. & Harris, J. (1994) "A monopsonistic market – or how to buy and sell human organs, tissues and cells ethically," in: Robinson, I. (ed.) *Life and Death Under High Technology Medicine*. Manchester: Manchester University Press in association with the Fulbright Commission, London, pp. 134–153.

Erin, C. & Harris, J. (2003) "An ethical market in human organs," *Journal of Medical Ethics* 29, pp. 137–138.

Hanna, J.K.M. 2010 "Revisiting child-based objections to commercial surrogacy", *Bioethics* 24(7), pp. 341–347.

HFEA // Human Fertilisation and Embryology Authority (2022) Surrogacy, [online] Available at: www.hfea.gov.uk/treatments/explore-all-treatments/surrogacy/ (Accessed: 2 May 2023).

Horsey, K. (2015) "Surrogacy in the UK: Myth busting and reform," Report of the Surrogacy UK Working Group on Surrogacy Law Reform, Surrogacy UK. Available at: https://surrogacyuk.org/wp-content/uploads/2015/03/SurrogacyUK-Mythbusting-and-Reform.pdf (Accessed: 2 May 2023).

Horsey, K. (2016) "Not withered on the vine: The need for surrogacy law reform," *Journal of Medical Law and Ethics* 3, pp. 181–196.

Humbyrd, C. (2009) "Fair trade international surrogacy," *Developing World Bioethics* 9(3), pp. 111–118.

Kleeman, J. (2019) "Having a child doesn't fit into these women's schedule: is this the future of surrogacy?" *The Guardian*, 25 May, Available at: www.theguardian.com/lifeandstyle/2019/may/25/having-a-child-doesnt-fit-womens-schedule-the-future-of-surrogacy (Accessed: 2 May 2023).

McLachlan, H. and Swales, J. (2000) "Babies, child bearers and commodification: Anderson, Brazier et al., and the political economy of commercial surrogate motherhood," *Health Care Analysis* 8, pp. 3–4.

Overall, C. (2012) *Ethics and Human Reproduction*. Abingdon: Routledge.

Parry, B. (2018) "Surrogate labour: Exceptional for whom?" *Economy and Society* 47(2), pp. 214–233.

Panitch, V. (2013) "Global surrogacy: Exploitation to empowerment," *Journal of Global Ethics* 9(3), pp. 329–343.

Pateman, C. (1988) *The Sexual Contract*, Cambridge UK: Polity Press.

Phillips, A. (2013) *Our Bodies, Whose Property*? Princeton, NJ: Princeton University Press.

Radin, M.J. (1987) "Market-inalienability," *Harvard Law Review* 100(8), pp. 1849–1937.

Radin, M.J. (1994) "What, if anything, is wrong with baby selling," *Pacific Law Journal* 26, pp. 135–158.

Rathmell, J.M. (1966) "What is meant by services?" *Journal of Marketing* 30(4), pp. 32–36.

Richards, J.R. (2006) "Consent with inducements: The case of body parts and services," in Miller, F. & Wertheimer, A. (eds.) *The Ethics of Consent: Theory and Practice*. Oxford: Oxford University Press, pp. 281–304.

Satz, D. (1992) "Markets in women's reproductive labor," *Philosophy & Public Affairs* 21(2), pp. 107–131.

Steinbock, B. (2004) "Payment for egg donation and surrogacy," *The Mount Sinai Journal of Medicine* 71, pp. 255–265.

Surrogacy UK (2018) "Surrogacy in the UK: Further evidence for reform," Second report of the Surrogacy UK Working Group on Surrogacy Law Reform, https://surrogacyuk.org/wp-content/uploads/2018/12/Surrogacy-in-the-UK-2nd-Report-20181230.pdf

Wertheimer, A. (1992) "Two questions about surrogacy and exploitation," *Philosophy & Public Affairs* 21(3), pp. 211–239.

Wilkinson, S. (2003) *Bodies for Sale: Ethics and Exploitation in the Human Body Trade*. London: Routledge.

Wilkinson, S. (2013) "Is the HFEA's policy on compensating egg donors and egg sharers defensible?" *Medical Law Review* 21(2), pp. 173–212.

Wilkinson, S. (2016) "Exploitation in international paid surrogacy arrangements," *Journal of Applied Philosophy* 33(2), pp 125–145.

22
ADOPTION
A mosaic of market and non-market elements

Martha M. Ertman

Introduction

Commodification in adoption has upsides and downsides. The well-known downside is outright baby-selling, a practice currently banned in virtually every U.S. state and abroad. The upsides are evident in exceptions that allow commodification in adoption. For example, legal, medical, and social work professionals routinely get paid in adoptions, and birth parents often receive monetary payments for expenses such as psychotherapy, maternity clothes and living expenses. Another form of monetary exchange takes the form of state subsidies that enable people to adopt children out of foster care (Hansen, 2007). But commodification, as understood in this chapter, also occurs in exchanges of value that do not involve money. For example, bartering a baby for a car – or for anything else of value – constitutes commodification. Other non-monetary exchanges of immensely valuable interests are common in adoption. Birth parents shop catalogues of adoptive parents and obtain promises about how the adoptive parents will raise the child – in a particular religion, for example – in exchange for the birth parents selecting them. Open adoption is structured by post-adoption-contact-agreements (known as PACAs), in which birth parents agree to relinquish legal parenthood in exchange for continuing contact with the children through, for example, email, letters, pictures, and even in-person visitation (Pertman, 2011).

Two-dimensional approaches to commodification – described by Viviana Zelizer (2005) as "Nothing But" and "Hostile Worlds" – view monetary exchange in intimate spheres as either inherently beneficial or wrongful. A better approach to those two extremes of complete commodification and market-inalienability is a more nuanced focus on who controls and benefits from contracts in contested contexts such as intimacy and body parts.[1] Accordingly, this chapter suggests that the "Mosaic" theory of commodification that I have articulated elsewhere best explains the range and implications of adoption contracts (Ertman, 2020, p. 186). As a regulatory matter, the "Mosaic" approach would support bans on outright baby-selling and also allow courts to enforce PACAs even when they involve some elements of commodification because those agreements often benefit birth parents, the children, and even adoptive parents. Consistent with U.S. family law, courts could enforce PACAs to order visitation unless that contact runs contrary to a child's best interests, but breach of a PACA would not empower a court to un-do the adoption.

DOI: 10.4324/9781003188742-27

These exchanges among birth parents, adoptive and foster parents, states, and private agencies have changed over time. Historically, the legal regulation of adoption has moved among the extremes of treating parenthood as essentially "Nothing But" a market transaction or seeing markets and parenthood as "Hostile Worlds," as well as the third analytical category – "Mosaic" – that captures a mélange of market and non-market elements. "Mosaic" also describes the mix of markets and intimacy in other parenthood contexts such as the sale of sperm and eggs, adult relationships such as cohabitation and marriage, and at-work caregiving that is sometimes called "office housework".[2]

This chapter both identifies the right moniker for the role of markets in adoption and argues in favour of some commodified practices on normative grounds. It begins by charting the emergence of today's conventional wisdom that modern adoption does not involve exchanges of value. First it describes the commonplace nineteenth century practice of taking in children who need care in exchange for the children's work for a family or institution, which is about as close as U.S. law has come to treating adoption as "Nothing But" an economic exchange. It then surveys the polar opposite view that adoption and monetary exchange are "Hostile Worlds" that cannot overlap without contagion and coercion. Finally, it discusses scholarly work recognizing that market and non-market domains overlap in adoption (as they do in other instances of contested commodification) (Zelizer, 2005, p. 20, p. 22, p. 29). It concludes that adoption is most accurately described as a "Mosaic" of emotional elements and exchanges of value – both monetary or non-monetary – and that the monetary elements can be beneficial or harmful to children, families, and the wider society depending on whether the transaction treats the children as goods sold like any other commodity or as social beings embedded in genetic as well as socio-economic relations.

This framework echoes the story of *Goldilocks and the Three Bears*. In the fairy tale, a hungry and tired Goldilocks stumbles on the bears' cabin and finds three bowls of porridge: one is too cold, one is too hot, and the third is just right. Likewise, assertions that adoption is "Nothing But" a market exchange are too cold, and "Hostile Worlds" assumptions that adoption and exchanges of value are mutually exclusive are too hot.[3] Fortunately, the "Mosaic" approach is just right because it captures the mix of market and non-market elements that co-exist in adoption. While space constraints preclude a detailed description of best practices, post-adoption contact agreements (PACAs) are illustrative. Courts in about half of U.S. states enforce PACAs, providing birth families with the remedy of visitation or other contact with the child, but only if that contact is consistent with the child's best interests. Moreover, adoption remains permanent even after adoptive parents breach a PACA; the breach would not lead a court to set aside the adoption.

Adoption as a contract

Adoption is essentially a legally binding agreement in which the original parents agree to relinquish parental rights and duties and adoptive parents agree to take on legal and social parenthood, but the terms of that transaction have changed dramatically over time and in different places. In other words, adoption involves exchanges of value. Commodification is obvious when money changes hands. But it is also present in barter transactions that swap some valuable interest or item for another without any monetary payments, such as a birth parent selecting adoptive parents because they agree to keep the name that the birthparent chose for the child.

Adoption did not exist at common law.[4] In the US, it came into existence in the nineteenth century via state statutes, replacing long-standing practices for dealing with children whose parents died or lacked the resources to raise them.

Adoption's evolution from relatively open market to masked commodification

U.S. adoption as we know it today emerged alongside the birth of modern childhood. For much of U.S. history, many children were valued by their families, society, and law for the work they did for wages, in apprenticeships, or indentured servitude. More privileged children, in contrast, got the benefit of an education, often through private tutors since free public schools were not widely available until the early twentieth century. Until 1865 enslaved children toiled alongside adults in fields and households, and even after Reconstruction many African American children worked instead of attending school. Gradually, reformers changed childhood into a stage of life focused on school instead of wage labour, which in turn led family law to start helping the most vulnerable children – orphans and the children of single mothers – by providing them loving and permanent homes.[5] Modern adoption did not emerge until the early decades of the twentieth century.

Before that, adoption was a buyer's market due to norms and law against unwed motherhood, limited options for women to engage in wage labour or to own property, and the lack of a social safety net. People taking in children often preferred the older ones who could perform work over infants who required greater care. The social valuation of babies whose parents could not raise them was so low that many birth mothers had to pay people known as "baby farmers" to take the children off their hands. In the custody of baby farmers, the low value of children translated to low survival rates. Children who survived were put to work, and older children were routinely hired out for domestic or farm work. At the age of twelve to fourteen they were apprenticed out to domestic or farm labour, and at eighteen, many were cast out into the world, illiterate, with just a little money, some clothes, a new Bible, and for the lucky ones, perhaps some cattle (Zelizer, 1985, p. 174).

But industrialization and other factors caused a sea change between the 1870s and 1930s, as children went from being valued for the work they could perform to financially worthless but sentimentally priceless (Zelizer, 2011, p. 62). That shift manifested in multiple social and legal developments, including the growing willingness of adoptive parents to pay to adopt. In the late nineteenth and early twentieth centuries, newspaper classified advertisements commonly listed children for adoption along with a price (Zelizer, 1985; Herman, 2008, p. 37). One ad stated bluntly, "For Adoption at Birth, Full Surrender, No Questions Asked". An early twentieth century ad in the *Boston Globe* was silent about the price of a child, and used sentimental terms in its query: "Who wants to take a little girl, three years old, the picture of health and a smart, handsome child? Only those who can give a comfortable home need answer" (Herman, 2008, p. 37). Perhaps that reference to a "comfortable home" hinted at a price paid to adopt. But rhetoric had changed by 1927, when an adoptive father told *Good Housekeeping* magazine, "Talk about children owing their parents anything! We'll never be able to pay what we owe that baby" (Zelizer, 1985, pp. 192–193).

Alongside these changing adoption practices, law evolved to treat adopted children as permanent members of a new family. In 1851, Massachusetts became the first state to enact a modern adoption law. The new statute made an adopted child a permanent part of the new family and also required a judge to determine that the adoptive parents were "of sufficient ability to bring up the child and furnish suitable nurture and education" (Cahn,2004, p. 19, p. 23). Other states soon followed suit, as norms and policies in law and society gradually evolved to protect children's best interests.

In 1917, Minnesota became the first state to require judges to investigate a child's adoptability and adoptive parents' suitability and also to protect children from stigma by eliminating the word "illegitimate" from birth certificates. Other states likewise began to incrementally obliterate birth parents from the public record. By 1948, nearly every state issued entirely new birth certificates for adoptive children, literally papering over their origins, to create what came to be known as "forever families" (Ertman, 2015a, p. 90). Consistent with the law's increasingly sentimental view of children and childhood, by the 1930s adoptive parents were making substantial payments to adoptive agencies to adopt infants and toddlers (Zelizer, 2011, pp. 62–65).

Just as the phrase "forever family" covers up the existence of the birth family, adoption professionals today mask the role of money in adoption by relabeling the payments made by adoptive parents. Some states let adoptive parents reimburse the birth mother for her living expenses during the pregnancy and to cover her medical and legal fees, while others make it a crime for adoptive parents to pay even modest amounts for a birth mother's maternity clothes unless she can produce a doctor's note certifying that she is too sick to work.[6] U.S. family law is mostly state law, so each state can allow or prohibit a range of exchanges, depending on the policy preferences of legislators and other law-makers.

Adoption as "nothing but" a market exchange: "Too cold"

The "Nothing But" understanding of adoption captures both historical patterns of children being valued for their work for families and institutions, and also the approach of leading law-and-economics scholars over the past few decades. Consistent with Zelizer's description of "Nothing But" approaches as following a "simpler principle … [that] actually explains what is going on" (Zelizer, 2005, p. 29). Chicago-school legal economists contend that parenthood – as well as marriage, friendship, and sex – can be viewed as "Nothing But" rational economic transactions (Becker, 1991 [1981]; Landes and Posner, 1978; Posner, 1992).

A leading example is Nobel laureate and University of Chicago Economists Gary Becker, who in his 1981 book *A Treatise on the Family* staked a claim for economic tools to understand family forms. Speaking within the framework of supply and demand, Becker suggests that on the supply-side birth parents are more likely to put what he calls "inferior" children "up for sale or adoption" (Becker, 1991 [1981], pp. 140–141). On the demand side, he postulates a "taste for own children, which is no less (and no more) profound than postulating a taste for good foods or any other commodity entering utility function", and that adoptive parents demand information about children's "intrinsic characteristics" before investing the "effort, emotion, and risk" to raise those children (Becker, 1991 [1981], p. 45). Elisabeth Landes and Richard Posner's 1978 article *The Economics of the Baby Shortage* famously – or infamously – applied this line of reasoning to identify the "potential gains in trade from transferring the custody of the child to a new set of parents" and catalogued the pros and cons of a "free baby market" in comparison to black or gray markets that would and perhaps do persist in part because of legal constraints on payments in adoption (Landes and Posner, 1978, p. 323, p. 339; Lucas, 2000, p. 553).

Other economic analysts have built on that foundation to propose reforms such as requiring women who were considering abortion to hear a pitch from an adoption provider about the "economic incentives" should the birth mother "produce a child for the market", and a national database detailing the characteristics and requirements of adoptive and birth parents and children on a platform akin to the Multiple Listing Service used by real estate agents (Balding, 2010, p. 1076). Another economist proposed establishing an "all-pay simultaneous ascending auction with a bid cap" with prospective parents submitting sealed bids, so that profits generated by placing healthy white infants could be used to place the children they call "less-desirable" (Blackstone et al., 2004, p. 1044; Blackstone et al., 2008, p. 221).

Landes and Posner's 1978 proposal is fairly limited, but their rhetoric – such as comparing children in foster care to "unsold inventory stored in a warehouse" (p. 327) – made their article shorthand for icy proposals voiced in the language of economics. Consequently commodification theorists frequently treat Landes and Posner's so-called "baby-selling article" as the go-to example of arguments in favour of free-markets in everything, including parenthood (e.g., Williams, 1995, p. 218; Goodwin, 2010, p. 2, pp. 4–6; Radin and Sunder, 2005, pp. 8–10; Rose, 2005, p. 407). Commodification sceptics thus frame baby-selling as evidence of how "Nothing But" thinking will lead to a culture in which everything and everyone is for sale, essentially using the most extreme example of commodification as a club to fight against less extreme forms of markets in intimate contexts.

This pigeon-holing can overlook economic aspects of adoption that can be beneficial to the children involved, rather than undermining their personhood and sacred value by failing to distinguish between people and mere things. For example, economic and technological developments catalyzed the emergence of modern adoption with its concern for a child's best interests and placement of a child as a permanent member of the adoptive family with equal status to genetically related kin. Early twentieth century limits on child labour and increased life spans due to Progressive reforms such as improved living conditions and health-related innovations such as pasteurization, vaccination and antibiotics made it economically efficient to invest in children's human capital by, for example, educating them instead of sending them into the work force (Ertman, 2015b).

Adoption and market exchange as "hostile worlds": "Too hot"

The "Hostile Worlds" view maintains sharp, impermeable boundaries between money and contested commodities like love, babies, and body parts. According to Margaret Jane Radin, a leading commodification sceptic, "payment in exchange for relinquishing a child for adoption [is] a nodal case of contested commodification" (Radin, 1996, 131). So, it is not surprising that the 1988 surrogacy case *In re Baby M* generated international press coverage and intense scholarly inquiry when the New Jersey Supreme Court refused to enforce a surrogacy contract that would have required Mary Beth Whitehead to relinquish the child she conceived and carried for payment to the "intended parents", William Stern and his wife Betsy Stern. The court reasoned that "There are, in a civilized society, some things that money cannot buy" (In re Baby M., 1988, p. 1249).

That view is consistent with a rich strand of "Hostile Worlds" analysis among philosophers. Michael Walzer would block monetary exchanges in the family context because he viewed money and family as completely separate spheres (Walzer, 1984, pp. 13–17). Along similar lines, Michael Sandel articulates a value he called "giftedness" to argue against commodification where it would corrupt something sacred (such as love) or result from a coerced exchange (such as poor people selling their organs) (Sandel, 2007, p. 33; Sandel, 2000, p. 95).[7] At a policy level, that view would translate to a ban on adoptive parents paying any of a birth mother's medical, housing, or other expenses (Carroll, 2011).

Others take more nuanced positions. Debra Satz, focuses on equality among the people involved, contending that we ought to limit markets where "their operation undermines or blocks the capacity of the parties to interact as equals, even if such markets arise through voluntary individual consent and on the basis of an initial equality of conditions" (Satz, 2010, p. 65). Radin, for her part, sees the boundaries between market and intimate realms as more porous than hardline "Hostile Worlds" proponents. She asserts that "conceiving of any child in market rhetoric harms personhood", which could justify legally banning paid surrogacy, but would allow adoptive parents to pay a birth mother's "reasonable out-of-pocket expenses" (Radin, 1996, p. 139, p. 144).

"Hostile Worlds" views predominate both in and outside of the academy (Titmuss, 1970; see also Radin, 1987; Gordon, 1992, p. 257; Havighurst, 2009; Landes and Posner, 1978, p. 98; Rose-Ackerman, 1985, pp. 945–946; Rao, 2000, p. 365). Law professor Patricia Williams' braided her experiences as an adoptive parent with her expertise in critical race theory. She began: "When I decided to adopt, I was unprepared for the reality that adoption is already a pretty straightforward market" (Williams, 1995, p. 218). Yet she was surprised by the adoption agency's query about whether she would pay the "standard" fee that reflected administrative costs, or the "special" half-priced rate for "older, black, and other handicapped children" (Williams, 1995, p. 223). Williams recoiled: "Suddenly what had been a price system based on services rendered became clearly, sickeningly, a price system for 'goods,' a sale for chattel, linked … to the imagined quality of the 'things' exchanged" (Williams, 1995, p. 223). She concluded, "I was unable to choose a fee schedule. I was unable to conspire in putting a price on my child's head" (Williams, 1995, p. 225).

Radin's concept of the "domino effect" expresses a related concern that commodification in a particular context – adoption, for example – could swallow up any non-commodified elements both for the people involved and for third parties:

> Perhaps babies could be incompletely commodified, valued by the participants in the interaction in a nonmarket way, even though money changed hands. Perhaps. … . [But then] how could any of us, even those who did not produce infants for sale, avoid measuring the dollar value of our children? How could our children avoid being preoccupied with measuring their own dollar value?
>
> (Radin, 1996, p. 138)

Similarly, Elizabeth Bartholet would retain legal bans on paying pregnant women to relinquish parental rights, or to induce a woman to become pregnant for that purpose (Bartholet, 1993, p. 227). Yet in the context of international adoption at least, Bartholet defends as "entirely legitimate" the "high fees" that adoptive parents pay agencies and intermediaries, attributing the fees to the complexity of the adoption process and largely ignoring that birth parents' desperate financial circumstances – and adoptive parents' ability to pay those high fees and support the children in question – underwrite the adoption process (Bartholet, 1993, p. 154).

Zelizer's critique of these "Hostile Worlds" views reveals the fallacy of seeing adoption as something that either is or should be entirely altruistic, given the reality that exchanges of value are present throughout the adoption process. In other words, it is simply inaccurate to say that some things and relationships are essentially inside or outside of the market (Zelizer, 2000; see Williams and Zelizer, 2005, p. 362). Today adoption agreements entail exchanges of social and economic value as people contract in and out of parenthood, even in jurisdictions where courts claim to reject parenthood by contract (Ertman, 2015a, pp. 25–63; Ertman, 2003; see also T.F. v. B.L., 2004).[8]

But norms are another matter. Patricia Williams, Margaret Jane Radin, and other commodification sceptics speak both to ideal justice and the world we actually live in. Even if parenthood is for sale in some contexts, maybe law and society should enforce "Hostile Worlds" boundaries in adoption. Maybe parenthood should be relinquished only as a gift from the birth parents to the adoptive parents, without strings such as raising the child Catholic or an annual letter with pictures.

"Mosaic" of markets and non-markets in adoption: "Just right"

Commodification theorists have long pointed out that things go in and out of the market (See, e.g., Almeling, 2011; Ertman and Williams, 2005, p. 9; Clement, 2006, p. 1; Goodwin, 2006a; Zelizer,

1985, pp. 169–170; Zelizer, 1997, p. 7; Zelizer, 2005, pp. 18–19; Cohen, 2012, p. 1983). For example, marijuana was not criminalized until the early twentieth century. Yet now, after decades of being banned, marijuana has gradually re-entered the market, first for medicinal purposes, and now for recreational use in more than a third of the states.[9] Likewise, as described earlier in this chapter, children and parenthood have gone in and out the market.

As discussed above, adoptive parents routinely – and legally – pay adoption agencies, doctors, and lawyers (Ertman, 2015a, p. 67).[10] In some states they may also pay birth parents for such things as living expenses, maternity clothes, and psychotherapy. Likewise, non-pecuniary exchanges such as Post Adoption Contact Agreements (PACAs), get different treatment in different states.

Some of these exchanges involve information sharing. For example, agencies routinely require that adoptive parents promise to tell children that they are adopted. Two other types of non-pecuniary exchange similarly sustain some form of connection between the birth and adoptive families.

First, birth parents – usually birth mothers – select adoptive parents from catalogues that list the adoptive parents' traits such as religion, sexual orientation, or the financial means to pay for private schooling or travel. Prospective adoptive parents' listings are essentially ads that urge birth parents to pick them based on the home they could provide for the child, i.e., a large extended family, good health, a spacious home, economic stability, or engagement in musical activities or team sports. Accordingly, many if not most U.S. adoptions involve the birth parent relinquishing parenthood in exchange for adoptive parents implicitly agreeing to raise a child in a particular type of household that obviously costs a good deal of money to sustain. The birth parent may also insist on more explicit albeit less financial promises such as not changing a child's name. In addition, birth and adoptive parents may make a post-adoption-contact-agreement, known as a PACA, that requires the adoptive parents to provide the birth parent periodic updates about a child's development and welfare through, for example, social media, emails, letters, and even in-person visits.

Another kind of adoption commodification frequently occurs after a couple with children divorces, and one of the parents wants her new spouse to adopt the child. A large percentage of U.S. adoptions fall into this category. Generally speaking, a step-parent can adopt his spouse's child only if the child's other legal parent – often the non-custodial father – consents. If the father is behind in his child support obligations, it is not uncommon for him to charge a "price" for his consent to the step-father adoption in the form of the mother agreeing not to pursue the father for unpaid child support (Hollinger, 2004, p. 41). Courts will not enforce that promise, because the child holds the right to that support and the child's mother cannot waive the right to child support. Nevertheless, the agreements are common.

These examples make clear that it is too simple to say that a particular relationship or exchange – be it adoption or some other contested transaction – is truly inside or outside the market, as both "Nothing But" and "Hostile Worlds" views insist. The better question is who controls and benefits from the transaction (Williams and Zelizer, 2005, p. 362). While many commodification scholars largely agree on this analysis, they lack a shared shorthand to describe the phenomenon. Elsewhere I first offered the term "Mosaic" in the context of "office housework" and other non-remunerated labour (Ertman, 2020, pp. 206–215).

The phrase "office housework" refers to tasks such as food management (i.e., shopping, cooking, cleaning up, or at-work lunch orders), event planning and supervision (i.e., birthday and holiday parties), and managing technology (i.e., wi-fi access, cell phone plans, and printer glitches). This caretaking labour occurs in many contexts, including workplaces as well as households. At the office, non-billable tasks known as "glue work" build and sustain trust and community, cultivate talent, and decrease attrition through activities such as onboarding new employees, mentoring, retreat planning and administration. In households, these kinds of caretaking tasks likewise generate tremendous value by sustaining health, education, and welfare.

Yet family law, employment law, and social norms systematically ignore or devalue caretaking labour at both work and home. "Hostile Worlds" reasoning drives that under-commodification, in the form of assertions that the caretakers perform that work because they care, not in expectation of remuneration. (See Chapter 16 in this volume by Jennifer Nedelsky on care work). But if we recognize that emotional labour as a "Mosaic" of market and non-market elements in both caretaking labour done in families and workplaces, that recognition can help law and society recognize the mélange of market and non-market elements in the more contested context of adoption.

The remainder of this chapter explores that possibility in the context of PACAs – post-adoption-contact-agreements – with a particular focus on who benefits when they are not legally binding. PACAs are a principal component of open adoption, meaning adoptions in which birth parents, adoptive parents, and the children know information about each other. PACAs come into play at the high-end of information sharing, and can include letters shared through the adoption agency, social media posts, and in-person visits.

Sex columnist Dan Savage's candid and moving account of his and his husband Terry's open adoption of their son DJ illustrates what a high-contact PACA can entail. DJ's birth mother Melissa chose them because the straight couple she initially chose passed on the prospect of an open adoption with a homeless-by-choice teenager who had been drinking early in the pregnancy. Dan, Terry and Melissa negotiated "pictures a few times a year and the occasional visit" (Savage, 2005b, 35–36). Savage explained why he and Terry imagined that their son would want and need that contact:

> [i]t seemed to us that all adopted kids eventually want to know why they were adopted, and sooner or later they start asking questions. "Didn't they love me?" "Why did they throw me away?" In cases of closed adoptions there's not a lot the adoptive parents can say. Fact is, they don't know the answers. We did.

They got those answers, at least for a while:

> For the first few years after we adopted DJ his mother made a point of coming up to Seattle during the summer so we could get together. When she wasn't in Seattle she kept in touch by phone. Her calls were usually short. She would ask how we were, we'd ask her the same, then we'd put DJ on the phone. She didn't gush. He didn't know what to say. But it was important to DJ that his mother called.

Calls and visits became rare, and often included worrisome news about a boyfriend's death of alcohol poisoning or that Melissa was in jail. DJ begged for her to move in with them, so she could use their bathroom and washing machine. But Melissa refused, reminding Dan of their initial deal:

> I gently suggested that maybe it was time to get off the streets, stop drinking and using drugs and think about her future. I could hear her rolling her eyes.
>
> She'd chosen us over all the straight couples, she said, because we didn't look old enough to be her parents. She didn't want us to start acting like her parents now. She would get off the streets when she was ready.

After a few more years, the visits and calls continued, if irregularly, as did their benefits:

> As DJ gets older, he is getting a more accurate picture of his mother, but so far it doesn't seem to be an issue for him. He loves her. A photo of a family reunion we attended isn't complete, he insisted, because his mother wasn't in it. He wants to see her "even if she smells," he said.

Savage confessed to wanting Melissa's "slo-mo suicide to end, whatever that looks like". Yet he concluded with the hope that it was enough for DJ to know that his mother "left him somewhere safe, with parents she chose for him, even though it broke her heart to give him away, because she knew that if he were close, she would hurt him, too" (Savage, 2005a).

Dan and Terry stuck to their PACA, as did Melissa. But in about half of US states PACAs are not legally binding. In the family law context, my book *Love's Promises* distinguishes between legally binding "contracts", and not-legally-binding "deals".[11] As discussed earlier, adoption historically was more of a deal, and gradually evolved into a legally binding contract in which the birth parents permanently relinquished legal and social parenthood and the adoptive parents took on those roles. Along the way the law went from largely ignoring outright baby-buying and selling to criminalizing it.

PACAs like the one between Dan, Terry and Melissa have evolved from being mere "deals" to being legally binding contracts. In the early twentieth century, courts refused to hold adoptive parents to their promises to send letters or pictures or facilitate visits between the children and their birth families (Stickles v. Reichardt, 1931, p. 720). PACAs were mere "deals" that adoptive parents could honour or not as they wished. That changed quite a bit in the 1970s, due to monumental changes in law and society that greatly increased birth mothers' bargaining power in adoption transactions.

The reasons that PACAs evolved from not-legally-binding "deals" to legally binding contracts in many jurisdictions illustrate the perhaps-surprising upside of commodification. A series of court cases and activism greatly increased availability of birth control and abortion, which reduced the number of unwanted pregnancies and babies available for adoption. Legal and social changes also improved the economic circumstances of women who otherwise were facing the prospect of relinquishing children in adoption proceedings. Family law began to require non-married fathers to financially support their children, and employment law as well as social reforms greatly increased women's options for well-remunerated wage labour. Consequently, single mothers as a group enjoyed much greater economic stability and could afford to raise their children. The birth mothers who did relinquish their children for adoption came to the table with vastly improved bargaining power, able to choose the adoptive parents and even insist on a continued – if small – role in the children's' lives via exchanges of pictures and letters.

The PACA between Dan Savage, Terry, and Melissa and their entire relationship, despite its difficulties, may be more amicable than many post-adoption contact arrangements. For example, many birth mothers agree to PACAs only because circumstances force their hands. If the state is about to terminate a mother's parental rights and duties due to her abuse or neglect of the child, she might be able to prevent that catastrophic result with the only slightly less unwanted outcome of an open adoption with a PACA (Sanger, 2012, p. 324). That kind of coerced exchange is precisely the circumstances that "Hostile Worlds" views of commodification decry.

A range of scholarly proposals seek to leverage the "Mosaic" of market and non-market elements in adoption to improve longstanding problems. My own work urges the states that still treat PACAs as mere deals to legally enforce them (Ertman, 2015a, pp. 104–107). That change could benefit birth parents, the children, and even adoptive parents. Birth parents would enjoy more certainty, and potentially less extended grief over adoption's losses. The children generally benefit from knowing their birth parents as flesh-and-blood people who operated under constrained choices instead of fantasized angels or monsters. Perhaps most surprisingly, adoptive parents often benefit from knowing that the birth parents really chose them and are not off plotting to take the children back.

The advantages of PACAs tell us a lot about the commodification of adoption and the appropriateness of taking the "Mosaic" view. Since adoption is a mix of market and non-market elements, law, policy and norms can specify conditions in which exchanges are beneficial instead of toxic. Toxicity exists when money is exchanged under circumstances that look or feel like the sale of a child. But pooling and ear-marking funds can skirt that danger. For example, a Texas adoption agency strongly encourages adoptive parents to contribute to a tuition fund for birth parents. The agency pools funds from all adoptive parents and uses the money to support the education of any birth parent. That structure protects the people involved from feeling that a child has been sold, but also acknowledges in a small, symbolic, way the birth parents' loss. It also operates as a form of reparations or restitution for the imbalance in socioeconomic status between birth and adoptive parents that underlies many, if not most, adoptions. As a practical matter, the fund increases birth parents' ability to care for themselves and their families and may also help the birth parent support any children she has in the future so that she does not have to relinquish them for adoption. In short, adoption law and policy could correct some harms of under-commodification by explicitly authorizing practices such as the Texas agency's tuition fund, or perhaps even make adoptive parents promise to pay a birth mother's tuition or vocational training legally binding (Hasday, 2005).

Foster care is another context where exchanges of value could reduce suffering. Approximately 400,000 children languish in foster care in the United States, often enduring trauma from being moved from one foster family to another, with attendant instability in their social and educational lives (Beam, 2013, p. xi). Since the 1970s the federal government has enacted subsidies to encourage these adoptions out of foster care, and empirical research has demonstrated the positive and statistically significant effect of subsidies on the rate of those adoptions (Hansen, 2007). Subsidies sometimes continue after the adoption to offset the costs borne by adoptive families who care for children with special needs (often due to early adverse experiences that landed them in foster care, or abuse in earlier foster care placements). Family law is largely state law, so this subsidy varies among states, with some states issuing payment based on the type of adoptive family instead of the needs of the child (Hansen, 2008). That uneven expenditure of funds could be ameliorated by a state-imposed 10% tax on adoption expenses in high-price private adoptions to subsidize adoption of and care of children in foster care (Goodwin, 2006b).

Conclusion

Conventional wisdom reflects the "Hostile Worlds" reasoning that commodification in adoption is always harmful, and perhaps unlawful because parenthood and money cannot overlap without contagion, corruption, and coercion. But a closer look shows that exchanges of value already structure adoption processes. Moreover, the variety of ways that law and society have viewed adoption in the past, and differences in American adoption law today across state lines, show that at the very least reasonable minds can differ about the role of economic exchange in adoption. Nor do "Nothing But" assumptions that adoption is or should be a market like any other provide a descriptive or normative framework of regulation and practices. Instead, adoption – both as it is practiced and as it should evolve to be more just – is a "Mosaic" of market and non-market elements. Law and policy should abandon the myth of "Hostile Worlds" and embrace the reality that adoption has long been a mix of market and non-market elements. That change of analysis could guide reforms to address long-standing problems such as unequal bargaining power of birth and adoptive parents, the losses inherent in any adoption, and the abysmal conditions suffered by many children living in foster care. In addition, recognizing adoption as a "Mosaic" of market and non-market elements could prevent some forms of commodification in adoption from causing – like one domino knocking down all the other dominos – the complete commodification of children and parenthood.[12]

Notes

1 For example, the conditions of a transaction matter as well as the goods or services exchanged. Public health insurance could cover expensive fertility services such as in vitro fertilization only for low-income people who could not pay for those services on their own (Panitch, 2015).

2 Commodification scholars use a range of terms to describe this mid-point, none of which enjoy widespread use. Zelizer uses the phrases "differentiated ties" or "economic lives" (Zelizer, 2011, p. 4) and other scholars have used the terms "incomplete commodification", "civic propert", "hybrid commoditization", "nuanced alienability", and "altruistic exchange" (Ertman, 2020, p. 200).

3 Contract technically denotes a legally binding agreement. However this chapter uses "contract" in its colloquial sense, sometimes calling attention to monetary aspects of adoption with the phrase "financial exchange".

4 Common law is a set of judge-made rules that first emerged around 1,000 years ago in England and later migrated to the U.S. and Commonwealth countries such as Canada, India, and Australia. Statutes enacted by a legislature can alter or change common law provisions.

5 The change was gradual. For example, Massachusetts passed the first U.S. child labour laws in 1836 and 1842, requiring children under fifteen to merely attend school three months a year and then banning children under twelve from working more than ten hours a day. A century later, in 1938, the federal government enacted the Fair Labor Standards Act to sharply limit child labour across the nation.

6 Compare Ind. Code § 35-46-1-9 (2013) with Md. Code Ann., Fam, Law § 5-3A-45 (2013); In re Adoption No. 9979, p. 591 A.2d 468 (Md. 1991).

7 Richard Titmuss's classic book *The Gift Relationship* (1970) likewise champions altruism and worries that allowing for blood sales could crowd out generosity in other contexts.

8 Family law, through the Uniform Parentage Act in its various iterations, allows gamete donors to sell their parental right and duties and allows recipients of that sperm or those ova to purchase parenthood (Ertman, 2015a, pp. 46–47, pp. 52–59).

9 For discussion see Laurie Shrage's contribution to this volume (Chapter 20).

10 Md. Code Ann., Fam. Law § 5-3A-45 (LexisNexis 2013) (stating that adoptive parents cannot pay for birth mother's maternity clothes unless the birth mother has a note from doctor that she cannot work); Md. Code Ann., Crim. Law § 3-603 (LexisNexis 2002).

11 "Contracts" in U.S. law are legally binding agreements. In other work I use the term "deals" to describe non-legally-binding agreement that can nevertheless profoundly shape people's lives at home and at work. (Ertman, 2015a, pp. xii-xiii)

12 For further discussion of the domino effect in commodification, see Radin, 1996, pp. 95–101.

References

Almeling, R. (2011) *Sex Cells: The Medical Market for Eggs and Sperm*. Berkeley: University of California Press.

Balding, C. (2010) "A modest proposal for a two-sided market clearing institution under asymmetric supply constraints with skewed pricing: The market for adoption and abortion in the United States," *Journal of Public Economic Theory* 12(6), pp. 1059–1080.

Bartholet, E. (1993) *Family Bonds: Adoption and the Politics of Parenting*. New York: Houghton Mifflin.

Beam, C. (2013) *To the End of June: The Intimate Life of American Foster Care*. Boston: Houghton Mifflin.

Becker, G. (1991 [1981]) *A Treatise On the Family*, enlarged ed. Cambridge, MA: Harvard University Press.

Blackstone, E.A., Buck, A.J., and Hakim, S. (2004) "Privatizing adoption and foster care: Applying auction and market solutions," *Child and Youth Services Review* 26(11), pp. 1033–1049.
Blackstone, E.A., Buck, A.J., Hakim, S., and Spiegel, U. (2008) "Market segmentation in child adoption," *International Review of Law and Economics* 28(3), pp. 220–225.
Cahn, N. (2004) "Perfect substitutes or the real thing?" In: *Families by Law: An Adoption Reader,* Cahn, N.R. and Hollinger, J.H. (eds.) New York: New York University Press, pp. 19–24.
Carroll, A.B. (2011) "Reregulating the baby market: a call for a ban on payment of birth-mother living expenses," *University of Kansas Law Review* 59(2), pp. 285–330.
Clement, E.A. (2006) *Love for Sale: Courting, Treating, and Prostitution in New York City 1900–1945.* Chapel Hill, NC: University of North Carolina Press.
Cohen, I.G. (2012) "Can the government ban organ sale? recent court challenges and future of U.S. law on selling human organs and other tissue," *American Journal of Transplantation* 12(8), pp. 1983–1987.
Ertman, M.M. (2003) "What's wrong with a parenthood market? A new and improved theory of commodification," *North Carolina Law Review* 82(1), pp. 1–60.
Ertman, M.M. (2015a) *Love's Promises: How Formal and Informal Contracts Shape all Kinds of Families.* Boston: Beacon.
Ertman, M.M. (2015b) "Adoption," in Marciano, A. and Ramello, G.B. (eds.) *Encyclopedia of Law and Economics,* Springer Science + Business Media. https://link.springer.com/referenceworkentry/10.1007/978-1-4614-7883-6_586-1
Ertman, M.M. (2020) "The cost of non-billable work," *Texas Law Review Online* 98, pp. 184–215.
Ertman, M.M. and Williams, J.C. (2005) *Rethinking Commodification: Cases and Readings in Law and Culture.* New York: New York University Press.
Goodwin, M. (2006a) *Black Markets: The Supply and Demand of Body Parts.* New York: Cambridge University Press.
Goodwin, M. (2006b) "The free market approach to adoption: the value of a baby," *Boston College Third World Law Journal* 26(1), pp. 61–80.
Goodwin, M.B. (2010) "Baby markets," in Goodwin M.B. (ed.) *Baby Markets: Money and The New Politics of Creating Families.* New York: Cambridge University Press, pp. 2–22.
Gordon, W.J. (1992) "On owning information: Intellectual property and the restitutionary impulse," *Virginia Law Review* 78(1), pp. 149–282.
Hansen, M.E. (2007) "Using subsidies to promote the adoption of children from foster care," *Journal of Family Economic Issues* 28(3), pp. 377–393.
Hansen, M.E. (2008) "The distribution of a federal entitlement: the case of adoption assistance," *The Journal of Socio-Economics* 37(6), pp. 2427–2442.
Hasday, J.E. (2005) "Intimacy and economic exchange," *Harvard Law Review* 119(2), pp. 491–530.
Havighurst, C.C. (2009) "Trafficking in human blood: Richard Titmuss (1970) and products liability," *Law & Contemporary Problems* 72(3), pp. 1–16.
Herman, E. (2008) *Kinship by Design: A History of Adoption in the Modern United States.* Chicago: Chicago University Press.
Hollinger, J.H. (2004) "State and federal adoption laws," in Cahn, N.R. and Hollinger, J.H. (eds.) *Families by Law: An Adoption Reader.* New York: New York University Press, pp. 37–42.
In re Baby M, 537 A.2d 1227 (N.J. 1988).
Landes, E.M. and Posner, R.A. (1978) "The economics of the baby shortage," *Journal of Legal Studies* 7(2), pp. 323–328.
Lucas, M. (2000) "Adoption: distinguishing between gray market and black market activities," *Family Law Quarterly* 34(3) pp. 553–564.
Panitch, V. (2015) "Assisted reproduction and distributive justice," *Bioethics* 29(2), pp. 108–117.
Pertman, A. (2011) *Adoption Nation: How the Adoption Revolution is Transforming America.* New York: Basic Books.
Posner, R.A. (1992) *Sex and Reason.* Cambridge, MA: Harvard University Press.
Radin, M.J. (1987) "Market-inalienability," *Harvard Law Review* 100(8), pp. 1849–1937.
Radin, M.J. (1996) *Contested Commodities.* Cambridge, MA: Harvard University Press.
Radin, M.J. and Sunder, M. (2005), "Introduction: the subject and object of commodification," in M.M. Ertman, M.M. and J.C. Williams (eds.) *Rethinking Commodification: Cases and Readings in Law and Culture.* New York: New York University Press, pp. 8–29.
Rao, R. (2000) "Property, privacy, and the human body," *Boston University Law Review* 80(2), pp. 359–460.

Rose, C.M. (2005) "Whither commodification?" in M.M. Ertman and J.C. Williams (eds.) *Rethinking Commodification: Cases and Readings in Law and Culture.* New York: New York University Press pp. 402–427.

Rose-Ackerman, S. (1985) "Inalienability and the theory of property rights," *Columbia Law Review* 85(5), pp. 931–969.

Sandel, M. (2000) "What money can't buy: the moral limits of markets," in G.B. Peterson (ed.) *Tanner Lectures on Human Values, vol. 21.* Salt Lake City: University of Utah Press, pp. 87–122.

Sandel, M. (2007) *The Case Against Perfection: Ethics in The Age of Genetic Engineering.* Cambridge, MA: Belknap Press.

Sanger, C. (2012) "Bargaining for motherhood," *Hofstra Law Review* 41(2), pp. 309–340.

Satz, D. (2010) *Why Some Things Should Not be For Sale: The Moral Limits of Markets.* New York: Oxford University Press.

Savage, D. (2005a) "DJ's homeless mommy," *New York Times.* Sept. 11. www.nytimes.com/2005/09/11/style/modern-love-djs-homeless-mommy.html

Savage, D. (2005b) *The Commitment: Love, Sex, Marriage and My Family.* New York: Dutton.

Stickles v. Reichardt, 234 N.W. 728 (Wis. 1931). T.F. v. B.L., 813 N.E.2d 1244 (Mass. 2004).

Titmuss, R.M. (1970) *The Gift Relationship: From Human Blood to Social Policy.* New York: Pantheon Press.

Walzer, M. (1984) *Spheres of Justice: A Defense of Pluralism and Equality.* New York: Basic Books.

Williams, J.C. and Zelizer, V.A. (2005) "To commodify or not to commodify: that is *not* the question," in M.M. Ertman and J.C. Williams (eds.) *Rethinking Commodification: Cases and Readings in Law and Culture.* New York: New York University Press, pp. 362–382.

Williams, P. (1995) "In search of Pharaoh's daughter," in Williams, P. (ed.) *The Rooster's Egg: On the Persistence of Prejudice.* Cambridge, MA: Harvard University Press, pp. 218–225.

Zelizer, V. (1985) *Pricing the Priceless Child: The Changing Social Value of Children.* New York: Basic Books.

Zelizer, V.A. (2000) "The purchase of intimacy," *Law & Social Inquiry* 25(3), pp. 817–848.

Zelizer, V.A. (2005) *The Purchase of Intimacy.* Princeton, NJ: Princeton University Press.

Zelizer, V.A. (2011) *Economic Lives: How Culture Shapes the Economy.* Princeton, NJ: Princeton University Press.

Zelizer, V.A. and Rotman, V.A. (1997) *The Social Meanings of Money: Pin Money, Poor Relief, Paychecks, and Other Currencies.* New York: Basic Books.

PART 5

Non-human nature and environment as contested commodities

23

NATURAL CAPITAL AND BIODIVERSITY

Money, markets and offsets

John O'Neill

Introduction

This chapter is concerned with the commodification of biodiversity, and in particular with the development of offset markets as a means to achieving "no net loss" or "net gains" in biodiversity. The first section places the arguments about commodification of biodiversity in the context of wider debates about the commodification of environmental goods. What are the sources of environmental problems such as biodiversity loss? Market-endorsing arguments in neo-classical welfare economics claim that their source lies in the incomplete commodification of environmental goods and the solution in their commodification. In contrast, market-sceptical positions are critical of arguments for commodification and more strongly claim that the generalised commodification of environmental goods is itself a source of environmental problems. The second section focuses specifically on the commodification of biodiversity and offset markets. It argues that environmental problems such as biodiversity loss have their source not in incomplete commodification, but, rather, in their commodification.

Some initial clarification is required here about the concept of commodification used in the chapter. Commodification is the process of transforming a good into a commodity. Two senses of the concepts of "commodity" and "commodification" can be distinguished:

1. In its primary sense, a good is a commodity if it is the object of market exchange. A commodity is a good that has exchange value. Correspondingly, commodification in its primary sense involves the transformation of previously non-commercial goods into objects of market exchange. Typically this will require the definition and assignment of a set of rights over the goods that render them possible objects of market exchange.
2. A good is a commodity in a secondary sense if it is conceptualised and valued as a marketable good. Commodification in this sense involves the extension of relationships, attitudes and forms of valuation typical of the market to objects which were previously characterised by non-market modes of value and spheres of activity constituted by non-market relationships. Consider for example the account of commodification offered by Anderson. Markets are characterised by impersonality, the freedom to pursue individual advantage, goods that are exclusive and non-rival, want-regarding attitudes to goods, and the exercise of exit rather than voice as an

DOI: 10.4324/9781003188742-29

expression of dissatisfaction with a good. Market modes of valuation are contrasted with other modes of valuation, for example those characterised by attitudes of respect for intrinsic value, by personal attachment and by shared values (Anderson, 1993, ch.7).

The secondary sense of commodification is parasitic on its primary sense. The social sphere of market exchange is constituted by particular social meanings and modes of valuation. Commodification in the secondary sense occurs when goods that are not actually marketed are conceptualised and valued according to these social meanings and modes of valuation. Both senses of commodification are at play in conflicts about the commodification of environmental goods.

Commodification and the environment

Environmental goods are currently the object of incomplete commodification. Much of non-human nature has long been commodified. Land, timber, crops, domesticated animals, fish, coal, oil, minerals and other inputs into manufacturing are exchanged in local, national and international markets. They are typically conceptualised as market resources and valued as such. However, much of non-human nature has been hitherto uncommodified. Commons and publicly held land and resources are typically inalienable and not subject to market exchange. The atmosphere and its absorptive capacity, clean air, and many water resources have not previously been an object of exchange. Neither have much wild animal and plant life. Biodiversity – biological diversity at the various genetic, species, habitat and ecosystem levels at which it is described – has been until recently uncommodified. However, these items of previously uncommodified nature are being subject to commodification. Their commodification has been a site of conflicts. The conflicts raise questions about the relationship between commodification and environmental problems. Those questions and conflicting answers to them have been subjects of debate that have a long history between market-endorsing and market-sceptical positions (O'Neill, 2016; Neuteleers, 2022).

Market endorsing positions

Arguments for the claim that the solution to environmental problems requires a more complete commodification of environmental goods take various forms (O'Neill, 2016). The most influential on policy is that from neo-classical welfare economics (Pearce and Moran, 1994; Helm and Hepburn, 2012). This approach assumes a preference satisfaction account of well-being. An attraction of the account is that it brings well-being under the "measuring rod of money". A person's preference for some marginal change in a bundle of goods can be measured by their willingness to pay for that change. On the neo-classical approach, the source of environmental problems lies in the fact that preferences for environmental goods, such as biodiversity, and preferences to avoid environmental harms, such as pollution, are not captured in market transactions. These "market failures" entail that markets do not realise the Pareto optimal outcomes of the "ideal markets" described in welfare economics. They are "externalities", costs and benefits that are not captured within market exchange (see Bertrand's contribution in Chapter 3 of this volume). The solution to the problem is to internalise them within market exchange through the extension of market prices to unpriced environmental goods. This can be achieved directly through commodification of environmental goods in its primary sense: the construction of markets for the goods, through definition of rights such as rights to pollute (see Chapter 24 by Berta in this volume) or biodiversity offset credits that can be the object of exchange. It can be achieved indirectly through commodification in its secondary sense – through the practice of placing shadow prices on environmental goods through individuals' willingness to pay at the margin for such goods if there were a market. Shadow prices are inferred either through market behaviour (e.g. travel costs or property markets), or through stated preferences in some hypothetical market contexts (e.g. contingent valuation). The shadow prices can enter into cost-benefit analysis that mimics the outcome of ideal markets. The criterion of choice used is an efficiency criterion, potential Pareto improvement – "the Kaldor-Hicks compensation test": a situation S1 is an improvement over S2 if the gains are greater than the losses, so that the gainers could compensate the losers and still be better off. An outcome is optimal if it maximises gains over losses. Commodification in either the primary or secondary sense is a condition for the solution of environmental problems.

Market sceptical positions

Against the view that the solution to environmental problems lies in the commodification of environmental goods stand various positions that challenge arguments for expanded commodification, some of which, more radically, hold that the very commodification of environmental goods is a major source of environmental problems.

Commodification, growth and environmental destruction

One central argument against increasing commodification is that it fails to address, and indeed exacerbates, one of the major underlying structural causes of environmental damage, the systemic imperative to economic growth. Particularly influential here is Marx's characterisation of capitalism as a form of society in which "commodity production is generalised" (Marx, 1970, ch.24. section 1): both labour power and nature are commodified and subordinated to the end of the accumulation of capital, to "production for production's sake" (Marx, 1970, ch.24. section 3), to the detriment of both the labourer and the natural world (Marx, 1970, ch.15. section 10). The forces that drive accumulation are systemic: the capitalist is forced by market competition to continually recycle surplus value into expanding production (Marx, 1970, ch.4). The expansion of the commodity frontiers for the extraction of resources for accumulation puts increasing pressure on biodiversity and habitats, and the dispossession of those whose livelihoods depend on them (Moore, 2000; Temper et al., 2015). In the absence of an absolute decoupling of economic growth from increasing greenhouse gas emissions and material throughputs in the economy, it will continue to drive climate change and biodiversity loss.

Commodification, commensurability and compensability

A central set of arguments against both primary and secondary forms of commodification are those that reject the claim that there is a single measure of value, specifically a monetary measure, through which different options, states of affairs and goods can be ordered.[1] The assumption that there is a single monetary metric is grounded within neo-classical welfare economics through a preference satisfaction account of human well-being. Against this view stand versions of value-pluralism that hold that there exist a variety of different values, irreducible to each other or some super value, which cannot be captured by a single metric of value or more specifically a monetary metric of value. One form value pluralism might take is that other things matter apart from human well-being. A pluralist account of value might appeal to the intrinsic value of the flourishing of non-human beings and states. However, a pluralist view can also be sustained within a framework concerned with human well-being, given a pluralist understanding of well-being according to which there is a plurality of constitutive dimensions of well-being – physical health, personal relations, wider social relationships, autonomy, knowledge, aesthetic experience, accomplishment and achievement, sensual and intellectual pleasures, a well-constituted relation with the non-human world, and so on. Pluralist objective accounts of well-being that appeal to needs (Wiggins, 1998, essay I) and capabilities (Sen, 1993; Nussbaum, 2000) offer influential examples. No single monetary measure is able to capture these different dimensions of well-being. Some central dimensions of well-being are indeed constituted by a refusal to treat them as tradable commodities that can be bought or sold. For example, certain social relationships such as friendship and love are such that they cannot be the objects of market exchange (Raz, 1986: 345ff.; see Panitch's contribution in Chapter 4 of this volume). Correspondingly, those with whom we stand in such relationships are the object of non-market modes of valuation. Constitutive incommensurability is evident in refusals to place monetary values on environmental goods discussed below.

These claims about incommensurability have implications for the possibilities of compensation for the loss of particular goods. The concept of compensation is used in economics to describe relationships between losses and gains with respect to well-being. A loss in a good *A* is compensated for by a gain in a good *B* for some agent if the agent is not worse off after the loss and gain. The state after the gain of *B* is at least as good as the state before the loss of *A*. The good *B* is a substitute in a welfare sense for the good *A*. However, given the existence of plural and incommensurable constitutive dimensions of well-being, some losses in goods central to well-being will not be compensable in this welfare sense. The end of a central relationship in a person's life, such as a loss of a close friend or family member, cannot be compensated for by some gain in some other dimension of well-being. The loss has no substitute. The existence of such blocks on substitutability has implications for the commodification of environmental goods discussed further below.

Distributional objections

There are a number of distributional objections to the use of a monetary metric of the value of environmental goods.

i. Willingness to pay is income dependent. If a raw monetary willingness to pay metric of preferences is used, the preferences of those with lower incomes will count for less than those with higher incomes. Monetary metrics might be weighted relative to incomes in response (Kolstad et al., 2014, 3.6.1). In practice, cost-benefit analysis employs unweighted metrics. The consequence is that the preferences of the poor count for less, and the most "efficient" siting of developments, such as a road or mine or of an environmental offset with negative impacts, will fall on those with lower incomes. Similarly, "efficient" markets will tend to allocate goods disproportionately to the wealthy and burdens disproportionately to the poor.
ii. Monetary metrics of goods fail to distinguish the ethical significance of the satisfaction of vital needs as against the satisfaction of trivial preferences. A monetary metric simply measures the strengths of preferences. It does not capture vital needs at stake, such that if the need is unsatisfied a person is harmed, falling below some minimal threshold of human well-being. An agent is not necessarily harmed if their preferences are not satisfied. They are harmed if they are unable to satisfy a vital need (Wiggins, 1998, essay I; O'Neill, 2010).
iii. The criteria that define optimal outcomes in neo-classical defences of market solutions to environmental problems are premised on forms of aggregative consequentialism. The optimal

outcome is that which most efficiently improves total welfare. Serious harms are justifiable if they lead to an aggregate improvement in well-being. Given a preference satisfaction account of well-being, environmentally damaging projects that threaten vital needs can be justified in cost-benefit analysis through the satisfaction of numerous but relatively trivial preferences (Wiggins, 2006).

iv. The interests of future generations and non-humans cannot be captured directly in either actual or shadow prices which reflect the preferences of current generations of market actors. At best they are captured indirectly and precariously to the degree that willingness to pay of current consumers reflects ethical concern for the well-being of future generations and non-humans (O'Neill, 1993, ch.4). Injustice to future generations is exacerbated by the practice of discounting.

v. Markets facilitate injustice through displacement. The claim is central to Kapp's criticisms of the concepts of "externalities" and "market failure". On the standard view, environmental problems are "market failures". The concept of "market failure" is founded on the claim that, in the absence of a series of imperfections such as externalities, transaction costs and imperfect information, markets lead to ideal welfare improving outcomes, specifically to Pareto optimal outcomes. Externalities that are the source of environmental problems are grit in an otherwise efficient social machinery. The solution is to "internalise" those externalities by extending market prices to previously unpriced goods. Kapp's criticism of the concept of "externality" and his replacement with that of "cost-shifting" contests these assumptions. The shifting of costs from those who produce them to other individuals or society in general are not "minor disturbances" in an otherwise ideal market, but rather systemic features of market economies (Kapp, 1963, 1978, p. 13). They result from the acts of rational agents in markets who, to compete, need to lower their production costs relative to competitors (Ibid, p. 14). Environmental problems are not market failures that could be resolved by being internalised into markets. Rather they are problems that are the result of the way that markets operate. Kapp's argument points to a wider set of arguments around ways commodification can facilitate injustice through displacement. Offset markets are particularly prone to this for reasons discussed in the section below on the distributional objections to offset markets.

Deliberative criticism

The marketisation of environmental goods takes the formation of environmental policy outside of the domain of public deliberation to which it properly belongs. Willingness to pay and monetary valuations are reason-blind. They express the strength of persons' preferences for some good. They do not reflect the soundness of the reasons they have for those preferences (O'Neill, 2007, ch.1). The preferences do not need to pass the test of being able to survive deliberative scrutiny. In contrast, judgements expressed in public deliberation do have to survive being made public. Hence, participants are forced to offer reasons that appeal to general rather than particular interests. As such, the interests of future generations and non-human nature are more likely to be represented in deliberative as against market-based modes of governance (Goodin, 1996, pp. 846–847).

Natural capital, biodiversity and offset markets[2]

Environmental policy making at local, national and international levels has been increasingly articulated in the language of natural capital. The various environmental goods that matter to people, such as woodlands, wetlands, rivers, rural and urban landscapes, biological variety at the different levels it is described – eco-system, habitat, species and genetic – are conceived of as forms of capital and are valued as such. What is it to value environmental goods as natural capital? A number of different claims need to be distinguished (O'Neill, 2017, pp. 3–5):

1. Ecosystem services: The core claim that all accounts of natural capital share is an account of how environmental goods should be conceptualised and valued. Like "produced capital" (machines, roads, buildings, etc.) and "human capital" (health, education, skills) they are to be conceptualised as assets to be managed and valued for the services they provide for human well-being (Dasgupta, 2021, ch.1). Natural capital provides a series of "ecosystem services": provisioning services, such as inputs into food production, water, plant-based medicines; regulating services, such as carbon sequestration, waste assimilation, pollination; cultural services, such as recreation or aesthetic enjoyment; supporting services, such as soil formation and photosynthesis (Millennium Ecosystem Assessment, 2005; TEEB, 2010; Chapter 25 by Martin-Ortega and al. in this volume).
2. Compensation and substitutability: The claim that environmental goods should be valued for their services grounds a second set of claims about compensability and substitutability. Given that goods are valued for their services, the loss of one component of capital can be compensated by a gain in another component of capital if the services they provide either maintain or improve total well-being. As Helm puts it "the aggregate of natural capital should be non-decreasing" but "there can be substitutability between different types of natural assets" (Helm, 2014, p. 111). The approach to sustaining an overall level of "natural capital" is influential through "no net loss" or "net gain" approaches to environmental policy. Policy should aim at maintaining or improving total aggregate levels of natural capital through compensation of loss in one component of natural capital with gains in another. The loss of one habitat can be compensated for example through the protection, restoration or the creation of another.
3. Monetisation: The claim that environmental goods should be understood as natural capital, valued for the services they provide for human well-being, grounds their monetisation, given the further assumption that well-being consists in preference satisfaction where the strength of preferences can be measured through agents' willingness to pay. The determination of this monetary value can be ascertained either through revealed or stated preference methods for ascertaining a shadow price or through the construction of markets for the goods (see Chapter 25 by Martin Ortega et al.).
4. Marketisation: The use of markets, and in particular offset markets, is defended as the most efficient and effective means to maintain aggregate natural capital. Given "unavoidable" environmental losses through development, offset markets are taken to offer an effective route for compensation for that loss: payments by the developer causing damage for environmental gains elsewhere leave aggregate levels of natural capital as good or better than they were before the trade. Payments can take a variety of forms. The developer might directly pay a third party, for example an NGO, to create an offset: consider, for example, the payments made by Rio Tinto Zinc to environmental NGOs to protect forest discussed below. The developer might make payments to a central government offsetting fund, such as the Indian Compensatory Afforestation Fund discussed below. Finally, a conservation bank might assign credits to landowners or environmental organisations for preserving, creating, restoring or enhancing a site of biodiversity which can be bought by developers to offset environmental damage. Market

transactions ensure that aggregate levels of natural capital are sustained efficiently at sites where the cost of maintaining aggregate natural capital is lower.

The claim that environmental goods should be understood as natural capital involves a number of distinct claims, involving forms of both primary and secondary commodification. The first three claims involve potential and actual forms of secondary commodification. The first core claim, that environmental goods should be understood as assets to be valued for their services, reconceptualises nature in an instrumental and impersonal manner and is a presupposition of the stronger claims about substitutability and compensability. The monetisation of environmental goods can take either a secondary form of commodification, where the good is the object of shadow pricing, or a primary form where the good is priced in a market. Marketisation involves primary forms of commodification.

Offsets, accumulation and the creation of a perverse asset set

One of the promises of biodiversity offsetting is that it overcomes the potential conflicts between the protection of biodiversity and continuing economic growth. Offsets are presented as part of a "mitigation hierarchy." Development should first attempt to avoid or reduce biodiversity loss, then mitigate losses on site where possible, but where avoidance, reduction and on-site mitigation are not possible, offsets allow for the compensation of the loss of biodiversity through payments for its maintenance or enhancement at another site. The result is claimed to be no net loss or net gain in biodiversity. It is a policy mechanism that renders the goal of "preserving the aggregate level of natural capital" consistent with "major increases in consumption that economic growth will bring" (Helm, 2014, p. 109).

This argument is open to the objection noted in the previous section, that the source of environmental problems lies in the systemic imperatives within a capitalist economy for growth and capital accumulation. The extension of the commodification of nature through offsetting does not address these systemic imperatives. It rather attempts to shift the boundaries of nature and sites of biodiversity to accommodate them to the growth imperatives (Spash, 2015). Indeed, the monetary value of biodiversity as an asset becomes structurally tied to the continuation of economic growth and the environmental losses this brings.

Offset markets create a perverse asset class: the economic value of an environmental good becomes dependent on the existence of environmental losses. For example, the economic value of a site of biodiversity as an offset is dependent on the loss of biodiversity elsewhere. Without that loss it is economically worthless. Offset markets create a structural dependence of nature conservation on the existence of environmental losses. Correspondingly, environmental organisations engaged in biodiversity market transactions find themselves structurally dependent on companies engaged in the destruction of sites of biodiversity (Seagle, 2012). One consequence is the limits this places upon their capacity to respond to environmental damage on which their own finances have become dependent (O'Neill, 2017).

Valuation, compensation and substitutability

The core claims about environmental goods as natural capital involve a particular conceptualisation and mode of valuing those goods. Biodiversity, habitats, landscapes and other environmental goods are valued for their ecosystem services. What is it to value goods for their services?

Consider the following influential characterisation of services and their place in economic theory offered by Ayres and Kneese:

> Almost all of standard economic theory is in reality concerned with services. Material objects are merely the vehicles which carry some of these services, and they are exchanged because of consumer preferences for the services associated with their use or because they can help to add value in the manufacturing process.
>
> (Ayres and Kneese, 1969, p. 284)

Ayres and Kneese make three claims about the concept of services that can be distinguished (O'Neill, 2017, p. 6):

1. Instrumental value: To value goods for their services is to value them instrumentally, as a means for some specified end.
2. "Mere vehicle": The good is valued "merely as a vehicle" that provides those services.
3. Scope: The ends for which the goods are valued are the direct satisfaction of consumer preferences through their use, or their indirect satisfaction through their role in manufacture.

The concept of ecosystem services widens the scope of services, including for example through the regulating and supporting role that environmental goods offer. However, in standard economic literature, the assumption that well-being understood as preference satisfaction is the end for which services are valued remains. So too are the first two claims. Environmental goods are valued instrumentally as mere vehicles for the provision of services.

The valuation of environmental goods for their instrumental value for human well-being is open to objections concerning the value of those goods that are independent of human well-being. It fails to capture the value that non-human beings or states have independent of their contribution to human well-being. These are important objections, but they will not be those I consider here. Both the instrumental value assumption and the mere-vehicle assumption are open to objections where we simply consider the relationship between environmental goods and human well-being.

Consider first the mere vehicle assumption. A good is valued "merely as a vehicle" that provides services. For what class of objects is the mere vehicle claim true? A starting point for an answer to this question is the distinction between *de re* and *de dicto* valuations. A joke about the socialite Zsa Zsa Gabor illustrates the distinction:

> Zsa Zsa: "Ah! People misunderstand me! They think that I am just a creature of leisure, that I do nothing useful, but they are wrong. I am constantly finding new ways to do good for people."
>
> Interviewer: "Like what?"
>
> Zsa Zsa: "I have found a way of keeping my husband young and healthy, almost forever."
>
> Interviewer: "Eternal youth… that is quite a discovery! How do you do it?"
>
> Zsa Zsa: "I get a new one every five years!"
>
> (Hare, 2007, p. 514)

The statement "Zsa Zsa Gabor values a husband who is young and healthy" is ambiguous. On a *de re* reading what is valued is a particular person – the husband of Zsa Zsa Gabor – who is young and healthy. Under the *de dicto* reading what is valued is that whoever falls under the description, "the husband of Zsa Zsa Gabor," is young and healthy. The joke plays on the ambiguity. When Zsa Zsa claims that she is doing good in keeping her husband young and healthy we assume a *de re* reading. The object of her concern is a particular person. It turns out her claim is to be given a *de dicto* reading – that whoever falls under the description "the husband of Zsa Zsa" is young and healthy.

To value some object for being merely a vehicle that provides services is to value it *de dicto* and not *de re*. It is to value the object in virtue of falling under the description of "provider of services, $\alpha_{1\ldots}$ α_n." Consider the statement "P values a site which has biodiversity properties $\beta_{1\ldots}$ β_m." The statement is ambiguous. It has a *de re* reading – P values a particular site which has biodiversity with properties $\beta_{1\ldots}$ β_m. It can be given a *de dicto* reading – P values that a site falls under the description of having biodiversity properties $\beta_{1\ldots}$ β_m. No net loss and net gain policies and the practices of biodiversity offsetting markets assume *de dicto* valuations. The loss of one site can be compensated by its replacement with another with the same properties. Those who defend particular sites of biodiversity often value them *de re*. It is the particular place that they are concerned to preserve. Another site that falls under the description of having properties $\beta_{1\ldots}$ β_m does not compensate for its loss.

The distinction matters to how far substitutability is possible between different objects. *De dicto* valuation does entail a specification of acceptable substitutes. Zsa Zsa Gabor's husband must have the properties of being young and healthy. A site of biodiversity that is valued *de dicto* as a site with biodiversity properties $\beta_{1\ldots}$ β_m is replaceable with another only if it also has those properties. Much of the debate about offsetting turns on the description under which a site of biodiversity is valued. If the description is general – for example that the site is deciduous woodland – then substitution by another woodland may not be difficult. If the description is detailed, for example through the specification of a particular species-mixture that a site exhibits, then the replacement with another site with the same qualities is more difficult and might be impossible. Correspondingly, a central debate about offsets turns on the descriptions under which different sites are considered equivalent (Carver and Sullivan, 2017). The valuation of an object *de re* entails stronger limits on the possibility of replacement without loss. If the object of Zsa Zsa Gabor's love is a particular person, his loss will not have a substitute in another person with similar properties. Similarly, if a community values a site of biodiversity as a particular place, then the existence of another with similar biodiversity properties will not be a substitute. The question arises therefore about what objects are the proper objects of *de re* valuations and for what objects *de dicto* valuations are appropriate.

There is a wide range of goods for which *de dicto* valuation is appropriate. A tool is typically valued *de dicto* for its properties that serve the job it does. Another with the same properties will be a substitute. The possibility of sustainability relies upon the fact that many goods are valued *de dicto*. A source of energy valued as such – as a source that provides energy that satisfies needs for warmth, mobility, the cooking of food, and so on – is valued *de dicto*. Any source of energy that meets those needs will be valued as such (Brand-Correa and Steinberger, 2017). Valued for such services, a source of energy with high greenhouse gas emissions can be replaced without loss or with gain by another with lower emissions.

However, there are many objects and beings that are the proper objects of *de re* valuations. Close relationships between persons are valued *de re*. Love is a *de re* attitude towards a particular person (Kraut, 1986, p. 421). What grounds these valuations? What value do relationships to particular persons have for our lives? An answer to that question has implications for the instrumental value assumption above. A distinction needs to be drawn between goods that are of instrumental value to well-being and goods that are of constitutive value for well-being (Wiggins, 1998, essay VI; James, 2022). A good has instrumental value for well-being if it is a causal means for well-being. A good has constitutive value for well-being if it is a constituent of well-being. Consider the increasingly pervasive language of social capital used to describe social relations such as friendship. While it may be true that a network of friends brings various goods typically mentioned as benefits of social capital – better physical and mental health, employment prospects etc. – the characterisation of friendship as simply a form of social capital misses the place of friendship in a good life. It treats friends simply as having instrumental value – as an external causal means to other goods that matter for well-being. However, friendship is not simply an external means to other goods that matter to well-being. Friendship is itself a central constitutive component of well-being. And friendship involves a concern *de re* for another as a particular person valued as an end in themselves, not simply as a means to other goods. This significance of *de re* valuation in personal relations is grounded in the objective pluralist accounts of well-being outlined earlier. Certain relationships are central constituents of a good life. They are not merely capital, the instrumental causal means for some other end. Correspondingly, when close friends, lovers and kin die, their loss is a loss for which there is no substitute or compensation.

De re valuations might be central to our relationships to other human beings. What of environmental goods? Here also relationships to particular places can matter and matter not simply as external instrumental means to well-being, but as constitutive components of a good life (O'Neill, 1993, pp. 23–24; 2020). They do so in part through the personal and community histories that they embody. Many conflicts over environmental goods and their loss turn upon the significance that a particular place has for a community – for the way that it embodies the life and work of a community. What is at stake is a particular place that is valued as such and which does not have a substitute in another that provides the same "services." They involve *de re* rather than *de dicto* valuations. These valuations can be revealed in refusals to accept monetary compensation. Consider an example that I have discussed before, a refusal to accept an offer of compensation by an adivasi community in India whose home is threatened by a dam:

> You tell us to take compensation. What is the state compensating us for? For our land, for our fields, for the trees along our fields. But we don't live only by this. Are you going to compensate us for our forest?…Or are you going to compensate us for our great river – for her fish, her water, for vegetables that grow along her banks, for the joy of living beside her? What is the price of this? …How are you compensating us for fields either – we didn't buy this land; our forefathers cleared it and settled here. What price this land? Our gods, the support of those who are our kin – what price do you have for these? Our adivasi (tribal) life – what price do you put on it?
>
> (Bava Mahalia, 1994)

Some goods mentioned here might be understood as "provisioning services" offered by the fields and river – the vegetables, fish and water. However, thus understood the question "what is the price of this?" has an obvious answer. It is the price of vegetables, fish and water in the market. What is threatened with loss here is not simply the provision of those goods. Activities such as fishing and growing vegetable are not simply instrumentally valuable for the goods they produce. They are activities that are themselves significant human goods constitutive of the well-being of members of the community. They involve social relationships and the exercise of skills passed across generations that are components of a good life lived by the river. What is threatened by the dam is the life of a community that is embodied in the landscape to be submerged beneath water. It is this particular place with its history and projected future that matters. It is valued *de re*. There is no compensation for its loss.

This way that particular places matter is true of more ordinary landscapes and habitats threatened with loss. Consider the successful campaign by a local community to protect Smithy Wood, an 800-year-old woodland of 20 acres that was part of a larger coppiced wood in Sheffield, UK, threatened by loss to build a motorway service station. The development was to be offset by the creation of a larger woodland. One objection to the development is that the new woodland would lack the particular flora and fauna of the ancient woodland (Barnes, 2017). However, even if it were possible to reproduce the particular mix of flora and fauna, this would not compensate for the loss of an embodiment of a particular evolutionary and social history and the historic sense of place it has for the community. It is the particular place with its history that is valued. To put it in terms noted earlier, the specific biodiversity properties $\beta_{1\dots}$ β_m of the woodland might already make substitution difficult if valued *de dicto* under that description and not under a more minimal description as a deciduous woodland. However, the woodland is also valued *de re* by a community as a particular place with its particular history.

To make these points about *de re* valuation and constitutive values is not to claim that such values are trumps in public decision-making. Where other vital needs are at stake (as opposed to trivial interests typified by a service station) then a development might be justified. However, the claim that the needs can be met with "no net loss" or "net gain" is false. The goods lost have no substitute.

Distributional objections to offset markets

Biodiversity offsetting and the no net loss or net gain policies they are used to implement are aggregative. Total levels of biodiversity are to be maintained or improved. Offset markets achieve this by shifting sites of biodiversity. As such, they raise distributional questions at two different sites: the site in which biodiversity loss takes place and the site in which the compensatory gain in biodiversity is made. Injustice can occur at both sites.

The site of biodiversity loss is that at which injustice is most immediately evident. It is no compensation to a community who loses a site of biodiversity that matters to them that another site elsewhere has a gain in biodiversity. The problem is true of ordinary urban and rural landscapes that matter to people. However, it is most clearly evident in cases in which, through a development, a community loses livelihood and a way of life that realises significant human goods. Consider for example the loss of access to common land and forests for communities affected by the Compensatory Afforestation Fund Act (CAFA) in India. CAFA involves a form of offsetting through a central fund: projects that destroy forests, such as mining, pay monetary compensation into a Compensatory Afforestation Fund based on the estimated monetary value of the forest. The funds are to be used to fund forest protection, restoration or development that compensates for the loss of forest. Communities who lose access to the forest and common land for livelihood can suffer losses in basic livelihood resources and at the same time associated forms of community, practice and culture (Saxena, 2019, p. 31; Ghosh, 2017; Worsdell and Shrivastava, 2020). For a community suffering those losses though a development of a place valued *de re*, no additional offers can compensate for that loss.

The site at which the offset takes place is also liable to problems of injustice by displacement of burdens and responsibilities. The responsibilities and burdens associated with an environmental loss are shifted from the agent causing the harm to the agent assigned with mitigation.

Notable injustices occur where those burdens are shifted from developers to marginal communities excluded from offset lands. Consider again the impacts of CAFA in India. The places in which the offset projects are implemented often involve the loss of use rights to forests (Saxena, 2019, pp. 31–33; Ghosh, 2017; Worsdell and Shrivastava, 2020, p. 14). The losses here again include loss of access to the means to satisfy basic needs and the loss of relationships to particular places that are valued as particulars that embody the life of a community. A quote from a woman losing use rights to forest affected by mining captures both dimensions of loss: "What do you do when your home and resources are both taken away?…We have totally lost our way of life" (Nagaraj, 2022; see also Larrère's Chapter 29 on parks and forests in this volume).

Similar examples are evident in other cases of offset regimes. Consider for example the offsetting projects associated with the Rio Tinto QMM's ilmenite mine in the Anosy region of Madagascar. The development of the mine causes the loss of littoral forest habitat. Working with the International Union for the Conservation of Nature, Birdlife International and other environmental NGOs, Rio Tinto promises that the mine will have a "net-positive impact" on biodiversity (Temple et al., 2012). The promise is to be realised partly through offsets to protect threatened habitats elsewhere in the region thereby "reducing the high background rate of deforestation" (Ibid., p. 2). It is claimed that through forest protection and restoration, the ratio of gain in littoral forest to loss to mining will be 2:1 with a ratio of gain to loss to all forest types of 4:1 (Ibid., p. 30). Who carries the burden and responsibility for the gains? At the offset site, Bemangidy-Ivohibe, run with a local NGO partner associated with Birdlife International, the answer is that a community which relies upon forests for their livelihoods loses customary rights for the use of the forest resources. The agent who causes the losses – a major corporation, Rio Tinto – shifts the burdens and responsibilities for sustaining forest to those with marginal livelihoods (Kill and Franchi, 2016). The additional burdens fall on those who are already among the worst off, affecting their capacity to meet their basic needs.[3] Two additional observations can be made of the case. First, claims to net gain rely upon counterfactual claims about rates of forest loss in the absence of the development, which themselves depend on a set of contestable claims about the causes of forest loss and how they can be best rectified. Second, the route to preserving forest creates the perverse asset class of biodiversity offsets noted earlier. The economic value of maintaining the forest is tied to its loss through mining. The consequence is that environmental organisations themselves are rendered structurally dependent on environmental damage.

Conclusion

This chapter has focused on offset markets as examples of the commodification of environmental goods. The examples illustrate some of the more general problems with the commodification of environmental goods: environmental governance is rendered consistent with systemic growth imperatives that are a source of environmental problems; modes of valuation foster ubiquitous substitutability; forms of injustice result through the displacement of burdens and the loss of places and livelihoods that meet vital biological and social needs. These problems are related. The design of systems of environmental governance consistent with continuing economic growth requires places and habitats to be substitutable so their destruction can be compensated with "no net loss". The shift in location shifts burdens and impacts. Where it is most "efficient" to shift them is to the poor.

The sources of environmental problems do not lie in their incomplete commodification, but rather in the generalisation of commodification noted in first section, in particular the commodification of wider domains of nature. Their solution lies in forms of decommodification. The forms these might take require larger debates. At the level of decision-making, it entails not the use of monetary valuation within cost-benefit analysis, but deliberative democratic procedures concerned with meeting the plurality of human needs within environmental constraints (O'Neill, 2007). At the level of larger economic structures, writers such as Neurath offer forms of generalised decommodification of goods, replacing markets with non-market economic institutions (Neurath, 1925; O'Neill, 2021). Less radical is the view of Polanyi, which takes social and environmental problems to have their source in the disembedding of markets from social and ethical constraints through the creation of fictitious commodities in labour, land and money (see Chapter 2 by Postel and Sobel in this volume). As such their solution lies not in a generalised decommodification but rather in the re-embedding of markets (Polanyi, 1957; Dale, 2010). It is on the various possible alternatives to commodification that deliberation on solutions to environmental problems needs to focus.

Notes

1 The concept of value commensurability is used in different senses. On one usage, different options are commensurable if their value can be measured on a cardinal scale of value, such as money (Chang, 1997, pp. 1–2; Aldred, 2006). On this use, "commensurability" is distinct from "comparability", the claim that options can be ordered under some value. Others use the terms interchangeably (Raz, 1986, chapter 13). This chapter focuses on criticisms of monetary measures of value.

2 This section draws on arguments in O'Neill (2017; 2020).

3 Other offset projects in Madagascar offer similar examples of injustice by displacement (Bidaud et *al.* 2017, pp. 7–11).

References

Aldred, J. (2006) "Incommensurability and Monetary Valuation", *Land Economics,* 82, pp. 141–161.

Anderson, E. (1993) *Value in Ethics and Economics.* Cambridge Mass., Harvard University Press.

Ayres, R.U., and A.V. Kneese (1969) "Production, Consumption, and Externalities", *American Economic Review*, 59(3), pp. 282–297.

Barnes, S. (2017) "For an Ancient Woodland near Sheffield, Spring will Herald a Carpet of Bluebells – or the Construction of a Giant Car Park", *Sunday Times*, March 19.

Bidaud, C., Schreckenberg, K., Rabeharison, M., Ranjatson, P., Gibbons, J., and Jones, J.P.G. (2017) "The Sweet and the Bitter: Intertwined Positive and Negative Social Impacts of a Biodiversity Offset", *Conservation and Society,* 15(1), pp. 1–13.

Brand-Correa L. and J. Steinberger (2017) "A Framework for Decoupling Human Need Satisfaction from Energy Use", *Ecological Economics*, 141, pp. 43–52.

Carver, L. and S. Sullivan (2017) "How Economic Contexts Shape Calculations of Yield in Biodiversity Offsetting", *Conservation Biology*, 31, pp. 1053–1065.

Chang, R. (ed.) (1997) *Incommensurability, Incomparability and Practical Reason.* Cambridge, MA: Harvard University Press.

Dale, G. (2010) *Karl Polanyi: The Limits of the Market.* Cambridge: Polity Press.

Dasgupta, P. (2021) *The Economics of Biodiversity: The Dasgupta review*. London: HM Treasury.

Ghosh, S. (2017) "Compensatory Afforestation: 'Compensating' Loss of Forests or Disguising Forest Offsets?", *Economic & Political Weekly,* 52(38), pp. 67–75.

Goodin, R. (1996) "Enfranchising the Earth, and Its Alternatives", *Political Studies,* 44, pp. 835–849.

Hare, C. (2007) "Voices from Another World: Must We Respect the Interests of People Who Do Not, and Will Never, Exist?", *Ethics*, 117, pp. 498–523.

Helm, D. (2014) "Taking Natural Capital Seriously", *Oxford Review of Economic Policy*, 30, pp. 109–125.

Helm, D. and Hepburn C. (2012) "The Economic Analysis of Biodiversity: An Assessment", *Oxford Review of Economic Policy*, 28(1), pp. 1–21.

James, S. (2022) *How Nature Matters.* Oxford: Oxford University Press.

Kapp, K.W. (1963/1978) *The Social Costs of Business Enterprise*. Nottingham: Spokesman.

Kill, J. and Franchi, G. (2016) *Rio Tinto's Biodiversity Offset in Madagascar,* World Rainforest Movement and Re-Common.
Kolstad C., Urama, K., Broome, J., Bruvoll, A., Carino Olvera, M., Fullerton, D., Gollier, C. Hanemann, W.M., Hassan, R., Jotzo, F., Khan, M.R., Meyer, L. and Mundaca L.(2014) "Social, Economic and Ethical Concepts and Methods", *Climate Change 2014: Mitigation of Climate Change. Contribution of Working Group III to the Fifth Assessment Report of the Intergovernmental Panel on Climate Change.* Cambridge, Cambridge University Press.
Kraut, R. (1986) "Love *De Re*", *Midwest Studies in Philosophy*, 10, pp. 413–430.
Marx, K. (1970) *Capital I.* London: Lawrence and Wishart.
Millennium Ecosystem Assessment (2005) *Millennium Ecosystem Assessment, General Synthesis Report.* Island Press, Washington D.C.
Moore, J. (2000) "Sugar and the Expansion of the Early Modern World Economy: Commodity Frontiers, Ecological Transformation, and Industrialization", *Review* (*Fernand Braudel Center*), 23(3), pp. 409–433.
Nagaraj, A. (2022) "India's Forest-planting Push Leaves Indigenous Women out in the Cold", Reuters https://news.trust.org/item/20220201170707-upki6
Neurath, O. (1925) "Economic Plan and Calculation in Kind", in Neurath, O. (2004), *Economic Writings 1904–1945*, T. Uebel and R.S. Cohen (eds), Dordrecht: Kluwer, pp. 405–465.
Neuteleers, S. (2022) "Trading Nature: When Are Environmental Markets (Un)desirable?", *The Journal of Political Philosophy,* 30, pp. 116–139.
Nussbaum, M. (2000) *Women and Human Development: The Capabilities Approach.* Cambridge: Cambridge University Press.
O'Neill, J. (1993) *Ecology, Policy and Politics: Human Well-Being and the Natural World.* London: Routledge.
O'Neill, J. (2007) *Markets, Deliberation and Environment.* London: Routledge.
O'Neill, J. (2010) "The Overshadowing of Need", in F. Rauschmayer, I. Omann, J. Frühmann (eds), *Sustainable Development: Capabilities, Needs, and Well-Being*, London: Routledge, pp. 25–42.
O'Neill, J. (2016) "Markets, Ethics and Environment", in S. Gardiner and A. Thompson (eds), *Oxford Handbook of Environmental Ethics.* Oxford: Oxford University Press, pp. 40–50.
O'Neill, J. (2017) *Life Beyond Capital.* Centre for the Understanding of Sustainable Prosperity www.cusp.ac.uk/wp-content/uploads/Life-beyond-capital-online.pdf
O'Neill, J. (2020) "What is Lost through No Net Loss", *Economics and Philosophy,* 36, pp. 287–306.
O'Neill, J. (2021) "Neurath on Political Economy", in T. Uebel, and C. Limbeck-Lilienau (eds), *The Routledge Handbook of Logical Empiricism,* Abingdon: Routledge, pp. 266–275.
Pearce, D.W., & Moran, D. (1994) *The Economic Value of Biodiversity*. London: Earthscan.
Polanyi, K. (1957) *The Great Transformation.* Boston: Beacon.
Raz, J. (1986) *The Morality of Freedom*. Oxford: Clarendon.
Saxena, K. (2019) "Compensatory Afforestation Fund Act and Rules: Deforestation, Tribal Displacement and an Alibi for Legalised Land Grabbing", *Social Change,* 49, pp. 23–40.
Seagle, C. (2012) "Inverting the Impacts: Mining, Conservation and Sustainability Claims Near the Rio Tinto/QMM Ilmenite Mine in Southeast Madagascar", *The Journal of Peasant Studies*, 39, pp. 447–477.
Sen, A. (1993) "Capability and Well Being", in M. Nussbaum and A. Sen (eds), *The Quality of Life.* Oxford: Clarendon Press, pp. 30–53.
Spash, C.L. (2015) "Bulldozing Biodiversity: The Economics of Offsets and Trading-in Nature", *Biological Conservation,* 192, pp. 541–551.
TEEB (2010) *The Economics of Ecosystems and Biodiversity: Mainstreaming the Economics of Nature: A synthesis of the approach, conclusions and recommendations of TEEB.* Available at: www.teebweb.org/wp-content/uploads/Study%20and%20Reports/Reports/Synthesis%20report/TEEB%20Synthesis%20Report%202010.pdf
Temper, L., del Bene, D. and Martinez-Alier, J. (2015) "Mapping the Frontiers and Front Lines of Global Environmental Justice: The EJAtlas", *Journal of Political Ecology*, 22, pp. 255–278.
Temple, H. J. et al. (2012) *Forecasting the path towards a Net Positive Impact on biodiversity for Rio Tinto QMM* https://portals.iucn.org/library/efiles/documents/2012-049.pdf
Wiggins, D. (1998) *Needs, Values, Truth*, 3rd edition. Oxford: Clarendon Press.
Wiggins, D. (2006) "An Idea We Cannot Do Without", in S. Reader (ed.), *The Philosophy of Need.* Cambridge: Cambridge University Press, pp. 25–50.
Worsdell, T. and Shrivastava, K. (2020) *Locating the Breach: Mapping the Nature of Land Conflicts in India.* New Delhi: Land Conflict Watch.

24

EMISSIONS TRADING

Commodification of pollution—From resistance to proliferation

Nathalie Berta

Introduction

Since the Kyoto Protocol of 1997, emissions trading has become a favoured way to manage climate change, as evidenced by the proliferation of carbon markets (for instance in Europe, Japan, Canada, and more recently China). Yet, when this idea first emerged, in the 1960s, it was largely regarded as "an impractical and cumbersome product of the convoluted minds of academia" (Baumol and Oates, 1979, p. 252). This chapter provides a history of this idea, mainly concerning the United States, where emissions trading first took off. It focuses both on its reception and its subsequent roll-out in the 1980s, and on the justifications for it put forward by mainstream economists.

The idea of emissions trading is rooted in the economic concept of externalities (on which see Chapter 3 by E. Bertrand in this volume). It has been promoted since the 1960s by environmental economics, a new academic field which quickly became a branch of neoclassical economics. Environmental economics regarded pollution as an environmental externality and claimed that it could be managed by economic instruments. Within neoclassical economics, the concept of externalities carried a strong normative content, which had two important consequences. First, as a market failure inducing inefficiency, an externality requires state intervention, the primary goal of which is to reach economic efficiency. So considering pollution in terms of environmental externalities requires first that we make pollution an economic issue, rather than the health or environmental one it used to be. Thus, from a historical point of view, the idea of emissions trading is part of a larger movement of economicization of environmental issues, of subjection of environmental policies to economic criteria.

Second, since from the 1960s onwards an externality has usually been defined as an unpriced individual interdependence (Berta, 2017), the solution, which obviously falls directly out of the definition, calls for the introduction of the missing price. The concept of externalities was originally used to demonstrate that markets fail, and potentially could have led to a strong criticism of competitive markets; instead, it has become a justification for the creation of new markets. But within the theoretical framework of neoclassical economics, the internalization of externalities does not necessarily call for their commodification. It calls for the introduction of prices or "incentive-based" policies, but the latter can also rely on administered prices, that is, taxes. This

DOI: 10.4324/9781003188742-30

is why the idea of emissions trading is part of a larger academic debate: first a debate between incentive-based policies versus direct control (standards, norms, or specific technology enforcement); second, a debate concerning the kind of incentive-based policies to be used, namely market prices versus taxes.

Within such a framework, emissions trading can refer to two kinds of trade, which raise different issues and pursue different theoretical objectives. First, following Coase (1960), tradable property rights on the externality ought to be created and allocated between the emitter and the receptor, who are expected to bargain over them and agree upon an optimal level of emissions. The negotiated price is expected to reflect their individual preferences for pollution, through a balance of its marginal benefit (for the polluter) and damage (for the receptor). Coasean bargaining is not considered relevant for most pollution control policies, since they involve a large number of agents. According to neoclassical theory, which assumes rational individual choices, such bargaining inevitably raises "free riding" issues because depollution or clean air has a public good dimension: while emitters have incentives to sell their rights for their own profit, receptors, as soon as they are more than one, have no incentives to purchase them since they could benefit from the others' purchases. Coasean bargaining is rather used to justify payments for environmental services or voluntary markets for compensation where the polluter directly pays someone else to offset the emissions (see Chapter 25 by Julia Martin-Ortega et al. in this volume).

The second kind of trade, following John Dales (1968), refers to a market for emissions rights—today labelled "cap-and-trade" instruments (CAT). Contrary to Coasean bargaining, the emissions level or the environmental goal—the cap—is exogenous to trade, since it strictly follows from a political decision. Tradable emissions rights are issued by public authorities according to this cap. They are auctioned or freely allocated to the emitters who are then expected to trade them in order to reach a cost-efficient allocation. Trading is used to allocate the burden of depollution among emitters depending on the marginal costs of depollution. More precisely, each polluter is supposed to bring his or her marginal cost in line with the market price; in a competitive framework where they all face the same price, it is expected that they will all equalize their marginal costs, which is the theoretical condition for total cost minimization. As a consequence, the price is a political price emerging directly from the political constraint (from a purely theoretical point of view, the more restrictive the cap, the higher the price). For instance, the price obtained in a "carbon market" does not give the social value of carbon as a perfect reflection of individual preferences. According to Dales (1968, pp. 803–804),

> the market in pollution rights is not a 'true' or 'natural' market [...] It transmits the government-owner's decisions [...] The price signals that the government gets from the market are 'false' in the sense that they are largely echoes of its own arbitrary decision about the supply of rights.

The commodification involved in CAT is very specific. What is traded is not nature or the environment, nor even the damage or the pollution—despite the ambiguous use of the term "carbon" markets or "sulphur" markets to designate such instruments. The exchanged commodity is an emission right, a legal license to pollute, today called "allowances". Sometimes, when emitters are allowed to offset their emissions, instead of reducing them or using allowances, trading is extended to another commodity: a certified emission reduction (CER), a legal certification that pollution has been reduced (or avoided). With both assets, the issue at stake is not the monetary valuation of nature or pollution, as it is for cost–benefit analyses or "optimal" solutions that claim to balance—and thus to monetize—the damage and benefit of pollution.[1] These assets raise the issue of the monetization of the polluters' legal obligation to abate, and thus the issue of the political flexibility they are offered: in the name of cost efficiency, they are afforded the possibility, through purchases of allowances or CERs, to transfer depollution to others and thus to postpone or avoid their own depollution requirements.

The first part of this chapter is devoted to the early history of the idea of emissions trading, the 1960s and 1970s. The idea followed from a twofold project: finding an alternative to optimal solutions whose attempts to equalize cost and benefit were considered unrealistic, and at the same time "rationalizing" present environmental regulation, that is, introducing incentives instead of direct pollution control, in the name of cost efficiency. Most environmental economists at the time promoted the use of taxes. But introducing taxes required an economicization of environmental policy, a conceptualization of pollution as an economic issue rather than the health issue it used to be, which raised strong resistance outside academia. More precisely, virtually everybody except economists considered taxes as "licenses to pollute": the idea that one could put a price on pollution and that paying this price could free one from any effort to clean up was considered immoral.[2] Such moral resistance to their tax approach explained why environmental economists received Dales's idea of a market for emissions rights quite cautiously.

The second part is devoted to the spread of both the idea and practices of emissions trading from the 1980s onwards. From the first incremental experiments in the late 1970s, to the Kyoto Protocol, "the concept of harnessing market forces to protect the environment has gone from being politically anathema to politically correct" (Stavins, 2002, p. 1). The moral resistance crumbled at the same time as the resistance of industry to existing regulation became organized and grew in strength. Policy makers started to consider CATs as a political compromise between environmental concerns (through the cap) and economic interests (since emissions trading offering opportunities for profit as well as political flexibility). Controversies partially shifted to design and implementation issues, challenging the practical ability of CATs to fulfil their theoretical promise to deliver both environmental effectiveness and economic efficiency.

The early history of the idea

The 1960s was a decade of growing awareness of environmental issues, especially concerning air and water pollution. In the United States, the existing regulatory framework mainly relied on technological and health-based standards, as evidenced by the 1963 Clean Air Act (CAA) and the 1972 Clean Water Act (CWA). The young field of environmental economics, which was just taking off, understood pollution as an externality. It started to promote the rationalization of environmental regulations, stressing the cost savings that the use of prices could achieve (influential in this respect were Kneese, 1964; Kneese and Bower, 1968). Dales's proposal for a market for emission rights was part of this movement.

The promotion of cost efficiency

Two "optimal" ways of internalizing costs were already on the table in the 1960s. First the Pigovian tax, understood here as an optimal tax which attempts to equalize the marginal benefit and damage at the optimum. Second, Coase's bargaining solution, although its influence remained thin in the environmental literature of the 1960s and 1970s (Medema, 2014). As already stressed, it did not seem a good fit with diffuse externalities like pollution, and it was also criticized on ethical grounds.[3]

By the mid 1960s the tax approach dominated the economic literature. But, to be optimal, the Pigovian tax required perfect knowledge of the marginal damage function and thus its monetary valuation. This raised the contentious issue of pricing what were called the "intangibles"—like recreational uses of water, health issues, or aesthetic values. Some environmental economists (Dales, 1968; Baumol and Oates, 1971) criticized solutions that attempted to balance the costs and benefits of pollution (Berta, 2020). At the same time, being strongly attached to the introduction of prices or incentives, they also criticized the existing regulation based on direct control as too costly. They suggested a strategic fallback position: separating the environmental goals—standards or emission levels—from their means, that is from the issue of their implementation. Environmental standards must follow from a political decision: they are arbitrary from the standpoint of economics, which means that standards do not necessarily have to balance damages and benefits to be optimal, so that the idealized and controversial monetary valuation of damage is no longer required. And pollution trading (through markets) or pricing (through taxes) must be organized in order to meet such standards at the lowest cost.

In this spirit, Dales (1968) proposed a market for emissions rights in order to organize trading between emitters. Emissions rights, issued according to exogeneous political standards, were to be auctioned and traded among polluters. Theoretically, cost efficiency—which requires the equalization of all marginal abatement costs to the market price—is thus expected to be reached at competitive equilibrium (Montgomery, 1972).[4] Meanwhile, Baumol and Oates (1971) suggested using uniform taxes to reach the same criterion of cost efficiency: the taxes then have to be adjusted ex post to achieve the given standards of environmental quality. The theoretical equivalence—in terms of cost efficiency—with Dales's market approach was quickly recognized.[5]

From the late 1970s the focus of economists and policy makers shifted from the costs of pollution to the costs of regulation; they started to compare the costs of the several policy options in pollution control. Baumol and Oates's proposal, and more generally the use of charges, was quickly favoured by many environmental economists (see, for instance, Freeman and Haveman, 1972; Tietenberg, 1973). But things were different with regards to Dales's proposal. It was well known within the relatively small community of environmental economists, but its initial reception among them was cautious. Influential economists often relegated his idea to footnotes without discussion—or at least until the mid 1970s (Baumol and Oates, 1971; Baumol and Oates, 1975; Freeman and Haveman, 1972). When Baumol and Oates finally discussed Dales's proposal for the first time, more than a decade after its publication, they stressed that "it does not seem to have a high degree of political appeal" (1979, p. 252).

This cautious reception of Dales's idea can be explained by the context at that time. The tax system that economists were intensely promoting was widely rejected by Congress, environmentalists, and industry. And, as we will see below, this rejection was based mainly on ethical grounds. So the political acceptance of a market proposal appeared highly unrealistic.

The wider resistance to the use of incentives

The still growing public concern for environmental quality and pollution urged President Nixon to declare the 1970s "the decade of the environment" (Meidinger, 1985; Andrews, 2010). The policy agenda considerably expanded and led to ambitious bipartisan amendments of the 1970 CAA and the 1972 CWA. Congress drafted the CAA amendments with the express goal of protecting public health. The Environmental Protection Agency (EPA) was asked to set health standards accordingly and to exclude cost considerations, according to the idea that public health could not be compromised by other considerations. The CAA regulatory strategy relied on "the best available technology": performance standards were based on the most effective technology already in use in each industry, and this technology was imposed in order to accelerate its diffusion among polluting installations.[6] The CWA was based on the same kind of regulatory framework and also ignored the economists' promotion of incentives. During the debate prior to their adoption, Senator Proxmire's bill proposed to impose effluent charges on industrial polluters. Many pro-tax economists, like Kneese or Haveman, testified before various congressional committees between 1971 and 1975 to advocate the advantages of such a policy. But the tax approach was consistently rejected by Congress.

In fact, there was no appetite for the tax approach, except among economists (Meidinger, 1985). Congress, environmentalists, and even policy-makers all resisted the idea. More generally, they rejected making pollution an economic issue. While the economic nature of pollution seemed obvious to economists, Congress and environmentalists considered pollution primarily a health issue, and feared that if environmental quality was decided on economic grounds, economic efficiency would take precedence over other considerations like enforcement (when choosing the policy instruments) and health (when choosing the policy goals). Perhaps because economists were aware of this reluctance, they regularly emphasized the economic dimension of pollution (see e.g., Freeman and Haveman, 1973, p. 59). Ruff's (1970) influential paper in favour of the tax approach, entitled "The Economic Common Sense of Pollution", is emblematic of the exasperation that economists sometimes evinced regarding this issue: "We are going to make very little real progress in solving the problem of pollution until we recognize it for what, primarily, it is: an economic problem, which must be understood in economic terms" (p. 69). And the "real progress" hoped for here was that, once the economic dimension of pollution was acknowledged, the balance of costs and benefits in policy choices would seem more obvious, and the use of incentives harder to resist. But this would have required an important change in narrative, since the economic "common sense" they evoked was common only to them. What Andrews (1984) called "a climate of economic reasoning" had not yet arisen.

Many Congressmen and environmentalists thought of taxes as unacceptable and immoral "licenses to pollute" (Kelman, 1981). Several arguments were linked in this "licenses to pollute" debate. They rejected the monetary valuation of pollution and the associated damage. Again, this issue is raised by cost–benefit analyses which claim to find an optimal level of pollution—as would be reflected by the Pigovian tax. But Baumol and Oates's fallback approach (1971) was intended to avoid this issue, since their proposed tax did not require any economic balance or valuation, but rather was meant to be adjusted ex post according to a political goal (Berta, 2020). This point, however, was not sufficiently stressed at the time, and this fed the confusion.[7] Nevertheless, the tax approach was also subject to other ethical criticisms. Environmental quality and health issues, it was argued, must remain "priceless" because they should be valued for their own sake. The pricing of "priceless" goods corrupts their value since any determinate price is less than priceless—a kind of ontological corruption argument (see Vida Panitch's Chapter 4 in this volume). Moreover, opponents of the tax also used a consequentialist argument, stressing that the use of incentives can crowd out intrinsic motivation (see Frey, 1986)—a kind of normative corruption argument (on Panitch's framework).

Third, a tax is not a fine, and endorsing self-interest with incentives fails to stigmatize or condemn polluting behaviour: "how many people would feel that by paying their money they're absolved of guilt?" (environmentalists quoted in Kelman, 1981, p. 110) Implicitly, this issue raises the distinction between consequential and deontological ethics. Economists, according to their utilitarian framework, focus on outcomes and consider pollution abatement as pollution abatement, irrespective of the motives behind it (making profit, complying with regulation, caring for the environment, etc.). For non-economists, some emissions are morally wrong, and some duties are inalienable. They want polluters to do their best—an obvious contradiction with the economic principle of marginal depollution costs equalization, according to which a high-cost polluter could efficiently do nothing. The debate also raised the distinction between a "legalist" approach, which relies on inalienable rights and duties, and the new "economistic" approach, which relies on incentives. As stressed by Goodin (1994), taxing emissions—and even more so trading them—could be compared to the selling of medieval indulgences (on which see Chapter 7 by Januard and Lapidus in this volume).

To sum up, making pollution an economic problem, and more specifically an environmental externality, raised moral issues: relying on incentives and self-interest instead of intrinsic motivations, balancing costs and benefits instead of rights and duties, focusing on efficiency rather than moral standing. Economists failed to understand these moral issues, which nonetheless constituted the most important resistance they had to face (Berta, 2023). They usually considered taxes to be an uncontroversial proposal, "a relatively neutral device" (Kneese and Schulze, 1975, p. 91) which just stressed that if one policy could achieve an environmental goal at less cost than another one, the cheaper should be chosen. And when they narrowly compared incentives and regulation, economists tended to address costs, as well as technical and sometimes distributional issues (see e.g., Baumol and Oates, 1975; Kneese and Schulze, 1975), but did not engage in what they sometimes called with disdain the "licenses to pollute cliché".[8]

This early reception of the tax approach explains why even mainstream economists did not promote Dales's CAT proposal while they were trying at the same time to "rationalize" direct regulation, using the argument of cost efficiency. Oates, who had become a promoter of CATs, would later stress: "I must admit that when I first read the Dales' essay, although I found the basic economics of the argument quite sound, I simply shook my head when thinking about the political feasibility of the proposal" (Oates, 2002, p. viii). This early reception also shows how resistance to market-based instruments and pollution pricing has eroded ever since. Prices have by now become rhetorical devices used to persuade, a language that policy makers listen to and that pragmatic environmentalists also adopt (O'Neill, 2006; Neuteleers and Engelen, 2015)—a change that owes much to the conceptualization of pollution as an externality (Spash, 2021). Such a change led progressively to the subjection of environmental policies to economic criteria, and to the growing disqualification, in the name of theoretical cost savings, of policies based on direct control rather than incentives.

The spread of cap-and-trade, in theory and in practice

The 1970s was a decade that saw strong economic growth, relative public confidence in the federal government, scepticism towards industry, and growing concern for environmental issues. After the oil shock, this large consensus started to unravel and opposition to regulation grew, especially from targeted industries who circulated the idea of a "growth ban" and "overregulation". Concern shifted from the costs of environmental degradation to the costs of environmental regulation. The idea that more flexibility should be given to industry progressively spread and market-based instruments found new support in the political arena. Regarding emissions trading, the debate changed after the first experiments in the late 1970s. Most criticisms now focused on the tax versus market debate. And as new experiments developed, they started to raise design or implementation issues, challenging the environmental and economic effectiveness of CAT and its ability to fulfil their theoretical promises.

The EPA's first—and unexpected—experiment

In the late 1970s the EPA implemented what would later be considered the first experiment in emissions trading (Meidinger, 1985; Andrews, 2010; Voß, 2007). Indeed, it quickly appeared that many sources would not be able to comply with the federal pollution standards set by the CAA, leading to there being areas where these standards were not achieved. In such "non-attainment areas", the Act prohibited new polluting installations—a prohibition which could lead to growth restriction. However, with the economic crisis, the political and economic context had changed and such a restriction now appeared unacceptable. The Carter administration had to face up to the rising contestation of regulation by industry and became interested in instruments that could circumvent these claims of a "growth ban". The EPA was urged to take measures that would not directly contradict economic efficiency. At the same time, within the agency, young economists tried to introduce incentives and flexibility despite the internal resistance of lawyers and engineers, of which the EPA staff was largely constituted (Cook, 1988; Meidinger, 1985). It was quickly decided to give firms flexibility by allowing emissions compensation among installations through several mechanisms.[9] For instance, a new installation could enter a non-attainment area provided that it offset its new emissions by a reduction in another installation, whether the latter was owned by the same firm—through internal compensation—or by another firm—through trading.

The irony of the story is that this first experiment in emissions trading was adopted when prominent environmental economists were mainly promoting taxes, considering emissions trading unrealistic. In fact, it did not owe much to the economists' promotion of cost efficiency and was rather an unintended consequence of the 1970 CAA; furthermore, it was more like a marginal and pragmatic breach in the CAA regulatory framework rather than a change in its spirit (Meidinger, 1985). Besides, the trades between firms were very marginal: first, they were subject to EPA approval; next, industry was reluctant and mainly secured its offsets internally; and, finally, they were repeatedly challenged in court by environmental groups.[10] But although trading remained quite rare, this reform introduced a flexibility mechanism which would pave the way for commodification: the possibility of offsetting emissions led to the creation of a new entity, the CER. Broadly defined, offsets allow polluters to avoid an abatement requirement by transferring the latter to someone else somewhere else. Even if offsetting does not necessarily induce trading (when it is done internally), it produces a kind of disassociation of the emission from the source that is decisive in the commodification process (see Chapter 23 by O'Neill in this volume). Both offsetting and trading require an abstraction: the separation of the emission (through allowances) or the reduction (through CER) from the emitters. This would be decisive in the future rise of "carbon" markets. This abstraction of emissions from their physical, temporal, and spatial dimensions—that is, from their material conditions of production—led to the creation of a homogenous unit of measurement, the ton of CO_2 equivalent (tCO_2e), on which both CATs and voluntary markets for carbon compensation rely today (Bumpus, 2011).

The spread of the idea

The caution in the reception of emissions trading among environmental economists was temporary; and from the early 1980s they started to promote the idea. Tom Tietenberg, primarily pro-tax, wrote a positive evaluation of the EPA trading scheme (Tietenberg, 1985; see also Hahn and Helster, 1989) which would become seminal. Within the EPA, the strong internal resistance encountered in the late 1970s finally crumbled, due to a higher concentration of economists. The agency wrote its own positive report, claiming to have saved several companies with these flexible mechanisms. An influential bi-partisan report, "Project 88" (Stavins, 1988), proposed the creation of offset markets for almost every pollution issue, and, for the first time, promoted an international "carbon" market.

Within environmental economics, the debate was no longer about the choice between incentives or direct control: the latter was disqualified for being inefficient and costly; the pejorative term "command-and-control" became widespread; and arguments became more ideological, contrasting "decentralized trading programs" with "omniscient bureaucracy" (Dudek and Palmisano, 1988). The theoretical debate now focused on the kind of incentives to be favoured, tax versus market. Both are expected to be cost efficient (to achieve marginal abatement costs equalization), but given that public authorities do not know the polluters' abatement costs, each faces a specific uncertainty: either the price is set (under a tax system) and the quantity (the level of emissions induced by the tax) is uncertain, or the quantity (the cap) is set (under CAT) and the market price is uncertain. Market proponents usually criticized the administrative adjustments required by a tax system—since it must be adjusted *ex post* to fit the environmental goal—a process regarded as "cumbersome and politically unattractive" (Montgomery, 1972, p. 411); at the same time, they optimistically assumed that "the market makes the necessary calculations independently in the course of reaching equilibrium" (ibid.). But this argument is not theoretically substantiated and relies on an implicit assumption: that the least-cost allocation, i.e., the competitive equilibrium which theoretically equalizes all marginal abatement costs, is reached efficiently. And it is only under the heavy assumption of costless market adjustments towards equilibrium that the inferiority of the tax approach, associated with high administrative adjustment costs, can be sustained. Such bias was decisive in empirical evaluations of CAT which tried to quantify the expected cost savings; the equalization of marginal costs at market equilibrium was simply assumed (as if the least-cost allocation was actually reached at no cost), which makes it possible to argue for high cost savings.

These arguments of economists in favour of CAT helped build a successful narrative for emissions trading (Lane, 2012). But the role of economists should not be overestimated. As already stressed, a shift also occurred in the political arena. While in the early 1970s emissions trading was politically unacceptable, by the 1980s it appeared to be a realistic compromise between regulation and flexibility. This movement was initiated under the Carter administration, which put "regulatory reform" on the political agenda, but it was overtly accelerated under the Reagan administration, which favoured pro-market activities and deregulation. Policy makers started to see CATs as a compromise for both industry and some environmental groups, like the Environmental Defense Fund which also supported Project 88. The latter were convinced by the cap, which theoretically could ensure a certain level of environmental quality, while the former were convinced by the trade, which promised to ensure flexibility and profit opportunities. So what emerged during the 1980s was a coalition of NGOs, industry, policy makers, and academic in favour of emissions trading (Voβ, 2007).

The spread of emissions trading in practice

This shift during the 1980s led to the decisive adoption of a large experiment with CAT. The United States had to manage the rise of sulphur dioxide emissions, which were responsible for acid rain. The 1990 CAA amendments gave birth to the "Acid Rain Program". Relying both on the theoretical justifications of economists and their positive evaluations of the EPA trading system, a CAT was created for sulphur dioxide emissions. It was the first emissions trading system created, not as an incremental experiment within a regulatory framework, but designed *ex nihilo*, as suggested by economic theory. It was thus presented as a paradigmatic shift (Voβ, 2007). It was immediately deemed a great success, "a living legend of market effectiveness" (Burtraw and Palmer, 2004), despite serious issues. In reality, it exhibited low prices and minimal exchanges, while the observed cost savings were mainly due to the falling costs of rail transport used for low-sulphur coal rather than to the market itself.

Nonetheless, this experiment paved the way for the Kyoto Protocol (Lane, 2012; Voβ, 2007). It helped to demonstrate that carbon markets could be technically implementable and politically acceptable. Ratified in 1997, the Protocol inaugurated an international market for CO_2, and, as a flexibility mechanism, it introduced the Clean Development Mechanism (CDM), which allowed polluters to offset carbon emissions with CERs obtained by investment in reduction projects in developing countries. This framework inspired the creation of national CATs for carbon emissions—the first and emblematic one being the European Union Emissions Trading System (EU ETS).

Like most CATs, the EU ETS saw low prices with recurrent collapses and high volatility. Thus, it failed to provide the steady high prices expected to drive polluters to low-carbon technologies. On the contrary, it allowed the postponing of the decisive investments urgently required in many industrial sectors since it provided them with cheap allowances. After more than 15 years of existence, the EU ETS had failed to reduce pollution: many studies showed that, although emissions had indeed declined, this was mostly due to the 2008 economic crisis, which mechanically decreased industrial pollution (by 30%), and to other measures against climate change taken by the EU at the same time—like the imposed increases in renewable energies and energy efficiency (which reduced emissions by 60%).[11] Meanwhile, the market experienced a constantly cumulating surplus of allowances, also fed by the emissions offsetting with cheap CER through the CDM. As a consequence, the market design has since its creation been subject to recurrent reforms, all trying *ex post* to palliate these pitfalls.

Several lessons can be drawn from the setbacks of the EU ETS. CATs require constant administrative adjustments to stabilize their prices faced with deeply uncertain changes in demand. So the usual arguments regarding their simplicity and low cost compared to the "cumbersome and costly" adjustments of a tax system, in addition to being theoretically questionable, also appear empirically contestable. Furthermore, the price volatility is inherent to the construction of these markets; compared to the consistency and predictability of a tax, they create significant price uncertainty for emitters. This price risk has justified their financialization in order to provide risk hedging and more market liquidity. So, they are actually financial markets which involve the development of new assets: what is traded is not allowances, but futures and derivatives of allowances, subject to speculation by purely financial actors (not necessarily regulated) who take advantage of the volatility. And this speculation feeds the volatility (see Berta et al., 2017 for an evaluation and a critical study, see also Lohman, 2009 for a more general survey). For instance, after a decade of low prices (around 5 Euros), the EU ETS has experienced a tenfold increase in price during the last few years. But given the remaining surplus of allowances in circulation, whether this spectacular increase has come about from recent reforms of the market—like a higher cap stringency—or from speculation, remains an open question.

Nevertheless, since their development in the mid 1980s, CATs have been insulated from criticisms regarding their poor effectiveness, for several reasons. First, exhibiting a methodological bias, economists often compare a theoretical CAT as it would be in an idealized world of perfect competition, to practical regulation, as it actually is with all its imperfections. Second, the debate became confined to implementation issues: if markets fail, it is claimed, this is primarily because they have been poorly designed, and they just need further reforms. But, as evidenced by the EU ETS, the practical setbacks of CAT are not unexpected and fixable disruptions, but are intrinsic to its construction: CAT systems require constant adjustment according to unexpected changes in demand for allowances; prices are volatile due to unavoidable uncertainty and speculation; and the postponement of abatements of entire polluting sectors through cheap allowance purchases is the very essence of the flexibility offered to industry.

Conclusion

After a period of moral contestation, the idea of CAT is now considered to be an acceptable compromise between necessary regulation and flexibility for industry. This owes much to the rhetoric of prices, or discursive commodification, that has permeated environmental policies since the 1980s. Pollution today is considered as an economic issue, and the idea that it can be managed by price adjustments (market prices or taxes) rather than a more stringent regulatory framework is widely accepted. From a practical point of view, despite the gap between the outcomes that were theoretically expected and the empirical problems CATs actually face, their usage still continues to expand. For instance, Europe has recently adopted a new market, EU ETS II, to regulate new sectors, namely road transportation and the heating of buildings.

The spread of carbon markets could lead in other directions, like the growth of tradable CERs. International agreements on climate change now focus on carbon neutrality (targets are formulated in terms of zero *net* emissions rather than *gross* reductions). This change encourages carbon offsetting. For instance, Europe is committed to achieving carbon neutrality by 2050, and in order to offset its actual emissions is now seeking to improve carbon storage in agricultural soils through the adoption of specific practices (like crop rotation). Such new agricultural carbon management, called "carbon farming", raises two main issues. The first is a funding problem: such new agricultural practices could be funded by subsidies or payments for environmental services (see Chapter 25 by Julia Martin-Ortega et al. in this volume); but it could also result in voluntary markets for CERs (sold by farmers to industry, for instance), whose prices could be connected to actual carbon markets. The second is that it challenges the political relevance of offsetting: one could decide to use carbon farming to achieve new reduction goals in this sector, which is not targeted by any specific policy; or one could choose to use it to offset actual emissions, as suggested by carbon neutrality commitments. More generally, the international account in terms of carbon ton equivalents (tCO_2e) inherited from Kyoto allows an unlimited expansion of carbon markets, which may be more or less compartmentalized. And this often comes with the same justification: making pollution control more flexible, even at the cost of postponing efforts to decarbonize the economy and the risk of high price volatility and uncertainty.

Notes

1 "Optimal" solutions—among which we may count the Pigovian approach—try to find an "optimal" level of pollution or externalities that would equalize the marginal cost and benefit.

2 Distributional issues are not addressed here (but see O'Neill's Chapter 23 in this volume). The way allowances are usually allocated among industries mainly depends on political reasons, and especially on the possibility to relocate the production outside the regulated area. Distributional options raise more ethical issues for consumers than for industry, and thus are out the scope of this chapter.

3 First because Coase's reciprocal principle would allow the receptors to bribe the polluters; second because the introduction of transaction costs could justify the status quo.

4 Dales acknowledged Coase's (1960) influence on the issue of the definition of property rights but he did not evoke Coasean bargaining at all. Crocker (1966) is often credited as being the father of emissions trading, along with Dales. Actually, their proposals were not the same: Crocker suggested organizing trading between polluters and receptors, in order to reach environmental standards in a very Coasean spirit.

5 Whether polluters equalize their marginal cost to a market price or to a tax, it is supposed to guarantee the minimization of the total abatement costs.

6 An installation is a source of pollution. A firm can own several installations.

7 Kelman (1981, p. 146) stressed that many environmentalists confused taxes and cost–benefit analyses. More generally, the theoretical arguments in favour of cost efficiency actually took a back seat in the tax debate.

8 Ruff stressed that tax approach has the advantage that no one has "to determine whom to blame or who should pay" (Ruff, 1970, pp. 80–81), while this was precisely the criticism levelled at taxes by Congress and environmentalists.

9 These mechanisms, named netting, offsets, bubbles, and banking—were all giving polluters the flexibility to avoid stringent limits, through the transfers in time or location of their abatement requirements. See Cook (1988) for a more detailed presentation.

10 But finally upheld by the US Supreme Court in 1986. Environmental groups opposed the fact that emissions could grow in non-attainment areas—even if compensated: the latter were precisely areas where no flexibility should be allowed. They also raised technical issues: for instance, offsetting new emissions required strong monitoring that rarely existed and was quite uncertain; furthermore, proving that a reduction had been done somewhere required a counterfactual scenario, called a baseline scenario, which was very hypothetical.

11 The market was responsible for less than 10% of the emissions reductions (Gloaguen and Alberola, 2013).

References

Andrews, R.N.L. (1984) "Economics and environmental decisions, past and present", in Smith, V.K. (Ed.), *Environmental policy under Reagan's executive order: The role of benefit-cost analysis*, Chapel Hill and London: University of North Carolina Press, pp. 43–85.

Andrews, R.N.L. (2010) "The EPA at 40: An Historical Perspective", *Duke Environmental Law and Policy Forum*, 21, pp. 223–258.

Baumol, W. and Oates, W.E. (1971) "The use of standards and prices for protection of the environment", *The Swedish Journal of Economics*, 73(1), pp. 42–54. https://doi.org/10.1007/978-1-349-01379-1_4

Baumol, W. and Oates, W.E. (1975) *The Theory of Environmental Policy*, Cambridge: Cambridge University Press.

Baumol, W. and Oates, W.E. (1979) *Economics, Environmental Policies and the Quality of Life*, London: Prentice Hall.

Berta, N. (2017) "On the definition of externality as a missing market", *European Journal of History of Economic Thought*, 24(2), pp. 287–318. doi:10.1080/09672567.2016.1169304

Berta, N. (2020) "Efficiency without optimality: environmental policies and pollution pricing in the late 1960s", *Journal of the History of Economic Thought,* 42(4), pp. 539–562. https://doi.org/10.1017/S10538 37219000579

Berta, N. (2023) "Thinking like an economist? The (temporary) resistance to market-based policies in pollution control", mimeo.

Berta, N., Gautherat, E. and Gun, O. (2017) "Transactions on the EU ETS: a bubble of compliance in a whirlpool of speculation", *Cambridge Journal of Economics*, 41(2), pp. 575–593. https://doi.org/10.1093/cje/bew041

Bumpus, A.G. (2011) "The matter of carbon: understanding the materiality of tCO2e in Carbon Offsets", *Antipode,* 43(3), pp. 612–638. doi.org/10.1111/j.1467-8330.2011.00879.x

Burtraw, D. and Palmer, K. (2004) "SO2 Cap-and-Trade Program in the United States. A Living Legend of Market effectiveness", In Harrington, W., Morgentern R.D. and T. Sterner (Ed.), *Choosing Environmental Policy*, Resources for the Future, Washington DC, pp. 41–66.

Coase, R.H. (1960) "The problem of social cost", *Journal of Law and Economics*, 3, pp. 1–44.

Cook, B.J. (1988) *Bureaucratic politics and regulatory reform. The EPA and emissions trading*, Greenwood Press, New-York: Westport and London.
Dales, J.H. (1968) *Pollution, Property and Prices. An Essay in Policy Making and Economics*, Toronto: University of Toronto Press.
Dudek, D.J. and Palmisano, J. (1988) "Emissions trading: Why is this thoroughbred Hobbled?", *Columbia Journal of Environmental Law*, 13(2), pp. 217–256.
Freeman, A.M. III and R.H. Haveman (1972) "Residuals charges for pollution control: a policy evaluation", *Science*, 177(4046), pp. 322–329. https://doi.org/10.1126/science.177.4046.322
Frey, B.S. (1986) "Economists favour the price system–who else does?", *Kyklos*, 39(4), pp. 537–563. https://doi.org/10.1111/j.1467-6435.1986.tb00677.x
Gloaguen, O and Alberola, E. (2013) "One billion tonnes of CO2 avoided since 2005 in Europe: half due to energy-climate policies and half due to economic context", CDC CLIMAT Research, Climate Brief n°32, October.
Goodin, R.E. (1994) "Selling Environmental Indulgences", *Kyklos*, 47(4), pp. 573–596.
Hahn, R.W. and Helster, G.L. (1989) "Where did all the markets go? An analysis of EPA's Emissions Trading Program", *Yale Journal on Regulation*, 6(1), pp. 109–154.
Kelman, S. (1981) *What price incentives? Economists and the environment*, Boston: Auburn House.
Kneese, A.V. (1964) *The economics of regional water quality management*, Baltimore: John Hopkins Press.
Kneese, A.V. and Bower, B.T. (1968) *Managing water quality: Economics, technology, Institutions*, Baltimore: John Hopkins Press for Resource For the Future.
Kneese, A.V. and Schulze, C.L. (1975) *Pollution, Prices and Public Policy*, Washington, D.C.: The Brookings Institution.
Lane, R. (2012) "The promiscuous history of market efficiency: the development of early emissions trading systems", *Environmental Politics*, 21(4), pp. 583–603. doi.org/10.1080/09644016.2012.688355
Lohmann, L. (2009) "Regulatory challenges for financial and carbon markets", *Carbon & Climate Law Review*, 2, pp. 161–171.
Medema, S.G. (2014) "The curious treatment of the Coase theorem in the environmental economics literature, 1960–1979", *Review of Environmental Economics and Policy*, 8(1), pp. 39–57. https://doi.org/10.1093/reep/ret020
Meidinger, E. (1985) "On explaining the development of 'Emissions trading' in the US Air Pollution Regulation", *Law and Policy*, 7(4), pp. 447–479.
Montgomery, W.E. (1972) "Markets in licenses and efficient pollution control programs", *Journal of Economic Theory*, 5(3), pp. 395–418. https://doi.org/10.1016/0022-0531(72)90049-X
Neuteleers, S. and B. Engelen (2015) "Talking Money: How Market-based Valuation can Undermine Environmental Protection", *Ecological Economics*, 117, pp. 253–260. https://doi.org/10.1016/j.ecolecon.2014.06.022
O'Neill, J. (2006) *Markets, Deliberation and Environment*, London: Routledge.
Oates, W.E. (2002) "Foreword". In J. Dales, *Pollution, property and prices: An essay in policy making and economics*, Cheltenham, UK: Edward Elgar, pp. vii–x.
Ruff, L. (1970) "The Economic Common Sense of Pollution", *The Public Interest*, 9, pp. 69–85.
Spash, C.L. (2021) "The contested conceptualization of pollution in economics: Market failure or cost shifting success?", *Cahiers d'Économie Politique / Political Economy Papers*, 79(1), pp. 85–122. https://doi.org/10.3917/cep1.079.0085
Stavins, R.N. (1988) "Project 88. Harnessing Market Forces to Protect Our Environment. Initiatives for the New President", Technical Report, Washington D.C.
Stavins, R.N. (2002) "Lessons from the American Experiment with Market-Based Environmental Policies", *Nota di Lavoro*, 30, Milano: FEEM. https://dx.doi.org/10.2139/ssrn.285998
Tietenberg, T. (1973) "Controlling pollution by price and standard systems: a general equilibrium analysis", *Swedish Journal of Economics*, 75(2), pp. 193–203. https://doi.org/10.2307/3439389
Tietenberg, T. (1985) "Emissions trading: An Exercise in Reforming Pollution Policy", Technical Report, Washington DC/ Resources for the Future.
Voβ, J.-P. (2007) "Innovation Processes in Governance: The Development of 'Emissions Trading' as a New Policy Instrument", *Science and Public Policy*, 34(5), pp. 329–343. https://doi.org/10.3152/030234207X228584

25
ECOSYSTEMS
Ecosystem services and the commodification of nature

Julia Martin-Ortega, Paula Novo, Erik Gomez-Baggethun, Roldan Muradian, Ciaran Harte, and M. Azahara Mesa-Jurado

Introduction

This chapter examines the way commodification processes are playing out in the domain of human-nature relationships. More specifically, we look at how and to what extent this phenomenon has been facilitated by the concept of ecosystem services, a generic term of wide use in environmental sciences and policy to denote the tangible and intangible benefits humans obtain from nature, including for instance food, air and water regulation, energy, recreation, and cultural and spiritual fulfilment.

Ecosystem services as a way of framing human-nature relationships

The ecosystem services framework is one of the many ways of conceptualising the relationship between humans and nature. Ecosystem services are defined as the benefits humans derive from natural ecosystems and are often classified in four main categories (Millennium Ecosystem Assessment, 2005): i) *provisioning services,* referring to goods produced by nature, such as timber, fibre, food and medicines; ii) *cultural services,* referring to the intangible benefits humans derive from their interaction with non-human nature, such as aesthetic values, recreation, and sense of place and belonging or spiritual connection with nature, iii) *regulating services,* which include the indirect benefits humans obtain from an ecosystem's regulatory processes, such as clean air and clean water, and iv) *supporting* or *habitat* services, that sustain all other ecosystem services, such as soil formation, nutrient cycling and primary production.[1]

Conceptualising and valuing ecosystem services

The notion of ecosystem services emerged in the late 1960s with the aim of raising awareness on the social and economic impacts of biodiversity loss. Attention to the notion increased through the 1990s, notably through Daily's influential book *Nature's Services: Societal Dependence on Natural Ecosystems* (1997), which defined ecosystem services as "the conditions and processes through which natural ecosystems, and the species that make them up, sustain and fulfil human life" (p. 3).

DOI: 10.4324/9781003188742-31

She also highlighted that failure to foster the delivery of ecosystem services undermines economic prosperity, forecloses options, and diminishes other aspects of human well-being.

Proponents of the notion of ecosystem services argued that as most of those services that nature provides are not exchanged in markets, their values are not properly considered in public or private economic decision-making. *Correcting* for this *structural* economic under-valuation of ecosystem services was seen as critical to reversing environmental degradation and the decline of biodiversity. Those benefits that nature gives to humans needed to be accounted for in decision-making, connecting in this way the notion of ecosystem services to environmental economics and monetary valuation.

Environmental economics assumes that values and benefits derived from nature can ultimately be expressed as "change[s] in human well-being arising from the provision of [an environmental] good or service" (Bateman et al, 2002, p. 1). Under this paradigm, rooted in neoclassical economic theory, values are expressed as changes in well-being that can be conveyed in monetary terms. These can be determined through formal economic valuation exercises that estimate relative values through people's willingness to exchange money to secure a certain level of provision of the ecosystem service. Benefits of ecosystem services calculated in this way can then be internalised in public or private decision-making. Like this, the *undervaluation* of ecosystem services can be *corrected* through e.g., the incorporation of monetised values into cost-benefit analysis. Using a basic example: the cost-benefit analysis supporting the decision of building or not a road through a forest would need to include not only the construction costs of the road, but also the costs associated with the loss of ecosystem services resulting from the damage to the forest (e.g. habitat loss, damage to climate and water regulating functions and lessening of recreational or spiritual fulfilment possibilities), measured against the benefits that the road would bring to society.

An array of methodologies has been developed to calculate the monetary value of ecosystem services. These include conventional market-based methods; for example, the flood-protecting value of an upstream forest could be monetised through the avoided costs of property loss if a flood were to occur in an inhabited area downstream. Other methods attempt to reveal the value of ecosystem services by looking into associated markets (representing *revealed* preferences). For example, the value of cleaner air could be revealed through the housing market by comparing the prices of houses subject to different levels (or lack) of air pollution. For ecosystem services whose values cannot be associated with current markets (for example, the value of biodiversity, or for certain forms of regulating and spiritual services), *stated* preferences valuation techniques have been developed. These techniques are survey-based and consist in asking the public how much they would be willing to pay for such services in hypothetical markets.

In a milestone publication from 1997, Costanza *et al.* assigned a monetary value to the world's ecosystems and estimated an aggregated value of the entire biosphere of $33 trillion USD per year. While criticised at the time, Costanza et al.'s work contributed significantly to placing the valuation of ecosystem services high on the research and policy agendas. Since then, application of monetary valuation techniques has continued to expand in a multiplicity of environmental domains within and beyond the academic realm.

In this way, what started as an attempt to raise awareness about the benefits that humans obtain *freely* from nature, moved into conceptualising those benefits as changes in well-being that could be monetised through a measure of the public's willingness to pay for them. The purpose of economic valuation is not necessarily to get the public to pay for the provision of ecosystem services (either in existing or hypothetical markets), but to use their willingness to pay as an indication of how much they value them.

The turning point in the world's environmental policy agenda

From the late 1990s onwards, the literature on ecosystem services grew rapidly (see Martin-Ortega et al., 2015 for a review). These publications provided the foundation for the Millennium Ecosystem Assessment, which is undoubtedly the turning point in the popularisation of the ecosystem services concept. In 2000, the Secretary-General of the United Nations called for this worldwide initiative to assess the consequences of ecosystem change for human well-being and the scientific basis for action needed to enhance the conservation and sustainable use of those systems. The Millennium Ecosystem Assessment (2005), emphasised the need to incorporate the value of ecosystem services into decision-making to reverse the increasing degradation of ecosystems and explicitly promoted using the notion of ecosystem services for decision-makers across the globe.

An explosion of academic work on the conceptualisation and application of the ecosystem services followed, including various frameworks to understand, classify, quantify, and operationalise the impacts of ecosystem change on human well-being. Several international and national assessments were published, such as e.g. The Economics of Ecosystem Services and Biodiversity (TEEB, Kumar, 2010) and the UK National Ecosystem Assessment (UK NEA, 2011); all attempting to provide a current snapshot and vision for the future state of ecosystems, including monetised ways of representing the value that such ecosystems have for humans and the value loss that their degradation would bring if existing trends were not reversed. Policy interest on the notion grew rapidly and extensively.

Beyond academia and the policy domain, businesses and corporations have also engaged with the notion of ecosystems services. Growing pressure on businesses to consider ecosystems was reflected in the official petition for the business community to contribute to the Convention on Biological Diversity in 2006, highlighting the need for businesses to develop best practice guidelines to reduce the impact of their activities on biodiversity. Initiatives highlighting the opportunities for businesses to engage in ecosystem services management aslo grew. For example, the United Nations Climate Change Conference of the Parties (COP26, in 2021) reflected the increasing efforts to demonstrate the value of ecosystem services to activate private investments in ecosystem services restoration.

Ecosystem services in markets and payment schemes

One of the clearest ways in which ecosystem services and their monetary valuation has entered environmental governance has been through the promotion of so-called market-based instruments (MBIs) to address environmental challenges. The term MBI has been used to refer to a broad array of policies, including fiscal policies (e.g., carbon taxes or agri-environmental subsidies), certification schemes, carbon markets, tradable rights or permits such as cap-and-trade systems for green gas emissions or Individual Transfer Quotas for fisheries (see Chapter 24 by Berta in this volume).

The most salient formulation of environment related MBIs in our context is Payments for Ecosystem Services (PES). PES schemes, which have been defined in various ways (Martin-Ortega and Waylen, 2018), provide economic incentives for land management practices that are expected to enhance or secure the provision of ecosystem services. One of the most influential framings of PES is based on the Coasean postulate by which negative environmental externalities can be internalised and the social optimum may be attained via bargaining between those producing the service and those benefiting from it.

While the notion of PES and its actual *on the ground* implementation is still very much subject of debate, they have popularised worldwide, with an estimated over 550 active programmes around the globe and an estimated US$36–42 billion in annual transactions, as per an analysis made by Salzman et al. (2018). The authors identify the watershed PES sector as the most mature in terms of transaction value and geographical distribution (present in 62 countries in 2015). These often includes programmes by which a downstream community pays upstream land managers for changes of practice that mitigate poor water quality or flooding. Another prominent PES sector is that of forest and land-use carbon, where PES have grown exponentially owing to the development of funding mechanisms for climate change mitigation, including REDD+,[2] promoting payments for forestry and land use practices that sequester carbon. Other sectors using PES include biodiversity and habitat off-setting to ensure no net loss on development projects. Unlike in water PES, for which the beneficiaries of clean water and flood protection are generally easily identifiable and local, the beneficiaries of biodiversity are widespread and the benefits tend to be indirect or non-material, making it a less developed sector so far.

The ecosystem services concept and its derivatives (such as PES) have inspired novel avenues for environmental research and have clearly contributed to placing environmental degradation (and the need to reverse it) more firmly in international agendas, with evidence of cases in which monetary valuation assessments of ecosystem services have led to investments in nature protection.

But the practice of monetary valuation of ecosystem services has also led to the emergence of new debates and criticism. Of direct interest to this book are the concerns that have been raised about ecosystem services reasoning converting nature into a tradable commodity. The remainder of this chapter explores such concerns by first presenting the theoretical basis for it, then discussing the process of nature commodification, and finally presenting some reflections on the de-commodification of nature.

Ecosystem services and nature commodification

Criticism around the notion of ecosystem services can be understood firstly in the light of the philosophical debate about the nature of values, i.e., whether something (in this case nature or the environment) has a value for its own sake (i.e., an intrinsic value), autonomously and independently of any other entity or whether all values are inherently instrumental, and ultimately decided by humans. If nature has an inherent value, rather than an instrumental value, that cannot be captured by price, then assigning it a price or even an instrumental use value, is corruptive of its true value (what Panitch calls ontological corruption in her contribution to this volume, Chapter 4).

The notion of ecosystem services stands unequivocally on an anthropocentric and utilitarian (instrumental) view of the relationship between humans and nature, by which nature *serves* humans to fulfil their needs and desires rather than having an inherent value of its own. The environmental ethics literature has long emphasised the inherent value of the natural world. But new developments in this field now show that people articulate the importance of their relationships with non-human others in diverse ways that are not fully captured by the dichotomy between instrumental and intrinsic values. This further leads to the question about whether these values can and should be expressed as exchange values through monetisation and whether this necessarily leads to harmful commodification.

The process of nature commodification

Gómez-Baggethun and Ruiz-Pérez (2011) explain how the economic framing and conceptualisation of nature's value as monetised exchange value can lead to the formalisation of property rights on specific ecosystem services or the land producing such services. This appropriation can in turn lead to the creation of institutional structures of sale and exchange in the form of markets; a process of commercialisation that, it is argued, often involves privatisation. Some scholars raise an alarm about the spreading of this phenomenon through the growing trade of previously un-marketed ecosystem functions (e.g., carbon sequestration, watershed regulation, habitat provision) in PES schemes. Gómez-Baggethun et al. (2010) argue that ecosystem service commodification is a gradual process involving various interrelated practices. First, a change in the discursive domain, by which utilitarian and anthropocentric framings of nature are adopted, such as that of ecosystem services – i.e. nature *serving* humans. Then, in the evaluative domain, where nature's benefits get expressed in monetary terms. And finally, in the institutional domain, such as articulating ecosystem services through markets and payment schemes.

While some authors have argued that we can monetise ecosystem services for awareness-raising purposes while avoiding their commodification (e.g. Costanza 2006; 2017), the case has been made that these practices are to be seen as interrelated rather than independent processes, where the utilitarian framing of nature paves the way discursively for its monetisation, which in turn paves the way for its commodification, in what Gómez-Baggethun and Ruiz-Pérez (2011, p. 624) have referred to as "the tragedy of well-intended valuation".

Degrees of commodification

Some scholars argue that commodification should be looked at from the perspective of its different purposes and degrees. Hahn et al. (2015, p. 76) refer to degrees of commodification as "the extent to which the value of biodiversity or an ecosystem services has become a tradable commodity". These range from "no commodification" (degree zero), which includes intrinsic appreciation of ecosystems, in which the rationale for protecting nature is nature itself; followed by varying degrees in which commodification arises under the instrumental framing of nature without valuation but with "new property rights and liabilities which involve measurement" (degree 1), and with valuation (degree 2). The third degree involves "deliberate efforts to express or 'demonstrate' the value of nature in monetary terms". Degree 4 involves the use of price signals such as taxes and subsidies to "internalize externalities and evoke behavioural change but do not create markets". Degree 5 comprises the use of market-traded instruments such as biodiversity offsets and other markets resembling cap-and-trade systems, conservation banking and user-financed PES. Finally, degree 6 covers financial instruments referred to as "complete commodification" as a traded commodity is "re-packaged and re-sold as financial instruments (e.g., biodiversity bonds or derivatives)". A study of environmental professionals in Mexico provides an illustration of the presence of all six degrees of commodification in the Mexican environmental policy discourse (Martin-Ortega et al. 2019), ranging from level zero (e.g. natural protected areas), to wildlife management plans (level 1), valuation studies (level 3), a national PES scheme (level 4) and voluntary carbon markets (level 5). Level 6, complete commodification in the form of green bonds and forest carbon bonds in the stock exchange, is considered in the study to be anecdotal, isolated or at early stages of planning, but still present in the debate.

Ecosystem services institutions and commodification

Institutions are important for commodification because they shape the different ways humans relate to and exist in their respective environments. Local and community level institutions such as pre-existing common property structures and community decision-making organisations, shape the way local communities interact with each other and with nature. For example, local institutions and associated class relations influenced the commons enclosure processes that made industrialisation possible in Europe (see Crétois's Chapter 6 on land in this volume) and that would have affected the way people could enjoy the ecosystem services that they provide.

Institutions at the national level, such as the state, legal systems, and academia, are also key in the process of ecosystem services commodification. Science and economics are legitimising institutions (Corbera and Brown, 2010) that have played a vital role in providing the technical capacity for the identification and measurement of ecosystem services, and have, through their input in large global initiatives such as the above mentioned Millennium Assessment and The Economics of Ecosystem and Biodiversity, contributed to transmitting "knowledge of market opportunity, assess project feasibility, and perform technical work to bring projects to market" (Kelly and Schmitz, 2016, p. 103).

The state plays a particularly active role in commodification by developing conducive frameworks to enable it. Higgins (2015) analysed this in his examination of UK biodiversity offset development. States develop regulatory frameworks and allocate property rights in close concordance with legal systems that facilitate the functioning of markets. They can also use discursive power to proliferate market-optimistic narratives that legitimise and encourage market participation. For instance, in the context of the regulatory framework for peatland restoration in the UK, the Peatland Code, a voluntary certification standard for projects wishing to market the climate benefits of peatland restoration, is inducing an explosion of interest from private investors, raising concerns over large corporations occupying the space of local communities and not-for-profit nature conservation organisations as nature stewards.

There are also international institutions that are said to have influenced the commodification of nature. In particular, the implementation of market-based governance is often mediated through international initiatives such as REDD+. These often relate to the work of international development agencies and global organisations advocating market-based environmental governance. Private corporations, banks and NGOs can also be important international institutions seeking to implement commodification. For instance, Ni'am et al. (2021) provide an example of the commodification of nature through elephant-based ecotourism promoted by international financial institutions such as the World Bank, NGOs as Fauna and Flora International, donors as United States Fish and Wildlife Service and public-private partnerships. In their study, Ni'am et al. analyse the commodification process through which captive elephants are transformed into lively commodities that embody "encounter value" (here commodification takes place in the encounter and not in the being itself).

Why is nature commodification a problem?

Since some ecosystem services such as food and timber have been already commodified for centuries, controversies around the commodification of nature revolve primarily around where to set the limits of money and markets in environmental governance. Beyond certain limits, commodification can be problematic for a number of reasons.

Firstly, there are equity concerns associated to changes over property rights and access to resources. There is evidence showing that in some cases the implementation of ecosystem services markets has led to increased inequalities (Corbera et al., 2007). Moreover, they can promote unequal access to ecosystem services by privileging those with ability to pay (Zografos et al., 2014), they may conflict with customary rights of access to land and resources (Ibarra et al., 2011), or benefit primarily landowners and rural elites (Corbera et al., 2007).

Secondly, from a conservationist perspective, there are misgivings that shifting to an economic framing may lead to the crowding out of moral motivations in the long term. That is, monetary payments could erode motivations for conservation that stem from the intrinsic rather than instrumental value of nature (what Panitch refers to as normative corruption in Chapter 4 of this volume) and result in changes in mind-sets, affecting motivations for environmental protection. It is argued that this could induce changing the conservation logic "from moral obligation or community norms towards conservation for profit" (Rode et al., 2015, p. 273), undermining ethical and moral arguments for conservation.

Furthermore, ecosystem services framing is seen as a risk for marginalising non-anthropocentric non-Western utilitarian frameworks for nature conservation. For example, Western dualistic constructions of human-nature relations have driven the enactment of enclosure-based policies (national parks, protected areas) by legitimising human separation from nature. This worldview often confronts the nature-culture mutualistic beliefs of local and indigenous cultures.

This clash of worldviews was made very evident specifically in relation to the ecosystem services framing during the discussions of the Intergovernmental Panel for Ecosystem Services and Biodiversity (IPBES), an expert advisory institution formed in 2012 and aimed at tackling the loss of biodiversity and the degradation of ecosystem services. From the beginning of IPBES, some countries, notably Bolivia and other South American countries, questioned the concept of ecosystem services. They argued that the notion of ecosystem services only represents the views and approaches of modern Western society and does not reflect other traditions and worldviews, such as the indigenous notion of Mother Earth and systems of life, shared by the indigenous peoples of the South American Andes, or expressed in concepts such as sēnluó-wànxiàng (vast forest and every manifestation of nature) and tien-ti (Heaven and Earth) of Taoism shared by East Asian peoples (Diaz et al., 2015).

In addition, it has been argued that monetary valuation privileges the visible and known (e.g., charismatic species) over what is invisible and unknown (e.g., ecological processes). This can lend itself to the underestimation of values, exposing biodiversity and ecosystems to "the vagaries of the market" (Silvertown et al., 2015, p. 645), particularly when used for making the case for conservation initiatives opposing large development projects.

At a more fundamental level there is the argument that the concept of ecosystem services cannot capture all the dimensions of value that are central to human well-being (O'Neill's Chapter 23 in this volume). Ecological economists have long debated the incommensurability of ecosystem values (Martinez-Alier et al., 1998), noting that there are multiple ways in which people attribute meaning and importance (value) to nature, and that these cannot be reduced to a single (monetary) metric. Imposing a monetary logic to the framing of the relationship risks changing the relationship itself. For example, it is noted that when the importance of something is perceived to reside primarily in its symbolic, cultural, or spiritual value or in its ecological or intrinsic value, market valuation can downgrade and demean such values by conveying the notion that they can be replaced by market substitutes with equivalent exchange value (Chapter 23 in this volume). Some argue that such ethical concerns are not necessarily equally relevant for all ecosystem services (Gomez-Baggethun and Muradian, 2015). For example, the emotional bonds we may develop in relation to wildlife may not be comparable to those we develop with carbon stocks.

Another issue relates to the extent to which a certain ecosystem service is essential to cover a basic human need. For example, whatever the intrinsic value of water is, we need it to survive and if markets disrupt this, that alone might be an argument against commodification (see Walsh's contribution to this volume in Chapter 26).

Ecosystem services as a symptom of a broader trend?

The frame shifting brought by the notion of ecosystem services has been related to a broader process of neoliberalisation of nature conservation. Monetising ecosystem services and related market environmentalism have been advocated as ways to reconcile economic growth, allocation efficiency and environmental conservation, that some associate with the expansion of neoliberal ideology since the 1980s (Igoe and Brockington, 2016).

The fact is that the vast majority of Payments for Ecosystem Services (PES) schemes are run by states under public regulation frameworks. Funds are typically collected through taxes and the level of payments is politically set, mainly based on opportunity costs or negotiations with concerned stakeholders. Many PES schemes operate as green rural subsidies where states pay landholders and communities to either reward their stewardship or compensate opportunity costs of conservation. Despite this, it is argued that they still reflect a *market logic* or *rhetoric*, with some scholars explicitly arguing that the promotion of PES responds to an agenda of global corporate interests (Fletcher and Büscher, 2017).

Some scholars take issue with these views arguing that PES do not *have to* require commodification. For example, arguing that propertization of ecosystem services does not have to mean privatisation since property rights may still be held collectively; or that nature valuation does not necessarily need to be orientated to profitability. Others have argued that seeing PES as neoliberal tools neglects the agency of local people in shaping them. Critics, however, insist that PES are *innately* neoliberal, and that they just perpetuate a trend that implicitly accepts neoliberal capitalism as both the problem *and* the solution to the ecological crisis.

Nature de-commodification

Commodification is not an irreversible process and commodities can undergo a process of de-commodification. In this section, we elaborate on the potential modes of action for nature de-commodification, and reflect on the scope of a more fundamental change in the conceptualisation of human-nature relationships possibly serving de-commodification.

Empirical evidence of de-commodification processes

One of the potential routes to de-commodification is found in changes to the property rights structure (e.g., de-privatisation through nationalisation). On a basic level, a re-transition to some form of common ownership may present an effective route to de-commodification. For instance, Benjaminsen and Kaarhus (2018) observed objections by local communities to private property exclusion in Zanzibar, as it contradicted their local "ndugu" relations based around nature-culture mutualism and reciprocity. A useful way to conceptualise this transition in the property rights structure is the distinction between property and possession presented by Heinsohn et al. (2013) in their theory of ownership. While possession can be referred to as the physical control of resources, property can be denoted as the representation of an entity in terms of its non-visible qualities – its representations or title – which allows it to become abstracted from its supporting ecological and social context. A property-oriented system allows for the commodification of entities (including nature). By contrast, in a possession-based system, entities cannot have their social and ecological contexts conceptually extracted. This means that in relation to nature, the processes of abstraction and valuation are unable to bundle and disaggregate ecosystems through commodification. A transition from a property to a possession-based economic system thus presents a potential route to de-commodification. Gerber and Gerber (2017) illustrate how forested land in Switzerland is one of the best examples of de-commodification through a possession-based logic in which 70% of the total forest area belongs to public bodies and everyone has the right to enter public and private forests for recreation and collection of non-timber forest products, thus remaining outside the land market (see Larrère's contribution to this volume in Chapter 29).

Another way to approach de-commodification might be through delegitimising commodities. Market proponents utilise win-win logic or promise coupled economic, social, and environmental outcomes (e.g., sustainable development, market environmentalism) to cloud discourse with morally-charged rhetoric that obscures the negative outcomes of commodification from the international public sphere. This essentially depicts what Tsing (2000) terms an "economy of appearances", by which market developers and proponents create and establish a reputation that becomes crucial for commodity functioning. Efforts to de-commodify nature could thus centre around challenging the ethical basis upon which commodification is legitimised. An interesting illustration of this is the case of the Atacameño people who, Prieto (2016) argues, have subverted the Chilean pro-water market by relying on their water-related cultural values. The author found that in some Atacameño communities the water market has not operated to ensure that water rights are put to those uses with the highest economic value (e.g., mining or urban water consumption). On the contrary, internal rules of the community forbid the sale of water rights to the mining sector and impose barriers to other transactions (those few who did sell their water rights to mining or other uses have seen themselves delegitimised, outcast, from the communities). These rules, the author argues, form part of an alternative moral economy of water based on shared values and affective connections opposed to market rules (See also Walsh's contribution in this volume in Chapter 26).

A more fundamental de-commodifying change in sight?

Recent international initiatives give cause to consider whether we might be witnessing the beginning of a shift in the hegemony of the ecosystem services paradigm in environmental sciences and policy.

Partly in response to the commodification criticism, alternative conceptualisations of human-nature relationships have been put forward and are gaining increasing prominence in the global conversation. The Intergovernmental Panel for Ecosystem Services and Biodiversity (IPBES) mentioned earlier initially responded to the challenges made by countries asking that non-Western anthropocentric and instrumental perspectives be considered by putting forward the notion of *Nature's Contribution to People* (NCP) as a (partial) alternative to the term ecosystem services (Diaz et al., 2015). NCP is conceptualised as a broad category that encompasses material and non-material benefits humans derive from nature and that contribute to *leading to a good life* in a broad sense that may widely differ across cultures (such as living in harmony with Mother Earth (Pascual et al., 2017)). Embedded in this proposition is a shift in the focus from exchange values towards *relational values*, defined as ethical and moral principles that guide *good* human-nature relationships (Chan et al., 2016). Relational values are not "present in things" (whether intrinsically for their own worth, or instrumentally for people) but are "derivative of relationships and responsibilities to them" (Chan et al., 2016, p. 1462). Relational values also resonate with the idea put forward by O'Neill in this volume: that relations (with nature) are not simply the instrumental means to well-being specified independently of these relations, but rather *constitutive* of well-being. According to Chan et al. (2016), relational notions of values are present in classic Western philosophies (both classical and contemporary), as well as in Indigenous (e.g., Tsawalk, Sumak kawsay) and Eastern philosophies (e.g., Confucian, Buddhist). Notions of a good life rooted in relationships are expressed in diverse worldviews, such as Ubuntu in South Africa, the Gandhian Economy of Permanence in India, Buen Vivir in several Latin American countries, and North American Back to the Land movements (ibid.).[3]

Since, the IPBES discourse has continued to evolve and the panel has recently produced a Value Assessment to help policy-makers better understand the different ways in which people conceive and value nature (IPBES 2022). The Value Assessment puts forward a typology of values which is intended to highlight how different worldviews and knowledge systems influence the ways people interact with and value nature. The typology is based on four general perspectives: living from, living with, living in, and living as nature.[4] The IPBES value assessment acknowledges more than 50 valuation methods and approaches, originating from diverse disciplines and knowledge systems, including academic, indigenous, and local knowledge systems embodied in different worldviews. It distinguishes between *broad values* – the moral principles and life goals that guide people-nature interactions – and *specific values* – judgements regarding the importance of nature in particular contexts, including *instrumental values* (i.e., means to a desired end, associated with the notion of ecosystem services), *relational values* (i.e., the meaningfulness of human-nature interactions), and *intrinsic values* (i.e., independent of people as valuers). It also acknowledges multiple value indicators as the quantitative measures and qualitative descriptors used to denote nature's importance in terms of biophysical, monetary, or socio-cultural metrics (IPBES, 2022).

Parallel to the IPBES conversation, other initiatives have been put forward, further challenging the instrumental and anthropocentric take on human-nature relationships. For example, since 2016 a number of rivers across the world (the Atrato River in Colombia, Ganga and Yamunai rivers in India, Wanghanui River in New Zealand, the Muteshekau-shipu in Canada and all rivers in Bangladesh) have been granted personhood as part of an increasing global trend to recognise and grant rights to nature (Eckstein et al., 2019; Hall, 2011; O'Donnell, 2018). Cohen et al. (2023) argue that this marks an important potential starting point for the restoration of a conceptualisation of human-nature relationships in terms of kinship. While with respect to indigenous and non-Western contexts this might simply represent ceasing to marginalise existing views, Cohen et al. (2023) suggest that this proposition might not be quite as strange and improbable as it could first appear also for the Global North. Offering the UK and its rivers as a paradigmatic example, the authors show how animistic (pre)historic representations of water as *kin* can be seen reflected in place names, and in other cultural memories and practices. Reviving and reinventing these memories and cultural practices, while cultivating other meanings, community relations and well-being through for example, swimming, angling, or simply being near waters in everyday practical ways, can reactivate the notion of water bodies as kin. Cohen et al. (2023) propose the notion of *Riverkin* as the "constituents of environments that reciprocally nurture, and contribute to the substance of, one another's life and well-being" (p. 3). This shift in relations is already starting to be visible: in the last two years, Britain has awarded its first designated bathing sites – in Oxford and Yorkshire – thanks to grassroots campaigns that have put pressure on the government's environment agency and forcing water companies to address pollution problems. Re-connecting with the river through a safe swimming environment can enable a narrative of change to emerge.

Conclusions

The notion of ecosystem services, which has dominated the environmental governance discourse during the past two decades, reflects a dualistic, anthropocentric and utilitarian way of perceiving and understanding human-nature relations. Such worldview facilitates the process of commodification of the natural environment by emphasising instrumental values measured in monetary units. In this chapter, we have provided an account of the foundations of the concept of ecosystem services, its history and applications in environmental governance, as well as the risks associated with the commodification of nature.

We have argued that commodification is not an irreversible process since it can be both constrained by social mobilisation and reversed by policy will. While there has been a significant increase in the use of market-based policy instruments in the socio-environmental field during the past two decades, these might be less consolidated than they appear. For instance, the fact that the actual performance of the so-called market-based environmental policy tools has been, in general, below the high expectations with which they had been promoted as win-win solutions some decades ago might erode their prospects.

Furthermore, alternative conceptualisations of human-nature relationships, acknowledging non-dualistic and relational values, including kinship, are gaining prominence. These could become turning points in reversing commodification trends. For that, efforts would need to be directed into embedding them in the policy and regulations spheres, and protecting them from being co-opted by neoliberal forces.

Notes

1 In further references, the category supporting services is often excluded from ecosystem services classifications, particularly in the context of their valuation. It is argued that supporting services are reflected in the other three (provisioning, regulating and cultural) and therefore should not be valued separately to avoid double counting.

2 REDD+ is a United Nations-backed framework that aims to curb climate change by stopping the destruction of forests in developing countries. It stands for "Reducing Emissions from Deforestation and forest Degradation"; the "+" signifies the role of conservation, sustainable management of forests and enhancement of forest carbon stocks. REDD+ is a mechanism through which countries, the private sector, multilateral funds and others can pay developing countries to protect their forests. It can take the form of direct payments or can be in exchange for "carbon credits", which represent reductions in greenhouse gas emissions to compensate for emissions made somewhere else.

3 It is to be noted that upon publication it was still criticised for maintaining the original anthropocentric perspective and for not representing a fundamental improvement on the way we conceptualise human-nature relationships, failing to recognise their non-dualistic nature. Kenter (2018, p. 40) voiced this criticism arguing the concept of nature's contribution to people "ditches the baby (the successful term ecosystem services), whilst keeping the dirty bathwater (the problems with the term)".

4 Living from nature emphasises nature's capacity to provide resources for sustaining livelihoods, needs and wants of people, such as food and material goods. Living with nature has a focus on life *other than human* such as the intrinsic right of fish in a river to thrive independently of human needs. Living in nature refers to the importance of nature as the setting for people's sense of place and identity. Living as nature sees the natural world as a physical, mental and spiritual part of oneself.

References

Bateman, I. (2002) *Economic valuation with stated preference techniques: A manual*. Cheltenham: Edward Elgar. Vol. 50.

Benjaminsen, G., & Kaarhus, R. (2018) "Commodification of forest carbon: REDD+ and socially embedded forest practices in Zanzibar." *Geoforum*, 93, pp. 48–56.

Chan, K.M., Balvanera, P., Benessaiah, K., Chapman, M., Díaz, S., Gómez-Baggethun, E., ... & Turner, N. (2016) "Why protect nature? Rethinking values and the environment." *Proceedings of the national academy of sciences*, 113(6), pp. 1462–1465.

Cohen, J., Dannreuther, C., Fraundorfer, M., Mackie, C., Martin-Ortega, J., Mdee, A., & Sutil, N. (2023) "Riverkin: seizing the moment to remake vital relations in the United Kingdom and beyond." *People and Nature*, 00, pp. 1–16.

Corbera, E., & Brown, K. (2010) "Offsetting benefits? Analyzing access to forest carbon." *Environment and Planning A*, 42(7), pp. 1739–1761.

Corbera, E., Kosoy, N., & Tuna, M.M. (2007) "Equity implications of marketing ecosystem services in protected areas and rural communities: Case studies from Meso-America." *Global Environmental Change*, 17(3–4), pp. 365–380.

Costanza, R. (2006) "Nature: ecosystems without commodifying them." *Nature*, 443(7113), pp. 749–749.

Costanza, R., D'arge, R., De Groot, R., Farber, S., Monica, G., Hannon, B., Limburg, K., Naeem, S., O'Neel, R., Paruelo, J., Raskin, R.G., Sutton, P., Van Den Belt, M. (1997) "The value of the world's ecosystem services and natal capital." *Nature* 387(6630), pp. 253–260.

Costanza, R., De Groot, R., Braat, L., Kubiszewski, I., Fioramonti, L., Sutton, P., ... & Grasso, M. (2017) "Twenty years of ecosystem services: how far have we come and how far do we still need to go?" *Ecosystem Services*, 28, pp. 1–16.

Daily, G. C. (1997) *Nature's services: societal dependence on natural ecosystems*. Island Press, Washington, DC.

Díaz, S., Demissew, S., Carabias, J., Joly, C., Lonsdale, M., Ash, N., ... & Zlatanova, D. (2015) The IPBES Conceptual Framework – connecting nature and people. *Current Opinion in Environmental Sustainability*, 14, pp. 1–16.

Eckstein, G., D'Andrea, A., Marshall, V., O'Donnell, E., Talbot-Jones, J., Curran, D., & O'Bryan, K. (2019) "Conferring legal personality on the world's rivers: A brief intellectual assessment." *Water International*, 44(6–7), pp. 804–829.

Fletcher, R., & Büscher, B. (2017) "The PES conceit: revisiting the relationship between payments for environmental services and neoliberal conservation." *Ecological Economics*, 132, pp. 224–231.

Gerber, J.D. & Gerber, J.F. (2017) "Decommodification as a foundation for ecological economics." *Ecological economics*, 131, pp. 551–556.

Gómez-Baggethun, E. & Muradian, R. (2015) "In markets we trust? Setting the boundaries of Market-Based Instruments in ecosystem services governance." *Ecological Economics*, 117, pp. 217–224.

Gómez-Baggethun, E., & Ruiz-Pérez, M. (2011) "Economic valuation and the commodification of ecosystem services." *Progress in Physical Geography*, 35(5), pp. 613–628.

Gómez-Baggethun, E., de Groot, R., Lomas, P.L., & Montes, C. (2010) "The history of ecosystem services in economic theory and practice: from early notions to markets and payment schemes." *Ecological Economics*, 69 (6), pp. 1209–1218.

Hahn, T., McDermott, C., Ituarte-Lima, C., Schultz, M., Green, T., & Tuvendal, M. (2015) "Purposes and degrees of commodification: Economic instruments for biodiversity and ecosystem services need not rely on markets or monetary valuation." *Ecosystem Services*, 16, pp. 74–82.

Hall, M. (2011) *Plants as persons: A philosophical botany*. Suny Press.

Heinsohn, G., Steiger, O. & Decker, F. (2013) *Ownership economics: On the foundations of interest, money, markets, business cycles and economic development*. Routledge.

Higgins, C.T. (2015). *(Un) Fixing Biodiversity: Nature, State, and the Techno-politics of Offsetting in the United Kingdom* (Doctoral dissertation).

Ibarra, J.T., Barreau, A., Campo, C.D., Camacho, C.I., Martin, G.J., & McCandless, S.R. (2011) "When formal and market-based conservation mechanisms disrupt food sovereignty: impacts of community conservation and payments for environmental services on an indigenous community of Oaxaca, Mexico." *International Forestry Review*, 13(3), pp. 318–337.

Igoe, J., & Brockington, D. (2016) 30. Neoliberal Conservation. In The Environment in Anthropology (Second Edition) pp. 324–331. New York University Press.

IPBES (2022): Summary for policymakers of the methodological assessment of the diverse values and valuation of nature of the Intergovernmental Science-Policy Platform on Biodiversity and Ecosystem Services. U. Pascual, P. Balvanera, M. Christie, B. Baptiste, D. González-Jiménez, C.B. Anderson, S. Athayde, R.

Chaplin-Kramer, S. Jacobs, E. Kelemen, R. Kumar, E. Lazos, A. Martin, T.H. Mwampamba, B. Nakangu, P. O'Farrell, C.M. Raymond, S.M. Subramanian, M. Termansen, M. Van Noordwijk, & A. Vatn (eds.). IPBES secretariat, Bonn, Germany. 37 pages.

Kelly, E.C., & Schmitz, M.B. (2016) "Forest offsets and the California compliance market: Bringing an abstract ecosystem good to market." *Geoforum*, 75, pp. 99–109.

Kenter, J.O. (2018) "Don't throw out the baby whilst keeping the bathwater; Put people's values central, not nature's contributions." *Ecosystem Services*, 33, pp. 40–43.

Martinez-Alier, J., Munda, G., & O'Neill, J. (1998) "Weak comparability of values as a foundation for ecological economics." *Ecological Economics*, 26, pp. 277–286.

Martin-Ortega, J., & Waylen, K.A. (2018) "PES what a mess? An analysis of the position of environmental professionals in the conceptual debate on payments for ecosystem services." *Ecological Economics*, 154, pp. 218–237.

Martin-Ortega, J., Ferrier, R.C., Gordon, I., & Khan, S. (Eds.) (2015) *Water Ecosystem Services: A Global Perspective* (International Hydrology Series). Cambridge: Cambridge University Press.

Martin-Ortega, J., Mesa-Jurado, M.A., Pineda-Vazquez, M., & Novo, P. (2019) "Nature commodification: 'a necessary evil'? An analysis of the views of environmental professionals on ecosystem services-based approaches." *Ecosystem Services*, 37, 100926.

Millennium Ecosystem Assessment (2005) *Ecosystem and Human Wellbeing: A Framework for Assessment*. Washington, DC: Island Press.

Ni'am, L., Koot, S., & Jongerden, J. (2021) "Selling captive nature: Lively commodification, elephant encounters, and the production of value in Sumatran ecotourism, Indonesia." *Geoforum*, 127, pp. 162–170.

O'Donnell, E.L. (2018) "At the intersection of the sacred and the legal: rights for nature in Uttarakhand, India." *Journal of Environmental Law*, 30(1), pp. 135–144.

Pascual, U., Balvanera, P., Díaz, S., Pataki, G., Roth, E., Stenseke, M., … & Yagi, N. (2017) "Valuing nature's contributions to people: the IPBES approach." *Current Opinion in Environmental Sustainability*, 26, pp. 7–16.

Prieto, M. (2016) "Transando el agua, produciendo territorios e identidades indígenas: el modelo de aguas chileno y los atacameños de Calama." *Revista de estudios sociales* (55), pp. 88–103.

Rode, J., Gómez-Baggethun, E., & Krause, T. (2015) "Motivation crowding by economic incentives in conservation policy: A review of the empirical evidence." *Ecological Economics*, 117, pp. 270–282.

Salzman, J., Bennett, G., Carroll, N., Goldstein, A., & Jenkins, M. (2018) "The global status and trends of Payments for Ecosystem Services." *Nature Sustainability*, 1(3), pp. 136–144.

Silvertown, J. (2015) "Have ecosystem services been oversold?". *Trends in Ecology & Evolution*, 30(11), pp. 641–648.

TEEB (2010) *The Economics of Ecosystems and Biodiversity Ecological and Economic Foundations*. Edited by Pushpam Kumar. Earthscan: London and Washington.

Tsing, A.L. (2000) "Inside the economy of appearances." *Public Culture*, 12(1), pp. 115–144.

UK National Ecosystem Assessment (NEA) (2011) *The UK National Ecosystem Assessment: Synthesis of the Key Findings*. Cambridge: UNEP-WCMC.

Zografos, C., Rodriguez-Labajos, B.A.O., Aydin, C.A., Cardoso, A., Matiku, P., Munguti, S., … & Živčič, L. (2014) "Economic tools for evaluating liabilities in environmental justice struggles, the EJOLT experience." In EJOLT Report No. 16.

26

WATER

Distributive justice and the commodification of water

Adrian Walsh

Introduction: What, if anything, might be wrong with the commodification of water?

What should we think about commodifying the natural resource of water? In many parts of the world today, processes of commodification of water resources are well under way—so much so that, in some areas, water can only really be accessed as a commodity. The commodification of water involves the buying and selling of water resources for domestic, agricultural, and industrial purposes as well as the buying and selling of the commercial organisations that trade in these resources. Such commodification is increasingly common. To be sure, there are some well-known exceptions to this tendency: for instance, the city of Paris remunicipalised water in 2009, but such cases are rare.[1] Furthermore, in some parts of the world there are water markets in which significant quantities of water are bought and sold on markets by large international corporations. This comes at the same time as there is increasing competition for water resources (more of which below) and when many people face restricted access because of water scarcity. Climate change has only exacerbated the pressures on existing water suppliers.

How should we regard any moves towards further commodification? What grounds might there be for *blocking exchanges* in water? Thinking through the issues raised by the commodification of water is (perhaps unsurprisingly) a complicated matter, in part because water has a number of different modes of normative significance. We can frame this significance under three distinct headings:

a) as a public resource which is primarily understood as being of instrumental value;
b) as a cultural good, such as when water is found in rivers and lakes which have cultural meanings for groups and;
c) as an ecological good which many regard as having intrinsic value.

In this chapter I shall concentrate primarily on water as a *public resource* and, in particular, the implications commodification has for access to commodified goods and, subsequently, for the justice or otherwise of the patterns of distribution that ensue.

DOI: 10.4324/9781003188742-32

Discussions of distributive justice need to consider the specific nature of the goods involved. After defining commodification and its distributive implications in section 2, I shall outline several normatively salient features of water as a *distributive good*. After that I shall consider some moral objections one might have to the commodification of water understood as a public good: these objections primarily concern issues of distributive justice. In this context, as we shall see, *expressive* or *attitudinal* concerns are not really germane.[2] Ultimately, I shall argue that the most important distributive reason for concern involves the implications for access to water for the satisfaction of basic human needs. I argue that:

> In so far as commodification gives rise to a lack of access to a basic human need then it is morally wrong.

The argument defended is, in essence, *sufficientarian* in that priority is given to ensuring the satisfaction of fundamental human needs (Benbayi, 2009; Huseby, 2010).[3] In the final section of this chapter I shall outline a more general claim about what this sufficientarian approach might mean more generally for questions of how we should set the "moral boundaries of commodification".

Defining commodification and the commodification of water

What do we mean by the "commodification of water"? In this chapter I shall define commodification in terms of *actual* buying and selling in a market. By "commodification", I simply mean the transformation of an object or practice into a market good (or a commodity); that is, a thing that is bought and sold. The canonical philosophical definition of a commodity comes from the work of Aristotle. In the *Politics* Aristotle notes that any object has two possible uses, namely as an object of use and as an object of trade or exchange (Aristotle, 1946 [1257a]). Thus, an article that is sold on the market can be said to have both a use-value and an exchange-value, while an article that is made for consumption alone, is said to have use-value alone. Following this line of reasoning, marketisation can be defined as the transformation of a thing which possesses *only* use-value into a good with both use-value and exchange-value. A good comes to possess an exchange value when it is bought and sold in a market for money or some relevant equivalent. On my account—unlike those of Elizabeth Anderson (1993) and Margaret Jane Radin (1996)—practices such as cost-benefit analysis, in which there is no actual buying and selling, but which simply involve shadow prices applied to non-market goods, do not count as commodification or at least commodification proper.

Let us turn to water itself. Water has, as a matter of historical fact, been subject to a wide range of mechanisms for allocating entitlements to its use. The three primary mechanisms have been *riparian legal rights*, *state allocation* and *market allocation* (Getzler, 2004). Under a system of riparian rights, landholders who own property adjoining watercourses are granted rights to use: these rights are occasionally unlimited, but typically involve some constraints upon usage. The other two mechanisms involve the allocation of rights to use water either by the State or the market. In the former case water is owned by the State which then grants rights of use to citizens. In the latter case, allocation on the market assumes private property. If we follow the definition endorsed above, then the commodification of water refers simply to the transformation of water into a good that has both use-value and exchange value and that is bought and sold, typically for money, on a market. Sometimes such commodification will involve water that was *previously owned by the State* (or some other collectivist public institution) and at other times it will involve water *that was part of the commons and not subject to specific ownership rights*. In both instances, whilst the water in question always possessed use-value, it now also possesses exchange-value.

This is still rather imprecise, however, since the analysis covers a range of different possible social phenomena. The phrase "commodification of water" might ordinarily be thought to refer to any one of the following cases, each of which involves a shift away from water being conceived of as a non-commercial entity to one which is in some sense a commodity. Firstly, it might refer to the provision of a pricing mechanism for water. This usage of the term simply concerns cases where state agencies decide to charge a price, with the aim typically of cost-recovery—that might or might not reflect the potential market value of the water—to citizens for the domestic water they use. Secondly, it might refer to the commodification of water-utilities that provide water to its citizens; that is, where state water utilities are privatised and become proper capitalist enterprises aiming to generate profits in their supply of municipal water or alternatively where private companies enter into the provision of water for citizens. Finally, the term might refer to the creation of full-scale water markets where water is bought and sold by commercial entities: that is, where it is not only municipal water and water utilities that are being bought and sold but where this is part of a broader pattern of marketisation of all (or at least most) water resources and in which water is a commodity in the fullest sense.[4] This means simply that (i) all access to water is via the market; (ii) the cost of water reflects the determinations of market processes and (iii) rights to the ownership of commercial water providers are bought and sold on the market.

Commodification also affects entitlements. The shift to a market system for the allocation of water—indeed a shift from any one mode to another—will affect the system of entitlements and this raises questions of distributive justice.[5] Given that water is both a basic necessity of human life and an important resource for agricultural and industrial activity, then the problem of which users obtain access for such purposes is a critical issue of social justice. Equally, water policy has significant implications for the environment and, consequently, for the environmental values we express through such policy. For instance, if a government increases the allocation of water to industry, then this can affect ecosystems from which that water is diverted. This, in turn, raises the issue of what value we place on ecosystem health as opposed to industrial outputs. Or again governments might well develop policies that would limit agricultural activities near sensitive riverine environments. But it raises the question of how we should do so. How do we compare environmental values, such as river health, against the commercial opportunities that such bodies of water provide? For many people, certain water systems have spiritual and aesthetic values that commercialisation potentially threatens. If we increase the marketisation, to what extent will that impinge upon the health of our water systems? These are all significant questions regarding our engagement with water systems that are fundamentally normative and, furthermore, require philosophical reflection for their solution. However, these are not directly distributive questions and, thus, most of the focus will be elsewhere, although these concerns will appear at various points in the discussion.

We should note that, any project aiming to commodify water also confronts various practical and conceptual difficulties that are *peculiar* to this good itself. For any form of commodification, if the good is to become a commodity *tout court*, then there are legal, practical and cultural obstacles) that must be overcome. With respect to the cultural obstacles to the commodification of water I have in mind such phenomena as social resistance to *the very idea* of treating some goods as commodities, which rely on similar intuitions to those which animate Anderson and Radin when they define commodification in terms of a specific mode of regard. The attitude in this instance involves a rejection of commodification, in my sense, as well as Anderson and Radin's concerns with *normative corruption* (see Panitch's contribution to this volume).[6]

But it is not just cultural attitudes which are relevant. In the case of water there are some *special difficulties* for those who wish to commodify. Firstly, practical problems arise with respect to the so-called security of the resource. One might, for instance, buy the right to access certain quantities of water each year, only for the occurrence of a drought to render the right meaningless. This makes for a highly unusual commercial right. Secondly, if one is to charge for the use of a resource, then there is a justificatory requirement for that impost to be universal in the sense that if any person consumes the good they must pay for it and this applies to all users. However, such universality is hard to enforce since, in many isolated regions, use of water is difficult to police and, further, not all interception activities are immediately obvious as interception activities. Many in more remote locations are able to make significant use of water, free of charge, without that use being detected. Thus, a rice farmer, living by a river in a remote region, might well be able to pump water into his fields without detection.

The third difficulty concerns the so-called "unbundling" of land and water rights. Traditionally, in many jurisdictions, water that flowed through a portion of land, or fell on it as precipitation, was considered lawfully the property of the landowner. Rights to the water of a plot of land were typically regarded as concomitant with the rights to the land itself. However, these sets of rights have usually been disconnected by legislatures (or "unbundled") in the process of creating water markets. Thus, the water that runs off a property is regarded as being owned by the holders of the catchment title. In some places, such as, for instance, Arizona, landholders do not even have the right to collect the water that runs off the roofs of their houses since all such water is owned by those with downstream water rights (Western States Water Law: Arizona). Unsurprisingly, such unbundling is often anathema to landholders who regard the water that falls on their properties as rightfully theirs. Resistance to unbundling is particularly marked amongst traditional landowners, such as Indigenous Australians, for whom the idea that one could separate land and water rights, in this way, conflicts with their spiritual relationship to the land itself (Jackson and Altman, 2009).

The urgency of the water crisis

One of the most pressing problems facing humanity at the present time is the Water Crisis. It is a crisis that concerns both the *quality* and the *quantity* of water available to people for individual domestic consumption, agriculture, the environment, and industry. Human over-exploitation of resources, significant increases in the human population and, finally, ecological shifts associated with climate change are all affecting both the amount of water available and the value of the water for human consumption or agricultural purposes. At the time of finishing this piece (May 2023), Europe had been suffering what some experts claimed was the most severe drought in 500 years (Henley, 2022). Climate change also means that water calamities, where water is a burden rather than a benefit, are increasing. (Here water is of negative instrumental value.) In many flood-prone parts of the world—which are in low-lying or otherwise vulnerable areas—water is a burden and brings with it damage, destruction, and disease and, as such, raises questions of distributive justice in terms of how those affected might be recompensed, or if they should be recompensed at all.

If we focus, in the first instance, on the *quality* of water available, we discover that in many parts of the world safe drinkable water is something that only the wealthy can afford. Indeed, much of the world's surface water has been degraded by pollution and salination to such extent that the water in some cases is no longer safe to drink or bathe in and it harms any crops or other vegetation that it is intended to nurture. If we direct out attention to the *quantity* of water available, again we find massive shortages in many areas and concerns about how to conserve water in the face of increasing temperatures and lower levels of precipitation.[7] For instance, because of over-extraction, the Dead Sea has shrunk by more than one third in the last four decades. More worryingly, the Aral Sea is now less than 30% of its original size and has lost its title as the fourth largest lake in the world and now is ranked as the 31st in terms of size (Hernandez, 2010). One striking feature of this phenomenon of water scarcity is that there are often conflicts between both *competing users* and *competing uses* (Chellaney, 2013; Barlow, 2013): it is not simply a matter of competition between people wishing to use water for the same kind of activity. In the case of irrigation, we have competition between users who have the same purpose in mind, namely watering their crops; however, conflict also arises over different *uses* of water (Joshi and Kapadia, 2010). So, for example, miners who want water for their mining operations will often lead to conflict with farmers who desire water for growing crops like cotton. Equally water for environmental flows will often be in competition with water for recreational purposes such as water-skiing.

In both these examples, the use of water for one specific purpose might well lead to it not being available for some other, quite distinct, purpose. As competition for water increases, water-users will increasingly seek out alternative sources to the surface water in lakes, dams and rivers which have been the mainstay of much domestic, agricultural, and industrial uses of water (and, indeed, have already been doing so). Recent years have seen an increased focus on ground water as surface water dries up or alternatively is insufficient to meet rising demand.[8] Again it is highly likely—given the demand for water—that access to reliable groundwater has been, and will continue in the future to be, a significant source of regional and national conflict (Christopher, 2013; Busby, 2017) For instance, since the 1950s, the Jordan River Basin has been a source of conflict among Israel, the West Bank, Lebanon, Syria and Jordan. The main point of contention has been the extraction of water for irrigation purposes and the effect this has upon downstream riparian nations (Hernandez, 2010).

It goes without saying that water scarcity is, in part, a consequence of *increased demand*, and such demand derives from increases in both users and forms of use.[9] The scarcity has been exacerbated primarily by beliefs within Western industrial societies—which one might well regard as naively utopian—about the extent to which water systems can sustain ever increasing amounts of use. Population growth and increased demand are not the only source of the intensification of competition for water resources and, especially, for good quality water—there are also effects on *the supply-side*. The value of a significant portion of the world's water for human use has been degraded through pollution and other effects of human activity. A less dramatic form of degradation of water, which is a less direct consequence of human activity, is salination (i.e. the phenomenon of increasing the salt level in a water way or in soils). In many parts of the world—and notoriously my own home country of Australia—clearing of deep-rooted perennial vegetation and heavy irrigation practices have caused a subterranean saline water table to rise closer to the surface, making a great deal of the land unusable (Selby, 1981). All of these pressures are being intensified by climate change.

Six salient features of water as a distributive good

Assuming that the principles appropriate to just distribution should be determined in part by the unique features of the good in question, I would like us to consider in this section some distinctive features of water as a human good that affect questions of distribution and of commodification. Below I identify some salient features of water as a human good as are relevant to its role in our systems of production and distribution.[10] (As we shall see, some of these features are also highly relevant to the *sufficiency principle* that is defended in the last section.)

1. Water is both a *distributive benefit* and a *distributive burden*. It is a benefit when it is used for human purposes, such as for agriculture, recreation, industry or navigation. Equally, it is a burden (or a public "bad") when, for instance, flooding occurs.[11] It is also burdensome when it is found in the form of wastewater.[12]
2. With respect to its role as a benefit, access to water has an *urgency* unmatched by a great many other distributive goods. When we reflect on how necessary water is for such activities as drinking, cooking, bathing, and sanitation, we soon realise that it is a fundamental human good that must be placed in the category of those goods without which we cannot do.
3. Water has a *multiplicity of uses* and, hence, a diverse range of distributive goods associated with it; that is to say, it counts as a distributive good under a variety of distinct descriptions. It is instrumentally useful in agriculture and industry and for recreation and domestic consumption as well as being a vital element of ecosystems considered as a whole.
4. Water also has a *multiplicity of meanings and values* associated with it and these meanings and values will affect and impinge upon our distributive policies and practices. If we go beyond a straightforward (and possibly crude) utilitarian framework in which we only consider the utility or instrumental uses of water, there is also a range of meanings, both religious and cultural, associated with water.[13] The meanings associated with water are remarkably diverse and, in this way, render water a very different distributive good to most others over which distributive principles and distributive theories are applied. This multiplicity of meanings and values leads to the fact that any distributive decisions by policy makers do not only involve access to a consumptive item—as would typically be the case if we were discussing the allocation of a food staple like flour—but will oftentimes also have significant social and cultural effects (Linton, 2010; Strang, 2004).
5. The use, consumption and destruction of water are not always aligned which means, in some cases use has little destructive effect upon water and in others it does—that is to say, in some cases water is durable and in some cases it is not. We know that with many distributive goods, consumption entails destruction; however, this is not the case when we use water for say transport or for electricity production.[14] Even in the case of irrigation, much of the water remains in the land-based system and, hence, its consumption does not entail its destruction.
6. Finally, "distributively-relevant" uses of water are not always obvious. Unlike many other goods, the use or consumption of water is not always immediately apparent, nor therefore are its beneficiaries. For an Australian example consider the case of the different water resource-use of pine forests versus blue gum plantations. Blue gums have a much deeper root system and, thus, are able to tap into the Great Artesian Basin, whereas pine trees cannot do so because their roots are not deep enough. In this case, the different water resource use is known and because blue gums do in fact extract water from the Basin, blue gum plantation owners are required to pay a licence fee for that use. In this case, government authorities are aware of the use, but the more general point is that it is not always obvious who is benefiting from water usage. Hence, determining who is gaining benefits from water is not always straightforward. This is very different from, what is the case for instance, when we allocate food to people.

Some key normative objections to the commodification of water

Commodification involves, amongst other things, a transformation of the mechanism by which water is allocated. There are a number of potentially undesirable aspects of such a transformation, but below I highlight four, all of which demonstrate how the commodification of water might affect important normative values. It is the conjunction of commodification itself and of water's idiosyncratic features that creates many of these difficulties.

The first objection—which is sufficientarian in nature—concerns our access to the basic goods that water provides. Recall that one feature of commodification is that it can make access to a good *contingent upon* possession of sufficient financial resources.[15] If one does not have adequate resources—and this is a rather obvious observation I suppose—then one cannot access a good. If we also consider the way in which water realises fundamental goods in the domestic sphere, such as for instance, washing, drinking and cooking, then it also follows that not having the necessary financial wherewithal means that one is denied access to a set of fundamental goods realised by water. The argument that is defended here regarding how one should respond to any distributive problems created by commodification is—as was noted earlier—sufficientarian in nature and is underpinned by the idea that individuals have, *inter alia*, a right to basic human goods and, conversely, society has an obligation to provide those goods (Gosserries, 2011; Huseby, 2010). Hence, a system which opens the possibilities that people do not have access to fundamental goods—that is to sufficiency in resources—also opens up the possibility of violating the society's obligations to provide basic goods. It is morally wrong for agents *not to have access* to basic water resources. I assume this to be a fundamental tenet of a decent political formation.

This then is the "objection from basic need" which I formulate as follows:

a) *The Objection from Basic Need*: in cases in which the commodification of water leads those without adequate financial resources to be excluded entirely from access to water then it is morally objectionable.

In commodifying, we discriminate against those with little economic power. The aim of the "water sufficientarian" argument is to ensure that basic water needs of everyone are met, not only those with the requisite financial resources. The emphasis, in this model, is upon the realisation of a sufficient amount of access to water. At the level of basic needs, the approach of the sufficientarian might be regarded as egalitarian. Since everyone is equal in the sense that all should have such water resources. However, the sufficientarian is open to the idea that once such needs are met, other non-egalitarian principles can come into play.

What might such principles be? In the first instance, I suggest that there are good utilitarian reasons for allowing markets to determine allocations once basic water needs have been met. In so doing, we harness the productive energy of the market whilst ensuring that everyone has their basic water needs met. Notice that this is a very different approach to that of the egalitarian who would presumably allocate all water on egalitarian principles. Of course, an egalitarian approach would also ensure that those who lack basic financial resources would have access to basic water resources, but it would also entail limiting the possibilities of commercial uses of water, through activities such as horticulture or industry, that are of considerable social benefit.[16]

The second objection to the commodification of water to be considered briefly here concerns the violation of expressive norms (or what some critics also refer to as the "corrosion of value").[17] This line of critique is most clearly articulated by Elizabeth Anderson (1990) who begins by noting that, in markets, commodities are treated via the impersonal modes of valuation of use. A mere commodity is something one "regards as interchangeable with any other item of the same kind and quality" and it is something that "one is prepared to trade with equanimity for any other commodity at some price" (Anderson, 1990, 181). Notice that this approach does not rule out the market and forms of commodification entirely. Only sale of goods which should not be regarded instrumentally need to be categorised as blocked exchanges. If we apply this to water, we can formulate an objection from expressive violation which would run as follows.

b) *The Objection from Expressive Violation*: insofar as the commodification of water leads us to regard water systems which *should be regarded* in a non-instrumental manner, as mere means to the realisation of profit, then such commodification raises moral concerns.

While this is an important objection to some forms of commodification, it is not clear how relevant it is to the topic under discussion. Clearly, there will be some water systems or waterways which should be regarded as intrinsically valuable, although I doubt this holds for water as a whole. Moreover, our topic is distributive justice and, again, the concerns of the expressivist seem orthogonal to questions of what the just or fair way of allocating water might be. To be sure, there is a place for expressive critique when determining the moral boundaries of commodification, but it is not obvious that it is relevant to questions of water and distributive justice. Indeed, one might well argue that it cannot capture all the concerns one might have with commodification (Panitch, 2020). A related concern with the non-consequential intrinsic value of particular entities—as opposed to all things—is also to be found in the work of certain environmental ethicists, such as for instance the so-called "deep ecologists". They might object to the instrumental treatment of water systems as part of a more general critique of our anthropomorphism (Bhagwat, 2009). But without wanting to sound too shallow or glib, it must be noted that there will necessarily be an instrumental element to our dealings with water—we cannot avoid it. Humans use water and need water and do so instrumentally. Any theory that rules out instrumental modes of regard for water entirely is naively other-worldly.

The third objection to be considered is what I shall call the "Objection from Environmental Integrity". Recall the earlier claim that, when we commodify, we transform the system of product and distribution so that decisions about the direction of activity are determined by the demands of the market. Moreover, the market system is so constituted that pressures of competition will often force producers to adopt *only* the most profitable path at the expense of less profitable choices, because if they do not, they might well be forced out of business. But the most profitable way of using water might well be at odds with what is required for ecological sustainability and environmental integrity. This objection we can be formulated as follows:

c) *The Objection from Environmental Integrity*: insofar as commodification leads to decision-making processes that typically favour the realisation of profits whenever a conflict arises between financial interests and significant environmental interests, then commodification is morally objectionable.

This is a significant objection to the commodification of water, especially insofar as the water is located within an ecological system of significant value, such as a river or lake. The thought is that we cannot allow choices to be made, based on profit alone, at the expense of the ecological systems upon which we rely. However, again, while it is clearly an important objection to commodification, it is not directly related to questions of distributive justice at the current time, although if we consider the question of resource allocation between present and future generations then clearly there are questions of distributive justice. However, the concern within this chapter is with distributive justice *at the present time* and, hence, the Objection from Environmental Integrity is not an objection that I will pursue in further detail herein.

The focus for the rest of the chapter will be upon the Objection from Basic Need and what such an objection might mean in terms of public policy and, most importantly, the extent to which we should prohibit or prescribe the buying and selling of water. However, before moving to the question of how one might implement public policy based on the Objection from Basic Needs, we should note one final plausible moral objection to one aspect of the commodification of water. Insofar as such commodification requires the unbundling of water and land, then it will be radically at odds with the spiritual values and relationship to land of many traditional peoples (Bhagwat, 2009).[18] Any process that imposes rules according to which land and water are to be treated separately might be said to ignore the spiritual values of traditional landowners. This objection applies to the commodification of water in regions where there are traditional owners *in situ* and who have a spiritual relationship with the water ways in question. This, however, does not provide us with a *general critique* of the commodification of water, but raises issue which are of relevance—and should be considered—when discussing the commodification of water in places where such spiritual relationships are in place. In the next section I consider what the Objection from Basic Need means at a practical policy level.

Prohibition or regulation? A sufficientarian approach

One initial general point to make is the mere fact that a process or activity has some negative consequences does not mean that there are not also potentially overwhelmingly good consequences outweighing the negative ones. A second point—which arises out of the sufficientarian model—is that it need not be the case that we either block all goods or none; rather it might be that we block all trades up until the point where basic human needs are met. Notice that this is the way that some extant water markets operate. In Australia, for instance, in the Murray Darling Basin, water can be traded once what the Murray Darling Basin Authority calls "critical human water needs" have been met (Commonwealth of Australia, 2007).[19] Here it is not a matter simply of categorising water as being, in all instances, a blocked exchange. The blocking of exchange might only be partial—that is, up to the point where basic needs are met. Furthermore, if we remember that water realises many different goods and has many different uses, then this claim makes the question of blocking or regulating even more complicated and, therefore, requires more detailed analysis to determine which uses are primary. Notice also on this model, allowing a good to be commodified does not rule out government intervention that regulates how commodities once commodified are bought and sold. Radin (1996) refers to this as "incomplete commodification".

Herein our primary concern is with access to basic goods and the relative probability that some persons will—because of the establishment of a marketised system of distribution—be denied access. Accordingly, priority must be given to those uses of water that realise basic human goods and in such a way that all users have access to these goods. Note that Panitch (2020, and Chapter 4 in this volume) makes a similar point with respect to healthcare and education. There must be a system of public provision of water for basic human goods in place, which could, for instance, involve various pricing mechanisms to regulate supply, and which ideally ensures that all have access. However, once those needs have been met to an appropriate level of sufficiency, it is then an open question as to which distributive mechanisms might be employed.[20] It might well be decided—as noted above when referring to the Australian case—that when basic needs have been met, water resources beyond sufficiency can be commodified. These are what we might refer to as "second-tier" markets. If basic needs are met, then the reasons defended above for opposing commodification are quietened. As Panitch (2020) notes: "[B]ecause necessary goods must only be met sufficiently, not equally, markets in necessary goods are perfectly defensible once the social minimum has been attained" (p. 73). Hence, in determining which water exchanges should be blocked, we need to consider (i) the role that the good plays in the satisfaction of basic human needs, (ii) whether those needs have been met and (iii) whether placing the good on the market, in a particular case, will hinder the realisation of those needs. On this conception of when to block exchanges, it is not simply a matter of *either* allowing *or* prohibiting trade in the good in question. Sometimes the sale of a good will be blocked and other times prohibition will not be required from a normative perspective.

This sufficientarian approach is remarkably different from critiques in which there are *expressive* or Kantian, rather than straight-forward *distributive* reasons for prohibiting sale. Think, for instance, of the sale of human organs. If one endorses the Objection from Expressive Violation or adopts a Kantian critique of the commodification of human organs (Chadwick, 1989; Munzer, 1993), according to which selling those organs expresses the wrong values or fails to treat human beings with the requisite dignity, then it must be the case that commodification is always wrong. That is simply not the case with the sufficientarian model outlined here. This model need not lead to *absolute prohibition* (or water being regarded universally as a blocked exchange), but it does leave open the possibility of there being different spheres where some water is commodified and other "tranches" of water are not. Priority here must be given to uses of water that satisfy basic human needs and—within those spheres—to those *users* who lack sufficient access to the basic goods. Once basic needs have been met, then the commodification of water is an option (although not in any sense a requirement). Hence, there is an acceptance of some forms of commodification, *contingent upon* the prior meeting of basic needs; commodification is only permissible if such needs have been met.

Of course, there might be concerns in some quarters that private second-tier markets undermine the integrity of first tier public provision. The thought is that permitting private commercial water companies to sell water alongside the publicly provided resource could plausibly lead the public (perhaps via explicit marketing on the part of commercial suppliers) to regard the commercial variant as preferable or more socially desirable or indeed safer. To be sure, there might well be such pressures and some poorer members of society might come to believe that the water they obtain is lesser. We must accept this as a possibility; the important thing is for the government to remain vigilant in ensuring that the market does not interfere with sufficiency in ways that limits the quantity or the quality of water available for domestic purposes.

Finally, one might wonder whether sufficientarianism provides a general model beyond the case of water for determining which goods should be blocked as commodities. An obvious candidate for a similar philosophical treatment would be healthcare. I think we do need to be exercise some caution at this point. Firstly, as has been noted several times in this chapter, water is an unusual good due to the multiplicity of uses and the ways in which one can commodify some uses and not others. Moreover, if we restrict our attention to one particular use—for instance, water used for drinking, we might well say that it can be commodified, once all the needs for potable water are satisfied. But it is not so easy with many other goods, to separate out different tranches of the good.

Further—as Panitch correctly notes—there are reasons for blocking exchange which are *not distributive* in nature. Think of selling human bodies or the sale of votes in an election. The reasons for opposing these sales are not because they violate norms of distributive justice. The sale of human bodies violates the dignity with which human beings should be treated, while vote-selling threatens to corrupt meaningful and valuable democratic processes. In such cases, sufficientarianism—as outlined herein at least—does not tell us what is wrong with commodification. Nonetheless, there is something distinctive about the approach developed herein for determining the scope of blocked exchange that is relevant to more general debates about the moral and political boundaries of commodification. In the distributive realm the sufficientarian model potentially provides a mechanism for determining whether specific bundles of goods should be commodified, where goods can be separated in the ways that water can. Importantly—and water provides a very useful case study for making this very point—we need not think that we are always faced with a stark choice between blocking a specific exchange in a particular good or alternatively enabling the good to be sold on the market. This, I suggest, sheds new light on the idea of blocked exchange and how we might determine which goods should be outside the range of the market.

Concluding remarks

In this chapter I have focused upon a set of normative concerns one might have with the commodification of water; namely with the distributive consequences or commodification and the extent to which this constitutes a significant form of injustice. I defend a sufficientarian model according to which the commodification of water is morally undesirable when it significantly limits access to the water resources required for the satisfaction of basic human needs. In developing this position, I outlined two key points that must be considered. The first concerns the water crisis (that is being exacerbated by climate change). This crisis renders struggles over access to water resources all the more intense (and discussions of reduction of access to water via commodification all the more relevant). Secondly, water itself has various distinctive idiosyncratic features that affect normative questions about the rightness or wrongness of commodification as well as its status as a distributive good. We must consider when discussing the morality of the commodification of water. Insofar as commodification gives rise to a lack of access to a basic human good, then this provides one set of grounds for moral critique. It is important to reiterate here that these distributive worries are not the only reasons for concern with the commodification of water. I have restricted attention to distributive questions but there are also important questions of environmental integrity and potential effects upon the cultural and religious meanings associated with certain water systems that are relevant to commodification and which should also be explored as part of the project of considering the normative implications of commodification.

What my sufficientarian approach entails with respect to water policy is that full-scale commodification should only be permitted once all basic water needs have been met. This might be achieved either (i) via state provision or (ii) by state intervention in markets, so that water is in Radin's sense "incompletely commodified". The state has an obligation to ensure all such needs are satisfied. Once such basic provisions are met, then it is permissible to commodify the excess water that exists over and above critical human water needs, so long as such commodification can be shown to generate important social benefits. Notice here that it is not that all water becomes a blocked exchange or is incompletely commodified, but rather the restrictions on water's commodification operate up until the point that all basic needs are met. This I take to be a distinctive, significant, and meaningful response to the specifically distributive consequences of the commodification of water.

Notes

1 https://corpwatchers.eu/en/investigations/cities-versus-multinationals/leaving-water-privatisation-behind-paris-grenoble-and-the-advent-of-the-water?lang=en

2 Although, of course, such concerns will often arise when one considers water as either a cultural good or if one approaches normative issues about water from a deep ecological perspective.

3 For an excellent overview of sufficientarianism as a theory of distributive justice see Gosseries (2011).

4 The divisions between "kinds" of water is, in many ways, artificial and, moreover, not always *normatively* relevant. Hydrologists often distinguish, for instance, between *ground* and *surface water*. But these are not different species of water, simply water located at different stages of the hydrological cycle. Similarly, policy makers often distinguish between industrial, municipal and agricultural water but again this does not track any intrinsic features of the water itself but simply distinguishes types of human use of water.

5 Robert Nozick famously suggests in *Anarchy, State and Utopia* that if goods fell like "manna from heaven", then they could be treated as public goods to be distributed according to some patterned theory of justice (Nozick, 1974, p. 198). In one sense water does fall like manna from heaven and, in another, it does not. The water we consume in our homes typically did not just fall from heaven but was provided by government utilities. Equally the water used in industrial processes or for agricultural purposes has typically been made available through human intervention in the form of dams, channels and pipelines. The bucolic vision of water falling naturally from the sky and running wildly in rivers often obscures the fact that much of the water we use is a product of human intervention in natural processes.

6 In Chapter 4, Panitch distinguishes between *normative corruption* (which includes concerns with motives) and *ontological corruption* which is a worry about corrupting a goods inherent value or meaning.

7 As Barlow noted in 2013:

> Close to two billion people now live in water-stressed parts of the planet and almost three billion have no running water within a kilometre of their homes. The global population tripled in the twentieth century, but water consumption jumped sevenfold … [B]y 2050, we will need an 80 % increase in water supplies just to feed ourselves. No one knows where this water is going to come from.
>
> (Barlow, 2013)

8 See Wolff, Yoffe and Giordano (2003).

9 For an interesting discussion of the role of scarcity in the justification of private property rights obtained through mixing one's labour with un-owned natural objects, see Bogart, 1985, and see Chapter 1 of this volume.

10 I am not claiming that this list is somehow exhaustive—although it might be—but these are at least some of the features one needs to consider when debating both the *concept* of just water and various *conceptions* of it.

11 This is a serious issue in for instance England now where flooding is affecting housing, mainly in poorer areas, and commercial insurance brokers are becoming increasingly unwilling to insure in such flood-prone districts (O'Neill and O'Neill, 2012).

12 And matters are far worse in some under-developed countries. In Bangladesh for instance flooding during the monsoon season from June until September affects millions of peoples, causing loss of property, crops and lives. Bangladesh is situated on the Ganges River Delta where waters flow into the Bay of Bengal and more than 80% of the country is on floodplain. Every year, as a consequence of its topography, around 18% of the country is flooded, killing on average more than 5000 people. It goes without saying that such flooding causes enormous damage to property and threatens the food security of the country. In this sense, flooding is a distributive burden.

13 As Nelke Doorn (2013) notes:

> A last aspect which is typical for water is the multitude of meanings attached to water…In its most simple form the debate on water scarcity is about prioritising different kinds of water use. In this discussion the value of water is primarily instrumental, a basic human need indeed yet a relatively tangible one … However, other values are still excluded from the debate about priorities for water use and water management. In many cultures and religions water has a symbolic meaning or value as well … In many religions the symbolic meaning of water is associated with its ability to remove sin and impurity.

14 There is an interesting question regarding the point at which severe contamination has the same effect as destruction. For example think of tailings dams on mine sites. Here it might signify a shift from a benefit to a burden. Or has the resource ceased to be water and become a toxic sludge?

15 Here we are solely concerned with cases of commodification at the endpoint for the user. There will sometimes be cases of monopsony where the state buys a good on the market and then distributes it for free. The good still has a market price—and hence an exchange value—but in this case our access isn't dependent on the market. Attention is therefore restricted to commodification at the point of use.

16 There are other related concerns. Debra Satz, for instance, in *Why Some things should not be for sale* (2010) focuses on the ways in which some markets are noxious because they impede the conditions that are required if we to relate as equals (2010, p. 94). The concern in Satz's work is not with expressive violations of corrosion of value but rather with the impediments to the realisation of egalitarian human associations.

17 And this is not the end of the terminological variety. For instance, Brennan and Jaworski (2015) rather dismissively refer to arguments like Anderson's as "semiotic" objections.

18 See Crétois' contribution on land in this volume (Chapter 6).

19 Critical human water needs (CHWN) are defined in the Commonwealth Water Act 2007 passed by the Australian Federal Parliament, as the minimum volumes of water that can reasonably be provided from Basin resources to meet core human consumption requirements that, if not met, would cause prohibitively high social, economic, or national security costs. This public policy essentially involves a sufficientarian model, in spirit at least, if not explicitly in name.

20 There are interesting and puzzling questions here about what the thresholds might be and how we might determine when sufficiency has been achieved, but those questions can wait for another time. For now, what matters is the idea in principle that there is a need to achieve sufficiency.

References

Anderson, E. 1990, "Ethical limitations of the market," *Economics and Philosophy* vol.6, no.2, pp. 179–205.

Anderson, E. 1993, *Value in Ethics and Economics*. Harvard University Press, Cambridge, Mass.

Aristotle. 1946, *The Politics*. trans. E. Barker, Clarendon Press, Oxford.

Barlow, M. 2013, *Blue Future: Protecting water for people and the planet forever*, New Press, New York.

Bhagwat, S.A. 2009, "Ecosystem Services and Sacred Natural Sites: Reconciling Material and Non-material Values in Nature Conservation," *Environmental Values*, vol.18, no.4, pp. 417–427.

Brennan J. and Jaworski P.M. 2015, "Markets without symbolic limits," *Ethics*, vol.125, no.4, pp. 1053–1077.

Busby, J. 2017, *Water and U.S. National Security*. New York: The Council on Foreign Relations. www.cfr.org/sites/default/files/pdf/2017/01/Discussion_Paper_Busby_Water_and_US_Security_OR.pdf

Chadwick, R. 1989, "The market for bodily parts: Kant and duties to oneself," *Journal of Applied Philosophy*, vol.6, no.2, pp. 129–140.

Chellaney, B. 2013, *Water, Peace, and War: Confronting the global water crisis*, Rowman & Littlefield, Lanham, MD.

Christopher, M. 2013, "MIWS_07—Water Wars: The Brahmaputra River and Sino-Indian Relations," *CIWAG Case Studies*. 7. https://digital-commons.usnwc.edu/ciwag-case-studies/7

Commonwealth of Australia, 2007, *Water Act*. Australian Government Publishing, Canberra. http://classic.austlii.edu.au/au/legis/cth/consol_act/wa200783/s86a.html

Doorn, N. 2013, "Water and Justice: Towards an Ethics of Water Governance," *Public Reason* Vol. 5, no.1, pp. 97–114.

Getzler, J. 2004, *A History of Water Rights at Common Law*, Oxford University Press, Oxford.

Gosseries, A. 2011, "Sufficientarianism," *Routledge Encyclopedia of Philosophy*, DOI 0.4324/9780415249126-S112-1

Henley, J. 2022, "Europe's run dry as scientists warn drought could be worst in 500 years," *The Guardian*. www.theguardian.com/environment/2022/aug/13/europes-rivers-run-dry-as-scientists-warn-drought-could-be-worst-in-500-years

Hernandez, N.E. 2010, "Water security Conflict: A Regional Perspective," *Small Wars Journal*, http://smallwarsjournal.com/jrnl/art/water-security-conflicts-a-regional-perspective.

Hoekstra, A. and Chapagain, A. 2007, *Globalization of Water: Sharing the Planet's Freshwater Resources*, Wiley Blackwell, Chichester.

Huseby, R. 2010, "Sufficiency: Restated and Defended," *The Journal of Political Philosophy*, vol.18, pp. 178–197.

Joshi, M.B. and Kapadia V.P. 2010, "Sharing Water in the 21st Century: Rethinking the Rationale?" *Irrigation and Drainage*, vol.59, no.1, pp. 92–101.

Lindley, S. and O'Neill, J. 2013, "Flood Disadvantage in Scotland," *The Scottish Government*. Edinburgh.

Linton, J. 2010. *What is Water? The History of a Modern Abstraction*, UCB Press, Vancouver and Toronto.

Munzer, S. 1993, "Kant and property rights in body parts," *Canadian Journal of Law and Jurisprudence*, vol. 6, no.2, pp. 319–341.
Nozick, R. 1974, *Anarchy, State and Utopia*. London: Basil Blackwell.
O'Neill, J. and O'Neill M. 2012, "Social Justice and the Future of Flood Insurance: What would be a fair model of flood insurance?" *Joseph Rowntree Foundation*. www.jrf.org.uk/report/social-justice-and-future-flood-insurance
Panitch, V. 2020, "Liberalism, Commodification, and Justice," *Politics, Philosophy, and Economics* vol.19, no.1, pp. 62–82.
Radin, M.J. 1996, *Contested Commodities: The Trouble with Trade in Sex, Children, Body Parts and Other Things*. Harvard University Press, Cambridge Mass.
Reiss, J. 2021, "Public Goods," *Stanford Encyclopedia of Philosophy*. HTTPs://plato.stanford.edu/entries/public-goods/s
Satz, D. 2010, *Why Some Things Should Not be For Sale*. Oxford University Press, New York.
Selby, J. 1981, "A salty problem for the River Murray," *New Scientist*, 25 June 1981, Vol.90, pp. 402–408.
South African Constitution, www.thehda.co.za/images/uploads/unpan005172.pdf
Strang, V. 2004, *The Meaning of Water*. Oxford: Berg.
Walsh, A. 2011, "The Commodification of the Public Service of Water: A Normative Perspective," *Public Reason*, vol. 3 no.2, pp. 44–60.
Walsh, A. 2001, "Are Market Norms and Intrinsic Valuation Mutually Exclusive?" *Australasian Journal of Philosophy*. vol. 79, no.4, pp. 525–543.
Walsh, A.J. and Lynch, A. 2008. *The Morality of Money: An Exploration in Analytic Philosophy*. London: Palgrave Macmillan.
Walzer, M. 1983, *Spheres of Justice: A Defence of Pluralism and Equality*. Oxford: Basil Blackwell.
Western States Water Laws: Arizona. www.blm.gov/nstc/Waterlaws/arizona.html
Wolff, A., Yoffe, S. and Giordano, M. 2003, "International Waters: Identifying Basins at Risk," *Water Policy*, vol. 5, no.1, pp. 29–60.

27
ANIMALS
Ending cruelty through markets

Aksel Braanen Sterri

Introduction

Farm animals are, legally and socially, thoroughly commodified: they are bought and sold, dead and alive. But they are not *mere* commodities. They are sensing, feeling creatures with a will of their own. It therefore matters how we treat them. Harming animals is morally wrong unless we have overriding reasons to do so.

Despite these undeniable moral claims, most of us are complicit in commodification and market exchange that harm animals. Around 80 billion farm animals are slaughtered every year around the world (Ritchie & Roser, 2017), primarily to please our palates and comfort our bodies.[1] A further 1–2 trillion—a thousand billion—fish are slaughtered every year (Fishcount, 2019). Paradoxically, death may be a salvation for many farm animals, given the immense suffering they endure while alive. Many farm animals live lives not worth living (Browning, 2022, p. 40). They are better off dead than alive.

In this chapter, I ethically assess the practice of farm animal commodification and examine novel ways to prevent animal harm. "Farm animal commodification" refers to the fact that farm animals are owned, treated as slaves, exploited for their flesh and reproductive capacities, and bought and sold dead and alive.

In the first part, I examine reasons for abolishing the market for farm animal products. I argue that although *decommodifying* animals is a bulletproof way of preventing harm, it has the unfortunate side-effect of preventing animals from living lives worth living.

In the second part, I explore an alternative and under-examined approach I call *animal welfare commodification*. According to this approach, animals are treated poorly because market participants do not account for their interests. By pricing or commodifying animal welfare, we can make animal welfare matter economically. I examine and improve on several specific proposals for animal welfare commodification, such as a meat tax and a market for animal welfare. I also defend two novel proposals, a tax on suffering and a death tax.

Animal welfare commodification is complementary to animal welfare regulation, the dominant way to improve animal welfare. While regulation improves animal welfare, few observers believe it does so sufficiently. We should therefore explore other strategies.

 DOI: 10.4324/9781003188742-33

Decommodifying animals

There are many reasons for decommodifying animals. Farm animals contribute to global warming, harming current and future generations (Errickson et al., 2021), and are a leading risk factor for epidemics and pandemics among humans (Bartlett et al., 2022). By displacing natural habitats, they are also a leading cause of the extinction of wild animal species and the disruption of ecosystems (Pendrill et al., 2019; Ritchie, 2019). Although these reasons are crucial, the one that will concern us in this chapter is the harm to the farm animals themselves.

Farm animal-related reasons to favour decommodification come in two forms, rights and interests. According to the *animal rights view*, defended by Tom Regan (1983), Gary Francione (1995), Steven Wise (2000), and Christine Korsgaard (2018), animals have a right against being treated as commodities. In its most ambitious form, this right bars us from treating animals as commodities no matter how much we want or need animal products or how well animals are treated on farms.

In this chapter, I will focus on the animals' interest in avoiding suffering and death and living good lives. On this "animal welfarist" view, animals count morally, but they do not have the same rights as humans against being owned, commodified, and killed (Singer, 2009). When assessing the practice of animal commodification, we should compare the interests both humans and animals have in commodification and decommodification, respectively. We should decommodify animals if and only if more and weightier interests are satisfied by decommodification. Despite a difference in approach, I hope animal rights proponents will welcome animal welfare commodification as a supplement to regulation to improve animal welfare.

The benefit of existence

Whether to decommodify or commodify animals is often construed as a conflict between humans' interests and animals' interests. But this misses a crucial insight. If animals on farms necessarily live lives *not worth living*, we would be required to decommodify animals. The pleasure humans get from consuming animal products is too insignificant to justify imposing immense suffering on animals (DeGrazia, 2009).

On the other hand, if farm animals live lives *worth living*, decommodification may be undesirable even for the animals themselves. The British historian Leslie Stephen's (1896) famously argued that "[t]he pig has a stronger interest than anyone in the demand for bacon. If all the world were Jewish, there would be no pigs at all". From Stephen's remarks, we may glean an argument for *Beneficence*: We ought to commodify animals because it is in the animals' interest to live good lives (Singer, 2011, p. 88).

Criticisms of Beneficence are as old as the view itself. Henry S. Salt (1914) famously ridiculed Stephen's argument by calling it the "logic of the larder", as it implausibly implies that the person with the biggest larder is the greatest benefactor. He also believed it nonsense to talk about benefiting someone by bringing them into existence. "The moment [one] begins to argue as if from the abyss of the non-existent", Salt (1914) argues, "[one] talks nonsense, by predicating good or evil, happiness or unhappiness, of that of which we can predicate nothing".

Despite its rhetorical force, Salt is overstating his case. It is perfectly appropriate to say that one would *harm* someone by bringing them into a life of utter misery, even if it entails arguing "as if from the abyss of the non-existent". Some philosophers have taken this to suggest that Salt is half right. There is an asymmetry between harms and benefits. Avoiding harm is a reason against bringing someone into existence, but a happy existence is no reason for procreation (McMahan,

2009). Proponents of Beneficence, of which I am one, believe Salt is wrong altogether. If someone can be harmed by being brought into a miserable existence, they can also be benefited by being brought into a happy existence (Singer, 2011, p. 88). According to Beneficence, a world with happy beings is better than one without, and the more beings that live good lives, the better. If animal commodification leads to miserable lives, it is ruled out by Beneficence. However, if commodification is necessary to bring happy lives into existence, one should support commodification on this view.

Early death as the price of existence

Commodification may provide farm animals with the benefit of a worthwhile existence, but it comes with a catch: the animals are killed when they are no longer maximally profitable. Dairy cows could live for 20 years but are killed when they are five. Pigs get to live 1.8 years but could live up to 27 years (Hoffman & Valencak, 2020). The harm of killing is another powerful reason for decommodification. It is difficult to believe that our interest in bacon and milk can outweigh the animals' interest in continuing to live for 15 or 25 more years.

Epicureans might respond that death is no harm since there is no subject in death that can experience the harm. Although they are correct that death is not a harm anyone can experience, felt harm is not the only harm worth caring about. Death is a comparative harm. It deprives us of a valuable future we would otherwise have (Bradley, 2016; DeGrazia, 1996; Harman, 2011).[2]

Another response is that animals do not have the temporally extended selves necessary for death to be a deprivation. If the animal lives only in the here and now, its death seems to be on par with never coming into existence. And one could arguably make up for the death of one such creature by bringing a new one into existence (Singer, 2011, pp. 106–107). Even if this *replaceability argument* could work for animals without an extended sense of self, such as perhaps fish, it is unlikely that it applies to most farm animals. Cows, pigs, and other farm animals arguably possess a sufficient temporally extended self for death to be bad for them (DeGrazia, 1996).

A better response is to adopt a stance I call *Holism*, according to which an otherwise impermissible action can be permissible if necessary for bringing about an overall desirable outcome (Gauthier, 1984; Quinn, 1985). From the farmer's perspective, bringing animals into existence would make no sense unless they could be killed when that is profitable. If life is an existential benefit and killing is required to ensure the animal gets this benefit, the killing could be justified on two related but conceptually distinct grounds. One is a *hypothetical contract*. If the only way one can get to live is to be killed, the animal would presumably prefer this over non-existence. Another is as a *hypothetical imperative*. The killing is justified if the practice is beneficial and the killing is required to produce the benefit.

However, Holism has its problems. It seems to suggest that we would be justified in bringing people into existence to serve as organ donors if their lives were worth living, and they would not exist if it were not for the practice. But most of us believe that when someone exists, they have claims "even against those whose purpose in creating him was to violate those claims" (Nozick, 1974, p. 38).

To avoid this unappealing implication, we might be forced to adopt an alternative view. According to *Reductionism*, "the permissibility of individual acts is determined by the considerations that favour them at the time of action" (McMahan, 2008, p. 74). Reductionists could only justify killing if it is necessary at the time to bring about a more important outcome. Saving the life of a human would qualify, but our interest in a tasty meal would not.

Although intuitively plausible, Reductionism is not without its problems. One problem in the case of farm animals is that it is self-defeating. The reason for endorsing Reductionism is to protect the animals' interest in living by preventing their premature death. However, it promotes no such interest if it precludes animals from living. Indeed, it ensures there will be no animal and no life to protect. Reductionists may object that there could be a market for animals that die natural deaths or are killed mercifully when necessary to avoid too much suffering. But this market will be drastically smaller than one that allows killing animals in their prime.

Jeff McMahan (2008, pp. 73–74) offers another solution for reductionists. If we could genetically engineer farm animals to die when that is most profitable for farmers, their early death would necessarily follow from procreation and thus be permitted if their lives were well worth living. But this *bundling solution* reveals another problem with Reductionism. It seems to imply that we should be willing to pay to ensure that actions get *metaphysically* bundled to achieve beneficial outcomes that would have been cost-free if we allowed ourselves to *perceive* the actions as bundled. Suppose gene editing is a costly affair. Is metaphysical bundling through gene editing a sufficient moral improvement over painlessly killing animals to justify spending scarce resources on gene editing? Suppose we must choose between improving and extending animal lives on the one hand and investing in gene editing on the other. In that case, I find it hard to believe we should bundle procreation and death instead of improving and extending animal lives.

Whether animal commodification is justified depends on whether Holism can be rescued. That, in turn, depends on whether we can explain why it is wrong to bring humans into existence to serve as organ donors without appealing to Reductionism. One plausible candidate is that we have obligations to treat humans as equals that we do not have towards farm animals (McMahan 2008, pp. 74–75; Anderson, 2004). Bringing humans into existence to serve as organ donors would violate this obligation. Bringing animals into existence in exchange for an early death does no such thing.

Beneficence and Holism provide sufficient justification for commodifying farm animals if their lives are sufficiently good. Below we will return to the content of the bargain: how good and long their lives must be to justify bringing them into existence. Before that, we turn to why the farm animal market produces so much suffering and what we can do about it.

Market failures in the farm animal market

Animal welfare commodification is an economic approach to accommodate the interests of animals and humans (Cowen, 2006; Norwood & Lusk, 2011). Its *diagnosis* is that the market in animal products suffers from "market failures" that predictably cause excessive harm to animals. Its suggested *treatment* is to rectify these failures not by decommodifying animals themselves but by commodifying animal welfare.

Animal welfare commodification starts from the premise that markets are good because of and to the extent they promote welfare and respect autonomy (Daou and Marciano's Chapter 1 in this volume). Markets perform this role by facilitating mutually beneficial trades between informed, consenting parties. But for markets to optimally serve their purpose, the effects of trade must be internalized, that is, born *only* by the trading parties. If market participants are rational and informed, and all effects are internalized, markets will lead to a *Pareto optimal* outcome, that is, an outcome that cannot make anyone better off without making someone worse off.

Often all effects are not born by the market participants. Instead, some burdens and benefits of trade are imposed on third parties without their consent. Some effects are thus externalized rather than internalized. Markets that produce externalities suffer from a market failure: they produce too much of the goods that impose harm on third parties and too little of the goods that impose benefits (see Bertrand's contribution to this volume in Chapter 3).

A classic case of a "negative externality" is carbon emissions (see Chapter 24 by Berta in this volume). More carbon is emitted than would have been agreed to if everyone affected was included in the market or the cost to third parties reflected in the prices. The farm animal market also produces large negative externalities, including emitting too much carbon (Errickson et al., 2021). Of interest to us here is the harm to animals.

Harm to farm animals is rarely considered an externality in economists human-centric models (Espinosa & Treich, 2021). But the same logic applies in this area as in the case of climate change. The participants in the farm animal market are farmers and consumers. Still, most burdens are born by animals that neither can veto treatments that are not to their liking nor demand compensation. Predictably, their interests are neglected when farmers and consumers satisfy their own.

Markets with externalities suffer from a market failure that could be rectified by a targeted intervention (Baumol, 1972). One intervention that is sure to prevent negative externalities is decommodification. However, it rarely leads to a better outcome. If we were to prevent harm from carbon emissions by taking all products with a carbon footprint out of the market, this would lead the world economy to grind to a halt with immense negative consequences.

Economists tend to favour three more targeted approaches to internalize externalities. One, which I will leave aside, is regulation. Another is to create new markets to capture all affected interests. The market for animal welfare that I examine below is an example of this *market creation approach*. The third approach, which I also explore below, is *Pigovian taxes*: a tax on trades that reflects the cost to third parties of engaging in the trades.

In a narrow sense, Pigovian taxes do not commodify animal welfare. One cannot buy and sell it or bargain over its price. However, taxes entails commodification in a broad sense because one is free to impose the externality if one pays. Moreover, this cost can be financialized and affect the prices of consumer goods. Commodifying animal welfare in either of these ways could make it economically beneficial to treat farm animals well. It thus promises to be a targeted and reliable way to serve the interests of farm animals.

The animal welfare market

According to Tyler Cowen (2006) and Jayson Lusk (2011), there is market failure in the current market for farm animal products. The market produces a negative externality on *animal friends* who have no way of paying other consumers to stop demanding products that involve harm to animals.

To include the interests of animal friends, Lusk (2011, p. 565) suggests "giving farmers property rights over an output called animal well-being units (AWBUs)" and creating a market where these units are "bought and sold independent of the market for meat". It is voluntary to join, but if a farmer participates, an independent agency will assess the level of animal welfare on the farm and award well-being units. The number of well-being units awarded per farm is a function of the number of animals and how well their life is; in short, the farm's total aggregate welfare. Animal friends can then buy well-being units without purchasing animal products, like "climate friends" can pay companies to reduce their carbon emissions through voluntary carbon markets without paying for their products (Lusk, 2011, pp. 572–573).

The animal welfare market has several strengths. It is a decentralized way of dealing with farm animal welfare that does not require a government agency to dictate the appropriate level of animal welfare. It will make animal-friendly products cheaper for consumers and provide farmers with an economic incentive to develop novel and cost-effective ways to improve animal welfare that, in turn, can spread to other farmers (Lusk, 2011, p. 565).

Despite the strengths of the proposal, it faces several objections. One is that the market for farm animals, although an improvement, still produces externalities. The animal welfare market presupposes that the appropriate level of animal welfare is dictated by what animal friends are willing to pay. That the market decides the right level of animal welfare could mean that the way we ought to treat animals is *constituted* by what people are willing to pay. Or it can mean, more plausibly, that people's willingness to pay for animal welfare *reveals* how we ought to treat animals. In this sense, the animal welfare market is a tool to express moral beliefs about the importance of satisfying farm animal interests. The more farm animals matter the more people should be willing to pay.

However, there are several problems with the animal welfare market as a tool for deciding the value of farm animals. One is that people's "willingness to pay" to prevent harm tends to be substantially lower than their "willingness to accept" said harm (OECD, 2006). One reason is that animal friends' level of care for animals is constrained by their purchasing power (Cowen, 2006, p. 40). Another problem is that animal welfare is a public good. Since animal friends care about animal welfare simpliciter, they benefit from other animal friends' investments in animal welfare. They will therefore invest less in animal welfare than they would agree to if they could coordinate their bidding (Cowen, 2006, p. 40).

The fundamental weakness in the animal welfare market, however, is that it is implausible that humans' willingness to pay for animal welfare improvements sufficiently captures the animals' interests. Compare with carbon emissions. It would be absurd to suggest that we could fully capture all externalities from carbon emissions on future generations and people in distant countries through a voluntary carbon market in polluter countries. People's sympathy with others in distant countries and the far future is too limited to reflect the interests of everyone affected, particularly when expressing sympathy comes with a substantial cost to the participants in the market. The lack of compassion applies to animals to an equal, if not greater, extent. Thus, even if the animal welfare market could capture the externalities imposed on people who care about animals, it would not sufficiently capture the harm inflicted on animals.

A market that used "willingness to accept" instead of "willingness to pay" to measure the appropriate animal welfare level could solve some of these problems (Cowen, 2006, p. 41). Instead of giving the property right in animal welfare to farmers, one could allocate the property right to organizations for animal friends. Farmers would thus have to bid for the right to impose harm on animals. This "flipped" animal welfare market would likely result in a significantly higher animal welfare level than Lusk's original proposal. It would remove the purchasing power constraint on animal friends and solve the coordination problem that plagues the animal welfare market. On the other hand, it may suffer from an alternative "hold out problem", where animal organizations would require substantially more animal welfare investments than what is optimal for animal welfare since it may radically depress the number of animals that come into existence (Cowen, 2006, p. 41).

Pigovian taxes

Could Pigovian taxes be a better alternative? Pigovian taxes are costs on activities with negative externalities that reflect the harm to the affected third parties in monetary terms (Baumol, 1972). This approach joins a burgeoning literature in including animals directly in our economic assessments (Budolfson & Spears, 2020; Carlier & Treich, 2020; Espinosa & Treich, 2021; Johansson-Stenman, 2018; Kuruc & McFadden, 2023; Stawasz, 2020). I will examine several versions of such a tax in the following subsections.

Tax on meat and animal products

The most well-known version of a Pigovian tax in the farm animal market is a meat tax, proposed by organizations such as People for the Ethical Treatment of Animals. A meat tax would increase the price of meat relative to substitutes. Since consumers are price-sensitive, a meat tax shifts demand from meat to other products.

Unfortunately, if our concern is animal welfare, a meat tax might worsen matters. If consumers strongly prefer animal protein, a meat tax may shift consumption from beef cattle to dairy products and eggs. Since beef cattle live better lives than dairy cows and egg-laying hens (Norwood & Lusk, 2011, pp. 225–230), a meat tax might therefore increase animal suffering (see also Cowen, 2006, pp. 42–43).

Tax on animal products

We could mitigate this perverse consequence of a meat tax by taxing all animal products instead of just meat. If one could do this without shifting consumption between animal products, it would reduce demand for all animal products. Although this proposal is better than the meat tax, it is still limited and possibly harmful. Notice that an effective tax on animal products is a form of *limited decommodification*. By depressing demand for animal products, one only ensures that fewer animals get to exist. The welfare of the animals that get to live remains unchanged.

A solution to this problem is to use the income from the tax to subsidize animal welfare improvements. This proposal is under serious consideration in Germany (Pistorius, 2021). Although an improvement, it is inadequate. Unless the tax reflects the differences in the animals' living conditions, the tax will not satisfactorily internalize the externalities. It will not shift consumption in the desired way, away from animals treated poorly, towards animals treated well.

Tax on suffering

A more promising approach is a tax that captures the suffering imposed on animals translated into monetary terms. Ideally, one would set the tax to reflect the magnitude of the animal's suffering, how sensitive consumers are to changes in price, and the relative disvalue of the suffering compared to human interests. This requires work by economists on the price elasticity for different animal products, animal welfare scientists on how different rearing practices impact animal welfare (Browning, 2020, 2022; Lusk, 2011; Norwood & Lusk, 2011), and philosophers on the relative value of animal and human interests.

The tax on suffering shares many of the strengths of the animal welfare market. It provides farmers with an incentive to reduce animal suffering since products from animals that are treated worse will become more expensive. Consumers will also have a monetary incentive to shift their consumption to products from animals that are treated better. The tax will also generate income that could be spent on animal welfare investments or transfers to consumers.

A tax on suffering would also avoid many problems with the animal welfare market. Since the tax affects the production of all animal products, farmers cannot choose whether to be exposed to the tax. This is morally apt. If farmers harm animals, they should not be free to opt out of a scheme that seeks to prevent or mitigate this harm. Second, it ensures that consumers and farmers who are complicit in harming animals pay for improving their welfare. This is a fairer way to distribute the burden than the (unflipped) animal welfare market, which requires animal friends to pay. A tax on suffering is thus in line with the belief that the people responsible for a problem should fix it. Finally, since the tax is set to reflect the cost to the animal rather than what animal friends are willing to pay, it could, in principle, be set to capture all the harm to animals.

One might object that consumers owe the animals nothing beyond ensuring that they live lives worth living. According to this *minimal beneficence objection*, only animals that live negative lives suffer from a negative externality. Lusk argues that because "[s]ome farm animals, such as beef cattle, arguably live an overall good life, [this] means that a positive—rather than negative—externality potentially exists for some animal products". This "positive externality" may be "in need of subsidy rather than tax" (Lusk, 2011, p. 563; see also Cowen, 2006, p. 42).

However, this objection sets an implausibly low bar for what counts as a negative externality. We would not be satisfied by a pet owner who justified routinely beating their dog by saying that the dog's life is worth living and that they would not have brought the dog into existence unless they could treat it however they liked (Nozick, 1974, p. 38). And we would find it extortionate if they demanded a subsidy to stop mistreating the dog. Admittedly, the cost of harming the animal is small in this case, but the point is more general. We should not harm animals if the cost of avoiding said harm is reasonable, and a tax on suffering should reflect this verdict.

We may even think that procreators have additional duties to care for the animals they brought into existence (DeGrazia & Sebo, 2015). Parents have special responsibilities to their children, which their role as procreators could explain. That we have procreative duties to animals in our care also explains that we have stronger obligations to avoid harm to farm animals than to wild animals. Given that farm animals are utterly dependent on us and would not exist if it was not for consumer preferences, consumers (and, by extension, farmers) have procreative duties to protect them from harm (Anderson, 2004).

These considerations give rise to another objection to a tax. According to the *sufficiency objection*, the tax allows too much suffering by failing to reflect that we must treat animals sufficiently well to be justified in bringing them into existence (Blackorby et al., 1995; Nussbaum, 2023). This objection could arguably be met by setting the tax so high as to deter treatments of animals below a certain level of welfare. But one might argue that this is better achieved by regulations that prescribe a floor for animal welfare.

Although I share the basic appeal of the sufficiency objection, it is implausible that animal welfare beyond a threshold should count for nothing. We should improve animal welfare whenever we can do so at a reasonable cost. Another problem is that adopting a high threshold for animal welfare may radically depress the number of animals that live lives worth living. Finally, even if we accept the sufficiency objection as an ideal, a tax on suffering might still be the best thing we can do to move towards the ideal. The tax could be gradually adjusted upwards to achieve progressively higher levels of welfare without creating too much resistance from farmers and consumers.

Death tax

Above, I argued that we might be justified in killing farm animals if killing is the price they must pay to exist. But an early death is still worse for the animal than a later death if their life is worth living. And we might think this harm should be accounted for in an optimal tax system. One way to do this is to capture the harm of death with a *death tax* that reflects the badness of life lost. The more valuable the future for the animal, the higher the tax. One way to come closer to setting the correct tax on death is to start with the economic value we put on a human life year in cost-benefit analyses. Then, use an appropriate discount rate for the relative importance of continuing an animal's life compared to human life. Finally, estimate the value of an animal's life year by multiplying the two numbers.

Many issues must be solved for such a tax to work appropriately. The most important thing is to settle on the appropriate discount rate. The discount rate will partly depend on one's view on the relative importance of satisfying human and animal interests. According to the *Equality View*, equal interests count the same, regardless of species membership: It is equally important to avoid a chicken's pain as a human's pain, all else equal (DeGrazia, 1996; Singer, 2009). According to the *Hierarchy View*, we should *discount* animal interests relative to human interests: It is more important to avoid a human's pain than a chicken's pain, even if it is equally painful for both creatures (Kagan, 2019).

Recently, Mark Budolfson and Dean Spears (2020, pp. 607–610) have suggested using the number of neurons as a proxy for "the well-being capacity" of different species and, thus, the importance of satisfying animal and human interests in cost-benefit analyses. According to this measure, it is 390 times as important to satisfy human interests as the similar interests of chickens (Shriver, 2022). Although there are several problems with using neuron count as a proxy for the weight we should put on someone's interests, as Adam Shriver (2022) points out, it might nevertheless be a decent first step when assessing the relative badness of death.

Notice that one does not have to be a proponent of the Hierarchy View to use neuron count or a similar proxy for assessing the importance of preventing death. Since humans have a more temporally extended self and a larger capacity for well-being, proponents of the Equality View could agree that it is more important to prevent the death of a human than an animal. What they will rightly deny, however, is that we should use the same discount rate when assessing the importance of avoiding animal suffering (Rachels, 2004; Singer, 2009). The badness of pain and suffering count the same on the Equality View, and this should inform the tax on suffering.

Conclusion

I have defended several claims in this chapter that I will briefly review here. We are not justified in commodifying animals if their lives are not worth living. We might be justified in commodifying animals if their lives are good. Farm animals suffer because of market failures in the farm animal market. These market failures can be rectified by regulation and commodifying animal welfare. Taxes on suffering and death are good ways of commodifying and thus improving animal welfare. Settling on the correct tax for suffering and killing requires much work in economics, animal welfare science, and philosophy.

Animal suffering and death are merely two types of externalities that should be reflected in the prices of animal products. The effects on the climate, extinction risk of wild animals, displacement of nature, and pandemic risks are all effects that should be internalized and accounted for in the market. But the opposite is also true. A tax on animal suffering and death is important in countering unintended side effects from tackling these other issues, including measures to prevent climate change. If people replace beef with chicken and farmed fish to reduce their carbon footprint, this may come at an immense cost to animal welfare, especially if chickens and farmed fish live net-negative lives, as many experts believe (Browning, 2022, p. 40; Kuruc & McFadden, 2023). Avoiding severely harmful unintended side-effects of efforts to prevent climate change is just one reason for getting the price of animal welfare right.

Acknowledgments

I'm grateful to Kida Lin, Sadie Regmi, Borgar Jølstad, Peder Skjelbred, Ole Røgeberg, Ole Martin Moen, the reviewer, and the two editors, Vida Panitch and Elodie Bertrand, for constructive comments on the chapter at different stages. While working on this chapter, I have received funding from the Norwegian Research Council, grant number 315957.

Notes

1 Two other reasons for eating animals are nutritional needs and sustaining traditions. The first is for the most part a myth. Most people do not need meat or dairy products to fill their nutritional needs (Melina et al., 2016). The role food plays to sustain traditions, may be a more important reason, see (Hasty et al., 2022). But "it is broadly recognized that there are moral limits to deference to tradition" (DeGrazia, 2009, p. 156). See also Elisa Galgut (2019).

2 Admittedly, there are difficult problems specifying what future the animals "would otherwise have" (Solis, 2021).

References

Anderson, E. (2004) "Animal Rights and the Values of Nonhuman Life". In C.R. Sunstein & M.C. Nussbaum, *Animal Rights: Current Debates and New Directions*. Oxford University Press, pp. 277–298.

Bartlett, H., Holmes, M.A., Petrovan, S.O., Williams, D.R., Wood, J.L.N., & Balmford, A. (2022) "Understanding the relative risks of zoonosis emergence under contrasting approaches to meeting livestock product demand". *Royal Society Open Science*, 9(6), 211573. https://doi.org/10.1098/rsos.211573

Baumol, W.J. (1972) "On Taxation and the Control of Externalities". *The American Economic Review*, 62(3), pp. 307–322.

Blackorby, C., Bossert, W., & Donaldson, D. (1995) "Intertemporal Population Ethics: Critical-Level Utilitarian Principles". *Econometrica*, 63(6), pp. 1303–1320. https://doi.org/10.2307/2171771

Bradley, B. (2016) "Is Death Bad for a Cow?" In P. Singer, T. Višak, & R. Garner (Eds.), *The Ethics of Killing Animals*. Oxford University Press, pp. 51–64. https://doi.org/10.1093/acprof:oso/9780199396078.003.0004

Browning, H. (2020) *If I Could Talk to the Animals: Measuring Subjective Animal Welfare* [The Australian National University]. https://doi.org/10.25911/5F1572FB1B5BE

Browning, H. (2022) "Assessing measures of animal welfare". *Biology & Philosophy*, 37(4), 36. https://doi.org/10.1007/s10539-022-09862-1

Budolfson, M., & Spears, D. (2020). "Public Policy, Consequentialism, the Environment, and Nonhuman Animals". In D.W. Portmore (Ed.), *The Oxford Handbook of Consequentialism*. Oxford University Press, pp. 592–615.

Carlier, A., & Treich, N. (2020) "Directly Valuing Animal Welfare in (Environmental) Economics". *International Review of Environmental and Resource Economics*, 14, pp. 113–152. https://doi.org/10.1561/101.00000115

Cowen, T. (2006) "Market failure for the treatment of animals". *Society*, 43(2), pp. 39–44. https://doi.org/10.1007/BF02687369

DeGrazia, D. (1996) *Taking Animals Seriously: Mental Life and Moral Status*. Cambridge University Press.

DeGrazia, D. (2009) "Moral Vegetarianism from a Very Broad Basis". *Journal of Moral Philosophy*, 6(2), pp. 143–165. https://doi.org/10.1163/174552409X402313

DeGrazia, D., & Sebo, J. (2015) "Necessary Conditions for Morally Responsible Animal Research". *Cambridge Quarterly of Healthcare Ethics*, 24(4), pp. 420–430. https://doi.org/10.1017/S0963180115000080

Errickson, F., Kuruc, K., & McFadden, J. (2021) "Animal-based foods have high social and climate costs". *Nature Food*, 2(4), pp. 274–281. https://doi.org/10.1038/s43016-021-00265-1

Espinosa, R., & Treich, N. (2021) "Animal welfare: Antispeciesism, veganism and a 'life worth living.'" *Social Choice and Welfare*, 56(3), pp. 531–548. https://doi.org/10.1007/s00355-020-01287-7

Fishcount. (2019) *Numbers of fish caught from the wild each year*. Fischcount.Org.Uk. http://fishcount.org.uk/fish-count-estimates-2/numbers-of-fish-caught-from-the-wild-each-year

Francione, G.L. (1995) *Animals, Property, and the Law*. Temple University Press.

Galgut, E. (2019) "A Critique of the Cultural Defense of Animal Cruelty". *Journal of Animal Ethics*, 9(2), pp. 184–198. https://doi.org/10.5406/janimalethics.9.2.0184

Gauthier, D. (1984) "Deterrence, Maximization, and Rationality". *Ethics*, 94(3), pp. 474–495. https://doi.org/10.1086/292561

Harman, E. (2011) "The Moral Significance of Animal Pain and Animal Death". In T.L. Beauchamp & R.G. Frey, *The Oxford Handbook of Animal Ethics*. Oxford University Press, pp. 726–737.

Hasty, J., Lewis, D.G., & Snipes, M.M. (2022) "Food and Cultural Identity". In *Introduction to Anthropology*. OpenStax. https://openstax.org/books/introduction-anthropology/pages/14-3-food-and-cultural-identity

Hoffman, J.M., & Valencak, T.G. (2020) "A short life on the farm: Aging and longevity in agricultural, large-bodied mammals". *GeroScience*, 42(3), pp. 909–922. https://doi.org/10.1007/s11357-020-00190-4

Johansson-Stenman, O. (2018) "Animal Welfare and Social Decisions: Is It Time to Take Bentham Seriously?" *Ecological Economics*, 145, pp. 90–103. https://doi.org/10.1016/j.ecolecon.2017.08.019

Kagan, S. (2019) *How to Count Animals, More or Less*. Oxford University Press.

Korsgaard, C.M. (2018) *Fellow Creatures: Our Obligations to the Other Animals*. Oxford University Press.

Kuruc, K., & McFadden, J. (2023) "Monetizing the externalities of animal agriculture: Insights from an inclusive welfare function". *Social Choice and Welfare*. https://doi.org/10.1007/s00355-023-01451-9

Lusk, J.L. (2011) "The market for animal welfare". *Agriculture and Human Values*, 28(4), pp. 561–575. https://doi.org/10.1007/s10460-011-9318-x

McMahan, J. (2008) "Eating animals the nice way". *Daedalus*, 137(1), pp. 66–76. https://doi.org/10.1162/daed.2008.137.1.66

McMahan, J. (2009) "Asymmetries in the Morality of Causing People to Exist". In M.A. Roberts & D.T. Wasserman (Eds.), *Harming Future Persons: Ethics, Genetics and the Nonidentity Problem*. Springer Netherlands, pp. 49–68. https://doi.org/10.1007/978-1-4020-5697-0_3

Melina, V., Craig, W., & Levin, S. (2016) "Position of the Academy of Nutrition and Dietetics: Vegetarian Diets". *Journal of the Academy of Nutrition and Dietetics*, 116(12), pp. 1970–1980. https://doi.org/10.1016/j.jand.2016.09.025

Norwood, F.B., & Lusk, J.L. (2011) *Compassion, by the Pound: The Economics of Farm Animal Welfare*. Oxford University Press.

Nozick, R. (1974) *Anarchy, State, and Utopia*. Basic Books.

Nussbaum, M.C. (2023) *Justice for Animals: Our Collective Responsibility*. Simon & Schuster.

OECD. (2006) "Willingness to Pay vs. Willingness to Accept". In *Cost-Benefit Analysis and the Environment Recent Developments*. OECD Publishing, pp. 155–167. https://read.oecd-ilibrary.org/environment/cost-benefit-analysis-and-the-environment/willingness-to-pay-vs-willingness-to-accept_9789264010055-12-en

Pendrill, F., Persson, U.M., Godar, J., & Kastner, T. (2019) "Deforestation displaced: Trade in forest-risk commodities and the prospects for a global forest transition". *Environmental Research Letters*, 14(5), 055003. https://doi.org/10.1088/1748-9326/ab0d41

Pistorius, M. (2021) *Germany eyes new animal welfare levy to help raise standards in livestock farming*. Euractiv. www.euractiv.com/section/agriculture-food/news/germany-eyes-new-animal-welfare-levy-to-help-raise-standards-in-livestock-farming/

Quinn, W. (1985) "The right to threaten and the right to punish". *Philosophy and Public Affairs*, 14(4), pp. 327–373.

Rachels, J. (2004) "Drawing Lines". In C.R. Sunstein & M.C. Nussbaum (Eds.), *Animal Rights: Current Debates and New Directions*. Oxford University Press, pp. 162–174. https://doi.org/10.1093/acprof:oso/9780195305104.003.0008

Regan, T. (1983) *The Case for Animal Rights*. University of California Press.

Ritchie, H. (2019) *Half of the world's habitable land is used for agriculture*. Our World in Data. https://ourworldindata.org/global-land-for-agriculture

Ritchie, H., & Roser, M. (2017) Meat and Dairy Production. *Our World in Data*. https://ourworldindata.org/meat-production

Salt, H.S. (1914) *The Humanities of Diet*. The Vegetarian Society. www.animal-rights-library.com/texts-c/salt03.htm

Shriver, A. (2022) Why Neuron Counts Shouldn't Be Used as Proxies for Moral Weight. *Effective Altruism Forum*. https://forum.effectivealtruism.org/posts/Mfq7KxQRvkeLnJvoB/why-neuron-counts-shouldn-t-be-used-as-proxies-for-moral

Singer, P. (2009) *Animal Liberation: The Definitive Classic of the Animal Movement* (Updated edition, original 1975). Harper Perennial.

Singer, P. (2011). *Practical Ethics* (Third edition). Cambridge University Press.

Solis, C. (2021) "How Much Does Slaughter Harm Humanely Raised Animals?" *Journal of Applied Philosophy*, 38(2), pp. 258–272. https://doi.org/10.1111/japp.12483

Stawasz, A. (2020) *Why and How to Value Nonhuman Animals in Cost-Benefit Analyses*. SSRN. http://dx.doi.org/10.2139/ssrn.3643473

Stephen, L. (1896) *Social Rights and Duties: Addresses to Ethical Societies* (Issue v. 2). S. Sonnenschein & Company, limited.

Wise, S.M. (2000) *Rattling The Cage: Toward Legal Rights For Animals*. Hachette Books.

28

SEED

Commodification, decommodification and commoning

Fabien Girard, Christine Frison, and Christine Noiville

Introduction

We could start with a paradox: a growing body of literature that draws on the ontological turn in anthropology emphasizes the *agency* of non-humans, including seeds (Congretel and Pinton, 2020). And yet, more than ever, one might say, seeds are hardly perceived as anything other than a resource base, a production tool or an input for food and agriculture production. Hence, this resource base is no longer "self-controlled" (van der Ploeg, 2010, p. 4) nor supplied from circuits of reproduction that are "located *outside* of the agricultural markets" (van der Ploeg, 2010, p. 9). On the contrary, it depends almost entirely on the *market*.

What does that mean precisely? That the market has completely occupied all spaces where seeds are exchanged. As for farming, this means that over time small farmers and peasants have been integrated into "fully working markets" for the provisioning of seeds (van der Ploeg, 2010, pp. 9–10).

This change has implied a transfiguration of seeds. Seeds do not pre-exist the market, in the sense that, by their nature, they "[…] are not created in a profit-oriented production process subject to the competitive pressures of market forces" (Peukert, 2019, p. 1175). In other words, they are not actively and originally "produced for sale on the market" (Polanyi, 2001[1944], p. 75).

The transfiguration process has constructed seeds institutionally as a commodity by means of complex technical and legal devices, notably intellectual property rights (IPRs) (Tordjman, 2008, p. 1341). This is what Polanyi was referring to when he said of the land (i.e., the "natural environment"), labour and money that they are "fictitious" or "false" commodities (as opposed to "genuine commodities"), built at the price of erasing the ties of reciprocity and redistribution between humans, on the one hand, and between humans and non-humans, on the other (Polanyi, 2001[1944], p. 76). The ties between landraces, peasant seeds, peasants, land and *terroirs*, were unravelled precisely at the end of the twentieth century just as Mendel's laws were being rediscovered and Soviet and European genetic science was becoming triumphant: nature became a "universal store of genes" (Bonneuil, 2019). This then led to the "disqualification of farmers' landraces as *obsolete* and *unproductive*" (Bonneuil, 2019, p. 3 – emphasis in the original). These were concurrently re-labelled as "gene stores" (ibid.).

 DOI: 10.4324/9781003188742-34

The historical context is important: it allows us to grasp that by "seed" we should understand not only all "plant propagating materials"[1] and resulting plants, i.e., "farmers' varieties" – also called "landraces" or "folk varieties" (Jarvis et al. 2016, p. 1)[2] – or, on the professional plant breeders' side, elite or modern varieties or cultivars; but also "plant genetic resources for food and agriculture", "genetic material", "germplasm" or "genetic resources". Indeed, if we want to take account of seed market(s) in all its/their complexity, i.e. including the entire value chain, it is necessary to pay attention to the way genetic resources are today constructed as commodities that circulate on the international germplasm market, in addition to being "technical objects", i.e. material entities that have been given stable and reliable properties through their entrenchment "in a wider field of epistemic practices and material cultures, including instruments, inscription devices, model organisms" and so on (Rheinberger, 1997, p. 29).

The size of the seed market gives an idea of the scale of the phenomenon at play: USD 52 billion in 2014 for the global commercial seed market (which includes public commercial varieties) (OECD, 2018, p. 25), and a cross-border seed trade worth USD 10 billion according to the statistics of the International Seed Federation (OECD, 2018, p. 30). At the same time, if we distinguish between peasant farming and the "opposite forms, entrepreneurial and capitalist farming" (van der Ploeg, 2010, n. 1, p. 1), a non-negligible part of those participating in the agricultural production process have not been *completely* integrated into the seed market. This applies to the Global South, but it is also valid for many industrialized countries where a phenomenon of repeasantization (i.e. the emergence of a new peasantry) has been seen (van der Ploeg, 2018). In concrete terms, a substantial portion of peasants are still sourcing seeds through farmer seed networks. These networks "transfer seed [...] from domesticated or undomesticated plants via farmer-to-farmer gifting, swapping, bartering, or purchase, and also via trading or sale which occurs outside of the commercial seed sector and formal regulation" (Coomes et al., 2015, p. 42).

These are a reminder that seed exchanges have long been organized through other forms of economic integration, in particular institutional reciprocal gift or market relations but tightly enmeshed in non-economic institutions (e.g., community-based, religious, professional) (Polanyi, 2001[1944]). Although non-negligible in the Global North, the place held by these farmer seed networks is still considerable in the Global South where estimates suggest that 80–90% of seeds are sourced through them (Coomes et al., 2015, p. 43). But these networks now only represent, as it were, pockets of resistance or beleaguered citadels: modern agriculture, with its specialization of tasks (the breeder breeds "elite" varieties and the farmer plants and harvests them) and the increasing use of artificial growth factors and technology for precision agriculture, is inseparable from market relations as the only mode of economic exchanges, and their progression seems inexorable.

For their proponents, these changes in the nature of agricultural production and economic integration are the only possible way forward. They believe that only through the coupling of modern agriculture and market tools we will be able to meet the needs of increased yield and nutritional value of crops and ensure the sustainability of agricultural systems in times of climate change.

Depending on whether these promises appear likely to be fulfilled or not, another paradox arises: more and more, the peasantry of the southern hemisphere is perceived as a credible model of more resilient agriculture. Local and sustainable peasants' practices are thought to cope better with climate change and the management of crop genetic diversity, whose paramount importance in terms of plant breeding, food security, nutrition and quite simply our (viable) life on earth (IPBES, 2019, p. 42) is no longer challenged. In a few decades, these systems have become the standard bearers of "transnational agrarian movements" (Claeys and Peschard, 2020), places of struggle and "laboratories" reflecting on decommodification. The right to seeds (Haugen, 2020; Le Teno et al., 2022), as now enshrined in the United Nations Declaration on the Rights of Peasants and Other People Working in Rural Areas (UNDROP), and the concept of "seed sovereignty" (Kloppenburg, 2010; O'Grady Walshe, 2020), reflect this reverse dynamic that reminds us that seeds are "the irreducible core of agricultural production" (Kloppenburg, 2014, p. 1225). More than just a commonplace commodity, seeds involve complex ties to territory, cultural heritage, identity and the autonomy of populations (Howard, 2010; Toledo, 1990) – ties that are essential, even though they have been rendered totally invisible, if not destroyed, by market society.

The rest of this chapter attempts to re-contextualize what is today a polarity between commodification and decommodification of seeds. It should be repeated at this point that this polarity is primarily the result of reactions or resistances to the penetration of market pressure, what the anthropologist Stephen Gudeman calls "debasement", i.e. the loss of all that, immaterial (ethnicity, religion) and material (communal land), which ensures group reproduction (Gudeman, 2016, pp. 17–22). It is then a question of creating distance from market relations. At the same time, this polarity has a heuristic value: it signals everything that the market is incapable of apprehending or everything that it destroys when certain resources, labour and social relations are joined with capital. Finally, the polarity raises the issue of coexistence between market society and peasant farming and farmers seed networks, sometimes judged impossible (because, as the argument goes, the market ends up destroying the commons) (Jodha, 1985), sometimes judged possible (Sengupta, 1995) and even desirable, as when, for example, plant breeders use commons-based innovations in order to retain control over their innovations and their model of agriculture production without giving up commodification.

The chapter begins with an account of how the seed market came into being and its main drivers: the biotechnological revolution, intellectual property and the consolidation of the seed industry. In a second section, the chapter shows how the debate has been largely focused on market failures – and not on restricting market transactions – as a way to keep up certain public goods, primarily innovation and crop diversity. The third section explores proposals to radically decommodify seeds, a more recent move that speaks more directly to research in ethics and economics on noxious markets.

Drivers of seed commodification

How have seeds, as the nexus of agricultural production activity and part of complex "biocultural" networks (Girard et al., 2022) left behind a "moral" economic model (Rogan, 2019) and become integrated into a market society in which they are no more than a commodity, defined only by their price?

What an abundant literature (see, e.g., Rangnekar, 1996; Bonneuil and Thomas, 2009) now demonstrates is that the commodification of seed has relied mainly on the use of industrial property. This sweeping intellectual property-driven commodification of seed has raised particular difficulties linked to the structure of the global market, which is highly concentrated.

The biotech revolution and patentability

The conceptualization of seed as a commodity has been constructed by a set of technical, political and legal mechanisms. The classification of seed as a "genetic resource" was the first step, cutting the age-old ties with the land and the peasantry. Additionally, the coupling between technical standards and regulation of the production, commercialization and use of seeds and varieties has been decisive. Whether the Soviet Union, the German National Socialist regime or later a large part of Europe, all States have supported and imposed agricultural modernization and productivism, thanks to a new division of labour, the specialization of activities and control over what peasants could plant (Pistorius and Wijk, 1999, p. 62; Bonneuil, 2019, p. 5). The catalogue of cultivated plants played a key role in the standardization necessary to this new division of labour by imposing the model of the distinct, uniform and stable (DUS) variety – a "fixed" variety cultivated in highly controlled environments (by mechanization, irrigation and the use of inputs). As an extra step indispensable to commodification, privatization was made possible in Europe by the International Convention for the Protection of New Varieties of Plants of 2 December 1961 (UPOV Convention, revised in 1972, 1978 and 1991). This Convention endorses the DUS criteria (Rangnekar, 2000; Llewelyn and Adcock, 2006) and guarantees a monopoly of exploitation to plant breeders that develop high-yielding elite varieties.

The United States, meanwhile, had already adopted the Plant Patent Act in 1930 for asexually reproducing varieties (fruits, nut trees and ornamental plants), but it had not been much used by the horticultural industry. A different path to intellectual property was initially chosen: hybrid varieties, which offer a technology lock-in and dispense with the need to rely on the law. Indeed, the progenies of the first generation (F1 hybrids) benefit from the heterosis effect and show excellent performance. However, genetic heterogeneity is created from the second generation onwards, and the associated loss of yield obliges farmers to buy seeds every season (Pistorius and Wijk, 1999, pp. 66–67). The fact remains that hybrids are no silver bullet: they can only be produced for a limited number of field crops – and breeders have therefore sought legal solutions, which they obtained with the passing of the Plant Variety Protection Act 1970 (PVPA–USC 2402 §7), to offer a form of protection similar to the plant breeders' rights (PBRs below) under UPOV (Llewelyn and Adcock, 2006, p. 81).[3]

Since the 1980s, the commodification of seeds has been underpinned by the considerable and rapid movement towards IP expansion in plant breeding. It followed the *Diamond v. Chakrabarty* ruling (447 U.S. 303 (1980)) by which the United States Supreme Court acknowledged the patentability of a bacterium, thereby expanding the utility patent (Calvert and Joly, 2011) to include living material. Unsurprisingly, the patentability of a variety of maize was recognized five years later by the United States Patent and Trademark Office (USPTO) (*Ex parte Hibberd* (227, USPQ 443 (1985)) (Llewelyn and Adcock, 2006, p. 86).

In Europe, whether under the European Patent Convention (EPC 1973, last revised in 2000) or Directive 98/44/EC of 6 July 1998 on the legal protection of biotechnological inventions, plant varieties are covered exclusively by PBRs and are not patentable (in the United States, conversely, a variety can be covered by both a PBR and a utility patent). On the other hand, driven by Article 27.1 of the Agreement on Trade-Related Aspects of Intellectual Property Rights (TRIPS, 1995), which opens the patent up to any invention in any field of technology, the scope of the patent has quickly expanded to take in plant innovation. In addition to DNA sequences or partial sequences, as well as processes for the production of plants, transgenic plants whose genome expresses a transgene liable to be integrated into an indefinite number of varieties can also be patented, as can "native genes", i.e. traits identified in nature (e.g. taste, salt tolerance, resistance), and then introduced into a target variety by means of essentially biological processes for obtaining plants, accelerated by modern methods (such as marker-assisted selection) (Godt, 2018). These patents, validated by the European Patent Office (EPO) (Girard, 2015), were considered so obstructive ("blocking" patents) that they led to an outcry in civil society, followed by a reaction at the

European Parliament and the Commission, which finally led the Administrative Council of the EPO,[4] and the Enlarged Board of Appeals itself,[5] to exclude the patentability of plants exclusively obtained by means of an essentially biological process.

PBRs, still widely used by medium-sized plant breeders, have been reinforced in response to the extension of the patent (Sanderson, 2017, p. 205).

Consolidation in the global seed industry

Today, IP is mainly used as a strategic tool. For example, a portfolio of patents may serve as a "bargaining chip" to acquire strategic technologies (Kock, 2021, p. 3), whereby company A negotiates at length with company B for the use of the patented gene C that the latter owns, in exchange for the use of technology D on which the former has a patent. This creates particular difficulties on the seed market, where operators are of different sizes, with profits consolidated around a few operators who are the only ones able to settle on the conditions of exploitation of their respective patents through cross-licensing agreements (Schenkelaars et al., 2011, p. 79), thereby creating real barriers to entering the market (Howard, 2015).

Indeed, the main problem remains the exceptional level of concentration in the seed industry, which is dominated by a handful of multinationals from the petrochemical sector (e.g. Bayer or Corteva) (Howard, 2009). Considering only the agrochemical sector, the figures speak for themselves. Following the recent raft of mergers involving ChemChina-Syngenta, Dow-DuPont (now Corteva) and Monsanto-Bayer (now Bayer) CropScience (Bonny, 2017), these three firms now control 70% of the sales in this sector (Hendrickson et al., 2017, p. 18).

Because of the world-wide oligopoly that has been dominating the seed market for quite some time, but perhaps also because of the market-centred approach towards agricultural production and seed provisioning that has been little questioned so far, discussions on production of and access to public goods have been able to emerge, but they have mainly remained focused on market failures and on how to overcome these failures.

Public and private responses to market failures

Whilst technological and biotechnological developments continue unabated in plant breeding, and with them the extension of the patent system (Metzger and Zech, 2020), intellectual property (especially in Africa: De Jonge and Munyi, 2016) and the rules on plant variety registration and seed certification keep expanding geographically (Herpers et al., 2017). This expansion is now spreading to countries where farmer seed systems remain the primary source of seeds (McGuire and Sperling, 2016), compromising further the provision of public goods (defined by their nonexcludability and nonrivalry: see, Hippel and Krogh, 2003) such as crop genetic diversity. There also remains the overall problem of the shift from agricultural research as a public good to the private investment model of innovation relying on the granting of temporary monopoly privileges. The growing number of, and overlaps between, intellectual property rights has tended to stifle research, and intellectual property-driven innovation has mainly resulted in orienting "research and development towards meeting the needs of farmers in rich countries, while the needs of poor farmers in developing countries have been comparatively neglected" (De Schutter, 2009, para. 34, pointing to the problem of "orphan crops"). Calls to remake innovation a public good via a different model of innovation (in which the state would play a central role) are increasing.

At minimum, dissatisfaction with the way the seed market operates is widely shared and, even if the arguments put forward vary from one actor to another, they all point to market failures.

Curiously enough, until recently there have been very few policy or private initiatives (contractual solutions) that have questioned the use and/or reach of the market in the field of seeds. One might expect such challenges given the harmful outcomes marketization can have on biodiversity or food security, and given the extreme vulnerability that may befall one of the parties to the negotiation (think of the contracts for access to genetic resources and traditional knowledge held by indigenous peoples: Bavikatte et al., 2015).

In the following section we present two examples, one relating to biodiversity, the other to innovation, which highlight the interventions of state actors on the one hand, and the private sector on the other.

Responding to crop genetic erosion

There is a consensus that the "widespread losses of landrace diversity over the past century, continuing to the present" is due to their replacement by elite varieties (Khoury et al., 2022, p. 9). Indeed, the "extension and expansion of formal seed systems" (ibid.) has enabled this substantial replacement, itself backed by intellectual property law and seed regulations which have been deployed in the Global South, and now goes as far as prohibiting and even criminalizing the exchange of non-certified seeds between peasants (Wattnem, 2016).

As early as the 1960s, the risks linked to the rapid dissemination of high-yield varieties (the "modernization bottleneck" – Louwaars, 2018, p. 2) were perceived by breeders and geneticists, who eventually managed to convince the international community to develop an international *ex situ* conservation network of crop genetic resources (Kloppenburg, 2005). Very favourable to the gene-poor North, the regime encountered resistance in the 1980s from the Global South, where countries were looking to take back control over their resources. After a failed attempt to adopt an international framework which would have placed all crop genetic resources (including those protected by intellectual property rights) under the "common heritage of mankind" regime (Mgbeoji, 2003), the principle of each State's sovereign right to exploit its resources was re-asserted in the Convention on Biological Diversity adopted in Rio de Janeiro in 1992.

This "appropriation" of resources by States was intended to counterbalance intellectual property rights on products developed using those resources. In reality, the "enclosure" validated by the Convention on Biological Diversity (Sievers-Glotzbach and Christinck, 2021) introduces a market based on "Access and Benefit-Sharing" – i.e. the conservation of genetic resources was now to depend on their use (Pistorius, 1997, p. 95).[6] Within this framework, the Global North retains access to resources in the intertropical zone, and countries of the South can expect incomes generated by intellectual property rights on "biodiscoveries" or "technology-for-nature swaps"[7] (Sedjo, 1992) to better protect nature while hoping to get a foothold on the path to "modernization".

At the same time, the international community recognized the high degree of crop interdependency between States and pleaded for a regime exempting crop genetic resources from the complex mechanism set up by the Convention on Biological Diversity (Khoury et al., 2015). Thus, the Multilateral System of the International Treaty on Plant Genetic Resources for Food and Agriculture (Seed Treaty 2001) established a virtual gene pool of plant genetic resources for food and agriculture to which the contracting parties have facilitated access via a Standard Material Transfer Agreement, i.e. a standardized contract between a supplier and a user of material (Frison, 2018, p. 167). Initially inspired by Global Public Goods theory (Kaul et al., 1999),[8] the Multilateral System is today described as a global seed commons (Frison, 2018). Furthermore, recognizing decades of research on on-farm conservation, the Seed treaty re-asserts the need to "[p]romote or support, as appropriate, farmers and local communities' efforts to manage and conserve on-farm their [plant genetic resources for food and agriculture]" (Art. 5.1(c)). The aim of the Benefit-Sharing Fund, in part funded by the benefits arising from commercialization of innovations protected by intellectual property rights which incorporate material from the Multilateral System, is to support these on-farm conservation activities in parallel to "farmers' rights" (Art. 9). The implementation of the Benefit-Sharing Fund has, however, been disappointing: the funds are very limited and not sufficient to widely sustain projects "designed to support farmers and breeders in adapting crops to changing needs and demands in the face of climate change" (Tsioumani, 2020, p. 18). As for farmers' rights (in particular Article 9, para. 3, which refers to farmers' rights to save, use, exchange and sell farm-saved seed/propagating material), their implementation depends entirely on national laws. Although it reports some progress, the first inventory of measures taken at national level (IT/GB-9/AHTEG-FR-3/20/2 (June 2020)) reveals some problematic biases: perpetuation of the commercial logic through intellectual property rights (Peschard, 2017); attempts to set up institutional steering of on-farm conservation through institutional incentives (Girard and Frison, 2021); and continuation of projects to "modernise" peasant communities, in particular through market-based incentives (see Jarvis et al., 2011).

In the final analysis, apart perhaps from the "commons" approach underpinning the Seed treaty, the trajectory of seed remains largely defined by the disembedded market, disregarding the biocultural embeddedness of seeds. For most people involved in mainstream commercial agriculture, it is inconceivable to extract seeds from the market, as non-tradable goods, as if pricing a variety was a *sine qua non* for any successful conservation strategy.

Circumventing intellectual property enclosure

For over twenty years, the role of intellectual property in plant innovation has been subject to close attention due to its incremental nature (Luby et al. 2015, p. 2481). Plant breeding is, indeed "a canonical example of sequential innovation, where continued progress may depend on the maintenance of a robust public domain (as some would put it) or at least on a set of carefully articulated and secure carve-outs from intellectual property protection" (Janis et al., 2014, para. 1.03). At the same time, these "carve-outs" have been challenged by the incursion and extension of the patent system. For example, patent law does not allow for "breeder's exemption" – and yet that is what enables breeders to use a protected variety, without the consent of the initial breeder, as a source of initial variation to obtain a new variety and to market it.

Today there is growing scientific consensus that patents stifle innovation (Halpert and Chappell, 2017, p. 4). Importantly, the development of "patent thickets" (the overlapping of intellectual property rights) (Heller and Eisenberg, 1998) has been described as the cause of a slowdown in innovation in certain crop sectors (Graff et al., 2004). And yet, to date, the public authorities have done little or nothing, except to include extended research exceptions in the unitary patent[9] and some domestic legislation (Prifti, 2015), but these measures are in no way to be equated with the breeder's exemption.

On this point, private actors have been left to fend for themselves[10] in a context where, with the development of genome editing techniques and the prospect of increasing trait stacking (the combination of different traits into a single plant to provide a response for a multitude of functions) the risk of new and formidable "patent thickets" looms large (Kock, 2021). This is a major issue, including for major players, as all breeders now run the risk of having to negotiate increasingly complex licensing agreements (Egelie et al., 2016; Gray and Spruill, 2017) and being sued for patent infringement (Kock, 2021, p. 6).

Various proposals have been suggested and even implemented to re-establish the "freedom to operate", such as "patent pools" or "patent clearing houses" (Girard and Frison, 2018; Kock and ten Have, 2016). Without challenging the genuine intent behind these proposals, they are stopgap measures at best because they do not proceed from the right question: given the negative outcomes the market may have on biodiversity, food security or the ability to innovate (whatever the meaning of this term) or given the extreme vulnerability that may beset one of transacting parties, should one not prioritize the elimination of the market or make the working out of its proper range a priority? Might not a first workable solution be to carry out a far-reaching overhaul of the IP system (Metzger and Zech, 2020), or even to abandon the patent altogether (Kock, 2021)? It is precisely this kind of questioning, echoing the work of commodification scholars, that forms the background to the following reflections on decommodification.

Decommodification

Decommodifiying through commoning

The foregoing shows that there is a systemic problem in the way the disembedded market reduces seeds to raw materials for breeding, as a standardized input. In relation to literature on commodification and ethics, the argument connects with some moral objections raised against so-called "noxious markets". Misallocations and rights violations (e.g., the right to food) are certainly at stake. But criticism of the commodification of seed also echoes what have been called "semiotic objections" to markets: "to engage in a market in some good or service X is a form of symbolic expression that communicates the wrong motive, or the wrong attitude toward X, or expresses an attitude that is incompatible with the intrinsic dignity of X, or would show disrespect or irreverence for some practice, custom, belief, or relationship with which X is associated" (Brennan and Jaworski, 2015, p. 1055).

Ongoing counter-movements proposing conceptual and political-legal innovations that seek to re-embed the seed market system into cultural and social fabrics illustrates this wide range of ethical objections to market and their meaning for seeds. Importantly, agrarian movements (Claeys and Peschard, 2020) aspire to bring about change in agricultural production: the objective is decommodification, understood to include all of the innovations aiming to free the "resource base" of agriculture from its virtually complete dependency on the market. This liberation emphasizes the noneconomic motives for exchanging seeds and their crucial role in the subsistence of populations, group reproduction and the protection of agroecosystems. By re-establishing agriculture as "co-production" (van der Ploeg, 2010, p. 13), it renders possible the expression of the multiple socio-cultural values that are attributed to seeds by social groups (Congretel and Pinton, 2020).

We will not go into the strategies of resistance seeking to block the deeper penetration of the market by means of mass protests and through political negotiations with the State, generally conducted within pre-established legal categories or through lawsuits (Claeys and Peschard, 2020). We will focus instead on practices based on "subaltern cosmopolitan legality", i.e. the local and *bottom-up* creation of law through resistance to cultural homogenization (Santos and Rodríguez-Garavito, 2005); a law that relies on "ingenious 'legal hacks' or anomalous innovations to transcend the epistemological premises of [Western] law" (Weston and Bollier, 2014, pp. 174–175).

A few examples include: the *Réseau semences paysannes* (RSP) in France (Demeulenaere and Piersante 2020), the *Red de Semillas Libres* in Colombia (Gutiérrez Escobar and Fitting, 2016), the *Red de Semillas: Resembrando e Intercambiando* in Spain (Reyes-García et al., 2018), or the open source seed movement. All these movements claim to be based on the "commons", less in line with Ostrom's theory and more with the "generative" (as opposed to extractive) approach to the commons, i.e. the search for a third way between a flawed self-regulating market and a State that has abandoned its protective functions with respect to the market (Capra and Mattei, 2015, pp. 184–186) (on commons, see also Chapters 6 and 29 in this volume). This third way pushes against the dominant legal-political system and believes in the generative *praxis* of "commoning", i.e. the practical science of "acting in common" or "common activity" (Dardot and Laval, 2019, p. 190) in order to create new forms of political, social, and economic organization. The idea is that of an "everyday politics" which takes place on the farm and in the fields, a "direct intervention in, and alteration of, labour and production processes" (van der Ploeg, 2010, p. 16), rather than open struggle or covert resistance.

The open-source seed movement aligns with this approach. Launched in 1999 by an American breeder, Thomas Michaels, the idea of a General Public License for Plant Germplasm (GPLPG) received double recognition: first through the "pledge" of the Open Source Seed Initiative (OSSI); then with the "OpenSourceSeeds" licence of the German association Agrecol (Kotschi and Horneburg, 2018). The complex trajectory of the OSSI, founded by Jack Kloppenburg, is interesting. Greatly inspired by the pioneers in open source software, Kloppenburg initially tried to get IP to make the same paradigm shift in plant breeding as had been achieved some decades earlier for software: to turn the logic of the copyright licence on itself, by using IP so as to place creation at the service of as many users as possible (Kloppenburg, 2014; Montenegro de Wit, 2019). However, technical difficulties (how to fit a complex license onto a packet of seeds?) and in particular a dispute concerning the meaning of the term "license" itself (is it about re-establishing free movement of the germplasm – "free seed license" – or about generating income by opening up new markets – "royalty-bearing license"?) led to the license and copyleft model being abandoned in favour of a pledge. This short pledge states a clear wish to recreate social norms in seed exchanges (Montenegro de Wit, 2019).[11]

Although the pledge is not enforceable (it is not a copyleft license – Luby et al., 2015, p. 2486), OSSI is nevertheless attempting to strengthen its social effectiveness by exerting control over the "moral" quality of the community members, i.e. their adherence to a certain vision of plant breeding. Indeed, seeds covered by the pledge must be *committed* to the "protected commons" (Kloppenburg, 2010), i.e. they must be "pledged" by a professional or freelance breeder, who thus becomes a member of the community (Montenegro de Wit, 2019) and undertakes to respect the exchange standards. OSSI retains the right of refusal and has for example already refused the offer to pledge a new genetically engineered variety (Ibid., p. 16).

Each member nonetheless retains the freedom to distribute their seeds at the price they have fixed, as long as she does not breach the open-source principle attached to the pledge. A breeder may even enter into a contract with a multiplier to multiply so-called "open source" seeds, and the two parties can share the income generated by the sale of these seeds. Likewise, breeders and farmers can draw up a "benefit-sharing" agreement with a seller (Montenegro de Wit, 2019).

Longing for sovereignty

The aim of the open-source seed movement is indisputably to decommodify, to counter the proprietary logic of modern agriculture and maintain the widest possible access to the pool of genetic resources available to breeders and farmers, by recreating a legal space for creative freedom and new rules for seed exchanges. This "freeing" of seeds (Demeulenaere, 2014, p. 55) is, however, only one approach among others. For example, it is rejected by the *Réseau semences paysannes* in

France, which considers "peasant seeds" to be inseparable from the project to "recreate communities of practices [of] sharing seeds, knowledge, know-how and new types of solidarity (between humans and plants)" (Demeulenaere and Piersante, 2020, p. 786). This is a "commons", closed by nature (Schlager and Ostrom 1992), that "has its own social norms and institutions" and is often "distinctively local", "tied to the land inhabited by a people, and shaped by their cosmological beliefs, spiritual beliefs and other fundamental aspects of their identity" (Hardison, 2009, p. 41). Hence, several strategies of decommodification via commoning can coexist, which contrasts with the application of a single, one-size-fits-all solution everywhere as the market tends to do.

Conclusion

This last point brings us back to the introductory question on the polarity between commodification and decommodification and on the place left to the "market" in the commons model. First of all, one thing is certain: none of the examples above show a total cutting off of commercial exchanges. The fruit and vegetables produced by the RSP's peasant seeds are on market stalls or even on supermarket shelves. Some RSP members plan to sell their seeds relying on the new "organic heterogeneous material" category as provided for in Regulation (EU) 2018/848, as the *Rete Semi Rurali* already does in Italy (Demeulenaere and Piersante, 2020, p. 777). Some OSSI pledged seeds are subject to licensing agreements with producers/distributors, which generate royalties and are sold by distributors.

While commercial exchanges contribute to reducing the resource to its market value by reintroducing the profit motive (Montenegro de Wit, 2019), market society should not be confused with marketplaces – in particular all these new markets (e.g., farmers'/peasants' marketplaces) construed as alternative responses to the global market and which remain embedded in noneconomic institutions (van der Ploeg, 2010, p. 18). If, in addition, the peasant model that these movements claim to be part of defines itself by a "partial integration into markets" (Friedmann, 1980, p. 166), that means there is plenty of space for "mechanisms that farmers can use to govern, adapt, and change the balance of commodity and non-commodity relation" (van der Ploeg, 2010, p. 111). These innovations based on commoning extend the repertoire of mechanisms which, through cooperation and reciprocity, allow control of material and social resources (traditional agroecological knowledge, breeding and seeds) to be taken back.

Nonetheless, these innovations remain fragile. They will only resist the pressure from globalized agrarian markets with a more favourable international legal framework. On this front, some positive signs can be discerned. First, the Nagoya Protocol (2010) has enshrined community protocols to protect Indigenous people, local communities and peasants as "stewards" of rich biocultural heritages of knowledge and resources (Girard and Frison, 2018). Secondly, the UNDROP has become established as the first instrument recognizing "seed sovereignty" (Kloppenburg, 2010) through the right to seeds – i.e. the entire bundle of rights necessary to enable peasants to maintain their farmer seed networks (Haugen, 2020) – but also through control of land and territory, the cultural heritage and through the protection of normative and institutional autonomy, all elements essential to ensuring the maintenance of crop diversity and subsistence activities (Alabrese et al., 2022). In this respect, UNDROP is an important milestone: it signals that decommodification, like many tightly intertwined contemporary issues (e.g. food, Indigenous peoples' rights, land grabbing), involves local sovereignty faced with the disembedded market and with States that are either passive or favourable to this market-focused model.

Notes

1 We are referring to true seeds, but also roots, tubers, bulbs, rhizomes, seedlings, propagules. Seeds differ from grain by their use and purpose. Grain is consumed by humans and animals and transformed into oils, biofuels or flours, whilst seeds are intended to produce plants.
2 Farmers' varieties and landraces are populations of a cultivated crop that are often genetically diverse. They have not undergone formal crop improvement procedures, but they are produced in using the traditional method of crossing and then selection of offspring in several generations.
3 In 1994, the PVPA was brought into line with the 1991 UPOV Convention.
4 EPO, Administrative Council CA/D 6/17 of 29.06.2017 (OJ EPO 2017, A56).
5 EPO, EBA, 14 May 2020, G 0003/19 (Pepper (follow-up to Tomatoes II and Broccoli II).
6 On land enclosures, see Chapters 6 by Crétois and 29 by Larrère in this volume.
7 UNEP/Bio.Div.3/6 20 June 1990, para. 9; taken from UNEP/Bio.Div.3/Inf.4, para. 40.
8 Non-rivalrous and non-excludable (even though they can become), these goods are public in consumption and above all in provision. Importantly, they are of nearly universal reach, *i.e.* costs and benefits are shared and enjoyed globally.
9 Agreement on a Unified Patent Court, *OJ* C 175, 20.6.2013, p. 1–40, Art. 27(c).
10 Even though it must be said that, so far, it has been the big players' interest (if not strategy) to ward off public interventions.
11 https://osseeds.org/about/

References

Alabrese, M. et al. (2022) *The United Nations' Declaration on Peasants' Rights*. 1st edn. London: Routledge. Available at: https://doi.org/10.4324/9781003139874

Bavikatte, K.S., Robinson, D.F. and Oliva, M.J. (2015) "Biocultural Community Protocols: Dialogues on the Space Within", *IK: Other Ways of Knowing*, 1(2), pp. 1–31. Available at: https://doi.org/10.18113/P8ik159704

Bonneuil, C. (2006) "Mendelism, Plant Breeding and Experimental Cultures: Agriculture and the Development of Genetics in France", *Journal of the History of Biology*, 39(2), pp. 281–308. Available at: https://doi.org/10.1007/s10739-006-0005-5

Bonneuil, C. (2019) "Seeing Nature as a 'Universal Store of Genes': How Biological Diversity Became 'Genetic Resources', 1890–1940", *Studies in History and Philosophy of Science Part C: Studies in History and Philosophy of Biological and Biomedical Sciences*, 75, pp. 1–14. Available at: https://doi.org/10.1016/j.shpsc.2018.12.002

Bonneuil, C. and Thomas, F. (2009) *Gènes, pouvoirs et profits: recherche publique et régimes de production des savoirs de Mendel aux OGM*. Versailles: Quae.

Bonny, S. (2014) "Taking stock of the genetically modified seed sector worldwide: market, stakeholders, and prices", *Food Security*, 6(4), pp. 525–540. Available at: https://doi.org/10.1007/s12571-014-0357-1

Bonny, S. (2017) "Corporate Concentration and Technological Change in the Global Seed Industry", *Sustainability*, 9(9), p. 1632. Available at: https://doi.org/10.3390/su9091632

Brennan, J. and Jaworski, P.M. (2015) "Markets without Symbolic Limits", *Ethics*, 125(4), pp. 1053–1077. Available at: https://doi.org/10.1086/680907

Calvert, J. and Joly, P.-B. (2011) "How did the gene become a chemical compound? The ontology of the gene and the patenting of DNA", *Social Science Information*, 50(2), pp. 157–177. Available at: https://doi.org/10.1177/0539018411399512

Capra, F. and Mattei, U. (2015) *The ecology of law: toward a legal system in tune with nature and community*. San Francisco, Calif.: Berrett-Koehler.

Claeys, P. and Peschard, K. (2020) "Transnational Agrarian Movements, Food Sovereignty, and Legal Mobilization", in Claeys, P. and Peschard, K., *The Oxford Handbook of Law and Anthropology*. Edited by M.-C. Foblets et al. Oxford University Press. Available at: https://doi.org/10.1093/oxfordhb/9780198840534.013.40

Congretel, M. and Pinton, F. (2020) "Local knowledge, know-how and knowledge mobilized in a globalized world: A new approach of indigenous local ecological knowledge", *People and Nature*, 2(3), pp. 527–543. Available at: https://doi.org/10.1002/pan3.10142

Coomes, O.T. et al. (2015) "Farmer seed networks make a limited contribution to agriculture? Four common misconceptions", *Food Policy*, 56, pp. 41–50. Available at: https://doi.org/10.1016/j.foodpol.2015.07.008

Dardot, P. and Laval, C. (2019) *Common on revolution in the 21st century*. London; New York: Bloomsbury Academic.

De Jonge, B. and Munyi, P. (2016) "A Differentiated Approach to Plant Variety Protection in Africa: A Differentiated Approach to PVP in Africa", *The Journal of World Intellectual Property*, 19(1–2), pp. 28–52. Available at: https://doi.org/10.1111/jwip.12053

De Schutter, O. (2009) *Report of the Special Rapporteur on the right to food. Seed policies and the right to food: enhancing agrobiodiversity and encouraging innovation*. A /64/170. United Nations, General Assembly.

Demeulenaere, É. (2014) "A political ontology of seeds: The transformative frictions of a farmers' movement in Europe", *Focaal*, 2014(69), pp. 45–61.

Demeulenaere, E. and Piersante, Y. (2020) "In or out? Organisational dynamics within European "peasant seed" movements facing opening-up institutions and policies", *The Journal of Peasant Studies*, 47(4), pp. 767–791. Available at: https://doi.org/10.1080/03066150.2020.1753704

Egelie, K.J. et al. (2016) "The emerging patent landscape of CRISPR–Cas gene editing technology", *Nature Biotechnology*, 34(10), pp. 1025–1031. Available at: https://doi.org/10.1038/nbt.3692

Friedmann, H. (1980) "Household production and the national economy: Concepts for the analysis of Agrarian formations", *The Journal of Peasant Studies*, 7(2), pp. 158–184. Available at: https://doi.org/10.1080/03066158008438099

Frison, C. (2018) *Redesigning the global seed commons: law and policy for agrobiodiversity and food security*. London: Routledge.

Girard, F. (2015) "'Though the treasure of nature's germens tumble all together': the EPO and patents on native traits or the bewitching powers of ideologies", *Prometheus*, 33(1), pp. 43–65. Available at: https://doi.org/10.1080/08109028.2015.1061258

Girard, F. and Frison, C. (2018) *The commons, plant breeding and agricultural research: challenges for food security and agrobiodiversity*. Abingdon, Oxon; New York: Routledge.

Girard, F. and Frison, C. (2021) "From Farmers' Rights to the Rights of Peasants: Seeds and the Biocultural Turn", *Review of Agricultural, Food and Environmental Studies*, 102, pp. 461–476.

Girard, F., Hall, I. and Frison, C. (2022) *Biocultural Rights, Indigenous Peoples and Local Communities*. London: Routledge.

Godt, C. (2018) "Technology, Patents and Markets: The Implied Lessons of the EU Commission's Intervention in the Broccoli/Tomatoes Case of 2016 for Modern (Plant) Genome Editing", *IIC – International Review of Intellectual Property and Competition Law*, 49(5), pp. 512–535. Available at: https://doi.org/10.1007/s40319-018-0710-6

Graff, G.D. et al. (2004) "Access to intellectual property is a major obstacle to developing transgenic horticultural crops", *California Agriculture*, 58(2), pp. 120–126.

Gray, B.N. and Spruill, W.M. (2017) "CRISPR–Cas9 claim sets and the potential to stifle innovation", *Nature Biotechnology*, 35(7), pp. 630–633. Available at: https://doi.org/10.1038/nbt.3913

Gudeman, S. (2016) *Anthropology and economy*. Cambridge: Cambridge University Press.

Gutiérrez Escobar, L. and Fitting, E. (2016) "The 'Red de Semillas Libres': Contesting Biohegemony in Colombia", *Journal of Agrarian Change*, 16(4), pp. 711–719. Available at: https://doi.org/10.1111/joac.12161

Halpert, M.-T. and Chappell, M.J. (2017) "Prima facie reasons to question enclosed intellectual property regimes and favor open-source regimes for germplasm", *F1000Research*, 6, p. 284. Available at: https://doi.org/10.12688/f1000research.10497.1

Hardison, P. (2009) "Appendix 2. Indigenous Peoples & the Commons", in E. Abrell and Natural Justice (eds) *Implementing A Traditional Knowledge Commons. Opportunities and Challenges*. Cape Town: Natural Justice, pp. 40–44.

Haugen, H.M. (2020) "The UN Declaration on Peasants' Rights (UNDROP): Is Article 19 on seed rights adequately balancing intellectual property rights and the right to food?", *The Journal of World Intellectual Property*, 23(3–4), pp. 288–309. Available at: https://doi.org/10.1111/jwip.12152

Heller, M.A. and Eisenberg, R.S. (1998) "Can Patents Deter Innovation? The Anticommons in Biomedical Research", *Science*, 280(5364), pp. 698–701. Available at: https://doi.org/10.1126/science.280.5364.698

Hendrickson, M., Howard, P.H. and Constance, D. (2017) *Power, Food and Agriculture: Implications for Farmers, Consumers and Communities.* SSRN Scholarly Paper ID 3066005. Rochester, NY: Social Science Research Network. Available at: https://doi.org/10.2139/ssrn.3066005

Herforth, A. et al. (2019) "Agrobiodiversity and Feeding the World: More of the Same Will Result in More of the Same", in *Agrobiodiversity: Integrating Knowledge for a Sustainable Future.* Cambridge (Mass.); London: MIT Press, pp. 185–211. Available at: https://cgspace.cgiar.org/handle/10568/101250 (Accessed: 24 April 2021).

Herpers, S. et al. (2017) *The support for farmer-led seed systems in African seed laws.* ISSD Africa: Synthesis paper. ISSD Africa, Wageningen University, KIT, Future Agricultures, Tegemeo Institute of Agricultural Policy and Development.

Howard, P.H. (2009) "Visualizing Consolidation in the Global Seed Industry: 1996–2008", *Sustainability*, 1(4), pp. 1266–1287. Available at: https://doi.org/10.3390/su1041266

Howard, P.H. (2015) "Intellectual Property and Consolidation in the Seed Industry", *Crop Science*, 55(6), pp. 2489–2495. Available at: https://doi.org/10.2135/cropsci2014.09.0669

Howard, P.L. (2010) "Culture and Agrobiodiversity: Understanding the Links", in S. Pilgrim and J.N. Pretty (eds) *Nature and Culture. Rebuilding Lost Connections.* London; Washington (DC): Routledge, pp. 163–184. Available at: https://doi.org/10.4324/9781849776455

IPBES (2019) *Summary for policymakers of the global assessment report on biodiversity and ecosystem services.* Zenodo. Available at: https://doi.org/10.5281/ZENODO.3553579

Janis, M.D., Jervis, H.H. and Peet, R. (2014) *Intellectual property law of plants.* First edition. Oxford, United Kingdom; New York, NY: Oxford University Press.

Jarvis, D.I. (2016) *Crop genetic diversity in the field and on the farm: principles and applications in research practices.* Yale University Press. New Haven.

Jarvis, D.I. et al. (2011) "An Heuristic Framework for Identifying Multiple Ways of Supporting the Conservation and Use of Traditional Crop Varieties within the Agricultural Production System", *Critical Reviews in Plant Sciences*, 30(1–2), pp. 125–176. Available at: https://doi.org/10.1080/07352689.2011.554358

Jarvis, D.I. et al. (2016) *Crop genetic diversity in the field and on the farm: principles and applications in research practices.* New Haven: Yale University Press. Available at: https://search.ebscohost.com/login.aspx?direct=true&scope=site&db=nlebk&db=nlabk&AN=1193647

Jodha, N.S. (1985) "Market forces and erosion of common property resources", in *Agricultural Markets in the Semi-Arid Tropics. Proceedings of the International Workshop held at ICRISAT Center, India, 24–28 October 1983.* Patancheru, Andhra Pradesh, India: ICRISAT, pp. 263–227.

Joseph, S.K. (2020) *Customary rights of farmers in neoliberal India: a legal and policy analysis.* New Delhi: Oxford University Press.

Juma, C. (1989) *The gene hunters: biotechnology and the scramble for seeds.* Princeton, N.J.: Princeton University.

Kaul, I., Grunberg, I. and Stern, M. (1999) *Global Public Goods.* New York: Oxford University Press. Available at: https://doi.org/10.1093/0195130529.001.0001

Khoury, C.K. et al. (2015) *Estimation of countries' interdependence in plant genetic resources provisioning national food supplies and production systems.* Rome: The International Treaty on Plant Genetic Resources for Food and Agriculture.

Khoury, C.K. et al. (2022) "Crop genetic erosion: understanding and responding to loss of crop diversity", *New Phytologist*, 233(1), pp. 84–118. Available at: https://doi.org/10.1111/nph.17733

Kloppenburg, J. (2010) "Impeding Dispossession, Enabling Repossession: Biological Open Source and the Recovery of Seed Sovereignty: Biological Open Source and the Recovery of Seed Sovereignty", *Journal of Agrarian Change*, 10(3), pp. 367–388. Available at: https://doi.org/10.1111/j.1471-0366.2010.00275.x

Kloppenburg, J. (2014) "Re-purposing the master's tools: the open source seed initiative and the struggle for seed sovereignty", *The Journal of Peasant Studies*, 41(6), pp. 1225–1246. Available at: https://doi.org/10.1080/03066150.2013.875897

Kloppenburg, J.R. (2005) *First the Seed: The Political Economy of Plant Biotechnology.* Madison; Chicago: University of Wisconsin Press Chicago Distribution Center. Available at: http://site.ebrary.com/id/10217039

Kock, M.A. (2021) "Open Intellectual Property Models for Plant Innovations in the Context of New Breeding Technologies", *Agronomy*, 11(6), p. 1218. Available at: https://doi.org/10.3390/agronomy11061218

Kock, M.A. and ten Have, F. (2016) "The 'International Licensing Platform – Vegetables': A prototype of a patent clearing house in the life science industry", *Journal of Intellectual Property Law & Practice*, 11(7), pp. 496–515. Available at: https://doi.org/10.1093/jiplp/jpw073

Kotschi, J. and Horneburg, B. (2018) "The Open Source Seed Licence: A novel approach to safeguarding access to plant germplasm", *PLOS Biology*, 16(10), p. e3000023. Available at: https://doi.org/10.1371/journal.pbio.3000023

Le Teno, S., Cogolati, S. and Frison, C. (2022) "The right to seeds: using the Commons as a sustainable governance scheme to implement peasants' rights?", in M. Alabrese et al. (eds) *The United Nations Declaration on the rights of peasants and other people working in rural areas in perspective. New international standards on natural resources and food systems*. Oxon, New York: Routledge, pp. 119–133.

Llewelyn, M. and Adcock, M. (2006) *European plant intellectual property*. Portland: Hart Publishing.

Louwaars, N.P. (2018) "Plant breeding and diversity: A troubled relationship?", *Euphytica*, 214(7), p. 114. Available at: https://doi.org/10.1007/s10681-018-2192-5

Luby, C.H. et al. (2015) "Enhancing Freedom to Operate for Plant Breeders and Farmers through Open Source Plant Breeding", *Crop Science*, 55(6), pp. 2481–2488. Available at: https://doi.org/10.2135/cropsci2014.10.0708

McGuire, S. and Sperling, L. (2016) "Seed systems smallholder farmers use", *Food Security*, 8(1), pp. 179–195. Available at: https://doi.org/10.1007/s12571-015-0528-8

Metzger, A. and Zech, H. (2020) *A Comprehensive Approach to Plant Variety Rights and Patents in the Field of Innovative Plants*. SSRN Scholarly Paper ID 3675534. Rochester, NY: Social Science Research Network. Available at: https://papers.ssrn.com/abstract=3675534

Mgbeoji, I. (2003) "Beyond Rhetoric: State Sovereignty, Common Concern, and the Inapplicability of the Common Heritage Concept to Plant Genetic Resources", *Leiden Journal of International Law*, 16(4), pp. 821–837. Available at: https://doi.org/10.1017/S092215650300147X

Montenegro de Wit, M. (2019) "Beating the bounds: how does 'open source' become a seed commons?", *The Journal of Peasant Studies*, 46(1), pp. 44–79. Available at: https://doi.org/10.1080/03066150.2017.1383395

O'Grady Walshe, C. (2020) *Globalisation and Seed Sovereignty in Sub-Saharan Africa*. Cham: Springer International Publishing.

O'Neill, J. (2007) *Markets, deliberation and environment*. London; New York: Routledge.

OECD (2018) *Concentration in Seed Markets: Potential Effects and Policy Responses*. Paris: OECD Publishing. Available at: https://doi.org/10.1787/9789264308367-en

Peschard, K. (2017) "Seed wars and farmers' rights: comparative perspectives from Brazil and India", *The Journal of Peasant Studies*, 44(1), pp. 144–168. Available at: https://doi.org/10.1080/03066150.2016.1191471

Peschard, K. and Randeria, S. (2020) "'Keeping seeds in our hands': the rise of seed activism", *The Journal of Peasant Studies*, 47(4), pp. 613–647. Available at: https://doi.org/10.1080/03066150.2020.1753705

Peukert, A. (2019) "Fictitious Commodities: A Theory of Intellectual Property Inspired by Karl Polanyi's 'Great Transformation'", *Fordham intellectual property, media & entertainment law journal*, 29(4), pp. 1151–1200.

Pistorius, R. (1997) *Scientists, plants and politics: a history of the plant genetic resources movement*. Rome: IPGRI.

Pistorius, R. and Wijk, J. van (1999) *The exploitation of plant genetic information: political strategies in crop development*. Wallingford: CABI publ.

Polanyi, K. (2001[1944]) *The Great transformation: the political and economic origins of our time*. 2nd edn. Boston: Beacon Press.

Prifti, V. (2015) *The Breeder's Exception to Patent Rights: Analysis of Compliance with Article 30 of the TRIPS Agreement*. Cham: Springer International Publishing (International Law and Economics). Available at: https://doi.org/10.1007/978-3-319-15771-9

Rangnekar, D. (1996) "Commodification of seeds", *Science as Culture*, 6(2), pp. 301–312. Available at: https://doi.org/10.1080/09505439609526469

Rangnekar, D. (2000) *Innovative appropriation: the role of law, economics and science in transforming plants into products – a case study of wheat breeding in the UK*. Kingston University.

Reyes-García, V. et al. (2018) "Governing landraces and associated knowledge as a commons: from theory to practice", in F. Girard and C. Frison (eds) *The commons, plant breeding and agricultural research: challenges for food security and agrobiodiversity*. Abingdon, Oxon; New York, NY: Routledge, pp. 197–209.

Rogan, T. (2019) *The moral economists: R.H. Tawney, Karl Polanyi, E.P. Thompson, and the critique of capitalism*. Princeton, N.J.: Princeton University Press.

Sanderson, J. (2017) *Plants, People and Practices: The Nature and History of the UPOV Convention*. Cambridge: Cambridge University Press. Available at: https://doi.org/10.1017/9781316411216

Santos, B. de S. and Rodríguez-Garavito, C.A. (2005) "Law, politics, and the subaltern in counter-hegemonic globalization", in B. de S. Santos and C.A. Rodríguez-Garavito (eds) *Law and Globalization from Below*. 1st edn. Cambridge University Press, pp. 1–26. Available at: https://doi.org/10.1017/CBO9780511494093.001

Satz, D. (2010) *Why Some Things Should Not Be for Sale*. New York; Oxford: Oxford University Press. Available at: https://doi.org/10.1093/acprof:oso/9780195311594.001.0001

Schenkelaars, P., de Vriend, H. and Kalaitzandonakes, N. (2011) *Drivers of Consolidation in the Seed Industry and its Consequences for Innovation | Forum Grüne Vernunft*. COGEM. Available at: www.gruenevernunft.de/meldung/drivers-consolidation-seed-industry-and-its-consequences-innovation

Schlager, E. and Ostrom, E. (1992) "Property-Rights Regimes and Natural Resources: A Conceptual Analysis", *Land Economics*, 68(3), pp. 249–262. Available at: https://doi.org/10.2307/3146375

Sedjo, R.A. (1992) "Property Rights, Genetic Resources, and Biotechnological Change", *The Journal of Law & Economics*, 35(1), pp. 199–213.

Sengupta, N. (1995) "Common Property Institutions and Markets", *Indian Economic Review*, 30(2), pp. 187–201.

Sievers-Glotzbach, S. and Christinck, A. (2021) "Introduction to the symposium: seed as a commons – exploring innovative concepts and practices of governing seed and varieties", *Agriculture and Human Values*, 38(2), pp. 499–507. Available at: https://doi.org/10.1007/s10460-020-10166-x

Toledo, V.M. (1990) "The Ecological Rationality of Peasant Production", in M.A. Altieri and S.B. Hecht (eds) *Agroecology and Small Farm Development*. Boca Raton, FL; Ann Arbor: CRC Press, pp. 53–60.

Tordjman, H. (2008) "La construction d'une marchandise: le cas des semences", *Annales. Histoire, Sciences Sociales*, 63(6), pp. 1341–1368. Available at: https://doi.org/10.1017/S0395264900038154

Tsioumani, E. (2020) *Fair and Equitable Benefit-Sharing in Agriculture: Reinventing Agrarian Justice*. 1st edn. Abingdon, Oxon; New York, NY: Routledge. Available at: https://doi.org/10.4324/9780429198304

van der Ploeg, J.D. (2010) "The peasantries of the twenty-first century: the commoditisation debate revisited", *The Journal of Peasant Studies*, 37(1), pp. 1–30. Available at: https://doi.org/10.1080/03066150903498721

van der Ploeg, J.D. (2018) *The new peasantries: struggles for autonomy and sustainability in an era of empire and globalization*. Abingdon [England]: Routledge.

Wattnem, T. (2016) "Seed laws, certification and standardization: outlawing informal seed systems in the Global South", *The Journal of Peasant Studies*, 43(4), pp. 850–867. Available at: https://doi.org/10.1080/03066150.2015.1130702

Weston, B.H. and Bollier, D. (2014) *Green governance: ecological survival, human rights, and the law of the commons*. New York, N.Y.: Cambridge University Press.

29

PARKS AND FORESTS

The question of the commons

Catherine Larrère

Introduction: Commodification, valuation, and the commons

Can public forests and national parks be considered commodities? If we approach this question solely in terms of the opposition between State and market, the matter is rather quickly settled, as there is no question of a real commodification of these natural spaces (they are removed from the market and all it entails, for reasons that will be recalled later), and only their economic valuation remains subject to debate. However, this is not the end of the matter, as the State's ability to effectively guarantee the protection of nature is not a given. The duality between private and public does not exhaust the possibilities: we must also take into account the commons and its relationships with both of those two poles. For while the commons clearly stands in opposition to the private, we may nevertheless not assimilate it to the public and the State. In this introduction, after showing that commodification is not simply a matter of putting things on the market, but raises the question of economic evaluation and its consequences, I explain why the bulk of this chapter will be devoted to the question of the commons.

From the second half of the nineteenth century onwards, national parks became established in North America, in Europe, and in other places around the world (Héritier and Laslaz, 2008; Larrère and Lizet, 2009). These parks were intended to protect vast natural expanses from the transformations engendered by human activity (urbanization, industrialization, intensive agriculture), and thus from the market. Such protected natural spaces are often invoked as the very exemplar of what must be defended from commodification. Considered virtually sacred (in this respect we might speak of them as "sanctuarized"), just as there can be no commercial traffic in the goods of the Church since God's blessings are not for sale (the sin of simony),[1] parks too cannot be commodified even if only by charging a fee for entrance: nature's blessings are not for sale either (Sandel, 2013, pp. 35–37, 41, 116). Having been established by and remaining under the protection of the State, national parks as such are not currently threatened by commercialization. Likewise, the status of public forests is comparable to that of national parks, and in France in particular there is a very long tradition of public forests belonging to the State. While these forests may certainly furnish marketable products, they are not, in themselves, commodities, and indeed such a thing is entirely ruled out.

DOI: 10.4324/9781003188742-35

Should we then conclude that, for national parks and public forests, the question of commodification has been settled: that they are not commodities? Unfortunately, however, commodification is not just a matter of actually being placed on the market; it also refers, more widely, to valuation in economic terms. And parks and forests are frequently so valued. This could be a matter of assessing the damage caused to them by a disaster (oil spill, fire, etc.). An assessment (by means of a contingent valuation) of what a park represents in economic terms is the sort of argument that carries weight for decision-makers. Yet there are two opposing positions on whether this kind of economic valuation is compatible with the protection of nature.

For Jean Gadrey and Aurore Lalucq (2015), valuation is inevitable, because, while nature has no price (in the sense that it evades full commodification, since nature cannot be bought), it does have a cost (notably since protecting nature incurs expenses), and hence we need to be able to value it. And this is not something that is done in a single stroke; rather, economic evaluation as a process can be broken down into a number of stages: quantification, monetarization, commodification, and financialization. This sequence is directed (each stage presupposes the previous), but it can be interrupted: one stage does not necessarily lead to the next, or so Gadrey and Lalucq argue. Following an oil spill that has caused ecological damage, if damages and interest are to be paid to the injured party (which may be nature), a monetary valuation of the loss suffered must be carried out, but this does not entail that anything is placed on the market. So, they insist, "we must not confuse monetarization, commodification, and financialization" (Gadrey and Lalucq, 2015, p. 115).[2] Handled with appropriate care, therefore, economic valuation can be a tool for protecting nature.

Quite the contrary, objects Virginie Maris (2014), and cites in this respect the "slippery slope" argument: from one stage to the next the progression is continuous, and begins indeed with the first stage, that of quantification, even before the economic evaluation itself takes place. Quantifying entails an act of homogenization that prepares – and heralds – economic evaluation and commodification, since the elements thus quantified are rendered intersubstitutable. This is the case with so-called ecosystem services: to consider that ecosystems provide services is to think of them solely from the point of view of their utility for humans (the function of the ecosystem, which is ecocentric, is transformed into a service that is anthropocentric), and to quantify these services (irrespective of whether the units of evaluation are monetary) is to prepare them to be inserted into the chain of commodification, which is one of substitutability. Evaluating ecosystem services is not about protecting nature, rebranded now as biodiversity, but about preparing to sell it.

With these two opposing positions thus set out,[3] the discussion can proceed indefinitely: we may ask whether a language of comparison is really necessary for protecting nature, and whether such language is really neutral. If, as Gadrey and Lalucq rightly remark, we must indeed find arguments to justify the protection of nature, is the language of economics, that of numbers, the most appropriate mode, or does its employment, as Virginie Maris argues, entail the exposure of nature to the very thing for which this language was invented: namely the market?

However important this discussion may be, it neglects an issue that I feel it should be the principal goal of this chapter to explore: that of the commons.[4] To reject commodification is to declare that protected natural spaces cannot be private property, and that they must be placed under the protection of the State. At the same time, however, this is to assume that the State is an effective guarantor of the protection of what is placed under its control. It is also to assume that there are only two possible statuses for goods: private or public. Yet the ecological debate – to which the question of protected natural spaces is tightly linked – has focused on the question of the commons, seen as a status that escapes the dualism between public and private. From Garett Hardin (1968) to Elinor Ostrom (1990), the debate on the commons has clarified this notion and demonstrated that the choice facing us is not restricted to the division between public and private: for the commons too must have its place. This will help us to make progress on the question of parks and forests because, as we shall see in relation to the activity of French foresters between the nineteenth and twentieth centuries, the reasons for opposing private management are not to be found solely in the debate on market value and private property, but particularly in a discussion of land use that connects more with the question of the commons than that of private property. This will lead us, in a third stage, to address the question of parks and forests, distinguishing between public domain and communal goods. To protect natural spaces properly and ensure that they escape commodification, ought they to be managed as commons?

The debate between Garrett Hardin and Elinor Ostrom on the question of the commons

Published in 1968 in *Science* magazine, Garrett Hardin's article "The Tragedy of the Commons" introduced the problem of the commons into ecological thought (Hardin, 1968). He offers a thought experiment, that of a pasture where farmers graze their animals. Each farmer, seeking to increase his profit, puts on it as many animals as he can: the result is overgrazing, which degrades the land to the detriment of all. This example of overexploited pasture has, for many, become a metaphor for humanity's overexploitation of the environment (the "commons"). The excess livestock can be taken to represent the growth of the human population (often considered, in the era in which Hardin was writing, to be the main cause of the environmental crisis) or can stand for the unlimited exploitation of unowned resources – the commons of water, air, and soil. In either case the lesson drawn is the same: free access to communal goods leads to irreversible depletion of resources, for the logic of individual action excludes cooperation. Thus posed, the problem admits of two solutions: state control, or the market. In the neo-liberal context of the 1980s, the idea spread that the generalization of the principle of the private appropriation of nature (water, forests, biological resources) would be the most appropriate tool by which to take account of the value of dwindling natural resources. Thus, at the 1992 Rio Earth Summit, the Convention on Biological Diversity did not accept the proposal to make biodiversity a common heritage of mankind, but made it dependent on the sovereignty of individual states, thus allowing it to be commodified. This also shows that the State is not sufficient to protect such goods from commodification. Considering them to be commons may offer better protection.

The work of Elinor Ostrom (and her team) on the governance of the commons, which earned her the 2009 Nobel Prize in Economics, has shown that the thought experiment to which Hardin's article appeals does not stand up to the test of fact: all over the world, there are and have always been communities that manage their resources collectively and govern themselves in a way that marries efficiency (resources are not depleted, but conserved or renewed) and equity (in the sharing of resources and the mode in which conflicts are resolved). Dispelling Hardin's confusion between the commons and lawless zones, Ostrom's work shows that the commons are not defined negatively, by the absence of private property, but have a positive existence which rests on three components: resources, community, and rules. *Community* is thus the condition for the existence of the commons; common *resources* are those resources that a community decides to render as such, by establishing rules to govern their use; and these *rules* concern the goods themselves, those to whom they are allocated (distribution of rights of use, and sharing of responsibilities), and finally the rules themselves and any modifications to them which might be made. Ownership does not refer simply to the relationship – of exploitation – between a person and a thing, but is rather a relationship between people with respect to certain things, concerning which there is a prior agreement as to who can use them and how. There is no single, exclusive right of ownership, but a "bundle of rights" (Orsi, 2015).

From the global environmental commons to which Hardin's article pointed, Ostrom shifts the focus to real communities that take charge of common resources, controlling their use without always being able to regulate access (what Ostrom calls "common pool resources"). This is the case with fisheries resources, Ostrom and her team having worked extensively on fishing communities. The emphasis here is on the community and its rules. This avoids an essentialist or naturalistic definition of the commons: resources are needed in order to make a commons, but it is not the resources that make the commons, but rather the people, and the rules on which they have agreed and through which they are brought together. This places Ostrom, as an economist, on the side of the institutionalists.

I emphasize, again, that the institutions she studies (communities and their rules) are not state-run. Whereas Hardin's article considers no alternative but the market or the State (under different modes of regulation, variously authoritarian or incentive-based), Ostrom demonstrates that there are other solutions that involve neither market nor State: these fishing communities do not hand themselves over to the market to regulate their relationships, but set their own rules for themselves, and do not call upon the state to settle quotidian conflicts. There are numerous examples of community practices of this type, notably in certain French communes where local residents still dispose of certain usage rights over forests (Vanuxem, 2020).

Ostrom thus shows that the commons represents a form of management of resources that allows it to escape commodification, without by the same token falling under the control of the State. This reinvigorates the discussion on why natural spaces should be protected from commodification. On the one hand, there is no essential reason – perhaps because they possess a defining characteristic (being "wild," constituting a "wilderness") which would remove them from human dominion – why natural spaces should not be transformed into commodities; it is the result of a human decision, an act of institutionalization. On the other hand, given that the commons introduces a third term relative to the market and the State, these now form the three vertices of a triad, private – commons – State, and any question concerning the governance of natural spaces must be situated within it. It is certainly within this triad that the arguments of the nineteenth century French foresters are to be found: if they defend the State in order to maintain the forests in the long term, this is not only through an opposition to private property, but also due to their criticism of the traditional practices that fall within the scope of the commons.

On the proper use of forests: The forestry controversy of the nineteenth and twentieth centuries

In the nineteenth century, the French foresters who made up the State body charged with the estate of public forests, developed a significant discourse on the benefits of forests and the catastrophic effects of deforestation. Their position was what we would today call ecological, and a number of their arguments in favour of forests or warning of the disasters their disappearance would entail are still employed by conservationists today. The benefits include climate regulation, hydrology, and the control of soil erosion. The disasters are the inverse: deforestation leads to soil erosion and flooding, but can also cause drought and desertification when the hydrology is completely out of balance. If foresters laid such stress on this contrasting picture, with an emphasis that in some cases amounted to exaggeration, it was because they believed that these natural phenomena had human causes. Hence the insistence with which they appealed to the State, whose officials they were, to give them the means to procure for the nation the benefits of the forest, as a guarantee against the disasters linked to deforestation (Larrère, 1981).

Among those they considered responsible for deforestation, they took aim at all who engaged in tree clearances or large-scale logging, including for expanding urbanization or the commercial exploitation of forests, without sufficient attention paid to their restoration. But principally, however, they called into question the agro-pastoral systems and the traditional usage of mountain forests, that is to say the rights of usage of the commons. To survive, in a period when the market economy was not universal, the mountain-dwellers were constrained to clear the slopes to make way for the plough and the fields necessary to overwinter their livestock. Needing animals for the manure they provided, they sent out their flocks to graze on the moorlands, mountain pastures, and undergrowth. Cleared, its capacity for regeneration compromised by the grazing animals, and sometimes even destroyed by the not-infrequent moorland fires, the forest was left in a sorry state. Continuing throughout the nineteenth century, this "deforestation" resulted in a slow degradation of the physical environment: stripped of its plant cover, the earth came away from the slopes, imperceptibly obstructing the mouths of rivers, or, through sudden mudflows, ravaging the crops and habitations of the valleys (Larrère and Larrère, 2009[1997], pp. 209–210).

Whether for the benefit of commercial practices aimed at private gain, or in order to sustain the traditional usage of the peasantry, the foresters upheld the capacity of the State to impose the general interest against particular interests over the long term. But interests can be considered particular, and hence as in opposition to the general interest, in two different ways. They can indeed be individual and private interests, those of rational agents; but "particular" can also be said of a part of a whole. The interest of a particular group is thus to be distinguished from the general interest. The arguments opposing the particular and the general are not the same in each case. The argument put forward against the harmful effects of individual private interests in forest management turns on the "myopia" of private interest, which sees only short-term profit and demands a rapid return on investment. We are thus witness to a kind of tragedy of commodification. Since the deforestation for which commodification is responsible has potentially catastrophic consequences, only the State, as the guardian of the public interest, can be the true defender of the forests (for which the foresters, as a State body, are the legitimate spokespersons). Given the long time period over which forests become established (centuries, if not millennia), only the State, which is undying, is capable of managing them with an appropriate eye to the distant future. And indeed the benefits of forests, from which all people benefit, render them a matter of the general interest, for which the State alone is the guarantor. We thus have an argument against commodification which is based on the well-known inability of economic calculus to take into account the long term, which cost–benefit calculations always discount (Ackerman and Heinzerling, 2002).

This may justify State intervention in ecological matters, on the grounds that only the State can impose the general interest without giving in to particular interests. Such were the arguments behind the intervention of the State forestry corps in the policy of mountain land restoration in France at the end of the nineteenth century (1881). But the foresters did not confine themselves to criticizing private commercial interests; they aimed also at the second type of private or particular interests. Their main target, namely the peasants and their traditional practices, called for a different kind of critique, one that was aimed not so much at short-sighted egoism as ignorance: here, then, the foresters mobilized the intellectual arsenal of the Enlightenment to denounce peasant practices as superstitious, archaic, and obscurantist, and to deny them any rationality. The State to which they appealed was not only the defender of the long-term general interest, but also the guardian of scientific knowledge (which for the foresters was the dialectical opposite of peasant obscurantism). It was therefore in the name of science that they called for a policy of restoring the mountain lands. We may thus see this policy as a kind of testing ground for the environmental policies of later eras: it raises questions about how to combine science and politics, and about how, through the intermediation of the State, to impose the general interest of the nation as a whole by subjugating the various divergent individual interests. Within the State, science and politics come to form a unity, which empowers the state discourse to counter not only the axiom of economic liberalism according to which "each person's interest is his own best guide," but also the want of culture in the peasants' routine. This justifies the foresters intervening on private land, in the name of the State, so as to "restore" it.

By criticizing the usage rights that allowed peasants to send their livestock into the forests or to gather wood, the foresters were attacking the remnants of communal practices surviving from the Ancien Régime. The critique of the foresters is in this sense a critique of the idea of the commons, even if the foresters themselves did not see it as such. Maintaining a strict distinction between private and public property, they condemned practices that they saw as dangerous for the forest and the soil. In so doing, they form part of a tradition of criticizing the communal holding of land, and their critique of common usage rights is all the more akin to Hardin's in that the latter borrowed many of his arguments – including the image of overgrazed pastureland – from the arguments advanced from the sixteenth to the eighteenth centuries by the supporters of the privatization of communal land, particularly in England – which has been dubbed the "enclosure" movement (Locher, 2013) (see Chapter 6 by Crétois in this volume). But the foresters' critique, unlike that of the apologists for enclosure, is aimed not at defending private property but of valorizing the role of the State. Because it promotes the general interest, but above all because it draws on science, the State is to be clearly distinguished from the private realm. But if the State stands opposed to the commons, does this not place it in the tradition of enclosure?

National parks: Public property or common land?

We thus find ourselves facing a paradox. In the wake of Ostrom's work, the "environmental commons" has become a reference point for ecologist movements: contrary to the destructive effects of private management, the governance of the commons (shared gardens, repair stores, etc.) combines caring for the environment with solidarist or collective action. The return of the commons, heralded by green movements, appears to be a way of "demarketizing" the economy to the benefit of both nature and humankind (Perret, 2015): but this valorization of the commons is limited to their opposition to private goods. The connection between common goods and public goods, between the commons and the State, is not called into question. Yet, on the contrary, it was precisely upon the presumed opposition between the commons and the State that the French foresters of the late nineteenth century grounded their argument. How do things stand with the protection of nature and the creation of national parks? As it unfolded in North America, in Europe, and in Europe's African colonies, then to spread over the rest of the world in the second half of the twentieth century, the history of the protection of nature is hardly a story of the commons. Although today's commons movement would present itself as a revival of the struggle against the enclosures that, in modern Europe, marked the triumph of private property over the collective usage of land, the history of nature conservation would be better understood as a continuation of the process of enclosure.

This, at least, is the thesis that emerges from Kenneth R. Olwig's historical study of the political dimension of landscape (Olwig, 2002). Encompassing Northern Europe, Great Britain, and the

United States, and covering a period from the sixteenth to the nineteenth centuries, his analysis of the historical transformations in the meaning and use of the word *landschaft* and its equivalents in Germanic languages shows how landscape went from being a political notion (*landschaft* signifying a form of political community) to becoming a national emblem, with nature as its object. This explains why *natural* parks, which are intended to protect nature, are also called *national* parks, and how, in such an institution, nature ceased to be seen as a common good and was entrusted to the State.

In the genesis of the idea that landscape has nature as its object and is an embodiment of the nation, as Olwig frames it, we can distinguish three stages, two occurring in the United Kingdom and one in the United States. The first, in the seventeenth century, consisted in expressing the political unity of the two kingdoms, England and Scotland, under the same king, James I, via a theatrical representation of a natural space (the "landscape," which then acquired the aesthetic meaning it has retained henceforth). This unificatory ambition, in its absolutist form, would fail, but after the "Glorious Revolution" (1688) the project of representing the unity of the kingdom via the landscape, understood as a natural setting, was in a second step taken up once more by the ruling political class. This was the English garden, the landscaped parks with which the English nobility embellished their country estates. The English park would be seen as an extension of the countryside, from which there is no visible separation. But it has its own independent existence nevertheless, and the enclosure movement not only privatized common land for productive purposes aimed to benefit the rich, but also brought nature into the parks and thereby enclosed it. In the pursuit of the "natural," entire villages had to be destroyed (Olwig, 2002, p. 101).

Olwig traces this dualism of the communal and the national, of political customs and nature seen as opposing ways of expressing political unity or of linking country and landscape, from the parks of the English gentry to the American national parks – this latter being the third stage of his study (Olwig, 2002, pp. 176–212). Frederik Law Omsted, the architect of Central Park, to which he transposed the principles of the landscaped English park which he so admired, was also the first chairman of the commission in charge of Yosemite Park, classified as a national park in 1890. Olmsted lamented that, in England, the country's most beautiful natural scenery was the monopoly of a very small number of the very rich. He rejoiced, therefore, that Yosemite had been made available to the American people as a whole. But while Yosemite's valley floor, with its meandering river and lush grasses, may recall the "village green" of the traditional English village commons, the mountain ridge that dominates the valley evokes an altogether different landscape, one of harsh, uninhabited nature. It was from here that John Muir, the lover of wilderness, contemplated the valley, and, according to him, the purpose of the American nature parks was to preserve nature's integrity. Having become the emblem of a nature that required protection, the wilderness was now to be enclosed in natural parks, designated as "fenced parks" (Cronon, 1996; Larrère and Larrère, 2015, pp. 25–49). To achieve this, it was necessary to evict the inhabitants who shared the use of the area with the rest of the living world. The Indians, who lived in Yosemite, were thus driven out. The local white inhabitants met the same fate, their traces being wiped from Yosemite as they were from many other parks (Cronon, 2008). In the same manner as in the English parks, between 1959 and 1963 the village in Yosemite's valley was razed, the only surviving structure being its church, built in 1879 (Olwig, 2002, pp. 115 and 207).

Such is the network of the American parks, at once both national and natural. Symbols of the American nation, forged by the virile settlers' confrontation with the wilderness, they are held up to the rest of the world as a model for the protection of nature. But in this meeting of the national and the natural, centred on the emblematic landscape of the wilderness, all trace of the commons has disappeared.

Does the same hold true in France? Unlike in the United States, in France nature is not identified with wilderness, neither as a national emblem nor as an image of authentic nature to be protected. The first natural areas in France to be protected, around the same time as in the United States, were the "artistic series," such as the Fontainebleau forest in 1853, intended to preserve the landscapes painted by the Barbizon painters. And when, in the 1960s, national parks began to be set up, particularly in the Alps to protect spaces and species threatened by the artificialization of mountains linked to the construction of facilities for winter sports, these were never based on the American model. Even if, as Jacques Lepart observed, "mountain parks have generally been established on former communal land" (2019, p. 100), it cannot be said that the history of enclosures is being recapitulated: for there is no radical opposition in these parks between the protection of nature and the pastoral usage of local populations. However, as the parks include state-owned forests and communal forests under state management, the Office National des Forêts (run by the forestry corps) continues to object to peasant practices, notably grazing in the forest, and the authorizations granted to local peasants must be negotiated between the managers of the park and the foresters on a case-by-case basis. The national parks have not inherited the criticisms of usage rights advanced by foresters of previous centuries, but the foresters are still there, which demonstrates the importance of the interplay between common management and state management.

Despite these difficulties, common uses of forest and grazing areas have been maintained, as have the traditional rules of access that regulate them. Doubtless, the Alpine parks (Vanoise, Écrins, Mercantour) are not inhabited all year round, but they do have temporary summer residents. Some parks are even permanently inhabited, as is the case both overseas (Reunion Island and French Guiana) and in mainland France: Port-Cros and Porquerolles, and above all the Cévennes. Clearly, wilderness (or whatever might take its place) is not the benchmark of French park policy.

Is a park inhabited permanently or for the summer, and still used by breeders (summer pastures) or shepherds (pastoralism), an inferior or bastardized form of nature protection? Or is it not rather a way of reconciling the protection of nature and of the commons, a way of linking land and landscape around a political unit (like the one that makes the Cévennes a historic land of resistance), and not merely an aesthetic one (for which the State would be the guarantor)? This requires us to revisit both the aesthetic goal of protecting nature by conceiving it as landscape, as well as the definition of the commons.

The definition we have adopted from Ostrom's work – that the commons is a set of resources, communities, and rules – does not correspond to the meaning of the term "commons" here. As Jacques Lepart points out, in protecting natural parks, we do not protect "resources that we consume, but rather things that we can degrade, or even lose, or take care of" (2019, p. 101). This land, which we want to hold in common, cannot be understood simply in terms of resources: it must be understood as an inhabited environment, whose productive utility (such as straw bales) can be appreciated, but to which it cannot be reduced.

Wouldn't the best way to protect nature from commodification be to treat it as a commons, a commons conceived not as a resource, but as an integral part of the Earth we inhabit?

Conclusion

Can protected natural areas such as national parks or public forests be considered as commodities? The examination of this question ultimately leads us back to Karl Polanyi's argument in *The Great*

Transformation: land, no more than money or labour, is not a commodity: "land is only another name for nature, which is not produced by man" (Polanyi, 2001[1944], p. 75) (see Chapter 2 by Postel and Sobel in this volume). But to reach this conclusion, we had to move away from the dualism of market and State, and introduce a third term, that of the commons.

How can we protect nature parks from commodification? We can, perhaps, sanctuarize them, set them outside the market by insisting on their sacred character. But the status they would thereby be afforded, and which would be guaranteed by the State, would not protect them from being subjected to economic valuation. Is this compatible with the protection of nature (its non-commodification), or does it precisely open up the possibility of commodification, because there is no way to resist the transition from quantification to commodification or financialization? The debate remains open, but one conclusion emerges: the State is not sufficient to guarantee natural spaces against commodification.

To advance the discussion, we need to introduce a third term, that of the commons. One of the points to retain from the debate (between Hardin and Ostrom, in particular) on the commons is that, if we presuppose a dualism between private/market and public/State, the commons cannot be reduced to one pole or the other. We are faced, therefore, not only with the question of the relationship between communal and private goods, but rather, in the case of parks and forests, with that of the relationship between public goods (under State control) and the commons (and the community that renders them commons). While the State – as we see in the case of forests in France in the second half of the nineteenth century, or, in the longer term, in the stages leading to the installation of national parks in the United States – may have destroyed the commons, even while claiming that it could better administer the areas it controlled in the general interest, this is not always the case. As we can see in France, public management of national parks does not exclude the maintenance of forms of commons and collective practices within the parks themselves. This association between public management and common management strengthens the protection of nature at the same time as it democratizes it. It is when these spaces are governed as commons – that is, treated not as resources, but as the natural surroundings within which every society exists (Polanyi, 2001[1944], p. 75), the place in which we live – that they are truly beyond the scope of commodification.

Notes

1 See on this issue Chapter 7 by Januard and Lapidus in this volume.
2 All translations from French texts are my own.
3 For references in English about this debate, see Chapters 25 by Ortega et al. and 23 O'Neill in this volume.
4 On historical forms of common property of land, see Chapter 6 by Crétois in this volume. And on modern forms of commons see Girard et al.'s contribution in Chapter 28.

References

Ackerman, F., and Heinzerling, L. (2002) "Pricing the priceless: Cost-benefit analysis and environmental protection," *Univ. of Pennsylvania Law Review*, 150, pp. 1553–1584.
Cronon, W. (1996) "The trouble with wilderness, or getting back to the wrong nature," in W. Cronon (ed.), *Uncommon Ground: Rethinking the Human Place in Nature*, London: Norton & Company, pp. 69–90.
Cronon, W. (2008) "The riddle of the apostle islands," in J. Baird Callicott and M.P Nelson (eds), *The Wilderness Debate Rages On*, Athens: University of Georgia Press, pp. 632–645.
Gadrey, J., and Lalucq, A. (2015) *Faut-il donner un prix à la nature?* Paris: Les petits matins.
Hardin, G. (1968) "The tragedy of the commons," *Science*, 162(13), pp. 1243–1248.

Héritier, S., and Laslaz, L. (eds) (2008) *Les parcs nationaux dans le monde – Protection, gestion et développement durable*, Ellipses.
Larrère, R. (1981) "L'emphase forestière: adresse à l'État," in *Recherches*, no. 45: *Tant qu'il y aura des arbres*.
Larrère, C., and Larrère, R. (2009[1997]) *Du bon usage de la nature, Pour une philosophie de l'environnement*, Paris: Champs Flammarion-Essais.
Larrère, C. and Larrère, R. (2015) *Penser et agir avec la nature. Une enquête philosophique*, Paris: La Découverte.
Larrère, R., and Lizet, B. (eds) (2009) *Histoire des parcs nationaux – Comment prendre soin de la nature?* Quae.
Lepart, J. (2019) "De la préservation de la nature à l'intendance du territoire," in P. Michon (ed.), *Les biens communs, Un modèle alternatif pour habiter nos territoires au XXIe siècle*, Presses Universitaires de Rennes, pp. 93–130.
Locher, F. (2013) "Les pâturages de la Guerre froide: Garrett Hardin et la 'Tragédie des communs'," *Revue d'histoire moderne et contemporaine,* 1(60–61), pp. 7–36.
Maris, V. (2014) *Nature à vendre, Les limites des services écosystémiques*, Versailles: éditions Quae.
Olwig, K.R. (2002) *Landscape, Nature, and the Body Politic: From Britain's Renaissance to America's New World*, Madison: The University of Wisconsin Press.
Orsi, F. (2015) "La propriété comme faisceau de droits," in B. Coriat (ed.), *Le retour des communs, la crise de l'idéologie propriétaire*, Paris: Les Liens qui Libèrent, pp. 53–60.
Ostrom, E. (1990) *Governing the Commons: The Evolution of Institutions for Collective Action*, Cambridge: Cambridge University Press.
Perret, B. (2015) *Au-delà du marché. Les nouvelles voies de la démarchandisation*, Paris: Les petits matins.
Polanyi, K. (2001[1944]) *The Great Transformation*, 2nd ed. with a preface by Joseph Stiglitz, Boston, MA: Beacon Press.
Sandel, M.V. (2013) *What Money Can't Buy*, London: Penguin Books.
Vanuxem, S. (2020) *Des choses de la nature et de leurs droits*, Versailles: éditions Quæ.

INDEX

Note: Endnotes are indicated by the page number followed by "n" and the note number e.g., 131n1 refers to note 1 on page 131.